WITHDRAWN

DANA GARDNER MUNRO has spent many years in the countries of which he writes, both as scholar and as government official, and is the author of *The Latin American Republics* as well as other works in this field. He is presently WILLIAM STEWARD TOD PROFESSOR OF HISTORY, Emeritus, at Princeton University.

INTERVENTION AND DOLLAR DIPLOMACY
IN THE CARIBBEAN

Intervention
and Dollar Diplomacy
in the Caribbean
1900-1921

BY DANA G. MUNRO

PRINCETON, NEW JERSEY

PRINCETON UNIVERSITY PRESS

42017

Copyright © 1964 by Princeton University Press
All Rights Reserved
L. C. Card: 63-18647
ISBN 0-691-04518-6

Second Printing, 1968
Third Printing, 1972

Printed in the United States of America
by Princeton University Press, Princeton, New Jersey

To My Wife

Preface

▶ The problems that confronted the United States in the Caribbean in the first two decades of the twentieth century were much like the problems that confront us there today. Disorder and economic backwardness in some of the West Indian and Central American republics were a standing invitation to imperialistic ventures by non-American powers and thus a danger to the security of the United States. The American government felt that it had to help its neighbors to do away with the conditions that exposed them to foreign intervention, but its efforts had unfortunate results. By 1921, after we had ourselves intervened by force in several Caribbean countries, and were ruling two of them under military occupation, we had aroused a resentment and fear throughout Latin America which still affects our relations with other American states.

The purpose of this study is to show how this happened and why it happened; how it came about, for example, that such a high-minded statesman as Woodrow Wilson felt compelled to order the military occupation of Haiti and the Dominican Republic, with all of the unhappy consequences that followed. The story can be understood only if it is told in what may seem tedious detail, for it was often the little incidents, the day-by-day developments, that gradually created a situation where radical action seemed the only solution. If we try to see how that situation appeared to the officials responsible for United States policy, and to see what considerations influenced their discussions of actions to be taken, we shall better understand some actions that would otherwise seem hard to justify. Motives are of course hard to determine, but the State Department's records reveal a rather definite, gradually evolving pattern of policy that did not change greatly when new individuals assumed responsibility or even when a different political party took control.

A study of this experience should be of some value at a time when we face a far more dangerous situation in the Caribbean than we did in 1900. We are acutely aware today of the importance of promoting stable, democratic government and improving living condi-

vii

tions in the region in order to check the further advance of communism, but we still seem uncertain about the best way to use the influence and the power of the United States to attain these purposes. We can at least perhaps profit from the lessons of history to avoid some of the mistakes that were made a half-century ago.

I have limited this study to the period between 1900 and 1921 because it was during that period that what might be called the intervention policy developed. After 1921 there was no abrupt reversal of the effort to improve conditions in the Caribbean, but there was definitely less disposition to seek control of the internal affairs of unstable Caribbean states. The change in policy was none the less real because the continued occupation of Haiti and the Nicaraguan intervention in 1927 tended to obscure the fact that it was taking place.

Since the purpose is to show how the intervention policy developed, and why the American government acted as it did, most of the material is drawn from the State Department's records in the National Archives and the papers of the Presidents in the Library of Congress. I have not attempted to write a general history of American relations with the Caribbean. Except for a brief account of the way in which the Republic of Panama became independent—an account that seemed necessary to give an adequate picture of Theodore Roosevelt's policy—there is no discussion of relations between it and the United States. These have been dealt with by other authors, and they involve many special problems arising from the existence of the Canal. I have also avoided any extended discussion of other matters, such as efforts to settle boundary disputes, which would have a place in a comprehensive study of Caribbean diplomacy but would have a less direct bearing on the development of the intervention policy.

To some extent, study of the written record has been illuminated by my own experience. As a student in Central America between 1914 and 1916, and later as an officer in the State Department, I knew many of the American officials and many of the Caribbean statesmen who figure in the story. In the State Department I had a minor role in the formulation of policy in the West Indies and Central America after 1919 and thus had an opportunity to learn something about the considerations that affected policy.

PREFACE

Leaves of absence and financial aid from Princeton University made possible much of the research on which the study is based, and the generous and competent assistance of the Diplomatic, Legal and Fiscal Branch of the National Archives made the research pleasant and profitable. I am also indebted to Mrs. Elizabeth Sangston, who helped me over the years with the preparation of the manuscript, and most especially to my wife, for her encouragement and sympathy and for her help in the dreary tasks of typing and proofreading.

D. G. M.

Waquoit, Massachusetts,
November 1, 1963.

Contents

	Preface	vii
1.	The Background	3
2.	Cuba and Panama, 1901–1905	24
3.	The Genesis of the Roosevelt Corollary	65
4.	Elihu Root's Policy	112
5.	Dollar Diplomacy and Intervention in Nicaragua, 1909–1913	160
6.	Dollar Diplomacy Elsewhere in the Caribbean	217
7.	The Military Occupation of the Dominican Republic	269
8.	Intervention in Haiti	326
9.	Wilsonian Dollar Diplomacy in Nicaragua	388
10.	Non-Recognition of Revolutionary Governments	426
11.	Relations with Cuba, 1909–1921	469
12.	Intervention and Dollar Diplomacy in Retrospect	530
	Index	547

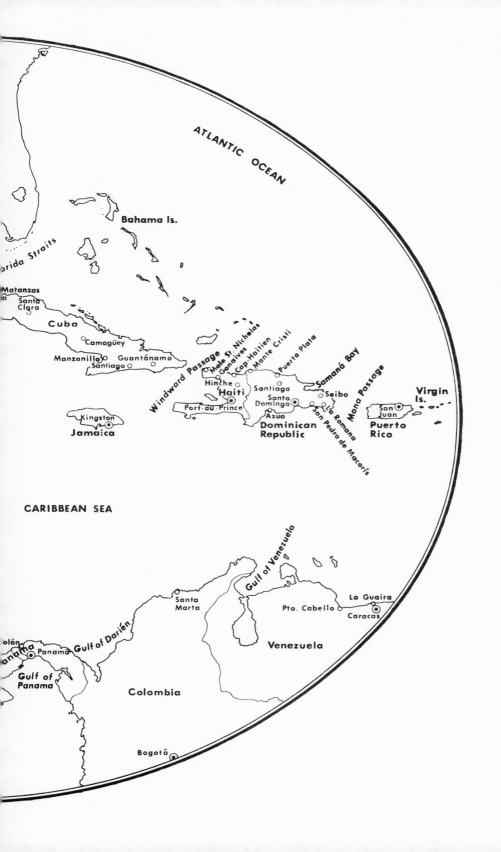

◄ 1 ►

The Background

The Caribbean Before 1900

🖌 The Caribbean was a theater of conflict between rival imperialisms long before the United States became independent. By the end of the sixteenth century, foreign smugglers and pirates, frequently supported by their own governments, were challenging Spain's claim to exclusive possession of America. Early in the seventeenth century interlopers were settling in the smaller islands and on parts of the mainland which the Spanish government had not effectively occupied. Tobacco, sugar, and illegal trade with the Spanish colonies soon made many of these settlements rich. They were coveted prizes in the frequent European wars between 1701 and 1815, and some of them changed hands several times. Spain, Britain, France, Holland, Sweden, and Denmark continued to hold colonies in the West Indies after the North American and Spanish American Wars for independence.

In the first decades of the nineteenth century, soil exhaustion and the abolition of slavery in the British and French possessions made most of these colonies less prosperous. European interest in the region declined. This was fortunate from the standpoint of the United States, for a continuance of the contest for territory and trade could not but have been dangerous to American security. The Monroe Doctrine—the assertion that no foreign government must be permitted to acquire new possessions in the Caribbean—was an expression of the American government's determination that the contest should not recommence.

There were occasions during the nineteenth century when it seemed possible that the territorial ambitions of other powers, or its own desire for expansion, would involve the United States in a conflict in the Caribbean. As Spain's internal troubles weakened her hold on Cuba, Britain and France were suspected of designs on the island, and there were North American statesmen who thought that it ought to become part of the United States. In 1854, in fact, in the "Ostend Manifesto" the three principal diplomatic representatives of the United States in Europe publicly advised their government

3

either to buy Cuba or to take it by force—a recommendation that was not accepted in Washington. The United States remained neutral during the unsuccessful ten-year revolt in Cuba between 1868 and 1878.

It seemed possible also that the Dominican Republic might pass into the control of another power. The Dominicans revolted against Spain in 1821, but they were immediately conquered by Haiti and were ruled by their French-speaking neighbors for twenty-two years. When they finally obtained their independence, they were so oppressed by fear of further Haitian invasions that many of their leaders looked to a European protectorate as a preferable alternative. Spain did reannex her former colony in 1861, but withdrew four years later after a bloody struggle with rebels in the interior. Soon afterward, the Dominican government sought annexation to the United States. President Grant supported the idea, but the annexation treaty was defeated in the United States Senate.

In Central America the United States was involved in a prolonged diplomatic controversy with Great Britain after 1848, when British agents took control of Greytown, at the mouth of the San Juan River, with the obvious purpose of controlling any transisthmian canal that might be built in Nicaragua. The British government was finally persuaded to withdraw from the town and from a few other points that it had occupied along the Central American coast, and the Clayton-Bulwer Treaty, signed in 1850, provided that neither the United States nor Great Britain would attempt to control any part of Central America or any canal that might be built there.

The Canal and the Monroe Doctrine

American Secretaries of State nevertheless showed only a sporadic interest in the affairs of the Caribbean states during the nineteenth century. The situation changed after the United States assumed responsibility for the future of Cuba and Puerto Rico and after some American statesmen began to think about the strategic problems that would arise from the decision to build an isthmian canal. President Roosevelt told the Congress in 1902: "The events following the war with Spain and the prospective building of the Isthmian Canal render it certain that we must take in the future a far greater interest than hitherto in what happens throughout the West Indies, Central

America, and the adjacent coasts and waters." [1] Aside from its commercial value, the canal would vastly increase the efficiency of the American navy, and it was of vital importance that no hostile power should be permitted to control its approaches.

The maintenance of the Monroe Doctrine in the Caribbean, however, promised to be not only more necessary but more difficult when the West Indian and Central American states found themselves close to one of the world's great trade routes. As Captain Alfred Mahan pointed out in 1890, the Caribbean, after the building of the canal, would no longer be a "comparatively deserted nook of the ocean," but a region in which all of the great powers would have a strategic interest. The fact that several positions of great strategic importance were in the hands of weak and unstable Caribbean governments seemed to Mahan a danger to the security of the United States. [2] This danger still existed after the Spanish American War did away with the always rather remote possibility that Spain might cede Cuba or Puerto Rico to another power. The existing British, French, and Dutch colonies gave little cause for apprehension, but it was possible that some less friendly government might endeavor to obtain a foothold in the Caribbean, if only to place itself on an equal footing with powers that already had West Indian bases. The recent history of Africa and China showed what might happen if the region became the scene of a contest for bases and spheres of influence.

The idea of such a contest seemed less far-fetched in 1900 than it would today. The Monroe Doctrine was still looked upon by Europe as an impertinence, and it was not clear that the United States would be able to maintain it against a challenge by another first-rate power. Though it was not probable that any European government would deliberately set out to conquer a Caribbean state, it was always possible that the chronic disorder and financial irresponsibility that prevailed in some of the West Indian and Central American republics would offer the pretext, or at least the occasion, for an intervention that would jeopardize a country's independence. At the turn of the century several of the great powers were beginning to show

[1] Special Message on Cuban Reciprocity, June 13, 1902, Richardson, *Messages and Papers of the Presidents* (Washington, D.C., 1896–1899), Vol. x, p. 458.
[2] Mahan, *The Interest of America in Sea Power* (Boston, 1897), p. 12.

an increased interest in foreign trade and investment and a disposition to be more aggressive in the protection of their nationals in less advanced countries. This was especially true of Germany and Italy, which had only recently achieved great power status. With increasing frequency, European warships appeared at Caribbean ports to protect foreigners in time of civil war or to compel the settlement of debts and claims. Such acts would inevitably influence the course of internal political affairs and could conceivably lead to the establishment of a more permanent political influence.

The country that was most often suspected of a disposition to challenge the Monroe Doctrine was Germany. Some German military leaders were openly unfriendly to the United States, and manifestations of this feeling during the Spanish American War had angered American public opinion. In the three years that immediately followed the war, there was much discussion of reported German designs to acquire territory or naval bases in Latin America. In 1901, when German warships were reported to be taking soundings around Margarita Island, off the Venezuelan coast, the United States remonstrated and was assured that the German government did not plan to acquire the island or any other port or coaling station in that part of the world. In 1902 it was suspected, perhaps mistakenly, that German intrigues prevented Denmark from ratifying a treaty for the sale of the Danish West Indies to the United States. There were persistent though apparently unfounded rumors of German intrigues to sabotage the ill-fated canal treaty with Colombia in 1902–1903,[3] and from time to time there was discussion in the American press of supposed German designs in southern Brazil.[4] Both Elihu Root and Theodore Roosevelt envisaged the possibility of a war with Germany in defense of the Monroe Doctrine,[5] and John Hay's hatred of the Kaiser seems to have been almost an obsession.[6]

The German navy would undoubtedly have been glad to acquire

---

[3] Miner, *Fight for the Panama Route* (New York, 1940), p. 312.

[4] *Literary Digest*, Vol. xxiv (1902), p. 510; Vol. 26 (1903), p. 696.

[5] See Root's speech at the Grant anniversary dinner in New York, April 27, 1900, reported in the Literary Digest, Vol. xx, p. 56; and Roosevelt's letter of March 27, 1901, to Henry Cabot Lodge in *The Letters of Theodore Roosevelt, Selected and Edited by Elting T. Morrison* (Cambridge, Mass., 1951–1954), Vol. i, p. 485. This will be cited hereafter as *Letters*.

[6] See Roosevelt's comment in his letter of July 11, 1905, to H. C. Lodge, *Letters*, Vol. iv, p. 1271.

a naval base or coaling station in the West Indies, because coal-burning warships could not operate effectively in a region where supplies of fuel were not available. The ships that it kept in the Caribbean to "show the flag" and protect German interests could obtain supplies only through the courtesy of the United States or other governments, and they would have been at a hopeless disadvantage in case of war. The navy, however, was restrained by the Foreign Office from embarking on adventures that might have brought on a conflict with the United States, and there seems to have been little basis for the suspicion that the German government, as a government, had any serious idea of acquiring territory in the Western Hemisphere.[7] Roosevelt himself seems to have modified his views after his first years as President, and by 1905 he thought that he had been able to persuade the Kaiser that any effort to acquire territory in the Caribbean would mean immediate war with the United States.[8]

The policy that the United States adopted after 1904 under Roosevelt's Corollary to the Monroe Doctrine was not directed solely against Germany. Its purpose was to avert intervention by any foreign power that might feel impelled to act for the protection of its nationals and their interests. Such intervention, even by a government friendly to the United States, could easily lead to a permanent control that would be repugnant to the Monroe Doctrine. It was impracticable, and at the time it would have seemed almost indecent, to insist that other governments should not use force to compel respect for what they considered their rights; but intervention could be averted if the Caribbean states could attain more stable governments and could pay their debts. It was this idea, made explicit in the Roosevelt Corollary, that shaped the policy of the United States in the Caribbean during the administrations of Theodore Roosevelt and Taft and Wilson.

Political Life in the Caribbean Republics

To understand the problems that faced Roosevelt and his successors, one must know something about conditions in the Caribbean states in the first years of the century. In 1900, few of the

[7] For a discussion of this matter, see Vagts, *Deutschland und die Vereinigten Staaten* (New York, c. 1935).
[8] Letter to Cecil Spring Rice, Nov. 1, 1905, *Letters*, Vol. v, p. 63.

Central American and West Indian republics had achieved the relative stability and economic prosperity that many of their South American neighbors were beginning to enjoy. They were small countries with scanty resources. Estimates of their population are unreliable, but Guatemala, the most populous, was thought to have somewhat less than 1,600,000 inhabitants in 1900. Cuba had about the same number. None of the others, except perhaps Haiti, had so many as one million, and Nicaragua, Honduras, Costa Rica, and Panama had considerably less than half a million. There had been some material progress in the quarter-century before 1900, when foreigners had begun to invest in a small way in railroads and mines and plantations, but in general the Caribbean area was one of the most backward parts of the Western Hemisphere.

The chief cause of backwardness was the continual internal strife that had discouraged economic activities of all sorts. Inherited political traditions, combined with the poverty and ignorance of the masses of the people, made it difficult to attain stable government under the republican constitutions adopted at the time of independence. In colonial times, the inhabitants had been ruled autocratically by officials sent from Europe and had had no opportunity to participate in governmental affairs. After independence, it had been difficult for them to operate unfamiliar institutions borrowed from people who had had centuries of experience in self government.

In most of the Caribbean republics, political affairs were dominated by a relatively few families who owned most of the large farms and cattle ranches. The members of this upper class, with their servants and dependents, lived a rather simple life in the towns and larger villages, without many of the amenities that their descendents enjoy today. Usually they left the actual management of their properties to overseers. Since their estates rarely produced large incomes, even in years when crops and cattle were not destroyed by revolutionary armies, few of them were wealthy. Many of the men practiced law or medicine, but these professions were overcrowded and usually unremunerative.

The upper class was avidly interested in politics because government employment did offer opportunities for profit as well as the prestige of holding office. As the only educated people in the community, and the only group that understood something of the complexities of public affairs, the members of the principal families held most of the positions in the government even when military leaders from other social groups occupied the presidency. In such a community, personal and family ties and private enmities played an important role in political life. Where the number of educated people was so small, a native leader or an unusually able foreign diplomat, or a small group that knew what it wanted, could have an extraordinary influence.

There was practically no middle class between the aristocracy and the illiterate and poverty-stricken masses. The great majority of the people were peasants, of Indian or Negro descent in some countries and of mixed blood in others. Most of these lived in small villages where the only contact with the outside world was in many cases by a journey of several days on foot or horseback over bad trails, and where, more likely than not, there was neither a school nor a priest. Their houses were dirt-floored, one- or two-room shacks, with little or no furniture. Some of them worked for a few cents a day on the farms and ranches of the upper class; others planted *milpas*—small clearings in the forest where a patch of corn could be grown for a few years before the land was exhausted. In Guatemala and a few other sections of Central America, the majority of the peasants were full-blooded Indians, who were practically slaves under a peonage system. Elsewhere the peasants were frequently oppressed and exploited by landowners and officials. The Indians, and the Negro peasants in Haiti, showed no interest in politics, but this was less true of the people of mixed blood in such countries as Nicaragua, Honduras, and Santo Domingo. There, the country people were often enthusiastic adherents of one of the parties that contended for power, and the monotony and poverty of their daily lives made them the more responsive to appeals to take up arms when the leaders appealed to them.

The political parties, though they might call themselves "conservatives" and "liberals," rarely represented any great differences over questions of policy. The Church, except perhaps in Guatemala, never had the wealth and power that made its relation to the government an issue in several of the larger Latin American countries, and there was rarely any clear-cut cleavage on other political or social problems. The groups that contended for control of the government were usually factions that supported a popular leader, and they were often called by the leader's name. A politician's importance depended on the number of adherents who were ready if necessary to take up arms to support him, and this was true whether he was a white aristocrat, popular among his fellow townsmen or among the people of the region where he had his estates, or an illiterate soldier who had attained an ascendency over his equally ignorant companions. When the leader's influence was particularly strong in one city or province it was reinforced by the traditional local rivalries that were one of the chief causes of civil strife.

Conflicts between rival leaders were normally settled by the use of force. Constitutional forms were preserved by holding elections at the end of each presidential term or after a successful revolution, but the party in power always won. The inexperience of the voters and the lack of any tradition of self-government made it easy for the group in power to control the electoral process, and leaders who seized power by force could see no reason to permit their opponents to oust them simply by obtaining a majority of the voters. Often the opposition party did not even contest the election, and, when it did, intimidation and fraud assured its defeat.

A political group could keep control of the administration only so long as it could prevent the opposition from waging a successful civil war or from inducing a part of the army to stage a *golpe de cuartel,* or military mutiny. Sometimes, to maintain an appearance of constitutional government, the presidency was passed from hand to hand among a group of leaders. More often, perhaps, the principal chief of the dominant group had himself reelected from term to term, or kept control by giving the presidency to a henchman who was little more than a figurehead. In either case, the man who controlled the army ruled the country, deciding who was to sit in Congress and giving orders to the courts in any case where political considerations were involved. If a leader were sufficiently ambitious and ruthless, he could maintain a despotic control over the country and its people for a long period.

If the president was a ruler of the more brutal type, he had his chief opponents shot or driven into exile, and he systematically persecuted their followers. Even if he wished to rule in a more civilized way, he could not usually afford to permit any overt political activity or any freedom of the press. He knew that political opposition could only have revolution as its goal, and that the toleration of public criticism would be regarded as a sign of weakness which could cost him the support of politicians and army officers who wanted above all to be on the winning side.

At the first sign of overt resistance, the principal members of the opposition party would be imprisoned or exiled. Even when there was no immediate threat of civil war, the lot of the opposition leaders was not a happy one. Lawyers who belonged to the wrong party found it difficult to get fair decisions from the courts, and planters were likely to have their workers seized for service in the army. The result was that the party out of power had to revolt in order to escape an intolerable situation, and it too often resorted to savage reprisals when it came into power. The cruelties practiced on political enemies engendered factional hatreds which were passed on from father to son and which helped to keep the revolutionary spirit alive.

Starting a revolution was a simple matter. In such small countries, a few hundred men were a formidable force. If the leaders did not have rifles that had been hidden since the last civil war, they could usually obtain them from foreign merchants willing to gamble on their success, or from the government of a neighboring country. Both in Central America and in Española, the governments continually interfered in one another's affairs in this way, partly because each ruler felt that he himself would be safer if a president indebted to him was in power in a nearby state. Frequently local commanders within the country could be induced by bribery or promises of preferment to join the revolutionary movement. An uprising might achieve important successes before the government could interfere because there were no roads for the rapid transport of troops. It was not necessary for the insurgents to be well trained or well equipped because the government had no well trained or equipped troops with which to oppose it.

The standing armies, made up of barefooted soldiers, recruited usually against their will from the most ignorant strata of the population and officered by men who had little or no professional training, were rarely formidable forces. Nevertheless, with revolution an ever-present possibility, the military establishment was the most important branch of the government. There were garrisons throughout the country, in each important town and village, and in the rural districts the *comandante*, though he might command only six or eight soldiers, was a petty despot, charged with police as well as military duties. In larger political subdivisions, civil and military jurisdiction were also combined in one official, so that the whole country was in fact under military rule. The army almost always consumed by far the largest part of the public revenue. All officers, from the Minister of War to the local *comandante*, expected to supplement their salaries by graft in the buying of supplies or by collecting money for the pay of non-existent soldiers, and important generals often demanded and received outright grants from the treasury as the price of continued loyalty. Even the most powerful dictators had to submit to this sort of blackmail because they could not hope to remain in office without military support.

Heavy military expenditures, and the graft that pervaded all other departments of the administration, usually kept the governments poor, even at times when internal disorders did not curtail their revenues. It was not unusual for civilian employees to go unpaid for months at a time, and frequently there was not even money to pay the soldiers. Very rarely were funds available for schools or road-building. Much of the money which the governments should have received was lost through smuggling and corruption in the custom-houses, which were the principal source of revenue.

Diplomatic Claims and Intervention

Revolution and misgovernment inevitably affected the Europeans and North Americans who were going to the Caribbean in small but increasing numbers in the latter part of the nineteenth century. Even in time of peace, foreigners were occasionally mistreated or despoiled by local officials or were unable to obtain justice in the courts. In time of war, they were exposed to physical danger, as the natives were, and their properties were sometimes looted or destroyed. Revolutionary governments frequently annulled concessions or repudiated other contracts made with their predecessors, and merchants who supplied goods to the governments were unable to obtain payment. Foreigners who suffered such injuries, or feared that they would be injured, were quick to appeal to their own governments for protection. "It is sometimes suggested," John Bassett

Moore wrote in 1905, "that, when citizens of a country go abroad and engage in business, they must be held to assume all the risks of disorder and injury in the country to which they go, and can look to the local authorities only, no matter how inefficient or malevolent they may be, for protection; but it suffices to say that no respectable government acts on any such theory." [9] When foreigners were murdered or mistreated, heavy punitive damages were demanded, and the demand was backed up, if necessary, by a show of force. Even demands for the adjustment of contract debts were sometimes pressed in the same way. Frequently, in fact, European or North American warships were sent to ports where there was disorder or a threat of disorder before any actual injury to foreigners had occurred, and occasionally they landed forces to patrol the streets or set up a neutral zone for the protection of noncombatants. Foreign governments were the more ready to take action of this sort in the Caribbean because an intervention in a small, weak state involved little risk or expense.

The collection of pecuniary claims by force often led to gross injustice. Some foreigners who did business in the Caribbean found it easy to take advantage of officials whose inexperience in the workings of international finance made it difficult for them to distinguish between sound and unsound proposals, and whose judgment could often be influenced by bribery or promises of participation in future profits. Goods were frequently sold to the local governments at outrageous prices, and unconscionable terms were exacted for small loans to meet urgent necessities. Concessions obtained through misrepresentation or corruption gave the promoters extraordinary advantages in grants of public property, monopolistic privileges, and exemptions from taxation. It was of course transactions of this type that were most likely to be repudiated when there was a change of government. It was often difficult to judge whether a given contract was so vitiated in its origin or so outrageous in its provisions as to make it unworthy of diplomatic support, because the evidence was apt to be unreliable and colored by partisan prejudice, and benefits obtained by the foreigner always had to be set off against the risks involved. Far too frequently, however, foreign governments supported claims without inquiring into the character and conduct

[9] *The Collected Papers of John Bassett Moore* (New Haven, 1944), Vol. III, p. 185.

of the claimants and without considering whether their demands might not be fraudulent or exaggerated. They tended to ignore considerations of fair play in their determination to teach the local authorities that they must respect their nationals simply because they were Germans, Italians, or Frenchmen.

An extreme example of this attitude was the Luders affair in Haiti in 1897. Luders, the son of a German and a Haitian woman, was sentenced to a month's imprisonment for allegedly assaulting a policeman who had entered his livery stable to arrest a Haitian employee. When he appealed the sentence, a Haitian court increased the term to one year and added a fine of $500. Through the good offices of the American Minister he was almost immediately released and permitted to leave Haiti, but the German government refused a proposal to arbitrate and demanded an indemnity of $20,000. The Haitian government agreed to pay this amount, but before it could raise the money two German warships arrived at Port au Prince and threatened to shell the public buildings and forts if $30,000 were not paid before noon of the same day. The money was hastily obtained from merchants in the town, and the Haitian government was compelled to apologize and to permit Luders to return.[10]

Aside from claims for injuries to individual foreigners, many of the Caribbean governments were perennially in default on bonds that had been sold in European markets many years earlier, usually on terms that were extremely disadvantageous to the borrowing state. In some cases the original loans had been scandalous affairs: the bankers who floated them had misappropriated part of the proceeds and used some of the rest to keep up interest payments while they unloaded more bonds on the investing public. Much of the money that the borrowing government did receive was usually dissipated in graft. When the loans went into default, however, those who suffered were not the bankers but investors who had bought the bonds in reliance on the credit of the borrowing government. The bondholders' governments consequently felt that they had a right to demand at least a partial settlement of the debts, even in cases where the character of the original transaction and the excessive amount of interest involved made it impossible to expect payment

[10] *Moore's Digest of International Law* (Washington, 1906), Vol. vi, p. 474. Vagts, *Deutschland und die Vereinigten Staaten*, Vol. ii, pp. 708ff.

in full. The use of force to collect on bonds was considered somewhat less respectable than intervention to collect claims based on torts, but the defaults were nevertheless dangerous because the bonds were usually secured by the customs revenues and other specific pledges that might conceivably be enforced by the seizure of ports or other military action.

The United States, like other powers, regarded the protection of its citizens abroad as a duty, but in practice it had been less aggressive than some of the European countries in exacting reparation for outrages and compelling the payment of claims. Americans living in backward countries bitterly criticized their government's seeming indifference to their welfare and often asserted that they had to pretend to be English if they wished local officials to respect their rights.[11] Claims for despoliation and personal injury were presented through diplomatic channels, after careful and sometimes protracted consideration by the legal officers of the State Department, and if no agreement could be reached for their payment the State Department usually eventually urged an arbitration. Many years might pass before a settlement was reached.[12] When claims arose from the violation of contracts, the State Department usually confined its interposition to an offer of diplomatic good offices. Roosevelt, in his message to Congress in 1905, said that the United States did not collect contract debts by force and wished that other governments would adopt the same point of view. Sometimes, however, the distinction between the formal espousal of a claim and the exercise of good offices seemed theoretical, for claims arising from contracts occasionally led to bitter diplomatic conflicts.

Under Theodore Roosevelt and his successors, the United States showed somewhat more concern for its citizens abroad. A desire to make the Caribbean safer for Americans and their interests and to encourage trade and investment there was one of the considera-

[11] This idea appears frequently in the literature of the period. For some characteristic expressions of it see the correspondence in connection with the Nicaraguan revolution of 1909, State Department file, Numerical Case 6369.

[12] The Solicitor of the State Department stated in October 1910 (State Department Decimal File 817.00/1432a), that the United States then had over 125 unliquidated claims against Nicaragua, some going back almost 100 years and many 50 years old. One reason, however, for the failure to press these was the United States' refusal to arbitrate Nicaragua's claims against the American government arising from Walker's expeditions and the bombardment of Greytown by an American warship in the 1850's.

tions that made the United States interested in the establishment of stable government in the area. It was a minor consideration, as compared with the desire to avert the danger that disorder would invite European intervention, but there were several cases where disputes involving American companies had an influence, and sometimes an unfortunate influence, on the American government's policy.

American Investments

American investments in the Caribbean were increasing considerably during the first two decades of the twentieth century. Cuba's great exports of sugar had been an important factor in world trade before her war for independence, and after 1900 they made her the wealthiest of the Caribbean states. At the time of the Spanish American War, American investments in the island were estimated at $50,000,000. The amount of British and Spanish capital was then much greater, but the relative importance of the American stake in the island, and especially the participation of American interests in the all-important sugar industry, rapidly increased. By 1911 it was more than $200,000,000 and by 1920 more than $500,000,000.[13] British investments, in 1918, were thought to total about $230,000,000.[14] Naturally concern for a vast amount of property and for the personal safety of the thousands of Americans in the island influenced the policy of the United States government, especially when revolutionary disturbances threatened them.

At the turn of the century, American investments in other parts of the Caribbean were relatively insignificant. It is difficult to find reliable estimates or even guesses as to the amount. It seems clear that European investments, while also small, were much greater. The bonds of the irregularly serviced foreign debts were held in England or on the continent of Europe, and British money had financed most of the railroads and many of the mining enterprises. Europeans or Asiatics controlled most of the wholesale and retail trade. The amount of American capital increased between 1900 and

[13] Jenks, *Our Cuban Colony* (New York, 1928), p. 165. R. W. Dunn, *American Foreign Investments* (New York, 1926), p. 120.

[14] Halsey, *Investments in Latin America and the British West Indies* (U.S. Dept. of Commerce, Special Agents Series, No. 169, Washington, 1918), p. 20.

1920 but continued to be far smaller than the amount invested in Cuba.

The largest investments in the island of Española were those of the San Domingo Improvement Company of New York, which for some years had carried on varied and sometimes questionable financial operations in the Dominican Republic. This concern was building railways and managing the National Bank, and it had distributed a large amount of Dominican government bonds in Europe, in a series of refunding operations. We shall have occasion to discuss its history in a later chapter. The Clyde Line was operating a steamship service to Dominican ports, under a monopolistic concession that gave rise to much controversy; and there was some American capital in the sugar industry. There was practically no American investment in Haiti until the National City Bank of New York and its associates began to finance railroad construction and bought a small amount of stock in the National Bank in 1910, almost immediately involving themselves and the American government in controversies with the Haitian government which took on an importance out of all proportion to the amount of money at stake.

In Central America, by far the most important American enterprise was the United Fruit Company, which was incorporated in 1899 to take over the West Indian banana trade of the Boston Fruit Company and the Central American plantations of Minor C. Keith.[15] Keith started to plant bananas in Costa Rica in 1872, to provide freight for the railway line that he was building from San José to the east coast, and he later established plantations in the western part of what is now Panama, near Santa Marta in Colombia, and on the east coast of Nicaragua. After the creation of the United Fruit Company, he continued until 1921 to manage its Central American interests and at the same time to press forward with his ambition to bring the railways of Central America into one system that would eventually connect all of the five republics. He seems to have been

[15] There are a number of books on the United Fruit Company, among them F. U. Adams, *Conquest of the Tropics* (New York, 1914), written from the Company's point of view; C. D. Kepner, Jr., and J. H. Soothill, *The Banana Empire* (New York, 1935), which is more critical; C. D. Kepner, Jr., *Social Aspects of the Banana Industry* (New York, 1936); and Stacey May and Galo Plaza, *The United Fruit Company in Latin America*, (National Planning Association, 1958).

more interested in railway building than in banana growing, but the two interests were not incompatible. The control of the railways not only assured prompt shipment of fruit from the farms to the seaports but also enabled the Fruit Company to divert freight to ports served by its own steamers. All of the railways in the eastern part of Costa Rica were operated by the Fruit Company after 1905, and in 1904 Keith obtained a contract to complete the partially built railroad between the capital of Guatemala and Puerto Barrios on the north coast. In 1912 the International Railways of Central America was formed to take over this line and the lines in southern and western Guatemala which had been operated by another North American company. In the same year the new company took over a short line in El Salvador which it later extended and connected with its Guatemalan system.[16]

The United Fruit Company meanwhile extended its banana plantations, moving into Guatemala in 1906, and into Honduras, where bananas had long been an important export, in 1912. By 1913, it had more than 100,000 acres under cultivation in Costa Rica, Guatemala, and Honduras and nearly 40,000 in Panama. Its large fleet of steamers carried passengers and general freight as well as fruit. Its total assets, which included one of the larger sugar properties in Cuba and banana plantations in Colombia and Jamaica as well as in Central America, increased from $17,000,000 in 1900 to more than $82,000,000 in 1913.[17] In the latter year, it shipped 60 percent of the bananas imported into the United States.

The United Fruit Company also seems to have had a substantial amount of control over the other companies that exported bananas from Central America. In the first years of the century it owned a considerable part of the stock of the Bluefields Fruit and Steamship Company in Nicaragua, and it helped to organize and finance Vaccaro Brothers and Company and the Hubbard-Zemurray Steamship Company, which were the principal banana producers in Honduras before the United Fruit Company started its own plantations in that

[16] For data on the Central American railroads see W. Rodney Long, *Railways of Central America and the West Indies* (U. S. Dept. of Commerce, Trade Promotion Series No. 5, Washington, 1925).

[17] The figures in this paragraph are from Adams, *Conquest of the Tropics*, pp. 297 and 332.

country. In 1913 the president of the United Fruit Company testified that his firm had sold its half interest in Vaccaro Brothers and its 60-percent interest in the Hubbard-Zemurray Company, but that it still maintained the friendliest relations with its former subsidiaries.[18] One factor that tended to discourage any real competition in the banana trade was the United Fruit Company's ownership of the Fruit Despatch Company, which virtually monopolized the transportation of bananas within the United States.

The fruit companies operated in districts where there had been few inhabitants before they arrived, and they obtained much of their labor by importing British West Indians. The communities that thus grew up on the Atlantic Coast of Central America were different in race and language and hardly seemed a part of the republics in which they were situated. The companies naturally dominated their economic life. The foreign firms paid good wages, as compared with those paid in the interior, and attempted to control the tropical diseases that had hitherto discouraged settlement in the coastal jungles. They also made it possible for many private planters to grow bananas in areas near their railroad lines. The planters, however, had to sell their product to the Company, and often complained that they were unfairly treated when market conditions made the Company less anxious to take their fruit.

The United Fruit Company maintained lobbyists in some of the Central American capitals to help obtain governmental favors or to head off unacceptable legislation, and it had friends and enemies among the native politicians. Occasionally, as we shall see, the Company or one of its associates was accused of helping a revolution. In general, however, it exercised less influence in internal political affairs than many observers thought. It had very little influence on the policy of the United States government. Secretary Root, on one occasion, expressed an interest in Keith's railroad projects, but in general the Fruit Company seems to have systematically refrained from asking diplomatic support and from giving American diplomats in Central America an occasion to interest themselves in its affairs.

---

[18] *Hearings before the Committee on the Merchant Marine and Fisheries, House of Representatives,* on H. Res. 587. January 7, 1913. Testimony of Andrew W. Preston, pp. 733ff. See also 63rd Cong., 2nd Sess. House Doc. 805, p. 193.

There were times during the Taft and Wilson administrations when its actions or reported actions aroused suspicion and resentment in the State Department.

Besides the banana plantations and the railways, there were small American-owned banks in Guatemala and El Salvador and American-owned mines in several parts of the isthmus. The largest was the Rosario mine in Honduras, which produced somewhat less than $1,000,000 worth of silver each year. Washington Valentine, who controlled this mine, also built a wharf at Puerto Cortés and for a time operated the short railroad line from that city into the interior. A number of North Americans, too, had come to the Isthmus as planters or merchants, especially on the Caribbean coasts of Honduras and Nicaragua, and several American companies were cutting hardwoods or exploiting other natural resources in this region. In 1911, however, it was estimated that there were less than 6,000 United States citizens living in the five Central American states.[19]

The State Department and the Foreign Service

In carrying out their policies in the Caribbean, Roosevelt and his successors had of course to work through the State Department and the Foreign Service. The State Department, though the volume of its work had been increasing rapidly in the past ten years, was still a small office, with only 63 clerks, in 1901.[20] Questions of policy were handled personally by the Secretary or one of the three assistant secretaries. All correspondence with embassies and legations in Washington and with American missions abroad was drafted in a Diplomatic Bureau, which had a chief, three divisional clerks, an assistant, six "typewriters," and a copyist.[21] There was no technical staff, except the Solicitor and the Assistant Solicitor, who advised on legal matters. There was no one whose duty it was to be specially informed about the problems of any given region or country until a Far Eastern Division was set up in 1908 and a Division of Latin American Affairs in 1909. In the latter year, Congress made

---

[19] E. B. Filsinger, *Immigration—a Central American Problem. Annals of the American Academy of Political and Social Science*, Vol. XXXVII, p. 745. Quoted by Callcott, in *The Caribbean Policy of the United States* (Baltimore, 1942), p. 291, f.n.

[20] *History of the Department of State* (Washington, 1901), pp. 4, 6.

[21] *Ibid.*, p. 47.

provision for eight "drafting officers," to help the higher officials of the Department in formulating and executing policy. Thereafter, the professional personnel was further increased, chiefly by assigning diplomatic officers to work in Washington. A number of economists were added to the staff in 1918–1919.

In the first years of the century, the lack of staff was to some extent made up for by the high quality of the officials who directed the Department's work. Elihu Root, especially, was a statesman of outstanding ability, and Alvee A. Adee, the Second Assistant Secretary of State from 1886 until 1924, was one of the great figures in the history of American diplomacy. Policy decisions made after personal study by men of this sort, or often by the President himself, were perhaps as likely to be sound as those reached by today's more complicated procedures. Certainly decisions could be made more promptly. It was hardly possible, however, for these high officials to give adequate personal attention to all of the questions that arose, particularly as the development of a new policy in the Caribbean led to the assumption of increasing responsibility in connection with the internal affairs of some of the Caribbean republics.

Much more serious was the deplorable state of the diplomatic and consular representation abroad. Richard Olney, in 1900, described the foreign service as "always inadequate and often positively detrimental to our interests." [22] Practically all chiefs of mission and consuls were appointed as a reward for political services. The extension of the civil service system had diminished the number of positions open to spoilsmen in other departments, so that the foreign service, as John Hay complained, had become "like the topmost rock which you sometimes see in old pictures of the Deluge. The pressure for a place in it is almost indescribable." [23] Few American ministers or ambassadors had any previous experience or any knowledge of the language and customs of the country to which they were accredited. The more important posts were filled by wealthy men, partly because salaries were pitifully inadequate and partly because one way to obtain an appointment was to contribute generously to a party campaign fund. The relatively unattractive posts in the Caribbean went to lesser politicians.

[22] *Atlantic Monthly*, Vol. LXXXV (1900), p. 289.
[23] Thayer, *Life of John Hay* (Boston, 1915), Vol. II, p. 193.

Roosevelt and Root attempted to change the "system, under which the Senators owned the places" [24] and to appoint better men to positions where competence was clearly required. During their tenure of office, and during the Taft administration, several of the abler men from the lower ranks were promoted to be ministers. Political considerations, however, continued to govern most appointments, and in 1913 the general level of competence was still low. In subsequent years it fell much lower, for Secretary Bryan frankly reverted to the practice of accepting the recommendations of the senators. Two or three of the men sent to the Caribbean by the Wilson administration were in their dotage and others had scandalous personal failings that made them worse than useless. A small minority were men of average, but rarely of outstanding ability. Parenthetically, it may be said that the situation did not improve greatly in the first years of the Republican administration after 1921. In countries where we had assumed heavy responsibilities by interfering in internal affairs, and where mistakes did infinite harm to our relations with all of Latin America, the United States was repeatedly represented by men who were untrained and lacking in judgment. Some who were notoriously unfit were allowed to remain at their posts for years after their unfitness had been demonstrated.

It would have been difficult to appoint trained men as chiefs of mission if the President had wished to do so, because of the situation in the lower ranks of the foreign service. Secretary Hay expressed a prevalent idea about the consular service when he wrote the President that a senator who had asserted the right to nominate a constituent for a vacancy "will require a little time to look through the Keely cures for a fitting candidate." [25] The character of the consular service was radically changed after 1906, when appointments and promotions were placed on a merit basis, but it was some years before the full effects of the reform made themselves felt.

The situation in the lower grades of the diplomatic service was somewhat different. The secretaries of embassy or legation were regarded as "career" diplomats, but low salaries made it virtually impossible for men without large private incomes to accept appointments. As late as 1920, the counselor of the Embassy at London, who

[24] Root to Seth Low, Dec. 24, 1906, (Root letter books, Library of Congress).
[25] Dennis, *Adventures in American Diplomacy* (New York, 1928), p. 521.

directed most of the work of the mission and who assumed charge in the absence of the Ambassador, was paid $3,000 a year, with practically no allowances. This represented but a small fraction of the expense which his position inevitably involved. Diplomatic appointments were thus reserved for young men who were able to serve the government at their own expense. Those who accepted them, moreover, had little hope of rising to higher rank unless they could count on strong political backing. Under these conditions the number of candidates seeking appointment was never very large, and many of those appointed did not stay in the service very long. Too often the secretary of legation or embassy was a spoiled young man, with little ambition but much interest in the purely social aspects of diplomatic life. It is rather surprising that several able men did enter the service under these conditions and did much to make the service the efficient organization that it became after its reorganization under the Rogers Act of 1924.

Neither the able nor the incompetent secretaries willingly went to posts in the Caribbean, where living conditions were uncomfortable and the social life was unattractive. Consequently, men were frequently sent to these posts as a punishment for misconduct or inefficiency. This practice had bad results when the Minister was absent and the secretary was left in charge.

Incompetent diplomatic representation was a major factor in many of the most unfortunate episodes in our Caribbean policy during the first decades of the century. The ablest Secretary of State cannot make wise decisions unless he has full, accurate information from his representatives in the field. He cannot get such information from diplomatic officers whose lack of experience and ignorance of the local language makes it impossible for them to understand what is going on. Furthermore, the wisest policy will be a failure if it has to be executed in the field by men without ability or judgment. This was especially true in dealing with the complicated questions that arose when the American government undertook to help bring about radical changes in the economic and political life of several countries where conditions were entirely different from those of the United States.

◂ 2 ▸

Cuba and Panama, 1901–1905

❧ In the first months after Theodore Roosevelt became President on September 14, 1901, two matters in Latin America demanded his attention. One was the situation in Cuba, where the United States, after two years of military occupation, was about to relinquish control of the island to the people. The other was to decide on the location of the projected isthmian canal and to make arrangements for its construction. Both of these matters must be discussed in any history of American policy in the Caribbean but since both have been rather fully dealt with by other historians, only a brief summary of what happened will be attempted here.[1]

Cuban Independence and the Platt Amendment

The principal decisions about Cuba had been made before Roosevelt took office. Of these, the most important was the decision to give the island independence. Many foreign observers had supposed that the United States would not relinquish a rich territory which was of such great strategic value. The McKinley administration, however, had been forced into the Spanish American War partly by public sympathy for the Cubans in their struggle for freedom. Congress, in the Joint Resolution of April 20, 1898, had declared that "the people of the island of Cuba are, and of right ought to be, free and independent." The pledge was honored even though some high officials in the American government wished that it had not been given, and even though the Spanish government, during the peace negotiations, expressed a wish that the United States would annex the island.[2] While the Military Government was completing

---

[1] There are many books that deal with the history of Cuba in this period, among them C. E. Chapman, *History of the Cuban Republic* (New York, 1927); W. F. Johnson, *History of Cuba* (New York, 1920); R. H. Fitzgibbon, *Cuba and the United States, 1900–1935* (Menasha, 1935); L. H. Jenks, *Our Cuban Colony;* and several important works in Spanish by Cuban historians. The most complete account of the events preceding the independence of Panama is D. C. Miner, *The Fight for the Panama Route*. Another excellent study is T. R. Favell, "The Antecedents of Panama's Separation from Colombia" (Ph.D. thesis, the Fletcher School of Law and Diplomacy.)

[2] Spain, *Ministerio de Estado. Spanish Diplomatic Correspondence and Documents* (translation), Washington, 1905, p. 209.

its work of reconstruction, under the direction of General Leonard Wood, the Cubans were asked to elect a convention to draw up a constitution for the new republic.

In freeing Cuba, however, the American government felt that it must have some arrangement that would give it a right to step in if the Cubans failed to maintain a stable and solvent government. The island's strategic importance made it imperative that there should be no excuse for other powers to interfere in the new republic's internal affairs. Secretary of War Root, who was chiefly responsible for American policy in Cuba, said later that suspicion of Germany was an important consideration in the decision to insist on the Platt Amendment. Root also thought that the United States had a moral obligation to Spain, arising from its promise, in the treaty of peace, to "advise" any government that might be set up in Cuba to afford due protection to Spanish interests. Many Spanish subjects remained in the island and owned properties and business enterprises there, and Root, when he visited Cuba, had been impressed by their fear of mistreatment at the hands of an independent government. Root seems to have felt little apprehension about the possible effects of independence on American interests in the island, and concern for their safety does not seem to have played an important part in determining the policy that the United States followed.[3]

The arrangement which the United States desired was embodied in an amendment proposed by Senator Platt to the Army Appropriation Bill, which was signed March 2, 1901. Congress stipulated that the occupation should not be withdrawn from Cuba until the provisions of this amendment had been incorporated in the Cuban constitution and until there was assurance that they would be incorporated in a permanent treaty with the United States. Cuba must agree never to enter into a treaty with a foreign power that might impair her independence nor to permit any foreign power to obtain "lodgement in or control over" any portion of her territory, nor to contract debts beyond her capacity to pay. Article III of the amendment gave the United States the right to intervene for the preservation of Cuban independence and for the maintenance of a govern-

---

[3] For an authoritative discussion of Root's attitude toward the Platt Amendment, see Jessup, *Elihu Root* (New York, 1938), Vol. I, pp. 313–315.

ment adequate for the protection of life, property, and individual liberty. Other articles provided for the establishment of American naval stations in the island, for the later determination of the status of the Isle of Pines, and for the continuation of the sanitation program inaugurated by the Military Government. The matter of sanitation was important because yellow fever, which had been endemic in Habana, had repeatedly been carried from there to North American ports, where it had caused much loss of life."

The Cuban constitutional convention was reluctant to agree on an arrangement that seemed to impair the new republic's independence. There was opposition especially to the provisions for American intervention and for naval bases. Root attempted to reassure the delegates by authorizing the Military Governor to state officially that the intervention described in Article III was "not synonymous with intermeddling or interference with the affairs of the Cuban Government but the formal action of the Government of the United States, based upon just and substantial grounds, for the preservation of Cuban independence and the maintenance of a government adequate for the protection of life, property, and individual liberty and adequate for discharging the obligations with respect to Cuba imposed by the Treaty of Paris on the United States." [4]

Later, in discussion at Washington with a delegation from the convention, Root emphasized the fact that the main purpose of the amendment was to preserve, not to impair, Cuba's independence; and he was quoted as saying that intervention would occur only to prevent a foreign attack or when a veritable state of anarchy existed within the republic. The naval stations were to be established solely to aid in the defense of both countries and not to serve as observation points or bases for interference in Cuba's internal affairs. The Secretary's arguments were reinforced by a letter from Senator Platt stating that the amendment had been carefully worded to avoid any possible idea that it would establish a protectorate or otherwise impair Cuba's sovereignty and independence. Unfortunately, Root made no record of these conversations, and later administrations at Washington sometimes interpreted the Platt Amendment in a way that was hardly consistent with the assurances that he had given. [5]

The convention finally accepted the Platt Amendment, and offi-

[4] *Report of the Secretary of War, 1901,* p. 48.
[5] The Cuban Commission's report is printed in the Cuban Senate's *Memoria de los*

cials who were to govern the new republic were elected in December 1901. The convention chose five of its members to supervise the counting of the votes. There were as yet no real political parties, but the Cuban leaders were divided, rather vaguely, into conservative and radical factions and somewhat more definitely into groups that opposed or favored cooperation with the United States. General Máximo Gómez, a hero of two wars for Cuba's independence, had been considered the strongest candidate for the presidency, although there was some doubt about his eligibility because he had been born in the Dominican Republic. General Gómez, however, refused to run, and threw his support to Tomás Estrada Palma, who had been president of the revolutionary government for a short time during the Ten Years War between 1868 and 1878 and had been the representative of the revolutionists in the United States during the more recent conflict. The only other candidate was General Bartolomé Masó, another war hero. Masó was supported by the groups that violently opposed the Platt Amendment, and the radical character of his campaign alarmed many of the Cuban conservatives.

All of the five members of the electoral commission, formally appointed by the Military Governor after the convention had chosen them, were among the large number of prominent Cubans that sponsored Estrada Palma's candidacy. They had apparently been selected without regard to their political connections [6] and before Masó had announced his candidacy; and General Wood refused to comply with demands that Masó be given a representative on the board and that the election itself be postponed to give him an opportunity to organize his campaign. Masó's followers thereupon decided not to participate in the election, and Estrada Palma, who had remained in the United States during the campaign, received all of the electoral votes for the presidency.

Estrada Palma was a man of distinguished family who had been a rich landowner at the beginning of the Ten Years War. During that conflict he had been taken prisoner by the Spaniards, and after his release he had become a school teacher in the United States. He was nearly seventy at the time of his election. His services to the

trabajos realizados 1902–4, published in Habana in 1918. Root later stated that the report was substantially accurate. See Jessup, Root, Vol. i, p. 318.

[6] Martínez Ortiz, Cuba, Los Primeros Años de Independencia, (Paris, 1929), Vol. i, p. 373.

revolution and his reputation for uncompromising honesty made him a popular candidate, even though he was thought to be more friendly to the United States than were most of the Cuban leaders.

There was much rejoicing in Cuba when the new President was inaugurated on May 20, 1902. The controversy about the Platt Amendment seemed temporarily forgotten in the festivities during the few days that elapsed between the transfer of the government and the departure of the Military Governor. On May 18 thousands of people joined in a great demonstration of appreciation to General Wood, and on the 21st the Cuban Congress resolved: "That a solemn vote of thanks be passed, a sincere expression of heartfelt gratitude to the Government and people of the United States of North America for their earnest sympathy, their efficient aid, and for the sacrifices made by them in behalf of the independence and freedom of Cuba." [7]

The new government took over as a going concern, with no debts and with substantial funds in the Treasury. The government offices were fully staffed, and General Wood had consulted with the President-elect about a number of recent appointments to make sure that there would be no occasion for wholesale changes in personnel. The economic and political outlook, however, was none too bright. Economic conditions were bad, because government subsidies to beet sugar producers in several European countries had depressed prices to a point where the Cuban mills could not operate at a profit. The great number of unemployed was a threat to public order. Many Cubans and North Americans were doubtful whether the new republic could maintain a stable government, and some businessmen and property owners hoped that the government would fail because they wanted to see the island annexed to the United States. At the same time resentment over the imposition of the Platt Amendment made it more difficult to deal with several diplomatic questions which had to be settled in the first years of independence, especially as political groups that had fought the amendment soon obtained control in the lower house of Congress.[8]

[7] *Papers Relating to the Foreign Relations of the United States, 1902*, p. 325. Hereafter this series, published by the Department of State, will be cited as *Foreign Relations*.

[8] Squiers to Hay, Nov. 11, 1902. Until Root introduced the system of filing by numerical cases, the instructions to and despatches from missions abroad and com-

Estrada Palma was friendly to the United States and apparently sincere in his determination to comply with the promises that the constitutional convention had made, but he resisted some of the proposals that the American government presented. On the American side, the negotiations were conducted by Herbert G. Squiers, who was sent to Habana as American Minister immediately after the new government's inauguration. Squiers had at one time been in the United States army, where his career had been marked by a series of refusals to obey orders from the War Department, and had later been secretary of legation at Berlin and at Peking. He had been officially commended for his conduct during the Boxer Rebellion, and was appointed to Habana because he seemed especially qualified for a difficult and important post. He was more competent than many of his contemporaries in the diplomatic service, but he was often tactless and sometimes indiscreet. During his first weeks in Habana he must have aroused misgivings among the Cuban leaders by his frequent expression of the idea that Cuba would eventually seek annexation to the United States. Nevertheless, he deprecated efforts to force annexation by causing disorder and economic chaos, and consistently urged support for Estrada Palma. He seemed to lose interest in the question of annexation, as most of the Cuban annexationists did, after the first two or three months of Estrada Palma's administration.[9]

The most urgent problem was to improve the situation of the sugar producers. The Military Government had urged a reciprocity arrangement which would reduce the duty on Cuban sugar imported into the United States; and a promise that Roosevelt and Root would support such an arrangement had apparently helped to overcome the constitutional convention's resistance to the Platt Amendment. Root, in his report for 1901, advocated "a reasonable reduction in our duties upon Cuban sugar and tobacco in exchange for fairly compensatory reduction of Cuban duties upon American products" and pointed out that this "would involve no sacrifice, but would be

munications to and from foreign diplomats in Washington were bound in separate volumes and will be referred to simply by date. Later papers will be cited by their numbers in the numerical case file or the decimal file. All of the State Department records cited are in the National Archives.

[9] For Squiers' attitude, see especially his despatches of June 7, June 23, June 24, June 28, and August 7, 1902.

as advantageous to us as it would be to Cuba." He continued: "Aside from the moral obligations to which we committed ourselves when we drove Spain out of Cuba, and aside from the ordinary considerations of commercial advantage involved in a reciprocity treaty, there are the weightiest reasons of American public policy pointing in the same direction; for the peace of Cuba is necessary to the peace of the United States; the health of Cuba is necessary to the health of the United States. The same considerations which led to the war with Spain now require that a commercial arrangement be made under which Cuba can live." [10]

In his first annual message to Congress, in December 1901, Roosevelt asked that he be authorized to negotiate a reciprocity agreement with the government that was about to be set up in Cuba. He again urged prompt action in a special message in June 1902, and Estrada Palma appealed for help before Cuba should be "financially ruined." The sugar producers in the United States were able to prevent action during the congressional session that ended in July 1902, but negotiations for a commercial treaty that would attain the desired objective were carried on during the summer and fall of that year.

The conclusion of a treaty was delayed by Estrada Palma's efforts to obtain greater advantages than the United States was prepared to concede. A rise in sugar prices, after the Brussels Conference of 1901–1902 agreed to abolish bounties to European producers, and a reluctance to increase Cuba's commercial dependence on the United States, made him less anxious to reach an agreement. The British Minister, Lionel Carden, who was later to be accused of opposition to American policies in Guatemala and Mexico, apparently encouraged him in his resistance, though the British government assured the State Department that Carden was merely negotiating an ordinary commercial treaty.[11] Estrada Palma was also accused of secretly urging the congress to change the tariff law so that the concessions granted to the United States would have less effect.[12] Friction over other matters made the negotiations more difficult. In October 1902, when the United States proposed that four naval sta-

[10] *Report of the Secretary of War for 1901,* p. 53.

[11] See Squiers' despatch of Oct. 10 and his telegrams of Oct. 10, Oct. 15, and Oct. 16, 1902, and the State Department's telegram of Oct. 16 and its instruction of Oct. 23 to Squiers.

[12] Squiers to Hay, Sept. 13, 1902.

tions be established under the Platt Amendment and the Cuban government refused to agree to more than two, Squiers made a veiled threat of intervention which brought on a discussion of the scope of Article III of the amendment. Estrada Palma's resistance to the American proposals for reciprocity nevertheless diminished as pressure for an agreement increased in Cuba; and a cigarmakers' strike, which caused serious disorders, emphasized the need for an improvement in economic conditions.

The commercial convention was finally signed on December 11, 1902. Its ratification was delayed for a year by opposition in the United States Congress, which insisted on amendments that were reluctantly accepted by the Cubans and which acted only after Roosevelt had exerted much pressure and called an extra session to obtain approval. The treaty provided that all products then imported free of duty in either country should remain on the free list, and that the duties on all other Cuban imports into the United States were always to be 20 percent less than those on similar imports from any other country. Cuban duties on imports from the United States, with the exception of tobacco, were also reduced by 20 percent, and in the case of a long list of commodities, by from 25 to 40 percent. Some of these were articles that could be produced very much more cheaply in Europe, so that a concession of more than 20 percent was necessary if American producers were to have a chance to compete. Others were goods already imported chiefly from the United States, and in these cases the purpose in reducing the duty was to encourage Cuban consumption.[13] In considering the value of the concessions made by each party, it should be noted that the actual reductions made by the United States averaged nearly twice as much, on an *ad valorem* basis, as those made by Cuba.[14] The treaty was to remain in force for five years, and thereafter from year to year until it was denounced by either party.

The treaty helped to put the Cuban republic on its feet at a time when help was much needed. Combined with the confidence that the Platt Amendment gave to native and foreign financial interests, it was undoubtedly responsible for much of the prosperity that the

[13] U.S. Tariff Commission, *Effects of the Cuban Reciprocity Treaty* (Washington, 1929), p. 28.
[14] U.S. Tariff Commission, *Cuban Reciprocity Treaty*, p. 46.

country enjoyed in the crucial first years of independence. Sugar production increased in value from $30,900,000 in 1902 to $123,900,-000 in 1912.[15] Until 1909, at least, the Cuban planters obtained practically the full benefit of the customs preferential, because the United States still imported a considerable amount of sugar from other countries and the price of sugar in the United States was based on the world market price plus the full amount of the duty that sugar from other countries had to pay. The reciprocity treaty was of less value to the Cuban sugar industry after it began to produce more than the American market could take.[16]

It is difficult to say how much effect the treaty had in other ways. The producers of tobacco, which was Cuba's other important export product, benefited relatively little, because the United States import duty, even with the preferential, was still very high. American exporters to Cuba were also disappointed in the results of the treaty, and even Root, after he became Secretary of State, felt that it should be revised in their favor.[17]

Some writers have argued that the reciprocity treaty in the long run did more harm than good to Cuba and have ascribed purely selfish motives to the American statesmen who negotiated it. One Cuban historian accuses the United States of deliberately restoring the "colonial economy" which had been destroyed by the war for independence and which might have been replaced by an economic system better adapted to the needs of a free nation; and he sees in the reciprocity treaty the means by which the United States hoped to complete its control over Cuba.[18] Other critics, without going quite so far, assert that the United States was seeking on the one hand to increase its own exports to Cuba and on the other to benefit an industry in which much North American capital was invested, and that the interests of Cuba received little consideration. Several authors have pointed to the obvious evils that resulted from making the island excessively dependent on sugar.

[15] Wright, *The Cuban Situation and Our Treaty Relations*, p. 108.
[16] For a discussion of this development, see U.S. Tariff Commission, *Cuban Reciprocity Treaty*, p. 78; and Wright, *Cuban Situation*, pp. 63–72.
[17] Jessup, *Root*, Vol. I, p. 527–528. See also Squiers' despatches of Septemebr 24 and September 28, 1904, and the State Department's instruction to the Legation at Habana, September 27, 1905.
[18] Portell Vilá, *Historia de Cuba en sus Relaciones con los Estados Unidos y España* (Habana, 1938–1941), Vol. IV, pp. 317, 379–380.

Neither the official record nor their private correspondence give any support to the idea that Roosevelt and Root had ulterior motives in pressing for reciprocity. Like most people in Cuba, they were convinced that the sugar industry must be revived if the new government were to have a chance for success. Their motives were not, of course, purely altruistic. Although they had a genuine interest in Cuba's welfare, they were also seeking to protect the political interests of the United States by creating conditions in Cuba that would afford no pretext for interference by other powers. They do not seem to have been greatly influenced by thoughts of any economic benefit that would accrue to the United States. In advocating the treaty, they advanced the perfectly sound argument that an expansion of trade would help both countries, but they emphasized much more the duty of the United States to help Cuba. American owners of Cuban sugar plantations, who probably controlled about 20 percent of the crop,[19] hoped to gain from the treaty, but cane and beet producers in the United States expected to lose by it.

The tremendous growth of the sugar industry after 1902 did have unfortunate aspects. The island's economy became excessively dependent on one commodity, which fluctuated in price and was often a drug on the market. A large proportion of the best agricultural land came to be owned by great foreign companies and worked by hired laborers, many of whom were unemployed for long periods each year. The *colonos,* the smaller farmers who grew cane, were almost equally dependent on the companies because they had to sell their crop to the nearest *central.* When prices were low and the *centrales* had to reduce costs, both workers and *colonos* suffered. On the other hand, with all its bad features, the sugar economy made Cuba richer than any of her West Indian neighbors. Conceivably, political and social conditions in the island would be healthier today if the reciprocity treaty had not been adopted, but it is difficult to say that the statesmen who were dealing with the situation in 1902 could or should have chosen to risk an immediate economic and political collapse in the hope that a more balanced economy would develop.

[19] U.S. Tariff Commission, *Cuban Reciprocity Treaty,* p. 170.

THE NAVAL BASES AND THE ISLE OF PINES

Before the signing of the reciprocity treaty, the American government proposed an agreement for the cession of the naval bases promised in the Platt Amendment. This seemed likely to be a troublesome matter, because cessions of territory are always particularly distasteful and there was still a fear that the naval stations might be used as bases for interference in Cuba's internal affairs. This fear had inspired much of the opposition to the Platt Amendment in the constitutional convention. The matter was settled, however, with less difficulty than might have been expected, partly because the American government made substantial concessions. In deference to Cuba's wishes, it accepted a long-term lease, instead of the outright cession that it would have preferred, and it agreed that there should be only two stations, instead of the four that it had asked. It also gave up its idea that one of the stations should be at Habana. Estrada Palma was thus able to proclaim publicly that he had won a diplomatic victory.[20] An agreement for the lease of areas at Guantánamo and Bahía Honda for coaling and naval stations was signed in February 1903; and after this had been approved by the Cuban Congress the details of the lease were fixed in a further agreement signed July 2. Cuba's sovereignty in the ceded areas was recognized, but the United States was given complete jurisdiction and control over them and was to hold them so long as necessary for coaling and naval purposes.[21] As it turned out, only the station at Guantánamo was actually established.

In the negotiations, the question of the naval stations, in which the United States was urgently interested, was closely linked with the question of the Isle of Pines, which was especially important to Cuba. The Isle of Pines, lying some fifty miles off the Cuban coast, had always been governed from Habana, but there was a question whether it should be regarded as a part of Cuba or as one of "the other islands now under Spanish sovereignty in the West Indies" which had been ceded to the United States by Article II of the Treaty of Paris. McKinley and his chief advisers seem to have considered

[20] See his messages to the Cuban Congress, April 6 and November 2, 1903. *Foreign Relations, 1903*, pp. 354, 361.

[21] For the text of the lease, see *Foreign Relations, 1911*, pp. 110, 111.

that the island was legally a part of Cuba, but in 1899 and 1900 officials in the War Department, without Root's knowledge,[22] informed several inquirers that the island belonged to the United States. North American real estate promoters proceeded to buy a considerable amount of land and some three hundred American citizens were induced to settle there. When the Senate Committee on Military Affairs was considering the Platt Amendment, representations by the colonists, and also perhaps a belief that the island might have military value, led the committee to insert an article in the amendment leaving the question of ownership to be adjusted at some later time by a treaty.

A treaty signed on the same day as the agreement for the lease of the naval stations provided for the relinquishment of any American claim to the Isle of Pines, and expressly stated that this concession was "in consideration of the grants of coaling and naval stations." The American government was thus placed in an embarrassing position when the United States Senate failed to ratify the treaty within the period fixed by its provisions. Another treaty, without a time limit, was signed March 2, 1904, but it too met with opposition and was not ratified until 1925, although successive administrations at Washington repeatedly endeavored to obtain its approval.

The three hundred Americans on the Isle of Pines were thus able through political pressure to prevent action in a matter that involved the good faith of the United States. Their unwillingness to submit to Cuban rule caused further complications between the two governments. They refused to admit that the island was not a part of the United States, and in November 1905 some of them attempted to set up a territorial government. Root told them emphatically that the territory would remain Cuban,[23] but Squiers, at Habana, was quoted in a newspaper interview as suggesting that it would be better for the United States to exercise control over the island until the treaty was ratified.[24] This indiscretion, which was the culmination of a series of incidents that had strained relations between the Legation and the Cuban government, led Estrada Palma to ask that the Minister be recalled.

[22] *Congressional Record*, 68th Cong., 2nd Sess., Vol. 66, pt. 2, p. 2019.
[23] 68th Cong., 1st Session, Senate Report, No. 2, p. 4.
[24] Portell Vilá, *Historia de Cuba*, Vol. IV, p. 415.

Despite considerable provocation, the Cuban government exercised commendable restraint in dealing with the settlers in the Isle of Pines, and there seems to have been less friction in the island after 1905. A United States Senate committee which investigated the situation in 1906 reported that the Cuban authorities had complied with several of the settlers' more reasonable demands by establishing a customhouse and a school at Nueva Gerona and by initiating action for the establishment of a registry of land titles and a court of first instance.[25]

THE PLATT AMENDMENT TREATY

The Platt Amendment had provided that its provisions be incorporated not only in the Cuban constitution but in a permanent treaty between the two governments. A draft of such a treaty, simply reciting word for word the provisions of the amendment itself, was presented to the Cuban government in January 1903 and was accepted after Estrada Palma had made a futile effort to obtain changes in the wording of Article III. The Cubans claimed that Root and Platt had promised that the scope of this article, dealing with intervention, would be restricted when the treaty was negotiated; but they were told that the language must be the same as that of the act of Congress and the Cuban constitution.[26] The treaty was signed on May 22, 1903, and was proclaimed, after ratification by both governments, on July 2, 1904.

SANITATION

One other question growing out of the Platt Amendment became a subject of diplomatic correspondence throughout Estrada Palma's administration. The Cuban government had obligated itself to carry out plans for the sanitation of the cities of the island, and one of these plans, specifically agreed to at the time of the President's inauguration, was a contract signed by the Military Government for sewers and paving in Habana. The American firm of McGivney and Rokeby had obtained the contract and had deposited $500,000 as a guarantee of good faith, but the municipality had been unable to raise the $13,000,000 needed for the work. The United States from

[25] *68th Cong, 1st Session, Senate Report, No. 2*, p. 211.
[26] Hay to Squiers, telegram, April 17, 1903.

time to time urged Cuba to arrange to have this contract carried out, and also complained of sanitary conditions in some of the other cities of the island. There was a recurrence of yellow fever in Habana in 1905, brought in this time from New Orleans,[27] and another in 1906. Estrada Palma repeatedly urged the Congress to provide funds to carry out the McGivney and Rokeby contract, but nothing was accomplished during his administration.

Panama and the Canal

During the Spanish American War the long voyage of the battle-ship *Oregon* around South America, at a time when she was desperately needed in the Caribbean, had dramatized the need for an isthmian canal. It was increasingly clear, too, that the canal would have to be built by the United States government. The failure of the French company at Panama and the ineffective efforts of a succession of foreign companies in Nicaragua had shown that private capital could not accomplish the task. A commission created by the United States Congress reported in 1897 that a canal in Nicaragua was practicable, and in his annual message of December 1898 President McKinley recommended that it be built. Disagreements between the Senate and the House, encouraged by those who wished to see the canal built at Panama rather than in Nicaragua, prevented definite action, and on March 3, 1899, the Congress set up a new commission which was to study both routes.

THE HAY-PAUNCEFOTE TREATY

Meanwhile the Secretary of State was negotiating with the British government to obtain changes in the Clayton-Bulwer Treaty of 1850, by which the two governments had agreed that neither would seek to control any canal that might be built on the isthmus. Though many American politicians had argued that the treaty was no longer binding, Hay felt that the United States could not honorably disregard it, and he was able, after protracted negotiations, to obtain the first Hay-Pauncefote Treaty, signed February 5, 1900. This treaty gave the United States a right to build and operate an isthmian canal, but it met with much criticism in the American press and in Congress

[27] *Report of the Provisional Administration of Charles E. Magoon . . . 1906–1908* (Habana, 1908–1909), p. 108.

because it provided for the neutralization of the proposed waterway and forbade its fortification. When the Senate consented to ratification, it was with amendments that were unacceptable to Great Britain; and Hay, much to his chagrin, was compelled to negotiate a new agreement. One of the most severe critics of the first treaty was Theodore Roosevelt, who became president while the second was being negotiated.

The second Hay-Pauncefote Treaty, signed November 18, 1901, said nothing about the fortification of the canal and omitted other provisions to which the Senate had objected. In operating the canal, the United States undertook to adopt rules similar to those governing the Suez Canal, guaranteeing free passage to vessels of all nations in peace or war. The Senate promptly approved the agreement by an overwhelming majority. The treaty not only removed an obstacle to the building of the canal but marked a change in the relationship of the two signatory powers in the Caribbean, for the withdrawal of British opposition to the fortification of the canal meant that the British navy was giving up the dominant position that it had always held in the West Indian region.[28]

THE QUESTION OF THE ROUTE

Before 1902 it was generally assumed that any canal built by the United States would be in Nicaragua, where the continental divide was very low and the San Juan River and a great lake provided a natural waterway to within a few miles of the Pacific. The Nicaraguan route was traditionally the "American" one, as opposed to the French project at Panama. There had been repeated efforts to obtain help from the United States Treasury for the Maritime Canal Company of Nicaragua, chartered by Congress in 1889, which started work on a small scale but was forced to suspend operations because of lack of funds; and there was a strong group in Congress, led by Senator Morgan of Alabama, which opposed any suggestion that any other route be adopted.

As a first step toward the conclusion of an agreement for the construction of a canal in Nicaragua, Secretary Hay signed protocols with the Nicaraguan and Costa Rican Ministers on December 1,

[28] See the article by J. A. S. Grenville, "Great Britain and the Isthmian Canal," *American Historical Review*, Oct. 1955.

1900, committing the signatories to negotiate more detailed agreements when the President of the United States should be authorized to acquire control of the territory needed for the canal. The protocols stipulated that the course of the canal and the provisions governing it should be in accord with the terms of the first Hay-Pauncefote Treaty, which was still pending in the Senate. It was necessary to negotiate with Costa Rica as well as with Nicaragua because part of Costa Rica's territory bordered on the San Juan River and an arbitral award handed down by President Cleveland in 1888, in connection with a boundary dispute, had enjoined Nicaragua to make no grants for canal purposes without consulting Costa Rica.[29]

The most active advocate of the alternate route at Panama was William Nelson Cromwell, the American counsel for French interests which faced heavy losses if Nicaragua were selected. A canal company headed by Ferdinand de Lesseps, the builder of the Suez Canal, had obtained a concession from Colombia in 1878 and had worked at Panama for several years before graft and extravagance and the terrific ravages of yellow fever had forced it into bankruptcy in 1889. Its concession had been transferred to the *Compagnie Nouvelle du Canal de Panama*, which had no funds to complete the work but hoped either to obtain new financing in the United States or to sell its rights and property to the American government. As its representative, Cromwell had worked indefatigably since 1896 to prevent any decision by Congress in favor of the Nicaraguan route.

The Canal Commission appointed in 1899 reported on November 16, 1901, that both routes were practicable and that each offered certain advantages. Nicaragua was nearer to the United States. Health conditions there were somewhat better, and there would be more probability of economic development in the country through which the canal passed. The construction of dams would be less difficult, and the work of excavation, being spread over a larger area, could be carried on more rapidly if enough labor were available. At Panama, on the other hand, the canal itself would be 134 miles shorter, and it would have fewer locks and fewer curves. It would be easier to obtain an adequate labor force, and since good harbors and a railroad were already available it would be possible to start work a year sooner than in Nicaragua. More was known

[29] The text of the two protocols is printed in *Foreign Relations, 1916*, p. 821.

about the country through which the canal would pass. Finally, the estimated cost of completing the waterway in Panama was only $144,233,358, as compared with $189,864,062 in Nicaragua; and the estimated annual cost of operation after completion was $2,000,000 in Panama and $3,300,000 in Nicaragua.

The commission evidently felt that the advantage lay with the southern route, but it pointed out that nothing could be done at Panama without an agreement with the French company, which still had the concession and a great amount of property. The company owned nearly all of the stock of the Panama Railroad, the trans-isthmian line which had been built by, and was still operated by, a North American company. The French, in fact, had done a substantial part of the work of digging the canal, for the commission estimated that only about half of the 77,000,000 cubic yards already excavated would be wasted through changes of plans and that only 94,863,703 cubic yards had still to be removed. The commission thought that $40,000,000 would be a reasonable price for the French holdings, including maps and records and the railroad stock. The canal company, however, asked $109,141,500; and since the payment of this amount would make the total cost in Panama considerably higher than in Nicaragua, the commission reported that Nicaragua offered "the most practicable and feasible route" for a canal to be built by the United States.[30]

Some days before the commission formally submitted its report, the State Department instructed William L. Merry, the American Minister at San José in Costa Rica, to go to Managua to discuss the terms on which the government of that country would agree to the construction of the canal. Captain Merry, who was accredited to Nicaragua and El Salvador as well as to Cost Rica, had had a long experience with Central American affairs, first as a steamship agent in Panama and Nicaragua and as captain of steamers serving isthmian ports, and later as a businessman in San Francisco. Since 1880, as he himself put it, he had been an "active commercial promoter" of the Nicaragua canal project.[31] In Nicaragua he had to deal with the dictator José Santos Zelaya, who had not yet embarked on

[30] The commission's report was printed as *Senate Document 54, 57th Cong., 1st Session,* and again as *Senate Document 222, 58th Cong., 2nd Session.*
[31] Merry to Hay, No. 692 of Feb. 25, 1902.

the policy of hostility to the United States which was to cause his downfall eight years later. The negotiations centered on the matter of price. The American government was prepared to offer $3,000,000 in cash, with a further payment of $100,000 per annum in perpetuity, while Zelaya at first demanded a total of $8,000,000 payable over a period of six years. On December 4, however, Merry cabled that the Nicaraguan government would accept one cash payment of $6,000,000 and would agree to all of the other important clauses of the Department's draft convention. He consequently signed a protocol which was intended to be the basis of a treaty to be drawn up after the United States Congress authorized the construction of the canal.[32]

When the protocol reached Washington, the State Department found it unsatisfactory in several respects and especially in its omission of a provision authorizing the United States to maintain courts in the canal district. Merry had been unable to persuade Zelaya to agree to this, and he had apparently not considered the matter sufficiently important to warrant his cabling for instructions before signing the protocol. Comments in several of his despatches suggest that he doubted whether the Department's proposal, which contemplated Nicaraguan and North American courts functioning side by side in the canal district, was workable. He pointed out that the French company had had little difficulty with the Colombian courts at Panama. The American government, however, felt that its officers and employees in the canal district must not be subjected to the jurisdiction of the Nicaraguan courts, and Merry was told that the protocol was unacceptable and that negotiations would be resumed with the Nicaraguan Minister in Washington.[33]

On January 9, 1902, the House of Representatives passed the Hepburn Bill, which appropriated funds for a Nicaraguan canal. Before the Senate acted on the measure, the French company decided to sell its rights to the United States at the price suggested by the Canal Commission. President Roosevelt hastily reconvened the commission and obtained a unanimous supplementary report recommending the construction of the canal in Panama. Senator Spooner

[32] The correspondence about these negotiations is in the volumes of despatches from and instructions to Costa Rica.
[33] Hay to Merry, Jan. 10, 1902.

then offered an amendment to the Hepburn Bill authorizing the President to build the canal in Panama if valid titles could be obtained from the French company and if satisfactory arrangements could be made with Colombia. If the necessary prerequisites for construction in Panama could not be arranged within a reasonable time the President was to proceed with the Nicaragua project. The amendment was accepted after a hard fight, and the Spooner Act became law on June 28.

The decision in favor of the Panama route represented a complete reversal of attitude by the leaders of the Republican party. As late as September 29, 1901, Secretary Hay had believed that the choice of any route expect Nicaragua was hardly conceivable.[34] Both Cromwell and Philippe Bunau-Varilla claimed credit for the change. Cromwell, in his efforts to protect the interests of the French company, had worked for years to persuade government officials and congressmen that the Panama route was superior. Bunau-Varilla had come from France for the same purpose. He had at one time been in charge of the French company's engineering work on the isthmus, and he was a stockholder in the new French company. He always asserted, however, that he was far from friendly with the new company's management and that his campaign was inspired solely by a sentimental, patriotic desire to see the completion of the work that his compatriots had started. He was a brilliant and persuasive advocate, and he had won over several influential people in the United States. One of his exploits, the distribution to all members of Congress of Nicaraguan postage stamps showing a smoking volcano, may have helped to change some votes, for disastrous eruptions of Mont Pelée and La Soufrière in Martinique and St. Vincent, which occurred only a few weeks before the final vote on the Spooner Act, had made the American public aware of the destructive capabilities of active volcanos. It seems hardly probable, however, that the strenuous lobbying of Cromwell and Bunau-Varilla was the chief factor in the victory of the Panama route. The actual decision was made by President Roosevelt and a few other Republican leaders, presumably on the basis of the Canal Commission's report that the southern route was the more feasible one.

[34] *Diplomatic History of the Panama Canal* (*Senate Document 474, 63rd Cong., 2nd Session*), p. 45.

NEGOTIATIONS WITH COLOMBIA

The Spooner Act did not definitely settle the question of the route, because the building of the canal at Panama was contingent on the prompt conclusion of a satisfactory agreement with Colombia. Under a treaty signed in 1846, the United States had been granted the right of free transit by any road or canal that might be built across the isthmus, and in return had guaranteed to New Granada, as Colombia was then called, the "perfect neutrality" of the isthmus and "the rights of sovereignty and property" over the territory. These provisions had become important when thousands of travelers began to cross the isthmus on their way to California, and especially after the completion of the Panama Railroad in 1855; and American forces were landed on the isthmus at least thirteen times between 1856 and 1902, usually at the request of the Colombian government, to keep open the transit route and to protect foreigners against disorder.[35] The treaty of 1846, however, did not give the United States specific authority to build the canal, and a special agreement would be needed for this purpose.

Colombia's consent would also be required for the transfer of the French company's concession to the United States. The original concession of 1878 had been amended in 1890 to provide that the canal must be finished in 1904. In 1900, President Sanclemente had granted the company six additional years in return for a cash payment of five million francs. His decree had been granted under the government's emergency powers at a time when there was no congress, and there were some Colombians who questioned its legality. The Colombian government itself did not raise this question, but it felt that it should receive a substantial payment from the company for its consent to the transfer.

The Colombian government was in no position in 1901–1902 to deal with so delicate a matter as the grant of canal rights to the United States. In 1899 dissensions within the dominant conservative party had encouraged the liberal opposition to start what proved to be the most destructive and costly civil war in the republic's history. The conflict, which was still going on, made it difficult for the leaders at Bogotá to consider other problems, however im-

[35] Parks, *Colombia and the United States* (Durham, 1935), p. 219.

portant, and the precarious situation of the government made it timid about committing itself on a controversial question of policy.

Any decision about the canal could have disastrous political consequences. On the one hand, Colombia had a vital interest in having the canal built in Panama. If the United States turned to Nicaragua, the isthmus, which had always been regarded as one of the nation's priceless assets, would become worthless. The territory might even be lost, for the resumption of work on the canal was all-important to the people of Panama and there was already talk of possible secession if the government failed to reach an agreement with the United States. Furthermore, the government desperately needed money to meet the expense of the civil war and to mitigate the effect of great issues of unsecured paper currency. On the other hand, the United States could not be expected to build the canal unless it were given a considerable measure of control over a part of the republic's territory, and this would be exceedingly distasteful to public opinion. The conclusion of an agreement would certainly be attacked as a betrayal of the nation's sovereignty.

The Colombian representatives at Washington repeatedly asked for instructions that would enable them to help Cromwell in his effort to have the Panama route selected, but with little result.[36] In the spring of 1902, however, it was clear that Colombia must show a willingness to negotiate if she wished to have the canal built at Panama; and Cromwell persuaded José Vicente Concha, the Colombian Minister, to act without instructions and to give Hay a draft treaty which the latter submitted to the Senate in May as evidence of Colombia's willingness to negotiate. The draft did not meet all the requirements of the Spooner Act, but it was a starting point for negotiations. These continued during the summer and fall of 1902. They made slow progress, partly because the Colombian government was reluctant to accept the terms proposed by the United States and partly because of poor communications between Washington and Bogotá. Mail took several weeks and the Colombian government's poverty often made it unwilling or unable to use the cable.

Late in 1902, the end of the Colombian civil war improved the outlook. In September, it seemed probable that a liberal army which had defeated the conservative forces on the isthmus would occupy

[36] Much of what follows is based on Miner, *The Fight for the Panama Route.*

Panama City and Colon. The government had already sought the good offices of the United States for the establishment of peace, and it now asked the United States to intervene under the treaty of 1846 to keep the transit route open. American forces were already on the isthmus, as they had been on many other occasions since 1846. At first they prevented the use of the railroad by either side, but when the State Department suggested that they change their attitude the government was able to reinforce its garrisons and the attack on the two cities was frustrated. The American intervention and defeats in other parts of the republic discouraged the liberals, and on November 21 they signed a treaty of peace on the *U.S.S. Wisconsin*. With the end of the war it became possible to elect a congress which could ratify any agreement that might be reached with the United States.

Marroquín, the Colombian president, had insisted that the canal question be submitted to Congress, because he was determined to avoid personal responsibility for the painful and dangerous decisions that would have to be made. He did not want to be accused of losing the canal by failing to reach an agreement with the United States, or of acceding to conditions that impaired the national sovereignty. He could not delay the matter until his Congress met, however, because the United States warned him that it would have to open negotiations with Nicaragua unless the prospect for an agreement with Colombia improved before the United States Congress met in December. He consequently instructed his representatives to sign the best treaty that they could obtain.

Concha refused to do so, but Tomás Herrán, as Chargé d'Affaires, continued the negotiations with Cromwell's assistance as intermediary. The only concession that he could obtain was a slight increase in the annual rental that the United States was to pay. Finally Herrán was instructed to obtain a written ultimatum from Hay and to sign a treaty when the ultimatum was received. When Hay informed Herrán that no further concessions would be considered and that the "reasonable time provided in the statute [the Spooner Act] for the conclusion of the negotiations with Colombia" had passed, the Hay-Herrán Treaty was signed on January 22, 1903.

By this treaty Colombia would authorize the French company to sell all of its rights and concessions to the United States. The

American government was to be given an exclusive right to construct and protect a canal, with the use and control of a canal zone ten kilometers wide. Colombia's sovereignty in this zone was explicitly recognized, but the United States was to have the right to maintain order and protect public health there, as well as other rights necessary for the construction and operation of the canal. Each government would establish courts to deal with civil suits between its own citizens, and there were to be mixed courts to settle controversies between Colombians and North Americans and to deal with all criminal cases. In general, Colombia was to provide any armed forces necessary for the protection of the canal, and American forces were to be used only with Colombia's consent. In cases of unforeseen or imminent danger, however, the United States was authorized to take action without Colombia's prior consent. Lands needed for the canal might be expropriated in accord with Colombian law, at prices to be fixed by a joint commission. The United States would pay Colombia a lump sum of $10,000,000 and an additional annual rental of $250,000.

On the whole, the treaty seemed a fair and reasonable arrangement. The canal promised great benefits to Colombia as well as to the United States. It would have been foolish to attempt to build it without obtaining a measure of control over the territory through which it passed. In the light of subsequent experience in building and operating the canal, in fact, we may question whether the limited authority granted to the United States in the zone, or the provisions for military protection, would have been adequate. The fairness of the indemnity was of course open to question, but here Hay's freedom of action was limited because a larger payment to Colombia would have given the still vociferous partisans of the Nicaraguan route a strong argument when the treaty came before the Senate. The Nicaraguan Minister in May 1902, had submitted a draft treaty which was unsatisfactory in some other respects but which proposed a lump sum payment of only $6,000,000 and an annual rental of $25,000.[37]

The Hay-Herrán Treaty was approved by the United States Senate

[37] For the text of the Nicaraguan proposal see *Diplomatic History of the Panama Canal*, pp. 565ff. The text of the Hay-Herrán Treaty is printed in the same volume, p. 277.

in March 1903, and in the same month the Colombians elected the Congress that would have to consider it. Marroquín, in a message to the nation in January, indicated that he did not expect his fellow citizens to like the treaty and that the Congress would have to take the full responsibility for accepting or rejecting it.[38] The officials at Washington later blamed him for taking an attitude that seemed to invite rejection, but it is not clear that a more courageous stand would have had a different result. Marroquín had few friends even in his own party, and the hostility of many of the local conservative leaders made it impossible for him to control the election as the Colombian government usually did. In spite of his effort to dissociate himself from responsibility, his enemies used the treaty as an issue in the campaign and stirred up a violent popular opposition to it.

While the campaign was going on, the Colombian government attempted to force the French company to pay for the privilege of selling its concession to the United States. It had always felt that it was entitled to a payment from the company, but Cromwell seems to have dissuaded the Colombian representatives at Washington from pressing the matter while the company and the government were working together to bring about the selection of the Panama route. During the negotiation of the Hay-Herrán Treaty, Cromwell had procured the insertion of the article that authorized the company to sell its rights and concessions to the United States. When the Colombian government, in February 1903, asked the company to send a representative to discuss the question of compensation, Cromwell appealed to Hay, and a strong protest was sent to Bogotá. Hay was justified in insisting that the Colombian government, after agreeing to the treaty, could not in good faith make further demands on the French company, but the rather harsh language of his note tended to embitter relations that were already rather strained.

Another communication that gave offense was delivered in June, when it became clear that the ratification of the treaty was in doubt, and when it was suggested in Bogotá that ratification would be easier if the amount paid by the United States were increased. Minister Beaupré was instructed to say that:

"The Colombian Government apparently does not appreciate the

[38] Favell, "Antecedents of Panama's Separation from Colombia," p. 220.

47

gravity of the situation. The canal negotiations were initiated by Colombia, and were energetically pressed upon this Government for several years. The propositions presented by Colombia, with slight modifications, were finally accepted by us. In virtue of this agreement our Congress reversed its previous judgment and decided upon the Panama route. If Colombia should now reject the treaty or unduly delay its ratification, the friendly understanding between the two countries would be so seriously compromised that action might be taken by the Congress next winter which every friend of Colombia would regret." [39]

In making this threat Hay probably had in mind the abandoning of the Panama route in favor of Nicaragua, but an article published in the New York *World* the day after the message was communicated to the Colombian government was calculated to give a different impression. This alleged that, if the treaty were not ratified, Panama would secede and would make a canal agreement with the United States. President Roosevelt and his Cabinet were represented as favoring this plan. It was later revealed that this article was inspired by Cromwell,[40] obviously in an effort to intimidate the leaders at Bogotá.

When the Colombian Congress met on June 20, the administration appeared to command a majority in the lower house but faced strong opposition in the Senate. Marroquín's enemies were more interested in embarrassing him than in considering the Hay-Herrán Treaty on its merits, and for some time the debate on the agreement centered on efforts to compel the President to assume full responsibility for it. Marroquín continued to insist that the Congress must take the responsibility, but he suggested to the United States that there would be less opposition to ratification if Colombia could receive $10,000,000 from the French company and $15,000,000 instead of $10,000,000 from the United States. This proposal was peremptorily rejected. A few weeks later, when a committee of the Senate reported the treaty with amendments which would have opened the way for financial demands on the French company and would have removed the provision for special courts in the Canal Zone, the Colombian government was again informed, forcefully

[39] Hay to Beaupré, June 9, 1903. *Foreign Relations, 1903*, p. 146.

[40] *The Story of Panama* (hearings on the Rainey Resolution before the Committee on Foreign Affairs of the House of Representatives, Washington, 1913), p. 344.

and rather tactlessly, that no amendments could be considered.[41]

On August 12, Marroquín took the wind out of his opponents' sails by a bold maneuver. The Senate had already been informed in secret session about the notes received from the American Legation, but on August 12 several of Beaupré's rather offensive and threatening communications and the government's dignified replies were read in public session. The government's friends thereupon joined with its opponents in unanimously rejecting the treaty.

Beaupré reported that the government had permitted the defeat of the treaty in the hope that there would be a reaction of public opinion which would make it possible to ratify the agreement without amendments. On August 15 he wrote that there was "an almost hysterical condition of alarm and uncertainty in Bogotá as to the future action of the United States." [42] It soon appeared, however, that both Marroquín and his opponents were disposed to let the matter remain where it was for the time being. Though a new and ominous note was interjected when a committee of the Colombian Senate suggested that the Congress consider the validity of the most recent extension of the French company's concession and pointed out the advantages that Colombia would derive if it were decided that the company's rights expired in 1904 rather than in 1910, the Congress took no further definite action before its session ended on October 31.

THE PANAMA REVOLUTION

What followed has been the subject of much controversy, and we cannot be sure that we know the full story. When the rejection of the treaty became a virtual certainty in August, the higher officials of the American government were clearly in doubt whether they should turn to Nicaragua or, as Hay put it, undertake "the far more difficult and multifurcate scheme of building the Panama Canal *malgré* Bogotá." [43] They were aware that there might be a revolution in Panama, but they were not counting on it.[44] By October, in fact, Roosevelt had decided that the best solution would be simply

[41] Miner, *Fight for the Panama Route,* gives a full account of this correspondence.
[42] *Foreign Relations, 1903,* p. 180.
[43] Hay to Roosevelt, Aug. 16, 1903. Quoted in Miner, *Fight for the Panama Route,* p. 340, and Dennis, *Adventures in American Diplomacy,* p. 342.
[44] See Hay's letter to Roosevelt of Sept. 3, 1903, quoted in Hill, *Roosevelt and the Caribbean* (Chicago, 1927), p. 57.

to seize the isthmus and start work. He thought that "to go to Nicaragua would be against the advice of the great majority of competent engineers—some of the most competent saying that we had better have no canal at this time than go there." [45] The President apparently found justification for the plan which he adopted in a memorandum sent him by John Basset Moore, which argued that the United States had guaranteed Colombia's sovereignty over the isthmus under the Treaty of 1846 for the specific purpose of obtaining a canal, and consequently had a right to demand Colombia's consent to build one. Moore, perhaps, did not intend to suggest the use of force, but in October Roosevelt prepared a draft message to Congress urging that the United States should either begin work immediately in Nicaragua or purchase the rights of the French company and complete the Panama canal "without any further parley with Colombia." He proposed to leave the matter to the judgment of Congress, but with a strong recommendation that the latter course be adopted. Fortunately, perhaps, the revolution in Panama took place before the message could be submitted.[46]

The connection between the department of Panama and the rest of Colombia had always been tenuous. The isthmian settlements were for all practical purposes nearer to New Orleans and New York than to the inaccessible capital at Bogotá, and most of their contacts were with the outside world. They had attempted to secede on two or three occasions in the first decades of independence, and between 1855 and 1886 they had had a practically autonomous government under a very weak federal system. After Rafael Núñez set up a centralized regime at Bogotá, however, the isthmus, like the other Colombian provinces, was ruled rather autocratically from the capital. Many Panamanians felt that the interests of the isthmus were neglected. Their discontent had been increased by the depression that followed the suspension of the French company's work; and the recent civil war, in which the isthmus had been the scene of much fighting, had left an aftermath of bitterness.

The communities on the isthmus owed their very existence to the transit route. In the sixteenth and seventeenth centuries all of the

[45] Roosevelt to Dr. Albert Shaw, Oct. 10, 1903. Roosevelt, *Letters*, Vol. iii, p. 628.
[46] For the text of the draft message, see Roosevelt's *Autobiography* (New York, 1919), p. 530.

legal trade of the rich Spanish colonies on the west coast of South America passed through Panama, and in the nineteenth, especially after the completion of the Panama Railroad, thousands of travelers crossed there on the way to and from California. The operations of the French company had brought another wave of prosperity, which ended when the company failed. The Panamanians would face a bleak future if the United States decided to build the canal in Nicaragua.

It is not surprising that a number of prominent Panamanians should have begun to discuss the idea of setting up an independent republic early in 1903 when the development of opposition at Bogotá made the ratification of the Hay-Herrán Treaty seem doubtful. Several of the conspirators were connected with the Panama Railroad Company, which was still an American corporation with its head office at New York though it was now a subsidiary of the French canal company. In June they made contact with Cromwell and were evidently promised his support. Cromwell probably thought that the threat of revolution would help to bring about favorable action on the treaty at Bogotá, and it was soon after his meeting with the conspirators' emissary that he brought about the publication of the New York *World* story mentioned above. He reiterated his promise of help late in August, when the group at Panama sent Dr. Manuel Amador Guerrero to New York in an effort to obtain more definite assurances from him and to ascertain what the United States government would do. A few days later, however, he suddenly dissociated himself from the conspiracy because he realized that reports of his activities had reached the Colombian Legation at Washington. Amador was about to return to Panama, completely discouraged, when Philippe Bunau-Varilla again appeared on the scene.

Up to this time, it seems probable that Roosevelt and the State Department had had no contact with the conspirators and had given them no encouragement. Roosevelt could contemplate taking the isthmus from Colombia by force, basing the action on what he knew to be a questionable interpretation of the treaty of 1846,[47] but he thought it would be dishonorable to foment a revolt surreptitiously.

[47] In his letter of Aug. 19, 1903, to Hay, cited above, Roosevelt wrote "If under the Treaty of 1846 we have a color of right to start in and build the canal, my offhand judgment would favor such proceeding."

51

Both Roosevelt and Bunau-Varilla always maintained that the United States government scrupulously refrained from giving the conspirators any encouragement at any time before the revolution, but even Bunau-Varilla's detailed account of what happened leaves some uncertainty about the accuracy of this contention.[48]

It was later charged that Cromwell had sent for Bunau-Varilla when he himself decided to withdraw from the conspiracy. The French engineer, on the other hand, insisted that he had come to the United States for purely personal reasons and that he knew nothing of the conspiracy until he met Amador by chance in New York. However this may be, he at once took charge of the movement. As a distinguished foreigner who had influential friends in the United States, he was able to see Roosevelt and Hay and other high officials and to discuss with them the probability of a revolution in Panama. From these conversations, he gathered the impression that Roosevelt intended to build the canal in Panama with or without the consent of Colombia, and that if the revolutionists could seize Panama City and Colon they might count on the United States to intervene under the treaty of 1846 to prevent further fighting. Bunau-Varilla consequently persuaded Amador to return to Panama to start the revolution at once and promised $100,000 out of his own pocket for expenses. In return, he was to be the first Minister of the new Republic of Panama in Washington.

Amador and his associates could hope to seize control of the isthmus with little difficulty. The governor, José Domingo de Obaldía, was a close friend, though apparently not a party to the plot, and the commander of the Colombian troops at Panama City had promised his support. It would be more difficult to resist the forces that the Colombian government could send to suppress the movement. The conspirators were consequently much alarmed in the last days of October when they learned that a Colombian force was approaching Colon by sea. They were somewhat reassured when Bunau-Varilla cabled that American warships were on their way to the isthmus. Bunau-Varilla later asserted that he was merely gambling on the assumption that the United States would send ships which he knew to be in the vicinity.

[48] P. Bunau-Varilla, *Panama. The Creation, Destruction, and Resurrection* (New York, 1914).

American warships were in fact on their way, and on November 2 their commanders were sent secret orders to "maintain free and uninterrupted transit. If interruption threatened by armed force, occupy the line of railroad. Prevent landing of any armed force with hostile intent, either Government or insurgent, either at Colon, Porto Bello, or other point. . . . Government force reported approaching the Isthmus in vessels. Prevent their landing if in your judgment this would precipitate a conflict." [49]

Before these orders reached the commander of the *U.S.S. Nashville,* which arrived at Colon on the same day, a Colombian warship had already landed 400 men. If these had crossed the isthmus, there would probably have been no revolution. There was no way to cross, however, except by rail, and Colonel Shaler, the superintendent of the Panama Railroad, made sure that no cars were available for the transport of a large force. Whatever Cromwell's relation to the revolutionary plot, it is clear that the local officers of the railroad were deeply involved in it. Shaler persuaded the Colombian commander to go to Panama with a few of his staff, promising that the troops could follow later, but throughout the day of November 3 no transportation was provided. The commander of the *Nashville,* still without orders, took no action until evening, when he formally prohibited the passage of troops in either direction.

Most of the leaders at Panama were ready to abandon their plans when they learned that the Colombian force had arrived at Colon. They were clearly still doubtful about Bunau-Varilla's promises of aid from the United States. The decision, however, was taken out of their hands when a mob gathered late in the afternoon of November 3 and marched on the barracks. The local garrison arrested the newly arrived Colombian officers, and the independence of Panama was declared. The revolutionists then proposed to send forces to attack the Colombians at Colon, but the American naval commander, in accord with the time-honored policy of preventing fighting along the transit route, prohibited them from doing so.

On the Atlantic side, meanwhile, the officer who had been left in charge of the Colombian troops threatened to burn the town and kill all Americans if his superiors were not released at Panama. Since the *Nashville,* which was a very small gunboat, could land only 42

[49] *Diplomatic History of the Panama Canal,* pp. 362–363.

men to oppose him, the American women and children took refuge on steamers in the harbor. The landing force and the American men in the city were concentrated in the railroad station, where they were for some time in apparent danger of attack. Fortunately, emissaries of the revolution and officials of the railroad company were able on November 5 to persuade the Colombian commander to leave with his troops on a British steamer.[50]

On the next day, November 6, the United States recognized the Republic of Panama. In informing the Colombian government of this action, the Legation at Bogotá was instructed to say that the President of the United States "most earnestly commends to the Governments of Colombia and of Panama the peaceable and equitable settlement of all questions at issue between them. He holds that he is bound not merely by treaty obligations, but by the interests of civilization, to see that the peaceable traffic of the world across the Isthmus of Panama shall not longer be disturbed by constant succession of unnecessary and wasteful civil wars."

Five days later, in reply to a specific question from the Colombian government, Secretary Hay telegraphed to Bogotá: "It is not thought desirable to permit landing of Colombian troops on Isthmus, as such a course would precipitate civil war and disturb for an indefinite period the free transit which we are pledged to protect." [51] Several American warships were by this time patrolling the coast of the isthmus to prevent a Colombian attack, and men were even put ashore in the remote Darién region to guard against an invasion overland. The Colombian government soon gave up any plans that it had for an attempt to reconquer Panama.

The Colombian government did attempt to reach an agreement with the United States. General Rafael Reyes, the dominant figure in the conservative party, proposed on November 6 to settle the canal question satisfactorily if the United States would uphold Colombia's sovereignty on the isthmus. He said that his government could declare martial law and ratify the canal treaty by decree, or that it would call a special session of Congress in May, with new and

[50] There are accounts of the revolution in Miner, *Fight for the Panama Route,* pp. 359ff. and in *The Story of Panama,* pp. 386–399, 439–464; Arango's *Datos Para la Historia de la Independencia* is a good account by a participant.

[51] For these communications, see *Foreign Relations, 1903,* pp. 225, 228.

friendly members, if the United States preferred. This offer merely confirmed Roosevelt and Hay in their belief that the Colombians had acted in bad faith in permitting the treaty to be rejected.

On November 18, 1903, Hay and Bunau-Varilla signed a treaty by which the United States guaranteed Panama's independence and Panama gave the United States the right to build a canal. Bunau-Varilla, in his enthusiasm for the completion of the waterway, proposed provisions that gave the United States far more freedom of action and a greater control in the Canal Zone than the Hay-Herrán Treaty would have done. The Frenchman acted without instructions from the new government at Panama, and the agreement was rushed to completion just before the arrival of a commission that the Panamanians had sent to participate in the negotiations. Nevertheless, the governing *junta* at Panama, without seeing the actual text, promised to ratify it as soon as it reached the isthmus. Both parties evidently felt that it was urgent to place the United States in a position where it would have a legal basis for resisting any Colombian attack on the isthmus. Nonetheless, it would have been more decent, and wiser, to give the new Panamanian government an opportunity to consider the terms of a document that so fundamentally affected the life of the republic and the lives of its citizens.

Though we may agree with Roosevelt's conviction that the canal was necessary for the safety of the United States and may sympathize with his exasperation at the Colombians' treatment of the Hay-Herrán Treaty, there are probably few North Americans today who would attempt to defend the way in which the President, to use his own words, "took the Canal Zone." [52] Roosevelt, however, always maintained that his action was proper. He was proud of it and took full responsibility for it. He wrote Henry Cabot Lodge in 1909: "The vital work, getting Panama as an independent republic, on which all else hinged, was done by me without the aid or advice of anyone, save in so far as they carried out my instructions; and without the knowledge of anyone." [53]

Roosevelt vigorously defended his action in a special message to Congress on January 4, 1904. He flatly denied any "complicity" of the United States in the revolution. He argued that the chief pur-

[52] Speech at the University of California, Berkeley, March 23, 1911.
[53] *Letters*, Vol. vi, p. 1491.

pose of the Treaty of 1846 had been the building of a canal and that Colombia had had no right to refuse permission for its construction. In rejecting Colombia's request to intervene to restore her authority on the isthmus, and in recognizing Panama, the United States, "instead of using its forces to destroy those who sought to make the engagements of the treaty a reality, recognized them as the proper custodians of the sovereignty of the Isthmus." His action, he said, was further justified by the fact that the prompt construction of the canal was imperative from the standpoint of "our national interests and safety." The events of the past five years had made the establishment of easy and speedy communication between the Atlantic and Pacific a matter "of vital necessity to the United States." Furthermore, if Colombia had been permitted to delay action until it could be claimed that the canal company's concession had lapsed, there would have been grave danger of complications with France.

The story of Panama raises ethical questions which are not easily answered. One serious charge against Roosevelt—that he instigated or helped to plan the revolution—was probably unfounded. The conspirators, up to the moment of the revolt, obviously doubted whether they would receive any help from Washington. If there had been any coordination between their plans and Roosevelt's preparations for dealing with an emergency on the isthmus, the United States would probably have had a more adequate force in isthmian waters at the time set for the revolt. One small ship, capable of landing about 40 men, was obviously inadequate, and its weakness endangered the lives of many American civilians.

Later, much was made of the fact that the State Department, some hours before the revolt actually occurred, sent a cable to the consulate at Panama reading: "Uprising on Isthmus reported. Keep department promptly and fully informed"; and that the consulate replied: "No uprising yet. Reported will be in the night. Situation is critical." The Department's inquiry, however, is explained by an Associated Press report, published on November 3, indicating that a revolution was imminent, and by a more explicit report from the consulate at Colon. Another suspicious circumstance was the visit to Panama in September 1903 of two army officers who had been making a tour of Venezuela and Colombia. Roosevelt later said [54]

[54] In his message to Congress of January 4, 1904.

that their report, combined with reports in the press, had led him to order several warships to the isthmus in the first days of November. It seems possible that these officers were sent to Panama after Roosevelt had begun to consider the idea of simply seizing the Canal Zone, but they apparently had little or no contact with the conspirators in Panama, for their information about the plot was inaccurate in several respects.[55]

While we cannot be satisfied that we know the whole story, there seems to be little reason to doubt the sincerity of Roosevelt's statement, made repeatedly in private letters as well as publicly, that he would have considered it dishonorable to foment a revolt in another country. At this distance, however, the difference between what he indignantly denied doing and what he admittedly did does not seem so great as it apparently did to him. It is clear that both he and Hay tacitly encouraged Bunau-Varilla, if only by receiving him and permitting him to discuss his plans. Bunau-Varilla was able to learn from them, and probably from other friends in Washington, what he needed to know. As Roosevelt wrote one of his friends, the Frenchman was "a very able fellow, and it was his business to find out what he thought our Government would do." The President had "no doubt that he was able to make a very accurate guess, and to advise his people accordingly. In fact he would have been a very dull man if he had been unable to make such a guess." [56]

We have seen how the American government prevented Colombia from restoring her control on the isthmus when the revolt occurred. The argument that this action was justified under the Treaty of 1846 is not convincing. There was certainly little basis for the assertion that the treaty obligated Colombia to permit the United States to build a canal. It did guarantee to the United States the right of free transit across the Isthmus of Panama "upon any modes of communication that now exist or that may be hereafter constructed," and promised American citizens the same treatment as the citizens of New Granada with respect to tolls or charges when "passing over any road or canal that might be made by the government of New Granada or by the authority of the same." In return,

---

[55] Excerpts from their report are quoted in *The Story of Panama* and in the President's Message to Congress of Jan. 4, 1904.

[56] Roosevelt to John Bigelow, January 6, 1904. *Letters*, Vol. III, p. 689.

the United States guaranteed to New Granada "the perfect neutrality" of the isthmus "with the view that the free transit from the one to the other sea may not be interrupted or embarrassed . . ." and further guaranteed "the rights of sovereignty and property which New Granada has and possesses over the said territory." The purpose of the treaty was to facilitate the construction of a canal, or a railroad, but it hardly required Colombia to permit a canal to be built.

The intervention of North American forces to prevent fighting along the transit route was not in itself unusual or improper. The United States had repeatedly taken similar action in the past under the treaty. Usually it had acted at the request of the Colombian government, though it had always been understood that the treaty did not obligate the United States to maintain Colombia's sovereignty on the isthmus against internal revolt.[57] What was difficult to justify was the use of force to prevent Colombia from suppressing a revolt. It would be hard to imagine that the makers of the Treaty of 1846 had contemplated that it would ever be invoked in a way that caused Colombia to lose the territory.

On the other hand, one may ask whether the United States had a duty to discourage or oppose the Panamanians in their bid for independence. Though persons connected with the French canal company had helped to promote the conspiracy for their own selfish purposes, and though its success was made possible by the bribery of some Colombian military officers, the revolution was nevertheless a real popular movement, supported by most of the leading citizens and by the mass of the people, at least in Panama City. The inhabitants of the isthmus felt that the rejection of the Hay-Herrán Treaty, as Hay wrote, "threatened their most vital interests with destruction. . . ."[58] Their livelihood had always depended on the transit route, which would become a thing of the past if the canal were built elsewhere.

The revolt would probably not have occurred, however, if the United States had attempted to discourage it. Roosevelt had alternative courses of action after the treaty was rejected at Bogotá. One was to continue negotiations with Colombia. With patience and

[57] See Admiral Chester's article in the *American Journal of International Law*, Vol. viii (1914), p. 443.

[58] *Foreign Relations, 1903*, p. 302.

more skillful and flexible diplomacy it might well have been possible to reach an agreement. The Colombians' fear that the United States might turn to Nicaragua could have been more effectively exploited, and the treaty could have been made more acceptable by increasing the amount of the indemnity. Roosevelt, however, was too exasperated by what he considered the incompetence and bad faith of the Marroquín administration. He never fully realized the difficulty of the Colombian President's position and thought of him as a dictator who could have forced ratification had he wished to do so. Furthermore, Roosevelt regarded as "blackmail" any suggestion of more generous financial terms. It would have been difficult in any case to defend an increase in the indemnity when the advocates of the Nicaraguan route knew that Nicaragua had agreed to accept a smaller amount.

Roosevelt was also little inclined to accept a further delay. On July 1, 1902, he had written John Hay that "the great bit of work of my administration, and from the material and constructive standpoint one of the greatest bits of work that the twentieth century will see, is the Isthmian Canal." [59] We can imagine that he was eager to see the work begun before he left office, which, so far as he knew, would be on March 4, 1905. Furthermore, he considered the immediate construction of the canal "imperative" for military reasons. [60] It would be difficult to refute his argument on this point, even though no one could have foreseen that a world war would begin just after the canal was opened.

To adopt another alternative, and turn to Nicaragua, would have entailed not only delay but also some loss of face politically, for some of the advocates of the Nicaragua route had been among the President's severest critics. The idea was the more unattractive because Zelaya had persistently refused to accede to what the United States considered essential requirements. [61] It also seemed doubtful whether an agreement could be reached with Costa Rica about

[59] *Letters*, Vol. II, p. 284.
[60] Roosevelt, *Autobiography*, p. 523.
[61] In this connection see Hay's letter to Senator Morgan, April 22, 1902 (quoted in Dennett, *John Hay* [New York, 1933], p. 367 and also in Thayer, *Life of John Hay*, Vol. II, p. 300), and Merry's later review of the situation in his despatch of Oct. 4, 1905, in which he expressed the opinion that no agreement with Nicaragua would have been possible.

her rights in the San Juan River. The President of that country had insisted that a constitutional amendment was necessary before an agreement could be negotiated, and the Congress had rejected the amendment in May 1903.[62] The decisive argument against the Nicaraguan route, however, was probably the fact that the engineers thought the Panama route better.

The third alternative—to seize the Canal Zone from Colombia by force—was the one that Roosevelt had decided to recommend before the Panama revolution offered an easier way to achieve his purpose. We may be thankful that the revolution averted so flagrant an act of aggression.

On the whole, in the light of hindsight, both the interests and the reputation of the United States might have been better served if Roosevelt had persisted in an effort to reach an agreement with Colombia. General Reyes, who succeeded Marroquín, was outspokenly in favor of an agreement, and his political position was much stronger than his predecessor's. If necessary, the United States could well have afforded to offer a larger payment. In the long run, after years of strained relations and difficult negotiations, the American government did pay Colombia an indemnity of $25,000,000.[63]

RELATIONS WITH THE REPUBLIC OF PANAMA

The treaty of November 18, 1903, gave the United States more extensive rights than it would have had under the treaty rejected by Colombia. Bunau-Varilla, who apparently suggested many of its provisions, was anxious to see the canal built, and he foresaw more clearly than did Hay or Roosevelt some of the problems that would arise when one government attempted to carry out a great engineering enterprise in the territory of another. The treaty gave the United States perpetual control over a zone ten miles wide, where it was to have all the rights, power, and authority which it would possess if it were the sovereign of the territory. The United States, furthermore, could take any additional lands that it needed for canal purposes. The cities of Panama and Colon, at either end of the proposed

[62] For the negotiations, see Merry's despatches of March 22, June 10, and Nov. 2, 1902; and May 6 and May 24, 1903.
[63] A treaty containing an expression of regret and providing for the indemnity was signed in 1914 but not ratified until April 1921.

canal, were not included in the zone, but the United States was given the right to intervene in either city to enforce sanitary ordinances or to maintain order. Panama, in return, received $10,000,000 in cash and the promise of an annuity of $250,000, to begin nine years after the exchange of ratifications.

The treaty created a situation in which many difficult and complicated problems were certain to arise. All of Panama's economic and political life centered in two cities which were entirely surrounded on the land side by Canal Zone territory and which formed continuous urban areas with the North American communities that soon grew up in the zone. The Panama Railroad, operated by the canal authorities, provided the only means of travel between them, and the railroad company owned nearly all of the real estate in Colon and much land in Panama. The future of the two cities would be shaped by the policies that the United States adopted in the zone, and conditions in the two cities, where many of the canal employees lived, would directly affect the tremendous task which the United States was undertaking.

Though they had no opportunity to participate in the negotiation of the treaty, the leaders in Panama seem to have raised no very serious objections to the provision authorizing the United States to intervene to maintain order in the terminal cities. Early in 1904, in fact, they incorporated in their constitution an article giving the United States the right to intervene not only in the terminal cities but in any part of the republic. This was adopted at the suggestion of the American Minister but against the wishes of the Department of State, which feared that it might impose an obligation which the United States would not wish to assume.[64] Later in 1904 President Amador asked the moral support of the United States in disbanding the Panamanian army, which had assumed a threatening attitude toward his administration.

[64] Assistant Secretary Loomis had apparently approved the Minister's idea in his cable of January 6, 1904, but Second Assistant Secretary Adee had characterized it as unwise and short-sighted because it would impose on the United States an obligation to intervene. Secretary Hay's instruction of January 19, sent by mail, told the Minister that he preferred that the constitution contain nothing incompatible with the widest liberty of action on the part of the United States and pointed out that the adoption of the proposed provision at the instigation of the United States would impose an obligation on the American government. Minister Buchanan reported the adoption of the article in his cable of January 28.

The new government's readiness to cooperate was also evident in the field of public health. If the canal were to be built, it was imperative to eliminate the yellow fever and malaria which had been so important a factor in the failure of the French effort. The canal treaty provided that the United States might build and operate sewers and water-supply systems in Panama City and Colon and might prescribe sanitary ordinances for the two cities, with the right to enforce these ordinances itself if the local authorities failed to enforce them. When yellow fever broke out in January 1905, the Panamanian government asked the United States to take over the enforcement of the sanitary code immediately, and public health work in Panama City and Colon was entrusted to the health officer of the canal. Though this involved constant inspection of private dwellings, accompanied by inflexible severity in the imposition of fines on offenders, the arrangement worked well, and the isthmus almost immediately ceased to be one of the most notoriously unhealthful places in the world. The change was effected under the leadership of Dr. William C. Gorgas, who had been responsible for the sanitation of Habana a few years earlier, and who was health officer of the canal during much of the construction period.

Inevitably, however, the peculiar situation established by the canal treaty gave rise to disputes and friction. The Panamanian leaders had their full share of national pride, and the American officials, as Roosevelt put it, had "the utmost difficulty in meeting [their] susceptibilities." Unfortunately, too many of the North American officials did not even attempt to meet them and were impatient or contemptuous of Panamanian protests or representations that threatened to interfere with their complete freedom of action in the Canal Zone. It was often difficult for them to see any merit in complaints or demands that seemed important from the Panamanian point of view, and many questions that could have been easily settled by the use of common sense gave trouble because they involved questions of principle on which neither side felt that it could afford to yield.

The most serious controversies arose from disputes about the interpretation of the canal treaty. Article III, as we have seen, stated that the United States would have all rights in the Canal Zone which it would have if it were the sovereign of the territory. The American government insisted on a literal interpretation of this article because it felt that it must have a free hand to carry on the work of construction and to provide for the welfare of the thousands of employees and laborers who were brought to the zone as the work got under way. The Panamanian government, on the other hand, maintained that the object of the treaty was to provide for the "construction, maintenance, operation, sanitation and protection" of the canal and that it had ceded only such rights in the zone as were necessary for these purposes. It denied that the United States had a right to treat the zone as though it were its own territory.

The first important dispute began in June 1904, when President Roosevelt issued an executive order opening the Canal Zone to commerce and ordering the establishment of customhouses in the zone ports. The Panamanian government had apparently agreed to these measures, but it reversed its attitude when local businessmen pointed out what would happen to them if commercial enterprises were established in the zone, where they would pay no Panamanian taxes and would presumably be able to import goods free of duty. The merchants were already worried about the operation of the commissaries which the United States was setting up for its own officers and employees. Panama consequently objected vigorously to the opening of the zone to trade and also to the establishment in the zone of post offices using United States stamps.

Secretary Hay, in his reply to this protest, insisted on the right of the United States to do what it saw fit in the Canal Zone. A few months later, however, William Howard Taft, the Secretary of War, visited the isthmus and arranged a compromise which was embodied in executive orders issued under the authority of the President of the United States. These provided that imports into the Canal Zone should be restricted to articles for the use of the canal or for persons connected with the enterprise, or for sale to ships passing through the waterway. The merchants of Panama were thus assured that private businesses would not be set up in the zone and that the commissaries would not be open to the general public. It was also agreed that the post offices in the zone should use surcharged Panamanian stamps purchased by the zone at 40 percent of their face value. The arrangement thus protected Panama's economic interests and also satisfied her national pride. The "Taft Agreement" was intended to be in effect only while the canal was under construction, but it was not abrogated until 1924, and the principle which it established with regard to imports into the zone governed American policy in the zone for a much longer period. Unfortunately the application of the principle was not always easy, and the operation of the commissaries, especially, gave rise to continual disputes in later years.

◄ 3 ►

The Genesis of the Roosevelt Corollary

▨ The basic idea that inspired the Caribbean policy of the United States in the first two decades of the twentieth century was Theodore Roosevelt's corollary to the Monroe Doctrine: that the United States, if it wished to prevent European intervention, must help the Caribbean republics to do away with the chronic disorder and financial mismanagement that invited intervention. This idea was not wholly new, for several statesmen and writers in Europe and in the United States had suggested that the United States could not maintain the Monroe Doctrine without assuming some responsibility for the conduct of the states protected by it.[1] The Corollary itself was foreshadowed by the Platt Amendment, which sought to make sure that Cuba's independence was not imperiled by inability to protect foreigners and to pay debts. Cuba, however, was an exceptional case. It was not until after the Anglo-German blockade of Venezuela in 1902–1903 that the Corollary became a part of the American government's general policy in the Caribbean.

It is sometimes difficult to determine the real motives that lead a government to adopt a policy. It is less difficult in the case of the Roosevelt Corollary because the policy reflected the President's own philosophy. It was formulated at a time when he was devoting much time and effort to foreign affairs and especially to Latin American problems. Roosevelt's ideas about international relations were perhaps not very profound, but they were positive, and he expressed them vigorously in public documents and personal letters. He was determined that the United States should be recognized as a great power and that it should conduct itself as a great power. He would probably have considered it his duty to take any action that seemed necessary for the security of the United States, even though the action, as in the case of the Panama revolution, involved some disregard of the rights of another nation, but at the same time he would have insisted that nations, like individuals, must be honest and decent in their relations with one another.

[1] For several examples, see Rippy, *The Caribbean Danger Zone* (New York, 1940), pp. 46ff.

Roosevelt had an intense dislike for disorder and financial irresponsibility, and he had no doubts about the right and even the duty of strong nations to impose the benefits of good government and civilization on weaker and less advanced peoples. He admired the British accomplishment in India, and he was proud of what the United States was doing in the Philippines. He was even prouder, however, of what the United States had done in setting up an apparently successful independent state in Cuba. He did not feel that it was right or profitable to take foreign territory simply for the sake of expansion, and he repeatedly emphasized his belief that the United States should never seek to expand at the expense of one of the other American republics.

Roosevelt was equally certain that the United States could never permit any other power to acquire new possessions in America. When he first took office, however, he does not seem to have shared the feeling, long traditional in the Department of State, that the use of force by a European power against an American state must be distasteful to the United States even though no occupation of territory was involved. "If any South American state misbehaves toward any European country," he wrote to a German friend in July 1901, "let the European country spank it." [2] It was apparently the European intervention in Venezuela in 1902 that caused him to realize that conflicts between European countries and American states were always potentially dangerous to the United States.

The Anglo-German Blockade of Venezuela

Venezuela offered a good example of the diplomatic complications that could arise from internal disorder and financial mismanagement. Since its independence, the republic had been ruled by a series of dictatorships that had risen and fallen in bitterly fought civil wars. There had been a period after 1870 when conditions seemed somewhat more stable, and many foreigners had settled or made investments in the country, but a new civil war began in 1898 and continued for some years. Disorder, as always, gave rise to claims, and when the foreign claimants appealed to their governments for help the country's new ruler, General Cipriano Castro, arrogantly rebuffed diplomatic efforts to obtain redress.

[2] To Baron Speck von Sternburg, *Letters*, Vol. III, p. 116.

Influential German trading firms, and the powerful *Diskonto Gesellschaft* of Berlin, had been among the chief sufferers. The *Diskonto Gesellschaft* had financed the Great Venezuelan Railway Company, built under a concession granted to Krupp of Essen and an English company in 1883. The Venezuelan government had guaranteed a minimum return on this investment but had failed to make good on the guarantee, and in 1896 the railway company and various other German and foreign creditors had accepted government bonds in satisfaction of their claims. These soon went into default, and in 1902 the total of principal and unpaid interest was about $12,500,000. In addition, Germans had some hundreds of thousands of dollars of damage claims for personal injuries and losses during the civil war. These, rather than the default on the bonds, were the ostensible reason for the German intervention, but pressure from those interested in the bonds undoubtedly helped to persuade the Foreign Office to act.

There is no reason to suppose that the German Foreign Office had any motive more sinister than to protect the German investments and to show that Venezuela and other disorderly countries could not safely mistreat German interests. There was probably no serious thought of obtaining any political control or territory in Venezuela,[3] and no deliberate purpose to challenge the Monroe Doctrine. The imperial government was at the time making an effort to improve its relations with the United States, which had been somewhat unfriendly since the Spanish American War, and it endeavored to handle the affair in a way that would not arouse American suspicion.

Germany had in fact reason to believe that a show of force against Castro would not be displeasing to the government at Washington. In his message to Congress in December 1901, Roosevelt declared that the Monroe Doctrine ". . . has nothing to do with the commercial relations of any American power, save that it in truth allows each of them to form such as it desires. . . . We do not guarantee any State against punishment if it misconducts itself, provided that punishment does not take the form of acquisition of territory by any non-American power." The President evidently had Venezuela in mind, and he could hardly have been surprised when the German

[3] In this connection, see the detailed account in Vagts, *Deutschland und die Vereinigten Staaten*, Vol. II, pp. 1525–1635.

Ambassador, a few days later, informed the State Department that his government was considering a blockade or a temporary occupation of Venezuelan ports in order to compel Castro to settle German claims. He gave assurance that no permanent occupation of territory was intended. Secretary of State Hay, in reply, quoted the President's recent message and indicated that the United States would not object.[4]

The German government nevertheless took no action for the time being. It apparently realized that public opinion in the United States was likely to react unfavorably to an attack on another American country, and did not wish to run the risk of arousing bad feeling before Prince Henry's goodwill visit to the United States, which took place early in 1902. Furthermore, the naval authorities needed more time for preparation and thought it better to postpone the operation until after the Venezuelan rainy season.[5]

In the meantime, the British government grew equally exasperated with Castro and decided to join the proposed blockade. British-Venezuelan relations had been strained to the breaking point by a series of disputes arising from Castro's belief that officials in Trinidad and other British islands were helping his enemies in a civil war that threatened his regime in 1901–1902. Several small British West Indian vessels had been seized by Castro's forces in Venezuelan waters or on the high seas or at Patos Island, which was claimed by both governments. In some cases, probably, these seizures were justified, but Castro's arrogant and offensive attitude made the demand for redress a matter of prestige. The amount involved was less than £10,000, but the British, like the Germans, clearly hoped to force Castro to settle other debts as well as the claims which were the ostensible reason for the intervention.

The principal British investment in Venezuela was in government bonds. The debt originated in a loan made by British bankers to Great Colombia in the first years of independence, and it had been increased by bond issues sold by unscrupulous bankers to unwary investors in 1862 and 1864. There had been few intervals when any of the debt was regularly served, and after several readjustments, in which the bondholders had to accept losses, the total amount

[4] *Foreign Relations, 1901*, pp. 192ff.
[5] Vagts, *Deutschland*, Vol. II, p. 1547.

outstanding, excluding unpaid interest, was £2,638,200 in 1902. The bonds, like those sold in Germany, were in default.

On November 13, 1902, the British Ambassador wrote Hay that Venezuela had refused even to discuss British complaints about unjustifiable interference with the liberty and property of British subjects, and that the British government would have to consider what steps it should take to protect British interests. Hay replied that ". . . the United States government viewed with regret any resort to force on the part of European powers against the Republics of Central and South America, but they could not object to any action taken by them with the view of obtaining redress for injuries inflicted on their subjects, provided such action did not contemplate any territorial acquisition." [6]

While the German and British governments were making plans for intervention, a group of bankers in London and New York came forward with a project for a peaceful adjustment of Venezuela's financial problems. This had been under discussion for some months between representatives of Venezuela and the republic's European creditors, but it is not clear that Castro had approved it or that either the German or the British government had been greatly interested in it. Its details were still vague, but the plan apparently contemplated the establishment of a bank and a customs collectorship with enough foreign control to make possible a new bond issue for the payment of claims. The plan's sponsors hoped for vigorous support from the United States.[7] When a representative of J. and W. Seligman and Company discussed the matter with Roosevelt and Hay in the first days of December, however, he was told that they would welcome a settlement that would avert the use of force, but that the United States ". . . would assume no obligation whatever in the nature of a material or moral guarantee of the liabilities created by the transaction." [8]

[6] *Venezuelan Arbitration . . . Appendix to Case of Great Britain,* Senate Document 119, 58th Congress, 3rd Session, pp. 782–783.

[7] See the interview with Isaac Seligman in the New York *Herald* for December 11, 1902, and the statement of the Venezuelan Consul at London in the same paper for December 13. Also Vagts, *Deutschland,* Vol. II, pp. 1549ff., 1578ff., and 1627, and Callcott, *The Caribbean Policy of the United States,* p. 130.

[8] See Hay's cable to the Embassy at Berlin, December 5, 1902, *Foreign Relations, 1903,* p. 418.

By this time the intervening governments were ready to act. On December 7, 1902, a Sunday, the German and British Ministers at Caracas peremptorily demanded the immediate settlement of the claims that they had presented. The next day, without awaiting a reply, they left the city. On December 9 German and British warships seized several small Venezuelan vessels, sinking two of them, and on December 13 they bombarded two forts at Puerto Cabello in retaliation for the alleged mistreatment of the crew of a British ship. There was no loss of life, but it was reported that the theft of twenty pedigreed fighting cocks by British sailors was a cruel blow to the local community.[9]

Castro's first reaction to the ultimatum of December 7 was to order the arrest of all British and German subjects in Venezuela, but Herbert W. Bowen, the American Minister, soon persuaded him to release them. On December 9 Castro proposed that the claims of the intervening powers be submitted to arbitration, and asked Bowen to represent Venezuela in negotiations for a settlement. Secretary Hay, at Castro's request, cabled this proposal to London and Berlin on December 12. He did not urge its acceptance, and it was apparently received rather coldly by the intervening governments.

Within a very few days, however, the German and British governments found it advisable to change their attitude. Roosevelt, as he later admitted to the German Ambassador,[10] had been mistaken in his estimate of the reaction of American public opinion to a European attack on Venezuela. Even before the attack began, there had been reports that the situation was being watched with increasing uneasiness in official circles in Washington,[11] and the sinking of Venezuelan ships and the bombardment of Puerto Cabello had aroused all the traditional American sensitiveness to European aggression in the Western Hemisphere. On December 16 rumors that American warships were being ordered to Trinidad and that Roosevelt was preparing a special message to Congress caused a flurry of selling on the New York stock exchange.[12] The *Literary Digest* reported on December 20 that "an apprehension that England and

9 New York *Herald,* Dec. 18, 1902, p. 3.
10 Vagts, *Deutschland,* Vol. II, p. 1626.
11 New York *Herald,* Dec. 4, 6, 7, 1902.
12 *Ibid.,* December 17, 1902.

Germany will overstep the limits prescribed by the Monroe Doctrine is apparent in the American press as a whole." Roosevelt himself thought that ". . . the chances of complications from a long and irritating little war between the European powers and Venezuela were sufficiently great to make me feel most earnestly that the situation should be brought to a peaceful end if possible," [13] though he was still "bound that we should not be put in the position of preventing the collection of an honest debt." [14]

It was probably in response to the pressure of public opinion that the American Ambassadors at London and Paris were instructed on December 16 to urge the acceptance of Castro's proposal for arbitration. They found both governments disposed to come to an agreement. Neither wished to offend the United States, and the British Cabinet was facing severe criticism at home, where cooperation with Germany was unpopular and public opinion was shocked by the events in Venezuela. Both governments were also probably concerned by the widespread hostile reaction in South America.[15] When the American Ambassadors made their representations they were told that the powers had already decided to ask Roosevelt himself to act as arbitrator. The President was at first inclined to accept this invitation in order to forestall any award that might be inconsistent with the Monroe Doctrine,[16] but his advisers dissuaded him, and after some difficulty he persuaded the parties to the dispute to agree to submit the matter to the Permanent Court at the Hague.

On December 19, Hay cabled Bowen that several important financial institutions would like to finance the payment of the claims against Venezuela and instructed the Minister to ascertain whether the Venezuelan government wished the United States to use its good offices in that direction. The Minister for Foreign Affairs replied that the idea of an arrangement with a financial syndicate seemed premature "at present." [17]

The intervening powers maintained their pressure on Castro while the conditions of the proposed arbitration were being discussed, and

[13] Letter to Albert Shaw, Dec. 27, 1902, *Letters,* Vol. III, p. 396.
[14] Letter to G. W. Hinman, Dec. 29, 1902, *ibid.,* Vol. III, p. 399.
[15] The New York *Herald* published a number of stories on this subject between December 13 and 19.
[16] Letter to Albert Shaw, cited above, n. 13.
[17] Hay to Bowen, Dec. 19, 1902; Bowen to Hay, Dec. 20, 1902.

Italy, which had miscellaneous claims amounting to about $560,000, now associated herself with them. On December 20 the three governments proclaimed a blockade of the Venezuelan coast. This was avowedly an act of war, for the British government had raised legal objections to Germany's proposal for a "pacific" blockade, and the United States had indicated that it would not recognize the right of other powers to stop American ships in time of peace.

In accepting arbitration, furthermore, England, Germany, and Italy insisted on conditions that amounted to a surrender. Castro was compelled to abandon his contention that his government was not liable for damages done by revolutionists. The German and British governments also demanded that their "first line" claims should be excluded from the arbitration and that Venezuela should give satisfactory guarantees for their prompt payment. In the case of Germany, these were all of the claims resulting from the civil war of 1898–1900, amounting to $325,000. Great Britain demanded immediate payment of £5,500 for the seizure of vessels and the mistreatment of British subjects. The two governments refused to raise the blockade until a full settlement was reached.

Castro asked Bowen to represent him in the negotiations, which began at Washington in January 1903. The blockading powers accepted Bowen's proposal that all except the first line claims be dealt with by mixed commissions with neutral umpires, rather than by the Hague Court, and that Venezuela should set aside 30 percent of the customs revenues at La Guaira and Puerto Cabello to assure payment of the awards. But the negotiations were deadlocked when Bowen insisted that the claims of all nations, including countries that had not participated in the blockade, should be treated equally. The blockading powers insisted that not only their first line claims but all their other claims must be paid first. Germany was particularly intransigent, and even after it was agreed that the general question of priority should be submitted to the Hague Court she delayed signature of a protocol by demanding that her first line claims be paid at once in cash—a demand that seemed unreasonable in view of the relatively large amount involved and the poverty of the Venezuelan treasury.

At this point, apparently, Roosevelt took an action which he frequently mentioned in later years but which does not appear in the official record. As the ex-President told the story in 1916, when Germany refused to agree to arbitration, he became convinced that she intended to occupy and fortify one of Venezuela's ports. He consequently assembled the American fleet in the Caribbean and told the German Ambassador that he would send it to the Venezuelan coast if no agreement were reached within a specified period. Receiving no reply, he repeated the threat and said that he would advance the date when Admiral Dewey would be ordered to sail. Thereupon the German government acceded to his demand.[18]

In 1916 Roosevelt apparently thought that this incident had occurred in December 1902, when the powers first moved against Venezuela. Several historians have argued that it could hardly have taken place then, because the German government in fact accepted arbitration very promptly when the United States urged it. There were indeed reports that Germany was reluctant to agree to Castro's first offer to arbitrate,[19] and it is possible that Roosevelt may have sought to exert pressure at that time, but there is very little evidence of any disagreement between Germany and the United States in December. On December 26, in fact, Roosevelt wrote to Albert Shaw that "nothing England and Germany have done or threatened to do so far has in any way conflicted with our contention as to what the Monroe Doctrine means."[20]

There was a sharp disagreement in February 1903. Roosevelt wrote to one of his sons on February 9: "My chief difficulty at the moment is the Venezuelan matter, in which Germany takes an impossible stand."[21] Admiral Dewey was still in the Caribbean with the bulk of the fleet, which had been carrying on maneuvers planned many months earlier; and on February 3 the German representative, Baron Speck von Sternburg, reported to his government that the President had told him that Dewey had been given secret orders "to be ready" (*sich bereitzuhalten*).[22] On the 19th, after an agree-

[18] Roosevelt told this version of the story in a letter to W. R. Thayer, written August 21, 1916; J. B. Bishop, *Life and Times of Theodore Roosevelt* (New York, 1920), Vol. I, p. 221.

[19] New York *Herald*, Dec. 16 and 17, 1902.

[20] *Letters*, Vol. III, p. 396.

[21] *Ibid.*, Vol. III, p. 423.

[22] Vagts, *Deutschland*, Vol. II, p. 1611.

ment was reached, the Baron expressed relief that possible trouble with the United States had been avoided.[23] It seems quite probable that it was in February that Roosevelt took a vigorous stand to break the deadlock and bring about the lifting of the blockade.

At any rate, Germany made the rather slight concession of agreeing that most of her first line claims should be paid in five monthly installments. Bowen signed protocols with the blockading powers on February 13 and with the United States and several other creditor governments a few days later, and the blockade was lifted. The protocols provided that Venezuela should set aside 30 percent of the customs receipts at Puerto Cabello and La Guaira for the payment of the awards of the mixed commissions that were to adjudicate the unsettled claims, and that the Hague Court should decide whether the blockading powers should receive preferential treatment. Belgian officials were to take charge of the customhouses at Puerto Cabello and La Guaira if Venezuela did not comply with her agreements.[24] Venezuela also promised to make arrangements that would assure the regular service of the bonded debt. It is interesting to note that Roosevelt apparently saw no objection to the provision that might have given a European government control of the customs. At a later period this would almost certainly have been objectionable to the United States.

On February 22, 1904, a tribunal of three judges selected by the Emperor of Russia from the panel constituting the Permanent Court upheld the blockading powers in their contention that they should have preferential treatment. It said that the Venezuelan government had recognized in principle the justice of their claims but had not done so in the case of the neutral powers, and that neither Venezuela nor the neutral powers had protested the demand for preferential treatment when it was first put forward. The court held that "the neutral powers, having taken no part in the warlike operations against Venezuela, could in some respects profit by the circumstances created by these operations, but without acquiring any new rights." [25] This reasoning was not very convincing, because both

[23] *Ibid.*
[24] For the texts of the protocols, see Senate Document 119, 58th Cong., 3rd. Sess., pp. 23ff. The protocol of Feb. 17 with the United States is printed in *Foreign Relations, 1903*, p. 804.
[25] For the text of the decision see Senate Document 119, cited above.

Venezuela and the United States had resisted the demand for preferential treatment during the negotiations leading to the signature of the protocols.

The protocols did bring about the settlement of most of the outstanding claims against Venezuela. With the money set aside from the customs receipts, the blockading powers' claims were paid off in full by 1907, and those of other countries by 1912.[26] In 1905 the outstanding British and German bonds were refunded—at par in the case of the 1896 bonds and at 72½ percent of face value in the case of the older British issue—in a new "Diplomatic Debt" on which the interest was reduced to 3 percent. The entire foreign debt was paid off during the Gómez regime. The blockade, however, did not bring about any marked change in Castro's general attitude toward foreign interests, and he was involved in new disputes with other governments, and especially with the United States, until he fell from power in 1908.

The Consequences of the Venezuela Blockade

Roosevelt thought that "getting England and Germany specifically to recognize the Monroe Doctrine" in the Venezuela affair had been an important achievement.[27] It was the first occasion when European powers had notified the United States and asked its acquiescence before taking action against a Latin American government.[28] Nevertheless, the reaction of American public opinion and the realization that any European military action against an American state could cause embarrassment to the United States led the President to feel that similar episodes should be prevented in the future. The Hague Court's decision, especially, had troublesome implications for American foreign policy.

The decision made it more rather than less probable that similar episodes would occur. If a state that used armed force to collect claims was to have a preferred position in any general debt settlement, interventions would inevitably become more frequent. There would always be the possibility that a punitive expedition would

[26] *Report of the Council of the Corporation of Foreign Bondholders* (London), 1912.
[27] Letter to Grover Cleveland, December 26, 1902, *Letters*, Vol. III, p. 398.
[28] Dexter Perkins, *The Monroe Doctrine, 1867–1907* (Baltimore, 1933), p. 394.

lead to the more or less permanent occupation of territory, or that the intervening power would interfere in internal affairs in a way that would give it political control. Aside from these dangers there was the fact that the principle established by the Court's decision would place at a disadvantage the citizens of countries like the United States which did not use force to collect claims. As one unnamed "prominent official" of the State Department told the press, it put "a premium on violence" and tended "to discourage nations which are disposed to settle their claims by the peaceful methods of diplomacy." [29]

Even before the Court's decision was handed down, Roosevelt seems to have been giving thought to the steps that the United States might take to prevent a repetition of the Venezuela affair. In March 1903, when the German Ambassador suggested the establishment of an international financial control in Venezuela, Roosevelt said that he did not think that the American people would approve such an arrangement. He had been mistaken, he said, in thinking that public opinion would not object to the recent intervention. A second attempt by foreign powers to collect debts by force would simply not be tolerated. Perhaps the establishment by the United States of a protectorate over South and Central America was the only way out, though he himself regarded this idea with repugnance.[30] Eleven months later, when he was considering the Dominican Republic's request for help to avert threatened European intervention, Roosevelt wrote one of his sons that he had reluctantly been obliged to take the initial step of interference; that he hoped that he would not have to go farther for a "good while" but that he thought it inevitable that the United States sooner or later "should assume an attitude of protection and regulation in regard to all these little states in the neighborhood of the Caribbean." [31] On February 26, 1904, he wrote to William Bayard Hále that his attitude toward the "weak and chaotic governments and people south of us" was based on the theory that "it is our duty, when it becomes absolutely inevitable, to police these countries in the interest of order and civilization." [32]

[29] *Literary Digest,* Vol. xxviii (1904), p. 318.
[30] Vagts, *Deutschland,* Vol. ii, p. 1626.
[31] To Theodore Roosevelt, Jr., Feb. 10, 1904, *Letters,* Vol. iv, p. 724.
[32] *Ibid.,* p. 740.

It seems probable that these ideas took more definite shape as a result of discussions with Elihu Root.[33] Root, who had been chiefly responsible for the policy of the United States in Cuba before his recent resignation as Secretary of War, was still a close friend and a trusted adviser, and the first statement of what came to be called Roosevelt's Corollary to the Monroe Doctrine appeared in a letter which Roosevelt asked Root to read for him at a dinner given in New York on May 20, 1904, to celebrate the anniversary of Cuban independence:

"I hail what has been done in Cuba not only for its own sake, but as showing the purpose and desire of this nation toward all the nations south of us. It is not true that the United States has any land hunger or entertains any projects as regards other nations, save such as are for their welfare.

"All that we desire is to see all neighboring countries stable, orderly and prosperous. Any country whose people conduct themselves well can count upon our hearty friendliness. If a nation shows that it knows how to act with decency in industrial and political matters, if it keeps order and pays its obligations, then it need fear no interference from the United States. Brutal wrongdoing, or an impotence which results in a general loosening of the ties of civilized society, may finally require intervention by some civilized nation, and in the Western Hemisphere the United States cannot ignore this duty; but it remains true that our interests, and those of our southern neighbors, are in reality identical. All that we ask is that they shall govern themselves well, and be prosperous and orderly. Where this is the case they will find only helpfulness from us." [34]

A few days later, in a personal letter to Root commenting on the criticism that his statement had aroused, the President expressed himself somewhat more explicitly: "If we are willing to let Germany or England act as the policemen of the Caribbean, then we can afford not to interfere when gross wrongdoing occurs. But if we intend to say 'Hands off' to the powers of Europe, then sooner or later we must keep order ourselves." [35]

[33] For Root's connection with the Roosevelt Corollary, see Jessup, *Root,* Vol. i, p. 469.
[34] *Letters,* Vol. iv, p. 801.
[35] *Ibid.,* p. 821.

The Foreign Debt of the Dominican Republic

In writing his letter of May 20, 1904, Roosevelt obviously had in mind the situation in the Dominican Republic, where European intervention to collect debts seemed imminent. His action in that country—the establishment of a customs receivership that made possible a general adjustment of foreign claims—was the first and perhaps the most important application of his corollary to the Monroe Doctrine. Because the apparent success of the Dominican experiment caused his successors to believe that customs receiverships would solve the worst problems of other Caribbean countries, it inspired the policies that led later to interventions in Nicaragua and Haiti. In the Dominican Republic itself the creation of the receivership was the first step in a chain of events that culminated in the establishment of an American military government in 1916.

Few people in the Western Hemisphere had a sadder history than the Dominicans. In the seventeenth and eighteenth centuries the Spanish colony of Santo Domingo had shared the island of Española with the fabulously rich French colony of St. Domingue, but the eastern end of the island, with a scanty population of Spanish settlers and Negro slaves, was poverty stricken and neglected. Their situation grew worse after the slave revolt in St. Domingue in 1791. The Spanish colony was conquered by Toussaint Louverture in 1800, and early in 1802 it was occupied by an army sent by Napoleon. The French forces remained in Santo Domingo after they were compelled to abandon Haiti, but in 1808–1809 Spain regained control with the aid of the British navy.

In 1821 a creole conspiracy overturned the Spanish regime and sought a union with Bolívar's Republic of Colombia, but the new government collapsed when a Haitian army invaded the country a few months later. During the next 22 years, the Dominicans lived under the authoritarian rule of a people of another race and culture. The families of Spanish descent found this situation especially unpleasant, and many of them left the island for good. The union ended in 1844, when disorders in Haiti gave the Dominicans a chance to revolt and set up an independent republic; but for many years afterward the Haitians attempted from time to time to restore their domination by force. The constant fear of another invasion and continual strife between the country's political factions made even independence a doubtful blessing. During the next quarter-century Dominican presidents repeatedly attempted to obtain foreign protection. Vigorous diplomatic representations by England, France, and the United States checked Haitian aggression after 1851, but projects for the establishment of a protectorate by one or another of the European powers were defeated by popular opposition and by the jealous intrigues of the other European consuls. Spain did reannex her former colony in 1861, but withdrew in 1865 after a long period of guerrilla warfare against groups that opposed her rule. Soon afterward the government in power at Santo Domingo and the Grant administration at Washington agreed that the republic should be annexed to the United States, but this plan was abandoned when the United States Senate failed to approve the treaty of annexation in 1870.

The chief reason for foreign interest in the republic was the fine harbor at Samaná Bay, on its northeastern coast, which was potentially one of the most important strategic positions in the West Indies. The United States, especially, had repeatedly attempted to obtain a naval base there. Its first effort, in 1854, was defeated by English and French opposition, backed by the appearance of warships. A renewed interest in the harbor was the most important consideration back of the annexation project between 1866 and 1870, and a third attempt to lease territory on the bay was defeated by premature publicity in 1892.

In the latter part of the nineteenth century fear of a Haitian reconquest receded and internal political conditions improved slightly. The country had its first long period of relative peace after 1882 under the heavy-handed and unenlightened dictatorship of Ulises Heureaux. Trade increased somewhat, and a number of foreigners set up businesses of various sorts. North American and Italian companies developed sugar growing, in which about $6,000,000 had been invested by 1905,[36] and the San Domingo Improvement Company of New York built some miles of railroad. This very limited economic progress, however, did little to ameliorate the country's backwardness and poverty, and its good effects were to a considerable extent offset by Heureaux's reckless and corrupt financial policies.

[36] Jacob H. Hollander, *The Debt of Santo Domingo* (Washington, 1905), p. 226.

The Dominican government already had a foreign debt arising from the "Hartmont" loan—one of the most notorious among several disgraceful financial transactions between British bankers and Latin American governments in the 1860's.[37] The Hartmont bonds, which were in default for many years, were refunded at less than a fifth of their face value when Heureaux obtained a new loan from the Dutch firm of Westendorp in 1888. As security for this loan, Heureaux agreed that the bankers should have a representative in each customhouse to receive all revenues collected. Westendorp attempted to float another loan for the Dominican government in 1890, but it was impossible to market the bonds at that time and the failure of the operation left the banker on the verge of bankruptcy. He consequently offered to sell his interests to the United States government. His offer was declined, but Secretary of State Foster suggested that an American company take over the bonds and the collection of customs, in order to forestall a reported plan to transfer them to French and German bankers.[38] It was thus that the San Domingo Improvement Company became the Dominican Republic's banker in 1893.

During the next six years the Improvement Company and Heureaux worked together in a close though not always harmonious partnership. The company floated new loans to refund the Westendorp bonds, which were in default, and to provide funds for the railroad construction that it undertook. In 1895 it came to Heureaux's assistance when the dictator's treatment of the French-owned national bank and the murder of a naturalized Frenchman caused the French government to threaten to seize the Dominican customhouses. The Improvement Company promised to guarantee the payments on the indemnity which the French government demanded, and a little later the company bought the stock of the bank and operated it as its own property.[39] In 1897, when the government again failed to meet the charges on its foreign debt, the company carried through another refunding operation.

[37] For the history of the Hartmont loan, see *Special Report from the Select Committee on Loans to Foreign States,* in House of Commons Sessional Papers, 1875, Vol. xi, Appendix No. 33.

[38] William H. Wynne, *State Insolvency and Foreign Bondholders* (New Haven, 1951), Vol. ii, pp. 212–213.

[39] John Bassett Moore, *Case of the San Domingo Improvement Company.* Collected Papers of John Bassett Moore, Vol. iii, p. 171.

When it floated bond issues, the company seems to have paid the government from 30 to 43 percent of the face value of the securities. It then sold the bonds to investors, mostly in Belgium and France, at such prices as it could obtain. A considerable proportion of the proceeds was always mysteriously absorbed in the expenses of the operation. Some, presumably, went into the pockets of the Dominican officials, and another portion was probably used for the bribery of stock exchange officials and newspapers which was customary in certain European countries when questionable bonds were being sold.[40] The success of such operations depended, of course, on finding gullible investors. It was later reported that a considerable number of the French holders of Dominican bonds were Catholic peasants in France who were under the impression that they were buying securities of the Dominican religious order.[41] Other investors were attracted by the promise of a large profit and by the supposed security afforded by the Improvement Company's customs collectorship.

This security was illusory. Though the loan contracts provided that the company might ask the Dutch, Belgian, British, French, and American governments to appoint a commission to take over the customs in case of default, no commission was set up when successive defaults occurred. The so-called *Regie*, through which the company collected the customs, was ineffective. The customs service was really controlled by Dominican officials, and until 1898 even the *Regie*'s representatives in the customhouses were Dominicans.[42] There was much fraud and much leakage. Heureaux himself was said to be the chief offender in the widespread smuggling that took place [43] and the customs receipts were further reduced by the government's practice of exempting merchants from the payment of duties in return for cash advances. The company frequently had to lend money to the government for the payment of interest on the bonds, and its refusal to continue these advances in 1896 led to a new default and to the refunding operation of 1897. This refunding, in which the bondholders were compelled for the third time in nine

[40] Hollander, *Debt of Santo Domingo*.
[41] *Ibid.*, p. 36.
[42] Moore, *San Domingo Improvement Company*, Vol. III, p. 154, and Dawson to the Secretary of State, Sept. 24, 1904.
[43] Hollander, *Debt of Santo Domingo*, p. 156. See also the *Report of the British Corporation of Foreign Bondholders for 1899*, p. 342.

years to accept a reduction in the interest that had been promised them, was a failure. It proved impossible to sell any considerable amount of new bonds, and the Republic was again in default when Heureaux was assassinated by political enemies in 1899.[44]

The San Domingo Improvement Company Claim

The conspirators who had planned the murder of Heureaux soon obtained control of the government, but Juan Isidro Jiménez, who became president, had to contend with rivalries within the revolutionary group and with the hostility of the still influential leaders who had been associated with Heureaux. Some sections of the Republic were dominated by local *caudillos* over whom the central government had little control, and the desperate condition in which Heureaux had left the national treasury made it impossible to keep these leaders quiet by bribery as the dictator had done. At the same time the new administration faced the urgent demands of native and foreign creditors for the payment of debts and claims inherited from its predecessor. The most difficult and dangerous question that confronted it was what to do about the Improvement Company, which was extremely unpopular because of its connection with Heureaux. It seemed politically impossible to permit the company to continue to collect the customs and control the National Bank and the railroads, but any action against it would cause trouble not only with the United States but with the various European governments whose nationals were clamoring for payments on their bonds.

In March 1900, despite the pressure of public opinion, Jiménez signed an agreement with the Improvement Company under which the latter would continue to operate the *Regie* in return for some concessions to the government. This arrangement was rejected by the French and Belgian bondholders, who would have been required to make new sacrifices, and in January 1901 the President removed the company's representatives from the customhouses. He ordered, however, that 46 percent of the customs receipts be turned over to a commission which was to include North American, Dutch,

---

[44] The best accounts of the Dominican Republic's financial history down to 1899 are Hollander's *Debt of Santo Domingo,* and the pertinent section of Wynne's *State Insolvency and Foreign Bondholders,* Vol. II. There is also much useful information in the Reports of the Council of the Corporation of Foreign Bondholders in London.

and Belgian consular officers and which would hold the money for the benefit of the bondholders. Jiménez then sent his Minister of Foreign Affairs to make separate arrangements with the Improvement Company and with the French and Belgian bondholders. The mission was successful, but new complications arose when the Dominican Congress approved the arrangement with the bondholders but not the settlement with the company.

Up to this point, the State Department at Washington had shown little interest in the Improvement Company's problems. Both sides had laid their cases before it when the company's representatives were ousted from the customhouses, but the Department had merely urged that the matter be dealt with by direct negotiations.[45] Presumably no one in the Department knew much about the real character of the Improvement Company's operations in the Dominican Republic, and even Jiménez was probably unaware of some of the unsavory facts that would come to light when Dr. Jacob Hollander looked into the situation a few years later at the request of the American government. If all the facts had been before him, Secretary Hay might not have given the company the support that he did when it again appealed for help.[46] As it was, he did what he would normally have done in a similar case in any foreign country and instructed the Legation at Santo Domingo to say that the American government "was not disposed to pass over unheeded the equities of the American companies" or to acquiesce in discrimination against them, and that it would expect that the parties would resort to arbitration if other methods of settlement failed.[47] He expected the Minister to make this statement "unofficially" and to make it clear that the United States was merely using its "good offices" on behalf of the Improvement Company.[48] He probably did not intend that the Legation take vigorous action in support of the company's claims.

The United States was represented at Santo Domingo by a Minister who was also accredited to Haiti and who spent nearly all of his time at Port au Prince. This was an unfortunate arrangment be-

[45] See memorandum attached to note from the Belgian Legation, August 11, 1903.
[46] See Roosevelt's comment on this, *infra.*, p. 87.
[47] Hay to Powell, January 20, 1902.
[48] Hay to Powell, May 14, 1902.

cause the Dominicans felt that he was more closely associated with their traditional enemies in the other end of the island. It meant also that the Department of State received relatively little information about what was going on in the Dominican Republic. Like nearly all of the American Ministers in Haiti before 1913, William F. Powell, who was there in 1902, was a Negro political appointee. He had held the position for five years. He was ardently patriotic and probably abler than many of the white political appointees who served in Caribbean posts, but he was over-zealous and his judgment was often poor. Just before Heureaux's death he had disturbed the State Department by negotiating, without instructions, a treaty that would have given the United States the use of all Dominican ports, including Samaná Bay, in return for a guarantee of American support—an arrangement that Hay peremptorily rejected.[49] When he was instructed to use his good offices on behalf of the Improvement Company, Powell sent the Dominican government a note that demanded in harsh language a settlement satisfactory to the company.[50] The State Department mildly rebuked him for failing to make it clear that the United States was only offering its good offices, but instructed him to continue his efforts to persuade the Dominican government to negotiate with the company.[51]

The negotiations were interrupted when a revolution ousted Jiménez in May 1902 and Horacio Vásquez, another leader of the revolutionary group, became president, but they were soon resumed. The chief point at issue—the amount that would be paid to the company for its rights and properties if it withdrew entirely from the country—was apparently settled when the company agreed to accept $4,500,000, instead of the $11,000,000 that it had been demanding, and agreed that the principal of the bonds that it owned should be reduced by 50 percent. This was the reduction that the French and Belgian holders had accepted. The company refused, however, to submit its accounts for the government's inspection and insisted on retaining control of the railroads until one-third of the total indemnity had been paid. The negotiations broke down on these issues.

[49] Powell to Hay, June 10, 1899. Hay to Powell, July 18, 1899.
[50] Powell to Hay, Feb. 22, 1902.
[51] Hay to Powell, March 12, 1902.

Since the French and Belgian bondholders were in the meantime receiving a part of the interest on their bonds, the American company had some cause to complain of discrimination. The discrimination also affected the British bondholders, whose interest the Improvement Company was representing, and the British government instructed its consul at Santo Domingo to cooperate with Powell in his negotiations.[52] The American and British creditors had a new cause for complaint when they learned that $400,000 of customs receipts which had been earmarked for them had simply disappeared.[53]

In July 1902, Powell was instructed to go to Santo Domingo to present a proposal that the whole question be settled by arbitration between the Dominican Republic and the United States.[54] After some weeks of negotiation, and after Powell pointed out that the parties had already agreed that the indemnity should be $4,500,000, the State Department modified its proposal and urged an arbitration that would merely decide how this sum should be paid. The Dominican government continued to insist that the company submit its accounts and immediately turn over the railroads, but on January 31, 1903, after what Powell described as a "fierce and obstinate contest," the protocol was signed.[55] The Dominican government agreed to pay the company $4,500,000 and the manner in which the money was to be paid and the conditions under which the company would turn over the railroads and other properties were to be fixed by an arbitration between the two governments. Pending the handing down of the award, the government was to pay the company $225,000 annually.

While the protocol was being negotiated, Powell had been vigorously pressing several other American claims. The most important was that of the Clyde Line, which was demanding compensation for the violation of a contract that promised it preferential treatment as to port dues. The others were based on business dealings with former Dominican administrations. In all of these matters,

[52] Powell to Hay, April 14, 1902.
[53] Powell to Hay, March 31, 1902.
[54] Hill to Powell, July 21, 1902.
[55] Powell to Hay, January 31, 1903. The text of the protocol is in *Foreign Relations, 1904*, p. 270. The *Foreign Relations* volume erroneously gives the date as Jan. 31, 1904.

Powell had merely been instructed to use his "good offices," but they were to be "strenuous good offices" [56] in the Clyde case. Instead of doing so he made such injudicious and threatening demands that the government called a meeting of distinguished citizens in February to discuss what should be done.[57] The State Department again rebuked the Minister for his excessive zeal, but it congratulated him in March 1903, when he proudly reported that all outstanding claims had been satisfactorily settled.[58] Settlement in most cases, however, merely meant that the government had promised to pay a specified amount at some future time.

When General Wos y Gil, who had been one of Heureaux's lieutenants, suddenly seized control of Santo Domingo City in March 1903, there was more trouble. Powell at first thought that the new President would be disposed to enter into the "closest political relations" with the United States and might even cede Samaná Bay,[59] but in September he was dismayed to learn that the government had proposed that Samaná and Manzanillo should be made free ports—a scheme which was intended, he suspected, to open the way for the establishment of a German coaling station. On his own initiative, he made a strong formal protest, saying that the establishment of a foreign coaling station would be an unfriendly act and that the creation of a free port would be a violation of the Clyde Line's concession. The Minister of Foreign Affairs, who had told Powell informally that the real purpose of the project was simply to end rumors that Samaná Bay might be ceded to the United States, replied that the government did not propose to give a port to any foreign power or to violate the steamship company's rights. Powell replied with another protest in rather intemperate language.[60]

Meanwhile, the Dominican government refused to appoint its arbitrator under the Improvement Company protocol on the ground that the agreement had not been ratified by the congress, and Powell, this time in accord with instructions, peremptorily demanded that the protocol be carried out. The Minister of Foreign Affairs suggested that the government would withdraw the free ports

[56] Hay to Powell, December 18, 1902.
[57] Powell to Hay, February 7, 1903.
[58] Powell to Hay, May 7, and Hay to Powell, March 31, 1903.
[59] See his despatches of March 28 and May 10, 1903.
[60] For this affair see Powell's despatches of September 12, 14, 18, and 26, 1903.

project if the United States would agree to negotiate a new protocol, but Powell flatly turned down this suggestion. The Dominican government finally withdrew the ports project, but it continued to urge that the Improvement Company matter be reopened, and on November 9 Powell, on his own initiative, took the extraordinary step of breaking off all relations with the government until the matter was settled. The Dominican arbitrator was appointed three days later.[61]

The First Request for Help

In its relations with the Dominican Republic in 1902–1903, the Department of State seemed chiefly concerned with the settlement of American claims. Assistance to American interests in such cases was a normal part of the Department's work, and it was not unusual to insist on arbitration when an agreement could not be reached through negotiation. There is no indication that Roosevelt or Hay thought of the Improvement Company case as an opportunity to obtain any control in the Republic's internal affairs, or that either of them paid a great deal of attention to the negotiations for its settlement. Roosevelt, in fact, felt at a later date that the support of the claim had been a mistake, which had occurred only because Hay was too ill to give adequate attention to the matter.[62]

In the first months of 1904, the American government's attitude changed. Roosevelt, as we have seen, was giving thought at this time to the need for policies that would prevent further incidents like the Venezuela blockade, and the Dominican Republic was the country where European intervention seemed most imminent. The weak administrations that had followed one another since Heureaux's assassination had had even more trouble with European governments than with the United States. In January 1900, French warships had threatened to blockade Santo Domingo City to compel the payment of an indemnity for the murder of a Frenchman, and Jiménez had been compelled to raise the money by public subscription.[63] Later there had been pressure from the French and

[61] Powell to Hay, September 18, 26, October 6, 8, 9, 12, November 3, 11, 12, 1903.
[62] See his letters to Dr. Hollander and to William Howard Taft, both written July 3, 1905, Letters, Vol. iv, p. 1259.
[63] Foreign Relations, 1906, Vol. i, p. 591.

Belgian bondholders, who received payments for only a short time under the agreement of 1901, and from a great number of other creditors who had claims of various sorts. After the Wos y Gil revolution, during which several foreign powers sent warships and landed troops to protect the lives and property of their nationals, the creditors became more insistent, and, in July 1903, the government was compelled to promise monthly payments on account of several claims that were vigorously pressed by the German, Spanish, and Italian governments. It did not have the money, however, to keep these up. The situation seemed hopeless when a new revolution in the latter part of 1903 started a civil war that continued well into the following year.

Wos y Gil was overthrown by a coalition of the *jimenistas* and the *horacistas,* or followers of Horacio Vásquez. The revolutionists entered Santo Domingo City on November 25. Jiménez expected to become president, but when the revolt succeeded Carlos Morales, the *jimenista* military leader, claimed the presidency for himself. Morales established a government at the capital, with the support of the *horacistas,* but for the next six months he had to contend with armed opposition from the *jimenistas* in parts of the country.

Without awaiting the end of the war, and without asking for instructions, Powell told Morales that he would not be recognized by the United States unless he promised that all agreements made by his predecessors with the American government would be "sacredly observed," and unless he gave permission for the erection of lighthouses on the Dominican coast—a privilege the United States had been seeking in anticipation of the opening of the Panama Canal. The State Department promptly instructed the Minister to withdraw this latter demand and also questioned the need for his insistence that Galván, who had been Wos y Gil's Foreign Minister, be continued as arbitrator in the Improvement Company case. This rebuff did not make Powell more cautious. Still apparently without instructions, he persuaded Morales not only to promise to respect his predecessors' agreements but to announce that he would send a commissioner to Washington to negotiate a treaty giving the United States Samaná and Manzanillo Bays and providing for a measure of American control over the Republic's financial administration. Thereupon he recognized Morales as Provisional President on January 20, 1904. His action came as a surprise to the State Department, which had been undecided whether to recognize Morales or Jiménez or neither of the two.[64]

For some years Powell had been advocating the establishment of some sort of American control over the Dominican Republic, and he had repeatedly expressed a belief that many of the country's leaders would welcome political and financial help from the United States. He thought that any opposition to American control came chiefly from German sources. How far he was correct in his interpretation of Dominican sentiment it is hard to say. There is no question but that a proposal for annexation to the United States would have been violently resisted by all parties,[65] but it seems probable that several of the short-lived administrations that succeeded Heureaux would have been glad to agree to some form of protectorate to bolster up their precarious tenure of power. Opposition groups, on the other hand, were always quick to make political capital out of any apparent readiness to surrender part of the national sovereignty.

There is nothing in the record to indicate that Powell knew that his government would be more willing to consider a treaty with the Dominican Republic in January 1904 than it had been when he submitted his unauthorized agreement with Heureaux in 1899. It seems probable that he was acting on his own initiative in urging Morales to propose a treaty, and that it was merely fortuitous that Morales' envoy arrived in Washington at a time when the American government was considering the desirability of a new policy in the Caribbean. The State Department, however, apparently welcomed Morales' action. An unsigned memorandum in the Department's files, bound with Powell's report of the Dominican commissioner's departure,[66] discussed the matter in terms that showed how much the thinking in the Department had changed.

The writer pointed out that the Dominican government's apparent purpose was to establish a relationship like that between the United

[64] Powell to Hay, Dec. 3; Hay to Powell, Dec. 3; Powell to Hay, Dec. 14; Loomis to Powell, Dec. 17; Powell to Hay, Dec. 17, 1903; Powell to Hay, Jan. 14, Jan. 20; Hay to Powell, Jan. 17, 1904.

[65] See Powell's despatch of March 13, 1904, discussing press reports about a bill for annexation that had been introduced in the United States Senate.

[66] Powell to Hay, Jan. 9, 1904.

States and Cuba, but he assumed that annexation or a reciprocity agreement were out of the question for the time being. He pointed out that the administration of the customs and American help in the maintenance of order, which were not dealt with in the Platt Amendment, were of "paramount importance" in the Dominican Republic but that the supervision of the customs would be useless unless the government were at the same time forbidden to contract new debts. If the customs were removed from exclusively native control and if the government and its enemies were prevented from borrowing on the public credit, the maintenance of order would be easier because there would be nothing left to fight over. The memorandum was very possibly the work of Francis B. Loomis, the Assistant Secretary of State. Loomis, in an interview published in the *Independent* of New York a few weeks later, stated that there was no question of annexing the Dominican Republic, but intimated that some arrangement like the Platt Amendment was under consideration as a means of putting an end to disturbances there. "The present state of affairs," he said, "cannot last much longer without attracting foreign attention in a way somewhat similar to the Venezuelan affair." [67]

Juan F. Sánchez, the Dominican commissioner, presented his proposals informally to Loomis on February 3.[68] He asked that the United States guarantee the Dominican Republic's independence and its sovereignty over all its territory and that it reduce import duties on Dominican products. In return for the lease of coaling and naval stations in Samaná and Manzanillo Bays, the American government would pay, directly to the creditors, a sum that would cover all of the Republic's foreign obligations. It would also help the Dominican government to maintain order by furnishing arms and helping to enforce blockades of ports held by rebels, and by preventing the departure of arms shipments and revolutionary expeditions from American territory. Finally, the United States was to have the right to build lighthouses on the Dominican coast.

Roosevelt felt that he should have more information before replying to Sánchez, and while the commissioner was still in Washington, he sent Loomis, with Admiral Dewey and an official of the

---

[67] The *Independent*, Vol. LVI (March 3, 1904), p. 467.

[68] His letter is bound with the communications from the Dominican Legation at Washington.

Department of Commerce, to look into the situation in Santo Domingo. During the visit, Loomis evidently discussed with the government the question of customs control, which Sánchez had not included in his proposals. Powell had reported earlier that members of the Dominican Cabinet had asked that American officers collect the customs at San Pedro de Macorís, which was in rebel hands, and that when he turned down this request the Ministers had asked whether the United States would take over the collection of all of the customs revenues, giving the government a fixed sum for its expenses and setting up a commission to examine all foreign claims. Powell suggested that Sánchez propose this in Washington, but the Dominican government evidently dropped the idea.[69] After Loomis' visit and return to Washington, however, Powell cabled that Morales had agreed to place the customhouses in the custody of the United States, as well as to lease the naval stations.[70]

Loomis was more interested in the proposed protectorate than was Roosevelt. The President wrote to a friend on February 23 that ". . . I have been hoping and praying for three months that the Santo Domingans would behave so that I would not have to act in any way. I want to do nothing but what a policeman has to do in Santo Domingo. As for annexing the island, I have about the same desire to annex it as a gorged boa constrictor might have to swallow a porcupine wrong-end-to. Is that strong enough? I have asked some of our people to go there because, after having refused for three months to do anything, the attitude of the Santo Domingans has become one of half chaotic war towards us. If I possibly can, I want to do nothing to them. If it is absolutely necessary to do something, then I want to do as little as possible. Their government has been bedeviling us to establish some kind of protectorate over the islands, [sic] and take charge of their finances. We have been answering them that we could not possibly go into the subject now at all." [71]

This letter suggests that the President was somewhat confused about what was actually happening in the Dominican Republic and makes it seem doubtful that he authorized Loomis' effort to obtain

[69] Powell to Hay, Jan. 26, 1904.
[70] Powell to Loomis, March 17, 1904.
[71] To Joseph Bucklin Bishop, Feb. 23, 1904, *Letters*, Vol. IV, p. 734.

control of the Dominican customs. His letter to Admiral Dewey, asking him to go with Loomis, merely requested a full report on the Dominican situation.[72]

There was much discussion of the Dominican situation in the American press, and several papers urged the need for some form of intervention.[73] Sánchez continued his effort to persuade the officials at Washington that his country needed help. At the end of March, however, when Morales was making some progress toward restoring order, Roosevelt decided to take no action for the time being. He asked Hay to say to Sánchez that the President saw "no way in which the United States could take part in the pacification of the Republic, without establishing precedents which would be equally inconvenient and undesirable for both countries." Hay told Sánchez this personally and also wrote to him that while the President regretted the unhappy conditions in the Republic and hoped that the recent improvement would be permanent, he "did not think the time opportune for such intervention in your administrative affairs as you invite." [74]

Roosevelt could apparently have had the Dominican government's cooperation in setting up a customs receivership and could also have obtained Samaná Bay, which the American navy had long coveted. His decision to discontinue the negotiations was evidently motivated by his belief that American public opinion would not support a policy of intervention. In a letter to Charles W. Elliot on April 4, he wrote that he felt that he ought to take "partial possession" of the Dominican Republic but that many honest people would misunderstand his motives if he did so and he must wait until the necessity for action was clear.[75] As a candidate for reelection in November, Roosevelt presumably did not wish to give ammunition to his opponents. There was less need for Samaná Bay since the United States had acquired bases in Cuba and Puerto Rico, and he probably realized the troublesome character of the responsibilities that he was being asked to assume. The civil war was still going on, and any effort to help the government restore order might easily

[72] February 20, 1904, *ibid:*, p. 734.
[73] See the *Literary Digest* for Jan. 2, 16, Feb. 20, and March 5, 1904, Vol. xxviii (1904), pp. 24, 68, 249, 319.
[74] Hay to Sánchez, March 30, 1904. Hay's memorandum of the President's instruction to him is bound with notes from the Dominican Legation.
[75] *Letters*, Vol. iv, p. 770.

lead to an armed intervention that would meet with violent Dominican opposition and with much disapproval in the United States. If American forces were landed, it was possible that they might have to fight not only Dominicans but Haitians, for Powell had reported that President Nord Alexis had sent a commission to tell Morales that the Haitian government would give active help to Jiménez unless Morales broke off the negotiations with the United States.[76]

If the State Department had informed Powell promptly of the President's decision, as it apparently did not, the Minister might have acted less precipitately when he learned in April that the Italian Minister was about to arrive to demand the payment of claims and that people in Santo Domingo thought that Italian naval vessels might seize some of the customhouses. On April 16, Powell telegraphed Washington that the Dominican government was ready to surrender its customhouses if the Italians demanded payment, and he asked that he himself be authorized to take them over. Without awaiting a reply, he wrote the Minister of Foreign Affairs that if the government were forced by the seizure of its ports to settle any claims he would be compelled under the recent decision of the Hague Court to take possession of the customhouses in order to assure equal treatment to all. He planned to place an armed guard at each customhouse, presumably from American warships then in Dominican waters, and he would deposit the collections to the credit of the United States, giving the Dominican government enough money for its expenses. Morales and the Minister of Foreign Affairs agreed to this action, but when the Department, in a rather prompt reply to his cable of April 16, told him to take no action without further instructions, Powell was compelled to withdraw his note. He explained to the State Department that he understood that the recent decision of the Hague Court in the Venezuela case gave any foreign power a right to seize and hold the ports of a country that could not or would not pay its debts. Secretary Hay did not reprimand him, but pointed out that he had misunderstood the significance of the Hague award.[77]

---

[76] Powell to Hay, March 17 and 18, 1904.

[77] On this incident, see Powell's telegrams of April 13 and 16, and his despatches of April 14 and 18, and the State Department's telegram of April 18 and instruction of May 6, 1904.

Powell seems to have exaggerated the danger of Italian intervention, for the American Ambassador at Rome reported that the government there assured him that it did not contemplate the seizure of any Dominican ports and that it would consult with the United States if any such action were undertaken.[78] In June, in fact, the Italian Legation reached an amicable agreement with the Dominican government under which regular payments on the claims were to begin on November 1.

The Establishment of the Dominican Customs Receivership

Despite the rejection of Sánchez' proposals, Roosevelt and his advisers continued to watch the Dominican situation closely. In April 1904, the President obtained authorization from Congress to appoint a Minister Resident at Santo Domingo and thus ended the unsatisfactory arrangement by which one man represented the United States in Haiti and the Dominican Republic. Thomas C. Dawson, who was appointed to the post on April 28, was an able career diplomat and a student of Latin American affairs who wrote one of the first histories of South America to be published in the United States. The State Department could hope that he would give it the full information that was needed for the formulation of its policy in the Dominican Republic.

When Dawson reached his post some weeks later, he found that the revolution was nearly over. By the end of April, Morales controlled all of the Republic except the port of Monte Cristi, and in June agreements signed on an American cruiser ended the war. It seems clear that Morales owed his success in part to the support of the American navy, which had sent ships to the Dominican coast to protect foreign life and property at places where fighting seemed likely. As was quite customary at the time, the naval forces had frequently forbidden or stopped fighting in towns where foreigners would be endangered, with the almost inevitable result of hampering the operations of one or another of the contending factions, and these actions seem usually to have helped Morales. Commander Dillingham of the *U.S.S. Detroit* asserted later in fact that he was "entirely responsible for the placing of Morales in power." [79] Dilling-

---

[78] Hay to Powell, May 9, 1904.

[79] Letter to Robert Bacon, Jan. 16, 1906, quoted by Rippy in his article on "The Initiation of the Customs Receivership in the Dominican Republic," *Hispanic Ameri-*

ham perhaps had in mind his successful effort to bring about the peace agreement in June 1904, rather than his intervention in the war itself, for Morales had come into the presidency before Dillingham arrived in the Dominican Republic and owed his victory chiefly to the support of the *horacistas*. The result of the war, furthermore, was by no means a clear cut victory for the government. In agreements that were signed through Dillingham's mediation, Morales was compelled to promise to pay the debts of the revolution and to leave Monte Cristi under the control of the local *jimenista caudillos*.[80] One of these was Desiderio Arias, who was to cause the United States an infinite amount of trouble during the next twelve years. Another semi-independent chieftain was left in control of the Azua district.

Though the treaties had ended the fighting, there was every prospect that it would soon break out again, and the government's own position was weakened by increasing dissension between Morales and the new Vice President Ramón Cáceres. Dawson reported that no one expected the peace to continue very long unless the United States intervened, and that practically everyone seemed to hope for some form of intervention.[81] He thought that there was no probability that the government would be able to pay its debts without outside help. As he wrote the State Department a few months later, the estimated revenue for the next year was only $1,850,000 and the payments that would be due during the next twelve months on "foreign and liquidated obligations" amounted to $1,700,000. There were $900,000 in arrears on promised payments, and the government must have money for its own running expenses, which were estimated at $1,300,000.[82] The government had not made the monthly payments due the Improvement Company under the protocol, and there was little hope that it could meet its solemn pledge to start payments to its Italian and French and Belgian creditors on November 1, 1904.

A showdown became inevitable after the arbitral commission announced its award in the Improvement Company case on July 14, 1904. The award provided that the $4,500,000 promised to the com-

can Historical Review, Vol. XVII (Nov. 1937), p. 419. Rippy's article summarizes the evidence tending to substantiate Dillingham's assertion.

[80] For the text of the peace treaties, see *Foreign Relations, 1904*, pp. 289–290.

[81] Dawson to Hay, July 6, 1904.

[82] Dawson to Hay, Sept. 12, 1904, quoted in *Foreign Relations, 1905*, p. 302.

pany should be paid to a financial agent appointed by the United States in monthly installments of $37,500, to be increased after two years to $41,666.66. The customs revenues of the ports on the Republic's north coast were assigned as security. In the event of default, the financial agent was to take over the collection of the customs at Puerto Plata, and then if necessary at other northern ports.[83] In August, John T. Abbott, an officer of the Improvement Company, was named as financial agent. This perhaps seemed a logical arrangement to the State Department, but it had an unfortunate effect on the Dominicans, who still hated everything connected with the company.

When Abbott reached Santo Domingo he found the officials there reluctant to accept the provisions of the award. They felt that the government could not make the stipulated monthly payments and that the arbitral commission had exceeded its powers in authorizing the financial agent to take over the customs in case of default.[84] When the government failed to make the first monthly payment, and Abbott demanded on September 21 that the Puerto Plata customhouse be turned over to him, Morales at first refused to comply.

Morales told Dawson that he still wished to turn all of the customhouses over to the United States, if he could make an arrangement that would assure his government $1,200,000 for its expenses.[85] He and his advisers, however, found it difficult to give the one customhouse at Puerto Plata to a man who, despite his appointment by the United States, was in reality a representative of the Improvement Company. Aside from the general popular resentment that would be aroused, the special situation in the North had to be considered. The President had little control over the officials and military leaders there, and he feared that they might revolt if the revenues of the most important port of the region were taken out of their hands. There might also be trouble with the local merchants who had made advances secured by the customs duties. Dawson nevertheless insisted that the award be complied with, and Abbott's representative was put in charge of the Puerto Plata customhouse on October 20. Morales felt compelled to issue a proclamation indicating that he

[83] For the text, see *Foreign Relations, 1904,* pp. 274ff.
[84] Dawson to Hay, Sept. 10, 1904.
[85] Dawson to Hay, Oct. 6, 1904.

was acting under duress, and to arrest several of his opponents as a precautionary measure, but only small disturbances occurred.[86]

When Morales found that he had to accept the award, he was disposed to give the United States immediate control of all of the northern ports and especially of Monte Cristi, where his enemy Desiderio Arias was in control. He changed his mind, however, when he met with strong opposition from his Cabinet and from other *horacista* leaders. The revenues at Puerto Plata were consequently seriously diminished by competition from other ports where smuggling was easier. Arias, in fact, encouraged imports at Monte Cristi by reducing the customs duties there.[87]

Most of the European creditors did not appear to resent what the United States was doing. In September Dawson reported that the French Chargé d'Affaires said that he and the Spanish, German, and Italian representatives at Santo Domingo had agreed to demand the appointment of a mixed commission to adjudicate claims arising from the recent revolution, and asked Dawson to join them. Dawson declined to participate, but he felt that the proposal would be very reasonable after the Morales administration had had a little time to get on its feet.[88] When the United States proceeded to enforce the award, the only serious protest seems to have come from the Spanish Chargé d'Affaires, who spoke also for German interests that had a share in the principal claim that he represented. Dawson thought that the other creditor governments wanted to see the award carried out, hoping that the efficient collection of the customs at one or more ports would improve the Dominican government's financial situation, and also, perhaps, hoping that the United States would take the lead in a general settlement.[89] The Dominicans, who hoped to profit by dissension among the creditors, repeatedly tried unsuccessfully to persuade the French and Belgian representatives to protest against the execution of the award.[90]

The European powers became more insistent in their demands for a settlement after the Dominican government failed to comply with its promise to make payments on the French and Belgian bonds

[86] For these events see Dawson's despatches of Oct. 21, 24, and Nov. 2, 1904.
[87] Dawson to Hay, Nov. 2, 1904.
[88] Dawson to Hay, Sept. 8, 1904.
[89] Dawson to Hay, Oct. 3, 1904.
[90] Dawson to Hay, Nov. 16, 1904.

and the Italian claims on November 1. The French and Belgian representatives at Santo Domingo indicated that their governments were considering the seizure of the customhouses at that city and San Pedro de Macorís to collect revenues that had been specifically promised them as security.[91] The Italian Embassy at Washington took the matter up more emphatically with the Department of State on December 24. It asserted that the Improvement Company award infringed upon the prior rights of Italian creditors and that the United States should either permit Italy to "collect the quota due her directly from the customhouses of the Republic assigned for this purpose" or assume the obligation to pay the Italian claims if the United States had already occupied these customhouses.[92] In apparent response to these representations Roosevelt decided to intervene to bring about a general settlement of the Dominican debt.

Roosevelt later told Congress that "there was imminent danger of foreign intervention" in the Dominican Republic and that only the opening of negotiations for an American customs receivership "prevented the seizure of territory in Santo Domingo by a European power." [93] This statement gives a somewhat exaggerated picture of the seriousness of the situation, for what the European powers apparently wanted was intervention by the United States. We do not know, however, what may have been said by the European representatives in oral discussions at Washington. Roosevelt wrote later in his autobiography [94] that he had been "notified" that two or three European powers intended to take and hold several Dominican seaports. Second Assistant Secretary of State Adee, who was always well informed about what went on, recalled six years later that a "rather positive" demonstration of the creditor governments, "with Germany in the van," was imminent, but that it was staved off by an Italian suggestion that the creditors might come to an under-

[91] Dawson reported on December 19 that the Belgian *Chargé* had spoken rather vaguely to him about this, but Hollander states definitely that the French government had threatened on Dec. 15 to seize the customhouse at Santo Domingo.

[92] In 1911, while advocating the treaty with Honduras, Secretary Knox told the Senate Foreign Relations Committee that Italy had sent a war vessel to Santo Domingo and would have seized customhouses if the United States had not intervened. (*Foreign Relations, 1912*, p. 586.) Knox evidently had in mind the reported threat of Italian intervention in 1904.

[93] Message to Congress, Dec. 5, 1905.

[94] P. 507.

standing with the Dominican government based on the collection and application of the customs revenues by the United States.[95] The reference to Germany is rather surprising because there is no other indication that the German government was taking an aggressive attitude.

In any event, it was not likely that the European governments would long acquiesce in a situation where an American claimant was collecting payments each month while other creditors got nothing. They had legitimate complaints about the operation of the Improvement Company award. The French and Belgians thought that the loss of revenue from Puerto Plata made it more difficult for the government to give them the income from the southern ports, and the Italians maintained that revenue from some of the northern ports, which would soon presumably be taken over by the United States, had been pledged as security for some of their claims. The United States could hardly enforce the award and at the same time refuse to permit other powers to collect debts due their nationals.

Dawson had been convinced for some time that the Dominicans would eventually have to accept a North American customs collectorship as the only way out of their difficulties.[96] Morales said early in December that he still wished to go ahead with the plan discussed with Hay and Loomis in March, but that the political situation made it impossible for the time being; and Dawson wrote Loomis privately on December 17 that ". . . our only policy for the present is to let the pressure of increasing financial difficulties bring about the inevitable result. Without our intervention they cannot pay, and unless they pay they cannot stay in power."

Roosevelt, however, evidently felt that further delay was impossible, and on December 30 Hay instructed Dawson to ". . . sound the President of Santo Domingo, discreetly but earnestly and in a perfectly friendly spirit, touching the disquieting situation which is developing owing to the pressure of other governments having arbitral awards in their favor and who regard our award as conflicting with their rights. Already one European Government strongly intimates that it may resort to occupation of some Dominican cus-

[95] Adee's memorandum of Jan. 10, 1911 about the Haitian loan, State Department Decimal File 838.51/215.
[96] See, for example, his despatch of Nov. 16, 1904.

toms ports to secure its own payment. There appears to be a concert among them. You will ascertain whether the Government of Santo Domingo would be disposed to request the United States to take charge of the collection of duties and effect an equitable distribution of the assigned quotas among the Dominican Government and the several claimants. We have grounds to think that such arrangement would satisfy the other powers, besides serving as a practical guaranty of the peace of Santo Domingo from external influence or internal disturbance." [97] Commander Dillingham was sent to Santo Domingo as a special commissioner to help the Minister in the ensuing negotiations.

Morales frankly admitted the necessity for American customs control. He said that he "was daily expecting a European demand, backed by a war vessel, and a demand from me [Dawson] for the four northern ports under the Improvement award." Morales realized that the powers would not accept further promises and that each would insist on payment in full, leaving the government no money for its own expenses.[98] His associates, however, were suspicious of the intentions of the United States, and several days of negotiation were necessary before the Cabinet and the principal *horacista* leaders consented to an arrangement. Differences about details, and especially about the proportion of the revenues to be allotted to the government for its expenses, were adjusted by compromise. So far as we can tell from the written record, the American representatives presented their proposals firmly but tactfully, without resort to threats or offensive pressure, and the Dominican officials accepted them because they realized that they had no real alternative.

The Dominican people were less ready to accept American intervention, and the secrecy with which the negotiations had to be conducted gave rise to wild rumors that the Republic was to be annexed to the United States or that Samaná Bay was to be ceded.[99] Both the American commissioners and the Dominican government feared that there might be a popular uprising, but the situation quieted somewhat when the terms of the proposed arrangement were given to the Dominican press.

---

[97] *Foreign Relations, 1905*, p. 299.
[98] Dawson to Hay, Jan. 2, 1905, *Foreign Relations, 1905*, p. 298.
[99] *Ibid.*, p. 305.

An agreement, dated January 20, 1905, was signed by representatives of the two governments on January 21. It provided that the United State undertake the adjustment of the Dominican Republic's debts, both foreign and internal, determining the validity of pending claims and the amount that should be paid to the creditors. The customs revenues were to be collected by the United States, which would give the government not less than 45 percent of the proceeds for its current expenses and apply the remainder to debt payment. The American government, at the request of the Dominican Republic, would "grant such other assistance as may be in its power to restore the credit, preserve the order, and increase the efficiency of the civil administration, and advance the material progress and the welfare of the Republic." The agreement was to go into effect on February 1.[100]

Dawson and Dillingham had apparently understood that they were to negotiate an executive agreement which would require no further ratification, and nothing in their instructions or in the correspondence exchanged during the negotiations suggests that this was not also the intent of the Department of State. When the text reached Washington, however, the propriety of this procedure was questioned, and Dawson was instructed to recast the agreement in the form of a treaty that could be ratified by the usual constitutional procedure. Apparently Roosevelt himself had not intended to bypass the Senate, but the incident aroused resentment in that body which probably contributed to the treaty's eventual defeat.

The Dominican government hoped that the establishment of a customs receivership would provide it with funds almost immediately, and it was dismayed at the prospect of an indefinite delay while the treaty was being considered by the United States Senate. To meet its most urgent needs, however, Dawson persuaded Santiago Michelena, a Puerto Rican banker doing business at Santo Domingo, to advance $75,000 monthly in return for permission to collect the customs at all of the ports except Puerto Plata. The continuing uncertainty also gave new encouragement to the government's enemies. There was talk of revolution, but when the *jimenista* leaders at Monte Cristi made difficulties about giving Michelena control of the customhouse there the United States took it over

[100] For the text, see *Foreign Relations, 1905*, pp. 311–312.

under the terms of the Improvement Company award. Governor Arias, after a visit from Commander Dillingham and Admiral Sigsbee, permitted an American naval officer to be installed as collector. This arrangement diminished the possibility of a *jimenista* uprising by depriving the party of its chief financial support.

Dawson had some difficulty in persuading the Dominican government to accept the relatively minor changes which the United States considered necessary in the text of the protocol, but his negotiations were probably facilitated when he was authorized to assure the Dominicans that the United States itself, and not the Improvement Company, would control the customhouses after the new arrangement went into effect.[101] He was able to allay Dominican fears on another point when the President sent word to the State Department: "of course put in anything the Dominicans want about our not annexing the Islands—the stronger the better." [102] A protocol containing virtually the same provisions as the agreement of January 20, but requiring approval by the United States Senate and the Dominican Congress, was signed on February 7.

A few days later Roosevelt submitted the protocol to the Senate with a long special message. He argued that the European governments had a right to insist on the payment of debts due their nationals, but that the only way in which they could obtain payment, in the hopeless financial situation of the Dominican Republic, was to occupy territory or at least customhouses. This, the United States could not permit so long as it maintained the Monroe Doctrine. On the other hand it was "incompatible with international equity for the United States to refuse to allow other powers to take the only means at their disposal of satisfying the claims of their creditors and yet to refuse, itself, to take any such steps." The President pointed out that a power that did intervene would be entitled to preferential treatment, under the decision of the Hague Court in the Venezuelan cases, and this would prejudice American claims and interests. He emphatically disclaimed a desire to exercise any control in Santo Domingo except that which was necessary for the Republic's financial rehabilitation. "It is supremely to our interest," he wrote, "that

[101] *Foreign Relations, 1905*, pp. 329–330.
[102] Loeb to Loomis, Feb. 6, 1905, bound with despatches from Dominican Republic.

all the communities immediately south of us should be or become prosperous and stable, and therefore not merely in name, but in fact independent and self governing." "This protocol," he concluded, "affords a practical test of the efficiency of the United States Government in maintaining the Monroe Doctrine." [103]

Although the Senate Foreign Relations Committee recommended approval, and although the President called a special session of the Senate to consider it, the protocol was not brought to a vote because it was clear that the two-thirds majority needed for approval could not be obtained. Roosevelt reluctantly agreed to let the matter go over until the regular session in December because he feared that an adverse vote would lead the European creditors to demand immediate action by their governments. The opposition came almost entirely from the Democrats, although Roosevelt also blamed a few of his enemies in his own party.[104] The public at large, to judge from editorial comment in the newspapers, showed relatively little interest.[105]

During the Senate debate, Morgan of Louisiana charged that Roosevelt's intervention had worked an injustice on a Mr. and Mrs. Reader, who had been on the point of making an arrangement with Morales for the adjustment of the Dominican debt. Mrs. Ella Rawls Reader, according to a biography published later in serial form in *Everybody's Magazine,*[106] had already, at thirty-two, had a colorful career as a financier and promoter in the United States and several foreign countries. Late in 1904 she had proposed to act as fiscal agent for the Dominican Republic, in return for a number of concessions for mines, railroads, steamship lines, and other purposes, and, in January 1905, she went to Santo Domingo to confer with Morales. She thought that Roosevelt had suddenly decided to intervene because he wished to defeat her project, and she charged that William Nelson Cromwell, whom she claimed to have consulted about her contracts, had betrayed her plans to the American govern-

---

[103] The text is printed in *Foreign Relations, 1905*, pp. 334–342.

[104] Holt, *Treaties Defeated by the Senate* (Baltimore, 1933), p. 220. Roosevelt, *Autobiography*, pp. 510–511.

[105] *Literary Digest*, Vol. xxx (1905), pp. 120, 157, 197.

[106] Juliet Tomkins, "Ella Rawls Reader, Financier: The Story of the Greatest Business Woman in the World," *Everybody's Magazine*, Sept., Oct., Nov., Dec. 1905.

ment. Cromwell denied this, and Morales, who at the time told Dawson nothing of his discussions with her, later said that he had not taken her project seriously.[107]

Though Dawson was instructed to tell them that the administration was confident that the protocol would be ratified when Congress met again in December,[108] Morales and his Cabinet were dismayed when the special session of the Senate adjourned on March 18 without action. Their opponents were openly discussing a revolt, believing, apparently, that the failure of the protocol would compel Roosevelt to withdraw the moral support that he had given the government by keeping warships in Dominican waters. The financial outlook was dark because Michelena was having difficulty collecting the customs duties and was threatening to stop his monthly advances. Worst of all was the prospect of renewed demands from other foreign powers. There was alarm in the Dominican administration, and joy among its enemies, when an Italian warship arrived on March 14 and its captain stated that he was instructed to inquire about the prospect for payment of Italian claims. The ship withdrew to Kingston after a brief visit, but returned after news of the Senate's adjournment was received. Meanwhile the principal Italian claimant was urging his demands on the government, and the Belgian Chargé d'Affaires on March 23 made a formal demand for the resumption of payment on the bonds. A new crisis was at hand.

Dawson reported that he was taking no action for the time being because he thought that the Dominican government and its creditors would soon have to come to him with proposals for some temporary arrangement.[109] He was probably aware that some of the creditors were already discussing such an arrangement with the government,[110] and when the Minister of Finance approached him on March 24 with proposals for a *modus vivendi* Dawson at once sounded out the representatives of the creditors and found that the European claimants and all of the principal American claimants except the Improvement Company were willing to accept the gov-

[107] Dawson to the Secretary of State, confidential, Oct. 7, 1905. For Morgan's charges and Cromwell's denial see the New York *Times*, March 19, 20, and 21, 1905.
[108] Adee to Dawson, March 25, 1905, *Foreign Relations, 1905*, p. 357.
[109] *Foreign Relations, 1905*, p. 357.
[110] For one version of what happened, see Rippy's article in the *Hispanic American Historical Review*, cited above, n. 79.

ernment's plan. Under this, the customhouses at all of the northern ports would be taken over under the Improvement Company award and those at the southern ports would be placed in the hands of a North American suggested by the United States. Fifty-five percent of the collections would be held in trust for the creditors pending the ratification of the protocol, and the government would receive the rest. Both the Dominican government and the creditors, including especially the French and Belgian bondholders' representatives, insisted that payments to the Improvement Company be suspended like other debt payments while this *modus vivendi* was in operation. Dawson had apparently resisted this part of the plan [111] and feared that it might make the proposals unacceptable to his government, but he nevertheless submitted the plan on March 25, pointing out that "some modus vivendi" was "absolutely necessary." [112]

Roosevelt approved the proposed arrangement but stipulated that persons nominated by the President of the United States should assume control at all of the ports. In other words, the northern ports would be administered for the benefit of all creditors rather than for the benefit of the Improvement Company under its arbitral award. He also proposed that the money set aside for eventual debt payment should be held for the time being in a New York bank. The funds would be returned to the Dominican government, if the protocol were finally rejected, or distributed among the creditors "in proportion to their just claims under the treaty," if it were approved. In the meantime, Dr. Jacob H. Hollander, who had been appointed as the President's confidential agent to look into the fiscal problems of the Dominican Republic, would investigate all claims, including that of the Improvement Company, to ascertain "the amount actually received by Santo Domingo, the amount of indebtedness nominally incurred, the circumstances so far as they are known under which the various debts were incurred, and so forth." [113] It was evident that the President no longer intended to support the Improvement Company in the privileged position that

[111] See the portion of his despatch of March 27, 1905, which is not printed in *Foreign Relations*.

[112] *Foreign Relations, 1905*, p. 359.

[113] Instructions to the Acting Secretary of State, March 28, 1905, *Foreign Relations, 1905*, pp. 360–361.

it had obtained under the arbitral award. Roosevelt's proposals were accepted, and the *modus vivendi* was put into effect by a decree which Morales signed on March 31.[114] A few weeks later Colonel George R. Colton, a retired officer of the United States Army who had had experience in the Philippine customs service, was installed as "General Receiver and Collector."

The internal political situation seemed better than it had been, but Morales' position was by no means secure. In the summer of 1905, Mrs. Reader's husband secretly visited Monte Cristi and offered to furnish the *jimenista* officials there with the means for an armed revolt. It was thought in Santo Domingo that the Improvement Company was back of this scheme, but Dawson did not take this idea seriously.[115] It was probably clear to the Dominicans that the United States would not permit a revolt, for Admiral Bradford, the American naval commander, was instructed to prevent any importation of arms and ammunition. Roosevelt wrote to the Secretary of the Navy on September 5: "As for the Santo Domingo matter, tell Admiral Bradford to stop any revolution. I intend to keep the island *in statu quo* until the Senate has had time to act on the treaty, and I shall treat any revolutionary movement as an effort to upset the *modus vivendi*. That this is ethically right, I am dead sure, even though there may be some technical or red tape difficulty."[116]

Roosevelt was criticized in connection with the *modus vivendi* for doing by executive action what the Senate had not authorized him to do by treaty. He insisted, however, that the arrangement was simply intended to cover the situation until the Senate acted one way or the other and that its purpose was to prevent occurrences that might make the consummation of the protocol futile or more difficult. The arrangement by its nature could only be a temporary one, because the creditors could not be expected to forego payment indefinitely. Before authorizing the *modus vivendi*, Roosevelt had consulted the leaders of both parties in the Senate and had obtained tentative approval, at least, from the Republicans.[117] All that he undertook to do was to nominate customs collectors for appointment

[114] For the text, see *ibid.;* p. 366.
[115] See Dawson's confidential despatch of Sept. 26, 1905.
[116] *Letters*, Vol. v, p. 10.
[117] *Ibid.*, Vol. iv, p. 1150.

by the Dominican government and to arrange for an examination of the Dominican debt.

Roosevelt's critics also questioned the sincerity of his statement that the United States took over the collection of the Dominican customs in response to an appeal voluntarily made by the Dominican government. It was said that Morales could not be regarded as a free agent because he owed his position to American intervention and was presumably acting under pressure from the United States. This assertion is hard to sustain if we look at the course of events and the way in which the situation actually developed. Morales, as we have seen, fought his way to the presidency. Such help as he received from American naval forces came after he had become president, and was probably not of decisive importance. He sought aid in dealing with his creditors because he desperately needed it. He would have preferred to have the aid without any surrender of national sovereignty, but when he was confronted by the choice between European intervention and the surrender of the customhouses to the United States under an arrangement that protected the Dominican government's interests, it is easy to understand why he chose the latter alternative, painful and unpopular though it was. The Dominicans, after all, had been used to foreign control of the customs service since the establishment of the *Regie*.

Roosevelt wrote one of his friends that he had negotiated the treaty of 1905 "after infinite thought and worry and labor," and with the advice of Root and Taft as well as that of Secretary Hay.[118] It seems clear that he felt that the establishment of a customs receivership in the Dominican Republic was the only means by which European intervention could be avoided. He, and most of his contemporaries, would have considered it morally wrong to prevent other powers from pressing their claims without offering some solution, and his hearty dislike for people who could not manage their own affairs and pay their debts made him the more ready to seek such a solution. He was undoubtedly influenced by his ambition to have the United States play the role of a great power and assert its hegemony in the Caribbean, but there is no reason to suppose that he regarded the customs receivership as a first step toward a more complete control of the Dominican Republic. On

[118] Roosevelt to J. B. Bishop, March 23, 1905, *ibid.*, Vol. IV, p. 1144.

the contrary, he and his advisers, to judge from frequent comments in the diplomatic correspondence, thought that the reorganization of the country's finances would bring nearer the time when it could govern itself without outside interference. Roosevelt was in fact somewhat troubled by the thought that the Dominicans would be the principal beneficiaries from his policy, for in a personal letter to Elihu Root, in September 1905, he wrote: "For the last six months most of what I have done in connection with foreign affairs, including the eastern war, Santo Domingo, Morocco, even Venezuela, not to speak of the Hague Conference, has been on an exclusively altruistic basis, and I do not want people to get the idea that I never consider American interests at all, or still worse, that I am posing as never considering them." [119]

In general, the American press regarded the establishment of the customs collectorship as a wise and necessary move.[120] Some papers, however, questioned its propriety. The Washington *Post* expressed an idea that was to find frequent expression in anti-imperialist literature in coming years when it said: "The proposition that a government has a right to tax its subjects to provide ships of war and fighting men to collect private debts, or that it has a right to risk the lives of any of its subjects in that kind of warfare is so self-evidently wrong that the simplest statement of it exposes its abhorrent character." [121]

It is true that the American government's efforts to protect American financial interests in the Dominican Republic helped to produce the situation that led to the establishment of the receivership. As was too often the case, the State Department had instructed the Legation to use its good offices on behalf of the Improvement Company and the Clyde Line and other American claimants without inquiring closely into the merits of their claims. Powell had gone beyond his instructions in the aggressiveness of his support for the claims. The result, in the case of the Improvement Company, had been an arbitral award which placed the United States in the position of collecting money for one American claimant, and which made a general scramble for the customhouses by other creditors almost

[119] Roosevelt to Root, personal, Sept. 14, 1905, *ibid.*, Vol. v, p. 26.
[120] See the *Literary Digest* during January, February, March and April 1905.
[121] Quoted by the *Literary Digest*, March 18, 1905.

inevitable. It should be noted, however, that the *modus vivendi* deprived the Improvement Company of the preferred position that it held under the arbitral award and cut off the small payments that it had been receiving. In the subsequent adjustment of the debt, the company was placed in the same position as other creditors, American and European.

Other American investors in the Dominican Republic, including especially some of the sugar producers, had been almost as active as the Improvement Company in urging the United States to protect their interests.[122] Their pressure, and the inconvenience caused by the frequent need to send warships to protect them in time of civil war, may have made the President more disposed to intervene, but there is no evidence that he was particularly influenced by them. There was, in fact, a noticeable tendency, after it became clear that the United States would have to assume more responsibility in the situation, toward caution in pressing American claims. Dawson was told that the State Department was disposed to exercise great care not to present claims that lacked real justification. He was particularly warned to go slow in supporting the Clyde Line, which was constantly complaining of violations of its monopolistic concession, and in supporting the sugar planters in their resistance to the export tax on sugar.[123] The planters claimed that they had obtained exemption from the tax in return for a money payment, but the State Department had doubts about the adequacy of the consideration.

The American representatives in the country had been reporting for some years that the "better people" would welcome American help, and it is probable that they honestly thought that this was true. Their associations were naturally with business people and property owners, who would gain from the establishment of peace, and with government officials who wanted American support. The idea that only "professional revolutionists" and their ignorant followers opposed American efforts to improve conditions appears repeatedly in the diplomatic correspondence from all of the more disorderly Caribbean countries, and it was many years before the

[122] Rippy, in "Initiation of Customs Receivership in the Dominican Republic," summarizes several of their letters.
[123] Hay to Dawson, Nov. 30, Dec. 1 and 2, 1904.

State Department began to realize that the people of these countries might prefer misgovernment under their own leaders to good government under foreign tutelage.

Most Dominicans probably regretted or resented the creation of the receivership. Dawson reported that the "fierce discussion" that followed the publication of the protocol with the United States soon died down,[124] but in November 1905 an incident showed that there was still much suspicion of American intentions. At a time when there seemed to be danger of an outbreak against Morales, Admiral Bradford, who had already caused some resentment by his tactless enforcement of the Navy Department's order to stop the import of arms, suddenly sent a large force from ships outside the harbor to one that was lying near the waterfront. This gave the populace the impression that American troops were about to land, and a mob invaded the President's palace and would have killed Morales if Vice President Cáceres had not dissuaded them. Another mob, which included many armed soldiers, rushed to the waterfront. There was terrific excitement and many threats to kill all Americans in the city. Fortunately Dawson, who courageously went to the waterfront himself, was able to convince the leaders that no landing was intended.[125] When civil war did break out in December, the French Minister offered to send for one of his own ships, if the United States wished him to do so, because he thought that a landing by American troops would imperil the lives of all foreigners.[126]

As a stopgap, the *modus vivendi* was a success. Colton's tactful handling of a situation that might have caused much friction helped to win support for the ratification of the protocol by the Dominican Congress.[127] As early as July 1, 1905, Dawson was able to send an encouraging report of the way the arrangement was working. Revolutionary plotting had ceased, and agriculture and cattle raising were again flourishing. Forty-five percent of the customs revenues had given the government more cash than it had had in the last five years, because local military and fiscal authorities could no longer get their hands on the collections at the various ports. The admin-

---

[124] Dawson to Hay, April 1, 1905.
[125] Dawson to Root, December 15, 1905.
[126] Dawson to Root, telegram, Dec. 29, 1905.
[127] Dawson frequently expressed this opinion. See, for example, his despatch of Nov. 18, 1905.

istration was paying its employees regularly and even had a small cash surplus which enabled it to think of road building and other public improvements. For the moment, at least, the country had been freed from the menace of foreign intervention. Dawson pointed out, however, that the long-term outlook would be uncertain until the agreement with the United States could be ratified.[128] The Dominican problem was one of the most important problems that Roosevelt turned over to Elihu Root when the latter became Secretary of State.

[128] Memorandum of July 1, 1905, *Foreign Relations, 1905,* p. 378.

◀ 4 ▶

Elihu Root's Policy

A New Approach to Inter-American Relations

▶ During the greater part of his first term, Roosevelt himself directed American policy in the Caribbean. He made the important decisions in connection with the Venezuelan blockade, the Panama affair, and the Dominican customs receivership, and directed the negotiations and actions which implemented these decisions. His correspondence with his friends indicates that he felt that these problems were as important as any with which he had to deal. In handling them, he seems to have asked for little advice from the Department of State. This was especially true during Secretary Hay's long illness, when the President felt that nothing was done in the field of foreign affairs unless he did it himself.[1]

The situation changed with the appointment of Elihu Root as Secretary of State in July 1905. From then until 1909 it was Root who formulated and carried out most of the administration's Latin American policies. Roosevelt, who was not prone to minimize the importance of his own role, was emphatic in giving credit to the Secretary of State for what was accomplished. "During the past three years," he wrote in February 1909, ". . . the bulk of the most important work we have done has been in connection with the South and Central American States. We have done more as regards these States than ever before in the history of the State Department. This work has been entirely Root's. My part in it has been little beyond cordially backing him up. It was he who thought of making that extraordinary trip around South America which did more than has ever been done previously to bring the South American States into close touch with us. It was he who made the Pan American Congress a matter of real and great importance for the Commonwealths of the Western Hemisphere. It was he who gave life to the Bureau of American Republics. It was he who brought about the formation of the international court for the Central American States. It was he who finally got the Senate to accept the Santo Domingo treaty,

[1] *Letters*, IV, p. 1259. See also the long and rather unfair letter to Lodge of January 28, 1909, *ibid.*, Vol. VI, p. 1489.

which secured an extraordinary increase in peace and prosperity in Santo Domingo and may prove literally invaluable in pointing out the way for introducing peace and order in the Caribbean and around its borders. No European statesman of whom I have heard has done as much for peace in any quarter of the world as Elihu Root has done in the Western Hemisphere during the last three years. No other American has rendered services to the cause of peace in any way comparable to his." [2]

Root's ideas about the Caribbean were basically similar to Roosevelt's. The policy he himself had sponsored in Cuba as Secretary of War foreshadowed the Roosevelt Corollary, and he participated, as we have seen, in the formulation of the Corollary. In January 1905, he had written to a friend that "The inevitable effect of our building the Canal must be to require us to police the surrounding premises. In the nature of things, trade and control, and the obligation to keep order which go with them, must come our way." [3]

Four years later, he wrote to Dr. Lyman Abbott: "In that region [the Caribbean] the United States must exercise a dominant influence. It is there that the true justification and necessity for the Monroe Doctrine is found. We must control the route to the Panama Canal, . . ." but he went on to say that the United States did not want any territory in the region because it would be inadvisable to "dilute the electorate" with people so different in race and customs.[4]

Root's general approach to Caribbean problems and his way of dealing with them were nevertheless quite different from those that had characterized Roosevelt's personal diplomacy. He showed more concern for the proprieties of international behavior and for the effect of his action on opinion in other countries. In his dealings with smaller states, he emphasized cooperation rather than coercion.

"I think the key of our attitude towards these countries," he said in January 1907, "can be put in three sentences:

"First. We do not want to take them for ourselves.

"Second. We do not want any foreign nations to take them for themselves.

"Third. We want to help them.

---

[2] To Andrew Carnegie, Feb. 26, 1909, *ibid.*, Vol. vi, p. 1539.
[3] Jessup, *Root*, Vol. i, p. 471.
[4] Root Papers, Library of Congress, Box 304.

"Now, we can help them; help them govern themselves, help them to acquire capacity for self-government, help them along the road that Brazil and the Argentine and Chile and Peru and a number of other South American countries have travelled—up out of the discord and turmoil of continual revolution into a general public sense of justice and determination to maintain order." [5]

In 1908 Root wrote Dr. Albert Shaw that he was "immensely interested in those poor people down in Central America, and it is delightful to see how readily and gratefully they respond to a little genuine interest combined with respectful consideration." If they were considerately treated, he believed that they would seek to conform to our standards of political conduct, "instead of considering that their dignity requires them to resent our supposed dictation . . . instead of wishing to hurt, they will strive to help American enterprise. . . . Patience, and a few years of the right kind of treatment I am sure will give us in that part of the world the only kind of hegemony we need to seek or ought to want." [6] He was one of the first North American statesmen to appreciate the potential importance of inter-American cooperation in world affairs. One practical demonstration of his interest was his successful effort, in the face of some European reluctance, to have all of the other governments of the hemisphere invited to the peace conference at the Hague in 1907.

The new Secretary of State was more interested than most of his predecessors in the economic aspect of international relations. He thought that the time had come when North American capital should invest in Latin America in the same way that British and French investors had aided the economic development of the United States. He pointed out that the United States had paid its debts to Europe and was beginning to have surplus funds to invest, just at the time when the South American countries were emerging from "the state of militarism" into "the state of industrialism" and were eager for foreign capital. He was equally interested in the problem of increasing inter-American trade, and his masterful discussions of the ob-

[5] Address at the National Convention for the Extension of the Foreign Commerce of the United States, at Washington, January 14, 1907. Root, *Latin America and the United States* (Cambridge, 1917), p. 275.

[6] Jan. 3, 1908, Root Papers, Library of Congress, Box 303.

stacles that American exporters faced, and of their own short-comings, show that he had given much hard-headed consideration to this matter.[7]

Most important of all, in marked contrast to Hay, Root genuinely liked Latin Americans as individuals.[8] He went out of his way to have cordial personal contact with the South and Central American diplomats at Washington, and he made many friends during his visits to South America in 1906 and to Mexico in 1907. In urging Harvard University to offer an honorary degree to President Estrada Palma of Cuba in 1906, he wrote that his close study of Latin American character during the past seven years had strengthened his impression that people in the United States "greatly lack in appreciation of their good qualities."[9] In 1907 he urged the Associated Press to give as much space as possible to speeches that the Mexican Ambassador and the Bolivian Minister were about to deliver.[10]

Root made his South American trip because he realized that "our relations with those countries will stand a good deal of improvement."[11] Some of Roosevelt's actions had intensified the misunderstanding and suspicion of the United States which was always latent in Latin America. To many people there, and to many in Europe, the Panama affair and the Roosevelt Corollary seemed to herald a new era of North American imperialism. As Roosevelt himself put it: "An idea had become prevalent that our assertion of the Monroe Doctrine implied, or carried with it, an assumption of superiority, and of a right to exercise some kind of protectorate over the countries to whose territory that doctrine applies. Nothing could be farther from the truth. Yet that impression continued to be a serious barrier to good understanding, to friendly intercourse, to the introduction of American capital and the extension of American trade."[12]

In South America the Secretary made a number of eloquent speeches in which he discussed the ideals upon which American

[7] For Root's views about economic relations, see his address to the Trans-Mississippi Commercial Congress, at Kansas City, November 20, 1906. Root, *Latin America and the United States*, pp. 245ff.

[8] Jessup, *Root*, Vol. I, pp. 473–474.

[9] To President Eliot, June 18, 1906, Root papers, Library of Congress, Box 303.

[10] To M. E. Stone, May 18, 1907, *ibid.*, Box 303.

[11] To Col. E. B. Buttrick, June 15, 1906, *ibid.*, Box 301.

[12] Annual Message to Congress, December 1906.

foreign policy was based. The most important of these, delivered before the Third Pan American Conference at Rio de Janeiro, was intended to set "a standard which the United States is bound to live up to" in the future.[13] One passage has often been quoted:

"We wish for no victories but those of peace; for no territory except our own; for no sovereignty except the sovereignty over ourselves. We deem the independence and equal rights of the smallest and weakest member of the family of nations entitled to as much respect as those of the greatest empire, and we deem the observance of that respect the chief guaranty of the weak against the oppression of the strong. We neither claim nor desire any rights, or privileges, or powers that we do not freely concede to every American Republic. We wish to increase our prosperity, to expand our trade, to grow in wealth, in wisdom, and in spirit, but our conception of the true way to accomplish this is not to pull down others and profit by their ruin, but to help all friends to a common prosperity and a common growth, that we may all become greater and stronger together." [14]

In other speeches at various cities, Root emphasized the common interest of the American republics in the peaceful settlement of international disputes, in the development of democratic government, and in economic and cultural cooperation. It was the first time that a North American Secretary of State had made such a trip, and it was to be many years, unfortunately, before another Secretary of State made an equally successful effort to establish friendly personal contacts with leaders in the other American countries.

The Dominican Customs Treaty of 1907

The situation in the Dominican Republic was one of the first problems that presented itself when Root took office. The *modus vivendi* was apparently working well, but it was only a stopgap, and the situation would be uncertain until the United States Senate took final action on the customs receivership treaty. Root was concerned about what would happen if Morales' enemies should attempt to overthrow him. He felt that it would be difficult to find constitutional justification for suppressing a revolt by force, if one should

[13] Jessup, *Root*, Vol. I, p. 480.
[14] *Speeches Incident to the Visit of Secretary Root to South America* (Washington, 1906), p. 12.

occur, but on the other hand he feared that the United States would lose prestige if the customs officers were compelled to yield to military force.[15] The riots of November 1905 [16] showed how tense the situation was. Roosevelt, as we have seen, had told the navy in September, to "stop any revolution," but Root after he received the navy's report of the riots, took a different position. Dawson was instructed that: "We cannot take any part in differences between factions or officers of Dominican Government. No troops are to be landed except when absolutely necessary to protect life and property of American citizens, and if landed they must confine themselves strictly to such protection, which will extend to the peaceable performance of duty by the Americans who are collecting revenue in the custom-houses so long as the Dominican Government desires them to continue that service." Several of the American warships in Dominican waters were withdrawn. Root told the Dominican government that it was free to terminate the *modus vivendi* if it wished to do so, but the government replied that it desired to continue the arrangement.[17]

The instructions about landing troops were reiterated in December 1905, when a revolution occurred. Morales' relations with the *horacista* leaders who had helped him to attain the presidency had been deteriorating, and opposition to the agreement with the United States made his position weaker. By November he had been compelled to give the *horacistas* practical control of the government, and he was reported to be seeking the support of the *jimenistas* in an effort to regain power. On December 24, the President left the capital secretly on foot and virtually started a revolt against his own administration. Despite some *jimenista* support, the movement failed, and Dawson had to interpose to save Morales' life.[18] Vice President Ramón Cáceres, the man who had fired the shots that killed Heureaux, became president. Cáceres, despite strong opposition in his own party, continued his predecessor's policy of urging

[15] Root to Taft, Nov. 16, 1905; quoted in Pringle, *Taft* (New York and Toronto, 1939), Vol. I, p. 274.

[16] See above, p. 110.

[17] Root to Dawson, Dec. 6, 1905, and Dawson to Root, Dec. 7, *Foreign Relations, 1905*, p. 408.

[18] Luis F. Mejía, *De Lilís a Trujillo. Historia Contemporánea de la República Dominicana* (Caracas, 1944), pp. 49ff.

the Dominican Congress to ratify the treaty with the United States.

By this time Professor Hollander had completed his detailed study of the Dominican debt. He reported that claims against the government, on June 1, 1905, aggregated more than $40,000,000, whereas the government's annual income, since 1901, had never been much more than $2,000,000. Bonds in the hands of the public abroad, chiefly in Belgium and Holland, where Westendorp had floated his loans, amounted with arrears of interest to more than $17,600,000. The government still owed the Improvement Company practically all of the $4,500,000 which was to have been paid under the arbitral award. In addition, there was a large internal and floating debt resulting from advances to the government by local merchants, unpaid bills, violated contracts, and miscellaneous items. Native Dominican creditors claimed about $10,000,000. The Italians were demanding $3,600,000, German and Spanish interests about $1,600,000, and American creditors other than the Improvement Company about $1,500,000. British investors held some of the external bonds and British bankers had a considerable interest in the Improvement Company's claim.

In the entire debt, there were few items that were not questionable. The foreign bonds had been issued almost entirely to fund earlier internal obligations, which had been contracted "under circumstances that smack always of extortion and often of fraud." The bonds had been sold at excessive discounts, and the principal of some issues had been "swollen by extravagant, and sometimes incredible, items for commissions, publicity, and kindred charges." Even the Improvement Company's arbitral award, Dr. Hollander thought, should not be recognized without investigating the Dominican government's plausible charges that there had been fraud and mismanagement in the issue of bonds and the administration of the customs *Regie* and the construction and operation of the railroad. The internal debt went back at least to the time of Heureaux and had been funded and refunded on terms extremely unfavorable to the Republic. There were "some particularly unsavory classes of indebtedness." One German claim which amounted to $15,970.24 in 1889 had grown with compound interest to $102,361.49 in 1902.[19]

Hollander's report was to have served as the basis for an adjust-

[19] Jacob H. Hollander, *The Debt of Santo Domingo.*

ment of the Dominican debt by the United States under the treaty, but, after the United States Congress met in December 1905, it became increasingly evident that the treaty would not be approved by the Senate. Some of the Democrats looked on the project as an improper scheme to help American and foreign financial interests, but the opposition centered chiefly on the proposal that the United States government take the responsibility for adjusting the Dominican Republic's debts. To meet this objection, Root began in May 1906 to work on a new plan under which the Dominican government would make its own arrangements with its creditors and then obtain a funding loan secured by the collection and application of the customs revenues by North American officials under a treaty that would impose less responsibility on the United States.[20] The change was hardly more than a matter of form, for Hollander was again employed as confidential agent of the President of the United States to cooperate with the Dominican Minister of Finance on a general plan of adjustment. Root nevertheless was able to obtain assurances of senatorial support.

During the next few months, Hollander and Federico Velásquez, the Dominican Finance Minister, worked out a general plan for the settlement of the debt. The French and Belgian bondholders, who had agreed in 1901 to accept a 50 percent reduction in their principal, were offered a cash settlement on this basis. The Improvement Company had to accept a reduction of 10 percent in the amount of its arbitral award. Other claims were scaled down from 10 to 90 percent, depending on their character. There was loud opposition from the foreign creditors when the plan was announced on September 12, 1906. The Improvement Company felt harshly treated, and the British and Italian claimants persuaded their governments to make protests in Washington; but none of the objections seem to have been taken very seriously in the State Department.[21]

At the same time, the Dominican representatives had been negotiating in New York for a $20,000,000 loan. This would make it possible to pay the Republic's debts in cash and would also provide a substantial amount for the roads and other public works which

[20] Jessup, *Root*, Vol. I, p. 546.
[21] For the correspondence, see Numerical Case 1199, in the State Department files in the National Archives.

the country so desperately needed. On September 11, Velásquez signed contingent contracts with Kuhn Loeb and Company and the Morton Trust Company, under which the former firm agreed to buy the proposed 5-percent bonds at a price of 96 if a customs collectorship were set up under a treaty with the United States. Another New York banker, James Speyer, complained that he had not been given a fair opportunity to compete for the business, but Root took the position that the negotiation of a loan contract, so long as its provisions conformed to any treaty that might be adopted, was not the concern of the American government.[22]

While these arrangements were being worked out, Root endeavored to allay the Dominicans' suspicion of the intentions of the United States. His instructions in connection with several pending questions in which American financial interests were involved authorized the Legation to use its good offices for a friendly adjustment, but with a scrupulous respect for the Dominican government's rights. He was careful not to press any claim where the equity was not clear. He was equally concerned that the arrangement with the United States should go no farther than necessary in impairing the Dominican Republic's independence. In December 1905, when the *horacistas* asked that the pending treaty be amended to provide that the Dominican president could not ask for United States help in maintaining order unless the Dominican congress approved the request, Root urged the Foreign Relations Committee to approve this provision. Its omission, he wrote, would give the United States an unconditional authority that "would practically destroy Dominican sovereignty, which of course none of us wishes to do." When the senators objected to the proposed change, he redrafted the article to provide merely that the United States should afford the customs officials "such protection as it may find to be requisite in the performance of their duties." [23] The same provision was incorporated in the new treaty of 1907.

The new treaty made it possible to carry out the plan of settlement and the loan contracts which the Dominican government had

[22] See the correspondence in Numerical Cases 1036 and 1199 and especially Root's personal letter to Minister McCreery, 1199/179a.

[23] Jessup, *Root*, Vol. I, p. 546–547. See also Dawson's despatch of Nov. 25, 1905, part of which is not printed in *Foreign Relations*, and his telegram of Dec. 5.

itself worked out with Hollander's help. It was negotiated rather hastily and signed on February 8, 1907. After reciting the fact that the Dominican Republic had effected an adjustment of its debt, contingent on the flotation of a foreign loan, and that the assistance of the United States in the collection of the customs revenues was necessary for the execution of the plan, it provided that the President of the United States should appoint a General Receiver of Dominican Customs and such subordinate employees as he deemed necessary, and that the General Receiver should pay $100,000 each month from the customs revenues to the fiscal agent for the loan. While any bonds of the new loan remained outstanding, the Dominican government promised not to increase its public debt or alter its import duties without the previous agreement of the government of the United States.

The treaty was promptly approved by the United States Senate, but it met with more opposition in the Dominican congress. Many of the government's creditors were bitter at the scaling down of their claims in the plan of adjustment and there was much opposition to the customs collectorship. A committee of the congress proposed amendments, but Root refused to consider them, saying that every negotiation must have a final stage, and that the United States Senate, where there was much feeling that the treaty was of no real benefit to the United States, would not be willing to consider it again. He said that the *modus vivendi* might have to be abandoned if the treaty were not ratified.[24] The Dominican congress, in approving the treaty on May 3, contented itself with attaching to it a series of "clarifications," which were generally acceptable to the United States and were made the subject of an exchange of notes at the time of ratification.[25]

Attempts in the Dominican congress to make changes in the contracts with Kuhn Loeb and Company and the Morton Trust Company caused more serious complications. The changes themselves were not especially important, but the panic of 1907 started while the congress was deliberating, and the amendments gave the bankers an excuse to withdraw their offer to purchase the bonds. Hollander

[24] Root to McCreery, April 24, 1907, Num. Case 1199/130.
[25] McCreery to Root, May 8, 1907, and Root to McCreery, May 9, Num. Case 1199/146; Root to McCreery, May 25, 1907, *ibid.*, 170–172.

was thus compelled to work out a new arrangement. Instead of selling the bonds for cash to the bankers, who would then have resold them on the market, the Republic offered each creditor new bonds issued under the treaty in an amount equivalent to 80 percent of his adjusted claim [26] and payment in cash of the balance. The cash was available from the funds impounded under the *modus vivendi*. The full $20,000,000 bond issue was authorized, in the hope that the unused balance could at some time be sold to provide funds for public works. Hollander, after some hesitation, entrusted the issuing of the bonds and the handling of the conversion operation to Kuhn Loeb and Company and the Morton Trust Company, paying each firm a commission of one half of 1 percent on the amount paid out. He explained to the State Department that he did so partly because these banks were in a position to influence a large group of troublesome British bondholders and partly because he hoped that they would market the remainder of the authorized $20,000,000 loan when conditions were more favorable.[27]

Root had avoided any participation in the negotiations with the bankers and the adjustment of the debt, but after the treaty went into effect he felt that the United States had an obligation to see that the customs revenues and the newly issued bonds were used in accord with its provisions and in accord with the Plan of Settlement. Several memoranda and instructions in the State Department files testify to the thought and the personal attention that he gave to the problem. The depositary was not allowed to pay out money or bonds without having evidence that both the American and the Dominican governments considered the payment to be in accord with the provisions of the treaty, a requirement that involved a tremendous amount of work in the State Department and in the Bureau of Insular Affairs of the War Department, which was given supervision over the customs receivership. One must appreciate how seriously both Departments took their responsibility in order to understand some of the later developments in the relations with the Dominican Republic.

[26] For the purposes of the settlement, the value of the new bonds was fixed at 98.5% of par, based on the amount that the government would have received under the loan contract plus the expense of the exchange.

[27] Root to Bacon, Dec. 6, 1907, Num. Case 1199/300.

The operation of the customs receivership does not, however, seem to have been regarded at this time as offering an opportunity for the extension of further control over the Republic's internal affairs. While Root considered the State Department obligated to see that funds were spent in accord with the treaty, he did not feel that it was required to interfere in matters of detail, or to impose its views on the Dominican government in doubtful cases. Occasionally, under this policy, American officials approved payments where there was at least a suspicion of graft. There was some friction with the Dominicans over payments that were not considered admissible under the treaty, and one very embarrassing affair occurred when it transpired that Dr. Hollander, who had severed his connection with the State Department and become an employee of the Dominican government in August 1908, had obtained $25,000 in cash and $75,000 in bonds from funds that had been set aside for the expenses of the loan. Hollander defended the payment as an honorarium for services being rendered and to be rendered in the future and claimed that some of the officials in the State Department had been consulted before he received it. This was probably true, but Root denied that he personally .had had any previous knowledge of the matter. The affair was the subject of some unpleasant publicity both in the Dominican Republic and in the United States.[28]

Colonel Colton was promoted to another post after the ratification of the treaty, and William E. Pulliam, who had been in the customs service in the Philippines, was appointed General Receiver. The office operated under regulations promulgated in an Executive Order by the President of the United States.[29] Because of the very general language of the treaty, there was from the first some uncertainty about the relationship between the American officials and the Dominican government. The latter was inclined to maintain that it should have the free appointment of most of the customs personnel, including the officials who appraised merchandise, and that the General Receiver should simply receive the amounts collected. Root apparently felt that it would be wiser not to have a showdown on the legal issue, but he talked with the Dominican Minister of Finance and pointed out that Pulliam must as a practical

[28] There is much correspondence about this affair in Num. Case 1199.
[29] Executive Order of July 25, 1907, copy in Num. Case 1199/326.

matter control the service and that the government should consult him on appointments. He thought that disputes could be adjusted through diplomatic channels. The Dominican government seems to have accepted this idea, and the customs service operated quite efficiently for some years. The unsettled legal questions nevertheless caused trouble for future Secretaries of State.[30]

Many of the foreign creditors continued to oppose the Plan of Settlement, especially after they were offered bonds instead of cash for the major portion of their claims. The principal Italian and Spanish-German claimants refused for several years to accept the settlement, and the British bondholders continued to object to it. The State Department nevertheless opposed any reopening of the plan. The Improvement Company, which was also dissatisfied, met with scant sympathy.

For the time being, the treaty of 1907 solved many of the Dominican government's worst problems. The public debt was reduced to manageable proportions, and the customs revenues under the new regime not only met the service on the new bonds but provided the government with more money than it previously had for its own running expenses. After settling most of the claims and reserving bonds for the claimants who did not accept, a considerable portion of the $20,000,000 bond issue remained at the government's disposal. Some bonds were used to buy a number of onerous concessions and others were sold from time to time to the sinking fund of the loan to obtain cash for public works, which were carried on under the direction of foreign engineers. Unfortunately, much of the money appropriated for public works was wasted, partly because the engineer in chief had little real authority.

The internal political situation seemed distinctly better. Horacio Vásquez, the leader of the party that came into control after Morales' flight, was unwilling to assume the presidency, in which he had had a hard experience some years before,[31] and Cáceres was consequently elected president in 1908. Though his position was weakened by a rupture with Vásquez, and by the unpopularity of Velásquez, who continued as Minister of Finance, Cáceres was able

[30] On the question of the functions of the American officials, see Num. Case 1199/244, 249, 265, 282, 293, 297, 301.
[31] Dawson to Root, Feb. 2, 1906.

to suppress occasional small revolutionary outbreaks and to give the country a longer period of relative peace than it had had since Heureaux's death. Thanks to the American customs receivership, revolutionary leaders could no longer seize a port and use the revenues there to finance further operations. It is not surprising that some of the officials in the State Department began to look on the arrangement with the Dominican Republic as a model to be followed in dealing with other disorderly Caribbean countries.

The Breakdown of Republican Government in Cuba

While the Dominican problem was thus being worked out to the satisfaction of both governments, and at the very time when the Secretary of State was making his trip to South America, the success of Root's efforts to improve inter-American relations was suddenly threatened by an outbreak of civil war in Cuba. The Cuban experiment had hitherto seemed a notable success. Thanks to the reciprocity treaty, the island's sugar industry was booming, and Estrada Palma's honest and efficient administration had apparently made the government respected and popular. The crisis might well have been foreseen, however, by a close student of the Cuban situation. There was little reason to suppose that the people of the island were better prepared for self-government than the people of other Caribbean republics, for the masses were still poverty-stricken and generally illiterate, despite the prosperity of the merchants and landowners. In one respect, indeed, the situation was worse than in other Caribbean republics, because in Cuba too many of the better educated and wealthier people refused to participate in politics. Many of the property owners, of course, were foreigners, but even those who were Cuban citizens showed a marked disinclination to enter public life and left the responsibilities of leadership to professional politicians. For the most part these were men who had risen to prominence during the war for independence and who were in many cases more accomplished as military leaders than as statesmen.

The political parties, at least until 1905, were essentially local groups, supporting individual leaders who formed more or less ephemeral coalitions at the national level. Some of the leaders were more conservative and others more radical, but in general there was little difference in their programs or policies. Estrada Palma attempted at first to govern with the support of both of the two strongest groups, but party squabbles frequently made it impossible for the congress to function effectively and prevented the enactment of the basic laws which were needed to implement the provisions of the constitution. The President repeatedly urged the need for legislation on such matters as the reorganization of the judiciary and the election of local officials, but with no result. He was no more successful in obtaining needed changes in the law governing national elections, which had been amended by congress in 1903 in a way that clearly encouraged fraud and violence. The defects of the existing law had become evident in the congressional elections, where each party won in the districts where it controlled the municipal government.

Political agitation increased as the time approached to choose Estrada Palma's successor. Late in 1904 some of the more conservative leaders formed a "moderate" party, which backed the President for a second term, and the President, after some hesitation, accepted their nomination. His opponent was General José Miguel Gómez, the powerful governor of Santa Clara Province, who had hitherto been considered a conservative but who now formed the liberal party to support his candidacy. As the campaign developed, both sides resorted to fraudulent and violent tactics. The administration was in a stronger position in such a contest, and it exploited its advantage to the utmost after the President was persuaded to appoint the so-called "cabinet of combat" in March 1905. All government employees were compelled to support the "moderate" ticket, and municipal officials who were friends of Gómez were systematically removed.

The government claimed the right to make these removals under the old Spanish law, because the congress had failed to make provision for the election of local officials and the officials elected during the American occupation had in most cases remained in office. Domination of the municipal governments was especially important, because these controlled the choice of the local electoral boards, which in turn controlled the registration of voters and the counting of votes. The government party was thus able to dominate the local boards when these were elected in September, and a few weeks later Gómez and his supporters withdrew from the contest. In October 1905, the local boards registered 432,000 voters, although the total number of citizens eligible to vote could hardly have exceeded 300,000.[32] When the presidential and congressional election was held on December 31, 1905, no liberal was successful in any province.[33]

The liberals began to talk revolution as soon as they realized that they had no chance at the polls, but minor disturbances that occurred after the election were easily suppressed. Estrada Palma was inaugurated for his second term on May 20, 1906. During the summer, it was an open secret that Gómez and his friends were planning a general uprising, but the government took few precautions. It could offer little resistance, therefore, when large but poorly armed bands of liberals took the field in the middle of August; it had practically no army and the rural guard of some 3,000 men was scattered about the island in small detachments. Efforts to recruit additional forces were not very successful. There was little fighting and little actual destruction of property, but commerce was paralysed and foreigners with interests in the island were much alarmed. The Spanish and British governments asked the United States to see that their nationals received protection.

Many patriotic Cubans who were not violent partisans realized that disorder would bring American intervention and tried to exert their influence for peace. The most active were a group of leaders of the veterans of the war for independence, who met at Manzanillo in the last days of August and appointed a delegation headed by General Mario García Menocal to treat with the government and the rebels. For a time it seemed that the veterans' effort might succeed. A truce was arranged, and both sides seriously considered their proposal that the President and the Vice President should remain in office but that the senators, deputies, provincial governors, and municipal councilmen elected in 1905 should resign and be replaced in new elections under an amended law. Estrada Palma, however, refused on September 8 to accept this proposal. On the same day he sent his Secretary of State to tell the American Consul

---

[32] Report of the Secretary of War, 1906. Appendix E, Cuban Pacification, p. 454 (59th Cong., 2nd Sess., House Doc. No. 2); cited hereafter as Taft's Report.

[33] Ibid., p. 455.

General that his administration could not put down the rebellion or protect life and property, and that he was convening congress to ask for intervention by the United States. He urgently requested that two warships be sent to Cuban ports.[34]

Estrada Palma's action reflected a belief, evidently shared by many other Cuban leaders, that the United States would step in to maintain order if the Cubans were unable to settle their own problems. Secretary Taft later reported, in fact, that there was reason to believe that the failure to take precautions against a possible revolt was explained by the thought that "the Platt Amendment and the intervention of the United States would supply the force needed to suppress any such uprising." [35] The moderates seem to have taken it for granted that the United States would uphold the constituted authorities. Many liberals, on the other hand, hoped that the United States would step in to help them. In October 1905, after it became clear that the government party would control the election, José Miguel Gómez had publicly suggested that the United States should intervene to assure fair play.[36] Colonel Asbert, another of the revolutionary leaders, expressed the same idea in a newspaper interview on August 29, 1906, after the revolt started. If the government did not yield, he said, the insurgents would soon start to destroy trains and burn property, without regard to foreigners, but they "preferred a new American intervention that will guarantee future legal elections." [37]

The American government apparently had not realized the seriousness of the situation that was developing. Minister Squiers had warned the State Department in July 1905 that a conflict over the election might compel the United States to intervene, and had later expressed his disapproval of the methods that the Cuban government was using; [38] but at the end of September he thought that the

[34] Secretary Taft later reported that Estrada Palma rejected the veterans' proposals because he learned that the *U.S.S. Denver* was being sent to Habana in response to his request (*Report*, p. 483); but the Cuban historians Martínez Ortiz and Collazo both state that the President rejected the proposals on the 8th and reiterated this refusal when he knew of the *Denver's* approaching arrival. Menocal's account, printed in Taft's *Report* (pp. 500ff.) is not precise as to dates.

[35] Taft's *Report*, p. 455.

[36] Chapman, *History of the Cuban Republic*, p. 190.

[37] *Foreign Relations, 1906*, Vol. i, p. 466.

[38] Squiers to Root, July 28 and October 7, 1905.

danger of revolution had passed.[39] The State Department had received no official reports about the political situation from Squiers' successor, Edwin V. Morgan. Morgan went to the United States on leave in July 1906 and, much to Roosevelt's disgust,[40] made no effort to return to his post when the revolution began. This left the Legation in the hands of an inexperienced secretary who had little standing with the Cubans or with the State Department; and when Estrada Palma appealed for help he addressed himself to Consul General Frank Steinhart, who had been one of Wood's staff during the occupation and had since become a prominent member of the American business community in Habana. Though the War Department had already prepared plans to send a considerable force to Cuba if the revolution should make intervention necessary,[41] Roosevelt was undecided about the course that he should follow. Letters to friends who were in his confidence show that he had no desire to intervene. Writing to Henry White on September 13, he expressed furious indignation at the conduct of the Cubans, who threatened to force him to take action that would convince the South Americans "that we do wish to interfere after all and perhaps have some land hunger!" To Whitelaw Reid, he wrote on September 24, "I earnestly hope I can persuade the Cubans to act decently and go on governing themselves. I shall make every effort to this end and intervene only when it is evident that no other course is open." [42]

In response to Estrada Palma's appeal, Acting Secretary of State Bacon cabled Steinhart on September 10 that two warships were being sent to Cuba but that "the President directs me to state that perhaps you do not yourself appreciate the reluctance with which this country would intervene." Public opinion, Bacon said, would not support intervention until the Cuban government had exhausted every effort to put down the revolt. At the moment, the American government was not prepared to say "what shape the intervention should take," and "before going into it we should have to be absolutely certain of the equities of the case and of the needs of the situation." Meanwhile, the Cuban government must endeavor to make

[39] Squiers to Root, Sept. 30, 1905.
[40] Roosevelt to Root, Oct. 3, 1906, Num. Case 1447.
[41] Roosevelt, *Letters,* Vol. v, p. 391. footnote.
[42] T. Roosevelt, Letterbooks, Library of Congress.

peace with the *insurrectos* if it could not defeat them. "Until such efforts have been made, we are not prepared to consider the question of intervention at all." [43]

Neither this message nor another that Bacon sent to Steinhart on September 11, saying that the President believed "actual, immediate intervention to be out of the question," seems to have shaken Estrada Palma's conviction, or Steinhart's own opinion, that the United States must intervene and that it would support the constituted authorities. On the 12th and 13th Estrada Palma sent further pleas for action, emphasizing his own inability to restore order. On the 14th, Steinhart cabled that the President and his colleagues would force the United States to take charge, by resigning their offices and leaving Cuba without a government.

Roosevelt was still determined to avoid intervention if possible, and on the 13th he indignantly ordered the reembarcation of a small force of marines which had been landed from the *Denver* at Habana. By the 14th, however, the situation obviously demanded some definite action by the United States, and the President made public a letter to the Cuban Minister at Washington in which he solemnly warned the Cubans that they were jeopardizing their independence by internal strife and urged an immediate cessation of hostilities. He also announced that he was sending Secretary of War Taft and Assistant Secretary of State Robert Bacon to Habana to aid in the restoration of peace.

Roosevelt's letter seemed to have a good effect. Most Cubans in both parties apparently accepted it as a friendly and timely warning. Hostilities were again suspended, and the moderate leaders not only resumed discussions with General Menocal but entered into direct negotiations with Alfredo Zayas, the head of the liberal party, who came out of hiding for the purpose. A number of political prisoners were released. Neither party, however, would change its basic position, and no agreement had been reached when the American commissioners arrived on September 19.

Efforts to Avoid Intervention

Taft and Bacon devoted the first four days of their stay to a study of the situation. After obtaining Estrada Palma's consent, they con-

[43] This and the subsequent messages were published in Taft's *Report* and in *Foreign Relations, 1906.*

ferred with the military and civilian liberal leaders as well as with members of the moderate party.[44] On the 21st they checked an imminent insurgent advance against Habana by threatening to land troops from the seven American warships which were by this time in Cuban waters. Two days later they proposed a set of rules to prevent violations of the truce that had been in effect before their arrival, and these were accepted by both sides. Their investigations had by this time convinced them that the liberals had real grievances in connection with the 1905 elections and that it would be inadvisable for the United States to attempt to support the weak moderate regime in the face of general popular opposition. They found on the other hand that the liberals were still ready to accept a compromise along the lines proposed by the veterans' committee early in September, and they based their own proposals on the veterans' plan.

The commissioners thought that the Cuban President would probably have been reelected even in a fair vote, and they consequently proposed that he remain in office but that he appoint a non-partisan Cabinet. The senators and congressmen chosen in 1905 should resign. The remainder of the congress would then enact a new electoral law and a new municipal law drafted by a bi-partisan commission on which there would be a legal expert appointed by the President of the United States. This would make it possible to hold new, fair elections not only for senators and congressmen but also for provincial governors and municipal councilmen. The same commission would draft a civil service law and a law making the judiciary independent. The rebels were to lay down their arms as soon as the resignations of the senators and congressmen were received.

Estrada Palma, who had apparently not been consulted about these proposals until they were put before him in definitive form, flatly rejected them, saying that they were "against my personal decorum and the dignity of the government over which I preside." When Roosevelt in a personal message urged him to reconsider, he replied that: ". . . the bases proposed by Mr. Taft and Mr. Bacon in order that the rebels should lay down their arms would, if accepted, simply be giving to these the victory, encouraging them, once they had put aside their arms, to continue in the same spirit

---

[44] The following account of the commissioners' activities is based mainly on Taft's *Report.*

of rebellion and laying the foundation for revolt in the future." [45] He reiterated his intention to resign, and the commissioners were informed that all of the other principal moderate officials would also resign, in order to force the United States to take control. The government party clearly felt that intervention was preferable to an arrangement that might bring the liberals into power.

By September 26 Taft had become convinced that the United States would have to assume full control and set up a provisional government. He had feared at first that action of this sort would mean a conflict with the liberal army, and Roosevelt had had to dissuade him from treating the insurgents as potential enemies. It now seemed evident that the liberals would not oppose a provisional government. Taft told the liberal leader Zayas "just what he would do; that is restore order and then hold new and fair elections and turn over the government and get out." [46]

Roosevelt, however, insisted that the commissioners make every effort to persuade the Cubans to agree to some other solution. Though he was prepared, as he cabled Taft on September 26, "to risk any political trouble here in order to do our duty in Cuba," he felt that intervention would be unpopular in the United States, especially if it involved fighting between Americans and Cubans. When Zayas and some of the moderates, in a last-minute effort at compromise, suggested that the congress choose a provisional president under whom new elections could be held, Roosevelt rather scornfully overruled Taft's objection that the plan was unconstitutional. Public opinion in the United States, he cabled, would demand that every possibility of a peaceful settlement be exhausted before intervention took place. Taft consequently encouraged the Cuban leaders to find any possible solution, despite some apprehension that a deal between the liberals and a part of the moderate party might be forcibly opposed by other factions in the government. He reported that there had been "an earnest effort" to agree on a provisional president, but that it had failed.

When the Cuban congress met on September 28, the moderates carried out the plan that they had been discussing during the past two weeks. Estrada Palma submitted his resignation and refused to

[45] *Ibid.*, p. 479.
[46] *Ibid.*

withdraw it when a committee of congress asked him to do so. The Vice President also resigned. Since the President had already accepted the resignations of the members of his Cabinet, who under the law would have been in line to succeed him, Cuba was left without a government. The congress could do nothing because the moderate senators and deputies prevented a quorum by refusing to attend. The government party had deliberately created a situation in which the American commissioners would be compelled to take over the government. On the evening of the 28th, at Estrada Palma's urgent request, Taft sent a marine guard to prevent any looting of the treasury.

The Establishment of the Provisional Government

On the 29th, Taft assumed control of the island as Provisional Governor. His proclamation stated that the new regime would be maintained only long enough to restore order and hold elections. The Cuban flag would continue to fly and the existing machinery of government would be maintained so far as possible. His action seemed to meet with the approval of all parties. Estrada Palma "expressed himself as very much pleased with the proclamation," and the liberals promised to lay down their arms. It was not an easy matter to disband the poorly disciplined and unruly forces which both sides had recruited, but the operation was successfully completed in about two weeks. A general amnesty, which was interpreted to apply even to some of the murders committed during the political campaign and the revolt, was proclaimed on October 10.

The Provisional Government was established without actually using force. A formidable fleet, which might have landed upward of 6,000 marines and bluejackets, assembled in Cuban waters soon after Taft's arrival, but no troops were landed at Habana during the negotiations, and only small detachments, chiefly for the protection of Americans, were landed at other points. The presence of the fleet doubtless discouraged breaches of the truce during the negotiations. After the Provisional Government was set up 2,000 marines were brought ashore, and a little later they were relieved by an army expeditionary force of 5,600 men. This garrisoned the larger towns, but left to the Cuban rural guard the task of preventing disorder in the countryside.

The intervention probably saved Cuba from an appalling disaster, but it was unfortunate from other points of view. It was easily misrepresented by unfriendly critics as new evidence of North American imperialism which belied the declarations that Secretary Root had been making in South America. Root himself felt that the affair might have been handled more skilfully.[47] It is possible that the outcome might have been different if the American commissioners had treated Estrada Palma with more tact. For several days after his first formal visit, Taft paid virtually no attention to the President, and the latter's refusal to cooperate in any compromise rose largely from a feeling that his personal dignity and the dignity of his office had been slighted. Bacon, who seems to have played a passive role in the affair, was probably suggesting his own opinion of the conduct of the negotiations when he wrote that he "was not satisfied," and that he would "be ashamed to look Mr. Root in the face." [48] Whether a compromise was in fact possible, when so many of the leaders in both parties preferred intervention to any arrangement that involved concessions by them, is of course debatable.

Many Cubans and many of the foreigners in the island thought that the attempt to reach a compromise with rebels would encourage revolutions in the future. Taft himself would have inclined to this view, in spite of the manifest unfairness of the 1905 elections, had it not been for the weakness of Estrada Palma's regime. "If the present government could maintain itself [he cabled Roosevelt on September 21], or if it had a moral support or following which would be useful in case of intervention, Bacon and I would be strongly in favor of supporting it as the regular and constitutional government, because the election was held under forms of law and has been acted upon and recognized as valid, but the actual state of affairs is such that we would be fighting the whole Cuban people in effect by intervening to maintain this government." [49] Roosevelt, too, thought that concessions to rebels in arms would set a dangerous precedent, but he felt that the Cuban government had forfeited any claim to support by its failure to defend itself and by the improper conduct of the elections. He was also unwilling to risk prolonged guerrilla war-

[47] Jessup, *Root*, Vol. II, p. 156.
[48] J. B. Scott, *Robert Bacon, Life and Letters* (Garden City, 1923), p. 118.
[49] Taft's *Report*, p. 470.

fare in which vast amounts of property could easily be destroyed. The recollection of Spain's unsuccessful effort to restore order in Cuba with an army of 200,000 men was still vivid, and there was much to be said for a solution that caused no bloodshed and no great resentment in Cuba. Fifty years after the event, it is difficult to think that the action of the United States government had any harmful effect on Cuba's political development. Subsequent experience, in Cuba and elsewhere, showed that supporting constituted governments without regard to the way in which they kept themselves in power did little to promote political progress.

There were two other alternatives. One was to turn the government over to the liberals. Taft was shocked when Roosevelt rather casually suggested this as a possibility. The insurrectionary force, he said, ". . . is not a government with any of its characteristics, but only an undisciplined horde of men under partisan leaders. The movement is large and formidable and commands the sympathy of a majority of the people of Cuba, but they are the poorer classes and the uneducated. The Liberal party, which is back of the movement, has men of ability and substance in it, but they are not titular leaders of the insurgent forces in whom such a government *de facto* must vest if in anybody." [50]

The other possibility was to let the parties fight it out. Roosevelt would probably have considered this a cowardly disregard of his obligations under the Platt Amendment, and it might have led to complications with the European powers, which were demanding that the United States protect the property of their nationals. We may be somewhat skeptical about the danger of actual European intervention, which Roosevelt mentioned in defending his action in his message to Congress in December, but the wholesale destruction of foreign property, which some of the liberals threatened, would very possibly have forced the United States itself to intervene under much more difficult conditions than those that confronted it in September 1906.

The second intervention might possibly have been avoided if the United States had exerted its full influence somewhat earlier to steer the Cuban government away from the course of action that brought on the civil war. Estrada Palma was personally honest and well-

[50] *Ibid.*, p. 477.

meaning, and an able and tactful American Minister might have been able to persuade him to check the abuses committed by his advisers, of whose worst misdeeds he was perhaps not fully aware. Unfortunately, Squiers' quarrels with the Cubans made it impossible for him to be of any great help, and his successor, as we have seen, did not even inform the State Department about what was taking place. In any event, Root, who had assured the Cubans in 1901 that the United States would not "intermeddle" in their internal affairs, would probably have hesitated to attempt to influence the Cuban government's conduct of elections.

Governor Magoon's Administration

Secretary Taft remained in Cuba until October 13, when he turned over the office of Provisional Governor to Charles E. Magoon. Magoon was a lawyer who had had several years of service in the War Department's Bureau of Insular Affairs and who had more recently held the combined offices of American Minister to Panama and Governor of the Canal Zone. As Provisional Governor, he reported to the Secretary of War rather than to the Secretary of State. He exercised legislative as well as executive authority, for Taft suspended the sessions of the Cuban congress because the annulment of the 1905 elections left it without a quorum. His most important duty was to prepare the way for the restoration of a Cuban government. This involved not only the pacification of the country and the holding of elections but also the formulation of the basic legislation which the Cuban congress had failed to enact before 1906. Most of the party leaders agreed that this legislation was essential to the establishment of a new government on a satisfactory basis.

Taft had hoped that the Provisional Government would not have to remain in Cuba more than six months,[51] but after conferring with Cubans of all shades of opinion he decided that it would be better not to hold the election until the sugar and tobacco harvests were over, in May. In April 1907, when he again visited Cuba, he found that the new electoral and municipal laws were not ready and that the Advisory Law Commission which was working on them thought that a census was needed to provide the basis for the registration of the voters. He consequently consulted again with the Cuban

[51] *Ibid.*

leaders and gave orders that the census should be taken. It was also decided that municipal and provincial elections should be held some months before the presidential election in order to try out the new electoral law. With the delays that this program involved, the Provisional Government did not get out of Cuba until January 1909.

Magoon's conduct of the government during this period has been severely criticized by Cuban historians. Some, animated by their resentment of the Platt Amendment and all its consequences, have accused him of dishonesty and incompetence and have even suggested that he was the author of many of the political evils from which Cuba has suffered since 1909. North American historians have not shared these extreme views and have shown that the charge of personal dishonesty, at least, was almost certainly unfounded. There is no real evidence that either Magoon or any of his principal American assistants profited financially from their positions.

The Provisional Government's financial record, in fact, was a creditable one. It found somewhat over $13,000,000 in the treasury, but there were outstanding commitments and appropriations totaling a much larger amount. During the next two years, a disastrous hurricane and the financial panic of 1907 seriously affected the revenues, and the government had extra expenses of several million dollars resulting from the 1906 revolution. In the same period, however, it appropriated about $33,000,000 for public works.[52] Magoon endeavored to provide employment for the thousands of laborers who were out of work during the dead season between cane harvests and to provide better transportation facilities which would reduce the cost of marketing products and increase the country's prosperity. The country's road mileage was doubled, many bridges were built, and ports were improved and opened to commerce. After paying off most of the government's outstanding bills, the Provisional Government turned over nearly $3,000,000 to President Gómez in 1909.

Other aspects of the provisional administration did merit criticism. As Roosevelt wrote Root in 1908, Magoon shrank "from following any course to which he [thought] any considerable number of Cubans would object, whether rightly or wrongly." It would be impossible to say how much graft and corruption occurred in con-

[52] Charles E. Magoon, *Report of Provisional Administration, from October 13, 1906, to December 1, 1908* (Habana, 1908–1909), p. 20.

nection with public works contracts without a more detailed examination of individual cases than is available, but it seems probable that the granting of contracts was not adequately supervised, and that in some cases political influence from the United States was brought to bear. The Provisional Governor could not always control his Cuban subordinates, and improper considerations were probably permitted to affect governmental business, especially in the matter of pardoning criminals. It had always been customary to use executive clemency rather freely in Cuba because the Spanish penal code, which was still in effect, prescribed harsh penalties for criminal offenses and allowed the judges little discretion in applying them.[53] It was charged, however, that Magoon granted an excessive number of pardons and that political pressure, exerted sometimes in return for bribes to Cuban politicians, was responsible for many of them.

In fairness to Magoon, it must be remembered that his situation was very different from that of Wood during the first intervention. Instead of building up an administration in which he could enlist the services of the ablest Cuban leaders, he had taken over one which was already functioning, but somewhat discredited and demoralized. Taft, before his departure, arranged that the various executive departments should be directed by their chief clerks, under the control of North American advisers, and he rejected a demand that some of the moderate officeholders be removed to make way for liberals. On the other hand, he promised that vacancies as they occurred would be filled by liberals. This perhaps seemed fair under the circumstances, but it dragged the Provisional Governor into politics to an undesirable extent, especially after the liberal party divided into two factions which could not agree on patronage. The efficiency of the administration suffered, and it was even alleged that new and unnecessary jobs were created to provide openings. Some Cuban writers, with little regard, it must be said, for historical accuracy, have accused Magoon of inventing the *botella,* or sinecure, which later became one of the flagrant evils of Cuba's political system.

If the Provisional Government erred in trying too hard to keep

[53] See Colonel Crowder's discussion on this point in his report to the Provisional Governor dated November 14, 1907, Magoon's *Report, 1906–1908,* p. 136.

the cooperation of the Cuban leaders, the responsibility was not entirely Magoon's. Taft feared that any serious dissatisfaction among the liberals might cause some of their followers to refuse to lay down arms, and it was he who formulated in broad lines the policy that was followed. It is difficult at this distance from the event to say that he was wrong, but the result illustrates the embarrassment that can come from assuming responsibility without insisting on untrammeled authority. The Cubans themselves would have had more respect for the Provisional Government if it had taken a firmer stand against questionable appointments and actions.

On balance, the shortcomings of the Provisional Government were more than offset by the efficiency with which it performed its two principal tasks. One of these was the preparation of a series of important laws. It was clear that the deficiencies in the laws governing elections and municipal and provincial government had contributed to the catastrophe of 1906, and all parties agreed that these deficiencies must be corrected if a new Cuban government was to be established on a sound basis. In accord with the peace settlement an advisory commission of six Cubans and three Americans was appointed in December 1906, to deal with this matter. In the next two years, under the energetic leadership of its president, Colonel E. H. Crowder, this group drafted new laws dealing with elections, local government, the organization of the executive power, the civil service, and many other subjects. These were promulgated by the Provisional Governor after public criticism of their text had been invited and after changes suggested by this criticism had been made.

The other chief objective of the Provisional Government was to hold elections and restore a constitutional Cuban government. The completion of the census, early in 1908, made it possible to compile accurate lists of the qualified voters in each district, and 60 percent of those eligible participated in the election for provincial and municipal officials which took place on August 1 of the same year. This proportion increased to 71 percent when the President and members of congress were chosen on November 14. Both elections were orderly and all parties expressed satisfaction with the way in which they were conducted.

The victor in the national elections was General José Miguel

Gómez, who had been the unsuccessful candidate in 1905. Alfredo Zayas, the leader of a rival group in the liberal party which had only agreed to support Gómez after both factions had made a poor showing in the local elections of August, was chosen Vice President. The defeated presidential candidate was General Mario García Menocal, who represented a new conservative party that included most of the former moderates. Gómez was inaugurated on January 28, 1909, and all American officials and troops were withdrawn.

Many European observers, who had been skeptical about the intentions of the United States after the war with Spain, found it even harder to believe that Cuba would be given a second chance as an independent state after 1906. In the United States also there was some talk of annexation in the first months of the intervention. The idea was not unwelcome to many property owners in the island, but it was opposed, as Magoon reported, by the overwhelming majority of the Cuban people.[54] Root refused to consider it: "There is a good deal of talk [he said in January 1907], about the annexation of Cuba. Never! so long as the people of Cuba do not themselves give up the effort to govern themselves. Our efforts should be towards helping them to be self-governing." [55] Roosevelt's attitude was equally unequivocal. He warned the Cubans, in his message to the United States Congress in December 1906, that they could not maintain their independence unless they learned to govern themselves in an orderly way, but he felt that the United States must honor the promises which had induced both parties to acquiesce in the intervention. In a personal note to Taft, on January 27, 1907, he wrote: "There can be no talk of a protectorate by us. Our business is to establish peace and order on a satisfactory basis, start the new government, and then leave the Island." [56] Later, he was disposed to offer the Cubans some temporary help in maintaining order and financial stability and in conducting elections [57] but no arrangements for such help were made when the new Cuban administration assumed office.

[54] *Ibid.*, p. 34.
[55] Address to the National Foreign Trade Convention at Washington, Root, *Latin America and the United States*, p. 275.
[56] *Letters*, Vol. v, p. 60.
[57] See his letters of April 4, 1908, to Magoon (*Letters*, Vol. vi, p. 993) and of July 20, 1908, to Root (*ibid.*, p. 1137).

Efforts to Maintain Peace in Central America

The policies of the State Department in the Dominican Republic and Cuba between 1905 and 1909 were shaped by earlier commitments that somewhat limited its freedom of action. In dealing with Central America, Root had a better opportunity to apply his own ideas, and to achieve what seemed at the time a notable success, without any appearance of arbitrary intervention. His efforts to lay the foundations for a lasting peace in the isthmus are perhaps the best example of the spirit in which he approached the problems of disorderly Caribbean countries. It was hardly his fault that they ultimately failed because the rulers of some of the Central American countries did not really want a lasting peace.

The five Central American states together had an area of less than 200,000 square miles, but they were quite dissimilar in the makeup of their population and their social conditions. In Guatemala, which was the most populous, the masses of the people were Indians, who still spoke their own languages and had little part in the country's political life. Most of them worked under a system of debt-slavery on coffee plantations owned by wealthy natives or foreigners. In Costa Rica practically all of the people were of European descent, and the majority were small farmers who owned their own land. In the other three countries the inhabitants were predominantly *mestizos,* of mixed white and Indian blood, mostly illiterate and living under primitive conditions, but somewhat less exploited by the land-owning upper class than were the Indians in Guatemala. El Salvador, like Guatemala and Costa Rica, enjoyed a measure of prosperity from coffee raising. Nicaragua and Honduras were poorer and more sparsely settled.

The five states had once been united in the Federal Republic of Central America, which the isthmian leaders set up when the breakdown of Spanish rule in Mexico in 1821 left them to their own devices. Though this union fell to pieces after several years of civil war, many Central Americans had always wished to see it restored. Unionist sentiment commanded lip-service even from presidents who had no real desire to give up their independent authority, and it was sometimes encouraged by rulers who aspired to head a new federal government. Several attempts to unite some or all of the states had failed. As recently as 1895, Nicaragua, Honduras, and El Salvador had set up a loose confederation which they called "The Greater Republic of Central America," but this collapsed after a revolution in El Salvador in 1898.

The party affiliations and rivalries formed during the first period of the union had survived, so that liberals and conservatives continued to fight each other across national boundaries after the five separate republics were formed. The governments consequently intervened frequently in one anothers' affairs, turning internal conflicts into international wars. The successive military dictatorships that ruled Guatemala repeatedly set up and overthrew governments in El Salvador and Honduras, and the presidents of those countries and of Nicaragua aided revolutions against one another. Only Costa Rica, which usually remained aloof from the quarrels of the other states, had been able to achieve a fairly stable government.

The isthmus' progress had also been retarded by isolation. The principal towns were on the western side, where they were cut off from the Caribbean by high mountains and jungles, and their commerce was carried on through ports on the Pacific Coast. Before the opening of the Panama Canal, these were rarely visited by steamers and were for all useful purposes thousands of miles from Europe or the eastern part of the United States. The transit route across Nicaragua, which was important for a short time in the middle of the nineteenth century, was abandoned after the building of the Panama Railroad. The Central Americans thus had little contact with the outside world, and there were few roads or railroads to encourage trade within the isthmus.

By the turn of the century, however, this situation was changing. All of the republics except Honduras had small railway lines that connected their chief cities with ports on the Pacific, and in 1890 Minor Keith completed a line that connected the principal towns in Costa Rica with Limon on the Caribbean Sea. The United Fruit Company, which Keith helped to found, was operating in Costa Rica and after 1906 in Guatemala, and other American companies were raising bananas in Honduras and Nicaragua. North Americans and Europeans were also interested in mines and banks and various sorts of commercial concessions.

As in other Caribbean countries, increasing contact with the outside world had some unpleasant results. Many of the earlier Central American railroads had been built with the proceeds of loans floated in London, often on terms scandalously unfair to the borrowers. The history of the foreign debt of Guatemala, Honduras, and Costa Rica, in fact, was much like that of Santo Domingo, and all three of these countries were in default in 1900. There had been disputes over the governments' failure to meet other obligations to foreigners and over injuries to foreigners in time of civil war. Episodes such as the British occupation of the Nicaraguan port of Corinto in 1895 and disputes over the lease to an American syndicate of a Honduran railroad in which the British bondholders claimed an interest suggested that the United States might at any time confront a situation like those which had caused so much embarrassment in Venezuela and the Dominican Republic.

Guatemala's treatment of its bondholders had been especially exasperating, and in 1901 the British, French, German, Belgian, and Italian governments united in demanding compliance with a recent promise to resume service. President Manuel Estrada Cabrera agreed to their demands when they threatened to seize some of Guatemala's ports. The other powers invited the United States to take cognizance of the arrangement, but were told that the American government was "indisposed to join in any collective act which might bear the aspect of coercive pressure upon Guatemala." It nevertheless reserved the rights of American citizens to participate equally in any adjustment of the Guatemalan debts.[58]

The United States had only two chiefs of mission in Central America before 1907, for Captain William Lawrence Merry, who was stationed in Costa Rica, was also accredited to Nicaragua and El Salvador, and Leslie Combs, in Guatemala, was accredited to Honduras. Its relations with the Central American governments had not been particularly intimate, despite its interest in the potential canal route in Nicaragua. After 1903, as a consequence of Roosevelt's growing realization of the strategic importance of the Caribbean region, it began to concern itself more actively with the internal political affairs of the isthmus. When it seemed probable in that year that there would be a war between Guatemala on one side and El Salvador and Nicaragua on the other, Roosevelt and Hay endeavored

[58] *Foreign Relations, 1902*, pp. 569ff.

rather cautiously to exert their influence for peace, "striving always," as Hay instructed Merry, "to avoid the slightest suspicion of compulsion or dictation." [59] This offer of good offices was not accepted, but the prospect for peace improved somewhat after representatives of the four northern Central American countries met at Corinto in August 1904 and pledged their governments not to permit political refugees to use their territory as bases for revolutions against one another.

All of the other countries, however, continued to be suspicious of Guatemala, which was ruled by one of the cruelest and most corrupt dictatorships in the history of the Continent. The Guatemalan President, Manuel Estrada Cabrera, was an exceptional figure in Central American political life. He had not been a military leader, and he had no friends or personal followers except the army officers and government officials who supported his regime for the sake of the license and graft that he permitted them to enjoy. Opposition of any sort was repressed with fiendish cruelty, and an extensive spy system made it dangerous even to mention politics. The dictator had little interest in the welfare of Guatemala, but he made elaborate efforts to convince foreigners that he was a benevolent and progressive ruler and he was occasionally able, by flattery or other means, to win the friendship of American diplomats. Estrada Cabrera's chief concern in his relations with his neighbors was his fear that they might give aid to Guatemalan exiles in organizing a revolution. He was especially suspicious of Mexico, because of the long-standing boundary dispute between the two countries, and there was bad blood between him and Tomás Regalado, the powerful War Minister of El Salvador.

Early in 1906 it appeared that war between Guatemala and El Salvador might break out at any time. Each government believed that the other was encouraging revolutionary movements against it, and Estrada Cabrera suspected that Porfirio Díaz of Mexico was supporting El Salvador in the hope of taking over some of Guatemala's territory on the northern frontier.[60] In May when the American Ambassador in Mexico was instructed to inquire about reports that political exiles were preparing to invade Guatemala from

[59] Hay to Merry, May 12, 1903.
[60] Combs to Hay, Feb. 22, 1905.

Mexico, the Mexican authorities assured him that they were doing what they could to prevent the invasion; but two revolutionary expeditions nevertheless crossed the frontier into Guatemala in May and June of 1906. Both were defeated, and President Díaz asserted that he had prevented the movement from becoming serious by dissuading El Salvador from attacking at the same time. Combs, however, reported that there had been revolutionary invasions of Guatemala from El Salvador and also from Honduras in the first days of June. It was impossible to be sure that any of the governments involved could have prevented small armed bands from crossing the poorly policed and sparsely inhabited frontiers, but it was evident that they had not tried very hard to do so. The situation remained tense, with large armies on each side of the Guatemala-Salvador frontier, and it became worse when President Bonilla of Honduras allied himself with El Salvador against Guatemala in June. Combs worked hard for peace in Guatemala, but it was impossible for the State Department to communicate effectively with the government of El Salvador until Merry, who had been on leave, was ordered to go there early in July.

Tomás Regalado, who was the dominant figure in El Salvador, had been president of that country from 1898 until 1903. He retained military control, as Minister of War, after he turned over the presidency to Pedro José Escalón. Regalado chose the night of Merry's arrival to go on one of his periodic drunken sprees, and started by announcing that the government was a "den of thieves" that should be wiped out and ordering two shells fired into the presidential palace. The President and other officials simply kept out of his way, and the next day Regalado, still drinking, went to the frontier and led an army into Guatemala. Escalón tried in vain to persuade him to return.[61] Fortunately Regalado was killed in battle in the first days of the war that ensued, and the United States and Mexico were able to persuade the belligerents to accept an armistice. A treaty providing for a general Central American peace conference later in the year was signed on board the *U.S.S. Marblehead* on July 20, 1906.[62]

Root was leaving for South America when the war started, but

[61] Merry to Root, July 10, 1906.
[62] For correspondence about these events, see *Foreign Relations, 1906*, pp. 834ff.

he had time to lay out the course of action that the Department followed. He was interested in maintaining peace in Central America, and he also thought that the United States should protect Minor Keith's railway projects in Guatemala and El Salvador.[63] He urged that President Díaz be asked to join with Roosevelt in offering mediation, because he thought that interposition by the United States alone might arouse suspicion. In carrying out Root's instructions, Acting Secretary Bacon told Merry to exercise great care "not to encroach in any way upon sovereign rights." Root himself wrote Roosevelt after the peace conference that Mexico's cooperation was "a good object lesson as to the way in which the stronger American states can be of service to the others and the way in which American affairs ought to be conducted." [64] Unfortunately the Secretary was somewhat over-optimistic. Though the peace conference, which met at San José, Costa Rica, later in 1906, framed an admirable set of treaties designed to lay the basis for a permanent peace, it was only a few months before new disturbances began.

Zelaya's Attack on Honduras

This time José Santos Zelaya, the dictator of Nicaragua, seemed to be the chief troublemaker. Zelaya had ruled Nicaragua since 1893 with the support of the powerful liberal party, violently suppressing every effort of the conservatives to regain power. He had more progressive ideas than Estrada Cabrera, and he did something to develop transportation and production, but at the same time he and his associates enriched themselves by setting up monopolies in many lines of business and selling concessions for the development of natural resources. He had already shown a propensity to interfere in the internal affairs of other countries by sending aid to revolutionists in countries as far away as Ecuador and Colombia, and he was regarded with suspicion and fear in Central America. The American Minister in Costa Rica reported in 1900 that Costa Rica and El Salvador had for some years had an agreement to support one another against any aggression that he might undertake.[65]

[63] See Root's letter to Roosevelt, quoted in Jessup, *Root*, Vol. 1, p. 501, and his letter of July 3, 1908, to Andrew Carnegie, Root Papers, Library of Congress.
[64] Jessup, *Root*, Vol. 1, p. 502, and Root to Roosevelt, Aug. 2, 1906, Root Papers, Library of Congress.
[65] Merry to Hay, June 24, 1900.

Zelaya had been having an unpleasant controversy with Merry over two American claims,[66] and he refused to be represented at the San José peace conference on the ground that he did not wish to recognize the right of the United States to interfere in Central American affairs.[67] Early in 1907 he permitted, and probably encouraged, a group of revolutionists to invade Honduras. When these were driven back across the frontier and attacked in Nicaraguan territory by Honduran forces, he threatened to declare war. Both governments agreed to submit the matter to arbitration, but when the arbitral commission demanded that all troops be withdrawn from the frontier during its deliberations Zelaya refused and the commission disbanded.

At this point Root suggested that the United States, Mexico, and the three neutral states in Central America make a joint effort to restore peace. As usual, he sought to avoid the appearance of North American dictation by letting Mexico take the lead.[68] Efforts to obtain a peaceful settlement were obstructed by Zelaya's insistence that Honduras first agree to pay reparations, and while the exchange of cables was still continuing, Nicaraguan troops invaded Honduras. President Bonilla's Honduran army and a large force that El Salvador had sent to help him were defeated on March 18 at the battle of Namasigue, where machine guns, used for the first time in a Central American war, caused a terrific number of casualties.[69] On March 27 Nicaraguan troops entered Tegucigalpa and set up a weak triumvirate as the provisional government of Honduras.

A general Central American war now seemed imminent because none of the other governments were willing to see Zelaya dominate Honduras. Costa Rica, which usually tried to stay out of Central American conflicts, asked Merry how the United States would regard a joint intervention by the neighboring governments. Root consulted the Mexican Ambassador and told Merry to reply that he would not feel at liberty to criticize any action that the Central American states might feel compelled to take. Somewhat later he

---

[66] The Emery and Weil claims, which will be discussed in Chapter v.

[67] Nicaragua, *Memoria de Relaciones Exteriores, 1907*, pp. xvii, 5.

[68] Root to Thompson, Feb. 4, 1907, Num. Case 3691/25B.

[69] Reported by the American Consul at Managua, April 1, 1907, Num. Case 3691/565–566.

also refused to advise Guatemala to remain neutral.[70] He evidently felt that the United States should not attempt to discourage the Central Americans from dealing with Zelaya in their own way when the United States was not prepared to stop him.

Root seemed equally reluctant to become actively involved in the situation when El Salvador and Honduras asked the United States and Mexico to propose an armistice, and he delayed his reply while the Mexican Ambassador and the Central American representatives at Washington discussed what Assistant Secretary Bacon characterized as "some indefinite plan of joint action by Mexico and the United States."[71] Second Assistant Secretary Adee, whose long diplomatic experience gave his views much weight, thought that "nothing short of some kind of constraining intervention by Mexico and the U.S. will accomplish any beneficial result," and that mediation would simply mean standing by while Nicaragua enforced her demands. He suggested that it might be "logically" proper for the United States and Mexico to intervene to prevent a prejudicial disturbance of the balance of power in Central America, just as the European powers had intervened between Russia and Turkey,[72] but this rather far-fetched idea probably had little appeal to Root.

While the other governments were still trying to decide what to do, Bonilla was making his last stand at Amapala, on an island in the Gulf of Fonseca. When the Nicaraguans prepared to attack the town, where most of the more valuable property belonged to Germans and other foreigners, Root asked that the U.S.S. *Princeton* prevent any bombardment until the civilian population had been evacuated. Roosevelt would have been glad to "stop the further destruction of life and property by Nicaragua" altogether,[73] but he left the decision in Root's hands. There seems to have been no effort to interfere with the Nicaraguan operations except in the interests of humanity, and on April 12 the surrender of Amapala was arranged through the good offices of the commander of the U.S.S. *Chicago*, who took Bonilla on board.

---

[70] Merry to Root, Feb. 28, and Root's reply March 2, Num. Case 3691/100. Root to Lee (Guatemala), Mar. 21, 1907, Num. Case 3691/202.

[71] Bacon's memorandum of March 29, 1907, Num. Case 3691/256.

[72] Adee's views were expressed in a memorandum attached to Num. Case 3691/295.

[73] Roosevelt to Root, April 1, 1907, Num. Case 3691/287.

Philip Marshall Brown, the American Chargé d'Affaires at Tegucigalpa, now intervened, on his own initiative, to bring about peace between Nicaragua and El Salvador. Through his efforts, the Foreign Ministers of the two countries met at Amapala on April 18. The negotiations nearly broke down over Zelaya's demand for an indemnity, but Brown, who was present unofficially, supported El Salvador in refusing one, and the Nicaraguan dictator finally yielded the point, after complaining bitterly to Roosevelt about Brown's attitude. A formal treaty of peace, which provided that any further disputes between the two parties should be submitted to arbitration by the Presidents of the United States and Mexico, was signed on April 23.[74]

In a secret treaty, of which Brown took no official notice, the two governments agreed on the establishment in Honduras of a government that would be acceptable to Guatemala and El Salvador as well as to Nicaragua. Zelaya was himself dissatisfied with the situation that had developed at Tegucigalpa, because neither the *junta* that he had installed nor his own discontented and unreliable troops had been able to maintain order there and a liberal leader named Miguel Dávila, whom he distrusted, had taken control of the government. The secret treaty provided that El Salvador should oust Dávila, since it would be embarrassing for Zelaya to attack a man who was still his ally, and that the two governments would then install General Sierra, a former president, as his successor.[75] There was evidently no thought of consulting the wishes of the people of Honduras. The secret treaty was not carried out because neither party gave Sierra enough support when he started a revolution in Honduras, and Dávila continued as President.

The Nicaraguan troops had been withdrawn from Tegucigalpa on April 17, but they continued to occupy some of the towns on the Honduran north coast. The American warships that had been sent to that coast during the fighting also remained there, and there were several unpleasant incidents because some of the commanders were over-zealous in protecting foreigners of various nationalities against

---

[74] For correspondence about the conference, see Num. Case 3691, including especially enclosures 422–453 and enclosure 589, which contains Brown's report.

[75] For the Nicaraguan government's account of the conference and the text of the secret treaty see its *Memoria de Relaciones Exteriores, 1907.*

alleged abuses by the local authorities.[76] This local situation improved when the Nicaraguan troops were withdrawn late in June and the United States and Mexico recognized Dávila's government in August 1907, but the general Central American picture did not. Zelaya was openly carrying on propaganda for the establishment of a Central American union, which he expected to dominate, and he was affording hospitality at Managua to several of the principal political exiles from Guatemala and El Salvador.[77] It seemed only a question of time before new troubles would begin.

A blunder in the State Department made matters worse. At the end of March, when the Nicaragua-Honduras-El Salvador war was still in progress, Washington Valentine, the president of the largest mining company in Honduras, persuaded Assistant Secretary Bacon that his long residence and wide acquaintance in Central America might make him useful in trying to straighten out the situation there. Ambassador Creel of Mexico supported him, and he was given letters of introduction to the American diplomats on the isthmus with a covering letter signed by Root himself suggesting that Valentine might be able to give them valuable advice and aid in their efforts to maintain peace. He was also permitted to travel from Costa Rica to Nicaragua on an American warship. Zelaya consequently had some justification for thinking that his advice reflected the State Department's views. What Valentine proposed, however, was far from what Root had in mind, for he urged Zelaya to set up a military government in Honduras and promised that the United States and Mexico would endeavor to prevent any interference by Guatemala or El Salvador. He seems also to have encouraged the Nicaraguan dictator in his ambition to establish a Central American union and to have suggested an attack on El Salvador as the first step.[78]

Valentine's cables reporting these actions horrified Root, but the Secretary's indignant disavowal came too late. Zelaya, who would probably have continued his career of aggression without encouragement, now had reason to think that he had the support of the

[76] For correspondence about these incidents, see Num. Case 3691/636–642.

[77] Report from Consul Ryder at San Juan del Norte, May 25, 1907, Num. Case 3691/661.

[78] The principal papers about the Valentine affair are Num. Case 3691/453, 547, 588, 607, 622, 633. See also the accounts in Jessup, *Root*, Vol. I, pp. 507–509, and in Nicaragua, *Memoria de Relaciones Exteriores*, 1907, p. xxi.

United States. In June 1907, he sent one of his gunboats, with a group of Salvadorean exiles and North American filibusters, to seize the port of Acajutla.[79] The expedition was repulsed, but El Salvador and Guatemala at once began to prepare for war.

Root described the Central American situation, as it appeared to him, in a letter to Assistant Secretary Adee on July 1, 1907. He was clearly discouraged. He blamed all the trouble in Central America on Zelaya's desire for conquest, and he felt that the Mexican-American effort for peace, though it must be continued, would be a matter of "mere form." He had no sympathy for Estrada Cabrera's brutally despotic regime in Guatemala, but he was inclined to support El Salvador, which had been "pretty decent," and he felt that Costa Rica was "so near Panama that we must not let her be overturned." So far as the rest of the isthmus was concerned, nothing would be of use except a long period of armed intervention "that we cannot undertake." The Central Americans would have to work out their own salvation, which would be a long process.[80] The letter shows that Root, at least, was not disposed to contemplate anything like the policy of interference that some of his successors were to follow.

The Washington Conference of 1907

The situation was not quite so hopeless as Root thought. Zelaya, who had sent his Minister of Foreign Affairs to Mexico and Washington to learn more about Valentine's proposals, was more ready to compromise when he found that he did not have the backing of either government. He faced an imminent attack from Guatemala and El Salvador, and he could expect no help from Honduras, where Dávila was trying hard to make sure that his country's neutrality would be respected. Probably at Zelaya's request, the Mexican government on August 21 suggested a joint effort to maintain peace,[81] and on August 28 Roosevelt and Díaz proposed that another Central American conference be held and that all warlike activities cease in the meantime. All five Central American presidents immediately agreed.

Adee, in Root's absence, skilfully conducted the rather compli-

[79] Merry to Root, June 20, 1907, Num. Case 6775/23.
[80] Num. Case 6775/82 2/11.
[81] Godoy to Knox, Aug. 21, 1907, Num. Case 6775/62.

cated negotiations that followed. One question was the place of meeting. Both Roosevelt and Root had wished that Mexico appear to be taking the lead in the peace effort, and that the conference should meet at the Mexican capital; but Guatemala, with the support of some of the other states, insisted on Washington. The Central Americans also suggested that the conference be postponed until hostile feelings had cooled somewhat and that a preliminary peace protocol be signed in the meantime. This course was adopted.[82] The protocol, signed on September 17, did not entirely put an end to the rumors of war, but early in November the Presidents of Nicaragua, El Salvador, and Honduras met at Amapala and reported that they had reached a cordial agreement on all outstanding problems.

The American diplomats in Central America strongly suspected that the real object of the Amapala meeting was to form a united front against any effort by the United States to increase its influence in Central America,[83] but there was little suggestion of anti-American feeling in the proceedings of the conference which convened in the Bureau of American Republics at Washington on November 14. Enrique Creel, the Mexican Ambassador, and William I. Buchanan, who had been appointed by Roosevelt "to lend his good and impartial offices in a purely friendly way," attended the sessions. The conference got off to a good start when each delegation, following the example of the representative of Salvador, announced that its government had no claims to present against any of the other republics. Harmony was temporarily disturbed when the Honduran delegation introduced a proposal for a Central American union, which was opposed by Guatemala and Costa Rica, but the crisis was smoothed over and the conference proceeded to draw up a series of treaties which were to influence the international relations of the Central American states for several years.[84]

The most important was the General Treaty of Peace and Amity. In this the five states agreed that all disputes between them should in the future be settled by a Permanent Central American Court

[82] For these negotiations see Num. Case 6775.

[83] This idea was expressed in several dispatches from Costa Rica and Guatemala and in a report from the American consul at San Salvador, all filed in Num. Case 6775.

[84] For the proceedings of the conference and the English text of the treaties, see *Foreign Relations, 1907*, Vol. ii, pp. 665–727.

of Justice. They also obligated themselves to prevent the use of their territory as a base for the organization of revolutionary movements against other states and to restrict the activities of political refugees from other states. This undertaking promised to do away with the chief cause of international wars in the isthmus and to make internal conflicts much less frequent. Another article, establishing the permanent neutrality of Honduras, had the same purpose, for Honduras' weakness and her central position in the isthmus had often made the control of her government an objective in conflicts between her stronger neighbors. Both the General Treaty and several separate conventions sought to pave the way for closer economic and cultural relations. They reflected the feeling that Central America was a political community whose members were bound to one another by special ties.

In an additional convention to the General Treaty, the five states agreed not to recognize a government coming into power by revolutionary means in a Central American country "so long as the freely elected representatives of the people thereof have not constitutionally reorganized the country." This provision seemed somewhat unrealistic, for in 1907 there had hardly ever been a free election in any Central American state except Costa Rica, but it was an expression of the delegates' faith in democratic ideals. It was little observed in practice while the 1907 treaties were in effect, but a similar provision in the Central American treaties of 1923 was to have more important results.

The Permanent Court of Justice was to decide controversies between the governments and certain classes of suits brought by citizens of one state against the government of another. Every effort was made to assure its independence. Though one of the five judges was to be elected by the legislature of each state, they were to be paid from the treasury of the Court, rather than by the governments, and they were to serve for five-year terms. They were to represent, not the countries that sent them, but the "national conscience of Central America."

The treaties, for the most part, represented the ideas of the Central Americans themselves, for many of their provisions were similar to those of conventions adopted at earlier meetings between the five republics. Root, however, may have been chiefly responsible for the provision establishing the permanent neutrality of Honduras. He later wrote that he had hoped to bring about a joint guarantee of Honduran neutrality by the United States and Mexico. This would give the President of the United States authority to use the navy to prevent violations, and he thought that the mere existence of the power would make its exercise unnecessary. The guarantee would be the "pivot upon which the whole political life of Central America would turn," because "the Zelayas and Cabreras, unable to get at each other and confined to their own dominions would be speedily disposed of by their own people." [85] He had hoped that such a guarantee would be spontaneously requested by the Central American governments. Since it was not, and since a mere treaty provision meant little to the "Zelayas and Cabreras," the neutralization of Honduras had no very important consequences.

Root was even more interested in the plan for the Central American Court, which reflected ideas that the American delegation, under his instructions, had unsuccessfully put forward at the recent peace conference at the Hague. It was at his suggestion that Andrew Carnegie gave the money for the erection of a building for the Court in Cartago in Costa Rica. Root had high hopes for what promised to be the first real permanent international tribunal. He probably did not fully realize how difficult it would be to create an independent international court in a region where the local courts, in most cases, took orders from the President in matters that involved political considerations. There were able and honest jurists in Central America, but it was not probable that rulers like Estrada Cabrera and Zelaya would permit them to be named to a body which would be dealing with questions of vital political importance.

Knowing that the prestige of the new treaties would be enhanced in Central America if they were discussed by the press in the United States, Root sent personal letters at the end of the conference to the editors of several newspapers and magazines urging that some attention be given them. He wrote that: "The great trouble with Central American efforts at peace hitherto has been that they have made general agreements of peace and empty promises which have been almost immediately broken. These treaties follow a different line, and contain a number of specific, practical provisions which I

[85] Jessup, *Root*, Vol. i, p. 510.

think are quite well adapted to begin a progressive growth of common sense conduct leading towards a real union. Of course the building of the Panama Canal puts these Central American countries in the front yard of the United States and their conduct is important to us, and the success of their appeal to us to act the part of a friendly neighbor in helping them to reconcile their differences may be of great value in the future." [86] He also proposed to the Mexican government that Buchanan and Ambassador Creel should be sent to Central America on a special mission of courtesy and congratulation, but this idea met with a very unenthusiastic reception from the Mexicans, partly because of their strained relations with Guatemala and partly, perhaps, because they were growing apprehensive of the influence that the United States was exercising in Central America. It was finally arranged that the two diplomats should simply attend the inauguration of the new court in Costa Rica.[87]

The First Test of the 1907 Treaties

The 1907 treaties would undoubtedly have improved conditions in Central America if their provisions had been respected. Unfortunately the statesmanship and the conciliatory spirit that had animated the delegates in Washington, while they were in contact with Root and Buchanan and Creel, was not reflected in the policies of their governments. Zelaya had not given up his ambitious ideas, and Estrada Cabrera was as determined as ever to stop him. Neither really intended to live up to their obligations under the treaties. Each wished to make his position more secure by controlling the governments of El Salvador and Honduras, and the weakness of the administrations in both of these countries continued to invite intervention in their affairs. In El Salvador, the government apparently had little popular support and was beset by revolutionary conspiracies. Since Zelaya was openly encouraging these, Fernando Figueroa, who became president in 1907, had reluctantly allied

---

[86] Num. Case 6775/275A.

[87] Num. Cases 6775/361A, 408, 413A, 432, and 7357.60. See also Daniel Cosío Villegas' *Historia Moderna de Mexico. El Porfiriato. La Vida Política Exterior, Parte Primera* (Mexico, 1960), pp. 680ff. Dr. Cosío Villegas' book gives a detailed account of the events of this period.

himself with Guatemala.[88] Dávila in Honduras also had little personal following. His cooperation with the influential liberal leader Policarpo Bonilla had made Zelaya less friendly but had not placated the hostility of Estrada Cabrera. Dávila's enemies in Honduras, most of whom were adherents of the former president, Manuel Bonilla, were constantly plotting against him.

Root apparently felt that the recently signed treaties brought the United States into a new relationship with Central America, which would justify more active interposition to maintain peace. At the end of 1907, when he learned that the famous American filibuster Lee Christmas was recruiting men in Guatemala for an invasion of Honduras, he expressed vigorous disapproval and asked the American Legation in Guatemala for a report on Christmas' activities.[89] In January 1908 Root asked the British government to prevent the organization of a filibustering expedition in Belize. He was probably the more determined to stop these movements because it was suspected in Honduras that the United Fruit Company, which was about to expand its operations into that country, was behind them.[90] In February 1908, when the American Ambassador in Mexico asked President Díaz to take action against Salvadorean revolutionists who were apparently organizing in that country, Root approved the request, saying "we wish to discourage in every proper way these continual revolutionary attempts." [91] Another evidence of increased interest was the establishment early in 1908 of separate legations in each of the five Central American countries. It was significant that there was some unfriendly comment in the tightly censored Mexican press when it was learned that Root had proposed this action to Congress.[92]

The whole structure created by the 1907 treaties seemed about to break down in July 1908, when a band of revolutionists invaded Honduras from El Salvador and another, led by Lee Christmas, attacked on the north coast. There was little doubt that the movement had been instigated by Guatemala and El Salvador as a way of

[88] See Merry's despatch of Jan. 8, 1908, from Costa Rica and Chargé d'Affaires Gregory's despatch of Jan. 24 from San Salvador, Num. Case 6575/300 and 305.
[89] Num. Case 7357/30–31.
[90] The evidence on this point is not clear. See Num. Case 7357/30–31, 41–42, 57A.
[91] Telegram to Thompson, Feb. 24, 1908, Num. Case 4598/22.
[92] Dispatch from Embassy, Mexico, March 12, 1908, Num. Case 6775/345.

striking at Zelaya, and the Nicaraguan dictator, despite his recent coolness toward Dávila, prepared at once to go to his assistance. To avoid a general Central American war, the United States and Mexico strongly urged all of Honduras' neighbors to keep out of the conflict, and Costa Rica by a happy inspiration asked the new Central American Court to interpose. The Court urged the four potential belligerents to submit their differences to arbitration, and a few days later, when Honduras and Nicaragua formally charged Guatemala and El Salvador with violation of the Central American treaties, the Court assumed jurisdiction in the dispute.

When the Court demanded that all of the governments withdraw their troops from the frontiers, the State Department and the Mexican Ambassador at Washington backed up its action by forceful representations to the Central American diplomatic representatives and discussed a proposal to send a strongly worded cable, signed by Roosevelt and Díaz, to demand respect for the Court's decisions. Root, who was away from Washington, telegraphed Assistant Secretary Bacon that he supposed "we are not at liberty to give the kind of guarantee that would have to be made good by military expedition," but he was willing to pledge the influence of the United States and Mexico to the fullest extent and to say that a failure to obey the mandate of the Court would be a violation of most solemn obligations upon which the United States and Mexico were entitled to insist and did insist.[93] The telegram was not sent, because the governments withdrew their forces and the revolution in Honduras soon afterward collapsed.

The Court had stopped the war, but it still had to render a decision on the complaint of Honduras and Nicaragua. This was a delicate matter. Dodge, the American Minister at San Salvador, feared that a decision in favor of either side would make the resumption of friendly relations more difficult and might cause the fall of one of the weaker governments. He thought that Honduras would be willing to drop the suit if a neutral power suggested such action. Buchanan went to Mexico to discuss this suggestion and an idea of his own for a general amnesty in Central America, but he found that President Díaz, though he was willing to go along with the United States, thought that any attempt to stop the suit would arouse criti-

[93] Root to Bacon, July 30, 1908, Num. Case 7357/273.

cism. The State Department decided not to take the initiative, and the proceedings continued.[94] In December, the Court dismissed the case against El Salvador by a vote in which each of the judges from the countries involved sided with his own government and the Costa Rican judge voted for the defendant. In the suit against Guatemala, all except the judge from Honduras voted to absolve Estrada Cabrera of responsibility for the Honduran revolt.[95]

Many persons felt that the judges' votes had been influenced by pressure from their own governments or by even more sordid considerations. The facts, however, were not entirely clear. Minister Merry, though he had no doubt that Guatemala and El Salvador were guilty, thought that the decision was justified by the lack of clear evidence.[96] Dodge, at San Salvador, had been inclined to think that President Figueroa had done what he could to police the frontier and to warn Honduras at the time of the invasion.[97] The American Minister at Guatemala, on the other hand, was convinced that both Figueroa and Estrada Cabrera had helped the Honduran revolutionists. He knew that several thousand copies of a Honduran revolutionary proclamation had been struck off in the Guatemalan government's printing office.[98] On the whole, the decision seriously hurt the Court's prestige even though the tribunal had proved its usefulness as an instrument to prevent a general Central American war.

When Secretary Root resigned in January 1909, he could look back on a substantial record of achievement. The Dominican customs treaty had been ratified, and the Dominican government was solvent and apparently more stable than at any time in the country's history. The intervention in Cuba was being terminated, and a new, freely elected government was taking office. It seemed reasonable to hope that the 1907 treaties and the permanent court would help to bring peace in Central America. On January 9, just before his retirement, he signed treaties with Colombia and Panama which

[94] Num. Case 7357/439, 457, 517, 532.
[95] *Corte de Justicia Centroamericana, Sentencia en el Juicio promovido por la República de Honduras contra las Repúblicas de El Salvador y Guatemala* (San José, Costa Rica, 1908).
[96] Merry to Root, December 20, 1908, Num. Case 7357/576.
[97] Dodge to Root, July 14, 1908, Num. Case 7357/202.
[98] Heimke to Root, July 25, 1908, Num. Case 7357/274.

promised to assuage Colombia's bitterness over the loss of the isthmus. In conjunction with a treaty signed at the same time between Colombia and Panama, these provided for the recognition of Panama by Colombia and for the transfer to Colombia of the first ten installments of the $250,000 canal annuity. The United States would begin the annuity five years earlier than it was required to under the treaty of 1903, so that it would contribute half of the money that Colombia would receive, and it would give Colombia special privileges in the Canal. Root had devoted much time and effort to these negotiations.

Most important of all, perhaps, was the fact that relations with the Latin American countries in general were friendlier than they had been for many years. Root's South American trip seemed to have dispelled much of the suspicion and ill-will caused throughout the hemisphere by the Panama affair. The Secretary had established cordial personal relations with many Latin American statesmen and had convinced them of his sympathetic interest in their problems.

Unhappily, this relatively satisfactory state of affairs was short-lived. The Colombians rejected the tripartite treaties and ousted the government that agreed to them. The Dominican Republic, after 1911, sank into a condition of anarchy, and conditions grew worse rather than better in Cuba. In Central America, efforts to compel observance of the 1907 treaties led to American armed intervention in Nicaragua. Root himself, however, had realized that even the wisest statesmanship at Washington could hardly bring about a rapid and lasting change in Caribbean political conditions. Writing to a Central American friend in December 1908, he expressed the conviction that the great obstacles to peace were the ambitions, the selfishness, and the disregard of public welfare on the part of a few individuals; and that no outside force could make these individuals less prominent. He thought that the problem was one that the Central Americans themselves must solve, and that the process would be a slow one.[99]

[99] Root to Policarpo Bonilla, December 16, 1908, Num. Case 6775/611.

◄ 5 ►

Dollar Diplomacy and Intervention in Nicaragua, 1909–1913

President William Howard Taft should have been well equipped to deal with Caribbean problems. His long residence in the Philippines, his intimate acquaintance with the people and the problems of Panama, and his mission to Cuba in 1906 gave him unusual experience. In general, he seems to have been successful in dealing with people of Spanish descent. He was cautious and conciliatory by temperament, and certainly had little predilection for an aggressive or imperialistic policy. After the Spanish American War he had opposed the retention of the Philippines, and as late as 1903 he had expressed doubts about the validity of the Monroe Doctrine.[1] His views had evidently changed during his service in Roosevelt's Cabinet, for he showed no misgivings about the Monroe Doctrine or about the Roosevelt Corollary to the Doctrine after he became President.

It was not the President, however, but the Department of State that was primarily responsible for the new administration's policies in Latin America. The Secretary of State, Philander C. Knox, was one of the ablest lawyers of his time, and is said to have had more influence with the President than any other member of the Cabinet.[2] Unfortunately, he lacked some qualities that were needed in dealing with Caribbean problems. Lord Bryce commented on his lack of "diplomatic and historical preparation," which made him inclined to be arbitrary in his decisions,[3] and Root later wrote that he was "absolutely antipathetic to all Spanish-American modes of thought and feeling and action, and pretty much everything he did with them was like mixing a Seidlitz powder."[4] Knox himself intimated that he found it difficult to cultivate "the delicate entente with the

---

[1] Pringle, *Life and Times of William Howard Taft* (New York, c. 1939), Vol. I, pp. 159–160, 256.

[2] *Ibid.*, Vol. II, p. 687.

[3] H. A. L. Fischer, *James Bryce*, quoted by Bemis, *American Secretaries of State and Their Diplomacy* (New York, 1928–1929), Vol. IX, p. 356.

[4] Jessup, *Root*, Vol. I, p. 251.

Latins which has been nourished and maintained largely in the past upon champagne and other alcoholic preservatives." [5]

During his frequent absences from Washington, and even when he was at his desk, Knox seems to have left the formulation of Caribbean policies largely in the hands of Huntington Wilson, the new Assistant Secretary of State. Wilson was an energetic and zealous career diplomat who had served for several years in the Embassy at Tokyo and then as Third Assistant Secretary under the preceding administration. He had apparently made a rather unfavorable impression on Root,[6] but seemed to have Knox's confidence. He had never been south of the Rio Grande, and like his chief he lacked the tolerant spirit and the genuine liking for Latin Americans that had marked Root's dealings with them.[7]

Both Knox and Wilson appreciated the growing importance and complexity of the American government's responsibilities in the Caribbean and made an effort to see that they were dealt with by competent personnel. Early in his term in office, Knox set up a Latin American Division which he placed under the direction of Thomas C. Dawson, who had served as American Minister in the Dominican Republic, Colombia, and Chile. New legislation made it possible to strengthen the Department's staff in other ways. Equally important was the appointment of career men with substantial Latin American experience as ministers in nearly all of the Caribbean republics. Though the career service still left much to be desired, both in quality and in training, and though only a few of the abler men in the service had any desire to work in Caribbean countries, the United States was better represented in the region than it had been earlier or than it would be for twelve years after 1913.

The basic ideas that shaped the Caribbean policy of the Taft administration were not very different from its predecessor's. Taft and Knox believed that the United States must promote stable government and economic progress as the best means of warding off European interference. Knox thought that the Monroe Doctrine "constantly [required] a measure of benevolent supervision over

---

[5] Handwritten letter to Taft, March 14, 1911, Taft Papers, Library of Congress.
[6] Jessup, *Root*, Vol. I, pp. 457, 563.
[7] For a good self-portrait of Wilson see his autobiography; F. M. Huntington Wilson, *Memoirs of an Ex-Diplomat* (Boston, 1945).

Latin American countries to meet its logical requirements." [8] The idea that the government had an obligation to protect American citizens in their lives and property rights was also emphasized, perhaps even more than under Roosevelt. Specific policies generally represented an effort to continue what the previous administration had been doing. The establishment of customs collectorships and the refunding of debts owed in Europe by loans from American bankers merely carried farther the experiment that Roosevelt had inaugurated in Santo Domingo, and even the armed intervention in Nicaragua was essentially an effort to make effective the machinery that Root had helped to create for maintaining peace in Central America. There was, however, a difference in the spirit and manner in which these policies were carried out. Where Root had made every effort to avoid any appearance of domination or coercion, Knox showed less concern for the amenities of diplomatic intercourse and a greater readiness to consider the use of force when diplomatic methods failed.

The new administration also went farther than its predecessor in its emphasis on financial reform as a principal objective of its Caribbean policy. In Nicaragua, Honduras, Guatemala, and Haiti, it attempted to have the old European-held bonded debts refunded by loans floated in New York or at least to have American bankers participate in international financial operations. It felt that the new role of the United States in the Caribbean required that American financial influence should be predominant there. The loan projects in Nicaragua and Honduras had an additional and more important purpose—the establishment of customs collectorships like that in Santo Domingo. The apparent success of the Dominican experiment led Taft and his advisers to look on American control of the customs almost as a panacea for the ills of disorderly Caribbean countries, a device which would discourage revolutions and would also make possible the payment of troublesome foreign claims and the construction of much needed public works.

It was this emphasis on loans and customs receiverships that led

[8] In his letter to Taft on March 14, 1911, cited above. For other statements of Knox's views see his speeches to the American Bar Association in January 1912 (quoted in Bemis, *American Secretaries of State and Their Diplomacy*) and at San Francisco, May 7, 1912, Knox Papers, Library of Congress.

the administration itself, as well as its critics, to describe its policy as "Dollar Diplomacy." To Taft, using dollars instead of bullets seemed humane and practical, but many critics, especially in Latin America, saw in the policy only a design to aid American bankers and other selfish interests in exploiting the countries where it was applied. This interpretation, as the story will show, was erroneous, but it has been accepted rather uncritically by many students of diplomatic history.

The idea that Knox was a servant of big business was hardly supported by his career in the public service. He had formerly been a prominent corporation lawyer, but as Attorney General under McKinley he had distinguished himself by his prosecution of the Northern Securities case and had helped to draft legislation giving the Interstate Commerce Commission effective control over railway rates. He had continued to take an interest in such legislation after he entered the Senate.[9] In dealing with bankers while he was Secretary of State, he showed that he was keenly aware of the responsibility that the Department was assuming in sponsoring loan contracts, and he took elaborate precautions to make sure that there could be no justified criticism of the terms of the contracts. The purpose of dollar diplomacy was to promote the political objectives of the United States, not to benefit private financial interests.

It is true that the bankers hoped to make a profit from their transactions. Though some of them insisted in later years that they had cooperated in the State Department's loan projects only as a patriotic duty, and because the United States government urged them to do so, the record suggests that they did not regard the projects as unattractive pieces of business. By 1909 several of the larger New York banks were taking an interest in foreign loans, even though it was still rather difficult to sell foreign bonds in the United States. J. P. Morgan and Company had made loans to Cuba, and at least two groups had shown an interest in the proposed Dominican loan before the panic of 1907 made its flotation impossible. Without any suggestion from the State Department three rival groups were working on a refunding loan for Guatemala and another group on a similar project in Costa Rica in 1909. The projects sponsored by the State Department were perhaps less attractive in one respect,

[9] *Dictionary of American Biography*, Vol. x, p. 478.

because the Department's officials insisted that the borrowing government be given the best possible treatment. One of the officers who had been closely connected with the Taft administration's loan projects recalled in later years that the bankers had been reluctant to make the loans on "moderate terms" and had agreed to make them only when they were asked to do so as a patriotic duty.[10] On the other hand the security offered by the customs receiverships made the bonds more attractive to investors. In most cases, more than one banking group showed a willingness to undertake the business.

The Breakdown of Cooperation with Mexico in Central America

One of the most troublesome matters that confronted Knox when he took office was the situation in Central America, where it seemed likely that war might break out again at any time. Estrada Cabrera had been foiled in his effort to upset Dávila, but there was reason to suppose that his success in the Central American court would encourage him to stir up further trouble in Honduras. His rival Zelaya was still fomenting revolutionary movements in El Salvador, and in March 1909 American warships on the Central American coast were instructed to use force if necessary to stop filibustering expeditions leaving Nicaraguan ports.[11]

Knox discussed Central American problems at Cabinet meetings on March 12 and March 16, 1909, and on the latter date, according to the Secretary of the Navy, he "read a paper which defined our policy in Central America in the future—all action to be in conjunction with Mexico. It ensures the neutrality of Honduras and con-

[10] G. T. Weitzel in *Annals of the American Academy of Political and Social Science*, Vol. cxxxii (July 1927), p. 115.

[11] I have been unable to find a record of these instructions, but Secretary of the Navy Meyer mentioned them in his diary for March 12, 1909. The entry suggests, but does not state, that the order had been given before he took office. (See M. A. DeW. Howe, *George von Lengerke Meyer*, New York, 1920, p. 427). An order in March is also mentioned by Philip Marshall Brown, who was at the time Minister to Honduras; P. M. Brown in *Supplement to the American Political Science Review*, Vol. viii (1911), p. 161.

Definite instructions to the Navy to stop all expeditions across the Gulf of Fonseca were sent at the State Department's request on April 24, 1909; Num. Case 18432/101A.

templates establishing its credit by their suggesting that we put in a financial agent such as we furnished to San Domingo.

"Much tact and diplomacy has got to be exercised in order to accomplish results and prevent armed interference on our part. President Taft endorsed the Secretary Knox action and said he would even make a show of force in order to maintain peace and stop revolutions." [12]

The statement reflected an intention to follow, in general, the policy that Root had developed. Taft's reference to possible armed intervention seemed to introduce a new and ominous note, but Adee had written Huntington Wilson on March 11 that Root himself had said a year earlier that the state of affairs in Central America would logically and necessarily end by the intervention of the United States and Mexico, ostensibly to preserve Honduras' neutrality, but practically to clip Zelaya's wings.[13] A proposal that the United States help to reorganize Honduras' finances had also received favorable consideration while Root was Secretary of State.[14] Knox accepted his predecessor's idea that the neutrality and stability of Honduras was the key to Central American peace, and he intended to continue the cooperation with Mexico by which Root had hoped to ward off suspicion of imperialistic designs on the part of the United States. Knox thought, however, that the relation of the United States and Mexico to Central American affairs must be more intimate if peace were to be maintained and that there should be a conventional right to intervene promptly, without awaiting outbreaks, when there was danger of civil war.

An unsigned intradepartmental memorandum of March 24 indicated more precisely what was contemplated. The writer suggested a new Central American treaty in which the United States and Mexico would "be charged with and assume the guarantee" of the peace of Central America and the neutrality of Honduras and would have judges in the Central American Court. The finances of Honduras would be reorganized under a plan like that adopted in the Dominican Republic, possibly with Mexican participation. He insisted on the right and the duty of the United States and Mexico to

[12] Howe, *Meyer*, pp. 427–428.
[13] Num. Case 18432/13.
[14] See Chapter VI.

stop warfare in Central America, by force if necessary. Most of these ideas were embodied in an informal letter which Knox sent to the Mexican Ambassador on March 26. The new treaty was to provide, among other things, that the Central American governments should agree to treat persons plotting against another state just as they treated their own opponents who engaged in revolutionary activities. Knox proposed that the Nicaraguan government, which he considered the chief troublemaker, should be excluded from the conference that was to draw up the new agreement.[15]

The Mexican government was unwilling to join in the policy that Knox suggested. Its approach to Central American problems, influenced as it was by a traditional hostility to Guatemala and an unwillingness to see North American influence in the isthmus increase, had always been different from that of the United States. Mexico had been willing to join in the use of good offices to preserve peace, but it was averse to the idea of compelling the Central Americans to behave themselves. Mexican misgivings about the direction in which North American policy seemed to be developing were evident in the sensitive reaction in April to an erroneous report that the American Admiral had asked one of the Mexican gunboats on the Central American coast to fire on a Nicaraguan filibustering expedition.[16]

In discussing Knox's proposals, the Mexican representatives did not flatly reject the idea of giving financial help to Honduras. They suggested that a commission of three experts, named by Mexico, Honduras, and the United States, might give financial advice if Honduras voluntarily requested it, provided that there was no effort to compel the Honduran government to follow the advice. They made it clear on the other hand that their government would not go beyond the use of moral influence in any attempt to maintain peace and insisted that Nicaragua be included in the proposed conference. The Minister of Foreign Affairs told Ambassador Thompson confidentially that President Díaz regarded Zelaya as a personal friend and felt indebted to him because Zelaya had offered active

---

[15] Knox to the Mexican Ambassador, March 26, 1909, Num. Case 18920. The intradepartmental memorandum is filed under 18920/13.
[16] Num. Case 18432/107,127.

military support against Guatemala at a time when Mexico's relations with that country were strained.[17]

Knox and Wilson regarded Mexico's attitude as a refusal to continue to work with the United States in Central America. Wilson, at least, seemed rather cheerful at the thought that the State Department would have more freedom in its Central American policy if it did not have to consider the Mexican point of view. From this time on, the State Department rarely consulted Mexico about steps it took in the isthmus, and it was only a few months before the two governments were working at cross purposes there. With the breakdown of cooperation, the Taft administration began to turn away from the course that Root had charted and to move toward a more active intervention in Central American affairs.

The Fall of Zelaya and the Nicaraguan Civil War of 1909–1910

One of the chief purposes of the proposals discussed with Mexico had been to check Zelaya's efforts to dominate Central America. Knox and Wilson blamed the Nicaraguan dictator for most of the trouble that had occurred in Central America since 1907. Estrada Cabrera, as Wilson told the Mexican Ambassador in April 1909, was equally "iniquitous," but he was "relatively quiescent" while Zelaya was "engaged in open defiance of international comity and conventional obligations." [18] It would perhaps have been more accurate to say that Estrada Cabrera showed enough respect for the State Department's opinion to pretend to cover his tracks, while Zelaya had gone out of his way to be offensive to the American government, not only by flouting the provisions of the 1907 treaties but in other ways.

One source of bad feeling had been disputes over two American claims. One of these originated in a loan that an American named Weil made to Zelaya in 1903 in return for the privilege of collecting the import duties on liquor on the Atlantic coast. The State Depart-

---

[17] Num. Case 18920/14. For a good account of these negotiations, see Cosío Villegas, *Historia Moderna de Mexico*, pp. 699ff. The State Department's record is in Num. Case 18920.

[18] Memorandum of conversation, April 17, 1909, Num. Case 18920/11.

ment would not ordinarily have supported a contract of this sort, but, when Zelaya arbitrarily canceled the concession, it urged that he pay Weil the $3,812 that the government apparently owed and release 960 cases of whiskey that it had confiscated. Minister Merry, though he was instructed only to use his good offices in the matter, was soon involved in an angry controversy about it. In March 1908, however, the State Department refused to press the matter farther, and Weil paid the government $17,000 to get his whiskey released. The Emery claim, where several hundred thousand dollars were involved, grew out of Zelaya's cancellation of a concession to cut lumber on the Nicaraguan east coast. The State Department had urged, unsuccessfully, that the matter be submitted to arbitration, but while Root was Secretary of State the claim was apparently handled as a routine matter by the lawyers in the State Department, and months sometimes elapsed between exchanges of communications. Nothing in the State Department's treatment of either claim need really have embittered the relations between the two governments, but the discussions at Managua had been made acrimonious by Zelaya's generally offensive attitude toward the representatives of the United States.[19]

This attitude had manifested itself in other ways. For several years, American diplomats at Managua had believed that the government was tampering with their mail and cables. Merry was especially irritated in 1907 when he found that messages in an unknown code were being sent over his signature to the American consul at San Salvador, who turned out to be conniving with Zelaya in subversive activities. In 1908 the new American Minister, John Gardner Coolidge, felt that he had been personally insulted when several conservatives, who had staged a political demonstration under the pretext of celebrating President Taft's election, were arrested while carrying American flags. The State Department did not take the matter very seriously, but Coolidge resigned, and the young secretary who took charge complained of continued unfriendly treatment.[20] Adee commented that Nicaragua might be a good place "to send people we are tired of" and suggested a politically influential

---

[19] The correspondence on the Weil claim is in Num. Case 146, and that on the Emery claim in Num. Case 924.

[20] For the "flag" incident see Num. Case 6369/36–57.

diplomat as a candidate. The man was appointed, but he did not go to his post because Knox, as one of his first acts in the State Department, ordered the withdrawal of the Chargé d'Affaires from Nicaragua and announced that he would not send a new Minister for the time being. This left a non-career vice consul as the representative of the United States at Managua—an arrangement that proved unfortunate in the months that followed.

At the same time Knox took a more vigorous stand on the Emery claim. On March 10 he told the Nicaraguan Minister at Washington that any further delay in agreeing to arbitration would be considered "unnecessary, unwarranted, and dilatory." [21] Negotiations were resumed two months later when Zelaya sent his Minister of Foreign Affairs to Washington to negotiate for a settlement, and on May 25 the two governments signed a protocol providing for arbitration. By mutual agreement, however, the recourse to arbitration was postponed while the parties made an effort to reach a settlement by further negotiation, and on September 18 Nicaragua promised to pay the claimants $640,000, in installments, for all of their interests in the republic. [22]

One reason for Zelaya's agreeing to the settlement was his desire to obtain a new foreign loan. Nicaragua's credit was better than that of most Central American governments because Zelaya had been paying interest regularly since 1895 on the small outstanding foreign debt; and in May 1909 the Ethelburga Syndicate of London and a French group agreed to float a loan of £1,250,000 to provide funds to build a railroad to the Atlantic Coast. Knox attempted to persuade the British and French governments to discourage the bankers, but neither took any effective action. The French government, however, prevented the new bonds from being quoted officially on the *Bourse* and told the bankers to urge Zelaya to settle his differences with the United States. Despite the State Department's expressed disapproval, the loan was successfully floated in London and Paris. [23]

The settlement of the Emery claim did little to improve relations between the United States and Nicaragua. The State Department

[21] Knox to Espinosa, March 10, 1909, Num. Case 924/185.
[22] The text of both agreements is printed in *Foreign Relations, 1909*, pp. 460–467.
[23] For the correspondence about the Ethelburga loan see Num. Case 5621.

still felt that Zelaya's ambition to dominate Central America was the chief obstacle to its efforts for peace. Even while Mexican and American warships were patrolling the Nicaraguan west coast to prevent further filibustering expeditions, Zelaya had kept the weak Salvadorean government on edge by maneuvering his warships provocatively, and on April 24, acting under the "moral right and duty which the United States shares with Mexico under the Washington Conventions," President Taft authorized the navy to "stop any expedition across Fonseca Bay." [24] Zelaya seemed more cautious for a time, but in August, when the American cruisers were temporarily withdrawn from the coast, there were again reports that he was making warlike preparations against El Salvador.[25] There was evidence, too, that he was attempting to interfere in politics in Costa Rica, where a presidential election was about to take place.[26] It still seemed likely that the rivalry between Zelaya and Estrada Cabrera might cause new disturbances at any time.

Philip Marshall Brown, the American Minister at Tegucigalpa, concluded that a Central American union set up with the help of the United States and Mexico might improve matters. In October 1909, the State Department was disturbed to learn that he and the Mexican representative at Tegucigalpa were publicly associating themselves with proposals to this end, and on the recommendation of Adee, who knew something of the "hideous record" of failure in previous attempts at union, the Minister was sent an instruction saying that the process of union must start from within and emphasizing the American government's continuing interest in the loyal fulfillment of the 1907 treaties.[27]

At the end of September, Knox reviewed the Central American situation in a letter designed to give Taft background for a meeting that he was about to have with President Díaz. He evidently thought that the situation had improved. The Emery claim had been settled, and there was a good prospect for American loans which would help to promote stability in Honduras, Guatemala, and El Salvador.

---

[24] Num. Case 18432/101A.
[25] Telegram of Aug. 30 from Consul at Managua, Num. Case 4598/96.
[26] Num. Cases 19865 and 6775/664,708.
[27] Brown to Knox, confidential, Sept. 9, 1909, Num. Case 6775/697–8; instruction to Brown, Oct. 23, 1909, Num. Case 6775/706,707.

Mexico's refusal to cooperate had made it impossible to carry out his plan for a new Central American treaty, but on the other hand the Mexican government's statement that it had no interests south of Guatemala was "of possible great importance to us in the future in view of our canal interests, certainly of enough possible importance to make it discreet not to challenge the statement at this time." The Secretary apparently did not have any new steps to suggest.[28]

A revolution which began a few days later in Nicaragua was to create new and more difficult problems. In Nicaragua, the political parties that had come down from the first years of independence had disputed the control of the government with an even more intolerant mutual enmity than in the other Central American states. Party loyalties were determined by geography rather than by political ideas. The liberals had their stronghold in Leon and the conservatives theirs in Granada, and each party was supported by allies in nearby towns. Virtually every Nicaraguan, whatever his station in life, was an ardent partisan, who carried his politics even into his social and business relations. Individuals rarely went over from one party to another, and though factional leaders might occasionally make deals with the opposite party, for patriotic reasons or for their own advantage, mutual dislike and ·distrust was apt to make such alliances precarious.

In the half-century before 1909 the Nicaraguan government had nevertheless been somewhat more stable than those of Honduras and El Salvador. Factional rivalries were temporarily subdued after both parties united to expel the American filibusters under William Walker in the 1850's, and for thirty years, from 1863 to 1893, there was relatively little internal strife. The capital, which had moved back and forth between the two chief cities with the fortunes of war, was permanently established at Managua, then a small town some distance from either. Throughout the period, the Granada conservatives controlled the government, passing the presidency in an orderly way from one member of their group to another. In 1893, however, they quarreled among themselves and a liberal revolution made José Santos Zelaya president.

In 1909, Zelaya had been in power sixteen years, with the support of the liberal party and of some prominent conservatives who had

[28] Knox to Taft, Sept. 28, 1909, Knox Papers, Library of Congress.

found it profitable to do business with him. He had been responsible for some progressive measures, such as the extension of the railway which connected the principal towns with the west coast and the establishment of steamer service on the Great Lake and the San Juan River, but the most striking feature of his economic policy had been the reckless granting of concessions to his Nicaraguan associates and to foreign businessmen. Monopolies had been set up for the sale of liquor, tobacco, and other commodities, and special privileges covering other branches of trade and industry had made legitimate business difficult and caused discontent among those who did not profit by them.

The east coast had been especially affected by these grants. This region had never had any close connection with the more thickly settled interior of the republic. The Mosquito Indians who occupied it had been under British protection for a time in the first half of the nineteenth century, and when the British withdrew in compliance with the Clayton-Bulwer Treaty they stipulated that the Nicaraguan government make the district an Indian reserve under a special regime. Zelaya had arbitrarily ended this regime in 1894. In 1909 most of the inhabitants were still Indians or West Indian Negroes who spoke little Spanish. Many foreign businessmen and planters had recently settled there. Bluefields, the principal town, was connected with the interior by a jungle trail, where the mud was apt to be so deep that pack bullocks rather than mules had to be used for transport, but travelers usually went by small boat to the mouth of the San Juan River, where a dangerous bar took a heavy toll of lives, and up the river, through several sets of rapids, to the great lake. Many in fact preferred to go by steamer to New Orleans and from there to Panama and up the west coast.

North Americans who lived on the coast had been complaining for some years about Zolaya's policies. One of the chief grievances was the monopolistic concession held by the Bluefields Steamship Company, which was accused of exploiting and oppressing the independent banana planters in the valley of the Escondido River. This corporation was closely connected with the United Fruit Company, which owned nearly half of its stock; but the Fruit Company asserted that it had no control over the admittedly unsatisfactory management of the Bluefields firm and that it was attempting in the fall of 1909 to divest itself of its interest in the firm.[29] The State Department had remonstrated with Zelaya about this concession and several other acts harmful to trade, but with little result.[30]

In May 1909 the resentment of the independent planters, both native and foreign, flared up in a "strike" against the Bluefields Company, during which much property was destroyed and the local authorities proclaimed martial law. The American government, at the company's request, sent a warship to Bluefields to protect American property, but it also sent an experienced consular officer to investigate, and the latter reported that the strike had been caused by the company's oppressive conduct and arbitrary actions.[31] It is not clear that the strike had any direct connection with the revolution which Zelaya's enemies were already discussing, but it was an expression of the general discontent with existing conditions.

The revolution of October 1909 was the work of a group of conservative leaders from the interior and of Zelaya's own governor at Bluefields, General Juan J. Estrada. Estrada and his brother Aurelio were influential liberal leaders who had apparently been hostile to Zelaya for some time,[32] and it is probable that Zelaya had left the governor at his post only because he feared to break with his faction. The governor was in a position to give the revolutionists immediate control of the east coast, and he was promised the presidency in return for his assistance. Money for the movement was obtained from a number of local Americans and from some of their associates in the United States.

It was later charged that the United States government instigated the revolt. The conspirators, who of course knew of Zelaya's bad relations with the State Department, certainly hoped for its help. They had had little success, however, in their earlier efforts to obtain assurances from American officials. In May 1909, for example, an American who said that he was an emissary of the conservative leader Adolfo Díaz told the commander of the U.S.S. Marietta that the conservatives and Estrada were ready to revolt if they could be

---

[29] Francis L. Hart to George von L. Meyer, Dec. 24, 1909, Num. Case 19475/94.
[30] Instruction to Merry, Jan. 13, 1905.
[31] From Consul Linard, June 2, 1909, Num. Case 19475/40.
[32] See, for example, the reports of his conversations with American naval officers in Num. Cases 3691/200, 6369/81, 6369/131.

assured that the United States would not interfere,[33] but the plan was abandoned when the commander refused to give any assurances. In July, Estrada himself told the American consul that he would start a revolution if he could be promised the disinterested moral support of the United States and could be given $50,000 in cash and 2,000 rifles.[34] He apparently got no such promises, for his army was handicapped in the early stages of the war by its failure to receive arms from any source. It is possible, of course, that the State Department's local representatives encouraged the revolutionists. Vice Consul Caldera, who was the only representative of the United States at Managua, was a Nicaraguan who was hostile to Zelaya, and Consul Moffat at Bluefields was later characterized by an American Admiral as "less an American consul than an agent for the Estrada faction." [35]

A careful study of the files, however, makes it seem doubtful that the State Department at Washington had any connection with the revolution in its earlier stages. Later, much was made of the allegation that Knox's law firm had formerly acted as counsel for one of the mining companies on the coast and that Adolfo Díaz, who was one of the leaders of the revolution, had been an employee of this firm. There is nothing in the record that suggests that this connection, if it existed, was of any real significance. It is true that Wilson openly sympathized with the revolution from the start. He made no secret of this feeling in conversations with the Central American representatives at Washington,[36] and his attitude probably encouraged Estrada Cabrera, who was sending at least a small amount of aid to the rebels. The American government noticeably failed to remonstrate with Estrada Cabrera about this [37] though it urged all of the Central American governments to comply with the provisions of the 1907 treaties that forbade intervention on either side in a civil war.[38] On the other hand, though most of Wilson's

[33] Comm. Hill to Secretary of Navy, June 8, 1909, encl. with Navy Dept.'s letter of June 22, Num. Case 6369/110.

[34] Consul Linard to Secretary of State, July 5, 1909, Num. Case 6369/131.

[35] Admiral Kimball's report of May 26, 1910, transmitted by Navy Dept. May 27, Num. Case 6369/985.

[36] See his memorandum of Oct. 21, 1909, Num. Case 6369/226.

[37] There are only casual references to Guatemala's aid in the State Department files.

[38] Foreign Relations, 1909, pp. 377, 453.

colleagues doubtless shared his hope that the revolution might eliminate Zelaya and were willing to encourage the revolutionists "up to the line of what was right and legal," [39] there was an effort to avoid action that could properly be criticized. Memoranda in the files suggest that Adee and probably Counselor Hoyt insisted on this, and often exercised a restraining influence on Wilson. Adee was skeptical about the success of the revolt and especially doubtful about the revolutionists' announced plan to set up an independent republic on the east coast if they failed to conquer all of Nicaragua.

There was no suggestion of partisanship in the formal action that the American government took. When Moffat reported from Bluefields on October 8 that a revolt was about to begin, Adee as Acting Secretary instructed all of the consuls in Nicaragua to "observe strict neutrality and abstain from any action or expression of opinion that might be imputed or construed as an indication of this government's opinion." [40] Later, Moffat was told "to do nothing whatever which might indicate the recognition of the provisional administration." [41] The commanders of the numerous war vessels that were sent to both coasts of Nicaragua to protect American interests seem to have understood that it was their duty to be neutral. [42]

Zelaya's own reckless action caused the American government to abandon its formal neutrality. Estrada's forces took control of the east coast with little trouble, but Zelaya foiled a plan for a simultaneous uprising in the interior by arresting the leaders. He then sent a force down the San Juan River to attack the rebels on the coast. Two Americans, Lee Roy Cannon and Leonard Groce, who were captured while allegedly trying to blow up a troop ship, were shot by Zelaya's forces, at his order, despite the efforts of the American consul to obtain a reprieve. Zelaya's action was especially exasperating because two Frenchmen who had been taken under the same circumstances were spared.

Zelaya asserted that Nicaraguan law authorized the death penalty for rebellion, but the State Department thought that regularly com-

---

[39] Counselor Hoyt to Knox, Nov. 19, 1909, Num. Case 6369/346.

[40] To Consul, Bluefields, Oct. 8, to Corinto and Managua Oct. 15, 1909, Num. Case 6369/202.

[41] *Foreign Relations, 1909*, p. 453.

[42] This statement is based chiefly on the Bluefields post reports in the Navy Caribbean Area file.

missioned officers in the revolutionary army were entitled to be treated as prisoners of war. It was not disposed to tolerate the murder of American citizens, even though it frowned on their participation in the revolt and knew that Cannon, at least, was a ne'er-do-well who had been involved in other Central American revolutions. Before deciding on a course of action, however, the Department spent several days making sure that it had accurate information and discussing the legal aspects of the case and the questions of policy involved.[43] Wilson wanted to announce that the United States would occupy Corinto, the chief port of Nicaragua, and possibly Managua also, until a government able to maintain order and assure respect for the 1907 conventions should be established, but this idea was apparently abandoned because it was felt that any such action should be approved in advance by Congress.[44]

Instead, the United States broke off all formal relations with the Nicaraguan government. A note that was handed to the Nicaraguan Chargé d'Affaires on December 1, and immediately published, condemned Zelaya in language rarely found in diplomatic communications: "Since the Washington conventions of 1907," Knox wrote, "it is notorious that President Zelaya has almost continuously kept Central America in tension or turmoil." It was "equally a matter of common knowledge" that his administration had done away with republican government in Nicaragua. His regime was described as "a blot upon the history of Nicaragua." The killing of two Americans was emphasized, but only as the most recent of a long series of offensive acts. The government of the United States was convinced that the revolution represented "the ideals and the will of a majority of the Nicaraguan people more faithfully then does the Government of President Zelaya." Both factions would be held strictly accountable for the protection of American life and property, but the United States would wait before demanding a heavy punitive indemnity for the execution of Cannon and Groce until it saw whether it would be dealing with a government "entirely dissociated from the present intolerable conditions and worthy to be

[43] On the legal question, see the Solicitor's memorandum of Nov. 18, 1909, Num. Case 22372/16.

[44] See the rough drafts and memoranda filed in Num. Case 6369, after enclosure /323.

trusted to make impossible a recurrence of such acts." It would also reserve for future consideration the question of requiring from a "constitutional" government in Nicaragua guarantees for the support of the 1907 treaties.[45]

The undisguised purpose of Knox's note, with its expression of moral support for the revolution and its threat that the United States might demand heavy punitive damages for the killing of Cannon and Groce if the liberal party stayed in power, was to force a change of government in Nicaragua. It should be noted that Knox emphasized Zelaya's obstruction of efforts to maintain peace in Central America and his dictatorial regime in Nicaragua rather than the murder of the two soldiers of fortune, as the chief reason for the United States government's action. President Taft took much the same position when he reported the action to Congress in his annual message of December 7, 1909. "Since the Washington Conventions of 1907 were communicated to the Government of the United States as a consulting and advising party," he wrote, "this Government has been almost continuously called upon by one or another, and in turn by all five of the Central American republics, to exert itself for the maintenance of the conventions. Nearly every complaint has been against the Zelaya Government of Nicaragua, which has kept Central America in constant tension and turmoil." The President referred to the numerous barbarities committed by Zelaya and to the death of Cannon and Groce. He reported the break in diplomatic relations and said that the American government "is intending to take such future steps as may be most consistent with its dignity, its duty to American interests, and its moral obligations to Central America and to civilization. It may later be necessary for me to bring this subject to the attention of the Congress in a special message."

The prospect of North American intervention in Nicaragua alarmed the Mexican government. When it became clear that the killing of Cannon and Groce would lead to trouble, President Díaz attempted to revive the policy of cooperation which had broken down some months earlier. President Díaz regarded Zelaya as a friend and Estrada Cabrera as an enemy, and he had no desire to

[45] For the text of the note, which is only briefly summarized here, see *Foreign Relations, 1909*, p. 455.

see a conservative victory in Nicaragua which might make the Guatemalan ruler the dominant figure in Central America. He was equally reluctant, probably, to see the United States increase its influence in Nicaragua. Late in November, he had the Mexican Chargé d'Affaires at Washington propose a peace plan under which Zelaya would resign in favor of some other liberal who would maintain good relations with the United States and would promise to hold free elections.[46]

The State Department received the proposal coldly. Wilson reminded Knox of the failure of earlier efforts to obtain Díaz' cooperation, saying that the Mexican government, after "playing with us for some months," had finally said that it had no interests south of Honduras in Central America and would endorse anything that the United States saw fit to do. He thought that Mexico was actuated by the most contemptible motives.[47] Wilson's statement about the earlier negotiations was not entirely accurate, but the attitude it reveals helps to explain why the policy of cooperation with Mexico had broken down. The Department gave the Mexican Chargé a noncommittal reply [48] and did not even inform him in advance of the contents of the note that Knox was just then sending to the Nicaraguan Legation.[49]

Meanwhile officials in the State Department had been discussing possible methods by which a popularly elected government that would respect the 1907 treaties might be installed in Nicaragua. The memoranda in the files show that they felt no commitment to support the revolutionists, as they presumably would have if they had instigated the revolt. Despite Wilson's attitude toward Mexico, the Department still seemed to hope to obtain its objective by joint action with that country and the other Central American states. It examined the Nicaraguan constitution and applicable precedents to see what could be done.[50] Merry, because of his earlier service in

[46] Copy of telegram left at State Department by Mexican Chargé d'Affaires, Num. Case 6369/326.

[47] Wilson to Knox, Nov. 26, 1909, Num. Case 6369/334.

[48] The reply and Wilson's memorandum to Knox are filed in Num. Case 6369/359A.

[49] The Minister of Foreign Affairs told the press that Knox's action came unexpectedly while Mexico was awaiting a reply to the peace plan. See press clipping enclosed with despatch of Dec. 3, 1909, from Mexico City, Num. Case 6369/377.

[50] See especially a memorandum of Dec. 14, 1909, Num. Case 6369/400 2/9.

Nicaragua, was asked to suggest possible candidates for provisional president, with the stipulation that they might be of any party so long as they were definitely opposed to Zelaya. Merry thought that Adán Cárdenas, the titular leader of the conservative party, was the only Nicaraguan who was not too bitter a partisan, and he seems to have approached Cárdenas, without instructions, and to have obtained his consent to serve.[51]

President Díaz also persisted in the hope that Mexico and the United States might work together for a solution, and on December 13 former Ambassador Creel arrived in Washington on a special mission to discuss the matter. Zelaya had already promised the Mexican government that he would resign and had ordered a suspension of hostilities pending negotiations.[52] Creel's proposal was that José Madriz, a generally respected liberal from Leon, who had formerly opposed Zelaya but had recently accepted appointment as the Nicaraguan judge on the Central American Court, should be made provisional president. This was unacceptable to Knox and Wilson, who thought that Madriz was too closely associated with Zelaya and who suspected that the real purpose was to set up a sort of joint protectorate in Nicaragua in which Mexico would play the leading role.[53] Creel's mission was consequently a failure.

The State Department's suspicion of Mexico increased when the Nicaraguan congress elected Madriz as provisional president after Zelaya resigned on December 16.[54] When Díaz permitted the ex-president to leave Nicaragua on one of his gunboats, the American government acquiesced but pointedly refrained from expressing approval.[55] It refused to recognize Madriz because it considered his regime merely a continuation of Zelaya's. It indicated that it would maintain its position of neutrality and deal with the representatives of both Nicaraguan factions on equal terms.

One of Madriz' first acts was to propose peace negotiations. The revolutionists agreed to talk, and the United States offered an Ameri-

[51] Num. Case 6369/398A, 424, 508.
[52] Copy of telegram from Mexican Foreign Ministry, Dec. 6, left at State Department by Mexican Chargé d'Affaires. Num. Case 6369/399.
[53] Memorandum of Creel's call on Knox, on Dec. 14, and his conversation with Wilson on Dec. 20, Num. Case 6369/400 2/9, 400 3/9.
[54] Madriz took office on December 22.
[55] *Foreign Relations, 1910*, pp. 739–742.

can warship as a meeting place.[56] Unfortunately the rebel emissary was drowned while on his way to Managua, and the conference did not take place. Soon afterward changes in the military situation made first one side and then the other less willing to negotiate.

Late in December the revolutionists won a victory at Rama, near Bluefields and prepared to invade western Nicaragua. Soon afterward, apparently, the State Department began to consider the establishment of an American customs collectorship in Nicaragua if the rebels won. It had been working for some months on a plan for a loan to Honduras, and in February 1910 it decided to yield to the bankers' insistence that this loan must be secured by a treaty providing for an American customs receivership. Wilson told Doyle of the Latin American Division to draft a letter, to be delivered by Estrada's representative when the revolutionists occupied Managua, committing the new government to the policies which the United States wished it to follow. Among these would be the rehabilitation of Nicaragua's finances by means of a customs-secured loan.

Both Doyle and Dawson seemed somewhat doubtful about the propriety of Wilson's plan. They thought that the recognition of the revolutionary government immediately after it took control would be contrary to the provisions of the 1907 treaties, and they suggested that the immediate announcement of the loan project might cause a new uprising. Their doubts, however, related principally to timing, and they apparently hoped as Wilson did that the success of the revolution would eventually make it possible to set up with Nicaragua the sort of relationship that had apparently been so helpful to the Dominican Republic.[57]

The revolutionists hoped that their invasion of the interior would be the signal for uprisings that would tie down a large part of Madriz' army. They apparently underestimated their opponent's strength, for no important uprisings occurred and their army was almost wiped out on February 22, 1910. After this disaster, Moffat reported on March 1 that the revolution had "practically collapsed"

[56] *Foreign Relations, 1910*, p. 740.

[57] State Department Decimal File, 817.00/1373. (All references to State Department correspondence hereafter, unless otherwise indicated, will be to the decimal file. For a time when the system was being changed, many papers were classified both in numerical cases and in the decimal file.)

so far as any hope of overthrowing the Managua government was concerned. At that time he thought that Estrada would probably be able to hold the east coast, but three weeks later he cabled that the revolutionary movement was rapidly disintegrating.[58] Admiral Kimball, the naval commander, who had never had much sympathy for the insurgents, recommended that the United States recognize Madriz.[59]

The State Department obviously had to reconsider its position. A liberal victory would be a serious setback to the whole policy based on the Washington treaties of 1907. Rightly or wrongly, the Department thought that Zelaya and his followers, working with what Dawson called the "anti-Cabrera factions" in other countries,[60] had been chiefly responsible for the frustration of its efforts to stop international war and revolution in Central America. It considered Madriz merely a creature of Zelaya, and its reluctance to recognize him was presumably not diminished by reports that Mexico was helping him with arms and money.[61] On the other hand, it was difficult to see how the United States could give the revolutionists any effective aid. There were several American warships in Nicaraguan waters, but the administration was still evidently reluctant to ask Congress to authorize actual military intervention. In March, in fact, when there seemed no prospect of further fighting in western Nicaragua, the navy withdrew 700 marines who had been encamped, with El Salvador's permission, on an island in the Gulf of Fonseca.[62]

Knox had given the revolution strong moral support by his denunciation of Zelaya and his continued refusal to recognize Madriz, but this had not materially weakened the liberal government. There is no evidence that surreptitious aid to the rebels was considered. The memoranda exchanged between the various offices of the State Department reveal a strong desire to help them, but at the same time a feeling that any action taken must be justifiable under international law and practice. Open military intervention or overt reprisals for injuries like the murder of Cannon and Groce could be so justified;

[58] Num. Case 6369/808, 932.
[59] Telegram to Secretary of the Navy, Num. Case 6369/843.
[60] Memorandum to Wilson, April 19, 1910, 817.00/907.
[61] See Merry's despatch of February 12, 1910, from Costa Rica, 817.00/776.
[62] *Foreign Relations, 1910*, p. 743.

clandestine aid to a revolution could not. There seemed to be little hope of bringing about peace by negotiation. The revolutionary leaders asked for American mediation on March 3, proposing that the United States designate a provisional president and then supervise the election of a permanent president who should be neither Madriz nor Estrada; but Knox was unwilling to make any suggestion for a settlement when only one party requested him to act.[63] He evidently felt certain that Madriz would reject any interposition.

For the time being, the State Department seemed to be waiting to see how the war would come out. On March 26, the agents of both factions were told orally that the United States would not recognize any government until it controlled the entire territory of Nicaragua and gave "tangible assurance" that a new president, preferably neither Estrada nor Madriz, would be chosen by a free election. The United States would also demand positive assurance of an effort to bring to justice the murderers of Cannon and Groce, and a pledge to fulfill the Washington conventions and to subscribe to such additional provisions as had been shown necessary by experience.[64] In April, when the British government indicated that it would recognize Madriz unless the United States objected, the State Department asked that such action be delayed.[65]

Two memoranda which Dawson wrote at Wilson's request on April 19 discussed the situation in some detail. Dawson asserted that Madriz was not Zelaya's legal successor because he was not one of the *designados* chosen by Congress, and he said that Madriz had shown little willingness to make reparation for the murder of Cannon and Groce. He suggested that a strong note, stating the American government's reasons for refusing to recognize the Provisional President should be handed to the latter's representative and made public. Madriz might then agree to the conditions that the United States had laid down on March 26. If he did not, the United States might at some later date seize the customhouse at Corinto to collect an indemnity for the murder of Cannon and Groce and the amount due on the Emery claim. Dawson suggested that this action might be delayed until after the Fourth Pan American Conference met

[63] *Ibid.*, p. 742–743.
[64] Unsigned memorandum of March 26, 1910, 817.00/851½.
[65] Knox to Embassy, London, April 14, 1910, 817.00/870.

in July. If Madriz, with Mexico's support, continued to work with the "anti-Cabrera" factions in the other republics, "wars and confusion" would ensue; but things would have to get worse in Central America before they got better, unless the United States should decide to let the anti-Cabrera and Mexican factions have "free swing" for a time. Dawson thought, however, that Mexico and Madriz would have to come to terms if the United States "showed its teeth." [66] It is interesting to note that Dawson apparently had no idea at this time that a rebel victory might solve the problem.

No action was taken on Dawson's proposal, probably because the Central American Court came forward on April 27 with an offer of mediation between the two Nicaraguan factions. The State Department welcomed the Court's action with an eagerness that suggested that it was ready to grasp at anything that offered a way out of its dilemma, and was evidently disappointed when Estrada turned down the proposal on the ground that he was still endeavoring to persuade Madriz to accept the mediation of the United States.[67] Madriz also rejected the Court's offer.

The turning point in the war proved to be the failure of a liberal attack on Bluefields, which began in May 1910. Bluefields was then the only important place still held by Estrada, and its fall would have meant the end of the war. Madriz' forces proposed to move against the city from the land side, while their warship, the *Máximo Jerez*, blockaded and bombarded it, but their plans were frustrated by a series of actions taken by the American naval commanders.

When the *Máximo Jerez* threatened a bombardment if the revolutionists did not surrender within twenty-four hours, Commander Gilmer of the *U.S.S. Paducah* told both sides that there must be no fighting in the city and landed 100 men to enforce his demand. The revolutionists were required to withdraw all but a small part of their forces from the city, but they profited from the situation because they could send all of their army to meet the attackers without worrying about protecting their base. Soon afterward, Madriz' forces took the bluff, where the Bluefields customhouse was, in order

---

[66] Num. Case 6369/906, 907.

[67] See Knox's telegram to the Court, *Foreign Relations, 1910*, p. 744, and the Department's telegram to Moffat, May 3, 1910, 6369/913. For the text of the Court's proposal and the replies of both Nicaraguan factions see *Anales de la Corte de Justicia Centroamericana* (San José, Costa Rica, 1911), Vol. I, pp. 146–151.

to cut off the supplies Estrada was receiving by sea, but the American commanders, at the request of the State Department, forbade them to interfere with the passage of ships to the new customhouse set up in territory under Estrada's control. Finally, the liberals' whole plan was disrupted when the American government refused to permit the *Máximo Jerez,* their one formidable warship, to blockade Bluefields. By the end of May it was clear that the attack on the city was a costly failure, and the liberal army withdrew into the interior.

What was done at Bluefields has frequently been criticized as an improper intervention in Nicaragua's internal affairs. It was not unusual for foreign naval officers to forbid fighting in towns where there were so many foreigners and so much foreign property as there were at Bluefields, and there was some justification for preventing interference with American merchant ships entering the port in the absence of a blockade. The refusal to permit the *Máximo Jerez* to establish a blockade was perhaps more questionable. Madriz had recently bought this vessel, then known as the British steamer *Venus,* and had had her loaded with a cargo of arms and ammunition at New Orleans. Estrada's agents in the United States had tried strenuously to prevent her departure, but neither the State Department nor the Commerce and Justice Departments had found any justification under the neutrality statutes for holding her, and after the captain swore that no armed expedition was contemplated she was allowed to sail. When she reached Greytown she was transferred to the Nicaraguan flag and renamed. The Madriz government insisted that the whole procedure had been open and legal, but the State Department took the position that: "a vessel which, by deceiving the authorities at a port of the United States, sailed therefrom in the guise of a merchantman, but had in reality been destined for use as a war vessel, by such act has forfeited full belligerent rights, such as the right of search on the high seas and of blockade." [68]

It is not clear that Knox and Wilson thought that they were actually departing from their policy of formal neutrality or that they hoped that the failure of the attack on Bluefields would bring about the fall of Madriz. They were presumably not sorry that the rebels

---

[68] *Foreign Relations, 1910,* p. 747. The most important documents about the events of May 1910 are printed in *Foreign Relations, 1910,* pp. 745ff. There is additional correspondence about the *Venus* in Num. Case 6369, beginning with enclosure 879.

profited by the Navy's action, but the real as well as the ostensible purpose of this action was probably to protect American lives and American trade. This at least was the understanding of most of the naval officers on the scene, whose reports often reflect a desire to be fair to both sides.[69]

Though the rainy season would protect them for several months, the rebels' situation still seemed hopeless. Commander Gilmer thought that Madriz must eventually win the war, unless the United States or someone else intervened,[70] and Moffat reported that the end might come at any minute, because there was no money and the revolutionary leaders were quarreling among themselves. He urged United States intervention as the only way out.[71]

Renewed diplomatic efforts to end the war brought no result. On June 3, Estrada appealed to the Central American Court to use its influence to persuade Madriz to accept the revolutionists' earlier proposal to request the mediation of the United States. When the Court replied by again offering its own good offices, Knox expressed a friendly interest in this suggestion,[72] but Estrada did not accept it. Meanwhile Madriz' Minister General sent cables to the principal European powers and to several Latin American governments complaining about the events at Bluefields and asking for help in persuading the United States to permit him to complete the pacification of Nicaragua. In response to this plea, President Díaz of Mexico urged President Taft to reconsider his policy, but was politely rebuffed.[73] Some of the Central American governments also approached the State Department informally, but were told that the United States would maintain its refusal to recognize Madriz.

Some of this activity was doubtless inspired by press reports that

[69] This statement is based on correspondence in the Bluefields post reports in the Navy Caribbean file and on some correspondence in the State Department Num. Case 6369. It should be noted however that General Smedley Butler who commanded a detachment of marines at Bluefields, gives a different impression in his autobiography, *Old Gimlet Eye* (New York, 1933).

[70] Acting Secretary of Navy to Secretary of State, June 27, 1910, Num. Case 6369/1084.

[71] Report of June 12, 1910, Num. Case 6369/1053.

[72] *Foreign Relations, 1910*, p. 755.

[73] Most of the correspondence about the action of the Court and Madriz' plea to other powers is printed in *Foreign Relations, 1910*, pp. 750–754. See also *Anales de la Corte de Justicia Centroamericana, Tomo I*, pp. 155–164, and *Hearings before a subcommittee of the Committee on Foreign Relations of the United States Senate pursuant to Senate Resolution 385*, 62nd Congress, 2nd Session. Washington, 1913.

the United States was considering armed intervention.[74] Knox did ask J. Reuben Clark, the Assistant Solicitor, to draw up a resolution by which Congress might have authorized intervention to set up a free and stable government in Nicaragua and memoranda defending the proposal.[75] These drafts, however, were apparently never used, and for the time being there was no change in policy. In August Adee was again insisting that the Department must "serve the same sauce for the Estrada gander as for the Madriz goose." [76] Adee was perhaps also the author of an instruction to the consul at Managua, cautioning him against too vigorous representations to the authorities there and saying that "the United States has recognized that a condition of armed unfriendliness exists in Nicaragua." [77]

Discouraging as the prospect for peace seemed in June, the end of the civil war was not far off. The reverse at Bluefields and the continued hostility of the United States hurt Madriz' prestige more than the American officials realized, and it encouraged his enemies to stage small uprisings in regions which he had hitherto controlled. Disorders in western Nicaragua in July encouraged the rebels to undertake another invasion of the interior. One of their armies won a decisive victory at Tipitapa on August 18, and a day or two later, when the liberals were again defeated at Granada, Madriz' regime collapsed. The leaders of the revolution entered Managua on August 28.

Political and Financial Negotiations, 1910-1912

With the victory of the revolution, Knox and his advisers could be more hopeful for the success of the Central American program which the Secretary had presented to the Cabinet in March 1909. Zelaya's fall had eliminated one of the chief obstacles to peace, and it seemed probable that customs collectorships, from which so much was expected, could now be set up in the two countries that seemed most in need of their stabilizing influence. Negotiations for a loan to Honduras were already well advanced, as we shall see in a subsequent chapter, and the State Department confidently expected the

---

[74] See for example the articles in the New York *Times,* June 1, 2, and 6, 1910.
[75] See 817.00/1486, 1487.
[76] Memorandum about shipment of arms on Panama Railroad steamers, 6369/1284.
[77] Instruction to Olivares, August 13, 1910, Num. Case 6369/1250.

POLITICAL AND FINANCIAL NEGOTIATIONS

new government in Nicaragua to ask for the same sort of help. The basis for this expectation is not clear, but the plan had probably been discussed with Salvador Castrillo, who was Estrada's agent in Washington, and there is a suggestion in one memorandum that some sort of assurance had been received from Estrada himself.[78]

The State Department's ideas were set forth in a cable that Castrillo sent to Estrada on August 28, giving the precise language that the Provisional President should use in a request for recognition. Estrada was to give assurances that he would hold elections within six months and that he would contract a loan secured by the customs. He should also promise to prosecute the murderers of Cannon and Groce and to pay a reasonable indemnity, and he was to ask the United States to send a commission to deal with any matter that might require a formal agreement between the two governments.[79]

Estrada was at first reluctant to commit himself to this program. For the moment he was not desperately in need of money because Madriz had left a considerable sum in the treasury. Probably neither he nor the other revolutionary leaders were anxious to accept outside financial control or to pledge themselves to early elections. Nevertheless, the new government desperately needed the recognition and the moral support of the United States, and on September 10 Estrada asked for recognition in virtually the language that Castrillo had suggested, except that he promised to hold elections within one year.[80] When the State Department made a friendly reply to Castrillo's note, the latter cabled that he had obtained recognition, and the provisional government celebrated by firing cannon every hour through the day. This caused some embarrassment, because the State Department had only intended to enter into *de facto* relations with the new regime pending the establishment of a constitutional government.[81] The Department nevertheless sent Dawson to Managua as special agent to help the new government carry out the policies to which Estrada had committed it.

[78] Dodge's memorandum of Sept. 6, 1910 (817.00/1404) said that the assurances that the Department was then requesting were not very different from what Estrada had already understood and agreed to.

[79] Telegram to American Consul at Managua, Aug. 28, 1910, 817.00/1370A.

[80] *Foreign Relations, 1910,* p. 762.

[81] 817.00/1400, 1422, 1427, 1428, 1431.

When Dawson reached Managua on October 19, he found that his first task would be to patch up dissensions among the revolutionary leaders, whose rivalries had brought the country to a condition that he described as "virtually anarchy." [82] Estrada, as a liberal, had few friends among the conservatives who made up most of the revolutionary forces, and the conservatives themselves were divided into factions. What was perhaps the majority were partisans of Emiliano Chamorro, the most popular leader in Granada, who had been the hero of several earlier revolts against Zelaya and a prominent general in the recent war. On the other hand, General Luis Mena, a soldier of humble origin who had also distinguished himself in the war, had a strong following in the army. It was clear that Estrada, Chamorro, and Mena each aspired to control any government that might be set up, and that their rivalries might well give the still strong Zelayista party a chance to return to power.

Dawson was instructed to urge the reestablishment of constitutional government "at the earliest possible date," through an election in which "absolute freedom" should be guaranteed.[83] But he soon realized that a popular election would be "dangerous to peace" [84] and also probably that absolute freedom could not be expected in any election which the Nicaraguans might conduct. He therefore accepted the traditional Central American device of a constitutional convention to give legal effect to the agreements that he persuaded the principal revolutionary leaders to sign. Under these, Estrada was to be elected as president for a two-year term and Adolfo Díaz, who was an influential conservative leader but a personal friend of Estrada, was to be Vice President.

The "Dawson Agreements" provided that the new constitution would abolish monopolies and that Estrada's administration would cooperate with the United States in setting up a commission to adjudicate all unsettled claims against the Nicaraguan government, including those resulting from the cancelation of monopolistic concessions. The new administration would also ask the American government's help in obtaining a customs-guaranteed loan. The murderers of Cannon and Groce were to be punished. All of these

[82] *Foreign Relations, 1910*, p. 765.
[83] Adee to Dawson, Oct,. 11, 1910, *Foreign Relations, 1910*, p. 763.
[84] Dawson's telegram of Oct. 28, 1910, *ibid.*, p. 765.

undertakings were formally communicated to Dawson on November 5 as an expression of the new government's policy. A separate agreement, signed by Estrada, Díaz, Chamorro, Mena, and the prominent conservative Fernando Solórzano, provided that Estrada would not be a candidate for reelection and that all the signers would support as his successor the candidate favored by a majority of them.[85] The constitutional convention was chosen late in November at an election in which *zelayista* liberals took no part,[86] and its members unanimously voted for Estrada and Díaz as president and vice president.

The United States formally recognized the new government when it was inaugurated on January 1, 1911, and Elliott Northcott was sent to Managua as American minister. Northcott was instructed to see that the Nicaraguan government carried out the full program contemplated by the Dawson Agreements.[87] He found, however, much opposition to the most important features of the program and reported that "an overwhelming majority of Nicaraguans" were "antagonistic to the United States." [88] The idea of a foreign customs collectorship was especially obnoxious, and the proposal for a claims commission became less palatable when the State Department changed its original plan and insisted that the Secretary of State of the United States should designate two of the three members.[89] Estrada, who knew that he must have the moral support of the United States and appreciated the need for a loan, was willing to go forward with both projects, but his cooperative attitude made him increasingly unpopular and gravely weakened his government's prestige.

In March, in fact, Estrada grew so concerned about his own situation that he proposed that the United States should set up a virtual protectorate over Nicaragua. He wished the American government to cooperate in holding elections and if necessary to help in suppressing insurrections, and at the same time to guarantee Nicaragua's independence. He suggested that Nicaragua withdraw from

[85] For the text of the Dawson Agreements, see *Foreign Relations, 1911*, pp. 652–653. The Nicaraguan government's note of November 5, 1910, is printed in the same volume, pp. 625–627.
[86] See 817.00/1474, 1482.
[87] *Foreign Relations, 1911*, p. 649.
[88] Northcott to Knox, February 25, 1911, *ibid.*, p. 655.
[89] Knox to Northcott, February 27, 1911, *ibid.*, p. 627.

the Central American Court to prevent the other states from using that body to defeat his plan. Northcott thought that this proposal was of "vital importance," but the State Department, in a friendly but noncommital reply, suggested that the best course was to carry out the Dawson Agreements and indicated that it still strongly supported the Washington treaties of 1907, which had established the Court.[90]

Unfortunately, the flimsy political structure created by the Dawson Agreements was already beginning to break down. Chamorro's friends, who controlled the constituent assembly, were doing everything they could to embarrass the President. When the new constitution was drafted, it gave the President no veto power and authorized the congress to appoint all high officials of the treasury —an obvious attempt to keep the proceeds of the proposed loan out of Estrada's hands. Estrada objected to these and other provisions, and on April 4, apparently with Northcott's moral support, he dissolved the assembly and called for the election of a new one. Chamorro thought it best to leave the country. The State Department approved Estrada's action, but it told Northcott to impress on the party leaders the fact that they had "assumed a responsibility toward this Government of working harmoniously and in a conciliatory spirit." [91]

Estrada gained little from the dissolution of the constituent assembly because Mena, who was Minister of War, was able to pack the new one with his own adherents. Further conflict seemed inevitable, in spite of the American government's appeals to good faith and patriotism, especially as the situation in the Legation at Managua made it more difficult for the American government to make its influence felt. Moffat, who had been transferred from Bluefields, was for a time the only officer on the staff who spoke Spanish, and Northcott relied heavily on his help and his intimate knowledge of the situation. Friction soon developed, however, and Northcott began to think that Moffat was unduly partial to Estrada and Vice President Díaz, while Moffat accused the Minister of being too friendly with Mena.[92] The Nicaraguan politicians quickly saw and

[90] Most of the correspondence on this episode is printed in *Foreign Relations, 1911,* pp. 655–659. See also 817.00/1546, 1548.

[91] *Foreign Relations, 1911,* p. 658.

[92] For Moffat's side of the story, see his despatch of May 27, 1911. See 817.00/1608.

tried to take advantage of these differences of opinion, and the situation was not greatly improved when Moffat left the Legation to become a member of the Claims Commission.

Northcott endeavored to persuade Estrada and Mena to work together, and at Mena's request he obtained Estrada's promise not to make any hostile move against the Minister of War. Nevertheless, on May 8, 1911, Estrada suddenly had Mena arrested and began to arm the liberals of Managua. The attempted *coup* failed when the conservative army officers refused to obey the President's orders, and, when Northcott intervened to save Mena's life and insisted that the prisoner be transferred to the British consulate, Estrada realized that the situation was hopeless and left the country.[93] Northcott insisted that Mena recognize Vice President Díaz as the new head of the government, and at the same time persuaded Díaz to continue Mena as Minister of War.

Adolfo Díaz was to play an important role during two periods when the United States was intervening in Nicaragua's affairs, but when he took office in 1911 the officials in the State Department apparently knew little about him.[94] He had been one of the civilian leaders in the Bluefields revolution, and his relations with some of the North American businessmen on the coast had been useful in raising funds for the movement. In politics, he was a moderate conservative, but not a member of the Granada group. He had little personal following, but his astuteness and his tolerant disposition, which made him less feared by opponents, gave him a special position in Nicaraguan politics. It was these qualities, and his sincere belief that Nicaragua would benefit from close relations with the United States, that later won him the confidence of most of the North American officials who dealt with Central American affairs.

The new President found himself in a difficult situation. With Mena in control of the army, he had little authority in his own government. He could not prevent arbitrary arrests or other discreditable acts by his subordinates, and even the members of his Cabinet paid little attention to his wishes. To retain Mena's support, he was compelled to promise in writing that he would permit Mena to make himself president for the next term.[95] A large part of the con-

[93] For the story see Northcott's despatch of May 15, 1911, 817.00/1607.
[94] See the memoranda filed under 817.00/1577.
[95] *Foreign Relations, 1911*, p. 664.

servative party opposed him, and there were frequent reports of liberal plots and rumors of filibustering expeditions from other Central American countries. On May 31, an unexplained explosion in one of the forts at Managua killed more than 60 of the garrison. Repeated assurances of moral support from the American Legation and the State Department gave Díaz little encouragement because they offered no hope of escape from the army's domination. Even when the State Department on June 1 told Northcott to say that "It would be the manifest duty of the United States Government to continue to recognize the constitutional authorities in case of irreconcilable differences between the Executive and any factions," it urged on him at the same time "the value of harmony with Mena." [96]

Díaz suspected, rightly or wrongly, that Northcott was more friendly to Mena than to himself, and he told his representative at Washington that the Legation was "either incapable or partial." [97] He consequently exasperated the Minister by refusing to talk frankly about his problems at a time when he was cabling complaints and threats to resign to Washington. The Legation's friendly attitude toward Mena seemed even more noticeable after Northcott left Nicaragua in June 1911.

Franklin Mott Gunther, the Chargé d'Affaires, was a 26-year-old officer who was to have a distinguished career in the Foreign Service but who had had only a few months of diplomatic experience in 1911, and the State Department found it necessary to caution him several times about his relations with the Minister of War. [98] In the Department, there was little sympathy for Mena, and there was even some serious discussion of supporting Estrada in returning to the presidency, which he had never actually resigned. [99] This came to nothing, and Díaz remained in office, working rather unhappily with Mena.

The State Department was far less interested in the political situation than in the realization of its program of financial reform. Since January 1911, Ernest H. Wands, whom it had selected as financial adviser to Nicaragua, had been making a study of the republic's

[96] *Foreign Relations, 1911,* p. 662.
[97] Castrillo so informed the Department. See 817.00/1624.
[98] See 817.00/1691, 1696, 1698.
[99] Latin American Division's memorandum of June 22, 1911, 817.00/1687; and Wilson's of July 10, 1911, 817.51/168.

economic problems. The plan was to negotiate a treaty providing for an American customs collectorship and at the same time to have Wands look into the republic's financial situation and outstanding debts in order to determine how large a loan was needed. When this study was completed, a contract would be drawn up and the loan would be awarded to the bankers who offered the best terms.[100] The negotiation of the loan treaty went ahead rapidly after Díaz became President, and on June 6, 1911, the treaty was signed at Washington.

The treaty was similar in every respect to an agreement which had been signed five months earlier with Honduras and which was already in the hands of the Senate Committee on Foreign Relations. It provided that Nicaragua should negotiate a loan to refund its internal and external debts and to provide funds for the development of the country's resources. The two governments would take note of the provisions of the loan contract and would consult with one another if difficulties arose. The bonds were to be secured by the customs duties, which were to be administered by a Collector General appointed by the government of Nicaragua from a list of names presented by the fiscal agent of the loan and approved by the President of the United States. The customs duties were not to be changed during the life of the loan without the agreement of the government of the United States. Both governments would give the Collector General of Customs any necessary protection in the exercise of his duties. The treaty differed from the Dominican convention of 1907 in the arrangement for the appointment of the Collector General and also in the omission of any provision requiring the consent of the United States for further increases in Nicaragua's public debt.[101] The treaty was at once approved by the Nicaraguan Assembly, and President Taft submitted it to the United States Senate to be considered at the special session which had been convened in May.

The treaty with Honduras had already met with opposition in the Committee on Foreign Relations, and Knox had appeared before

---

[100] Knox outlined this plan for Nicaragua in his statement to the Senate Committee on Foreign Relations defending the Honduran loan treaty, on May 24, 1911, *Foreign Relations, 1912*, p. 594.

[101] The text of the treaty is printed in *Foreign Relations, 1912*, p. 1074.

the committee on May 24 to urge approval of the agreement as an essential part of a broad policy for the maintenance of peace in Central America. He had told the senators that a similar treaty would soon be signed with Nicaragua. After his presentation, a majority of the committee voted to report the Honduran treaty favorably, but every Democrat present voted "no," and Senator Cullom wrote Knox on June 12 that he thought there was not "a ghost of a chance" for ratification during the session.[102] A few days later the State Department learned that the treaty would not even be called up for action.[103]

This made the outlook for the Nicaraguan treaty discouraging, but President Taft nevertheless sent it to the Senate with a message urging speedy ratification. On June 28 and again on July 15 the President renewed his request that the Senate consider both treaties, but with no result. The adjournment of Congress soon afterward made it impossible to hope for action before the end of the year.

Meanwhile, Wands was endeavoring to arrange the proposed loan. Several bankers showed an interest in the project even before the treaty was signed. Brown Brothers and Company, who were interested in Nicaragua because they were part owners of the Emery claim, approached Castrillo and the State Department in January 1911, after asking Senator Penrose to intercede with Knox on their behalf.[104] In February, Speyer and Company, who were associated with the Ethelburga Syndicate, which floated the loan for Zelaya in 1909, made a definite offer to the Nicaraguan government, but when they consulted the State Department a few days later they were told that they should not go ahead until Wands made his report.[105]

In anticipation of the signing of the treaty, Wands talked with both of these firms and with other bankers when he went to New York in April. There is no indication that the State Department took any part in the negotiations, except to urge that all reputable American firms have an equal opportunity to bid for the business. After

[102] 815.51/269.
[103] 815.51/269.
[104] Penrose to Knox, Jan. 26, 1911, 817.51/99; Brown Brothers to Knox, Feb. 2, 1911, 817.51/104; Latin American Division Memorandum, Feb. 9, 1911, 817.51/106.
[105] Northcott to Knox, Feb. 25, 1911, 817.51/112, and Latin American Division Memorandum of March 6, 1911, 817.51/118.

Wands decided to accept a proposal from Brown Brothers and Company and J. and W. Seligman and Company, however, Knox asked the New York law firm of Dexter, Osborn, and Fleming, which had no connection with the interested banks, to make an independent examination of the contract from the standpoint of Nicaragua's interests, to make sure that there could be no justified criticism of its terms.[106]

It is interesting to note that Nicaragua could apparently have obtained a loan, in the first months of 1911, without setting up an American customs collectorship. Speyer in February offered to take $15,000,000 in 5-percent bonds at 85 if the proposed treaty was concluded, or to make the interest rate 6 percent if Nicaragua agreed only to install an American customs collector in case of default.[107] Wands reported in June that Brown Brothers and Seligman would also make an offer, even though the convention were not ratified.[108] The State Department, however, was interested in the customs collectorship as an instrument of policy. It still believed that arrangements like the Dominican convention would be the best means to assure political stability and better financial administration in Nicaragua and Honduras. A loan that did not carry with it a more effective collection of the revenues would not achieve the same purpose.

The bankers were apparently not discouraged by the delay in ratifying the treaty, for on September 1 Brown Brothers and Seligman signed a series of contracts with the Nicaraguan government. These would have made possible a broad program of financial reform and economic development. They authorized a $15,000,000, 5-percent bond issue, of which the bankers would buy $12,000,000 at 90½ percent of face value when the treaty with the United States was ratified. The remainder was to be reserved for later use. The bankers undertook to refund the Ethelburga bonds and thus free for the Nicaraguan government's use about $1,500,000 still on deposit in London from the proceeds of the 1909 loan. This money, with a part of the $3,000,000 of reserve bonds, would be used for the payment of the awards of the Claims Commission. A National Bank,

[106] 817.51/202.
[107] Northcott to Knox, Feb. 25, 1911, 815.51/112, and Latin American Division Memorandum of Feb. 21, 1911, 817.51/113.
[108] Wands to the State Department, July 9, 1911, 817.51/176.

set up and managed by the two New York firms, would stabilize the depreciated and fluctuating paper money which was one of the pernicious legacies of the Zelaya regime. The bankers would also build and manage railroad lines to the Atlantic Coast and to the coffee region of Matagalpa.

If all had gone well, the contracts would probably have benefited Nicaragua and would at the same time have been profitable for the bankers. The price at which the bonds were to be taken was slightly more favorable to Nicaragua than that offered by J. P. Morgan and Company to Honduras, but a provision that the bankers should receive $450,000 for having the bonds engraved and for other relatively minor expenses promised an additional profit from the transaction. Brown Brothers would also benefit from the payment in full of the Emery claim. There were further possibilities for profit in the National Bank and the proposed railroad company. The bankers took an option on 51 percent of the stock of the bank, which would issue the new paper money and be the depository for all government funds, besides carrying on a regular banking business. In the case of the railroad company, they would furnish half of the cost of building the new lines. In return, they would receive first mortgage bonds to cover the amount of their contribution and also an equal amount of the railroad company's common stock. The Nicaraguan government, for its share of the cost of construction, would get 6 percent non-cumulative preferred stock. The railroad company's concession promised it about 335 acres of public land for each kilometer built, plus 247 acres for each family of colonists that it might bring into the country: grants that were generous but perhaps not unreasonable as an inducement to persuade capitalists to provide funds for a line through regions where there was little population.

Since several months would elapse before the United States Senate could again consider the treaty, the bankers agreed to make a short-term loan, which would be secured by the immediate establishment of a customs collectorship, under a Collector General nominated by themselves and approved by the Secretary of State. By buying $1,500,000 6-percent Nicaraguan treasury bills at par they made it possible to set up the new National Bank and to start work on the currency problem, which had to be dealt with if commerce were to revive and if the government's finances were to be put in order. They also undertook to seek an arrangement with the holders of the Ethelburga bonds, in order to obtain the money still on deposit in London. This temporary arrangement, which was the only part of the program that actually went into effect, was to involve the bankers and the State Department in troublesome responsibilities in Nicaragua, from which they did not extricate themselves for many years. The bankers later asserted that they entered into it much against their own inclinations [109] but the State Department's files do not indicate that the American government applied any pressure.[110]

While the loan contracts were being negotiated, the two governments had been discussing the organization of the mixed claims commission which had been provided for in the Dawson Agreements. Estrada, with some difficulty, persuaded the constituent assembly to authorize the establishment of a commission in April 1911. After the law was enacted, however, the State Department suddenly realized that some of its provisions would cause serious embarrassment. The law contemplated the immediate cancelation, by executive action, of all concessions granted by Zelaya and Madriz, and allowed an inadequate period within which claimants might appeal to the commission for compensation. Objectionable as the concessions might be, many of them had presumably been granted legally and had conferred rights on American investors which the State Department could hardly refuse to support. Americans who would be affected by the law were in fact already appealing to the Department for help, and some of them were urging their senators not to vote for the loan treaty unless the law were changed.

The State Department consequently insisted that the law be amended to provide that contracts and concessions should not be canceled unless they had been granted illegally in the first place, and that no decree of cancelation should take effect until it had been affirmed by the Claims Commission after a full hearing.[111] It sug-

[109] In a cable from their representative in Nicaragua, enclosed in a letter to the State Department from Mr. S. Mallet-Prevost, June 12, 1912. See 817.51/446.

[110] The texts of the loan contracts and of later contracts with the New York bankers were published in the annual reports of the Ministry of *Hacienda y Crédito Público* of Nicaragua, and later reprinted in César Arana's *Compilación de contratos celebrados con los banqueros de Nueva York, con el Ethelburga Syndicate de Londres y con el Banco Nacional de Nicaragua Inc.* (3 volumes, Managua, 1928). There are English copies in the State Department's files in the National Archives.

[111] Knox to Northcott, June 26, 1911, *Foreign Relations, 1911*, p. 633.

gested that legal but objectionable contracts should be expropriated. Díaz and his Cabinet accepted these proposals, reluctantly because they said that not more than three of Zelaya's concessions could actually be considered illegal,[112] but it was thought wiser not to ask the assembly to change the law until it had acted on the recently signed loan contracts.

Mena's followers still controlled the assembly, and it was becoming increasingly clear that the Minister of War would attempt to force the United States to approve his own presidential ambitions in return for his support of the State Department's financial program. Some of the deputies were openly asserting that they would not vote for the loan contracts unless the assembly were permitted to elect Mena as President for the term beginning in 1913, and Mena himself discussed the idea of such an election with Gunther. Gunther reported that he had attempted to discourage him, but he pointed out to the State Department that a "tacit assent" to Mena's plan "would result in immediate approval by the Assembly of the loan and mixed commission matters." [113] The State Department's reply deserves to be quoted as a classic example of diplomatic double-talk:

"You are instructed," Adee wrote, "that of the Nicaraguan matters under consideration by the Department the ratification of the pending loan contract and the amendment of the decree establishing a claims commission are of the first importance and should be disposed of before attention is directed to other subjects.

"Thereafter, in due time, the Department would be prepared to give deliberate consideration to such political questions as might concern it in pursuance of existing engagements and the principles of international law, and would consider, when opportune, making appropriate expressions in a proper case upon questions affecting the necessary steps to insure recognition by the Government of the United States of succeeding presidents in Nicaragua." [114]

Gunther's failure to take a strong stand against what would definitely be violation of the Dawson Agreements apparently encouraged Mena and his friends to go ahead, and on October 7, without

[112] Gunther to Knox, July 10, 1911, ibid., p. 636.
[113] Gunther to Knox, Sept. 5 and Sept. 29, 1911, ibid., pp. 666–667.
[114] Adee to Gunther, Sept. 30, 1911, ibid., p. 667.

waiting to learn the State Department's views, the assembly elected Mena as President and Fernando Solórzano as Vice President for the term which would begin nearly fifteen months later. Gunther persuaded Mena to withhold his acceptance until he learned the attitude of the United States, but reported that the election had been "well received." [115] A few days later the assembly approved the loan contracts and the new Mixed Claims Commission law.

It was now at least possible to make a start with the program of financial rehabilitation. The customs collectorship, from which so much was expected, was inaugurated in December 1911 under the direction of Colonel Clifford D. Ham. Colonel Ham had been nominated by the bankers and approved by the State Department in a letter in which Knox informed the bankers that this action did not indicate that they would receive any support or protection that would not be accorded to any legitimate American enterprise abroad.[116] The National Bank was organized, and two foreign experts were employed to draw up a plan of currency reform. Early in 1912, the Mixed Commission, with one Nicaraguan and two North American members, began to pass on unliquidated claims against the government, though no funds for payment were likely to be available until after the loan treaty was ratified.

The political situation was still bad. Though Díaz had told the State Department that he approved Mena's election, he was still unhappy in his relations with the Minister of War. In October, with Gunther's support, he was able to reorganize his Cabinet in a way that placed his own friends in control of some departments, but he complained to the State Department that Mena's friends were obstructing his policies and committing acts of violence against pro-administration newspapers.[117] He was also worried about the attitude of Emiliano Chamorro, who returned to Nicaragua in October. Chamorro's great prestige in the conservative party made him a formidable threat to the success of Mena's plans, and it seemed likely that he would start a revolution if the Dawson Agreements, which provided for a popular election at the end of Díaz' term, were not respected. It was reported that he would be aided by Estrada

[115] Gunther to Knox, Oct. 7, 1911, 817.00/1702.
[116] 817.51/256.
[117] Copies of cables from Díaz to Solórzano and Castrillo, Oct. 26, 1911, 817.00/1708.

Cabrera, whose efforts to sabotage the United States government's loan projects in Nicaragua and Honduras had already led the State Department to make vigorous representations to Guatemalan officials.[118] Díaz thought that the chances for peace might improve if the United States said that it accepted Mena's election,[119] but he received no reply to his inquiries about the American government's attitude.

On December 21, Díaz sent Gunther a letter in which he asked for more effective help from the United States. He complained that the other Central American governments were fomenting trouble in Nicaragua because they opposed the American policy there. In Nicaragua itself, he wrote, "the party leaders, filled with hatred by years of bloody struggle, will never confide the triumph of their cause to republican propaganda, but expect always to assert by force of arms the right to exercise power." The government consequently faced a continual struggle against conspiracy. The only solution that he could see, the President wrote, was the same sort of help from the United States that Cuba enjoyed, and he proposed the negotiation of a treaty that would give the United States the right to intervene in Nicaragua's internal affairs. Knox, in reply, indicated that such a proposal would require "deep and careful consideration," but he did not reject the idea.[120]

The American government had made the political situation more uncertain by continuing to maintain its equivocal attitude about Mena's assumption of the presidency. A new constitution, which the assembly sent to the Executive in December for promulgation, contained an article that formally confirmed his election, and also one that seemed to Gunther to be likely to interfere with the operation of the customs collectorship. When Gunther obtained Díaz' promise to delay promulgation until after the arrival of the newly appointed American Minister, the assembly, after an angry debate, adopted a resolution denouncing his intervention as "an insult to the national autonomy and the honor of the Assembly" and ordering the immediate publication of the constitution. The Department

---

[118] See the Department's .telegram to the Legation in Guatemala, Oct. 10, 1911, 817.51/248, and the memorandum of conversation between Adee, Heimke, and the Guatemalan Minister at Washington, Oct. 26, 1911, 817.51/256A.

[119] Gunther to Knox, Nov. 1, 1911, *Foreign Relations, 1911*, p. 669.

[120] *Ibid.*, pp. 670, 671.

instructed Gunther to "summon" Mena to the Legation and to inform him that the American government expected him to abide by the Dawson Agreements and that "Díaz must complete his term of office." When the new American Minister arrived in January, however, he reported that the objectionable provisions of the constitution did not seem sufficiently important to justify an attempt to force the assembly to rescind its action.[121]

The new Minister, George T. Weitzel, had been the Assistant Chief of the State Department's Latin American Division. He was thus well-informed about the Department's policy; but if the Nicaraguan leaders hoped that he would clear up the doubts about its stand on the question of the presidential succession they were disappointed. He made it clear when he arrived that he intended for the time being to devote all of his attention to financial matters.[122] These clearly required attention, because the Nicaraguan government's desperate financial situation was threatening to defeat all of the State Department's plans.

The revolutionary government when it took office had paid out large sums to conservatives who had suffered real or alleged losses from extortion or confiscation at Zelaya's hands. It had also paid many other claims, despite its promise that all of the floating debt should be adjudicated by the Claims Commission. The considerable amount of money left in the treasury by Madriz was soon dissipated, and the current revenues fell far short of meeting the government's expenses. All of the customs receipts had to be set aside for the service of the Ethelburga bonds and the treasury bills, and the internal revenues, which had been counted on to run the government, were greatly reduced by graft and administrative inefficiency. An agreement with the Ethelburga Syndicate, which would have released the funds held in London, had been rejected by the bondholders. Worst of all, when the foreign experts began to work on the plan for currency reform, they found that vast sums of paper money, increasing the amount outstanding by 50 percent, had been secretly issued since Wands had made his study of Nicaragua's finances in March, 1911.

To prevent the collapse of the whole program of financial reform,

[121] *Foreign Relations, 1912*, pp. 993–997.
[122] Weitzel to Knox, April 19, 1912, *Foreign Relations, 1912*, p. 1020.

the bankers were compelled to agree to open an additional credit of $500,000 for the retirement of the paper money and to advance $30,000 per month, up to a total of $255,000, for the government's current expenses. They charged 6 percent interest and 1 percent commission on both loans. The loans were nominally repayable in October 1912, but the bankers agreed to extend this period for twelve months, and also to extend the maturity of the treasury bills, if the government requested such action. They exacted a promise that no further claims should be paid without submission to the Mixed Commission.

As security for these advances, the bankers took a lien on all of the stock of a new company, incorporated in the United States, to which the government transferred the ownership of the railroad which connected the principal cities with the port of Corinto. At the same time they obtained an option to buy 51 percent of the company's stock and assumed the management of the railroad until all of their loans should be repaid. The bankers could hardly be criticized for demanding security for their loans, and the terms of the arrangement were fair to Nicaragua, but many Nicaraguans were dismayed to see their national railroad, as well as their National Bank, go into the hands of foreigners.

The Nicaraguan assembly approved the agreements with the bankers on March 20, 1912, after it found that it could not obtain the State Department's consent to Mena's election by delaying action.[123] This made it possible to go ahead with the monetary reform, so that a new currency, maintained at par with the dollar, was in circulation early in 1913. The bankers performed another service for Nicaragua when they negotiated an agreement with the London Council of Foreign Bondholders in May 1912, by which the interest on the Ethelburga bonds was reduced from 6 to 5 percent in return for the republic's promise that the customs would be collected by North American officials so long as any of the bonds were outstanding. This promised the eventual release of the funds held by the Ethelburga Syndicate, which were used in part to repay the bankers' recent advances. It also assured the indefinite continuance of the customs collectorship, even though the pending treaty with the United States were defeated.

[123] Weitzel to Knox, Feb. 28, 1912, 817.51/383.

In the first months of 1912, Knox made strenuous efforts to get action on the Nicaraguan and Honduran treaties, which were still in the hands of the Committee on Foreign Relations. In January he sent to every member of the Senate a copy of a speech that he made to the New York State Bar Association, discussing the bearing of the treaties on the Monroe Doctrine and the good results that might be expected from them. The replies that he received were not encouraging, for even those who supported the treaties feared that Democratic and Insurgent opposition would prevent approval.[124] When the Secretary visited Nicaragua in March, during his tour of the Caribbean, he was more impressed than ever with that country's need for help, and he cabled the State Department to urge his friends in the Senate to push the Nicaraguan treaty, which was not subject, he thought, to some of the objections that had been voiced against the agreement with Honduras.[125] At Wilson's request, Taft sent long letters to 57 senators.[126] Meanwhile, chambers of commerce and similar organizations had been persuaded to pass resolutions urging favorable action.[127] When the Foreign Relations Committee voted on both treaties on May 8, however, the result in each case was a tie, which defeated the motion for a favorable report. This practically ended any hope for ratification, although it was some time before the officials in the State Department were willing to admit that the projects were dead.

In the case of Nicaragua, it was too late for the bankers or the State Department to withdraw from the commitments that they had undertaken on the assumption that the treaty would be ratified. Instead of selling bonds to the public, the bankers had tied up a considerable amount of their own money in stopgap loans to a government that was still on the verge of bankruptcy. They could not refuse further help or give up the management of the National Bank and the Pacific Railroad without risking the loss of this investment. The American government was also committed to a new relationship with Nicaragua, through the customs collectorship and the Mixed Claims Commission, and it had at least some moral obliga-

[124] The letters and speech are printed in Foreign Relations, 1912, pp. 1082–1092. For the replies, see 817.51/297A.
[125] Telegram from Legation at Managua, March 11, 1912, 817.51/386.
[126] March 14, 1912, Taft Papers, Library of Congress.
[127] Many of these are in file 817.51.

tion to help the bankers solve their problems. The State Department had achieved some of its objectives in Nicaragua, but the failure of the loan treaty would prevent the rapid economic advance for which it had hoped. One embarrassing result would be the lack of funds to pay the awards of the Mixed Claims Commission.

While the new agreements with the bankers and the Ethelburga Syndicate were pending, neither Weitzel nor the State Department took a stand on the question of Mena's election. They thought that the agreements would meet with less opposition in the assembly if each faction hoped that it might eventually have American support. The State Department continued "to regard this whole question in the spirit of the Dawson agreements," and attached "full value" to a promise that Mena had made to Gunther to relinquish the presidency if the United States asked him to do so, but it had deliberately refrained from forcing the issue. It instructed Weitzel to say just enough, if necessary, to prevent its silence from being misinterpreted, but it thought that the success of the financial program was "of paramount importance," and in view of the possible need for further legislation it did not want to "precipitate political difficulties." [128]

Mena's election by the assembly was inconsistent with the Dawson Agreements, which had provided for a popular vote; but it could be argued that Mena and Díaz and Solórzano, the Vice President-elect, were a majority of the five leaders who were to have selected a candidate under the arrangement signed in 1910. Furthermore, the State Department thought that a refusal to accept Mena would lead to a more energetic intervention in Nicaragua's internal affairs than it wished at the time to contemplate. Its failure to take a positive stand, however, only made the situation worse. It is difficult to be sure that any action which the American government could have taken would have averted the disaster that ensued, but it seems strange that no real effort to avert the disaster was made.

The First Armed Intervention

By June 1912 a showdown between the rival conservative factions was imminent. Díaz had somewhat more control over his government after he reorganized the Cabinet in October, but he still had

[128] Telegram to Weitzel, June 7, 1912. 817.51/464.

little personal following. Emiliano Chamorro's influence had increased, so that he now had most of the conservatives behind him. In June 1912, a *chamorrista* was elected President of the assembly, which had continued to function as a legislature after it finished work on the constitution. This impaired Mena's influence, but the Minister of War still controlled the police and practically all of the army except the garrison at Managua, which was commanded by officers personally loyal to Díaz.

The crisis came on July 29, when Mena brought a band of his followers to Managua and attempted to occupy the fort of La Loma. Díaz gave orders to resist and appointed Chamorro General in Chief. In the fighting that ensued, the government clearly had the upper hand. Mena would probably have been captured and killed if Weitzel, at Díaz' request and at great risk to himself, had not gone to Mena to propose that he resign. Mena agreed to do so, but in the night, under cover of darkness, he slipped out of the city, taking the police force with him. Since he had already taken the precaution to ship most of the government's arms and ammunition to places under his control, and since much of the army still followed him, Díaz was at a serious disadvantage. The situation became worse when many liberals began to join the revolution.

North Americans were in real danger because Mena's followers as well as the liberals were resentful toward the United States. Other foreigners were also alarmed, and Weitzel was beset by demands for protection. In the first days of August, when Mena seized the lake steamers which belonged to the railroad company and were thus under the management of the New York bankers, the Minister formally asked Díaz for assurances that American property would be protected. The President replied by requesting that the United States "guarantee with its forces security for the property of American citizens in Nicaragua and that it extend its protection to all the inhabitants of the Republic"; and Weitzel immediately arranged to have 100 bluejackets from the U.S.S. *Annapolis* come to Managua as a legation guard. At the same time the State Department arranged to have substantial additional forces sent to Nicaragua.[129]

During the rest of August, the situation grew worse. An attempted

[129] The important documents about the civil war of 1912 appear in *Foreign Relations, 1912*, pp. 1027ff.

mediation by the diplomatic representatives of El Salvador and Costa Rica came to nothing when the armistice that they arranged was broken by a sudden rebel attack on Managua. The attack was repulsed, after four days of destructive bombardment, but the revolution continued to hold Granada and several other towns. When the liberals seized control of Leon and massacred the government's garrison there, the railway line from Managua to the coast was blocked. Major Smedley Butler had come through to the capital with 350 marines just after the rebel attack on that city, but on August 20 50 bluejackets and marines who were attempting to return to Corinto were attacked by a mob at Leon and forced to abandon their train and go back to Managua on foot. President Taft, who thought that the situation was "analagous" to the Boxer Rebellion in China, would have sent an infantry regiment to Nicaragua if the army and the navy had not both objected.[130] Instead, more marines were landed. Early in September the marines opened the railroad from Corinto to Managua, but the revolutionists still controlled the line between Managua and Granada.

The other Central American governments watched what was happening with increasing dismay. When the war began they were disposed to support the government at Managua, because they had no wish to see the *zelayistas* return to power. El Salvador and Honduras even considered sending troops to help Díaz.[131] When the American marines began to arrive in Nicaragua, however, the President of El Salvador cabled a mild protest to Taft and urged that an effort be made to persuade the Nicaraguan factions to agree on a neutral as president. In September, El Salvador again protested against the American intervention, and proposed Salvador Calderón as a person who could restore peace in Nicaragua. The United States rather coldly rejected these suggestions and referred pointedly to reports that El Salvador was sending aid to the rebels, in violation of her obligations under the 1907 treaties.[132] The other Central American governments also viewed the policy of the United States with increasing misgivings, and the Costa Rican government was

[130] Foster to Wilson, Aug. 27, 1912, 817.00/1904; Wilson to Taft, Aug. 30, 1912, 817.00/1940A.
[131] *Foreign Relations, 1912*, p. 1047.
[132] For these events see *Foreign Relations, 1912*, pp. 1037, 1042, 1046ff.

strongly suspected of giving secret help to the revolution, in defiance of the State Department's remonstrances.[133] When the Central American Court of Justice decided to send a peace mission to Nicaragua in August, the Legation at San José was confidentially told that they would probably work in the interests of the liberals.[134] The commissioners, however, were treated discourteously by both Nicaraguan factions, and had some disagreeable and dangerous experiences before they left the country.[135]

On August 30 Wilson, who was acting Secretary in Knox's absence, recommended to the President that the United States try to end the war.[136] He thought that vigorous action to eliminate the troublemaking groups in Nicaragua might restore some of the prestige that the American government had lost as a result of recent troubles in Mexico and Cuba and Panama. It might also offset the effect of anti-imperialist activities in the United States Senate. Wilson expressed some solicitude for the safety of the American citizens in Nicaragua but made no very definite suggestions about protecting them. The immediate action which he proposed, and which the President approved, was a public statement denouncing the revolutionists and promising support to the constituted government of Nicaragua. On September 4 the text of a statement was cabled to Weitzel with authorization to publish it at his discretion.[137]

The policy of the United States, the statement said, was to maintain an adequate Legation guard at Managua, to keep open communications, and to protect American life and property. "In discountenancing Zelaya, whose regime of barbarity and corruption was ended by the Nicaraguan nation after a bloody war, the Government of the United States opposed not only the individual but the system, and this government could not countenance any movement to restore the same destructive regime." Many Americans were in danger and at least two had been killed. There were American claims and concessionary interests to be considered. "Under the Washington conventions, the United States has a moral mandate

[133] Copies of cables from Díaz to Castrillo and Wilson's telegrams to American Legations at San José and Managua, Aug. 17, 1912, 817.00/1980.
[134] Langhorne to Knox, Aug. 8, 1912, 817.00/1875.
[135] Weitzel to Knox, Dec. 21, 1912, 817.00/2202.
[136] Wilson to Taft, Aug. 30, 1912, 817.00/1940A.
[137] For the text, see *Foreign Relations, 1912*, pp. 1043–1044.

to exert its influence for the preservation of the general peace of Central America, which is seriously menaced by the present uprising." The Nicaraguan government, unable to protect American life and property, had asked the United States to afford protection to Americans and to all inhabitants of the republic; and the United States proposed to protect its citizens and to "contribute its influence in all appropriate ways to the restoration of lawful and orderly government in order that Nicaragua may resume its program of reforms unhampered by the vicious elements who would restore the methods of Zelaya.

"The revolt of General Mena in flagrant violation of his solemn promises to his own Government and to the American Minister, and of the Dawson agreements by which he was solemnly bound, and his attempt to overturn the Government of his country for purely selfish purposes and without even the pretense of contending for a principle, make the present rebellion in origin the most inexcusable in the annals of Central America."

The "uncivilized and savage" conduct of the revolutionists, the statement asserted, gave the revolt "the attributes of the abhorrent and intolerable Zelaya regime."

After some hesitation, Weitzel gave out the statement on September 13.[138] Its effect was at first somewhat lessened by the policy of the American officers who commanded the marine force. Admiral Southerland had criticized Díaz for making little effort to suppress the revolt, and, when the marines had taken control of the railroad line to Managua, the Admiral refused to permit its use by the forces of either side, hoping in this way to compel them to make peace.[139] A few days later, he was reported to be discussing peace terms with one of the liberal leaders at Leon and assuring the latter that the American forces would maintain a strict neutrality.[140] Southerland's policy horrified Díaz, who cabled to Washington that he considered his own position hopeless.[141] It also distressed the State Department and Weitzel, who wanted to give Díaz every possible support. Weitzel was in fact so bitter against the rebels that he was

[138] Weitzel to Knox, telegram, Sept. 13, 1912, *ibid.*, p. 1048.

[139] See his telegram of Sept. 12, 1912, to the Secretary of the Navy, enclosed with the latter's letter to Knox, Sept. 14, 817.00/1976.

[140] Weitzel to Knox, telegram, Sept. 16, 1912, 817.00/1985.

[141] In his cables to Castrillo referred to above, 817.00/1980.

prepared to recommend that their leaders be tried and hanged by the American forces.[142] When Wilson laid the situation before Taft, the President backed the State Department,[143] and Southerland was instructed on September 24 to permit the Nicaraguan government, but not the rebels, to use the railroad line and to control all towns along the railroad which were not held by the government.[144]

Before Southerland received these orders, the rebellion had begun to collapse. The liberals at Leon could not take any effective part in the war because Mena had been unable and perhaps unwilling to send them adequate quantities of arms. The American forces had forbidden another attack on Managua, and Weitzel's statement had made many of the revolutionists feel that their cause was hopeless. For some time, Mena himself had been too ill to give the movement strong leadership, and on September 24, on receiving a promise of personal protection, he surrendered to American forces that had pushed through the rebel lines to succor the foreigners at Granada.

The liberals still held Leon, and a liberal leader named Zeledón was intrenched on two hills overlooking the railroad between Managua and Granada. Weitzel thought that Southerland should demand that Zeledón evacuate this position, to assure free use of the railroad. The Admiral had no desire to do the Nicaraguan government's fighting for it,[145] but Wilson took the matter up with the navy in Washington, and Southerland was ordered to act.[146] He waited a few days while the government's forces made an unsuccessful attack on the rebel position, and then on October 4 the American marines took the two hills in a battle in which they lost four dead and seven wounded.

After this, the rebels could see that further resistance was hopeless. Three more marines were killed in street fighting when American forces occupied Leon on October 6, after the liberals had agreed to surrender the city, but by October 8 the war was over and the government was beginning to disband its forces. American marines

[142] Weitzel to Knox, Sept. 17, 1912, 817.00/1988.
[143] Wilson to Taft, Sept. 23, 1912, 817.00/2003B, and Doyle's memorandum of conversation with President, Sept. 23, 817.00/2014.
[144] Wilson to Weitzel, Sept. 24, 1912, 817.00/2000A.
[145] Weitzel to Knox, Sept. 20, 1912, 817.00/2005.
[146] Wilson to Secretary of the Navy, Sept. 25, 1912, 817.00/2015.

occupied several towns for a short time, to restore order and also to prevent atrocities against the defeated party—a precaution that was justified by incidents that had already occurred. Mena was taken on an American warship to the Canal Zone, where he received medical treatment at the State Department's expense and was held in custody for a short time.

The greater part of the American expeditionary force left the country, but Weitzel insisted that 100 marines remain at Managua as a legation guard, at least until after the installation of Díaz' successor. He thought that a complete withdrawal would be "construed as the tacit consent of the United States to renew hostilities." [147] This legation guard was to remain in Nicaragua for thirteen years. Its presence caused serious problems for future administrations at Washington because it came to be regarded as the symbol of American support for the constituted order, and it could not be withdrawn without seeming to invite a revolution. A disastrous civil war did ensue when the United States ended its existence in 1925.

When the revolution ended, less than three months remained of Díaz' presidential term and it was necessary to consider the selection of his successor. Some of the conservative leaders urged that the choice be made by the assembly, in which Mena's influence was now eliminated, but Weitzel insisted that there be a popular election in accord with the Dawson Agreements.[148] Earlier, while the war was still going on, Wilson had asked Weitzel's views about the supervision of such an election by the United States, with a "stipulated exclusion from candidacy of those disqualified as representing the worst elements." Wilson thought it important to make it clear that the United States was not hostile to the liberal party but simply to Mena and the *zelayistas* who were "enemies of the peace and welfare" of Nicaragua. Weitzel replied, however, that any attempt at supervision would be unwise, because there was not enough time nor enough available personnel to set up an organization that could assure fair play.[149] The Minister was unquestionably right, but

[147] Weitzel to Knox, Dec. 14, 1912, *Foreign Relations, 1912*, p. 1069.

[148] Weitzel to Knox, Nov. 5, 1912, *ibid.*, p. 1063.

[149] Wilson to Weitzel, telegram, Sept. 25, 1912, 817.00/2017A, and Weitzel to Knox, telegram, Oct. 9, 1912, 817.00/2081.

the result was to leave the choice of the new president in the hands of the conservative leaders.

Chamorro was probably the strongest candidate for the conservative nomination, but he was opposed by the Díaz wing of the party and was feared and hated by the liberals. Weitzel consequently persuaded him to withdraw in Díaz' favor, in return for a promise of appointment as minister to Washington.[150] The election was a mere matter of form, as the liberals decided not to participate, and Díaz took office on January 1, 1913, for a four-year term.

During the last months of Díaz' provisional administration the government seemed nearer than ever to insolvency. Even before the civil war, government employees were threatening to stop work unless their salaries were paid, and Díaz was borrowing small sums locally at interest rates running up to 18 percent.[151] The administration still had for its own use only the product of the inefficiently administered internal revenues. Mena's revolt naturally made matters worse. After the fighting started, the bankers agreed that the National Bank, which opened for business under their management on August 1, 1912, should lend the government $100,000,[152] but this money lasted only a short time. Díaz asked the bankers for another loan, but they insisted on conditions which Weitzel considered unnecessarily complicated and unfavorable.[153] When the State Department pointed out to the bankers that any assistance, to be effective, must be immediate, they replied that they had already made proposals which Díaz had accepted, but that on September 23 the President had told them that he had decided to resign, because the United States government was giving him no support.[154] This of course was a reference to Admiral Southerland's policy.

The same proposals were finally put in the form of a contract signed on November 4. The bankers agreed to let the government

[150] The writer obtained this information from well-informed sources in Nicaragua in 1914. Weitzel did not report it to the State Department, but his despatch of November 5, cited above, shows that he took a hand in the selection of the conservative ticket.

[151] Weitzel to Knox, May 22 and June 29, 1912, *Foreign Relations, 1912,* pp. 1101, 1102. Mallet-Prevost to Wands, July 16, 1912, 817.51/480.

[152] The text of the contract is in Arana, *Compilación de contratos,* Vol. I, p. 275.

[153] Weitzel to Knox, Sept. 23, 1912, 817.51/503.

[154] Papers left with State Department by Mr. Mallet-Prevost. 817.51/504.

have $100,000 from the customs receipts and also to make available for current expenses over a period of months $400,000 of the Ethelburga money, which would otherwise have been available to relieve the bankers of their obligation, assumed in March, to provide an additional $500,000 for the currency reserve. In return for these concessions, which in effect postponed the repayment of amounts already lent, the bankers obtained an option to buy for $1,000,000 the 49 percent of the stock of the Pacific Railroad which was not covered by the option given them in March. They also insisted that the new National Bank take over the collection of the internal revenues. These concessions proved to be of very doubtful value, for the Nicaraguan congress refused to approve the railroad option and the collection of the internal revenues was soon abandoned because the Nicaraguan officials failed to cooperate in enforcing the fiscal laws.[155]

It was only a few weeks before the Díaz government was again attempting to borrow money. The President sent word to the bankers that he had an offer of financial backing from another source and proposed the immediate liquidation of his contracts with them, saying that he feared that the new administration at Washington would withdraw its support when it took office in March.[156] He had probably been talking with the local British bankers in Nicaragua, who had opposed the whole American program of financial reform. The State Department expressed its emphatic disapproval of this idea, and nothing came of it, although Weitzel reported on February 20 that an English syndicate had offered to arrange a large loan at once.[157] The State Department continued its efforts to get Nicaragua further financial help from New York, and several plans for the purchase of the Pacific Railroad stock by the bankers were discussed, but the bankers were unwilling to make any new commitments because they could obtain no information about the policy of the incoming administration at Washington.[158]

A stopgap arrangement was finally made just as the Taft administration was going out of office. When Weitzel cabled on March 2

[155] The text of the contract is in Arana, *Compilación de contratos,* Vol. I, p. 287.
[156] Wilson to Legation at Managua, Jan. 31, 1913, 817.51/522A.
[157] *Foreign Relations, 1913,* pp. 1034, 1037.
[158] Latin American Division memorandum of conversation with Mr. Strauss, Feb. 27, 1913, 817.51/532.

that there was imminent danger that the assembly would revoke all of the financial legislation passed since 1911, the bankers agreed to release to Nicaragua the customs receipts that should have been applied to the payment of the treasury bills during the next four months.[159] This assured Díaz of enough money to run the government until June 30. The new administration at Washington would have to deal with the problem after that date.

Another legacy to the incoming Secretary of State was the Chamorro-Weitzel canal option treaty, which was signed in February 1913. Early in 1912, during the negotiations for the short-term loans made in March, the Nicaraguan government had suggested to the bankers the possibility of making the San Juan and Tipitapa Rivers navigable for barge traffic, to provide transportation between the east coast and Managua. When a provision giving the bankers an option to do this was included in the draft of the loan contract, the State Department asked that a stipulation be added forbidding the transfer of the concession to any foreign company or government or the establishment of any transisthmian route at all without the consent of the United States.[160] The whole idea was dropped when the Nicaraguan assembly opposed it. One of Weitzel's comments at the time suggested that he at least was thinking about the possibility of a treaty giving the United States canal rights in Nicaragua,[161] and in December 1912 he elicited from Díaz a proposal that the United States buy for $3,000,000 not only an option to build a canal but also a right to establish naval bases in the Gulf of Fonseca and the Corn Islands off the Atlantic Coast.[162] A treaty containing these provisions was concluded on February 8, 1913, and rushed to the United States Senate even before the signed copies could reach Washington. It was too late, however, to obtain action before the end of the session on March 4.

The purpose of the treaty, as Weitzel later explained it,[163] was to show that the United States, despite the failure of the 1911 loan convention, was still giving Díaz its support and confidence. Later

[159] Weitzel to Knox, March 2, 1913, 817.51/534. Bryan to Weitzel, March 5, 1913, *Foreign Relations, 1913*, p. 1039.
[160] Wilson to Weitzel, Feb. 26, 1912, *Foreign Relations, 1912*, p. 1096.
[161] Weitzel to Knox, Feb. 14, 1912, *ibid.*, p. 1096.
[162] Weitzel to Knox, telegram, Dec. 15, 1912, 817.812/5.
[163] Memorandum to Assistant Secretary Phillips, Jan. 9, 1917, 817.51/914.

on, both governments seemed interested in the canal option chiefly as a means of solving some of Nicaragua's more pressing financial problems, but the original plan was to use the money received from the United States for education and public works rather than for debt payment. It was not clear that the treaty would be of any great benefit to the United States. The need for a second inter-oceanic canal seemed doubtful,[164] and the reports of foreign governments' intrigues to obtain canal rights, which were cited by the State Department in defense of the treaty, were, to say the least, vague. Weitzel cabled, for example, in December 1912, that a German company was said to be working in Costa Rica on a project to canalize the Colorado and San Juan Rivers,[165] but the story turned out to have little foundation. Later, he sent up documents showing that Zelaya's Minister for Foreign Affairs, some years before, had instructed the Nicaraguan Minister at Paris to sound out the Japanese Ambassador there about the possibility of Japan's building a canal in Nicaragua. The Nicaraguans had heard that Japan and Great Britain were both interested in the project, but the report was apparently baseless.[166] It was perhaps prudent to make sure that no foreign government could obtain canal rights in Nicaragua, but it does not seem probable that this was a major consideration. It is also questionable whether the Taft administration was really interested in the proposed naval bases. They would doubtless have been needed if a Nicaraguan canal had been built, but as matters turned out the provision for them merely involved the United States in unfortunate controversies which will be discussed in a later chapter.

The claims for the murder of Cannon and Groce were also adjusted in the last month of the Taft administration. Weitzel suggested in November 1912 that he be authorized to inquire what had been done about punishing the murderers and to intimate that the amount of the indemnity demanded would be influenced by the reply, but the State Department told him merely to present a formal claim for $10,000 in each case. Nicaragua promptly agreed to pay

---

[164] This was the opinion expressed by General Goethals to the War Department; letter of Jan. 14, 1913, 817.12/8.

[165] Telegram of Dec. 24, 1912, 817.812/6.

[166] Weitzel to Knox, Feb. 23, 1913, 817.812/18.

this sum,[167] but no effort to collect the money was made until 1918, when both claims were paid in full. In the meantime, however, the State Department continued the small payments that it had been making out of its own funds to Groce's widow, who was a Nicaraguan. The amount of the indemnity seems very moderate, when we consider how seriously the American government viewed the murders when they occurred.

The intervention in Nicaragua in 1912 marked a turning point in American policy in the Caribbean. Before 1912, the navy had frequently made a show of force to prevent fighting which would endanger foreigners or to discourage revolutionary activities. Sometimes, as in Nicaragua in 1910, such measures had influenced, or decided, the outcome of a civil war, but there had been no case before 1912 where American forces had actually gone into battle to help suppress a revolution. American public opinion, as reflected in the press, seemed on the whole to approve what was done, but many voices were raised in protest.[168] Senator Bacon, who had criticized previous actions of the State Department in Central America and had presented a resolution denying the right of the President to use the military forces in operations in a foreign country without the express consent of Congress, again spoke out when the marines first began to arrive in Nicaragua, pointing out that the State Department had gone ahead with its financial projects in spite of the Senate's refusal to approve them and that the power of the United States was being used to support private interests in profitable, speculative operations. The Senate unanimously approved his resolution for an inquiry.

The intervention intensified the already prevalent fear and mistrust of the United States in the other Central American countries. On the other hand, for several years after 1912 the recollection of what had happened to Mena's rebellion discouraged potential revolutionists throughout the isthmus. Except for a *coup d'état* staged by

[167] Weitzel to Knox, telegram, Nov. 21, 1912, 317.112G 89,131; Knox to Weitzel, Feb. 10, 1913, *ibid.*; Weitzel to Knox, Feb. 15, 1913, *ibid.*/137.

[168] For resumés of press comment, see the *Literary Digest* for Aug. 24, Sept. 28, and Oct. 19, 1912.

the Minister of War of Costa Rica in 1917, there was no case where a government was overturned by force in Central America between 1912 and 1919. When disturbances threatened, the appearance of an American warship was enough to restore tranquility. The belief that the United States would intervene to uphold constituted governments helped the groups in power in each country to remain in power with little regard for the rights of their opponents, but it at least gave Central America an era of much needed peace.

In Nicaragua, the continued presence of the legation guard was interpreted to mean that no revolution would be tolerated. This meant that the conservatives would stay in power, though everyone, including the State Department, knew that they were a minority party.[169] The arguments advanced in defense of this policy: the assertion that the liberals included a large proportion of the "ignorant mob," and that most of their leaders represented the evil zelayista tradition, were perhaps put forward in all sincerity by officials who had little contact with any except the conservatives, but they made little sense to anyone who had friends in both parties. The support of a minority government was inconsistent with the principles that governed American policy in the Caribbean, but for more than ten years no Secretary of State wanted to assume responsibility for the revolution that would almost certainly follow the legation guard's withdrawal.

[169] There are many reports in the State Department's files, from the Legation at Managua and from naval officers, emphasizing the liberals' numerical superiority.

◂ 6 ▸

Dollar Diplomacy Elsewhere in the Caribbean

Loan Negotiations in Honduras

✍ Before the revolution of 1909–1910 presented the opportunity to set up a customs receivership in Nicaragua, Knox and Huntington Wilson were endeavoring to establish one in Honduras. The chief purpose of the Central American policy proposals that they discussed with Mexico in March and April of 1909 was to safeguard the neutrality and promote the stability of Honduras, and financial reform was an essential part of their plan. The fact that the British government was at the time pressing President Dávila to resume payment on the republic's long-neglected foreign debt made the financial problem especially urgent.

Honduras had contracted three loans in London between 1866 and 1870, to refund her share of the old debt of the Federal Republic of Central America and to provide funds for a railroad to connect her principal cities with the Atlantic Coast. Only a few miles of railway were built because most of the proceeds of the bonds went into the pockets of bankers and government officials or were used to pay interest during the period when bonds were being unloaded on investors.[1] After complete default occurred in 1872–1873, a British parliamentary investigation revealed shocking fraud and mismanagement.[2] In 1909, the debt, with arrears of interest, amounted to more than $120,000,000. Since Honduras' total annual revenue was about $1,650,000, the bondholders' chance of recovering any substantial part of their claim was small.

The Council of Foreign Bondholders in London had nevertheless made several attempts to arrange a settlement, taking advantage of the fact that the bonds could claim a lien on the short railroad line running from Puerto Cortés into the interior, which the Hondurans had always hoped to extend to Tegucigalpa. This line became more important with the increase of banana growing on the north coast,

---

[1] Of the 57 miles in operation in 1911, only one-half had been built with the proceeds of the loans, *Foreign Relations, 1912*, p. 575.

[2] This was the same investigation that dealt with the Hartmont loan in Santo Domingo. The report is in *British Parliamentary Papers*, Vol. XI.

and Washington Valentine, an American who obtained a concession in 1896 to build and operate a wharf at Puerto Cortés, had long been interested in acquiring and extending it. Valentine's Honduras Syndicate had attempted on two or three occasions to work out an adjustment of the British debt. When these efforts failed, it leased the line from the government in 1900 making no provision for the bonds. This lease was canceled three years later, partly because of British pressure,[3] but Valentine obtained another in 1908, and was operating and extending the line when Lionel Carden, the British Minister at Guatemala, began to negotiate in the same year for a settlement on the British bonds.

To protect his own interests, Valentine, in January 1909, proposed to the Honduran government a general refunding of all of its debts through a new loan that would be secured by an American customs collectorship like that in Santo Domingo. Root wrote the American Minister that the United States could not suggest such an arrangement, but that the Minister would be safe in expressing a confidential opinion that any overture from the Honduran government "would be considered by the government of the United States with the strongest possible desire to be of service to Honduras and to contribute towards bringing about such a satisfactory result as has recently been obtained in Santo Domingo."[4] Secretary of State Bacon, after Root's resignation, thought that the idea was "the keynote of the solution of our whole Caribbean problem, and should not be lost sight of," and Adee, on March 9, in calling Huntington Wilson's attention to a memorandum by Hollander on Santo Domingo, wrote: "It is not at all unlikely that in the near future we shall have to undertake a similar office for Honduras and Liberia. Things are fast drifting that way."[5]

President Dávila seemed at first to favor Valentine's proposal, but he dropped it when popular opposition developed.[6] When Carden came to Tegucigalpa early in March 1909 to press the British demands, Dávila accepted in principle a plan of settlement which called for the payment of 40 annuities of £40,000 each. Bonds were to be drawn each year and paid off, with no accrued interest, at

---

[3] At least, according to Valentine. See Jennings' statement before the Senate Foreign Relations Committee in 1911, 815.51/233.

[4] Root to Dodge, Jan. 26, 1909, Num. Case 17624.

[5] Both memoranda are filed under Num. Case 17624/2.

[6] Brown to Knox, April 7, 1909, Num. Case 17624/12.

rates which would gradually increase from 20 to 40 percent of their face value. The needed funds would be provided from the net revenues of the railway and the wharf at Puerto Cortés and by a 15 percent surcharge on the import duties, which would be payable in certificates sold by an agent of the bankers.[7] An arrangement with Valentine, under which the government undertook to pay him for his interest in the railroad and the wharf, seemed to protect his interests.

Nevertheless, Philip Marshall Brown, the American minister, objected to the proposed settlement on the ground that it did not protect the interests of the republic's other creditors. The State Department, in spite of representations from the British Embassy at Washington, took the same position.[8] The Department's real motive, probably, was to block an arrangement that would perpetuate British financial influence in Honduras and thus prevent the establishment of financial control by the United States. The execution of the British plan was further imperiled when the Honduran government was unable to pay Valentine for the railroad and the wharf. The government was about to seize the properties without payment, but the timely arrival of the *U.S.S. Marietta* at Puerto Cortés dissuaded it from doing so, and, in June 1909, the Legation was instructed to say that the United States would not tolerate any arbitrary confiscation or obstruction of Valentine's business.[9]

The American government, however, could hardly oppose what seemed a reasonable settlement of the British debt without offering some alternative. The obvious alternative was an American refunding loan. Dávila told Brown in April that he would welcome such a loan if the interest of American bankers could be enlisted, and Huntington Wilson suggested to Knox the negotiation of a convention that would pave the way for a loan by providing for an American financial adviser or perhaps a customs receivership.[10] No action was taken, possibly because Knox felt that the initiative should come from Honduras or from interested bankers.

In the weeks that followed, when various bankers visited the De-

---

[7] For a copy of the British proposal, see 815.51/348.

[8] Memorandum from British Embassy, March 7, 1909, Num. Case 17624/7. For these events, see also *Foreign Relations, 1912*, pp. 550ff., and the *Report of the Council of the Corporation of Foreign Bondholders, 1909*, p. 15.

[9] Num. Case 15004/11, 14, 28A.

[10] Wilson to Knox, May 9, 1909, Num. Case 17624/79.

partment in connection with other matters, Wilson urged them to consider the possibility of a loan to Honduras, and in June he found that two firms were working on plans, each of them under the impression that it had the Department's support. J. P. Morgan and Company, who were associated with Valentine, had been negotiating with the British Council of Foreign Bondholders to obtain the bondholders' consent to a new arrangement, and James Speyer was preparing to send a representative to Honduras, in the belief that the Department had promised to support his firm to the exclusion of any other. The misunderstanding seems to have arisen from Wilson's anxiety to make sure that some American banker undertook the business and his cautious effort to avoid any appearance of favoritism. Both firms were disturbed, but Morgan, who had already reached an agreement with the British bondholders, was in a stronger position and Speyer withdrew, protesting angrily to the State Department and to the President.[11]

The Morgan firm proposed a loan that would make possible the purchase of the British bonds and provide some money for the internal debt and for public works. On July 15, the State Department telegraphed the American Legation at Tegucigalpa that the European creditors and Valentine had agreed to this arrangement, and Brown was told to suggest that the Honduran government send a representative to confer with the bankers in New York. He was told confidentially that the execution of the plan depended on an agreement between the governments of the United States and Honduras for some sort of financial control.[12] Dávila agreed to send commissioners to negotiate, but only after some hesitation. It was clear that there was much opposition to the proposal in Honduras because many people suspected that it was merely a revival of Valentine's earlier scheme for a customs receivership, and articles in North American newspapers discussing the loan as a step toward a protectorate made the project more unpopular.[13]

While negotiations for the loan were going on in New York, Brown grew more and more concerned about the political situation

[11] For Speyer's protest, see 815.51/97 and 151. Wilson's explanation of the misunderstanding with the bankers was published in *Foreign Relations, 1912*, pp. 549–554.

[12] Num. Case 17624/32.

[13] Brown to Knox, Aug. 19, 1909, Num. Case 17624/62.

in Honduras. He thought that Dávila was rapidly losing his hold on the country and was showing signs of mental disturbance, and in July he suggested that it might be better to delay the negotiations until a new government came in. The State Department, however, insisted that the matter be pushed.[14] Three months later, when the Minister had continued to send alarming reports about the political outlook, Wilson vetoed Adee's suggestion that J. P. Morgan and Company be informed of his views. Wilson, who thought that Brown was unduly pessimistic, did not wish to discourage the bankers, and he warned Brown that he should make every effort to "assist the American syndicate to success."[15]

On December 21, 1909, the Department of State was informed that the bankers had reached an agreement with the Honduran commissioners. Ten million dollars of 5 percent bonds were to be authorized, of which $7,500,000 would be issued immediately. Of this latter amount, $6,000,000 would be set aside for the external debt, and the balance would be used to pay internal claims and to rebuild and extend the railroad, which the bankers would operate during the life of the loan. The execution of the plan would depend on the execution of a treaty under which the United States would guarantee the independence of Honduras and assist in the collection and application of the customs revenues.[16] The Department later learned that Valentine and his associates would be paid $630,-000 for their interests, for which they had earlier claimed over $2,000,000.[17] The British bondholders would fare somewhat better than under the plan that Carden had negotiated in March, receiving 15 percent of their nominal principal in cash instead of a long-deferred payment of 20 to 40 percent.

The bankers' plan seemed likely to achieve one of the chief objectives for which Wilson, at least, had been working since March, but some of the State Department's officers were at first doubtful about the United States government's participation in the proposed customs receivership. Dawson, who was head of the new Latin American Division, suggested that the Department consider the

[14] Wilson to Brown, Aug. 5, 1909, Num. Case 17624/37.
[15] Brown's despatch of Oct. 6, 1909, and the Department's reply of Nov. 4, with the accompanying memoranda, Num. Case 7357/672.
[16] Jennings to the Secretary of State, Dec. 21, 1909, Num. Case 17624/91.
[17] McCreery to Knox, April 27, 1910, 815.51/103.

"numerous bearings" of the proposed arrangement, before giving instructions to the Legation at Tegucigalpa, because it seemed likely that a financial protectorate, if it was to be considered at all, should be considered in connection with similar arrangements in other Central American countries. He was not sure that a treaty was necessary, because he thought that the United States, under its general policy of protecting American citizens and property, could give adequate support to a customs collector appointed by the bankers.[18] Fenton McCreery, the newly appointed Minister to Honduras, also thought that it might be better to find some other method to secure the bonds in view of the Honduran opposition to a "Santo Domingo plan." McCreery discussed this idea with the bankers before going to Tegucigalpa, but received little encouragement.[19] By February 1910, Dawson had reached the conclusion that a treaty like the Dominican convention would be the best arrangement.[20] It is interesting to note that this was about the time when the first reference to a possible customs receivership in Nicaragua appears in the files.

After the loan contract was sent to Tegucigalpa, however, the negotiations made little progress for several months. Dávila was having trouble with his own hand-picked Congress, and he feared the political consequences of agreeing to a customs receivership. The bankers, however, insisted that control of the customs was essential. In August 1910, the State Department finally decided to intervene more actively in the negotiations and sent a telegram to the American Legation expressing "amazement" at Dávila's failure to give definite instructions to his commissioner in the United States. "The President and Government of the United States," it said, "are convinced that a just bankers contract supported by a convention are necessary." The United States could not be expected indefinitely to stand between Honduras and its creditors and must insist that Honduras go ahead with the negotiations, "already delayed to the limit of patience," or else accept the far-reaching consequences of its improvident course, abandoning the negotiations and thereby inviting a situation in which the United States might

---

[18] Memorandum attached to Jennings' letter of Dec. 21, 1909, Num. Case 17624/91.
[19] McCreery to Wilson, personal, Feb. 12, 1910, 815.51/95.
[20] Memorandum to Wilson, Feb. 21, 1910, 815.51/96.

be unable to prevent the imposition of a settlement by someone else with less scrupulous regard for Honduras' interests. The Legation was told to say that the bankers insisted on a customs arrangement and that the State Department appreciated the necessity for one.[21]

Dávila then sent his commissioner full powers to conclude the negotiations, and final drafts of the contracts and of the treaty which the bankers thought necessary were soon submitted to the State Department for consideration. Several weeks elapsed while the Department, with the aid of the Bureau of Insular Affairs, studied the documents. To make sure that the loan contract was fair to Honduras, Knox employed Charles A. Conant to make a study of its financial aspects and asked the law firm of Dexter, Osborn, and Fleming to give it the sort of scrutiny that they would if they were employed as counsel for Honduras.[22] Several changes were made to meet Conant's and the lawyers' suggestions. By December, though the terms of the contract were still being considered, the State Department was sufficiently satisfied to proceed with the signature of the treaty. The Honduran commissioner fled to New York at the last moment, in a desperate effort to avoid personal responsibility for the agreement, but he returned after Wilson sent word that the State Department felt that it had already wasted too much time because of his "trifling" and would not oppose the forcible occupation of Honduras' customhouses by the British if he refused to sign.[23]

The treaty, signed on January 10, 1911, was exactly similar to the one that was to be signed a few months later with Nicaragua. It provided that Honduras would negotiate a refunding loan secured by the customs duties. So long as the bonds were outstanding the customs would be administered by a Collector General appointed from a list of names presented by the fiscal agent for the loan and approved by the President of the United States. Both governments would give the Collector General any needed protection.[24]

President Taft submitted the treaty to the United States Senate on January 26, with a message that was drafted with great care in the State Department. As Wilson wrote Adee, Knox expected opposi-

[21] 815.51/112B.
[22] For their report, see 815.51/192.
[23] Wilson's memorandum to Dodge, Dec. 23, 1910, 815.51/150.
[24] For the text, see *Foreign Relations, 1912*, p. 560.

tion in the Senate, and he considered the treaty a test of the utmost importance, because its failure would doom in advance the State Department's plan for the financial rehabilitation of Nicaragua by a similar treaty, and because "the principle we seek to act upon in Honduras is one we are bound to have to resort to in still other cases." [25] The message stressed the importance of strengthening Honduras in order to assure peace in Central America and emphasized the idea that the United States could not prevent other powers from intervening to collect debts if it did not help its neighbors to put their finances in order. The President cited the benefits that the Dominican Republic had obtained from a similar arrangement and indicated that the agreement with Honduras was part of a broad policy designed to bring stability to all of Central America. Knox reiterated these arguments in another long communication on February 13, when he sent the Foreign Relations Committee a copy of the loan contract.[26] The committee reported the treaty favorably on March 1, but there was no time for final action before Congress adjourned on March 4.

Since Juan Paredes, the Honduran commissioner who had reluctantly signed the treaty, refused to sign the loan contracts, Dávila instructed his Minister at Washington to do so. Wilson wrote the Honduran Minister on February 8 that the State Department and its outside advisers considered the agreements "just and equitable," and on February 11 he sent him "final copies" with a statement that they were now acceptable to the bankers.[27] On February 15, the Minister signed a loan contract with J. P. Morgan and Company; Kuhn, Loeb, and Company; the National City Bank and the First National Bank of New York; and a fiscal agency agreement with the Guaranty Trust Company.

The contracts authorized a 5 percent loan of $10,000,000, of which $7,500,000 were to be issued immediately. The bankers would buy $6,354,000 of these at 88, giving in return $2,100,000 in cash and about $19,750,000 of the old British bonds, which they had under option at 15 percent of their par value. The balance of the $7,500,000 would be held to be exchanged for any other old bonds

[25] Wilson to Adee, Jan. 13, 1911, 815.51/207.
[26] The President's message and Knox's letter of Feb. 13 are printed in *Foreign Relations, 1912*, pp. 555ff. and 568ff.
[27] *Foreign Relations, 1912*, pp. 566, 567.

whose holders might subsequently accept the arrangement. Of the cash which Honduras would receive, about $700,000 would be used to pay internal debt, about $700,000 to buy Valentine's wharf at Puerto Cortés and pay his claims in connection with the wharf and the National Railroad, and the remainder to extend and improve the railroad. Payments on the internal debt and the payment to Valentine would be determined either by an agreement approved by an assessor named by the Secretary of State of the United States or by an arbitral board of which the chairman would be appointed by the Secretary of State. The price of 88, at which the bankers would take the bonds, was admittedly low, but Conant pointed out that conditions in the market were uncertain and that the price was higher than any which Honduras could hope to obtain without the cooperation of the United States. Conant did not appear to think that the allotment of $529,900 to the bankers for expenses was excessive, in view of the large amount of work that the operation had involved.[28] The chief benefit that Honduras would derive from the loan would be the rehabilitation of the republic's credit and the efficient collection of the customs revenues. The fact that little money would be available for any purpose except debt refunding was doubtless one reason for the government's reluctance to accept the arrangement.

The Honduran Revolution of 1911

In the last weeks of the loan negotiations a civil war began in Honduras. Dávila's position had naturally become precarious after the defeat of the liberal government in Nicaragua. In July 1910, he had repelled a poorly organized attack on the north coast led by Manuel Bonilla and Lee Christmas and supported by Estrada Cabrera, but Bonilla and Christmas immediately began to plan a new venture. Estrada Cabrera apparently promised to give arms and to permit the use of Guatemalan territory as a base of operations. He became more cautious after the State Department repeatedly reminded him of his obligations under the 1907 treaties, and he finally promised to expel the conspirators from Guatemalan territory. Bonilla and several of his followers then came to New Orleans.

This confronted the United States with the problem of maintain-

[28] For Conant's analysis of the contract, see *Foreign Relations, 1912*, p. 562.

ing its own neutrality. The State Department warned the Attorney General about Bonilla's presence, but the American government did not have the legal authority to take the sort of action that it demanded of Central American governments in similar circumstances. This became evident when some of Bonilla's North American friends procured for him a converted yacht called the *Hornet*, which had been used earlier in the year by a group in New Orleans to carry arms to the Nicaraguan revolutionists at Bluefields. Transporting arms did not violate American law, but the use of the ship for a military expedition such as Bonilla evidently planned would be illegal. It was impossible, however, to prove that any violation was contemplated, and the federal authorities were consequently compelled to permit the vessel to sail in ballast, with a few men on board, late in December. Bonilla and Christmas left New Orleans secretly about the same time. A few days later they appeared in the *Hornet* off the Honduran coast, and on January 10, 1911, the day the loan treaty was signed, they landed near Trujillo.

The State Department had little sympathy for either party when the war began. It considered Dávila weak and incompetent and knew that many of his followers were violently anti-American. It was by no means certain that his government would, or could, obtain ratification of the loan agreements. On the other hand, the Latin American Division thought that Dávila should have the moral support of the United States because he had agreed to the loan treaty and because the secret aid that Bonilla was getting from Estrada Cabrera was "sufficient reason why our sympathy should tend the other way." [29] F. B. Jennings, the counsel for the bankers and also for Valentine, expressed grave misgivings about Bonilla and urged that the revolution be stopped. [30] The State Department was not prepared to intervene, but it urged the other Central American governments to make sure that persons in their territory did not aid the revolutionists.

Knox also asked the Attorney General to investigate charges that the United Fruit Company was helping Bonilla in the hope of obtaining a monopoly of the Honduran banana trade. In 1910 the region back of Puerto Cortés was one of the few places along the Central American coast where independent railroad and steamship

[29] Weitzel's memorandum of Jan. 11, 1911, in which Doyle concurred, 817.00/974.
[30] Letter of Jan. 13, 1911, 815.51/168.

lines still made it possible for banana growers to market their fruit without selling it to the Fruit Company or one of its associates; and the State Department had received a number of communications from American planters in the area and other interested persons asking for protection against efforts to change this situation.[31]

It seems clear that Samuel Zemurray, who was at the time associated with the United Fruit Company,[32] was in fact giving Bonilla active support. Many years later an American magazine published a story about the *Hornet*, based apparently on material obtained from Zemurray or from one of his associates. According to this, Zemurray wished to prevent the establishment of a customs collectorship in Honduras because it would make it impossible for him to obtain a concession for the duty-free importation of railway material. He consequently lent Bonilla money for the purchase of the *Hornet*, and later took Bonilla and Christmas on his own yacht to board the *Hornet* after she reached the high seas.[33] The State Department perhaps did not know these facts at the time, but it did have a report from the captain of one of the American warships on the Honduran coast, who was indignant when one of Zemurray's steamers refused to load coal for his use but brought coal for the *Hornet*. Zemurray explained to the captain and to the American consul at Puerto Cortés that he had a financial interest in Bonilla's success, and he alleged that an official in the State Department had assured him that the United States would not interfere with the revolution. This assertion seems to have been based on an inaccurate report of a conversation between one of his representatives and Wilbur Carr, the Chief Clerk.[34]

As it usually did when fighting seemed imminent, the American

---

[31] Letter from banana growers and other Americans on north coast of Honduras, Jan. 30, 1911, 815.00/1127; from H. H. Haines, representing Galveston Chamber of Commerce and Galveston and Central American Banana and Steamship Co., Feb. 15, 1911, 815.00/1129; from group of north coast planters, Feb. 18, 1911, 815.00/-1145; petition forwarded by Consular Agent at San Pedro Sula, Feb. 19, 1911, 815.00/1151.

For Knox's letter of Feb. 6, 1911, to the Attorney General see 815.00/1049.

[32] For the relationship between the United Fruit Company and the other fruit companies in Honduras see Chapter i.

[33] *Fortune Magazine*, March 1933.

[34] Report from Consul at Puerto Cortés, Feb. 20, 1911, 815.00/1153. A memorandum attached to the report stated that Mr. Carr had talked very generally about Honduras with an American from La Ceiba, Honduras, who did not have a good record in the State Department.

government had sent warships to Honduras' north coast to protect American lives and property, and their commanders had been ordered to watch the adjacent Guatemalan coast to prevent Estrada Cabrera from sending aid to the rebels.[35] They were also to prevent the *Hornet* from engaging in hostilities pending an investigation of her alleged violation of the American neutrality laws. When Bonilla was told that he could not use the *Hornet* in military operations, he was so indignant and defiant that the commander of the *U.S.S. Marietta* felt compelled to seize the ship on January 21.[36] At the same time men were landed from the American warships and also from a British warship to set up a neutral zone for the protection of foreigners and other non-combatants at La Ceiba, which Bonilla was about to attack.

Bonilla took La Ceiba on January 25. On the 28th, Dávila cabled President Taft that his government was "resolved to approve convention and loan" and asked that the United States interpose its influence to end the war. He told the American Minister that he wished the United States to arbitrate between the two parties and that he would himself retire from the presidency, but only on condition that the United States name, or at least approve, his successor. McCreery suggested that "A convenient order of procedure would seem to be: Armistice, approval of convention by Congress; and an agreement as to the presidency";[37] but President Taft, in his reply to Dávila, repudiated the idea that the United States might take advantage of the situation to force approval of the loan. The American government, he said, was interested in the loan because it would be helpful to the people of Honduras and desired its consummation only with their "sanction."[38]

On January 31, Dávila made a desperate effort to obtain congressional approval of the loan treaty, but the deputies voted against it, 33–5. McCreery reported that the President's hysterical and threatening demand for immediate action was chiefly responsible for the result.[39] Most of the deputies, however, later signed a state-

[35] State to Navy Dept., Jan. 14, 1911, 815.00/984.
[36] Secretary of Navy to Secretary of State, Jan. 19 and Jan. 23, 1911, 815.00/1004, 1018.
[37] The three communications—Dávila to Taft, Jan. 28, and McCreery's two cables to Knox—appear in *Foreign Relations, 1911*, p. 297.
[38] *Ibid.*, p. 298.
[39] Despatch of Feb. 16, 1911, 815.51/229.

ment saying that they had opposed the treaty because it would violate the constitution and would transform Honduras "from a free country into an administrative dependency of the United States." [40]

Meanwhile, probably without intending to do so, the American naval commanders had taken action that forced the government's troops to abandon their last important position on the north coast. Because bullets had fallen in the neutral zone during the attack on La Ceiba, the commanders decided to permit no fighting in Puerto Cortés when the revolutionists moved against that town. They consequently announced that General Christmas must confine his attack to one area, and that the defenders would be forced to surrender if they refused to meet him there.[41] This created a bad tactical situation for the government's troops, and they decided to evacuate the town.

There was some difference of opinion in the State Department about Dávila's suggestion that the United States designate or approve a new president. Adee pointed out that it would not be practicable to do so without taking sides. The United States could hardly pick Bonilla or one of his partisans for the presidency, but it would be difficult to find a neutral; and if one were selected the United States would be under some moral obligation to support him. A makeshift, compromise government would be powerless. Adee realized that the navy's action at Puerto Cortés would make Bonilla's victory almost certain, but he thought that Bonilla would probably be the ultimate beneficiary of anything that the United States might do. He suggested that the United States "call a halt on both parties," as it had often done in Central America, proposing an armistice and offering the deck of an American naval vessel for a conference. It might thus be possible to obtain agreement on a "neutral, necessarily a Bonillista," to head the government until elections could be held, and thus to obtain Bonilla's good will.[42] Dodge, the chief of the Latin American Division, still distrusted Bonilla because of the foreign adventurers around him and the "concessions, promises etc. he has doubtless made," and because Estrada Cabrera would certainly attempt to control him,[43] but

[40] *Foreign Relations, 1912*, pp. 577–580.
[41] Secretary of Navy to Secretary of State, Feb. 9, 1911, 815.00/1106.
[42] Memorandum of Jan. 30, 1911, filed in 815.00.
[43] Memorandum of Jan. 30, 1911, 815.00/1116.

Adee's suggestion was adopted. On January 31 the United States urged an armistice and offered its mediation to restore peace. Pending acceptance of the proposal, Bonilla's troops were not allowed to enter Puerto Cortés.[44]

Both sides accepted, and Thomas C. Dawson was sent to preside over the peace conference that met on February 21. Just before the meeting, a grand jury at New Orleans indicted Bonilla and Christmas and several of their associates for violation of the United States neutrality laws. The State Department tried to assure Bonilla that this would not affect its impartial attitude, but Dawson feared that it would make the revolutionists more antagonistic.[45] Both sides in fact proved distrustful and uncooperative, and for several days it seemed unlikely that any agreement could be reached.

By March 1, Dawson had concluded that, while Bonilla's defiant attitude and his relations with the "New Orleans Syndicate" made him objectionable, the government party's hatred of Americans and its internal dissensions, combined with the fact that it could hardly recover the north coast without active aid from the United States, made it advisable to support the revolution.[46] As he was about to express this opinion to the Department, he received a message from the Secretary of State authorizing him to use the influence of the United States in favor of the candidate he believed best for the welfare of Honduras.[47] This strengthened Dawson's hand, and the conference immediately agreed that he should select a provisional president from lists of names submitted by the two factions. On March 3, Dawson chose Francisco Bertrand, who was one of the candidates proposed by the revolutionists. Dávila accepted the arrangement, and Bertrand was duly elected by the Congress as first designate, so that he assumed the presidency when Dávila and the Vice President resigned. The peace agreement provided for a general amnesty and an early free election and pledged the provisional government to divide positions in the government equally between the two parties.[48]

[44] Foreign Relations, 1911, p. 298.
[45] Ibid., p. 300, and 815.00/1134.
[46] Dawson's report on the conference, 815.00/1284.
[47] 815.00/1147.
[48] The text of the peace agreement is printed in Foreign Relations, 1911, p. 301.

The Failure of Dollar Diplomacy in Honduras

Neither Dawson nor the State Department seems to have tried to take advantage of the peace negotiations to obtain a definite commitment about the loan. The conference recommended "the settlement of the public debt," but in very general terms. Bonilla, however, had committed himself to the loan project in a message that he sent to the State Department through René Keilhauer, one of Minor Keith's associates, in August 1910, and in a more definite statement by his representative at Guatemala to the American Minister there on January 24, 1911.[49] With these assurances, neither the State Department nor the bankers seem to have taken very seriously the Honduran congress' rejection of the loan treaty when Dávila sought its approval in January.

The new government consolidated its position after some minor disorders. Despite the provisions of the peace agreement and the remonstrances of the American Minister, it filled all positions with *bonillistas*,[50] and there was little pretense of freedom in the election that took place in October. Bonilla, of course, became president. Meanwhile, the Department of Justice had *nolle prossed* the indictment against him, though not those against his American associates. Until the Honduran election in October and the reconvening of the United States Senate in December, little could be done about the treaty and the loan contracts. The bankers still seemed interested, however, and in April they suggested to the State Department that they might change the contracts to make $100,000 available for the use of the Honduran government,[51] which would make the loan more acceptable in Honduras.

In the meantime, Bonilla's public statements and the press comment in Honduras made it evident that the prospect for ratification of the treaty and the loan contracts was not bright. Bonilla, in fact, was thinking of obtaining financial aid from his friend Samuel Zemurray rather than from the Morgan syndicate, and it was perhaps to pave the way for an arrangement with Zemurray that Knox asked the Morgan firm in June 1911 if it would be willing to have the

---

[49] 815.00/960, 1092.
[50] 815.00/1262, 1277, 1281.
[51] See Jennings' letter of April 5, 1911, 815.51/253.

State Department announce that any other bankers that offered better terms might make a loan under the treaty. The bankers replied that they would be happy to withdraw if the Honduran government and the State Department would relieve them from their commitments, but that they would insist on retiring before any invitation was extended to another group. They reluctantly consented to the publication of their letter, coupled with a statement from Knox that the State Department's financial experts doubted whether any responsible banker would offer better terms.[52]

The State Department was evidently more interested in the establishment of the customs receivership than in having any particular banking group make the loan, and it is possible that Knox thought that some of the Democrats in the Senate might be more friendly to the treaty if New Orleans interests were involved. At an earlier stage in the negotiations, Wilson had insisted that the treaty be so framed that anyone who offered better terms could take advantage of it, and he had been amused to see the bankers' reaction to the idea that they might lose what they evidently considered a good piece of business.[53] In September 1911, when the State Department was informed that Zemurray was discussing a loan with the provisional government, it instructed the Legation at Tegucigalpa to emphasize the fact that the treaty and the loan contract were "separable"; the United States still considered the ratification of the treaty "essential," but if Honduras ratified the treaty it could modify the contract or even substitute a new one.[54]

Zemurray was working with the Whitney Central Trust and Savings Bank of New Orleans and William C. Sheldon, who was said to be connected with the Bethlehem Steel Company and to be interested in the Agalteca iron deposits in the interior of Honduras.[55] Zemurray's plan contemplated an immediate loan of $500,000 to meet the expenses of the recent war, to be followed by a $10,000,000 bond issue. The details do not seem to have been discussed with the State Department until the Whitney Bank and Sheldon presented their

[52] 815.51/277A, 279.
[53] Memorandum of conference of Sept. 26, 1910, 815.51/214.
[54] Instruction of Sept. 21, 1911, 815.51/297.
[55] Zemurray gave this information to the American Minister at Teguciagalpa, White to Knox, Feb. 4, 1912, 815.77/100.

project in January 1912.[56] At first, the new group contemplated an arrangement by which an American customs collector would be installed only in the event of a default, but after a talk with Knox they decided to tie their loan to the pending treaty and thought that they could help to obtain favorable action in the Senate.[57] The State Department was freer to cooperate with them after J. P. Morgan and Company formally withdrew their own proposal on February 3.

Valentine, who had initiated the 1909 loan project in an effort to protect his own investment in the railroad and the wharf at Puerto Cortés, seemed likely to be the chief loser from the change of plan, because the New Orleans proposal made no provision for any settlement with him. This was evidently not displeasing to the State Department, for when Knox wrote to the Senate Foreign Relations Committee on March 18 to tell it about the new plan he pointed out that the omission of any reference to the railroad and wharf concessions would remove one of the objections that had been raised to the Morgan contract.[58] The legal officers in the State Department had apparently by this time come to have doubts about the validity of Valentine's possession of the railroad, because his lease had never been approved by the Honduran congress.[59] Dávila had permitted him to operate the line while the Morgan loan negotiations were going on, but the new government refused to continue the arrangement.

The State Department consequently took no very vigorous action when Bonilla seized the railroad in February 1912. It urged the Honduran government to respect Valentine's rights,[60] but an American naval officer who attempted to prevent the seizure was ordered not to interfere.[61] The State Department gave Valentine somewhat more support in his efforts to obtain compensation when Bonilla canceled his wharf concession later in 1912.[62]

[56] Foreign Relations, 1912, p. 609.
[57] Latin American Division memorandum of Feb. 3, 1912, 815.51/324.
[58] Foreign Relations, 1912, p. 610.
[59] See J. R. Clark's memorandum of May 25, 1912, 815.77/130.
[60] Telegram to Tegucigalpa, Feb. 5, 1912, 815.77/78.
[61] 815.77/82, 89.
[62] Most of the correspondence about the railroad and the wharf in 1912 is printed in Foreign Relations, 1913, pp. 594ff.

In the meantime there was little progress in the loan negotiations. The bankers made the acceptance of their project less probable when they decided to tie it to the pending loan treaty, for Bonilla had repeatedly indicated to the local press in Honduras that he opposed the establishment of a customs collectorship. On April 13, 1912, in reply to an inquiry from the State Department, Bonilla said that he regarded the treaty's rejection by the Honduran congress as final, though he added that he was disposed to "make a loan convention, since a large loan is necessary but cannot be made except under such a guarantee." [63] The failure of the United States Senate's Foreign Relations Committee to report the treaty, in May, practically ended hope for its ratification by either government. The New Orleans group nevertheless continued their efforts, and in June Zemurray and his associates discussed with the State Department a proposal under which the loans would be made without establishing a customs collectorship. Bonilla, they reported, was willing to accept an arrangement by which any differences arising under the loan contracts would be submitted to an arbitral board headed by the Chief Justice of the United States Supreme Court.[64] The State Department raised no objection to this idea, but nothing came of it.

Early in June 1912, the government of El Salvador came forward with an offer of financial assistance to Honduras. President Araujo had for some time been scheming to unite El Salvador and Honduras, and perhaps Nicaragua, under his own leadership. He had discussed his idea with Knox during the latter's visit to Central America, and had suggested that the combined state might be able to obtain a loan that would take care of the Honduran debt. The Secretary had expressed interest but had been noncommital.[65] It was reported, without confirmation, that the money Araujo now offered would come from financiers in the Argentine Republic.[66] Minister White reported that a similar offer was being made to the government of Nicaragua. Neither the Honduran government nor the Nicaraguan government seems to have taken the proposal very seriously.

[63] *Foreign Relations, 1912*, p. 611. For the Department's inquiry, see 815.51/332.
[64] *Ibid.*, p. 615.
[65] Doyle to Wilson, June 28, 1912, 813.00/788.
[66] White to Knox, June 13, 1912, 815.51/341.

The State Department seemed definitely less enthusiastic about the New Orleans project after its backers discarded the idea of a customs collectorship, and it was still less disposed to support a plan which Minor Keith of the United Fruit Company proposed in the last weeks of the Taft administration. The plan was to settle the British debt partly with funds obtained from new taxes and partly by using a sum of $25,000–$50,000 each year which Keith promised to furnish in return for the cession to his company of the wharf and the railroad at Puerto Cortés. The American Consul at Puerto Cortés thought that such an agreement would cause disorder on the north coast, where the United Fruit Company was extremely unpopular, and the American Minister thought that it would be disadvantageous to Honduras.[67] As the Minister later pointed out, the United Fruit Company had already bought the railroad from Trujillo into the interior and Keith had recently obtained a concession to extend his Pan American railroad across southern Honduras from the Salvadorean to the Nicaraguan border, so that the possession of the Puerto Cortés line would enable him to dominate the whole country.[68] The State Department, on February 28, authorized the Minister "very discreetly and informally to discourage" the project on the ground that it would probably cause discontent among American residents in Honduras and might "even possibly cause injury to some Americans who already have vested rights." [69] The Minister did not have to act on this instruction because Bonilla's death diminished the Fruit Company's influence in the Honduran government.

The Refunding Loans in Costa Rica

In defending the Honduran treaty, Knox told the Senate Foreign Relations Committee, in May 1911, that he proposed "to make American capital the instrumentality to secure financial stability, and hence prosperity and peace, to the more backward Republics in the neighborhood of the Panama Canal." He said, however, that "such a degree of intimacy" as was involved in the proposed treaties with Honduras and Nicaragua would not be necessary in most of

[67] Consul Myers to the Secretary of State, Feb. 19, 1913, 815.77/166; White to Knox, Jan. 14, 1913, 815.77/164.
[68] White to Byran, March 5, 1913, 815.77/169.
[69] 815.77/166.

the other Caribbean republics. One of the countries that Knox probably had in mind, though it could hardly be called a backward country in 1911, was Costa Rica.

Costa Rica was the best governed of the Central American states, but its treatment of its foreign bondholders had been no better than its neighbors'. Its foreign debt went back to two loans issued in London in 1871 and 1872, which had almost immediately gone into default. Minor Keith, when he was seeking capital for his railroad projects, had arranged a refunding in 1885, but there had been further defaults, followed by settlements in which the bondholders in each case accepted a reduction in their claims. Payments had ceased again in 1901. By 1910 the amount of the debt, with arrears of interest, was about $15,000,000. As in the other Central American debtor states, the London Council of Foreign Bondholders, supported by the British government, had been insistently demanding a settlement.

James Speyer of New York negotiated a contract in 1909 under which the debt would have been refunded by a new bond issue of $13,250,000. The State Department took a friendly though not very active interest in this project, but it was opposed in Costa Rica because Speyer insisted on a provision authorizing the Secretary of the Treasury of the United States to appoint an agent to collect the pledged revenues in case of default. When it came before the Costa Rican congress in September 1909, the prominent political leader Ricardo Jiménez opposed it in what Merry described as an "anti-American" speech, and the contract was rejected.[70]

After Jiménez became President in 1910, Minor Keith negotiated a loan for £2,000,000 on terms that were more acceptable to the government. The British bondholders were asked to take a further reduction in their principal, and the interest rate was fixed at 4 percent for ten years and 5 percent thereafter. The loan would be secured by a first lien on the customs, and in case of default the American bankers would have the right to appoint a customs agency to sell certificates that must be used in paying customs duties. Keith would profit from the transaction through the refunding of a substantial amount of internal Costa Rican bonds which he owned and probably also by a generous allowance for expenses.

[70] For the correspondence on this contract, see Num. Case 8642.

Before the contract went to the Costa Rican congress, Keith's lawyers submitted it to the State Department, saying that the American government's approval would be helpful in persuading the British bondholders to accept an exchange. Speyer was said to be willing to participate and to conduct the necessary negotiations with the British. Under earlier administrations, the Department would probably have considered it improper to express an opinion about a business transaction of this sort, but Knox and his advisers had already departed from precedent in the case of the recent loan to Haiti,[71] evidently because they felt that the new relationship that they were establishing with the Caribbean states imposed a duty to see that these states did not make major mistakes in their dealings with foreign bankers. The Costa Rican contract was consequently referred to Charles B. Conant, the economist who was later employed to prepare the program for monetary reform in Nicaragua.

"The Department," Adee wrote Conant, "desires to ascertain from an expert financial point of view the real meaning and effect of this contract, and whether it appears to be fair and reasonable as regards the Government and people of Costa Rica, as well as in no way detrimental to American interests." Apparently Conant or the Department suggested several minor changes, which were accepted, and when Conant gave the Department a favorable opinion Adee wrote Keith's representative that the contract seemed "unobjectionable" and that the Department thought that the rehabilitation of Costa Rica's finances would be good for Costa Rica and for the United States. He stipulated, however, that the intermediary appointed to receive the money for the service of the bonds in Costa Rica, and the customs agent to be appointed in case of default, "should always be a responsible American citizen approved by this Department."

The Costa Rican congress approved the contract in February 1911, but with an amendment that would give the Minister of Finance somewhat more control over the customs agency that was to be set up in the event of default. This brought forth a protest from the British Council of Foreign Bondholders, which took the occasion to complain to the State Department about the treatment

[71] The Haitian loan will be discussed below.

it had received from American bankers in recent negotiations with several Latin American states. The Department, however, declined to express an opinion about the amendment, and the refunding operation was carried out.

Keith was less successful in 1911 in an effort to arrange a loan for the refunding of the Costa Rican internal debt. The State Department approved his project but there was a disagreement as to the way in which the liquor revenues, which were to be pledged for the service, would be administered in case of default. The National City Bank, which was to sell the bonds, insisted that it be given possession of the distilleries if a default occurred—a provision which Keith's advisers considered unnecessary and which was unacceptable to the Costa Rican congress. Apparently there were some officers in the State Department who hoped that this requirement might be withdrawn, but Knox personally directed that no effort be made to influence the Bank's decision. Later in 1911, consequently, a contract for the loan was signed with a French group.[72]

The Failure of Dollar Diplomacy in Guatemala

Another country where unpaid debts seemed likely to cause diplomatic complications was Guatemala. The Guatemalan debt dated back to a British loan made to the Central American Federal Republic soon after independence, and it had been increased by a small issue sold at 70½ percent of face value in 1869. The original bonds had been repeatedly refunded and scaled down, but there had been only a few short periods in the republic's history when the bondholders had received interest on them. Under a refunding operation in 1895, the government created a new coffee export tax which was specifically and irrevocably pledged to the bondholders, but Estrada Cabrera repeatedly violated the contract by reducing the tax or diverting the receipts to other uses. In 1901–1902, diplomatic pressure from several European governments, backed by a threat of force, compelled him to make new promises, which were soon broken.

Despite this unsavory record, several American bankers were interested in floating a loan for Guatemala. J. and W. Seligman and Company, who were later to be involved in Nicaragua, prepared a

[72] The correspondence about the Costa Rican loans is in 818.51/19–58.

plan for refunding the foreign debt and refunding the currency in 1906, but held it in abeyance until market conditions should make it possible to sell bonds. In 1909 they revived this project, working with Adolfo Stahl, an American banker in Guatemala City, who for years had had dubious financial dealings with Estrada Cabrera. At about the same time Minor Keith presented a separate project in connection with his efforts to consolidate and extend Guatemala's railway system. James Speyer was at first associated with Keith but early in 1910 joined the Seligman group. A third project was presented by the Windsor Trust Company and William Sulzer, who was interested in a mining concession in Guatemala.

None of the three groups seems to have given the State Department much information about its negotiations or to have sought any assistance. The State Department learned, however, that both the Seligman and the Keith plans contemplated at least a minor participation by the United States government in the collection of the pledged revenues in case of default, and in February 1910, when its plans for financial reform in Honduras and Nicaragua were beginning to take shape, the Department decided to ask that it be consulted about the Guatemalan projects. In letters to all of the bankers involved, Knox wrote that the United States government was much interested in the proposed loan, especially as it understood that the plan was to give it some relation to the security of the loan. He took occasion to state, "categorically and once for all," that the United States would give no support at a later time to any syndicate making a loan unless it were convinced, after examining the terms, that the arrangement was equitable and beneficial and protected American vested interests in Guatemala, but he said that the State Department would be glad to see the loan made, and he suggested a meeting of those interested.

Keith's representative accepted this invitation, but the other bankers declined on various pretexts. They probably knew that any appearance of a connection with the State Department would make their negotiations more difficult in Guatemala, and they were perhaps unwilling to admit the State Department's right to scrutinize and demand changes in their projects. Despite the bankers' attitude, Minister Sands at Guatemala City was instructed to tell Estrada Cabrera that the United States would view a financial arrangement with an American syndicate with special favor but would discourage one with a European syndicate.[73] The President replied that he would make a loan with an American syndicate if it offered favorable conditions, but that he considered the proposals then before him "onerous." [74]

Estrada Cabrera was suspicious of all foreigners, and he apparently distrusted the local representatives of Seligman and the Windsor Trust Company, who were carrying on a scurrilous campaign against each other through subsidized newspapers and resorting to other practices that did not raise American prestige. On the other hand, Sands thought, he was unwilling to increase Keith's already great financial influence in Guatemala.[75] In July 1910, when the President submitted the loan projects to his subservient congress, and a committee reported adversely on all three, it was clear that he did not intend to proceed with them.

During the next eighteen months the negotiations made little progress, though the State Department reiterated its interest in them and its complete neutrality as between the competing projects.[76] In the meantime the British Minister Sir Lionel Carden was pressing the Guatemalan government to resume service on the British bonds. Estrada Cabrera protracted the negotiations with his usual skill, but on January 1, 1912, Carden demanded that the pledged revenues be restored within thirty days. This was described as an ultimatum, but Estrada Cabrera avoided a showdown by telling the Minister that the government was working on a plan for the general rehabilitation of its finances and by promising to start direct negotiations with the British bondholders if the new arrangement were not concluded before the end of the forthcoming session of the National Assembly. At Washington, the State Department informed all the bankers of what had occurred and suggested that they take advantage of the opportunity which the situation presented.[77]

Both the Seligman group and Keith's representative wrote that they were already negotiating. Estrada Cabrera seemed by this time

[73] For the letter to the bankers and the instruction to Guatemala, see 814.51/55A.
[74] Sands to Knox, March 4, 1910, 814.51/62.
[75] Sands to Knox, Sept. 15, 1910, 814.51/106.
[76] Telegram of Oct. 29, 1910, 814.51/113.
[77] 814.51/150, 159.

to have decided to give preference to the Seligman plan, but he was still pretending to study the matter as the session of the assembly neared its end. On May 23, 1912, consequently, Knox told him, through his Minister at Washington and the Legation at Guatemala City, "that since January last the Government of Great Britain has assumed a firm attitude regarding a settlement of the claims of the British bondholders, and that unless steps be taken toward such financial reorganization within the period mentioned by the President of Guatemala this Government may find it impossible further to endeavor to dissuade the Government of Great Britain from adopting such means for the enforcement of its claims as under all the circumstances may be justifiable." Estrada Cabrera replied that he had nearly completed the examination of the various proposals but that the determination of the necessary changes in the most acceptable one would require sixty days. He promised to call a special session of the assembly when an agreement was reached.[78]

When three more months passed with no sign of progress the British government grew impatient. On August 28, it told the State Department that it was demanding that British claims against Guatemala be submitted to arbitration and asked that the United States support this demand.[79] The State Department made no immediate written reply, but two weeks later, after Wilson had talked roughly to the Guatemalan Minister about Guatemala's deceitful conduct,[80] it sent word to Estrada Cabrera that it would ask the British government to withhold its demand for arbitration for twenty days, to afford an opportunity to conclude an arrangement with American bankers. The British government consented to the delay, but at the same time said that it was not interested in any arrangement except one that would restore the coffee tax to the service of the bonds.[81] In other words, the British would not delay their demand for an immediate resumption of service pending a decision on a refunding plan.

Meanwhile, Estrada Cabrera was negotiating with the Seligman-Speyer group and was proposing several unacceptable amendments

[78] Both communications are printed in *Foreign Relations, 1912*, p. 500.
[79] *Ibid.*, p. 501.
[80] See Wilson's memorandum of Sept. 12, 1912, 814.51/187.
[81] Lord Bryce to the Acting Secretary of State, Sept. 29, 1912, *Foreign Relations, 1912*, p. 504.

to the proposed contract. The bankers consulted the State Department about one of these, which would have eliminated a provision giving the customs agency to be set up in case of default a right to invoke the protection of the United States, and were told that the Department deemed it advisable to retain the "American character" of the loan.[82] In October the situation in the Balkans was making the bankers themselves less enthusiastic. Nevertheless, the State Department continued to urge the British government to accept the idea of refunding the British bonds through the arrangement that the bankers were discussing, and at its suggestion the bankers, apparently for the first time, communicated the terms of a proposed settlement to the British Bondholders Council.[83]

The British government thought that the United States had promised to support its demand for arbitration if the twenty-day period expired without a settlement, and when Knox and Wilson failed to do so neither the Foreign Office nor the bondholders showed any further interest in the American project. The London Bondholders Council did not like the plan, because Estrada Cabrera had adamantly refused to make any provision for arrears of interest on the outstanding bonds, but it refused to discuss the plan with the American bankers on the ground that the matter was in the hands of the Foreign Office. The British government, as Lord Bryce wrote Knox on November 13, did not think that the plan offered a fair prospect for a satisfactory solution. The Ambassador referred to the Guatemalan government's failure to keep earlier promises and also to the British bondholders' disappointing experience with attempts to negotiate general settlements with other countries—presumably the Dominican Republic and Honduras and Costa Rica—and he urged that the United States support the demand for the restitution of the security pledged to the British bonds.[84]

Knox was still unwilling to abandon the refunding plan. The principal advantage that the United States hoped to obtain from it, presumably, was the elimination of unpaid European debts as a possible cause for foreign intervention in Guatemala, and it was the

[82] J. B. Wright's memorandum of Oct. 9, 1912, 814.51/184.
[83] This seems a fair inference from Wright's memorandum of Oct. 26, 1912, 814.51/191.
[84] *Foreign Relations, 1912*, p. 507.

political aspects of the project that Knox emphasized in his final efforts to obtain the British government's cooperation. On December 3, 1912, he wrote the British Ambassador that the United States had "the keenest interest" in the financial rehabilitation of Guatemala through the proposed loan and argued that the British bondholders would be better off under the new arrangement than if they simply obtained the restoration of the coffee tax. On the 6th, he instructed the American Ambassador at London to take the matter up with Sir Edward Grey, and to emphasize particularly "the fact that we have to deal with a general situation involving to a great extent the policy of this government towards a portion of the world where the influence of the United States must naturally be preëminent." The British government, however, insisted that the coffee tax be restored before any refunding operation was considered.[85]

On December 11 the Guatemalan Minister and the Speyer-Seligman group told the State Department that they had agreed on a contract and that the President would call a special session of the assembly to consider it.[86] Knox sent a copy of the agreement to London and instructed the Embassy to point out again that it offered the bondholders a better arrangement than they could hope to obtain by arbitration. The American Chargé d'Affaires was told to seek an interview with Sir Edward Grey and to urge him "to consider the question upon a broad basis of international policy," saying that "the Department considers that Great Britain should now show a fuller appreciation of this Government's deep and predominant interest in the region of the Caribbean." He was even to suggest discreetly "that the British government would doubtless be amazed if in some country correspondingly within a sphere of special British interest the Government of the United States should press arbitrarily for a specific solution of a question involving American citizens without any regard for the broad interests and policies of the State, in such a case Great Britain, in whose sphere of special interest the controversy had arisen." [87]

The Foreign Office nevertheless declined to urge the bondholders

---

[85] *Ibid.*, pp. 508ff.
[86] Wilson to Hitt, Dec. 11, 1912, 814.51/196.
[87] Knox to the Chargé d'Affaires in London, Jan. 7, 1913, *Foreign Relations, 1913*, p. 558.

to renounce their claims in return for a settlement which still had to be approved by the President and congress of Guatemala. It said that it was aware that neither "Guatemala in general," nor the President favored the proposed debt conversion and pointed out that the President for three and a half years had evaded accepting it. The British government was "bound to remember" how British bondholders had been induced to abandon an agreement that they had made with the President of Honduras, and had since received no payments at all. In reply to the State Department's allegation that the bondholders were now holding up the arrangement with Guatemala, the Foreign Office pointed out that for three and a half years the United States government had not thought it necessary to consult the wishes of the British bondholders at all. Under the circumstances, the British government would "have no option but to adopt such measures as may be best calculated to obtain satisfaction from the Guatemalan Government." [88]

While these exchanges were taking place, Estrada Cabrera was justifying British doubts of his good faith by urging new and unacceptable amendments to the loan contracts.[89] By January 29, the State Department and the bankers realized that the loan plan had been "killed at both ends," at Guatemala City and at London.[90] The American diplomatic representatives in both places suspected that uncertainty about the policy of the administration that was to take office at Washington in March had contributed to its defeat.[91] On February 7 Knox cabled the American Minister in Guatemala that the Department would take no further action for the time being.[92]

In May 1913, after Knox had left the State Department, a British cruiser appeared at Belize, and Sir Lionel Carden threatened to break off diplomatic relations if the coffee tax were not applied at once to the service of the bonds. Estrada Cabrera asked that the United States interpose its good offices, but then capitulated without waiting for a reply. He would have had little help from the

[88] Laughlin to Knox, Jan. 28, 1913. *Ibid.*, p. 565.
[89] Hitt to Knox, Jan. 25, 1913, 814.51/223; Feb. 4, 1913, 814.51/230.
[90] Note on letter from Strauss to Pierrepont, Jan. 29, 1913, 814.15/227.
[91] Hitt to Knox, Jan. 11, 1913, 814.51/215; Laughlin to Knox, Jan. 28, 1913, 814.51/225.
[92] *Foreign Relations, 1913,* p. 567.

United States if he had waited, for Bryan, apparently not fully understanding the situation, had instructed the Embassy in London merely to ask for a short delay which would give Guatemala time to arrange for payment. To the surprise of the American Chargé d'Affaires, the Guatemalan officials seemed quite cheerful about the matter after it was finally settled. While they asserted that they still hoped to arrange a loan from American bankers, it was evident that Estrada Cabrera had never really intended to accept any plan for financial reform. He had been able by playing off the British against the Americans to delay payments on the British debts for more than three years, and the agreement that he finally had to accept provided merely for the resumption of current interest payments and left the accrued arrears for further consideration.[93]

The Haitian Loan of 1910

While the Taft administration was promoting loans by American bankers in Central America as a means of assuring political stability and eliminating European political influence, it was also working in Haiti to block a loan project that would have given European bankers a large measure of control over that country's finances. The Haitian loan contracts of 1910 were the first step in a chain of events that led to the North American military occupation of Haiti five years later.

Haiti was different in many ways from its Spanish-speaking neighbors. In the eighteenth century the western end of Española had been a rich French plantation colony, where a small group of white planters and officials ruled over some hundreds of thousands of Negro slaves. France was unable to hold the country during the French Revolution and the Napoleonic wars, and practically all of the white inhabitants were exterminated in the savage fighting that started with a slave revolt in 1791 and went on with few intermissions until the Haitian leaders proclaimed the country's independence in 1804. The new state for many years had little contact with the outside world. France acknowledged its independence, in return for the promise of a large indemnity, but the United States did not recognize its government until 1862. The Haitians themselves were

[93] The important correspondence about the British ultimatum is printed in *Foreign Relations, 1913*, pp. 568–572.

distrustful of foreign influences, and successive constitutions forbade foreigners to own land in the country.

By 1900 there were nevertheless a number of foreigners resident at Port au Prince. The most influential were the French and the Germans. France was the principal market for Haitian coffee, and French bankers had floated the country's two external loans, in 1875 and 1896. French investors also controlled the National Bank, which was set up in 1881 to collect the principal revenues and to act as the government's depository and paying agent, an arrangement that facilitated the service of the foreign debt. The Haitian government took the "treasury service" from the Bank in 1905, after the discovery of large-scale frauds, but the Bank continued to collect certain revenues and to pay the service on the foreign debt. France also supplied the priests for the Haitian Church and most of the teachers in the schools which foreign religious orders maintained in several of the larger towns.

The Germans were for the most part merchants. Many of them were married to Haitians or, in the second generation, were the sons of Haitian mothers. They thus had close ties with the Haitian ruling class. The most important German group, which often posed as North American because some of its members were naturalized American citizens, owned the *Chemin de Fer de la Plaine du Cul-de-Sac*, the "P.C.S. Railroad," which ran from Port au Prince into the interior to the east and southwest. It also controlled the wharf, the electric company and the tramway at Port au Prince, and the electric company at Cape Haitian.

Most North Americans knew less about Haiti in 1909 than about the other Caribbean republics. Though disorder and conflicts with foreigners in Haiti were potentially as troublesome to the United States as in the other countries, the American government had not shown any very active interest in the country's problems. Roosevelt thought that American public opinion would oppose any intervention there.[94] Root realized that the Haitians' intense distrust of foreigners would make them peculiarly suspicious of any attempt to interfere in their affairs, though he hoped that the "psychological moment" to offer help might eventually arrive.[95] The American Min-

---

[94] Roosevelt to William Bayard Hale, Dec. 3, 1908, *Letters*, Vol. VI, p. 1408.
[95] Jessup, *Root*, Vol. I, p. 555.

ister at Port au Prince in 1909 was Dr. Henry Watson Furniss, a Negro physician educated at Howard University and Harvard, who had served for several years as American Consul at Bahia before replacing Minister Powell in 1905.

The American government's attitude changed after 1909. Just before the inauguration of the Taft administration, the French-controlled National Bank, which had had much trouble under the preceding administration, sought to persuade President Simon to restore the treasury service, in return for financial assistance. Under the proposed contract the Bank would collect practically all of the customs revenues. Furniss thought that this would give it an influence that would be "contrary to the spirit of the Monroe Doctrine," and Secretary of State Bacon authorized the Minister to say that the American government would regard the arrangement with concern.[96] Evidently the proposals seemed equally objectionable to the Haitian government, for they were not accepted, in spite of the active efforts of the French Minister. A few months later, however, a bank scheme that seemed equally open to objections was being urged on Haiti by both the French and the German Legations.

The scheme seems to have originated with the German Minister at Port au Prince, who took advantage of his home leave in the summer of 1909 to discuss with some powerful German financial institutions a project for a loan to Haiti, in return for which they would receive a concession for a new national bank. The German financiers were interested, but it was necessary to enlist the cooperation of French interests because France was the only likely market for the bonds of the proposed loan. Apparently they also thought it wise to attempt to avoid opposition from the United States, and to this end they offered a participation to Hallgarten and Company and Ladenburg Thalmann and Company, two firms in New York which had intimate connections with banks in Germany. Hallgarten's representative called at the State Department on September 14, 1909, with letters of introduction from J. P. Morgan and the First National Bank of New York, and discussed the possibility of a loan secured by a customs collectorship. Adee gave him "what informa-

<hr>

[96] Furniss to Bacon, Feb. 3 and Feb. 5, 1909, and Bacon to Furniss, Feb. 23, 1909, Num. Case 874/23–4, 31–2.

tion I could," but told him that a "Dominicanoid treaty was quite out of the question just now." [97]

In November, Furniss reported that the new group was proposing to set up a National Bank in which the Germans would hold 50 percent of the stock and the French and Americans each 25 percent. The bank would take over the treasury service and collect the customs, and the charter of the existing National Bank would be canceled unless its owners accepted the new group's terms. Furniss thought that the Haitians would never give up the control of their customs administration, but since the plan would imperil Haiti's sovereignty and raise questions connected with the Monroe Doctrine he intended to oppose it in accord with the instructions he had received in February. The State Department approved his action.[98] Knox made his views more explicit in a confidential letter in June 1910, when a representative of the National City Bank of New York asked whether the State Department would countenance the Franco-German plan for a loan to be secured by the collection of the customs by a commission representing French, German, and American interests. The United States, the Secretary said, would probably not favor this arrangement but would expect to control the customs itself, as in the Dominican Republic, with "subordinate representation of other interests." [99]

The National City Bank was interested in defeating the European plan because it was itself working on a project to set up a new bank in Haiti. It had joined with Speyer and Company of New York in making a loan of $800,000 to the P.C.S. Railroad early in 1909, and later in the same year the two firms had obtained a concession for a bank. As they were not entirely satisfied with the terms of the grant, they attempted to buy the concession of the existing National Bank, but could not reach an agreement with the French stockholders.[100] The two American firms do not seem to have pushed their project very actively in Haiti during the first six months of 1910, when the European group was busily promoting its own proj-

[97] Num. Case 874/52, 53, and Adee's memorandum of Sept. 21, 1909, Num. Case '2126/471.

[98] Furniss to Knox, Nov. 17, 1909, and the Department's reply of Dec. 24, Num. Case 874/62.

[99] Ailes to Knox, June 4, 1910, and Knox to Ailes, June 6, Num. Case 874/72.

[100] Speyer and Co. to the Secretary of State, Aug. 12, 1910, Num. Case 874/81.

ect, but in July they told the State Department that they were disposed to make a $12,500,000 loan to Haiti, secured by a customs collectorship controlled either by the United States or by a representative of the bankers. At their request, the Department asked the Embassy in Paris to see whether the bonds of such a loan could be listed on the Paris Bourse. The Embassy thought that the listing would be difficult if the National Bank of Haiti opposed it, but the American group nevertheless said that it was anxious to go ahead with its plans and asked the State Department's help.[101]

Up to this time, the State Department had opposed proposals for the control of Haiti's customs by European interests without giving diplomatic support, or being asked to give support, to the National City-Speyer group. There was some question of the propriety of helping this group when two other New York firms were interested in a rival project. It was also difficult to help the National City Bank and Speyer when they had not yet presented any definite proposition to the Haitian government. Nevertheless, Dawson commented in a memorandum written on August 12 that he and Furniss both felt that the State Department should support the National City Bank project in order to keep Haiti's finances out of German hands. Dawson questioned whether the banks connected with the German project were genuinely American.[102] On August 20 the Haitian government was told that the United States would expect to have an opportunity to assure itself in advance that any new financial arrangement was not detrimental to American interests, and that the United States would especially deplore any agreement with another group pending the outcome of negotiations with the American syndicate.[103]

This communication produced no visible result. A representative of Speyer and Company went to Port au Prince shortly afterward but apparently made no specific proposals. Furniss told the representative that there was no chance that the Haitian government would accept the American group's request for some measure of customs control, and the President of Haiti said that he was willing

---

[101] Num. Case 874/74, 81, 84.
[102] Num. Case 874/78.
[103] Aide Memoire to the Haitian Minister at Washington and cable to Port au Prince, Num. Case 874/120A.

to have a new bank established but that he planned to obtain a loan from the European group.[104] This group, meanwhile, had made a deal with the owners of the old National Bank, which in turn had obtained a satisfactory settlement of its disputes with the Haitian government. Early in September the Franco-German bank and loan contracts were before the Haitian congress.

The contracts provided that a reorganized National Bank would resume the treasury service, receiving all customs duties and disbursing them in accord with the contracts with the republic's various creditors. The bank would also have the sole right of note issue, and a part of the proceeds of the promised foreign loan would be set aside to retire Haiti's depreciated paper currency and replace it with the bank's notes. The arrangement would obviously impair Haiti's independence, and Furniss thought that the government's approval had been obtained by bribery and that intimidation was being used to force congressional approval.[105] Furniss, despite the protests of his French and German colleagues, earnestly pointed out to the Haitians the bad features of the contracts, and his representations were reinforced by messages from the State Department. President Simon promised to change some of the more objectionable provisions but took no definite action, even after the State Department authorized Furniss to say that the American government "would see conclusion of the bank and loan proposition . . . with such grave apprehension that it would be compelled to reserve all its rights for serious consideration in order to determine its future course of action." [106]

The State Department, meanwhile, asked financial experts in the Treasury and in the Bureau of Insular Affairs to make a detailed study of the contracts, and on October 12 it cabled Furniss that the United States must view with disfavor the collection of the customs duties by a French corporation because this might lead to European intervention in Haiti's political affairs. It also objected to monopolistic privileges granted to the National Bank and questioned the soundness and fairness of several provisions affecting the treasury service and the proposed currency reform. The government of Haiti, it said, would have no adequate voice in the man-

[104] Furniss to Knox, Aug. 27, 1910, 838.51/93.
[105] Furniss to Knox, Sept. 2 and Sept. 16, 1910, 838.51/97, 106.
[106] Sept. 27, 1909, 838.51/97.

agement of the bank. The loan contract was unfair because the bankers would take the bonds at a price of about 72, whereas the Dominican bonds had been issued at 98½. Finally, there was no adequate provision for the protection of American holders of Haitian internal bonds and unliquidated claims. The American government expressed entire disapproval of an arrangement "at the same time so detrimental to American interests, so derogatory to the sovereignty of Haiti, and so inequitable to the people of Haiti." [107] A paraphrase of the cable was sent to the German-American firms connected with the project, who had been questioning the propriety of Furniss' opposition to a project in which American interests were involved.

Despite the State Department's attitude, and despite a protest from the British government which objected to the granting of a monopoly to the National Bank and to the failure to make provision for British claims, a law approving the contracts, with only minor changes, was promulgated on October 26. The Franco-German group nevertheless seemed hesitant about proceeding in the face of the American government's opposition, which might well discourage prospective buyers of the new bonds. Ladenburg Thalmann and Company had approached the State Department on October 22 with a suggestion that the execution of the contracts might be delayed pending an effort to persuade the Department to withdraw its objections; and on November 9 they submitted a memorandum from their French associates arguing that the criticized portions of the bank contract merely reproduced the provisions of the existing concession and asserting that the prospective stockholders had no thought of asking for diplomatic intervention, because there was an arbitration clause in the contracts. About the same time, apparently, the Franco-German group offered the National City Bank and Speyer a participation in their project.

A statement by an official of the National City Bank, made twelve years later, gives the impression that Knox insisted on additional American participation in the contracts and arranged a meeting at which this participation was agreed to.[108] The story as it appears in the State Department's files makes it seem doubtful that this is ex-

---

[107] 838.51/119c.
[108] Testimony of Roger L. Farnham, *Hearings Before a Select Committee on Haiti and Santo Domingo, U. S. Senate, 67th Congress, 1st and 2nd Sessions*, Vol. I, p. 105.

actly what occurred. In October Counselor Hoyt was privately urging the National City Bank group to press their own projects so that Haiti would not be left without a loan if the State Department's opposition defeated the French plan.[109] The proposal that the American banks participate in the contracts which the Haitian government had already approved seems to have come originally from the Franco-German group. The American banks at first rejected it [110] but after some dickering reached an agreement. Under the new arrangement the French interests were to have a 50 percent participation and each of the other five interested banks—the National City, Speyer, Hallgarten, Ladenburg Thalmann, and the Berliner Handelsgesellschaft—a 10 percent participation in both the loan contract and the bank contract. To avoid the appearance of non-American control, however, the Berliner Handelsgesellschaft agreed to work in accord with the American group.[111]

The new arrangement seemed to lessen the possibility that Haiti's customhouses might come under European control, but it did not meet the State Department's other objections to the contracts. A representative of the National City Bank was told on November 18 that the Department had not yet modified its position in any way.[112] There was in fact a delay of several weeks, caused partly by the illness and death of Counselor Hoyt, before the Department was persuaded to withdraw its objections.

There was clearly much uncertainty and some difference of opinion about the propriety of opposing a private business transaction simply on the ground that it was disadvantageous to the Haitian government. J. Reuben Clark, the Assistant Solicitor, who drafted much of the correspondence on the matter, opposed the bank and loan contracts because he considered them unfair to Haiti, and he continued to oppose them after the American group became party to them.[113] Hoyt, too, felt that when such proposals were brought to the State Department's attention "we must pass upon them from the point of view of the rights and interest of the government in question and its people." He raised the question whether the De-

[109] Hoyt to Knox, Oct. 14, 1910, 838.51/198.
[110] Memorandum of Oct. 28, 1910, 838.51/147.
[111] Landenburg Thalmann to the State Department, No. 22, 1910, 838.51/180.
[112] Memorandum of Nov. 18, 1910, 838.51/174.
[113] See his memoranda of Jan. 4 and Jan. 9, 1911, 838.51/229.

partment should not also "inspect" the National City Bank's own project and the MacDonald railroad concession, which the National City Bank was financing, to make sure that they were not also unconscionable. He pointed out that some of the bankers in the Franco-German group claimed to be as American as the National City Bank.[114] Adee, on the other hand, "had misgivings" that the Department was "getting out of our depth" in its protests. He thought that the United States had a right to object to any discrimination against American interests but could not do more than offer kindly advice on such matters as the price of the bonds and the soundness of the plan for currency reform. He did not take seriously the idea that the bank contract might lead to French intervention.[115] None of the memoranda in the files suggest that the State Department's objections to the contracts would be met merely by giving American interests a larger participation.

The bankers argued that it was impracticable to insist on changes in contracts which had already been approved by the Haitian government and that the provisions of the bank contract were similar to those of the existing concession, which still had several years to run. Thus the real choice before the American government was between a bank completely controlled by French interests and one in which the American stockholders would have an equal voice. They argued further that the original participants in the Franco-German group were obligated to go ahead with the transaction whatever the attitude of the American government might be. Ladenburg Thalmann, in fact, signed a contract for an interim loan of $600,000 to Haiti on December 21, 1910. The National City Bank insisted that 72 was a fair price for the proposed 5 percent bonds because the outstanding 6 percent bonds were selling about par.

At a conference on January 9, 1911, the bankers apparently convinced even Clark that the State Department could not continue to oppose the contracts. The National City Bank and Ladenburg Thalmann assured the Department in a letter written the next day that the National Bank of Haiti would not collect the customs under the contract as amended and that it would have monopolistic privileges only with respect to the right of note issue and the treasury

[114] Hoyt to Knox, Oct. 14, 1910, 838.51/198.
[115] Memorandum to H. Wilson, Jan. 10, 1911, 838.51/215.

service. They promised to endeavor to see that American claims against Haiti were settled, and they indicated that they planned to take further steps for the development of Haiti with American capital. Furthermore they promised that the American group would maintain at least a 50-percent control and approximately a 50-percent participation in the National Bank. On January 11, Knox wrote the bankers and cabled Furniss that he no longer felt warranted in pressing his original objections to the contracts. He said, however, that the State Department did not waive its reservations as to the possible effect on American citizens and interests in Haiti, and that, while the contracts were perhaps as favorable as conditions in Haiti and the facts and circumstances permitted, he was not expressing a final opinion on them.[116]

It had clearly been a hard decision. Aside from the doubt as to the propriety of passing judgment on a private business transaction, it was difficult to determine whether the terms were fair or unfair in view of the risks involved in dealing with a country like Haiti. The contracts had desirable as well as undesirable features. It was better from a political standpoint that the National Bank should be at least partly controlled by Americans, and the restoration to the bank of the treasury service would protect Haiti's creditors and perhaps prevent controversies over foreign claims. The contemplated currency reform was much needed. On the other hand, both the treasury service and the currency reform would be inordinately profitable to the National Bank, if all went well, because the bank would collect a commission of 1 percent on money received for the government's account and ½ percent on sums disbursed, plus an additional ½ percent on payments in foreign countries. Furthermore it would replace the existing paper currency, at the government's expense, with its own not too adequately secured notes.

The bankers were to take the bonds of the new 65,000,000 franc loan at 72.3 percent of their face value. This promised a substantial profit, even after paying the bribes that the French press was said to exact for creating a favorable atmosphere in the market. The State Department suspected that some of the margin represented

---

[116] Knox to Furniss, Jan. 11, 1911, 838.51/203a; to the bankers, same date, 838.51/204.

graft to be paid in Haiti, and Clark, during the negotiations, obtained definite assurance from the National City Bank that no corruption was involved.[117] In March 1911, however, Furniss reported that the National Bank was paying large sums to high officials who had helped obtain approval for the contracts, and that some of the recipients had complained to him because they did not receive as much as they expected.[118] There was one report that President Simon and his associates would receive 5,000,000 francs in connection with the transaction.[119]

At first the new bank was managed by the same persons who had directed the old one, and Furniss reported that the principal officers were noticeably unfriendly to American interests; [120] but in August 1911, the National City Bank arranged to have a North American appointed as co-manager. Later this man became the local head of the National Bank, and Roger L. Farnham, a vice president of the National City Bank, became vice president of the Haitian institution. The control of the bank nevertheless continued for some years to be shared by two sets of owners, at New York and at Paris. This arrangement enabled each group to call on its government for support when trouble came; and a desire to avoid French intervention often made the American government more disposed to support the bank in its disputes with the Haitian authorities. The National City Bank continued to act as spokesman for the American group.

The National Railroad of Haiti

While the loan negotiations were going on, the National City Bank had also become interested in the projected National Railroad of Haiti. Its investment in this enterprise was to involve both the bank and the United States government in troublesome controversies for several years to come.

The concession for the National Railroad was obtained by an American promoter named J. P. MacDonald, who proposed to complete a line which had been begun but abandoned by other Ameri-

[117] See Clark's memorandum of May 13, 1911, 838.51/243.
[118] Furniss to Knox, March 31, 1911, 838.51/236.
[119] Latin American Division memorandum of Dec. 27, 1910, 838.00/513. See also Kelsey, *The American Intervention in Haiti and the Dominican Republic* (Annals of the American Academy of Political and Social Science, Vol. c, March 1922), p. 156.
[120] Furniss to Knox, Feb. 24, 1911, 838.51/231.

can investors. MacDonald offered to build lines from Port au Prince to Cape Haitian and from Gonaives to Hinche, serving most of the important towns in North and Central Haiti, if the Haitian government would help him to raise money by guaranteeing the service on bonds to be issued at the rate of $20,000 per kilometer of completed track. At the same time he asked that the government lease him all unoccupied public lands along the line and give him a monopoly of the exportation of bananas from the area north of Port au Prince. He promised that the export duty on bananas would cover the interest on the railroad bonds.[121] Furniss, apparently on his own initiative, vigorously supported the project. The German owners of the P.C.S. Railroad opposed it and financed newspaper articles playing up the danger of North American intervention,[122] but the Haitian government approved the contracts in July 1910. It was said in Haiti that President Simon's daughter, who was a powerful voodoo priestess, made the final decision for the government after MacDonald promised her an impressive string of pearls, which later turned out to be fake.[123]

Early in 1911 the National City Bank and Speyer formed a syndicate with W. R. Grace and Company and the Ethelburga Syndicate of London to finance the construction of the railway. The syndicate provided $2,000,000 in working capital and made arrangements in France to sell bonds, which would be issued with the Haitian government's guarantee as construction progressed. The bankers were not interested in the concession for growing bananas, and since MacDonald could not finance it the Haitian government was disappointed in its hope that export taxes on bananas would help it to meet its guarantee of interest on the bonds. MacDonald was soon excluded from any active participation in the railroad project,[124] and the National City Bank represented the railroad company in its dealings with the Haitian and American governments from the time when construction began in 1911.

[121] There are copies of the contracts in Num. Case 21210.

[122] Furniss to Knox, Aug. 14, 1909, Num. Case 21210.

[123] One version of this story is told by Frederick Douglass in the *Political Science Quarterly*, June 1927, Vol. XLII, p. 380.

[124] For MacDonald's account of what happened, see his letter of Oct. 14, 1915, to the State Department. 838.77/126.

Bank and Railroad Problems, 1911–1913

Cincinnatus Leconte, a leader of the mulatto *élite,* ousted Simon in August 1911. This revolution, like many others, was financed by German merchants in Port au Prince, and its "battle-cry," as Furniss described it, was "Down with MacDonald." The movement began in the North, and when the army approached Port au Prince, the diplomatic corps was able to prevent fighting in the city so effectively that the commander of an American warship who had been authorized to establish a neutral zone there to protect foreigners considered it unnecessary to do so. A German warship, however, landed forty men. This action aroused the State Department's ever-present suspicion of German designs and intensified its apprehension that the new government would be unfriendly to American and French interests. Furniss was consequently instructed to delay recognition until he obtained assurances that American interests would be safeguarded and that American claims for damages during the revolution would be paid.[125]

Leconte promptly made the necessary promises and was recognized, but throughout his administration his relations with the American companies were colored by mutual suspicion and dislike. The fault perhaps, was not entirely his, for neither the National Bank nor the National Railroad were tactful or conciliatory in dealing with the problems that arose.

Relations with the bank were complicated by the latter's efforts to force the government to accept a more effective control over the collection of the customs. Under its concession, exporters and importers paid the customs duties into the bank, but the examination of the merchandise and the fixing of the amounts due were in the hands of Haitian officials whose honesty and efficiency was open to question. When Leconte came in, the French directors of the bank refused to give him the financial help that he desperately needed unless he agreed to change this situation. Their attitude forced the President to turn to his German friends, who lent him $400,000 on unconscionably onerous terms.[126]

The Paris directors renewed their demands when the govern-

[125] *Foreign Relations, 1911,* pp. 282–290. See also 838.00/625.
[126] For Furniss' reports on this, see 838.51/264–267.

ment again needed money in September 1911, but the American directors apparently did not support them. There was still some doubt whether Leconte would do business with the bank at all, but Furniss, with the State Department's support, was able to prevent another recourse to the Germans. The "budgetary convention," which was signed with the bank in October, provided that the bank would advance money each month for the government's current expenses, an arrangement that was necessary because a great number of agreements with the republic's creditors provided that the proceeds of specific revenues be set aside for the creditors' benefit. Since the bank withheld the pledged revenues each year until the service of each debt had been covered, nothing was available for budgetary expenses during the greater part of each twelve-month period.[127]

Shortly afterward, when Leconte again needed money, the Americans interested in the bank offered a loan on condition that the United States government be asked to reorganize the Haitian customs service. Farnham, who was sometimes over-optimistic, told the State Department that Leconte had agreed to ask the United States for help, not only in connection with the customs but in the reorganization of the army and the navy. The State Department was interested, but it insisted that any initiative must come from the Haitian government. Leconte rejected the bankers' proposal.[128] It seemed unlikely that the French directors in the bank were in accord with their American associates, because Furniss had reported in August that the French Minister at Port au Prince was said to have instructions to oppose any North American control of the customs unless French interests participated.[129]

Leconte was especially unfriendly to the National Railroad. The railroad was, in fact, generally unpopular in Haiti, partly, Furniss thought, because of the "rough character" of the Americans who directed the construction work.[130] The company was allowed to continue with the building of the line, but when the first section south from Cape Haitian was completed in June 1912, and the company

---

[127] 838.51/276, 279, 281, 284.
[128] Latin American Division memoranda of Dec. 27 and 28, 1911, 838.51/297, 298.
[129] Furniss to Knox, Aug. 19, 1911, 838.51/267.
[130] Furniss to Knox, June 5, 1912, 838.77/38.

asked the Haitian government to accept it, a commission packed by Leconte with known enemies of the railroad made an unfavorable report. The government consequently refused to guarantee the bonds which the syndicate had been selling in France to finance its work. This threatened to destroy the whole enterprise, and the State Department instructed Furniss to ask that the section be accepted.[131]

On August 8, 1912, just before this instruction was sent, Leconte was killed by an explosion in the presidential palace, and the congress hastily elected Tancrède Auguste to take his place. Furniss reported that the new President was "a strong man and pro-American" and that "the German clique has received a severe blow." [132] It seemed possible that the change in government might make it easier to settle the dispute about the railroad, but the company's truculent attitude, inspired by a belief that any concession to Haitian desires would invite further demands, made it difficult for Furniss to work out an agreement. The State Department, without assigning any reason for the delay, withheld recognition of the new administration while the matter was under discussion. Finally, Furniss' persistent efforts brought success; Auguste was recognized on September 24, and the Haitian government accepted the railroad section four days later. The company was nevertheless soon involved in new controversies which complicated Haitian-American relations after the Wilson administration took office.

New Troubles in the Dominican Republic

In defending his dollar diplomacy in Central America, Knox had repeatedly pointed to the Dominican Republic as an example of the benefits conferred by an American customs receivership. Referring to the treaty provision that authorized the United States to give any necessary protection to the Dominican customs service, he told the New York Bar Association in January 1911 that "just this potential safeguard, unexercised and without any undue interference on the part of the United States, has cured almost century-old evils." [133] The Secretary almost seemed to suggest that peace had

[131] Knox to Furniss, Aug. 10, 1912, 838.77/41.
[132] Telegrams of Aug. 8 and Aug. 10, 1912, 838.00/690, 692.
[133] Foreign Relations, 1912, p. 1091.

been attained simply by keeping the customhouses out of the hands of revolutionists. He perhaps did not fully realize that President Cáceres' ability and popularity were at least partly responsible, and he must have been deeply disappointed when the Dominican Republic was again convulsed by revolution in 1911–1912. The resurgence of disorder did not mean that the customs receivership had been a failure, but it showed that customs control was not a complete remedy for the troubles of the more backward Caribbean states.

There had been minor outbreaks of disorder while Cáceres was President, and in February 1911 ex-President Morales and Desiderio Arias had attempted to organize a full-scale *jimenista* revolt. This disturbed the State Department because it threatened to make less plausible the arguments for the ratification of the Honduras loan treaty. The movement collapsed, however, after Morales was arrested in Puerto Rico, where he had been openly recruiting forces, and after the *U.S.S. Petrel* was sent to Dominican waters with orders to prevent any revolutionary expedition from landing. The affair seems to have caused more alarm in Washington than in Santo Domingo.[134]

Real trouble began when Cáceres was murdered by political enemies in November 1911. The assassin and about thirty other persons were executed, and the ex-President's Cabinet assumed executive authority, but it soon became clear that Alfredo Victoria, the *comandante de armas* in the capital, intended to dominate the new government. Victoria, according to the American Minister, was a "reckless and brutal young man," who had been one of Cáceres' closest friends.[135] He was too young to become President himself, but he forced Velásquez, who was the leading candidate, to take asylum in the Haitian Legation and persuaded the congress, by bribery and intimidation, to elect his uncle, Eladio Victoria. The nephew continued to act as though he were the ruler of the country, and his arbitrary conduct angered the other leaders of the *horacista* party as well as the *jimenistas*.

By January 1912, insurgent bands under various leaders were operating in several provinces. The State Department warned the

---

[134] *Foreign Relations, 1911*, pp. 171–172, and 839.00/331, 339, 350, 375, 380.
[135] Russell to Knox, Nov. 28, 1911, 839.00/421.

revolutionists that it was the practice of the United States "to refuse to recognize any government resulting from a revolution unless it appears to represent the will of the people and to be able and willing to respond to its international obligations";[136] and when this seemed to have no effect it consulted the American Minister in April about the advisability of sending a commission to attempt a conciliation of the warring factions. The Minister, W. W. Russell, replied, rather vaguely, that the revolution would soon either collapse or break out again and that the insurgents' "sole grievance seems to be that they are out and want to get in."[137] He was then instructed to advise the Dominican government to "make friendly overtures to the leaders of the revolution with a view to some arrangement or understanding" and to say that the United States expected the Dominican government to "take immediate, proper and effective steps to meet the present crisis." The Dominican government replied that it had already offered "guarantees" to the rebels and that the movement was now practically suppressed.[138]

Desultory fighting nevertheless went on for nine months. No one group was strong enough to take control, and the government's forces made little real effort to restore order because the state of war gave their commanders attractive opportunities for personal profit.[139] The State Department grew increasingly concerned about the situation along the Haitian frontier, where the Haitian government was surreptitiously helping the rebels and had occupied a strip of territory that was in dispute between the two governments. This conduct was especially irritating because the United States had been endeavoring since January 1911 to bring about a settlement of the boundary dispute, and had obtained from both sides promises to maintain the status quo. The fact that several customhouses along the frontier had had to be closed because of the disorders was still more disturbing, because it raised questions about the duty of the United States to protect the customs service under the treaty of 1907.

[136] Foreign Relations, 1912, p. 341–342.
[137] Russell to Knox, April 15, 1912, 839.00/551.
[138] The State Department's instruction of April 24 and Russell's rather inadequate telegraphic summary of the Dominican reply are printed in Foreign Relations, 1912, pp. 346–348. For the text of the Dominican reply see 839.00/577.
[139] Foreign Relations, 1912, pp. 360, 363.

The State Department consequently asked Russell on September 14 what "further suggestions" he had "in regard to definitely curing the present deplorable situation in the Dominican Republic, and restoring it to a condition in accord with what this Government has expected of its policy under the convention?" The Minister's only concrete suggestion was that the frontier custom posts be forcibly reoccupied. He thought that this might lead to the "supremacy" of the Victoria administration, which was "extremely unpopular and very detrimental to the country," but the success of the revolutionary leaders would be "disastrous." Even some of Victoria's cabinet officers had intimated that "an effective intervention by our Government would be good for the country," and "intelligent Dominicans in general" felt "that they had a right to expect that under the convention the existing conditions would not have arisen." "Only complete control by our Government," the Minister concluded, "would permanently insure order and justice, but any degree of control would be beneficial; indeed, without our effective control, one administration here would be just as good as another. Once having landed men for protection of the customhouses, in accordance with our rights under the convention, we might be able to dictate a policy beneficial to the country. The main evils to be remedied are: the absolute subservience of the courts; forced recruiting for the army; wholesale imprisonment without trial; peculation of public funds." [140]

Wilson recommended to President Taft a somewhat less extreme course of action. He proposed in the first place that the United States lay down a provisional boundary line between Haiti and the Dominican Republic and enforce it by a border patrol under the customs service. There was some justification for this step because both of the governments involved had indicated their willingness to have a provisional line established.[141] He further proposed that the Dominican President be urged to remove Alfredo Victoria, who was now Minister of War, and his brother, who was in command of the army, and to decree an amnesty. The recommendations should be backed up by sending a warship with a landing force. If they

---

[140] *Ibid.*, pp. 365, 366.
[141] The Dominicans had done so on June 27 (738.3915/125), and the Haitians a few days later (738.3915/129).

produced no result Wilson thought that the United States would either have to "sit by and see its whole Dominican policy fail and carry with its failure the wreck of the broad policy pursued in Central America, or else enforce its demands by such measures as the breaking of diplomatic relations, the forcible protection of the customhouses, and perhaps the withholding of the customs revenues." [142]

The President approved, and on September 24 the Dominican and Haitian governments were told that the United States had decided to regard as the provisional *de facto* boundary line between the two countries the line shown on a map of the island prepared some years earlier by the War Department at Washington. The United States would instruct the Receiver General of Dominican Customs to set up a border patrol to see that the line was respected. On the same day, Brigadier General Frank McIntyre, the chief of the War Department's Bureau of Insular Affairs, and William T. S. Doyle, the chief of the Latin American Division in the State Department, were ordered to go to Santo Domingo as special commissioners. They were accompanied by 750 marines, who were to reopen and protect the frontier customhouses if their help were needed. [143]

The Haitian government acquiesced in the provisional boundary line, with reservations, [144] and the Dominican government seemed pleased that it had been established. The Dominican authorities also welcomed the arrival of the commissioners. [145] President Victoria accepted their suggestion that he retire in 1914, at the end of the term for which Cáceres had been elected, and that he proclaim an armistice. He at first refused to remove the Victoria brothers from their positions but agreed to do so after the commissioners presented their demand in a stiff formal note.

It soon became evident, however, that both of the President's nephews were still in positions of authority. Furthermore, in spite of the armistice, the government continued to make political arrests and the fighting in the interior did not stop. On October 26, the

[142] H. Wilson to the President, Sept. 19, 1912, 839.00/659a.
[143] *Foreign Relations, 1912*, pp. 366–370.
[144] Furniss to Knox, Oct. 10, 1912, *ibid.*, p. 370.
[145] McIntyre, in a personal letter to Walcutt on Oct. 8, 1912, discussed the attitude of the Dominican government on both matters, 839.00/760.

State Department suggested that Alfredo Victoria be forced to resign immediately. The War Minister offered to withdraw if an agreement could be reached with the revolutionists, but peace negotiations, carried on through the Archbishop of Santo Domingo, produced no result.

The commissioners finally decided that President Victoria himself must go. They told the President that they could give him no help in restoring order, and at the same time they began to apply financial pressure. The government, which did not receive its share of the customs collections until the end of each month, had been living hand to mouth between payments on daily advances from Santiago Michelena, the Puerto Rican banker with whom the customs receipts were deposited; and when the commissioners told Michelena that they could no longer approve these advances Victoria was left virtually penniless. On November 13, the commissioners recommended to the State Department that the customs receipts be withheld altogether if the President remained in office and the revolution continued. The Department's reply, approving the proposal, was delayed by a failure in the cable service, but the commissioners seem to have withheld the funds without waiting for it,[146] and on November 18 Victoria issued a decree convoking Congress to name his successor. He resigned on November 26.

In the negotiations with the rebels, it had appeared that many of them would be willing to accept Adolfo Nouel, the Archbishop of Santo Domingo, as provisional president. The commissioners, though they had avoided any participation in the negotiations, seem also to have reached the conclusion that Monsignor Nouel would be the most available and satisfactory candidate. When the Dominican congress elected him, on November 30, the fighting stopped and the commissioners returned to Washington. The marines, who had spent almost two months in extreme discomfort on board their transport, were also withdrawn.[147]

The commissioners seem to have handled a delicate task with tact and self-restraint, and it would perhaps have been difficult to find a better solution. The apparent alternatives were to intervene

[146] Sumner Welles in *Naboth's Vineyard* (New York, 1929), Vol. II, p. 697 and Luis F. Mejía in *De Lilís a Trujillo*, p. 89, both state that the funds were withheld.

[147] Much of the correspondence about the commissioners' mission is printed in *Foreign Relations, 1912*. Other papers are in file 839.00. For the commissioners' report to the Secretary of State, see 839.00/775.

by force, as Russell had recommended, or to leave the Dominicans to their own devices. General McIntyre, who had followed the Dominican situation closely while supervising the customs service, had also favored intervention but had apparently been told that President Taft was against it.[148] To let the Dominicans fight it out would have entailed much misery and possibly international complications, with little prospect that any of the factional leaders would be able to set up a stable government. The election of Archbishop Nouel, who was generally liked and respected, seemed to offer the best hope for the reestablishment of peace and the holding of a free election from which a stable government could emerge.

Unfortunately, too many of the Dominican leaders were not interested in peace and free elections. All of the principal political parties had been in revolt against Victoria, and the end of the war left several factional leaders in control of various sections of the country. These pretended to recognize the provisional government's authority, but they insisted on offices and money for themselves as the price of support, and the Archbishop's emotional aversion to the use of force made it difficult to control them. Efforts to placate them simply increased their insolence. Within a few days of his inauguration, Mgr. Nouel was ill from overwork and discouragement, and in spite of assurances of support from the United States government he sent his resignation to congress on December 15. Russell, with difficulty, persuaded him to withdraw it.

The *horacistas* gave the government less trouble after Vásquez publicly announced that he was withdrawing from politics for the time being and giving the administration his support, but the *jimenista* leader Desiderio Arias continued to control a large section of the North. Arias had not been a party to the agreement for the election of Nouel. He had stopped fighting when the *horacistas* did, but he showed little willingness to recognize the Provisional President's authority, and in the last days of January 1913, Mgr. Nouel felt compelled to go to Monte Cristi to treat with him and to concede many of his demands as the price for his nominal support.

Since Arias' demands and those of other potentially troublesome military leaders were principally financial, keeping the peace involved a heavy drain on the treasury, which was already in bad shape. The customs revenues had increased greatly since 1905, but

[148] See McIntyre's personal letters filed under 839.00/760.

expenditures had increased even more rapidly, especially during the ten months of civil war, when the Victoria government, as we have seen, had continually borrowed ahead against anticipated receipts. It had also misappropriated a large sum that had been made available for public works by selling to the sinking fund some of the undistributed bonds of the 1907 loan. Doyle and McIntyre had recognized that the government must have some emergency aid, and had urged that $1,000,000 of the unsold bonds of the 1907 loan be marketed to provide it with funds, but the State Department's lawyers questioned the legality of such an operation. The Department did, however, agree to permit the government to obtain a new loan of $1,500,000, provided that the disbursement of the funds were controlled by a North American official.

This condition reflected a growing realization that honest and efficient collection of the customs revenues would not ensure financial stability if a government was improvident and irresponsible in spending money. The State Department considered that the Dominicans' accumulation of current deficits violated Article III of the 1907 treaty, which forbade increases in the public debt without the consent of the United States, and it had cited the violation of the treaty as one of the principal reasons for sending the commissioners to Santo Domingo in September. In October, before Victoria resigned, Wilson had cabled the commissioners that the Department was convinced that the Dominican Republic should appoint an American financial adviser, not only to control the disbursement of the proceeds of any new loan but to audit all of the receipts and expenditures.[149] This proposal, which was not followed up at the time, was to be pressed more vigorously by the Wilson administration.

Several bankers were interested in the new loan, which would be secured by a second lien on the customs revenues. Russell seems to have discouraged Mgr. Nouel from dealing with the Royal Bank of Canada, which was one of the first to submit a proposal.[150] Competition between American bidders caused the State Department

---

[149] Telegram of Oct. 26, 1912, 839.00/688.

[150] We may infer this from Russell's statement that the Royal Bank would not cooperate with the United States, and the State Department's telegram to Russell saying that Jarvis would meet the Royal Bank's terms, 839.51/914.

some embarrassment. Samuel Jarvis, who had recently established the "National Bank" in Santo Domingo City, was the first to come forward, and at Russell's suggestion the Bureau of Insular Affairs in the War Department worked out with him what it considered a satisfactory contract. A few days later the National City Bank submitted a proposal, which, with a few changes, also seemed satisfactory. The State Department cabled both draft contracts to Russell, making it clear that it did so simply as an accommodation to the bankers, without expressing any preference between them. Further negotiations were carried on by the bankers' representatives in Santo Domingo. When the Dominican government accepted the National City Bank's proposition in January 1913, Jarvis protested, first claiming that his proposal was a better one and then complaining, in a telegram to President Taft, that the National City's bid had been submitted after his own confidential offer had been published and after "the supposed period for closing bids" had expired.[151]

The State Department, always sensitive to the charge of favoritism,[152] held up the whole matter for some weeks, although it knew that the Dominican government desperately needed the loan. On February 12 it told Jarvis that the calculations of the Bureau of Insular Affairs indicated that the National City proposition was somewhat more favorable to the Dominican government; but on February 19 it insisted that the decision be made by the Dominican government, so long as the proposed contract was not onerous or otherwise improper. The State Department said that it did not feel that it was necessary for it to interfere as between rival American bidders. The Dominicans signed the contract with the National City Bank on February 22, and the United States, after insisting on minor changes, gave its formal consent to the loan on March 1, three days before the Taft administration went out of office.[153]

The proceeds of the new $1,500,000 bond issue were to be used to pay back salaries and expenses caused by the recent war and were to be disbursed only with the approval of the Secretary of the

---

[151] 839.51/941, 952.
[152] The fear of being accused of favoritism in connection with the Dominican loan is evident in several memoranda and cables in file 839.51.
[153] 839.51/965–967.

American Legation and the General Receiver of Customs.[154] This procedure, which had been proposed by Mgr. Nouel himself,[155] did not assure an effective audit, but it would give the Provisional President some protection in his efforts to prevent misuse of the money. Unfortunately, it also led to friction and invited newspaper attacks that increased the suspicion and resentment with which many Dominicans regarded any American interference. The loan itself did not materially improve either the financial or the political situation.

Mgr. Nouel felt that there was little hope for peace unless the United States would help to control the election of his successor and to establish "a government expressing the will of the people," and he asked Knox, through the American Minister, for a statement indicating that the United States would take such action if disorders recurred. Knox replied on January 22 with an expression of sympathetic interest in the Provisional President's effort to maintain peace and a warning that a recurrence of disorder would "make more onerous the duty of the United States under its conventional and moral obligations never to be indifferent to the peace and order of the Dominican Republic." At the same time Knox instructed Russell to point out informally the need for reforms in the electoral law and in some of the other laws that made electoral abuses possible.[156]

The Archbishop published Knox's statement, but his reply suggested that its tenor had disturbed him. He was "touched" by the "generous interest" of the American government and people, but he trusted that "the occasion may not arise for the Government of the United States to fulfill in a manner painful to the Dominican people its moral obligations and those imposed by the Convention of 1907." [157] The thought that he might find himself in the position of asking foreign intervention perhaps contributed to the Archbishop's growing disgust with his task, which he was to abandon soon after the advent of the Wilson administration.

[154] The text of the law authorizing the loan was enclosed with Russell's despatch of Jan. 4, 1913, 839.51/944.

[155] Russell to Knox, Dec. 16, 1912, 839.51/913.

[156] Knox to Russell, Jan. 22, 1913, *Foreign Relations, 1913*, p. 419.

[157] *Ibid.*, p. 420.

◄ 7 ►

The Military Occupation of the Dominican Republic

The Policy of the New Administration

🖉 It seemed reasonable to expect a radical change of policy in the Caribbean when Woodrow Wilson became President of the United States in 1913.[1] Foreign affairs had hardly been mentioned during the electoral campaign,[2] but for several years past the Democrats in the Senate had criticized the Republican administration's actions in the Caribbean and had opposed the treaties with the Dominican Republic, Honduras, and Nicaragua. William J. Bryan, the new Secretary of State, had publicly condemned dollar diplomacy.[3] Wilson had given no indication of his own views about Latin America, but his forcefully expressed liberalism seemed to promise that "imperialistic" policies would be abandoned. It would have been hard to foresee that his administration would go farther than any of its predecessors in intervening in the internal affairs of several Central American and West Indian republics.

We shall better understand what Wilson did in the Caribbean if we bear in mind what was happening during the same period in Mexico. Throughout his first term, continual civil war in that country created exasperating problems that occupied much of his time and had serious repercussions on relations with other countries and on domestic politics. His conflict with General Huerta, who seized power by treachery and was accused of the murder of his constitutionally elected predecessor, impressed on Wilson the evil aspects of tyranny and government by violence in Latin America. In April 1914, the dictator's conduct exasperated Wilson to the point where he ordered the navy to seize Vera Cruz, with the subsequent loss of some American and many Mexican lives. Huerta fell soon after-

---

[1] For a discussion of this expectation, which also expressed some shrewd doubts, see the anonymous article by "high Democratic authority" in the *Review of Reviews* (January 1913), Vol. XLVII, p. 83.

[2] R. S. Baker, *Woodrow Wilson, Life and Letters* (Garden City, 1922), Vol. IV, p. 56.

[3] Merle E. Curti, *Bryan and World Peace*, in *Smith College Studies in History*, Vol. XVI, Nos. 3–4, p. 140.

ward, but conditions in Mexico grew steadily worse. When North Americans and Europeans were robbed or murdered, Wilson was criticized at home and abroad for not intervening to restore order. In 1916, when Pancho Villa killed several persons on the American side of the border, he felt compelled to order General Pershing's rather futile invasion of northern Mexico.

One sinister aspect of the Mexican problem was the German effort to take advantage of the civil wars to make trouble for the United States. In 1915, German agents attempted to aid Huerta in organizing an invasion of Mexico from American soil. By fomenting a counter revolution, the agents could hope to create a situation which would make it more difficult for the American government to consider any intervention in the war in Europe, or even to install a friendly government which would permit the use of its territory for submarine bases. Huerta's arrest in Texas and his subsequent illness and death foiled the plot, but German efforts to fish in troubled waters in Mexico continued.[4] In 1917 these efforts culminated in the famous Zimmermann note, in which the Kaiser's government proposed a German-Japanese-Mexican alliance against the United States and offered to help Mexico recover New Mexico and California.

These events make it easier to understand Wilson's determination to impose political stability in the Caribbean. At a time when the United States faced the possibility of becoming involved in the war in Europe, disorder in Central America or the West Indies was almost as embarrassing and almost as dangerous to the security of the United States as disorder in Mexico. The American government was especially concerned about Haiti, where Germany had for some years openly opposed what the United States was trying to do, and the Dominican Republic, where the principal troublemakers were known to be pro-German. In 1915 Secretary Lansing wrote that German agents appeared to be working in Mexico and Haiti and Santo Domingo, and probably in other Latin American countries, to stir up trouble in the hemisphere which would prevent the United States from entering the war.[5]

---

[4] For an account of Huerta's activities, see George J. Rausch, Jr., "The Exile and Death of Victoriano Huerta," *Hispanic American Historical Review*, Vol. XLII, May 1962, p. 133.

[5] Lansing, "Notes," Vol. I, July 11, 1915, Library of Congress.

For Wilson, however, the improvement of political conditions in the Caribbean was by no means merely a matter of self-defense. Concern about hostile foreign influences was undoubtedly an important factor in his administration's policy, and particularly in his decision to intervene in the Dominican Republic, but most of the President's public statements gave more emphasis to his determination to promote constitutional government in the Americas. He considered that the United States had a moral duty to promote democratic government in the countries that lay within its sphere of influence. With little understanding of the political traditions and social conditions that made the immediate establishment of constitutional government impossible in many of the Latin American republics, Wilson attributed their troubles chiefly to the selfishness of bad men. "We can have no sympathy," he said in his first formal statement of Latin American policy, "with those who seek to seize the power of government to advance their own personal interests or ambition." [6] Some months later, in a message to Congress, he declared that "we are the friends of constitutional government in America; we are more than its friends, we are its champions." [7] He told a visiting British statesman: "I am going to teach the South American republics to elect good men!" [8]

Wilson was the more determined to oppose revolutionary activity and dictatorship in Middle America because he thought that these evils were made worse by European and North American economic interests that exploited political weakness for selfish purposes. He indicated his disapproval of dollar diplomacy anywhere in the world two weeks after his inauguration when he refused to approve further participation by American bankers in the proposed six-power loan to China, which the Taft administration had promoted. In his famous speech at Mobile, on October 27, 1913, he condemned foreign economic exploitation in Latin America:

"You hear of 'concessions' to foreign capitalists in Latin America. You do not hear of concessions to foreign capitalists in the United States. They are not granted concessions. They are invited to make investments. The work is ours, though they are welcome to invest in it. We do not ask them to supply the capital and do the work. It

[6] Circular telegram of March 12, 1913, *Foreign Relations, 1913*, p. 7.
[7] Message to Congress, December 1913.
[8] *Life and Letters of Walter H. Page* (Garden City, 1922), Vol. i, p. 204.

is an invitation, not a privilege; and States that are obliged, because their territory does not lie within the main field of modern enterprise and action, to grant concessions, are in this condition, that foreign interests are apt to dominate their domestic affairs, a condition of affairs always dangerous and apt to become intolerable. . . . The Latin American States . . . have had harder bargains driven with them in the matter of loans than any other peoples in the world. Interest has been exacted of them that was not exacted of anybody else, because the risk was said to be greater; and then securities were taken that destroyed the risk—an admirable arrangement for those who were forcing the terms!"

The President told his hearers that the United States would help the Latin Americans to emancipate themselves from these conditions, and that "we must show ourselves friends by comprehending their interest whether its squares with our own interest or not." The United States, he said, "will never again seek one additional foot of territory by conquest." [9]

One might question the accuracy of the picture that the President presented, for concessions, however iniquitous they might be in specific cases, were insisted upon by the Latin American governments themselves as a prerequisite to engaging in many sorts of business enterprises. Probably, too, few holders of Latin American bonds, after their painful experience with recurrent defaults, would have agreed with his remarks about the loans. The Mobile speech nevertheless seemed to Latin Americans a convincing statement of an enlightened policy. Its chief importance, perhaps, lay in the fact that the President's eloquence and evident sincerity convinced many people who had been skeptical when other American statesmen, probably with equal sincerity, had repudiated any idea that the United States sought to acquire additional territory or to obtain special advantages for private American interests in the Caribbean.

The objectives which Wilson sought to obtain in the Caribbean were in fact not very different from his predecessors', and his policy, in practice, was essentially a continuation of theirs. In his efforts to promote stable government and economic progress, he met the same obstacles and attempted to overcome them by much the same methods. Secretary of State Bryan, in the first months of the

[9] For the text of the Mobile speech, see *Congressional Record*, Vol. L, p. 5845.

new administration, attempted to introduce some new methods, but with little success. Even in the matter of dollar diplomacy there was no real change of policy; the new administration continued, however reluctantly, to work with and through American bankers for the achievement of its own purposes in Haiti and Nicaragua.

The Wilson administration did carry considerably farther the Taft administration's efforts for peace and economic progress in countries that were particularly disorderly. It had become clear by 1913 that a foreign customs collectorship would not by itself assure progress toward good government; and after some months of attempting to cope with troublesome situations in the Dominican Republic and Haiti Wilson and his advisers reached the conclusion that there must also be some control over expenditures and a reorganization of the armed forces to make them an element for stability instead of a constant danger to peace. They consequently demanded the appointment of American financial advisers and the creation of American-controlled constabularies. When these demands were resisted, and increasingly chaotic conditions frustrated their efforts to maintain peace, they resorted to armed intervention.

In general the problems of the smaller Caribbean states seem to have received less attention from the President than those in Mexico, which he handled himself. The President was consulted about important decisions, but the State Department dealt with the questions that rose from day to day, and it thus had the primary responsibility for the formulation of policy. Secretary Bryan, as the record shows, personally took over the handling of many important matters, but his frequent absences from Washington and his rather unsystematic ways of doing business were obstacles to his effectiveness. Under Bryan, in the first years of the administration, the chief responsibility fell on Boaz Long, the new chief of the Latin American Division, who was a newcomer to the State Department but had had some business experience in Mexico and spoke Spanish. Except for the veteran A. A. Adee, there was a complete change in the policy-making officers in the Department.

There was an equally complete change in the American diplomatic representation in the Caribbean, and not a change for the better. Wilson overruled Bryan's attempt to reintroduce the spoils system into the consular service and insisted on selecting able men for the larger diplomatic posts,[10] but he left appointments in smaller countries to the Secretary of State. Since the latter's chief concern was to provide jobs for deserving Democrats and to distribute them equitably among the states,[11] nearly all of the new chiefs of mission in the West Indies and Central America were politicians who had had no experience in diplomacy or in Latin America. Nearly all were incompetent and some had personal failings that soon made their removal necessary. Such appointments were disastrous at a time when the United States was assuming greater and greater responsibilities in the Caribbean.

Resurgent Disorder in the Dominican Republic

The development of President Wilson's policy in the Caribbean is perhaps best illustrated by the events in the Dominican Republic.

In March 1913, Archbishop Nouel, who had been made provisional president when the Victoria regime was ousted, was clearly about to give up his thankless task. He had been unable to maintain order or to cope with the exactions of the local *caudillos* who ruled many sections of the Republic. The American Chargé d'Affaires reported on March 14 that Nouel's resignation was expected at any time. President Wilson's cabled plea that he remain in office brought only a noncommittal response,[12] and before the end of March he resigned and sailed for Europe.

The congress again had to choose a provisional president. Federico Velásquez was one of the strongest candidates, but some of the other leaders announced that they would resist his election by force and held several hundred armed men in the suburbs ready to march into the capital if congress disregarded their warning.[13] Juan Isidro Jiménez withdrew his own candidacy when it was clear that he did not have enough votes to win, and Horacio Vásquez, the titular leader of the other principal political party, did not want the provisional presidency. Several ballots were necessary before José Bordas Valdés, whom Vásquez supported, was finally chosen, with the stipulation that elections for a constitutional president should take place within one year.

[10] Seymour, *Intimate Papers of Colonel House* (Boston, 1926–1928), Vol. I, p. 177.
[11] See Bryan's letter to Wilson, May 24, 1913, Bryan Papers, Library of Congress.
[12] *Foreign Relations, 1913*, p. 421.
[13] Curtis to Bryan, April 21, 1913, 839.00/840.

Bordas, who was inaugurated on April 14, was a professional soldier, fairly well educated, and reported to be a man of good character and high ideals.[14] His election seemed to meet with general approval. An attempted revolt by some of the *jimenista* leaders soon collapsed for lack of support. He had little more control over the provincial *caudillos* than the Archbishop had had, but for some months after his inauguration the country was relatively quiet.

During these months all of the principal American officials in the country, and many of their experienced and competent subordinates, were replaced by political appointees. In the customs service, Walter C. Vick, who had no special qualifications for the position, replaced Pulliam. The change was made without consulting the wishes of the Dominican government, which in fact urged that Pulliam be retained. It was to Vick that Bryan wrote his well-known letter of August 1913, which was published eighteen months later,[15] inquiring about other positions in the customs service "with which to reward deserving Democrats." Still more unfortunate was the choice of the new American Minister, James M. Sullivan, a lawyer-politician whose record, to say the least, was undistinguished. Sullivan wanted the position because the salary would enable him to pay his debts,[16] and his appointment seems to have been engineered by Samuel Jarvis, who had recently founded the so-called *Banco Nacional* of Santo Domingo. Ever since they had failed to get the contract for the $1,500,000 loan floated by the Nouel government, Jarvis and his associates had been carrying on a scurrilous campaign against the customs receivership and against some of the officers of the State Department, and the fact that they openly claimed credit for the new appointments in Santo Domingo did not help American prestige.

Though the country was relatively peaceful in the first months of Bordas' administration, there could be little hope that it would remain so. It was difficult for any of the principal political leaders to establish a stable government because none of them could command enough support. Horacio Vásquez and Juan Isidro Jiménez were still the nominal leaders of the two parties that had fought for power

[14] Secretary of Navy to Secretary of State, May 6, 1913, 839.00/842.

[15] New York *Times*, Jan. 15, 1915.

[16] *Santo Domingo Investigation. Copy of the Report, Findings and Opinion of James D. Phelan, Commissioner named by the Secretary of State, with the approval of the President, to investigate charges against the United States Minister to the Dominican Republic*, p. 7.

since 1899, but neither could count on the loyalty of all of the *caudillos* in his group. Though the *horacistas* had controlled the government since 1904, Vásquez had been at odds with Cáceres and had been in open revolt against Victoria. He had also opposed the rising influence of Federico Velásquez, whose administrative ability and reputation for honesty had given him a prestige in the party that made up for a lack of popular following. The *jimenistas* were more united because they were in the opposition, but their elderly chieftain, as events were soon to show, had little more control over his nominal followers than Vásquez had.

The real authority, outside of the capital, was in the hands of the local governors and military chieftains, many of whom had been virtually independent of the central government since the death of Cáceres. The establishment of the customs receivership had for a time strengthened the central government by keeping the revenues out of the hands of the local officials, but in recent years the provincial leaders had learned to finance themselves in other ways, by withholding the internal revenues from the national treasury and by many forms of graft and extortion, including blackmailing the central government by threats of revolt. The most powerful and dangerous of the local *caudillos* was Desiderio Arias, who during the next three years was to become the *bête noire* of Dominican politics in the eyes of the State Department.

Arias was nominally a follower of Jiménez, for whom he had once worked as an ox-cart driver. He had little education, but he was intelligent, sober, and frugal in his personal habits, and without the cruelty that often characterized Caribbean military leaders. He is said to have had little capacity for organization and little judgment in the selection of advisers, but he was a clever and tenacious guerrilla leader, with a large following in the northwestern province of Monte Cristi near the Haitian frontier. He was excessively generous with his friends, and seems to have distributed among them the large sums of money that he extorted from successive governments and from private individuals.[17] He was no less troublesome to Bordas than to Nouel. Relying on his possession of the government's best gunboat, which he had seized just before Bordas' election, he forced

---

[17] This description is based partly on Mejía, *De Lilís a Trujillo,* p. 113, and partly on various reports from American officials.

the Provisional President to accede to his demands for more money and for the control of the government in several provinces. The *horacistas* were especially irritated because some of these were in territory which they regarded as theirs.

The *horacistas'* resentment turned to exasperation when the government leased to a private individual the railroad line that ran from Puerto Plata into the interior. The successful bidder for the lease was a *jimenista* and presumably a representative of Arias, for no one else, as the American Chargé pointed out, would have contracted to pay the $130,000 which the government demanded. Arias could afford to assume the obligation because he knew that the government could not compel him to meet it.[18] Governor Céspedes of Puerto Plata, who had until then controlled the railroad line and used it to provide jobs and revenue for the *horacista* party, promptly started a revolution. The movement spread into several of the northern provinces, and on September 8 Horacio Vásquez proclaimed himself provisional president.

This was the first serious disturbance that had confronted the Wilson administration in the Caribbean and the first test of its announced policy of supporting constituted governments in the area. Three years later the officers of the State Department might have had more sympathy for rebels who were seeking to check Arias' rising power, but in September 1913 they saw only a rebellion against a properly elected provisional president who must be supported if the republic were not to sink again into anarchy. They seem to have obtained much of their information about the situation from Bordas' representative in Washington and to have acted, partly at least, on his advice.[19] Bryan at once instructed the American Chargé d'Affaires to communicate to Céspedes "the profound displeasure felt by this government at his pernicious revolutionary activity, for which this Government will not fail to fix the responsibility." [20] A few days later the Chargé was told to see that $300,000,

[18] Curtis to Bryan, Sept. 3, 1913, 839.00/880.
[19] This is apparent from Boaz Long's memoranda of Sept. 4 and Sept. 11, 839.00/-872, and from an undated memorandum from Bryan to the President, 839.00/961½, stating that a telegram, probably that of Sept. 12 mentioned below, was "prepared at the request of the Santo Domingo Chargé with a view to stopping a revolution that is starting over there."
[20] Bryan to Curtis, Sept. 4, 1913, *Foreign Relations, 1913*, p. 425.

which had recently been made available for public works by selling bonds of the 1908 loan, was spent entirely in territory controlled by Bordás.[21] The *U.S.S. Des Moines* was ordered to Puerto Plata to protect American lives and property.

Meanwhile Minister Sullivan was starting for his post with instructions that reiterated the American government's determination to support the lawful authorities and to discourage "any and all insurrectionary methods." The Minister was given a copy of the statement of policy for Latin America which Wilson had issued on March 11, which, as Bryan wrote, made clear: "First, that we can have no sympathy with those who seek to seize the power of government to advance their own personal interests or ambition; and, second, that the test of a republican form of government is to be found in its responsiveness to the will of the people. . . ."

The Minister was instructed to: "Say to any who may feel aggrieved or who may be disposed to resort to violence that the good offices of this Government can be counted upon at all times to assist in the establishment of justice, in the remedying of abuses, and in the promotion of the welfare of the people. We must depend, therefore, upon all the people of Santo Domingo, of whatever party or faction, to join together in securing justice through law and in the election by free and fair ballot of officials whom the people desire. You will make it known to those now in insurrection that this Government will employ every legitimate means to assist in the restoration of order and in the prevention of further insurrections, holding itself open at all times to advise with the government in behalf of those who feel that they have a grievance." [22]

On September 12, while Sullivan was still on his way to Santo Domingo, Bryan instructed the Legation to tell the revolutionists that the United States would not recognize a de facto government if the movement succeeded and would consequently withhold the government's share of the customs receipts. Furthermore, the United States would not consent to any increase of the Dominican debt to pay the expenses of revolutions and would look with disfavor on any tax increase for this purpose.[23] The State Department had

---

[21] Bryan tc Curtis, Sept. 6, 1913, 839.51/1091.
[22] *Foreign Relations, 1913*, pp. 425–426.
[23] *Ibid.*, p. 427.

realized that its consent to the use of the $1,500,000 loan to pay the expenses of both sides in the 1912 revolution had set a bad precedent.

Sullivan undertook his mission of peace-making with enthusiasm if not with discretion. Since his boat stopped at the northern ports before going to Santo Domingo, he talked first with the revolutionary leaders. In a series of flamboyant statements, he assured them and their followers that the United States would permit no more revolutions in Santo Domingo, and that they could rely on the American government to see that any wrongs were redressed. He reported to Washington that the revolutionists would lay down their arms if Céspedes was permitted to remain Governor of Puerto Plata and if Bordas promised to refrain from reprisals and to hold a fair election in the near future. He seems to have undertaken to have the Bordas government agree to these terms; but when he reached the capital he found that the President insisted on Céspedes' removal. Bordas was probably less, rather than more, inclined to make concessions when Sullivan assured him in writing that: "No revolutionary movement can prevail against you because the United States Government in the support of the integrity of your sovereignty will join hands with you in maintaining constitutional authority." [24]

Bordas, however, finally accepted a compromise by which another *horacista* would take Céspedes' place, and the American naval commanders and the consul at Puerto Plata were able to work out a peace treaty which some but not all of the rebel leaders accepted. Sullivan cabled on October 6: "The policy of the administration wins . . . Revolutionists yield to American declaration that force of arms can never again settle any question. It is agreed by all parties that the last civil war of the country is over. The revolutionists will rely on the assertion of our Government that a free ballot and fair elections will be insisted on." [25]

The Minister's jubilation was premature, because Céspedes had not agreed to the treaty. Four days later, Sullivan was reporting that "further negotiations would be worse than futile" and asking for instructions that would enable him to show the "malcontents" that the United States would use force if necessary to establish order.

[24] Sullivan to Bryan, Sept. 24, 1913, Enclosure 13, 839.00/911.
[25] 839.00/913. A part of the cable was printed in *Foreign Relations, 1913,* p. 432.

He wanted to take "the most drastic measures." [26] In another cable he announced his intention to advise the Dominican government to treat the rebel leaders as outlaws.[27] Bryan replied that it would be unwise to make threats but that the revolutionists should be told that "all the influence we can exert will be employed to support the Government against them." [28] Fortunately both Céspedes and Vásquez signed the peace treaty a few days later, and the war ended.

Consul Hathaway at Puerto Plata reported that the rebels had signed the treaty with the clear understanding that the United States would guarantee its execution.[29] The State Department does not seem to have specifically authorized its representatives to assume such a commitment, and it certainly did not fully appreciate what would be involved in enforcing the most important provision of the treaty, which stipulated that elections, first for a constituent assembly and then for a permanent president, should be completely free. Sullivan had to remind his superiors several times that the constituent assembly would be chosen on December 15 before Bryan asked him on November 21 how he thought that the American government's guarantee of a fair ballot could best be made effective. Sullivan in reply recommended a ". . . non-interfering scrutiny by open agents appointed by the Department at the principal towns and polling places upon whose joint report the Department will decide as to the validity of the constitutional election, the Dominican Government to be informed of our purpose with the assurance from us that unless the election of December 15 expresses the will of the people as a whole the American Government will take full control of the presidential election that follows." [30] The State Department was rather inclined to confine its action to giving good advice about electoral procedure, but Sullivan insisted that supervision was necessary, and barely two weeks before the election Bryan obtained Wilson's approval of the Minister's plan.[31]

When Bordas was told that the United States would send a com-

[26] *Foreign Relations, 1913*, p. 433.
[27] Sullivan to Bryan, undated, 839.00/920.
[28] Bryan to Sullivan, Oct. 13, 1913, *Foreign Relations, 1913*, p. 434.
[29] Hathaway to the Assistant Secretary of State, Oct. 31, 1913, 839.00/957.
[30] Sullivan to Bryan, Nov. 22, 1913, *Foreign Relations, 1913*, p. 435.
[31] Bryan to Wilson and Wilson's reply, Dec. 1, 1913, 839.00/1054.

mission to supervise the election, he objected vigorously, and Bryan and his advisers were tempted to drop the whole project. Boaz Long, the chief of the Latin American Division, had already expressed doubts about the efficacy of the proposed supervision and had suggested that the Department proceed with it only if it was requested by the opposition leaders, who, he thought, would hardly dare demand foreign interference of this sort.[32] President Wilson, however, thought that it would be better to go ahead, and he himself evidently drafted the telegram which was sent on December 7 instructing Sullivan to tell Bordas that the Department's representatives would go to the Dominican Republic, not as an official commission but ". . . only as individuals to lend by their presence moral support to the efforts that President Bordas has so freely pledged himself to make to keep the election free and uninfluenced in all respects, and in order that, if any question should arise as to the good faith of anyone concerned, undeniably impartial witnesses may be available."[33]

With the help of the Insular Government, the State Department hastily recruited twenty-nine "agents" in Puerto Rico to act as observers. To direct them, it appointed three commissioners—Hugh Gibson, J. H. Stabler, and F. A. Sterling—all young diplomats who were later to become prominent in the Foreign Service. The two groups arrived at Santo Domingo only three or four days before the election, and it was naturally impossible to give the agents any adequate preparation or instructions before they went out into the field.

Despite the bitter feeling between the contending factions, which had led to bloody clashes in Santo Domingo City followed by the arrest of many oppositionists, the election went off fairly well. The opposition parties withdrew from the contest in the capital after the first day of voting because the government arrested four more of their leaders on charges of conspiracy, but elsewhere the presence of the American observers had a good effect. The commission was on the whole satisfied with the result, and any doubts that the Department might have had were presumably allayed when Bordas

[32] Long to Bryan, Dec. 4, 1913. In file 839.00.
[33] Bryan to Sullivan, Dec. 7, 1913, *Foreign Relations, 1913*, p. 443.

promised to call a special session of Congress to consider complaints.[34] The opposition coalition, which included many of the *jimenistas,* as well as the *horacistas* and the *velasquistas,* seems to have won a majority of the seats in the constituent assembly.[35]

The American government's efforts for peace had thus far been successful, but it could be foreseen that the approaching presidential election would put the administration's policy to a more severe test. There could be little hope for a satisfactory election, even with North American observers present, if Bordas was free to use the methods that Dominican governments always had used to prevent opponents from organizing and campaigning: arbitrary arrest and imprisonment, forced induction in the army, discriminatory taxation, and intimidation in many other forms. The reforms that Knox had suggested to Nouel in January 1913 would have curbed some of these abuses, but the Archbishop had had no time to accomplish them. The meeting of the newly elected constituent assembly offered a new opportunity for needed changes in the laws.

In a cable sent to Sullivan on January 18, 1914, the State Department outlined in very general terms several reforms that it considered advisable, including the "establishment of habeas corpus, bail, military conscription, an electoral law and a law of government for the provinces." [36] To these proposals, Bryan himself added the suggestion that the governors of the provinces be elected by the people,[37] a change that would probably have produced more, rather than less disorder. Sullivan was to present these as "guarded and friendly suggestions." They seem to have received little attention either in the constituent assembly or in the congress.

The constituent assembly, in fact, did little work of any kind, because Bordas' supporters, who were in a minority, were able to prevent a quorum.[38] In the congress, the party leaders were interested only in jockeying for advantage in the approaching presiden-

---

[34] For the commission's report, see *Foreign Relations, 1913,* p. 449–453.

[35] The commissioners reported that the opposition parties had won 10 out of 24 seats, but other reports cast doubt on the accuracy of this statement.

[36] Most of the correspondence about political and financial affairs in the Dominican Republic in 1914 and 1915 is printed in *Foreign Relations* for the respective years. To avoid the accumulation of footnotes, documents so published will not usually be individually cited when they are referred to in the text by date.

[37] See 839.001/3.

[38] Mejía, *De Lilís a Trujillo,* p. 99.

tial election, and especially in thwarting any plans that Bordas might have for his own candidacy. Early in February, the Chamber of Deputies voted to impeach Bordas, but the move was defeated in the Senate when Sullivan opposed it.[39] Both political and economic conditions grew steadily worse during the next few months.

The State Department was especially concerned about the desperate state of the government's finances. Like all of his predecessors since the death of Cáceres, Bordas had failed to keep expenditures within what under better management would have been a fairly adequate income. By the beginning of 1914 the government owed $386,000 for back salaries and over $740,000 for what were described as immediately pressing, worthy claims. It would have had no funds for current expenses if it had not been able to borrow from Michelena against prospective customs receipts. Michelena, however, had become reluctant to make further large advances after he realized that Jarvis' influence might enable the Banco Nacional to take the customs depositary account away from him, and the Banco Nacional, which did take over the receivership account late in 1913, through Sullivan's influence, did not have the resources to give the government any substantial help.[40]

The State Department attempted to meet the situation by ordering the receivership itself to anticipate the payments which it would normally have made to the government at the end of each month. On January 7, 1914, when the congressmen threatened to "cause chaos" if their December salaries were not paid, the Department authorized an advance of $20,000. Two days later it authorized another $20,000 because Sullivan reported that the government would fall unless it received further help. Such stopgap measures, however, were clearly inadequate, and for the second time within a year the State Department found itself compelled to give serious consideration to the Dominican government's need for a substantial loan.

A loan, however, would be of little use unless there could be some assurance that it would make the government solvent. Nothing could be accomplished if the funds were dissipated as those from

[39] Sullivan to Bryan Feb. 3 and Feb. 5, 1914, *Foreign Relations, 1914*, pp. 204, 205.
[40] For an account of the receivership's difficulties with the Banco Nacional, see letter from War Department, June 4, 1914, 839.51/1338.

the earlier loan had been and if the government were left free to accumulate a new floating debt. The State Department had been convinced of the need for a thorough financial reform since it received a report from Pulliam in June 1913 describing the wreckage of the relatively efficient fiscal administration that had been achieved under Cáceres.[41] Bryan at that time had pointed out, in a long friendly note, that the continual increase of the government's indebtedness was a violation of the 1907 treaty and had urged that Bordas agree to the appointment of an auditor nominated by the United States.[42] Bordas seems to have made no reply and the matter was not pressed at the time, but the idea was now revived.

Sullivan was authorized on January 26 to suggest to Bordas and to the Dominican Congress that $1,200,000 of the 1907 bonds, hitherto set aside for public works, be sold to meet back salaries and pressing claims, with the proviso that the alcohol and tobacco taxes be increased and their proceeds set aside for a period of years to reimburse the Public Works Fund. The American government would approve this transaction if Bordas invited an American financial expert to come to Santo Domingo: "To aid the proper officials of that government in paying outstanding claims, in devising a proper system of public accounting, and in devising and putting into effect additional means of increasing revenues and adjusting expenditures to them with the object of assuring financial order and stability and preventing deficits."

Bordas accepted this proposal, after he had persuaded the American government to increase the amount of bonds to be sold to $1,600,000 and to agree that the financial expert should appear to be a commercial attaché in the Legation; but there was strong opposition in Congress, where Bordas' enemies were more than willing to see him continue in financial difficulties. Sullivan pointed out that congressional action would take weeks and that "in the meantime the government has not one dollar." The State Department consequently had the General Receiver advance $5,000 daily during February and an additional lump sum of $35,000 for the Dominican diplomatic and consular officers abroad, who had long been unpaid.

While these negotiations were going on, the country was rapidly

---

[41] Secretary of War to Secretary of State, June 4, 1913, 839.51/1027.
[42] Bryan to Curtis, June 13, 1913, 839.51/1053a.

drifting toward civil war. After the revolt of September 1913, Bordas had few friends. He had broken with the *horacistas* when he submitted to Arias' demands, and he could not count on Arias' support. The other party leaders became more hostile when it began to appear that the Provisional President planned to be a candidate to succeed himself, for none of them seemed to take very seriously either the promise of a free election or Sullivan's declarations that no further revolutions would be permitted. Their skepticism was to some extent justified by the fact that the American government was making no preparations to assure a free election and by their experience with Sullivan's ineptitude.

As the political conflict moved toward a crisis, the chief troublemaker, as usual, seemed to be Desiderio Arias, who still controlled several of the northern provinces. On February 12, Sullivan reported that Arias was "openly aspiring to the Presidency," and that he was supported by "Vidal, who aided in the assassination of Cáceres; Victoria, with whose reign of terror you are familiar; Epifanio, a man of blood; and Brache, an American baiter." The Minister thought that Arias' success would be "a disaster immeasurable"; he had blackmailed all governments, he was a smuggler, and he "openly declares for plunder." It was he and his friends who were blocking the State Department's loan proposal. He was now insisting that Bordas retire. Sullivan thought that the American government should take action to "eliminate Arias and his gang" by urging Bordas to proclaim him an outlaw.

In the same message, the Minister informed the Department that Bordas was about to launch his own candidacy. Sullivan thought that the American government should support him "as the best possible agency for implanting American ideas of good government in this country." His reelection would be assured, and he would be strong enough to deal with Arias, if the United States would arrange the proposed loan without continuing to insist that it must first be approved by the congress. "To remain passive," Sullivan said, "seems to me to be almost shirking our responsibility."

Sullivan's picture of the situation was not wholly accurate. He apparently did not realize that Bordas' attempt to bring about his own reelection would almost certainly encounter armed opposition from Vásquez and Jiménez, whom he mentioned rather casually as "oratorical candidates of the respectable type." Furthermore, it was not entirely clear that Arias seriously sought the presidency, for on February 21 Sullivan reported that Arias had given up the idea and would support the candidate that offered the greatest reward. With his control of the North, Arias could play a decisive part in the contest, and, as Bordas saw it, the question was whether to attempt to destroy his influence or to come to terms with him. In view of past experience, Bordas preferred to break with Arias if he could obtain enough support from the United States.

The State Department found it difficult to decide what position to take. It told Sullivan that it was "impressed that the basis of permanent improvement in Dominican affairs depends upon the Constitutional Convention and Congress adopting its recent suggestions for reforms," and asked whether the elimination of Arias would assure the adoption of the measures that it had urged in January. It also wanted to know whether Arias and his associates had interfered with the fulfillment of the 1907 convention. Bryan suggested to Wilson that Sullivan should talk to Arias to get his point of view and perhaps to bring him into line by some concession. He pointed out that "a revolution once commenced is not easily terminated, not to speak of the cost of money and lives." [43] On February 27 he authorized Sullivan to tell the factional leaders that the Department of State favored the existing government because it was the constitutional government and because it favored reforms which the Department considered indispensable.

Bordas, meanwhile, insisted to Sullivan that the American government must decide whether it wished Arias to be "eliminated" or "placated." If it wished him to proceed against Arias and push through the constitutional and legal reforms which the State Department desired, he must have a substantial sum to pay back salaries and other expenses. The State Department, however, could find no way to give him additional financial aid. It could not authorize the proposed sale of bonds without the consent of the Dominican congress, and neither the banks at Santo Domingo City nor the National City Bank of New York were willing to make a loan.[44] When Bordas

[43] Bryan to Wilson, Feb. 26, 1914, Bryan Papers, Library of Congress.

[44] Bryan to Sullivan, Feb. 27, and Sullivan to Bryan March 4, 1914, *Foreign Relations, 1914*, pp. 212, 214. See also Long's memorandum of a telephone conversation with R. L. Farnham on March 13, 839.51/1318.

found that he could not obtain unqualified moral support and money from the American government, he decided to negotiate with his opponents. The *U.S.S. Petrel* took him to a conference which met at Puerto Plata early in March.

Bryan at first authorized Sullivan to attend this meeting but, on second thought, instructed him not to do so. He did, however, tell the Minister to suggest what Bordas should say. "This Department" he cabled, "advises him to . . . point out to Arias (1) that the Government of the United States will not permit revolutionary methods to be employed in Santo Domingo, (2) that no money will be paid to him by the Dominican Government unless there is just claim for services actually rendered, (3) that patriotic services rendered to the people are the only bases upon which to seek public honors, (4) and that the influence of the United States Government will be used to reward those who show themselves deserving and will be used against those who attempt to misuse governmental power for personal ambition or private gain, and that (5) the only methods through which public office should be sought are those upon which the Constitutional Assembly is now at work in perfecting. You should further inform Bordas that in his interview with Arias he should assume that Arias is sincerely interested in his country's welfare and should talk to him as one patriotic citizen would talk to another. This attempt should be made to secure his support before forcible means are resorted to." If the conference failed to reach an agreement, Sullivan was to summon Arias to the capital for a talk with himself. If Arias should refuse to come, the commander of the *Petrel* was to tell him that the American government "will, if necessary, have to consider him as unfriendly to it and will take such appropriate action as is deemed expedient by the President of the United States of America." Arias later confirmed the State Department's low opinion of him by publishing this threat and his own defiant reply.[45]

Sullivan's reports give very little information about what happened at the meeting at Puerto Plata, where the political leaders evidently made a final effort to reach a peaceful agreement for the installation of a constitutional government. Besides Bordas and Arias, the governors of five northern provinces were present, some

[45] Bryan to Sullivan, March 1, and Sullivan to Bryan March, 22, 1914, *Foreign Relations, 1914*, pp. 213, 219.

of them, at least, as spokesmen for the other opposition parties. Jiménez, Vásquez, and Velásquez were all opposing Bordas' reelection. They had hitherto maintained that the Provisional President's term ended legally in April and that a new man should be chosen to serve until the constitutional government was inaugurated; but at the conference it was apparently agreed that Bordas should remain in office until June 30 and that the constitutional convention should in the meantime go ahead with the reform program that was before it.[46] The election would thus be held under Bordas, but there seems to have been no agreement about candidates or about the way in which the voting should be conducted.

For two weeks there was relative quiet; then Bordas provoked a crisis by announcing that the election would be held on April 1 and 2 and by removing the governors of Monte Cristi, Puerto Plata, Santiago, and Seibo provinces. All of these were Arias' men. Walter Vick gave the President some excuse for this action by complaining of the governors' failure to prevent wholesale smuggling, and Sullivan apparently also encouraged it,[47] but the obvious purpose was to make sure that Bordas could control the election. In choosing the new governors, Bordas made what proved to be an unsuccessful bid for support from some of the *horacistas*.[48]

The State Department did not go so far as Sullivan in feeling that it was necessary to support Bordas because Arias would be likely to dominate any government that the opposition parties might install. It felt constrained to warn the Minister to be cautious in discussing electoral matters and to impress on him the fact that the United States was interested only in a free and fair election. It was still endeavoring to help Bordas obtain a loan for back salaries, but when he suddenly called elections on such short notice, Bryan expressed doubts about the propriety of putting a large sum in the government's hands just before the voting took place.[49] The failure of the efforts to obtain a loan, however, made this question an academic one.

[46] A newspaper account of the conference was sent to the State Department by the Consul at Puerto Plata on April 19, 839.00/1112.

[47] This is an inference from the tone of Sullivan's cable of March 20, *Foreign Relations, 1914*, p. 218.

[48] Mejía, *De Lilís a Trujillo*, p. 101.

[49] Bryan to Sullivan, March 23, 1914, *Foreign Relations, 1914*, p. 220.

The opposition parties, when they laid down their arms in October, had understood that the American government would assure the holding of a free election for president at the end of Bordas' term. Their representatives in the congress and the constituent assembly had prevented the enactment of a new electoral law, which was one of the reforms that the State Department had urged, and without which decent elections could not be held; but they still accused the American government of failing to live up to its promises. Sullivan reported that there was much hostility toward the United States and toward himself. It was true that the State Department made no adequate preparations for supervision of the voting. On March 19, when the date for the election had been set, Sullivan inquired whether observers would be sent from the United States or whether he should employ Puerto Ricans already in the country, and was urged to follow the latter course, because the Department's emergency fund was running short.[50] The Minister recruited thirty men whom he considered satisfactory but there was no occasion to use them because Arias' followers started a revolution in La Vega and Santiago on March 30.

Bryan at once made clear his disapproval of the revolt and denounced Arias as "a smuggler and revolutionist" who had been "hampering the Government of the United States in the fulfillment of its obligations under the Convention of 1907." The daily advances by the receivership were increased by $2,000 and later temporarily by $1,500 more. With this help and the moral support of the United States, Bordas seemed for a time to have reestablished his control over most of the Republic's territory, but on April 20 the governor of Puerto Plata proclaimed himself in revolt. In May both the *horacistas* and the *jimenistas* joined the revolution, claiming that Bordas' term had expired on April 13 and that he no longer had any legal right to head the government.

In this situation, Bordas finally yielded to the State Department's demand for the appointment of a financial expert who would act as controller. The Department had been pressing him since January to agree to this, but he had refused to do so unless he could at the same time receive substantial financial help. The original plan for

[50] Sullivan to Bryan, March 19, and Bryan to Sullivan, March 21, 1914, 839.00/-1101.

the appointment of the expert as an attaché of the Legation had to be abandoned for legal reasons, and it was arranged that he should be attached to the customs receivership, but not subordinate to it. The new official was to have broad powers in connection with the government's financial administration. To fill the position, President Wilson designated Charles M. Johnston, who had had some years of experience in Mexico and the West Indies and who seems to have been chosen on the basis of competence rather than for political reasons.[51]

Meanwhile Bryan and the President had been watching the development of the political situation in Santo Domingo with growing concern. The State Department feared that the revolution might continue indefinitely, and it was doubtful about the propriety of permitting Bordas to hold an election while it was going on. On May 23 Bryan asked Sullivan whether it would not be possible for the contending factions to agree on a candidate of high standing and universal popularity to whom the people could turn for relief, but Sullivan replied that there was no such person and pointed to the experience with Archbishop Nouel as evidence of the futility of the idea.[52]

Nevertheless Bryan put forward his idea again when Bordas asked the United States on May 25 to prevent insurrectionary activities in the ports and customs towns and to "lend protection" to the presidential elections, which he had now set for June 7 and 8. Bryan responded with a proposal that all of the presidential candidates withdraw and give their support "to an honest and upright citizen of Santo Domingo who has no connection with politics or with the present situation and who should be able to give to the country civil and legislative reforms which are necessary." The Secretary did not suggest where such a citizen might be found, but he said that the United States could not remain passive any longer, and would be obliged to take "the most effective steps to restore order in those sections of the Republic where the operations of the customs houses are being affected and where the lives and property

---

[51] A memorandum by Johnston, dated Oct. 11, 1919, refers briefly to his past experience, 839.51/2078.

[52] Bryan to Sullivan, May 23, 1914, 839.00/1244a; Sullivan to Bryan, May 28, 1914, 839.00/1253.

of foreigners are in danger." He promised that "the United States will use all means in its power to aid in the holding of free and fair elections and will support the constitutionally elected president."

Sullivan apparently did not present this message very forcefully to Bordas, and he reported on June 1 that the Dominican government claimed that it was winning and was unwilling to agree to any mediation. The Dominicans had evidently learned that the State Department's threats were rarely followed by positive action. In this case, in fact, it is clear that the American government would have been reluctant to resort to force, for the naval commander in Dominican waters had been advised that the United States government wanted a settlement by agreement because it felt that the time was particularly inopportune for any drastic action.[53] It is not difficult to surmise why. An intervention in Santo Domingo might have made hopeless the effort that the United States was about to undertake to persuade the Haitians to accept a customs receivership,[54] and would certainly have been embarrassing at a time when Argentina, Brazil, and Chile were helping the United States to bring about a peaceful solution of the crisis caused by the American occupation of Vera Cruz. From a purely military point of view, moreover, the navy was finding it difficult to provide enough ships to handle so many troublesome situations simultaneously.

The Wilson Plan

The situation continued to grow worse. At the end of May the principal opposition parties agreed on a formal coalition against Bordas, and the elections, held in several provinces in June, made no change in their attitude. The Haitian government, despite vigorous protests by the United States, helped the rebels to obtain arms and ammunition. Bordas' waning prestige received serious blows when the American naval commander in Puerto Plata fired on his camp to enforce an order against bombarding the city, and when a Hamburg-American liner, under the protection of a German cruiser, entered Puerto Plata in violation of the government's blockade.[55] Soon afterward the United States demanded that the blockade be

[53] Secretary of Navy to Secretary of State, June 3, 1914, 839.00/1268.
[54] See Chapter IX.
[55] Secretary of Navy to Secretary of State, June 18, 1914, 839.00/1329.

raised because of its effect on the customs receipts. Bordas protested bitterly against the actions of the American officials, but to no avail. By July the revolution had spread to the South and was threatening the capital itself. J. C. White, who was Chargé d'Affaires because Sullivan had gone to Washington for consultation, told both sides that the *U.S.S. Castine* would prevent fighting in the city, and he arranged a short truce.

The provisional government refused to ask for American mediation, but on July 29 Bryan cabled White that President Wilson was about to present a plan for the restoration of peace, and asked that hostilities be suspended. The Dominican leaders signed a general armistice on August 6, and a few days later a commission, consisting of ex-Governor Fort of New Jersey, Mr. Charles Cogswell Smith, and Sullivan, was on its way to Santo Domingo.

The commissioners were instructed to demand immediate acceptance of what was described as "The Plan of President Wilson." The contending factions were to be told to lay down their arms and to select a provisional president; if they could not agree, the United States would name one and give him its support. The new government was to hold an election, which would be closely observed by the United States. If it was satisfactory, the United States would support the new constitutional government and would insist that there should be no more revolutions. If the vote was not free and fair, a new election would be held "at which the mistakes observed will be corrected." The commissioners were told to present the plan and "see that it is complied with." "No opportunity for argument should be given to any person or faction." The wording of the plan suggests that it was drafted by Wilson himself. When Bordas objected to being treated as a de facto, rather than a constitutional president, Wilson gave orders that the commissioners should yield nothing, that they should insist on full and literal compliance with the plan, and that Bordas should be given to understand that the United States "means business" and would brook no refusal.[56]

The American government backed up these peremptory demands by a considerable show of force. In July it had been announced that a detachment of marines was being sent to Guantánamo to be

[56] See the President's memorandum attached to the Department's cable of August 23, 1914, 839.00/1489.

available if it was needed to protect American interests in the Dominican Republic or in Haiti.[57] Marines were also sent to Santo Domingo with the commission but were held on board the transport during the negotiations. The commanders of the numerous naval vessels in Dominican waters were told to warn the local leaders that force would be used to prevent further fighting.[58] Fortunately most of the Dominican leaders were by this time tired of the war and seemed ready to accept any reasonable proposals for peace.

Within a week of the commissioners' arrival, all of the principal leaders except Arias had accepted the Wilson Plan, and Dr. Ramón Báez, a physician who had not hitherto been very active in politics, was chosen provisional president. The new administration was promptly recognized by the United States. One of its first problems was to deal with Arias, who remained in control of the Cibao, the rich region around Santiago. Bryan told the commissioners on August 31 that Arias must be "eliminated" and suggested that the Provisional President ask that American marines cooperate with the customs guard in arresting him on smuggling charges. Báez, however, preferred to deal with the situation in his own way and Governor Fort advised that he be permitted to do so. The result was that Arias nominally recognized Báez' authority but in fact remained virtually independent. Báez preferred to accept this situation because he was extremely unwilling to ask for the landing of marines.[59]

On September 8 the commissioners signed an agreement with Báez for the supervision of the presidential election by American observers. Governor Fort, who was ill, had to leave Santo Domingo the next day, and he wisely insisted that Sullivan be called back to Washington at the same time. Smith stayed to help the Chargé d'Affaires in carrying out the Wilson Plan.[60]

By this time the presidential campaign was well under way. Juan Isidro Jiménez and Horacio Vásquez, the leaders of the two historic political parties, were the principal candidates. Velásquez, who had

[57] See 839.00/1403a.
[58] Secretary of Navy to Secretary of State, Sept. 15, 1914, 830.00/1518.
[59] White to Bryan, Sept. 21, 1914, 839.00/1544.
[60] Phelan, Santo Domingo Investigation, p. 27.

headed a third party supported by Bordas' friends, withdrew in favor of Jiménez after being promised control of 25 percent of the jobs in the new government. Báez made a laudable effort to be neutral, especially in the important matter of making government appointments, but his sympathies were with the *jimenistas,* and the partisan activities of his ministers in the interior and justice departments gave that party at least a slight advantage.[61] The *horacistas'* chances were further impaired when Jiménez obtained Arias' support by promising him a Cabinet position.

The election took place on three days beginning October 25. Two Americans, in most cases naval personnel, were at each polling place to observe and to offer advice and good offices. At several ports there were American warships whose commanders were authorized to restore order if disturbances got out of control, but they had been instructed that the American government wished to avoid landing forces or giving the appearance of military interference.[62] There seems to have been a fairly satisfactory election in most parts of the country, despite the lack of any preliminary registration of voters and the insufficient number of polling places in the larger cities. There were, however, serious disturbances in Santo Domingo and also at Santiago, where the courts annulled the first election and ordered a new one, in which the *horacistas* refused to participate. Of a total popular vote of 80,000, Jiménez got 40,000 and Vásquez 35,000, and Jiménez had a substantial majority in the electoral college.[63]

The disputes about the election tempted Báez to try to remain in power, and he was encouraged in this idea by the *horacistas.* The latter appealed to the Supreme Court to declare the election invalid, and they proposed to prevent a quorum in congress when that body met for the final canvas.[64] Bryan, however, was not disposed to per-

[61] Mejía, *De Lilís a Trujillo,* pp. 106–112.

[62] For the instructions to the observers, see 839.00/1575.

[63] The final returns, as communicated to the State Department by the Navy Department, were:

Jiménez	337 electors	40,476 votes
Vásquez	246 electors	35,391 votes
Vidal	49 electors	4,244 votes
Velásquez	0 electors	186 votes
	632	80,297

[64] White to Bryan, Nov. 9, 1914, 839.00/1624.

mit such a maneuver. On November 14, he authorized the Chargé d'Affaires to say: "that this Government, fulfilling its promise, will actively support the President elected by the people whenever satisfied of people's choice, and will not tolerate further insurrections. The period of revolutions is past; law and order will be supported; necessary reforms will be urged through legislation. It is believed that under such a policy peace will be followed by prosperity and progress." On November 25 Bryan indicated that he considered that "the will of the people has been clearly and freely expressed." When the *horacistas* still threatened to prevent a majority in congress, he made it clear that the United States would recognize Jiménez in any event and would hold "personally responsible" any leaders who interfered. The *horacistas* were further discouraged when the Supreme Court upheld the validity of the election, and Vásquez ordered his followers to make no more trouble. Jiménez was consequently inaugurated on December 5, 1914.

The Jiménez Administration

Bryan thought that the Dominican situation had been "cleared up" and that the American government's policy had been "vindicated." [65] The American government had in fact attained one of its most important objectives: the establishment of a freely elected government at Santo Domingo which the United States would feel able to support by its moral influence and if necessary by force. The officials concerned with Dominican affairs in the State Department, however, realized that intervening to repress disorder would not by itself create a situation where democratic government could flourish, and they felt that reforms like those which they had been urging on the Dominicans since January were still essential to the existence of a stable republican government.

The most obvious and immediate need was better administration of the government's finances. One bad situation was remedied when the receivership account was restored to Michelena in the summer of 1914, after the Banco Nacional had on two or three occasions been unable to honor drafts sent to New York by the customs service; [66] but the European war and the revolution had made the condition of the treasury worse than ever. The customs receipts had

---

[65] Bryan to Wilson, Dec. 12, 1914, Bryan Papers, Library of Congress.
[66] Letter from War Department, June 4, 1914, 839.51/1338.

been reduced by a half, and the receivership's small daily advances to the government had been kept up only by drawing on the hitherto scrupulously conserved public works funds. There were practically no receipts from other sources because the Bordas government had sold a twelve-year supply of revenue stamps and a seven-year supply of postage stamps at a small percentage of their face value, and had persuaded all of the distillers to pay their taxes in advance at a reduced rate.[67]

Johnston, the new controller, had accomplished little. When he went to Santo Domingo in June 1914, Bryan told him to proceed slowly in asserting his authority,[68] and he made no real effort to do so until the end of the civil war. Báez cooperated with him and usually accepted his advice, but was unwilling to give him any official recognition. There had been much hostile comment in Santo Domingo when Báez published the correspondence about his appointment in September, and Johnston himself advised against pressing for any formal recognition of his authority before the advent of the new government.[69] His principal accomplishment had been to introduce somewhat more order into the government's system of making payments.

During the electoral campaign, all of the presidential candidates had assured the American commissioners that they were heartily in favor of establishing the controllership on a regular basis; [70] and in November, after the election, Jiménez and Velásquez assured the American Legation in writing that they would accept the controllership if the new administration was recognized by the United States. They also agreed to endeavor to obtain legislation placing the internal revenues under the customs receivership.[71]

On December 14, when Jiménez had hardly settled down in his new office, the State Department urged that he issue decrees placing the collection of the internal revenues under the receivership and giving Johnston official recognition as controller. In the same note the Department made other proposals which showed that it was considerably expanding its ideas about the sort of aid that it

[67] Johnston's report to the Department of State, Oct. 15, 1914, 839.51/1436.
[68] See Long's memorandum of Nov. 17, 1915, 839.51/1650.
[69] Report on Dominican affairs transmitted by navy, Oct. 3, 1914, 839.00/1547.
[70] White to Bryan, Oct. 23, 1914, 839.51/1429.
[71] White to Bryan, Nov. 16. 1914, 839.51/1452.

should press on Caribbean countries that seemed to need help. Jiménez was asked to give the Director General of Public Works, who was an American, a more definite tenure and more control over his subordinates; and was urged to reduce military expenses, as a step toward the ultimate complete disbanding of the Dominican army. He was offered the help of the American government in the reorganization of the police and the creation of a constabulary to replace the existing armed forces.

Jiménez showed little disposition to accept these proposals. He referred to congress the agreement reached in May 1913 about the appointment of the controller, and when that body twice refused to ratify it he took the position that Johnston could have no legal authority. The American Legation nevertheless insisted that Johnston continue to countersign all checks covering governmental expenditures; and the status quo continued for some months, with constant friction between the controller and the President and with little beneficial effect on the Republic's financial situation.

The State Department was also disappointed in its hope that a freely elected government would mean political stability. Jiménez, never a man of great ability, and now old and in feeble health, could not control the ambitious and mutually antagonistic leaders who had been given positions in the government in return for their support in the election. The most powerful of these was Arias, who controlled the army as Minister of War and had a large following in each house of congress. There were other leaders in the old *jimenista* party who were hostile to Arias, and most of the *jimenistas* were hostile to Velásquez.[72] Dissension within the administration encouraged the opposition parties to make trouble.

On January 9, 1915, Sullivan reported that the *horacistas* were "assailing the government with blackmailing" and that Arias was threatening to join the opposition. Bryan, after discussing the matter at a Cabinet meeting,[73] authorized Sullivan to say to Jiménez that the American government would "support him to the fullest extent in the suppression of any insurrection" and to warn Vásquez and Arias that they would "be held personally responsible if they attempt to embarrass the government."

[72] Mejía, *De Lilís a Trujillo,* pp. 115ff.
[73] This appears from Bryan's letter to Wilson, Jan. 15, 1915, 839.00/1382.

"The people of Santo Domingo," Bryan cabled, "will be given an opportunity to develop the resources of their country in peace. Their revenues will no longer be absorbed by graft or wasted in insurrections. This Government meant what it said when it sent a commission there with a proposal looking to permanent peace and it will live up to the promises it has made. . . . A naval force will be sent whenever necessary." At the same time the Secretary again urged the need for the reforms that the United States had proposed.[74] Bryan told the Dominican Minister that the United States would furnish any force necessary to maintain order if Arias made trouble.[75]

Two weeks later trouble threatened when Jiménez decided to remove an insubordinate governor at Puerto Plata. Sullivan thought that the governor's purpose was to "determine whether the professional revolutionist need fear American suppression," and advised "prompt and vigorous suppression of this disturbance by the Department." Jiménez preferred to maintain order with his own troops but asked for additional money, and Bryan agreed to allow him funds for the expedition. Ultimately, the governor withdrew peacefully, after negotiations in which the commander of the *U.S.S. Castine* seems to have played an important part.[76]

A problem of a different sort arose when Sullivan reported in April that there was a "political plot" to impeach Jiménez on the ground, among others, that the President had failed to remove Johnston after the congress had refused to approve his appointment. Bryan promptly replied that the American government ". . . will not permit any attack to be made upon President Jiménes for acting in good faith toward the United States. Notify the plotters, as you have the opportunity to do so, that President Jiménes, having been chosen President by the people, is entitled to and will receive from this Government, any assistance that will be necessary to compel respect for his administration. This support will be given whether the attacks made upon him are direct, or indirect, open or in secret." The effect of this communication, as critics have pointed

[74] Most of the important correspondence with regard to Dominican affairs in 1915 is printed in *Foreign Relations* for that year, pp. 279ff.

[75] Bryan to Wilson, Jan. 15, 1915, 839.00/1382.

[76] As is often the case, Sullivan's reports do not give full information about what occurred.

out,[77] was to prevent the congress, which had also been elected by the people, from exercising a power that it enjoyed under the Dominican constitution; but the American government evidently did not propose to let such considerations defeat its whole policy in the Dominican Republic. It was the more determined to support Jiménez because Sullivan had reported that the plotters planned to make Arias provisional president.

Congress' hostility to Johnston had been aggravated by an action that the controller took in March, when the Senate voted a budget contemplating expenditures far in excess of the probable revenues. Johnston announced that he would immediately suspend the payment of a number of budgetary items that he considered superfluous, and on his recommendation the daily advances from the receivership were suspended, presumably to impress on the government the need to live within its income. This weakened Jiménez' position; but when the President asked for further advances from the customs receipts, so that he could suppress an expected *horacista* uprising without calling for open assistance from the United States, Bryan replied that it would be better for the United States to give military aid immediately if trouble occurred.

Besides the disagreement about Johnston's position, there had been a revival of an old controversy about the customs receivership. The American government had always insisted that it had a right, under the 1907 treaty, to appoint all of the personnel of the customs service, but this right had not been exercised because Secretary Root had agreed in 1907 that the Dominican government might name the local collectors, subject to the General Receiver's approval, and with the understanding that any unsatisfactory employee would be removed. This arrangement had not worked well. Both Pulliam and Vick had attempted unsuccessfully to obtain more control over their personnel. Clarence H. Baxter, a political appointee who became General Receiver in September 1914 when a quarrel with Sullivan caused Vick's resignation, faced an especially difficult situation with the change of administration at Santo Domingo. When he attempted to set up a "civil service system" which would prevent the government from making removals, he met with vehement opposition. Jiménez and his associates had many political

[77] Welles, *Naboth's Vineyard*, Vol. II, p. 752.

obligations to meet, and they wished, as they told Baxter, to reward their partisans with customs appointments just as the administration at Washington did.[78] The State Department approached the question cautiously because it realized that some customs employees had been active opponents of Jiménez. It was willing to permit the dismissal of employees for political disloyalty, but it insisted that the General Receiver have authority to refuse to accept undesirable appointees and to reward efficient service by promotion. This was not satisfactory to the Dominicans.

Jiménez consequently sent a commission to Washington in April 1915, to discuss the question of customs appointments and the status of the controller. Wilson and Bryan made a special effort to give the commissioners a friendly reception.[79] In the ensuing negotiations, which continued for some weeks, the State Department made no further concessions in the matter of the customs service, but it sought to meet the Dominicans' objections to Johnston by transferring to the customs receivership most of the duties of the controller. Johnston himself was to have a post in the receivership, but there seems to have been an understanding that another customs official would act as financial adviser for the time being.[80] The Dominican commission accepted this arrangement, and represented it as a diplomatic victory.

Jiménez objected to Johnston's being given any position in the government, but the State Department refused to withdraw him unless formal charges were presented.[81] The Dominican President had deeply resented Johnston's actions, and the latter said later that Jiménez would have expelled him from the country if Arias had not supported him.[82] This rather surprising statement, though it was probably colored by Johnston's disapproval of the American government's treatment of Arias, shows that the State Department's information about the situation in 1915, derived from Sullivan's reports, was at least incomplete.

[78] Baxter to McIntyre, Feb. 19, 1915, 839.51/1825.
[79] See the letters exchanged between the Secretary of State and the President, May 6, 1915, 839.00/1706.
[80] See the memorandum filed with the letter of June 19, 1915, from the Chief of the Bureau of Insular Affairs, 839.00/1954.
[81] Foreign Relations, 1915, pp. 310–314. See also 839.51/1581.
[82] See Johnston's memorandum written in 1919, 839.51/2078.

In May 1915, Sullivan was finally compelled to resign. The State Department had realized much earlier that its Minister was incompetent and very unpopular in Santo Domingo, but the removal of a political appointee was always a difficult matter. In December 1914, the administration was compelled to take cognizance of charges that Sullivan had been guilty of gross improprieties in the conduct of his office. He was nevertheless permitted to return to his post after Jiménez' inauguration and to remain there while James D. Phelan, who was appointed as commissioner for the purpose, was making a formal investigation of his conduct. Meanwhile public hearings, held in the United States and at Santo Domingo, destroyed any prestige and usefulness the Minister still had. It is extraordinary that the American government should have attempted for several months to deal with so potentially dangerous a situation through a representative who was completely discredited.

Phelan's report, submitted on May 8,[83] showed that the most perfunctory inquiry into Sullivan's earlier career would have revealed his complete unfitness for a diplomatic post. It also showed that his appointment had been brought about by persons who had interests in the Dominican Republic and that these persons had profited financially by their relationship to him. There was no clear evidence that Sullivan himself had taken graft, but he had attempted in improper ways to use his official position to help friends and relatives, and his relations with the Banco Nacional, which he often used as a downtown office, had given rise to deserved criticism. His retention became completely impossible when a private letter from him, containing insulting remarks about the Dominicans, was produced and made public at the hearings.

The situation in the Dominican Republic continued to grow worse. Jiménez had a breakdown during the summer of 1915, and for a time left the direction of public affairs to his sharply divided Cabinet.[84] In July, there was a small uprising in the North and another near San Pedro de Macorís, where the owners of American sugar plantations urgently demanded protection. One group of rebels sacked the customhouse at La Romana, and another seized a revenue cutter. When the State Department threatened to use force

---

[83] *Santo Domingo Investigation.*
[84] Welles, *Naboth's Vineyard*, Vol. II, p. 757.

to restore order, Vásquez, as the leader of the chief opposition party, asserted his desire for peace but protested publicly against American intervention; and the Dominican government said that it did not desire foreign aid which might arouse "national sentiment." Jiménez restored order by bribes to both revolutionary groups, but it was clear that what the American Chargé called his "inconceivably weak and temporizing policy" could only lead to further trouble.[85]

Evidently stability could not be attained by the policy that the American government had been following. Bryan's resignation in June 1915 and the appointment of Robert Lansing as his successor seem to have strengthened the hands of those officials in the State Department who felt that the United States would have to exercise more control over the Dominican government's affairs. The Latin American Division had opposed even the small concessions that were made to the Dominican commissioners in June, for Long feared "that we have yielded the very thing [financial direction in Dominican affairs] which in time, if continued, would have caused revolutions there to cease."[86] Apparently the State Department's ideas of what ought to be done took more definite shape after the intervention in Haiti in July forced the American government to formulate a relatively definite program for that country. The provisions of the treaty with Haiti had their origin largely in the State Department's experience in Santo Domingo, and the main features of the treaty now became objectives of American policy in that country.

The new Secretary's approach to the problem was somewhat different from his predecessor's in another respect. Bryan had primarily emphasized a desire to maintain peace and promote constitutional government. Lansing, as a lawyer, was more inclined to base his actions on the specific provisions of the 1907 treaty. This was apparent in the instruction given in September 1915 to William W. Russell, who had been minister in the Dominican Republic before 1913 and who was now Sullivan's successor. The instruction was a long document, which was carefully considered by President Wilson before it was delivered.[87] It emphasized the failure of successive

[85] *Foreign Relations, 1915*, pp. 292–295. See also the report from the American consul at Puerto Plata, Sept. 30, 1915, 839.00/1764.

[86] Long's memoranda of June 6, 1915, 839.51/1580, and Aug. 6, 1915, 839.00/1731.

[87] Polk to Russell, Sept. 17, 1915, 839.51/1633a. An extract is printed in *Foreign Relations, 1915*, p. 321. For Polk's letter of Sept. 21 to Wilson see 839.51/1834. The

Dominican governments to comply with Article III of the 1907 treaty, which obligated the Republic not to increase its debt except by previous agreement with the United States, and said that the American government had "now, for the first time, determined that further violations of the obligations of the convention, which the Dominican Republic freely assumed, shall cease." The "wisest course" would be the adoption of an amended treaty. As outlined in the instruction, this would have been similar in many respects to the treaty that had just been signed with Haiti, with provisions for a financial adviser, for a constabulary officered by Americans, and for the appointment of American engineers to direct public works and sanitation. It would also have given the United States the same right to intervene in Dominican affairs that it enjoyed under the Platt Amendment in Cuba. One provision contemplated a land survey, to facilitate taxation and to eliminate the uncertainty about titles which was an obstacle to the country's economic development and especially to the expansion of the plantations of the large American sugar companies.[88]

If the proposed treaty could not be obtained, Russell was in any event to present a note informing the Dominican government ". . . that the United States interprets the convention of 1907 to give it the right:

"A. To compel the observation of Article III of the convention in the appointment of a financial adviser.

"B. To provide for the free course of the customs by the organization, on a much larger scale, of what is now known as the Dominican Customs Guard, or by the creation of a constabulary."

Russell became convinced soon after his arrival that the proposed treaty would never be ratified by the Dominican congress. Jiménez, in fact, did not dare to tell most of the members of his Cabinet about the American government's proposals, and he sent a personal letter to President Wilson explaining why he thought that any discussion of them would endanger his administration.[89] The State Department consequently told Russell to carry out his alternative instructions

instruction dated Sept. 17 was not sent until after Polk had consulted the President on Sept. 21.

[88] For the State Department's views on this point, see Polk's letter to Wilson, cited above, and Long's memorandum of Nov. 4, 1915, 839.51/1716.

[89] Russell to Lansing, Oct. 29, 1915, 839.00/1776.

and at the same time to say that an advance of $120,000 from the customs receipts, which the Dominican government was urgently asking, would be approved when the demands for the appointment of a financial adviser and the creation of a new police force were accepted.[90]

On November 19 Russell addressed a long note to the Dominican Foreign Office setting forth the American government's decision that unauthorized increases of the Dominican debt must stop and asserting the right of the American government to appoint a financial adviser and create a new police force. The very extensive powers and functions that the financial adviser should have were spelled out in detail, as was the authority to be conferred on the director of constabulary, who, like the financial adviser, was to be nominated by the President of the United States. The American government was willing to have the rights and duties of the financial adviser vested in the customs receivership provided that the receivership exercised "full budgetary control."

Reports of the contents of the note, as they leaked out, caused much excitement and intensified the anti-American feeling which had been growing since the intervention in Haiti in July. The proposal for a constabulary was especially objectionable. The Minister of Foreign Affairs asked if this could be eliminated if the government agreed to a more effective control of its expenditures, but the State Department said no.[91] Jiménez, after consulting the leaders of the opposition parties, consequently rejected both proposals on December 8, emphasizing the unanimous opposition of the Dominican people to foreign intervention.[92] Though the State Department had evidently intended to insist, this time, on the acceptance of its demands, no further action was taken immediately because President Wilson was unwilling to press the matter while the treaty with Haiti was before the United States Senate.[93]

Russell had warned the State Department that the presentation of his note might encourage the *horacistas* to revolt and might even

[90] Unless otherwise indicated, the correspondence that ensued is printed in *Foreign Relations* for 1915 and 1916.
[91] Russell to Lansing, Dec. 7, and Lansing to Russell, Dec. 9, 1915, 839.51/1653.
[92] Welles, *Naboth's Vineyard*, Vol. II, p. 761.
[93] Latin American Division memorandum of June 3, 1916, 839.00/1896. The Haitian treaty was approved by the Senate Feb. 28, 1916.

cause the resignation of Jiménez, which would mean the election of Arias as president. In January, Russell thought that there might be trouble in the near future, and Lansing instructed him to tell Jiménez that the United States would furnish forces to suppress insurrection and maintain order if requested to do so. Declarations of this sort were of doubtful value to Jiménez, because the opposition to the proposals for American control of the finances and the armed forces would have made it impossible for a government maintained in power by the United States to have any popular following.

While the State Department continued to embarrass Jiménez with unwanted offers of military support, it showed little disposition to help him in other ways. Though the receivership reported that the Minister of Finance was cooperating with Johnston, who had resumed his position as controller, Russell advised against giving the government the financial help that it needed, apparently because he thought that financial pressure would compel Jiménez to accede to the American demands.[94] The State Department's attitude on other matters was often unsympathetic. As early as November 1915, in fact, Lansing and his aides were contemplating with some equanimity the possibility that the Jiménez government might be overthrown in spite of their support, because they thought that such an event would justify the landing of American troops and the negotiation of a treaty like that with Haiti.[95]

There was little change in the situation until April 1916, when Jiménez, with the encouragement of the Velásquez faction in his Cabinet, decided to break with Arias who was still Minister of War. On April 14, the commander of the fortress at Santo Domingo City and the chief of the Republican Guard, who were Arias' chief lieutenants, were summoned to the President's country place and imprisoned. The troops in the fortress remained loyal to Arias, and the leaders of the opposition parties at once offered him their support. Russell, who thought that "the gang controlling the President" was principally to blame for what had happened, joined with Arch-

---

[94] Vance to the Bureau of Insular Affairs, Nov. 11, 1915, 839.51/1645; Russell to Lansing, Nov. 10, 1915, 839.51/1641.

[95] This seems evident from Long's memorandum of Nov. 18, 1915, 839.51/1716, and Lansing's letter to Wilson Nov. 24, 839.00/1776.

bishop Nouel in an effort to bring about an agreement.[96] For a time, he was able to prevent an open break, but on May 1 the House of Representatives, which was dominated by Arias' friends, began impeachment proceedings against Jiménez and the President retaliated by dismissing Arias from the Cabinet.

The State Department authorized Russell to give Jiménez "all support." Two American warships arrived at Santo Domingo City and landed men to protect the American Legation and also the Haitian Legation, where many foreigners had taken refuge. The provincial governors who were loyal to the President sent forces to support him, but when he attempted to take the capital on May 5 a shortage of ammunition prevented him from pressing the attack. Jiménez then asked the American forces to take the city for him, but a few hours later withdrew the request and resigned. This, according to Russell's interpretation of the constitution, left the four remaining members of the Cabinet in charge of the executive power, but Arias declined to recognize their authority. He still held the capital, and the congress would apparently have elected him provisional president if the *horacista* members had not prevented a quorum by refusing to attend.

In this situation, the government at Washington authorized Russell and Admiral Caperton to take such action as they considered advisable. It was not disposed to recognize the congress' impeachment of Jiménez because Russell reported that a quorum had been obtained only through intimidation by Arias. Jiménez was out, but Russell decided to support the Council of Ministers. On May 13, he and Caperton told Arias that the American forces would attack Santo Domingo if he did not at once surrender the city to them. Arias quietly withdrew into the interior, and the capital was occupied without bloodshed.

It was fortunate that Jiménez did not accept Russell's offer of armed support and that Arias decided not to resist. If Caperton had carried out his threat to bombard Santo Domingo City, his action would have shocked all Latin America. Russell had warned the State Department that even the government's forces might turn

---

[96] For these events, see Mejía, *De Lilís a Trujillo*, pp. 118–119. Russell gave a slightly different account of what happened in his dispatch of April 27, 1916, 839.00/ 1821.

against the Americans if the capital were attacked.[97] The attitude of the populace was distinctly hostile. American forces met with some resistance when they landed at Puerto Plata a few days after the occupation of Santo Domingo, and three American marines were killed when Caperton sent a detachment to occupy the principal cities of the Cibao in June and July. Arias, however, surrendered at Santiago without a fight.

Armed Intervention

The State Department evidently hoped to attain its objectives in Santo Domingo by somewhat the same course of action that had been successful in Haiti in the preceding year. Caperton, in occupying the Cibao, publicly announced that American troops would remain until peace was restored and until reforms that the American government deemed necessary were adopted. To achieve reforms, however, it was necessary to have a Dominican government that would cooperate, and Russell and Caperton were opposed to the immediate election of a president by the congress because they thought that Arias would be chosen. With the State Department's approval, they asked the congress to delay the choice of a provisional executive until more normal conditions were restored.

The congress ignored this request, though it was repeated from time to time,[98] and early in June the slow electoral procedure prescribed by the Dominican constitution had proceeded to a point where it seemed certain that Dr. Federico Henríquez y Carbajal, the chief justice of the Supreme Court, would become president. Russell thought that final action must be prevented, both because Henríquez refused to make any promises about the reforms desired by the United States and because several provincial governors were threatening to revolt if he were chosen. The Minister consequently suggested that the American forces arrest some of the senators. The State Department did not approve this idea, but it told Russell that the American government could not consent to the election of Arias or any of his friends, or even of Henríquez, in view of the latter's attitude. No candidate must be chosen who was not in sympathy

[97] Telegram of May 10, 1916. A part of this is printed in *Foreign Relations*.
[98] There is a copy of one of the letters that they addressed to the Congress in the Navy Caribbean Area File, May 1916.

with the American proposals for financial control and a constabulary. The Dominicans must be reminded that the United States would not recognize any unsatisfactory government and that recognition would be "absolutely necessary" because the United States would maintain complete control over the Republic's finances.[99]

Russell had already recommended that the customs receivership should take over the collection of the internal revenues as well as the customs duties and should disburse all government funds. Early in June, apparently without awaiting instructions, he told the Dominicans that this would be done. The Council of Ministers protested vehemently, and the Minister of Finance resigned, but Russell and Caperton proceeded with their plan. J. H. Edwards was appointed controller, because Johnston, who disapproved of the United States policy, had resigned.[100] Meanwhile the American naval forces were occupying more and more of the country, disarming and paying off the government troops with funds supplied by the receivership.[101]

The congress was still determined to elect a provisional president. The Council of Ministers, led by Velásquez and hostile to Henríquez because he was an *horacista,* arrested seven senators and one deputy on June 4, with Russell's acquiescence; but the next day both Russell and Caperton realized that this step had been ill advised and obtained the prisoners' release. By this time Russell was beginning to see that the Council of Ministers could not govern the country and to reconcile himself to the idea that a provisional president should be chosen even though it were impossible to obtain promises from the candidates before the election.[102]

The Senate went ahead with the electoral procedure, but when Henríquez withdrew his candidacy on June 12 the factions in the congress again had to begin the search for a candidate who could command a majority in both houses. In July the *jimenistas* and the *horacistas* agreed on ex-President Nouel, and Russell and Caperton informally expressed their approval of this idea, but the Archbishop

[99] Russell to Lansing, June 2, and Lansing to Russell, June 3, 1916, 839.00/1847.
[100] For Johnston's attitude see the Latin American Division memorandum of July 7, 1916, 839.00/2202, and a memorandum written by Johnston in 1919, 839.51/2078.
[101] Navy Caribbean Area File, July 1916.
[102] Russell to Lansing June 6, 1916, 838.00/1856.

emphatically declined to be a candidate.[103] Then, on July 25, apparently without consulting the American officials, the congress elected Dr. Francisco Henríquez y Carbajal, the brother of the chief justice, as provisional president for a term of five months.

Dr. Henríquez, who was at the time living in Cuba, had had no connection with recent political events. He was a man of constructive and statesmanlike ideas, and Russell considered him as good a choice as the Dominicans could have made. One American official said that he "poses as a scholar and writer but he is honest." [104] Russell, however, feared that he would be controlled by the Arias faction, with which he had formerly been associated, and doubted from the beginning whether he would agree to the reforms that the United States demanded.[105]

The American government was still determined that these reforms should be adopted. On Russell's recommendation, the State Department authorized the Minister to say that recognition would be withheld until its demands for financial control and the organization of a constabulary had been accepted and until the administration had shown itself to be free from the domination of Arias. Without making any prior effort to reach an agreement with the Provisional President about these demands, the American officials withheld from the government all of the customs and internal revenue receipts.[106] This would have made it impossible for the government to remain in office at all had it not been for the presence of the American forces. It caused serious hardship to the government employees and the local merchants and to the public in general.

This seemingly impossible situation continued for several weeks. Henríquez would not surrender, but he endeavored to reach a compromise. Late in August he told Russell that he was willing to acquiesce in the collection and disbursement of all revenues by the receivership, pending negotiations for a definite agreement, and willing to reorganize the army with the assistance of American officers. His proposal, which was made more explicit on September 5,

[103] Caperton's report of July 1, Navy Caribbean Area File, July 1916.
[104] For these opinions, see Pond's Report of Operations, July 23–31, 1916, Navy Caribbean Area File; and Russell's dispatch of Aug. 21, 1916, 839.00/1921.
[105] Russell to Lansing, July 25, 1916, 839.00/1900.
[106] Max Henríquez Ureña, Los Yanquis en Santo Domingo (Madrid, n.d.), p. 129.

contemplated the employment of one American officer under contract, with assistants from Cuba and other Latin American republics. He insisted that he could not constitutionally, on his own authority, bind the government in any formal way to the permanent continuance of these arrangements, but he would agree to enter into negotiations for a new treaty after his administration was recognized. The United States, however, insisted that the financial control and the establishment of a constabulary must be "definitely assured and made binding."

Henríquez then proposed a treaty that would give the United States the financial control it demanded and that would assure reforms in the army, most of which he had already disbanded. He was willing to employ American officers under four-year contracts, but on constitutional grounds he would not agree to the appointment of Dominican army officers by the President of the United States.[107] Admiral Pond, who had replaced Caperton in July, was impressed by the Provisional President's sincerity and thought that there was a good prospect of obtaining the reforms that the American government desired,[108] but the State Department considered Henríquez' proposals unsatisfactory.[109] Russell thought that nothing could be accomplished until the United States presented an ultimatum, and that the United States should "take charge" if the ultimatum were rejected.[110]

On August 29, while these negotiations were going on, a tidal wave wrecked the cruiser *Memphis* on the coast near Santo Domingo City. Forty men were lost, and the toll would have been greater had it not been for the heroic efforts of Dominicans on shore. The warm expressions of sympathy, to which both the Admiral and President Wilson responded, momentarily relieved the tension between the Dominicans and the North Americans, but the incident had no effect on the State Department's intransigence.

Early in October Russell obtained permission to go to Washington to confer with the State Department, leaving Admiral Pond and the clerk of the Legation to represent the United States. After the Min-

[107] Russell transmitted the text of the proposed treaty on Sept. 8, 839.00/1796. See also Henríquez Ureña, *Los Yanquis en Santo Domingo*, pp. 145ff.
[108] Navy Caribbean Area File, Sept. 1916.
[109] To Russell, Sept. 21, 1916, 839.51/1791.
[110] Russell to Lansing, Sept. 25, 1916, 839.51/1795.

ister's departure, Pond reported that an emissary of President Henríquez had proposed the appointment of a mixed commission of Dominicans and North Americans to consider changes in the Dominican constitution and laws to make possible the control of the constabulary by American officers. The Admiral felt that this plan deserved consideration,[111] but it apparently received little attention in Washington.

The State Department, in fact, had seemingly lost interest in any further effort to negotiate. Though Henríquez had shown a willingness to give the American government most of what it asked, the officials at Washington apparently doubted his good faith.[112] Furthermore, the ultimate value of any agreement with him would depend on the attitude of the Dominican congress and of any president who might succeed Henríquez at the end of the five-month term.

The prospect for cooperation with any future government did not seem bright. When Henríquez was elected, the Dominican leaders had reconvened the constitutional convention elected in 1914, with the idea that it would prepare the way for the reconstitution of the government, but this body had been unable to function because the *jimenista* members refused to attend.[113] In the absence of constitutional changes, the new president would be named by the electors chosen in 1914, a majority of whom, like most of the members of congress, were *jimenistas*. This made it seem more than possible that the next government would be dominated by Desiderio Arias, who was now the most influential leader in the *jimenista* party.

This was a prospect that the State Department could not contemplate with equanimity. For several years it had regarded Arias' ambition as the principal reason for the failure of its efforts for peace. He had been but one of several military leaders who had blackmailed every Dominican president during the past thirty years, but he had been the most prominent and most powerful. Furthermore—a consideration that weighed heavily in the latter months of 1916—he was outspokenly pro-German. The State Department had

[111] Navy Caribbean Area File, Nov. 1916.

[112] This is evident from a personal letter that Captain Knapp wrote to Admiral Benson on Nov. 23, Navy Caribbean Area File.

[113] Mejía, *De Lilís a Trujillo*, pp. 134–135. See also Russell's dispatch of August 8, 1916, 839.00/1913.

agreed with Russell on August 5 that the "permanent elimination of Arias from Dominican politics must now be accomplished," [114] and he had been kept under surveillance by the marines since September, when he had voluntarily asked for protection. The American government found itself, however, in an increasingly untenable position. The suspension of payments, which had been expected to bring the provisional government to its knees immediately, had merely brought on an intolerable economic situation for which the United States must assume the responsibility. The Dominicans were becoming increasingly resentful, and there was a distinct possibility of disturbances which the American marines would presumably have to suppress.

Ill-advised actions of the American representatives made matters worse. During the past three years, the State Department had repeatedly declared that persons disturbing the peace would be held "personally responsible" for their acts. In an effort to show that these threats had not been as meaningless as they seemed, Russell asked the naval commander to arrest the minor *caudillos* who had been responsible for the raid on the customhouse at La Romana and the seizure of one of the receivership's cutters in the summer of 1915.[115] One leader was seized in the interior without bloodshed by a marine patrol, but on October 24 an attempt to apprehend another, in the suburbs of Santo Domingo, resulted in the death of a marine captain and a sergeant. The next day another marine patrol was attacked, and three Dominicans were killed. After these incidents the State and Navy Departments were disposed to place Santo Domingo City or perhaps the entire republic under martial law, but Admiral Pond advised against any extreme measures.[116]

Pond was still optimistic about the prospect for an agreement, but a conference of high State Department and naval officials in Washington on October 31 reached the conclusion that the position of the American forces was "untenable" and that the American government must either withdraw them or "legalize" their position.[117] Russell and Herbert Stabler, who had succeeded Long as

[114] Lansing to Russell, Aug. 5, 1916, 839.00/1899.
[115] Admiral Pond's report of the incident is in the Navy Caribbean Area File, August 1916.
[116] *Foreign Relations, 1916*, pp. 238–239; and Report of Operations of Cruiser Force, Oct. 18–31, 1916, Navy Caribbean Area File.
[117] Stabler's memorandum of Oct. 31, 1916, 839.00/1952.

chief of the Latin American Division, thought that a formal military occupation would be the best way out of an increasingly embarrassing situation. They were doubtless influenced by the American experience in Haiti, where full military control had made it possible to obtain a treaty that gave the United States virtually everything that it wanted. The State Department was also influenced by the increasing probability of war with Germany.[118] Because Arias and the *jimenistas* in general were notoriously pro-German, a government controlled by them could endanger the security of the United States. Under martial law, the American naval commander would have a technical justification for compelling all concerned to accept any reforms that the American government might initiate. Payments could then be resumed and steps could be taken to alleviate the distress which the American policy had caused. Russell and Stabler realized that it would be difficult to establish martial law without more justification than the Dominicans had as yet provided, but they seemed to look forward with cheerful equanimity to the probability of disorders that would afford the occasion for a more drastic intervention.[119]

Henríquez himself provided the occasion when he issued a decree dated November 14 ordering the electoral colleges to choose new senators and deputies in place of those whose terms were expiring. The Provisional President feared that the absence of a congress would be taken by the United States as an excuse for further intervention,[120] but the State Department thought that the election would give Arias control of the legislature and that prompt action must be taken to prevent it. On November 22 Secretary Lansing laid the matter before President Wilson and asked for instructions. Lansing for some reason refrained in his letter from making any recommendation of his own, but he enclosed a memorandum from Stabler describing the situation that had arisen and recommending the proclamation of a military occupation as "the only solution of the difficulty." The President approved the proposed action on November 26 "with the deepest reluctance," "convinced that it is the least of the evils in sight in this very perplexing situation." He did,

---

[118] Herbert Stabler emphasized this consideration in a conversation with me a few years later.

[119] Russell's memorandum of Oct. 27, 1916, 839.00/1941; and Stabler's memorandum of Sept. 8, 1916, 839.00/1923.

[120] Henríquez Ureña, *Los Yanquis en Santo Domingo*, p. 170.

however, strike from the proposed proclamation a passage that explicitly authorized the commanding officer to remove Dominican judges, saying that "it may be necessary to resort to such extreme measures, but I do not deem it wise to put so arbitrary an announcement in the proclamation itself." [121]

There was no real effort to negotiate further with the provisional government. Captain (later Rear Admiral) H. S. Knapp, who replaced Pond in November, had one interview with Henríquez, in which the latter reiterated his belief that the decrees which the United States wanted him to issue would be unconstitutional and that any reforms would have to be approved by congress.[122] Four days later, on November 29, Knapp proclaimed the establishment of a military occupation, with himself as Military Governor.

The proclamation based the intervention on the Dominican government's violation of Article III of the 1907 Convention. It referred to the Dominican government's allegation that the unauthorized increase of the public debt had been caused by revolutions and to the unsuccessful efforts of the United States to maintain peace and to persuade the Dominicans to adopt reforms that would assure the maintenance of order. In order to assure the observance of the convention and the maintenance of tranquility, the Republic was "placed in a state of military occupation" and made "subject to military government." The occupation was undertaken "with no immediate or ulterior object of destroying the sovereignty of the Republic" but, on the contrary, was "designed to give aid to that country in returning to a condition of internal order that will enable it to observe the terms of the treaty aforesaid, and the obligations resting upon it as one of the family of nations." Dominican statutes were to remain in effect, and there was to be no interference with the Dominican courts, except in cases where a member of the forces of occupation was involved.

As Military Governor, Knapp immediately issued orders establishing a strict censorship of the press, telegraph, and mails, and forbidding the possession of firearms and explosives by individuals.[123]

---

[121] The letters and Stabler's memorandum are printed in *Foreign Relations, 1916*, pp. 240–242. Two memoranda which went to the President, which are not printed, are in 839.00/1952.

[122] Navy Caribbean Area File.

[123] Henríquez Ureña, *Los Yanquis en Santo Domingo*, pp. 180–182, gives the text of the orders.

The censorship was considered necessary not only to prevent the newspapers from inciting the public to resistance but also to check the activities of the recently formed National Press Association, which was endeavoring to present the Dominican point of view in other Latin American countries.[124] At the same time it was announced that budgetary payments would be resumed at once.

Russell, who returned to Santo Domingo in December, reported that the new situation had been generally accepted except by "disappointed petty politicians," and he recommended that the military government should continue for at least a year while needed reforms were worked out with the aid of "patriotic Dominicans." After that, he thought that there should be a period of control by a junta of the "best native element" to prepare the way for elections. The State Department expressed its general concurrence with these views.[125] As things turned out, the Dominican Republic was ruled by American naval officers throughout the remainder of the Wilson administration.

In setting up the military government as the best way out of their immediate difficulties, the State and Navy Departments apparently hoped to create a situation like that in Haiti, where Admiral Caperton had proclaimed a military occupation of Port au Prince and the surrounding territory and had assumed the power and responsibility of military government in September 1915. In Haiti, the President and the congress had continued to function, under the protection of the American forces, and the government had entered into a treaty with the United States providing for the same sort of American assistance and control that the American government had been demanding in the Dominican Republic. In Santo Domingo, however, by what the Navy Department later described as an "unexpected evolution," [126] the American naval authorities from the first assumed direct control of all branches of the central government. Knapp asserted that this was necessary because the members of the Cabinet simply deserted their posts, but it is not clear that he made a very earnest effort to obtain their cooperation. When he was told that the provisional government thought of staying in office in an effort to help, he sent word that its members might do so, but with-

---

[124] Brewer to Lansing, Dec. 6, 1916, 839.00/1958.

[125] Russell to Lansing, Dec. 14, and Lansing to Russell, Dec. 20, 1916, 839.00/1967.

[126] *Hearings Before a Select Committee on Haiti and Santo Domingo.* U.S. Senate, 67th Cong., 1st and 2nd Sess. Pursuant to S. Res. 112. Vol. I, p. 94.

out recognition or salaries.[127] Henríquez y Carbajal quietly went to Cuba, and when the members of the Cabinet also left their offices, Knapp declared their positions vacant and put naval officers in their places. His action was suspended, except in the case of the war and interior departments, under instructions from Washington,[128] but these instructions were soon changed and American naval officers were in charge of all of the executive departments throughout the occupation.

In theory, the Military Governor simply took the place of the Dominican government, "acting for and in behalf of that government—in a sense as a trustee."[129] Russell remained at Santo Domingo, and there was a Dominican Legation in Washington which reported to the American naval officer who served as Minister of Foreign Affairs. On occasion, as when the consent of the United States was needed for an issue of bonds, the two governments exchanged diplomatic communications. Most of the Dominican officials in the executive departments stayed in office, as did the provincial and municipal authorities and the judges, but the Military Governor made such changes as he saw fit. In October 1917, President Wilson authorized Knapp to remove judges in cases where the proper administration of justice required such action and where the removal could not be effected by the procedures provided by the Dominican constitution.[130] The Military Governor also "suspended" the congress and issued any laws that he considered advisable.

There was some opposition from guerrilla groups in the first months of 1917, but after this was put down the military government gave the greater part of the Republic a peace and tranquility which the inhabitants had not enjoyed for many years. Desiderio Arias was kept under surveillance but made no trouble. The systematic disarmament of the population decreased crime. In the province of Santiago, where it had been customary for fathers to give their sons revolvers at the age of puberty,[131] the number of

[127] Knapp to Navy Department, Caribbean Area File.
[128] See Brewer's two telegrams to Lansing on Dec. 9, 839.002/36,37.
[129] State Department Solicitor's Memorandum, July 10, 1918, *Foreign Relations, 1918*, p. 382.
[130] Navy Dept. to Knapp, Oct. 7, 1917, Navy Caribbean Area File.
[131] Mejía, *De Lilis a Trujillo*, p. 145.

homicides is said to have been reduced from 300 to 50 each year.[132] Throughout the occupation, however, the American forces had to deal with bandits in the sparsely settled eastern end of the island, where several leaders who had been operating during the disturbances of the past five years did not want to lay down their arms. The harsh measures taken by some marine officers during the fighting there, and a few atrocities committed by individual soldiers, gave the Dominican patriotic groups much material for propaganda when they began an organized movement to have the occupation withdrawn.

The organization of a constabulary, which had been an important objective of the American government's policy, was begun in 1917, but proceeded rather slowly. An act of the United States Congress authorized American officers to accept appointments in the Dominican service, but it was hard to persuade able marines to accept such appointments because the Navy Department was reluctant to approve extra compensation on the scale that was being paid in Haiti. Hostility to the occupation made it difficult to recruit qualified Dominican officers, and as late as February 1920, Russell reported that the *Guardia Nacional,* as the constabulary was called, was still inefficient. Its inadequacy forced the marines to carry on most of the operations against the bandits.

In other respects the military government seemed favored by fortune in its first years. High wartime prices for sugar and cacao made the country prosperous and caused a sharp rise in the customs receipts. The internal revenues, too, increased astonishingly after the receivership took over their collection. With the establishment of peace in most of the country, and with ample funds at its disposal, the military government was able to make improvements that had been beyond the reach of its predecessors. Knapp and his assistant, Colonel Rufus H. Lane, working with a commission of Dominicans, did an especially fine job with the public school system. New buildings were constructed, teachers' salaries were raised, and the number of pupils in attendance increased from 12,000 to more than 100,000.[133] This was one aspect of the occupation's work which the Dominicans accepted with some enthusiasm. Much was also ac-

---

[132] Kelsey, *The American Intervention in Haiti and the Dominican Republic,* p. 179.
[133] *Foreign Relations, 1920,* Vol. II, p. 130.

complished in the field of public health, though not always in a tactful way, and there were other public works of lasting value.

Among these the most important were the new highways. Though roadbuilding had been one of the principal objectives of the 1907 bond issue, the failure to market the bonds had given the Cáceres administration little to work with and the frequent revolutions had made it impossible to accomplish anything after 1911. In 1916 there was but one cart-road in the country, running a few miles west from Santo Domingo City. A short railroad connected Puerto Plata with Santiago in the north, but it was in such bad shape that it was unsafe to run trains. In general the only communication between the principal towns was by sea or by inadequate trails. This situation not only discouraged trade but made it difficult for the central government to exert its influence in the provinces, where the local *caudillos*, as we have seen, had often been virtually independent rulers. The military government undertook to connect all of the principal centers of population with the capital by roads crossing the island from north to south and from the Haitian frontier to Seibo Province. The work progressed slowly, partly because it was difficult to find enough labor to do the work, but the north-south road was at least made passable and the others were partly completed before the occupation was withdrawn. "The new arteries of the national life," as one Dominican historian wrote, "brought about the unity of the Dominican family." [134]

Another reform which the military government attempted to carry out was the improvement of the chaotic situation with respect to land ownership. A land court was set up to record titles and the imposition of a land tax encouraged the adjustment of titles and encouraged property-owners to use uncultivated land. Unfriendly critics pointed out that these measures also made it easier for the large foreign sugar companies to acquire land, but from the standpoint of the military government, and probably in the eyes of most contemporary Dominicans, the development of the sugar industry was good rather than bad. There was also criticism of the new customs tariff, effective January 1, 1920, which removed the duties on machinery and other articles needed for economic development and reduced those on many of the necessities of life. These changes

[134] Mejía, *De Lilís a Trujillo*, p. 151.

were clearly beneficial, but the Dominicans alleged that their real purpose was to encourage imports from the United States.

The floating debt, which had been accumulating since the general settlement of claims under the 1907 treaty, was adjusted by a commission in which two of the five members were Dominican. The commission's awards were paid in 5-percent bonds of an issue authorized in 1918. As there was little market for such securities in Santo Domingo, the military government sought to persuade investment firms in the United States to buy them and itself bought many from the holders of awards, for resale. In April 1920, it was estimated that $1,000,000 of approximately $3,000,000 that had been issued up to that time were held in the United States.[135] The total amount issued was somewhat over $3,500,000.

There was an unfortunate misunderstanding in connection with this bond issue. The State Department, when it was formally consulted in accord with the provisions of the 1907 treaty, gave its formal assent to an increase in the Dominican debt but apparently failed to realize the significance of a statement by the Military Governor that the decree authorizing the bond issue in effect extended the duration of the treaty of 1907 for the twenty years that the bonds would be outstanding. When the State Department was called on to assure prospective purchasers that the treaty was in fact extended, it took the position that the executive department could not extend the treaty or extend its provisions to cover the new issue. This caused great embarrassment to the military government, because it seemed probable that the 1908 bonds would be retired within a few years and that purchasers of the new issue would then not have the security afforded by the customs receivership. To prevent this from happening, 30 percent of the customs receipts in excess of $3,000,000 was pledged for additional amortization, and a substantial part of the bonds were thus retired with a rapidity that meant large profits for investors who had bought them at a discount. There were still some bonds outstanding when the United States withdrew the military government in 1924, but the convention of evacuation provided for their service by the customs receivership until they should be fully retired.

Despite its not insubstantial material achievements, the military

[135] *Foreign Relations, 1920,* Vol. II, p. 114.

government left much to be desired. Too many of the naval officers who held the higher positions had no training that qualified them for the delicate and complicated task. Few spoke Spanish or had any adequate understanding of local conditions, and frequent transfers prevented them from acquiring experience. The Navy Department gave them little guidance because it was not organized to do so, and the State Department knew little about what was going on. Russell made few reports, and it seems improbable that anyone in the Latin American Division read carefully the bad carbon copies of the Military Governor's reports or the files of the official gazette which arrived from time to time. There were occasions, as in the case of the 1918 bond issue, when the State Department suddenly realized that it had not been aware of an important action about which it should have been consulted.

With the end of the war in Europe, however, the State Department began to take more interest in the Dominican situation. Early in 1919 it put forward the idea of changing the purely military regime to a "provisional government" with more civilian participation, but this seemed impracticable from a legal point of view and was opposed by the navy.[136] Later in the same year Department officers had a series of talks with ex-President Henríquez y Carbajal, who urged that steps be taken to pave the way for a gradual withdrawal of the occupation. The State Department at this time accepted the navy's view that the occupation must continue for an indefinite period, to assure the correction of the conditions that had caused the intervention, but it was becoming increasingly concerned about some of the military government's policies and their effect on Dominican sentiment.

Hostility toward the occupation in Santo Domingo increased noticeably after Rear Admiral Thomas Snowden succeeded Knapp as Military Governor in February 1919. Many prominent Dominicans had at first been willing to cooperate, in the hope that the military government would effect needed reforms and then withdraw, and Knapp had often made good use of their services. Snowden showed less interest in maintaining contact with the local community. The

[136] Latin American Division memorandum of Jan. 27, 1919, 839.00/2114; Polk to Roosevelt, May 23, 1919, 839.00/2133; State Department Solicitor's memorandum, Dec. 13, 1919, 839.00/2226.

new Governor also dismayed those who had been inclined to be friendly by his public assertions that the occupation would have to continue for many years.[137] To most Dominicans the prospect of remaining indefinitely under foreign military rule was intolerable.

The prospect was made more unpleasant by the military government's treatment of those who opposed or merely criticized it. The press censorship, which had been instituted in 1916, was described by a reliable North American witness as stupid, arbitrary, and ridiculous. The newspapers were forbidden to comment on any act of the military government or to use such words as "national," "freedom of thought," "freedom of speech," or "General" as a title for Dominicans. Offenses against the censorship, and other acts that could be considered offenses against the military government, were tried by the American provost courts, which had the reputation of being unjust and cruel.[138] As public opinion in the United States and other American countries began to take more interest in the Dominican situation the censorship and the provost courts were the two features of the occupation's policy that attracted most unfavorable attention.

In the last months of 1919, in an effort to placate local feeling and to pave the way for an eventual withdrawal, the State Department suggested that the Military Governor appoint an advisory council of prominent Dominicans. Ex-President Nouel, Federico Velásquez, Francisco Peynado, and Jacinto de Castro agreed to serve on this, and a place was reserved for Dr. Henríquez y Carbajal, who, however, remained abroad. The group made a number of suggestions for legal and other reforms, most of which the Military Governor did not accept. The venture ended unhappily in January 1920, when the council resigned in protest against Snowden's refusal to follow their recommendation for the restoration of freedom of the press.[139]

The control of the press had been considerably relaxed in the last months of 1919, apparently as a result of pressure from the State Department,[140] and a few days after the council resigned Snowden issued a decree abolishing the censorship but providing penalties

[137] Welles, *Naboth's Vineyard,* Vol. II, p. 820.
[138] Judge Schoenrich's memorandum of Dec. 11, 1919, 839.00/2297.
[139] Brewer to the Secretary of State, Jan. 9 and Jan. 13, 1920, 839.00/2182, 2187.
[140] Navy Caribbean Area File.

for publications or public speeches calculated to incite unrest or disorder. The State Department approved this measure, though it obviously left the way open for abuses. The operation of the provost courts was also somewhat restricted. These partial reforms, however, did not satisfy people who did not want to live under an alien military rule.

At the end of 1919 the Dominican leaders were organizing a vigorous campaign against the continuance of the occupation. There were nationalist juntas in several cities, and Henríquez y Carbajal was carrying on an effective propaganda in other American countries. The friendly relations that had often existed between Dominicans and individual North Americans ceased, and North Americans were excluded from many social clubs. There was an increase in banditry which compelled the navy to send more marines to the country. In July 1920, there were many violently unfriendly articles and speeches during a "patriotic week" which the leaders proclaimed in order to collect funds for their movement, and several persons, including the poet Fabio Fiallo, were jailed and tried by military commission. The State Department, confronted by an outburst of criticism throughout Latin America, endeavored to have them released, but they were held for some weeks and then freed under surveillance.

The State Department was more than ever convinced that definite plans for an eventual withdrawal must be formulated. On June 3, 1920, it had instructed Russell to suggest that the Military Governor appoint a new commission of Dominicans to draft an electoral law and other needed legislation, but it had soon dropped the idea, apparently because of opposition from the navy. In July it was working on another plan under which several basic laws would be framed as a preliminary to the establishment of a Dominican government. It was not until November 1920, however, that Secretary Colby was able to obtain the President's approval for a definite program of action.[141]

Under this, preliminary steps toward withdrawal would be taken at once, but there would be no final relinquishment of control until the original purposes of the occupation had been substantially

[141] Colby to Wilson, Nov. 13, and Wilson to Colby Nov. 15, 1920, 839.00/2420a, 2478.

achieved. The Military Governor would be ordered to announce that the United States intended to begin to return to the Dominican people the government of their country; and he would appoint a commission of Dominicans to undertake a general revision of the country's laws, including especially the electoral law. At first it was suggested that the commission be composed of the members of the Senate elected in 1914, but this idea was dropped, after more mature consideration. After the laws were formulated, a congress and a constitutional convention would be elected, the local governments would be reorganized, and finally, when all needed reforms had been assured, the Military Governor would turn his authority over to an elected president. Among the reforms would be provisions giving the United States control over the Republic's finances and over the constabulary. The new Dominican government would be expected to sign a treaty ratifying all acts of the military government and giving the United States authority to assure the continued maintenance of a government adequate for the protection of life, property, and individual liberty.[142]

To create a more favorable atmosphere for the reception of its plan in Santo Domingo, the State Department on December 13 asked the navy to order Snowden to abolish the provost courts and to revoke the executive order of January 1920 which provided penalties for seditious speeches or writings. It did not know at the time that the Military Governor had published two new laws on December 6: a "sedition law," which prohibited criticism of the occupation or hostile comment on conditions in Santo Domingo, and a "defamation law," which authorized the punishment of insults to American officials. Both were promptly annulled when they were brought to the State Department's attention.

In accord with the plan which the President had approved, the Military Governor announced on December 23 that the United States believed that the time had arrived when it might "inaugurate the simple processes of its rapid withdrawal" from the Republic, and that a commission of Dominicans would be appointed to draft laws to be submitted to a constitutional convention and to a congress.

---

[142] The plan was described in a letter to the navy on Nov. 27, printed in *Foreign Relations, 1920*, Vol. II, p. 136, and in a telegram to the Legation at Santo Domingo on Jan. 8, 1921, 839.00/2290.

The proclamation did not indicate the character of the "reforms" that the American government would demand, but it was not hard to guess that they would impose restrictions on Dominican sovereignty. The response was an outburst of angry protest from the nationalists, who declared that nothing short of an immediate complete restoration of sovereignty would be acceptable. The Dominicans' distrust and dislike of the military government had reached a point where there was little hope for cooperation.

The execution of the plan of withdrawal was made more difficult not only by the Dominican's attitude but also by the strained relations between the military government and the State Department. By obtaining the President's approval of the plan, the State Department had resumed control over Dominican policy, and its rather brusque assertion of authority caused resentment in the Navy Department and perplexed and distressed the officers in Santo Domingo. Some of these felt that the more liberal policy which had been forced on them during the past year had placed them in an untenable position and had encouraged nationalist opposition and violence. They had no sympathy for the idea of an early withdrawal because they were convinced that the occupation must continue for a long period if it were to accomplish its purpose.

They also felt that the change in policy had come at a particularly inappropriate time. In the latter part of 1920, the postwar depression had caused a sharp drop in the prices of Dominican exports and a consequent drop in the government's revenues. Earlier in the year the government had adopted an ambitious public works program for which it had spent all of its surplus and had obligated revenues for some time to come. This of course had to be suspended, with much resulting unemployment and distress. Other expenditures had to be sharply curtailed, so that the constabulary, which was so important in the general scheme of American policy, was reduced to a small force and the educational work was curtailed. A well-meant but inept effort to support sugar and tobacco prices made the deficit in the budget larger and would have been more costly if the sugar companies had not been compelled, later on, to assume the loss on the sugar that was purchased. To extricate itself from some of its difficulties, and especially to resume the road work, the Military Governor wished to obtain a loan in the United States, but the State Department refused to give its consent because it knew that there would be strong Dominican opposition to an operation that would inevitably involve some extension of American financial control.

Under the circumstances, it is not surprising that there was little progress toward a withdrawal during the few remaining months of the Wilson administration. The nationalists' attitude made it difficult to persuade representative Dominicans to serve on the proposed commission, and though seven finally accepted, the commission did not organize for work until February 16. Nothing had been accomplished when President Wilson left office in March. The Harding administration attempted to go ahead with the same program but abandoned the effort when the Dominicans persisted in their refusal to cooperate. In 1922 a new plan, under which the United States retained the customs receivership, but gave up its other demands for control, was worked out with a group of Dominican leaders, and in 1924, after a popular election, Horacio Vásquez was inaugurated as president. For some years the Dominican Republic seemed to have entered a new era of peace and material progress. Vásquez' government, however, was overthrown in 1930, and soon afterward General Rafael Leonidas Trujillo established a dictatorship that continued for more than 30 years.

◄ 8 ►

Intervention in Haiti

🏴 In the Dominican Republic, and as we shall see in Nicaragua, the policy of the Wilson administration was shaped to a great extent by commitments made by its predecessors. A dominant consideration was to prevent the undoing of whatever good had been accomplished by earlier efforts to rehabilitate the finances and help establish stable government in those countries. This was less true in Haiti. The Taft administration's action in connection with the 1910 bank and loan contracts did not really impose new responsibilities on the United States. The intervention of 1915 in Haiti was the result of policies inaugurated by the Wilson administration to put an end to the increasing internal disorder in the republic.

These policies were inspired partly by the President's belief that the United States had an obligation to help its neighbors for their own sake and partly by the fear that disorder and financial mismanagement might invite European intervention. French and German interests were still more powerful in Haiti than in any other Caribbean state. The French were the republic's chief creditors and the best customers for its exports, and the National Bank, in which the French had an equal voice with the American directors, was constantly involved in politics because the government had to have its help in meeting the budget. Germans owned the most important public utilities, and German steamship lines carried most of the country's trade. The local German merchants had much political influence because it was they who usually financed the revolutions.[1] The State Department's concern about these European activities was the greater because the French and German governments manifested a rather special interest in Haitian affairs and resisted the efforts of the United States to increase its own influence. Their desire to participate in any customs receivership that might be established was perhaps understandable because their nationals held

[1] "Everyone knows of the complicity of the German merchants in Haiti in the Leconte revolution and they also know that the Germans financed the Simon revolution of 1908 and the others before it, and doubtless will finance all those to follow." Furniss to Knox, March 2, 1912, 838.00/682.

large amounts of Haitian bonds, external and internal; but it irritated the American government and, in the case of the Germans, it aroused suspicions of ulterior motives. Lansing, looking back on the story in 1921, cited the attitude of the Kaiser's government as one of the principal considerations that inspired American policy in the republic.[2]

Germany was suspected especially of wanting to obtain a naval base or a coaling station in Haiti. Since her navy, without such facilities, was at a disadvantage as compared with those of powers that had colonies in the Caribbean, this desire was not unreasonable, but the naval authorities at Washington thought that any large supply of coal, anywhere in the West Indies, might be dangerous to the United States. The State Department in 1910 and 1912 had opposed efforts by French and German steamship lines to obtain concessions for coaling depots in Haiti,[3] and it was of course especially sensitive to any project that seemed to involve the Mole St. Nicholas. Rumors and reports of such projects caused uneasiness from time to time, even after Assistant Secretary of State Osborne visited Haiti in the first months of the Wilson administration and obtained an oral promise that no concessions affecting the Mole would be granted to foreign interests.[4]

Haitian Politics Before 1915

The establishment of a stable, democratic government in Haiti promised to be even more difficult than in the other Caribbean states. After the white colonists and many of the mulattoes were exterminated during the war of independence, the vast majority of the remaining inhabitants were the former slaves, two-thirds of whom had been born in Africa.[5] During the next hundred years there was almost no immigration and little contact with the outside world. The black peasants, who made up some 95 percent of the popula-

[2] Letter to Senator McCormick, May 4, 1922, 67th Cong., 2nd Sess., *Senate Report No. 794*, Appendix B.

[3] See the correspondence in files 838.802 and 838.345.

[4] This promise is referred to in Hazeltine's despatch of July 16, 1916, from Port au Prince, 838.345/20, and in the State Department's instruction of Aug. 28, 1914, to Bailly-Blanchard, 838.15.

[5] This is the estimate of Moreau de St. Méry, whose *Description Topografique, Politique, et Historique de la Partie Française de Saint-Domingue* (Philadelphia, 1798), is the classic description of the French colony.

tion, spoke a primitive *patois*, partly French and partly African, and their religion was a mixture of African cults called *voudou*. They were a simple, peaceable people, ignorant of anything outside of their daily experience and universally illiterate. The great sugar and indigo estates of colonial days had long since disappeared, but coffee continued to grow half-wild in the hills, and the peasants supported themselves by selling the berries to merchants in the ports and by growing food in their little gardens. Except for a limited amount of trade, they had little contact with the mulattoes who formed the upper class.

The *élite*, as this upper class called itself, spoke French and lived in Port au Prince and a few smaller towns. Most of them were Catholics. Haiti had been completely cut off from Rome until a concordat was signed in 1860 under which missionary priests from France took over the country's churches and French religious orders established several schools. Through these, the upper class had kept in touch with the culture of the mother country, and some of its more fortunate members had studied in Paris. Though the mulattoes were a very small minority, they usually occupied most of the positions in the government. Few of them had any other lucrative occupation. They had to share political power, however, with black leaders who could command more support from the masses of the people.

Throughout the history of the republic the chief political issue had been whether blacks or mulattoes should rule. This was partly a regional matter, for the Negroes were stronger in the North and the mulattoes in the country around Port au Prince. There was a bitter hostility between the two groups, intensified by the *élite*'s social exclusiveness and their strong feeling of superiority; but in practice neither could control the government without help from some leaders in the other. In the first years of the twentieth century the blacks had had the upper hand, but mulatto influence was stronger in the governments of Leconte and Auguste between 1911 and 1913.

The American Minister in 1909 described Haiti as a military dictatorship, where both the congress and the courts did what the president ordered and opponents were shot without trial. The government was run solely for the benefit of the group in power. Salaries were ridiculously low, but graft was omnipresent, for it was said in Haiti that "taking from the state is not stealing." Elections, of course, were a farce.[6] "I have seen in Port au Prince," Furniss wrote in an earlier despatch, "the soldiers come up in companies and remain all day voting and repeating at the command of their officers, while none of the better or middle or common classes were trying to vote, if indeed, it had been possible." [7]

During the nineteenth century, a number of strong rulers had been able to maintain themselves in power for considerable periods before they were killed or forced to flee. The liberal party, to which many of the leaders of the *élite* belonged, tried from time to time to establish a better sort of government, but it rarely controlled the administration for any considerable period. After a civil war in 1902, in which the intervention of a German warship brought about the government's defeat, an uneducated octogenarian soldier named Nord Alexis ruled as a dictator until he was overthrown in 1908 by another soldier of humble origin named Antoine Simon. The latter was ousted by a revolution in 1911 and his successor, Cincinnatus Leconte, was killed some months later by an explosion in the national palace. When the next President, Tancrède Auguste, died suddenly in May 1913, his funeral was interrupted by a battle between rival generals who sought to control the election of his successor. The late President's friends won, and the congress chose Michel Oreste, a popular lawyer and orator, who is said to have been the country's first civilian president.[8] Furniss reported that each senator and deputy received a promissory note from the successful candidate and that these were later paid from the national treasury.[9]

The revolutions, which became more and more frequent after 1913, all followed much the same pattern. Madison Smith, the first minister appointed under the Democratic administration, wrote in 1914: "Practically no method of obtaining more than a bare living is open to the Haitian except through government position. Politicians who are at any time willing to inaugurate a revolution, are abundant, and with a comparatively small sum of money can obtain

[6] Furniss to Knox, April 20, 1909, Num. Case 2126/466.
[7] Furniss to Root, August 29, 1907, Num. Case 2126/12.
[8] H. P. Davis, *Black Democracy* (New York, 1929), p. 148.
[9] Furniss to Bryan, May 10, 1913, 838.00/72.

an army and take the field against the Government. In this emergency the man with the money appears—almost invariably a German merchant who looks upon the financing of a revolution as a straight business proposition. The revolutionary leader gives his paper for not less than double the amount borrowed, and when the revolution succeeds the merchant receives his money again with 100 per cent or more interest. As most revolutions succeed, there is little risk in such loans and they are easily obtained." [10]

Governments fell more easily because the standing army was so ineffective. Since generals were paid $10 to $20 per month, and captains $1, the officers supported themselves by taking part of the 50¢ per month that the privates were supposed to receive and by hiring out the privates as porters or for other non-military work. The privates had to work or steal to avoid starvation.[11] There was naturally little training or discipline, and little incentive to fight for the government. Revolutionists, on the other hand, could offer good pay and opportunities for plunder.

Insurgent armies, especially after 1913, were usually recruited among the *cacos*—peasants living along the northern part of the frontier between Haiti and the Dominican Republic. Time after time between 1913 and 1915, a *caco* army took Cape Haitian and marched south overland to Port au Prince. The president in office usually fled to Jamaica as the revolutionists approached the capital, and the congress, with its meeting place surrounded by troops, elected the revolutionary leader as president. The *cacos* were paid off and sent to their homes, where they were soon ready for a new adventure of the same sort.

Constant disorder and the irresponsible conduct of the courts and the local authorities had given rise to a great number of foreign claims which the short-lived governments were unable and unwilling to settle. Each revolution seemed to bring nearer the time when Haiti would face somewhat the same situation that had confronted the Dominican Republic in 1905. For some years before 1913, in fact, the American, British, French, German, and Italian governments had been vigorously demanding a general settlement of claims,

---

[10] Smith to Bryan, Feb. 21, 1914, 838.00/872.
[11] Furniss to Knox, April 20, 1909, Num. Case 2126/466.

and the Haitians had prevented a showdown only by making timely concessions to one power after another so as to prevent concerted action. European governments frequently sent warships to extort such concessions, and also to land forces for the protection of foreigners during the revolutions. Accepting, as it did, the principle of the Roosevelt Corollary to the Monroe Doctrine, the Wilson administration would have felt that reforms in Haiti were essential to the security of the United States, even though no American financial interests had been involved.

American Financial Interests

The existence of American interests and the annoyance at the Haitian government's unfriendly treatment of them doubtless made the need for reform seem more pressing. The amount of the American investment, however, was not very large. Four New York banks were said to have paid a total of $200,000 for 40 percent of the stock of the reorganized National Bank, and American interests in a syndicate headed by W. R. Grace and Company had half of the stock in the National Railroad, the rest being held by the Ethelburga Syndicate of London. This railroad company operated three short, unconnected lines, with a total length of barely over 100 miles. The cost of construction was being financed by selling in France the company's bonds, which were guaranteed by the Haitian government, but the Grace syndicate had had to advance about $2,000,000 against its underwriting obligation, and it had borrowed $500,000 from the National City Bank, which thus had a stake in the railroad as well as in the National Bank.[12] There was also an American interest in the German controlled Central Railroad of Haiti, the corporation which owned the P.C.S. Railway, the wharf at Port au Prince, and the electric light companies at Port au Prince and Cape Haitian. The National City Bank, Speyer and Company, and the Guaranty Trust Company held between them $215,600 of the corporation's $1,450,000 capital stock, and the Guaranty Trust Company was trustee for an issue of $800,000 of the corporation's bonds which

---

[12] Testimony of Roger L. Farnham in the *Hearings Before the Select Committee on Haiti and Santo Domingo*, pp. 106–107. Cited hereafter as *Hearings*.

had been sold on the American market and were apparently in the hands of small investors scattered all over the United States.[13]

The spokesman for the American financial interests in Haiti was Roger L. Farnham, a vice president of the National City Bank who had also become president of the National Railroad early in 1913. Farnham had been a frequent caller at the State Department since 1911, and during the Wilson administration he exercised an influence on policy which was rather surprising in view of Secretary Bryan's general attitude toward Wall Street. He was always able to give the Department's officers a plausible and fascinating picture of Haitian conditions and psychology, which were so different from those of other Latin American countries, and about which no one in the Department knew very much. Unfortunately, his unsympathetic attitude toward the Haitians and his undisguised determination to bring about American intervention in the republic made him a dangerous counsellor. He was especially adept at playing on the State Department's desire to avoid French or German interference in Haiti. If the American government seemed reluctant to support either of the companies that he represented, Farnham could always point out the probability that the European stockholders would invoke the protection of their own governments, and if necessary he could arrange to have these governments make representations to the United States or to Haiti.

The success of such tactics was evident in the first important controversy after the inauguration of the Wilson administration. In March 1913, the Haitian government made difficulties about accepting the railroad company's line from Port au Prince to St. Marc. It objected to the location of the station at Port au Prince, which was two miles out of town in a swampy area, and it alleged, with much justification, that the whole line was badly constructed.[14] Furniss reported that the dispute was aggravated by the aggressive and offensive attitude of the company's local representatives, who seemed more interested in provoking a controversy than in reaching a settlement.[15] Nevertheless, the State Department instructed the Min-

[13] The Central Railroad of Haiti to the Secretary of State, Jan. 6, 1915, 438.00/11C33.
[14] Farnham admitted this; Furniss to Bryan, July 24, 1914, 838.77/95.
[15] Furniss to Bryan, March 28, 1913, 838.77/73.

ister on May 22 to urge that the government accept the three sections involved, in order to avoid complications which, it was told, would otherwise immediately arise with the company's European creditors and "probably" with the French and German governments. It said that the company promised to remedy any defects.[16] The next month Assistant Secretary of State Osborne visited Haiti and worked out an agreement that closed the matter.

Increasing Disorder and Projects for Reform, 1914–1915

The chain of events that led to American armed intervention began with the revolt of one of Oreste's generals in northern Haiti in January 1914. The new minister, Madison Smith, reported that the situation throughout the republic was regarded as "exceedingly grave," and American warships were ordered to Haitian ports.[17] Bryan told Smith that the State Department was "disposed to do anything proper to support constituted government." When the revolutionists seized the customhouse at Cape Haitian and began to divert funds that should have been applied to the payment of the republic's debts, both the American stockholders in the National Bank and the French government took the matter up in Washington, and the French government also protested to Haiti.[18] Bryan told the consul at Cape Haitian to do what he could to protect the Bank's interests and told Smith to impress on the revolutionary leaders President Wilson's condemnation of revolutionary activities in Latin America as set forth in his statement of March 1913 and to "insist upon constitutional methods for the reform of any abuses." When Oreste resigned and went aboard a German cruiser on January 27, both the American and the German war vessels landed forces to maintain order, and Smith reported that British and French warships were about to arrive.

The foreign troops maintained order for some days before the revolutionists entered the capital in force. Davilmar Theodore, the original leader of the revolt, had been defeated before he reached Port au Prince by another insurgent force led by the Zamor brothers,

[16] Bryan to Furniss, May 22, 1913, 838.77/76.
[17] *Foreign Relations, 1914*, pp. 334–336.
[18] Hallgarten and Co., Ladenburg Thalmann and Co., the National City Bank, and Speyer and Co., to Bryan Jan. 24, 1914, 838.51/319; Jusserand to Bryan, Jan. 27, 1914, 838.00/784.

and it was the latter who took possession of the government. Smith went to some trouble to assure himself that constitutional forms were observed when the congress, in the presence of the revolutionary army, elected Oreste Zamor as president on February 8.[19]

It was at this time that the American government began seriously to consider the advisability of giving Haiti the same sort of help that it was trying to give to the Dominican Republic. It seemed doubtful whether Zamor could establish a stable regime without outside aid. Theodore was still carrying on guerrilla operations along the Haitian frontier, and the new administration's efforts to restore order were handicapped by lack of money. The interest on the National Railroad bonds due on February 1 was not paid until March 25, a default that seemed the more serious because Haiti had hitherto been punctual in servicing the foreign debt. The National Bank flatly refused any aid, and its attitude caused Smith to suspect that it was trying to create a situation where the United States would have to intervene.[20] As a matter of fact, Farnham had been discussing with some of the officials of the State Department the possibility of intervening to install a capable civilian as president and to support him while he carried out essential reforms.[21]

Neither Secretary Bryan nor President Wilson seem to have contemplated actual intervention, but they apparently thought that Zamor might voluntarily agree to some form of customs control in the hope of obtaining prompt recognition. Smith and Farnham both assured the State Department that many Haitians would welcome such a step.[22] On February 26 Smith was instructed to tell the Zamor government that the United States would probably be disposed to recognize it but to indicate that the United States wished to know its views about accepting American aid in administering the customs and in selecting locations for the lighthouses which

[19] Smith to Bryan, Feb. 16, 1914, 838.00/857.

[20] Smith to Bryan, March 6, 1914, 838.51/327.

[21] See Farnham's letter to Bryan, Jan. 22, 1914, 838.00/901; and J. H. Stabler's memorandum to Bryan, Feb. 3, 1914, 838.00/894.

[22] Smith to Bryan, Feb. 14, 1914, 838.51/323, and Feb. 21, 1914, 838.00/872, and Farnham's letter of Jan. 22 cited above. A Latin American Division memorandum of March 25 stated that the cable of Feb. 26 had been sent because private parties had represented that certain members of the Zamor administration had indicated a willingness to have the United States reorganize the customs.

would be important to shipping after the imminent opening of the Panama Canal. Bryan asked also for a renewal of the assurances that no power except the United States would be allowed to obtain a foothold at the Mole St. Nicholas. When Smith reported, however, that the Haitian government would make no definite reply to his communication until it had received recognition, Bryan promptly authorized him to recognize it.[23]

A few days later, Farnham told the State Department that Zamor was negotiating with French bankers for a loan secured by a customs receivership, and that he had been asked to ascertain whether the United States, if it was unwilling to take over the customs itself, would object to French administration and protection of the service.[24] Smith was at once instructed to say that the United States would be willing to consider assisting Haiti in the administration of the customs if the Haitian government wished such assistance. President Wilson, Bryan said, did not ask that Haiti make such a request, but was disposed to support the existing government against insurrections if it proved itself worthy of confidence by meeting its governmental responsibilities.[25] Neither Wilson nor Bryan probably foresaw the angry reaction that these suggestions would produce in Haiti, where Zamor himself convened a mass meeting at which members of the Cabinet accused the National Bank of trying to force the establishment of an American protectorate.[26]

At the same time both the French and German governments made it clear that they would oppose any unilateral action by the United States. The French Embassy at Washington told the State Department on March 12, 1914, that France would expect to participate in any reorganization of the Haitian customs, and alleged that T. C. Dawson had assured the French Ambassador in 1911 that such participation would be natural and desirable. Bryan replied more than three months later that Dawson had no power to bind the State Department, but that the Haitian government had not asked for any reorganization.[27] On March 14 the German Minister at Port au Prince

[23] Bryan to Smith, Feb. 26, 1914, 838.00/855; Smith to Bryan, Feb. 28, 838.00/864; Bryan to Smith, March 1, 838.00/864.
[24] Farnham's memorandum of March 6, 1914, 838.51/328.
[25] Bryan to Smith, March 7, 1914, 838.51/327A.
[26] Smith to Bryan, March 19, 1914, 838.51/334.
[27] Byran to French Embassy, July 21, 1914, 838.51/330.

formally advised the Haitian Foreign Office that his government would demand a share in any foreign customs control.[28]

The German merchants at Port au Prince helped Zamor out of his immediate difficulty by arranging a small loan locally, but the general situation grew steadily worse. Continued disorder along the frontier not only endangered foreign interests in Haiti but made more difficult the American government's efforts to establish peace in Santo Domingo, where the revolution against Bordas started in April. Zamor continued to borrow money, always on ruinous terms, from the local Germans, and his relations with the National Bank steadily deteriorated. In June 1914, the bank's manager told Smith that his directors would probably refuse to renew the "budgetary convention" when it expired in September, in the belief that this action would bring on a crisis that would compel Haiti to agree to the establishment of an American customs receivership.[29]

In the State Department there was a growing feeling that something must be done in Haiti, if only to check the growing German influence there. J. H. Stabler of the Latin American Division, in a memorandum written May 13, 1914, mentioned reports that German bankers and merchants were taking advantage of Zamor's situation, not only to make great profits from loans but to obtain "almost complete control of the financial and commercial affairs of the Island," and said that "unless some outside power immediately takes charge of the financial affairs of the Haitian people, it would appear that serious international difficulties will follow." [30] Boaz Long, the chief of the Division, thought that "the ever present danger of German control" was growing more serious because of the tragic political situation. The Haitian people, he said, were "virtually slaves; their owners a lot of low politicians. . . . If we are going to remove the hands of graft from their throats, we will have to be very firm, for our opponents are among the most skillful in the world." [31] It was probably Haiti that Robert Lansing, then counsellor of the Department, had in mind when he suggested to Wilson that the Monroe Doctrine might be broadened to cover situations where financial

[28] Government of Haiti, *Exposé Générale de la Situation, 1914* (Port au Prince, 1932).

[29] Smith to Bryan, June 9, 1914, 838.51/340.

[30] 838.00/1667.

[31] Memorandum of May 16, 1914, 838.00/1669.

control threatened to give a European state dominance over a Latin American country.[32] There were reports that the Zamor government might authorize the establishment of a German coaling depot at the Mole St. Nicholas, but Ross Hazeltine, a consular officer on special detail, investigated these and thought that they had been spread chiefly by interests that wished to provoke American intervention.[33]

The Americans interested in the National Bank continued to insist that a customs receivership was the obvious solution for Haiti's troubles, and some officers in the State Department agreed with them. Bryan had thus far taken the position that the United States should act only if the Haitian government asked for help, but late in June 1914 he accepted proposals that contemplated a somewhat more positive policy. These were described in the State Department as the "Farnham Plan." Just what the plan was is not entirely clear from the record, but it seems to have been based on a memorandum, apparently dictated by Farnham or based on his suggestions, which was presented to the Secretary on June 23 and which urged particularly that definite steps be taken to reorganize the Haitian customs service. The author wrote that he understood that Charles Zamor, who was "the guiding hand" in his brother's administration, would not oppose American control of the customs if the government were assured of adequate physical protection against those who would oppose it. If customs control were arranged, the National Bank would help the government financially. It was suggested that a special emissary of the State Department, working with someone from the bank, might be able to persuade the Zamors to accept the plan.[34]

Arthur Bailly-Blanchard, who had just been appointed to succeed Smith as minister, consequently took with him to Haiti a draft convention which would have established an American receivership. In general, this followed the language of the Dominican convention of 1907 but with additions which recent experience in Santo Domingo had suggested: a provision for an American financial adviser and an article authorizing the United States to prevent "any and all" interference with the customs service. The Minister was

[32] Memorandum of June 16, 1914, *Lansing Papers*, Vol. II, pp. 459ff.
[33] Hazeltine's Report No. 5, July 6, 1914, 838.345/20.
[34] 838.51/494.

asked to "sound the Government of Haiti for an expression of its attitude toward the proposed convention . . . and advise the Department of any objections." [35] No offer of military support was mentioned in the instruction, but the commander of the U.S.S. *South Carolina* and Farnham himself were apparently entrusted with the task of explaining the new plan to the American consul at Cape Haitian so that he could discuss it with the Zamors, who were in northern Haiti with their army. [36]

Consul Livingston and Farnham had an interview with the President's brother, Charles Zamor, and reported on July 12 that he accepted the plan in principle. [37] A few days later, however, Charles Zamor suggested that American forces occupy Port au Prince, so that the Haitian government would apparently be acting under duress. [38] Bryan was not prepared to go so far. The Department had indeed asked the navy on July 11 to assemble a force of marines at Guantánamo for possible use either in Haiti or in the Dominican Republic, and this action had been given publicity in an obvious effort to create an impression in both countries; [39] but on July 24 Bailly-Blanchard was told by radio that it was absolutely necessary that any request for the adoption of the proposed plan come from the Haitian government. [40]

If it seems strange that Bryan should have permitted a person in Farnham's position to help formulate and execute the State Department's policy, we must remember that Farnham was the only person with whom he had contact who seemed to be thoroughly well informed about Haiti. The Secretary should, of course, have been able to rely on the American Legation at Port au Prince, but Smith, a political appointee, was of little use. Smith had been given the post because Bryan insisted that a white man be sent to Haiti "until affairs there could be straightened out," and Wilson, who wished to appoint a Negro, had acquiesced with the understanding that

[35] The text of the instruction and draft convention is printed in *Foreign Relations, 1914*, pp. 347–350.

[36] Instruction to Consul Livingston, July 10, 1914, 838.00/947a.

[37] Telegram from Cape Haitian, July 12, 1914, 838.00/945.

[38] Telegram from Cape Haitian, July 18, 1914, 838.00/958.

[39] The correspondence about this was apparently withheld from the files at the time and placed later in file 838.00 without enclosure numbers.

[40] Letter to navy requesting that cable be sent, July 24, 1914, 838.00/967a.

Smith would remain for only a few months.[41] Smith had shown little interest in his work,[42] and Bailly-Blanchard, a white man and a career diplomat, had been picked to succeed him. The new Minister was a mild-mannered, elderly gentleman, whose chief qualifications were a fluent command of French and long experience with the formal and ceremonial aspects of diplomacy in large embassies, and he went to Haiti rather reluctantly but apparently with a promise that he would later be transferred to Paris as First Secretary.[43] As it turned out, he was Minister to Haiti for many years.

Soon after Bailly-Blanchard arrived at his post, he himself went to northern Haiti on the *U.S.S. Connecticut* to discuss the "Farnham Plan" with Oreste Zamor. The President, however, evaded him, and it was soon evident that he did not intend to accept the American government's proposals. The State Department thought that the German Minister and the local German merchants had been chiefly responsible for the failure of its plan.[44]

Neither the German nor the French government was willing to see the United States take control of Haiti's finances. In the last days of July 1914 both of them informed the United States that they would expect to participate in any customs receivership that might be set up.[45] The State Department merely took note of the French communication, which was received just as the war was beginning in Europe, but the reply to Germany, dated September 18, 1914, was drafted by President Wilson himself and was an important statement of his policy with respect to foreign economic interests in the Caribbean.[46]

The United States, the President said, welcomed participation by German interests in the economic development of Haiti, but it had long and invariably taken the position that "neither foreign mer-

[41] Bryan to Wilson, June 19, 1913, Wilson Papers, Library of Congress.
[42] Bryan to Wilson, Jan. 21, 1914, Bryan-Wilson Correspondence, Library of Congress.
[43] Bryan to Wilson, April 30, 1914, *ibid.*
[44] Bailly-Blanchard to Bryan, July 31, 1914, 838.00/970. For the State Department's belief that German influence defeated the plan, see Heimke's memorandum of October 23, 1914, 838.00/1630.
[45] The German Chargé d'Affaires to Phillips, July 25, 1914, 838.51/354; French Embassy to the Department of State, July 30, 1914, 838.51/343.
[46] Regarding the authorship of the note, see *Lansing Papers* (printed as part of Foreign Relations series, 1939–1940), Vol. II, p. 466. The text of the note is filed under 838.51/354.

cantile influences and interests, nor any other foreign influence or interest proceeding from outside the American hemisphere, could with the consent of the United States be so broadened or extended as to constitute a control, either wholly or in part, of the government or administration of any independent American state." German participation in a customs administration would be a serious departure from this principle. One of the grave dangers involved in certain sorts of concessions to Europeans was that the "legitimate and natural course of enforcing claims" might lead to measures imperiling the independence or at least the complete autonomy of American states "and might issue in results which the Government of the United States has always regarded it as its duty to guard against as the nearest friend and natural champion of those states whenever they should need a friend or champion." The President assured the German representative that anything that the United States might do in helping Haiti in her financial difficulties "would be done without intending to serve the interest of any citizen of the United States or the interest of the Government of the United States in preference to the interest of the citizens or government of any other country." The United States did not regard its insistence on an exclusive privilege to help Haiti as a course dictated by selfishness but, on the contrary, as one dictated by a desire for peace and for the exclusion of all occasion of unfriendliness with any nation of the other hemisphere. It was willing to give any pledges of disinterest and impartiality that might reasonably suggest themselves.

The outbreak of war in Europe made it easier for the State Department to disregard German and French opposition to its plans in Haiti but made worse the republic's internal problems. The merchants could not obtain credits for the movement of the coffee crop, and the National Bank, with a part of its funds tied up in Paris, had an excuse for reducing its advances under the budgetary convention —a step that aggravated its already bad relations with the Haitian government. Interest on the National Railroad bonds was defaulted on August 1, and in September the government announced its intention to seize the railroad line because the company had failed to complete the amount of construction required by its concession. Bailly-Blanchard was able, however, to obtain a stay in the proceedings which postponed the issue for the time being.

Meanwhile Theodore continued his guerrilla operations in the interior. The State Department was the more disturbed about his activity because he was apparently allied to Desiderio Arias, who was the chief obstacle to its efforts for peace in Santo Domingo. It was becoming more than ever clear that it would be difficult to establish stable government in either end of the island if disorder prevailed in the other; and when the American government made up its mind to take energetic steps to stop the civil war in Santo Domingo it renewed its efforts for reform in Haiti. In a telegram dated August 28, 1914, which he dictated himself, Bryan told Bailly-Blanchard of the successful execution of the "Wilson Plan," and said that "henceforth constitutional methods will prevail in Santo Domingo and peace and prosperity will follow." The Minister was instructed to tell the Haitians that he was authorized to negotiate the treaty that had been proposed in July, whenever Zamor was disposed to consider the plan, and that the United States would furnish any assistance necessary to enforce law and order and insure constitutional government in Haiti.[47]

Zamor showed no disposition to discuss the plan. For a time he seemed likely to defeat the revolutionists, and when he took Theodore's stronghold at Ouanaminthe in September the prospect for peace seemed so good that the United States withdrew two of the three warships that had been in Haitian waters. In October, however, the *cacos* resumed operations and took Cape Haitian. Zamor, finding his position desperate, begged for help from the United States and indicated that he would accept the American government's proposals. Two warships and 800 Marines were ordered to Port au Prince, but before they arrived the revolutionists took possession of the city. Zamor went on board a Dutch merchant vessel, and his brother Charles took refuge in the Dominican Legation.

Lansing, as Acting Secretary of State, authorized Bailly-Blanchard, at his discretion, to ask the commanding officer of the American warships to "take charge of Port au Prince" and to restore Charles Zamor to his Cabinet functions, saying that the State Department wished to negotiate with the Zamor brothers and that it was contemplating a convention like that proposed in July. The Minister

[47] Except where other sources are cited, the account that follows is based on *Foreign Relations* for 1914 and 1915.

was also to endeavor to bring about an agreement for a fair election, to be held within a specified time, like the agreement that had recently restored peace in Santo Domingo.

The complete collapse of the government and the flight of the Zamor brothers before the American warships could arrive made it impossible to carry out these instructions, and on October 30 Lansing told Bailly-Blanchard to endeavor to persuade the factional leaders to reach "a practical agreement for the restoration of permanent order and peace and the establishment of a stable constitutional government." The Minister was to warn them that the United States might have to "take steps necessary to prevent a period of disorder and anarchy which would menace the rights and property of Americans and other foreigners." The next day he was informed that the Department of State contemplated "conversations looking toward a customs convention and a free election under supervision of United States commissioners" when a *de facto* government was established.

Lansing evidently hoped to do in Haiti what the United States was doing in the Dominican Republic: to install a provisional government chosen by the party leaders, which would in turn arrange for the free election of a constitutional government worthy of vigorous support by the United States. On November 4, in fact, the State Department sent to Port au Prince, by mail, a copy of the "Wilson Plan," with "Dominican Republic" changed to "Haiti." It described this as a memorandum for the Minister's "information," but it said that it believed that only some such arrangement would assure the maintenance of public order and that it considered holding elections under American supervision to be as important as the negotiation of a customs convention. It is not clear that the State Department realized the futility of attempting to apply the "Wilson Plan" in Haiti. The plan had worked in Santo Domingo, where there were organized political parties with a substantial following, but in Haiti the contending leaders were little more than chiefs of mercenary bands, and the ignorance and political indifference of the masses made a popular election practically impossible. Under the Haitian constitution, furthermore, the president was chosen by the congress.

The American government did not go forward with the vigorous policy that Lansing's instructions had foreshadowed. The revolutionists established order in Port au Prince, and there was no need to land men from the American warships. The demand for a supervised election was apparently forgotten after the congress chose Theodore as president on November 7. Even the State Department's efforts to exact conditions from Theodore in return for recognition produced no result. Theodore was told that he would be formally recognized after he had agreed to a long list of demands, including the signature of a customs convention, the settlement of the questions pending with the National Bank and National Railroad, the arbitration of other American claims, and a promise never to lease Haitian territory to any European government for use as a coaling station. He was asked to send a commission to Washington to sign protocols covering these matters, and the State Department promised to use its good offices with the National Bank to obtain financial help while the commission was negotiating.

Theodore at first seemed willing to comply but then submitted a counterproposal, alleging that popular opposition would make it impossible to instruct a commission to negotiate about the customs. The counterproject would have provided for a measure of financial control and seemed to Bailly-Blanchard "possibly acceptable." It had to be abandoned, however, when the Minister for Foreign Affairs read its text and the text of the American government's draft convention to the Senate and barely escaped a beating by the irate senators. The proposal which the Haitian government finally submitted covered none of the State Department's specific demands but offered instead to "grant preference to the Government of the United States and citizens in commercial and industrial affairs," in return for assistance in Haiti's economic development. Bryan, in reply, disclaimed any intention of asking special privileges for Americans and pointed out that peace was the first requisite for economic development.

On December 12, Bryan instructed Bailly-Blanchard to say that "this nation has no desire to assume responsibilities in regard to Haiti's fiscal system except in accordance with the wishes of the Government." The question of recognition would be considered "on its merits," but the United States would want information about "the fiscal standing and general plans of the Government, its attitude toward foreigners, and its attitude in connection with the Mole St. Nicholas." This seemed a reversal of the policy Lansing had adopted a few weeks earlier when Bryan was away from the State Department. Bryan often seemed more hesitant than Wilson to use compulsion on a government that resisted plans for its improvement, but the change in policy was perhaps more apparent than real. It was clearly impracticable to insist further on the customs receivership for the time being, but the Haitian government knew what the United States wanted and might still be expected to endeavor to make a satisfactory proposal in order to obtain recognition and financial help. A few days later, in fact, the State Department suggested this. When Bailly-Blanchard and Louis Borno, the new Minister of Foreign Affairs, had worked out a tentative understanding that left the customs matter aside but dealt with several other matters that had been under discussion, the Department virtually ignored their proposals but reiterated its willingness to help Haiti as it had helped the Dominican Republic if the Haitian government would request such help.

The situation was complicated by bitter quarrels between the new Haitian government and the National Bank. Theodore inherited several unsettled disputes about the bank's privileges and duties under its concession. The currency reform, which was one of the chief purposes of the 1910 loan, had not yet been carried out because it had been impossible until late in 1913 to agree on a procedure for the replacement of the old paper money with the bank's own notes.[48] In 1914 the replacement was going forward, rather slowly, but new disputes arose when the bank refused to give Theodore the financial help he demanded. On November 24, Bailly-Blanchard reported that a new issue of government paper money was under consideration. The bank protested against this as a violation of its concession, and the State Department told the government that it would not consider the new money "legal," but Theodore went forward with the plan.

Against this background, an inicident occurred which has sometimes been given more importance than it deserves. Early in December 1914 the bank decided to return to New York about half of the gold which had been sent to Haiti a few months earlier for

[48] Farnham's memorandum of Dec. 23, 1914, 838.516/82.

the redemption of the paper money. In New York, the Haitian government would receive interest on the money, which was a part of the proceeds of the 1910 loan, but which was held by the bank under the loan contract exclusively for the currency reform. The money would also be safer. Since no merchant vessels were available, for few ships were calling at Haitian ports since the outbreak of the European war, the bank asked the State Department to have the gold transported on a warship, and the U.S.S. *Machias*, which was returning to the United States, was ordered to stop at Port au Prince to receive it. On December 17, a large number of marines, armed with stout canes and concealed revolvers, escorted about $500,000 in gold from the bank to the wharf, where it was embarked without incident. There was nothing illegal about the shipment of the money, but the move was probably ill advised. The Haitians saw it as an effort to put their own property beyond the reach of seizure, and they not unnaturally regarded it as an affront. The American Minister and the manager of the bank and the senior naval officer present were all doubtful about the necessity for the transfer and realized that it might cause trouble.[49] It was true, as the State Department pointed out in reply to the Haitian government's angry protests, that there had been attempts during the recent revolutions to seize the money and that the bank would have incurred a responsibility by not taking all proper measures to safeguard it; but the American officials thought that there was no imminent danger so long as United States warships were in Haitian waters.

When the bank refused to accept the government's new paper money, Theodore retaliated by forcibly taking $65,000 in gold from its vaults and attempted to seize other funds. Haitian officials even made threats of bodily injury to the American and other foreign employees, and the State Department felt compelled on January 4, 1915, to warn the Haitian government that they must not be harmed. On January 7, Bryan wrote Wilson that there was no progress toward a solution of the Haitian problem. Zamor and Theodore had each seemed willing to make a treaty with the United States but had done nothing. "The important matter of interest, however, is

[49] See the communications from Commander Willard filed with 838.00/1067 and 1075, and Bailly-Blanchard's two telegrams of Dec. 14, 838.516/18, 19.

the Bank." Bryan gave the President a rather vague account of the bank's difficulties. He made no specific recommendations but thought that there would be no peace in Haiti until there was some such arrangement as there was in the Dominican Republic. "There is probably sufficient ground for intervention," he wrote, "but I do not like the idea of forcible interference on purely business grounds." He asked for the President's instructions.

Wilson had less difficulty in deciding on a course of action. He was convinced, he wrote Bryan on January 13, that it was the duty of the American government to take immediately the action that it had taken in the Dominican Republic. He meant to send a commissioner who would say firmly that the United States would not permit revolutionary conditions "constantly to exist there." The United States would insist on a popular election and would support "to the utmost" the government that resulted. Bryan thought that the President's idea would put Haiti "on the highway to prosperity," and he suggested that Fort and Smith, who had carried out the Dominican mission successfully, be asked to undertake the assignment, with Minister Bailly-Blanchard as a third member of the commission.[50]

In the six weeks that elapsed before the commission sailed, the situation grew worse. By decrees issued late in January and early in February the government took the treasury service from the bank and ordered that the customs duties be paid to merchants at the various ports. This not only deprived the bank of one of its most valuable privileges but violated agreements with the republic's creditors and made a default on the foreign debt virtually inevitable. Bailly-Blanchard protested, but his protest was rejected by the Haitian government on the ground that the bank was a French corporation. There was also another revolution. Theodore had never been strong enough to replace the military chiefs who had controlled several districts under Zamor, and lack of money made it impossible for him to retain the loyalty of his own adherents. In December he had been forced to appoint General Vilbrun Guillaume Sam, who was a rival leader of his own group, as ruler of the Department of

[50] Bryan to Wilson, Jan. 7, 1915, Bryan-Wilson Correspondence; Wilson to Bryan, Jan. 13, 1915, 838.00/1378; Bryan to Wilson, Jan. 16, 1915, 838.00/1382.

the North, and when a *caco* army approached Cape Haitian in January 1915 Sam assumed the leadership of the revolution. There was little fighting. By February 19 the whole country outside of the capital was in the hands of the insurgents, and on February 22, after Port au Prince had been without food or water for three days, Theodore fled on a Dutch merchant ship.

President Wilson's plan changed somewhat when Bailly-Blanchard pointed out that it would be impracticable to hold a popular election in Haiti because the constitution provided that the president be elected by the congress and the leader of a successful revolution was always chosen as a matter of course. Members of the Chamber of Deputies were elected "by the people," but, he explained, "elections as understood in America do not exist in Haiti. Elections being simply a continuation of military system under which the country is governed. The population generally takes no part in elections, the voting being done by soldiers acting under instructions. Few voters who vote many times." The commission was consequently instructed not to follow the Dominican procedure but rather to report on Guillaume Sam's popularity, his qualifications for the presidency, and his views about international matters. It was told that the President of the United States wished to help Haiti but must have full information; and that the draft convention for a customs collectorship, proposed in July 1914, set forth the President's views as to the most desirable arrangement.[51]

There is no evidence that these vague written instructions were supplemented by more explicit oral instructions. At any rate, the commissioners accomplished little. The congress elected Guillaume Sam president on March 4, the day before they arrived. Fort reported on March 9 that "situation looks encouraging for quick results," but three days later he cabled that the commission had "full possession of facts" and could accomplish nothing by a longer stay. Apparently the shocking sanitary conditions at Port au Prince, which caused Fort and Smith to live on a warship, contributed to their eagerness to wind up their mission.[52] Perhaps the information that

---

[51] Bryan to the commission, Feb. 27, 1915, 838.00/1382.
[52] I was told this by a member of the Legation staff at Port au Prince. See also Fort's undated telegram to the State Department, 838.00/1138.

they brought home with them was of some value to the State Department in dealing with subsequent events.[53]

It seemed possible for a time that Guillaume Sam would establish a more stable government. He had more money than his predecessors because he used the revenues that would have been impounded for the benefit of the republic's creditors if the treasury service had continued in the bank. His administration was recognized by Germany, Italy, and France late in March. The commissioners advised against recognition by the United States, but Bailly-Blanchard recommended on March 25 that recognition be granted if the Haitian government would agree to the protection of foreign interests and the arbitration of claims, and would promise not to grant naval or coaling stations to a European power. The Minister thought that this would be the best way to obtain a later agreement about the customs and the Bank and the railroad, but he was rebuked for this suggestion by direction of President Wilson himself.[54]

Wilson and Bryan still felt that they must take some decisive step to put an end to the continual disorder in Haiti and to eliminate the foreign influences which seemed to be obstructing what they were trying to do there. The French government, on February 20, had again reminded the United States of its desire to participate in any financial reorganization and had asserted that "no other nation holds the peculiar situation that France occupies toward Haiti." When Bryan replied that the United States could not admit any European nation to partnership in any political control, France still insisted on a right to take part in a customs receivership if one were established.[55] Bryan thought that French and German influence was still undesirably strong in Haiti, and Farnham encouraged his suspicions by reporting that French interests were lending money to Guillaume Sam and that the European stockholders were making difficulties for the American interests in the National Bank. Farnham seems to have indicated that the Americans were thinking of selling their stock. Bryan hoped that they would not, but he did not see how he could ask them not to sell unless the United States was pre-

[53] The commissioners' report of March 13, to the Secretary of State, is in the Wilson Papers, Library of Congress.
[54] Bryan to Bailly-Blanchard, March 26, 1915, 838.00/1151a.
[55] The French note of Feb. 20 is printed in *Foreign Relations, 1915*, p. 514. For Bryan's reply and the second French note, see 838.51/385 and 394.

pared to protect them against the influence which the French and German interests were bringing to bear. Incredible as it seems when the two governments were at war, the Secretary thought that these interests were working together in Haiti and that they might even have designs on the Mole St. Nicholas.[56]

To Wilson also, the situation had "a most sinister appearance." He thought that the American interests should remain in Haiti and that the United States should assist them in every legitimate way. He asked Bryan to think out a "plan of controlling action" to take before things got worse. Bryan's reply, on April 2, was rather vague. He thought that Bailly-Blanchard, who had been a disappointment, should perhaps be replaced. The United States should obtain an agreement about the Mole and decide its whole course of action before recognizing Guillaume Sam. The American stockholders would be willing to buy the European holdings in the bank if they were assured protection, but "their idea seems to be that no protection will be sufficient that does not include a control of the Customs House." The Secretary thought that the time had probably come to decide on a more active supervision over Haiti but that perhaps an American adviser in the customs service might be enough, at least at the beginning. He thought that a demand backed by "a good sized ship" might produce results.

Bryan went on to say that he had been reluctant to approve the use of force but that some force might now be necessary. "Following the line of your Mobile speech," he wrote to Wilson, "we have as much reason to object to the control of a Latin American government by foreign financiers as by a foreign government, and there is no doubt that the foreign financiers have been a controlling interest in the politics of Haiti." Furthermore, the revolutions in Haiti were a menace to the stability of the Dominican Republic. These two considerations justified a more active policy on the part of the United States.[57]

Early in May, Paul Fuller was sent to Haiti to discuss the terms on which the United States would recognize Guillaume Sam. Probably because of the strong feeling in Haiti and fear of renewed European

[56] Bryan to Wilson, March 21, 1915, 838.51/395a; March 25, 1915, Bryan-Wilson Correspondence; March 27, 1915, *ibid.*
[57] Wilson to Bryan, March 21, 1915, *ibid.*; Bryan to Wilson, April 2, 1915, *ibid.*

opposition, the customs collectorship was not mentioned. The proposed agreement, however, would require the Haitian government to take advice from the American Legation, especially in connection with the removal of dishonest or inefficient officials, in order to assure the existence of an administration which the United States could support with any force that might be necessary. It would also provide for a general arbitration of foreign claims. Fuller was to say that the United States was willing to lease the Mole St. Nicholas, if the Haitian government wished, and that it must insist in any case that it be not granted to another power.[58]

Fuller embodied these proposals in a draft treaty he submitted to the Minister of Foreign Affairs on May 22. The Haitian government's response was typical of the methods of Haitian diplomacy. First it stalled, demanding formal recognition before making a reply. Then it submitted a counterproject, omitting Fuller's proposal that an American Minister Plenipotentiary be appointed for the specific purpose of advising the government, and accepting American help in maintaining order only on condition that the American troops be withdrawn at the first request of the Haitian government. Fuller could not accept this last stipulation and could not persuade the Haitians to relinquish it. Without definitely breaking off the negotiations he left Port au Prince on June 5.

It seems probable that Fuller suspended his negotiations because a different solution for the problem of customs control was under consideration. One of the American vice presidents of the National Bank informed the State Department on June 4 that the president and the general manager of the Bank had come to the United States to discuss the "Americanization" of the institution, which Bryan had suggested. If the bank was an American concern, it could cooperate with the United States government in a plan for the reorganization of Haiti's finances and the administration and collection of the customs. The letter stated that the Haitian government had indicated a willingness to let the bank control the customs, but the bank must have some assurance of governmental protection. The proposed arrangement would make it possible for Haiti to obtain a loan from the interests which would control the bank.

The State Department made a noncommittal reply, but it was

[58] For Fuller's instructions see 838.00/1393a.

evidently interested in this proposal. In a memorandum left with the State Department on June 25, the bank said that the Haitian government now advised it that it needed money and wanted American recognition; and, while it could not accept American military intervention, it would permit the bank to nominate a white man to take charge of each customhouse. The government wished the moral support of the United States and if necessary its military support, but only on the understanding that any forces sent to Haiti would be withdrawn when order was restored. This seemed still more encouraging, but it soon appeared that French law would make it impossible to transfer the bank to American control when a substantial number of the French stockholders opposed the transaction.[59]

Meanwhile Fuller had submitted his report to the State Department. He expressed the opinion that most Haitians wanted an arrangement such as he had suggested, or even a customs collectorship, but that individual officials were afraid to take the responsibility for an agreement. He thought that the existing situation could not continue. If the treaty he had proposed were not accepted, he recommended that the United States intervene with marines to impose a treaty along the lines of the Cuban Platt Amendment.[60] The report gave President Wilson "a great deal of concern." He felt that "Action is evidently necessary and no doubt it would be a mistake to postpone it long"; and he asked Lansing, the new Secretary of State, to read the report and to give him his opinion on what ought to be done and how.[61]

The American Intervention

The crisis came before the Secretary could present a plan of action. While Fuller was in Port au Prince another *caco* revolution was in progress in the North. Sullivan reported from Santo Domingo on March 28 that a Haitian leader named Ronsalvo Bobo, then at Monte Cristi, had proclaimed a revolution to prevent the establishment of an American customs collectorship and that he was being

[59] Wehrhane's letter of June 4, the Department's reply of June 10, and Wehrhane's memorandum of June 25, 1915, are filed under 838.516/87. With regard to the obstacle presented by French law see the Latin American Division's memorandum of Dec. 13, 1915, 813.516/98.

[60] Report of Paul Fuller, Jr., to the Secretary of State, June 14, 1915, 838.00/1197.

[61] Wilson to Lansing, July 2, 1915, 838.00/1197.

secretly aided by Desiderio Arias. President Jiménez had Bobo arrested and deported, but on April 25 a band of his followers occupied Cape Haitian, and on May 13 his forces administered a serious defeat to the government's army in the North. The government recaptured Cape Haitian on June 19, but the revolution continued. French marines were landed at the Cape during the fighting, and were still there when Admiral Caperton arrived on the *U.S.S. Washington* two weeks later and told both Haitian factions that there must be no fighting in the town. During the next month the outcome of the war seemed uncertain, but on July 27 there was a sudden successful uprising in Port au Prince and Guillaume Sam sought asylum in the French Legation.

As the President left the palace, and supposedly at his orders, there was a general massacre of the political suspects who were being held in the prison at Port au Prince. Approximately 167 persons, many of them members of the city's most prominent families, were killed in cold blood. The commander of the prison, who had carried out the massacre, took refuge in the Dominican Legation, but was almost immediately murdered there by relatives of some of the victims. The next day an organized mob, made up of members of the *élite* of Port au Prince, took Guillaume Sam from the French Legation and tore him to pieces in the streets.[62] The *U.S.S. Washington* entered the harbor as this occurred.

When it received word of the uprising at Port au Prince, but before it learned of the violation of the French Legation, the State Department had asked the navy to order Admiral Caperton to land marines immediately at Port au Prince and to ask the captains of the British and French warships that were present not to land forces, assuring them that the Americans would protect foreign interests. Caperton consequently landed marines and blue-jackets on the afternoon of July 28, much to the relief of the foreign residents, who had been terrified by the unprecedented violation of two foreign Legations. The Committee of Public Safety, which the local leaders had set up to maintain order, cooperated with him and agreed to disarm the Haitian soldiers in the city. Two American sailors were nevertheless killed by snipers.

[62] For a vivid account of these events, see R. B. Davis, Jr.'s memorandum in *Foreign Relations, 1916*, pp. 311ff.

The American government was now in a position where it might hope to obtain the control which it had been seeking to impose on successive Haitian governments, but both Lansing and Wilson found it difficult to decide what should be done. Lansing asked the navy on July 30 to instruct Caperton not to turn over the city government of Port au Prince to any Haitian authority for the time being,[63] but he wrote the President on August 3 that the situation in Haiti was "distressing and very perplexing. I am not at all sure what we ought to do or what we can legally do." He pointed out that the United States had no such excuse to take over the government at Port au Prince as it had had for example at Vera Cruz, where there was a question of reprisal, but he thought that it might base its action on the humane duty of relieving starvation. The control of the customs and the expenditure of the revenues for the benefit of the people could be justified on the same basis. If the situation were permitted to continue, another corrupt and irresponsible government might be established.

Wilson replied that he was equally perplexed and that he feared that "we do not have the legal authority to do what we apparently ought to do . . . , I suppose there is nothing for it but to take the bull by the horns and restore order." A more definite program would require legislation and a treaty. In the meantime, he felt that the United States must:

1. Send to Port au Prince a sufficient force to control the city and the surrounding country from which it drew its food.
2. Let the Haitian congress know that it would be protected, but that the United States would not recognize any action that did not put in charge of affairs men who could be trusted to end revolutions.
3. Make clear to all the leaders that the United States would take steps to prevent the payment of debts contracted to finance revolution. In other words, that the United States considered it its duty to insist on constitutional government, and would be prepared if forced to do so, to take charge of elections and obtain a real government which the American Government could support.[64]

---

[63] 838.00/1231a.
[64] For Lansing's letter and Wilson's reply see 838.00/1418.

Lansing asked the navy to send a sufficient force to control Port au Prince and the country from which it drew its food supply, and to have Caperton take charge of the principal customhouses in order to obtain funds for the organization of a constabulary and for starting a public works program that would relieve unemployment.[65] The Admiral occupied the port towns one by one as reinforcements arrived, and the customs receipts, which had been going into the hands of the military leaders who happened to be in control in each place, were deposited in the National Bank subject to his orders. In an effort to allay the suspicion these acts aroused, Caperton issued a proclamation on August 9 stating that "I am directed by the United States Government to assure the Haitian people that the United States has no object in view except to insure, to establish, and to help maintain Haitian independence and the establishment of a stable and firm government by the Haitian people.

"Every assistance will be given to the Haitian people in their attempt to secure these ends. It is the intention to retain the United States forces in Haiti only so long as will be necessary for this purpose."

Meanwhile, as Caperton reported on August 7, "all classes of Haitians" were clamoring for the election of a president. Bobo, who was the candidate of the Committee of Public Safety, expected to be chosen. He was supported by some fifteen hundred *cacos* who had remained in Port au Prince and were thought to have hidden arms and ammunition, and an intimidated congress would probably have elected him if Caperton had not requested a delay. As the congressmen became more confident that they would be protected by the American forces, however, a majority of them seemed more inclined to support Sudre Dartiguenave, the president of the Senate. Caperton had rather unfavorable reports about both candidates,[66] but Dartiguenave seemed more likely to cooperate with the United States. He and his colleagues assured the Admiral that they would gladly accede to any terms that the American government proposed, including control of the customs and a cession of the Mole St. Nicholas. They begged that they not be subjected to any unneces-

---

[65] Lansing to Secretary of Navy, Aug. 6, 1915, 838.00/1418.
[66] See for example the comments in Caperton's weekly report of August 13, 838.00/1269.

sary humiliation but said that no Haitian government could stand without protection from the United States.

The departments at Washington wished to delay an election until a more definite program could be worked out, but, when Caperton reported that this would require an undersirable use of force, he was authorized to let the Haitians choose a president whenever they wished to do so. He was told that the United States preferred Dartiguenave.[67] At the same time, the American Chargé d'Affaires was instructed to see that "the following things be made perfectly clear:

"First: Let Congress understand that the Government of the United States intends to uphold it, but that it can not recognize action which does not establish in charge of Haitian affairs those whose abilities and dispositions give assurances of putting an end to factional disorders.

"Second: In order that no misunderstanding can possibly occur after election, it should be made perfectly clear to candidates as soon as possible and in advance of their election, that the United States expects to be entrusted with the practical control of the customs, and such financial control over the affairs of the Republic of Haiti as the United States may deem necessary for an efficient administration.

"The Government of the United States considers it its duty to support a constitutional government. It means to assist in the establishing of such a government, and to support it as long as necessity may require. It has no design upon the political or territorial integrity of Haiti; on the contrary, what has been done, as well as what will be done, is conceived in an effort to aid the people of Haiti in establishing a stable government and in maintaining domestic peace throughout the Republic."

Bobo's friends in the Committee of Public Safety, which had been carrying on the civil government of Port au Prince, opposed the election of a president by congress and urged that a provisional government be set up instead. When they saw that the Americans would insist on compliance with Haitian constitutional procedure, they offered their support, successively, to several prominent citizens

[67] 838.00/1275D. The cable was sent by the navy after approval by the President and the Secretary of State.

355

in an effort to defeat Dartiguenave, but all of these refused to be candidates. On August 11, the committee attempted to prevent an election by ordering the dissolution of Congress. Caperton blocked this bid for power by terminating the committee's own existence, and the next day the congress met for the election.

The Admiral took precautions to make sure that the congressmen would not be intimidated. No Haitian was allowed to approach the building where they met unless he held a pass from a senator or deputy or from the American command, and all spectators were disarmed as they entered the building. All of the congressmen, on the other hand, were permitted, at their urgent request, to carry weapons. Caperton's chief of staff mingled with the congressmen on the floor of the house, and was apparently treated as a welcome guest. The first ballot gave Dartiguenave 94 votes, as against 16 for Bobo and about 30 scattered votes for other candidates.

Caperton, who later told the story of the occupation with a candor that somewhat dismayed the State Department, insisted that no pressure had been brought to bear to effect Dartiguenave's election. He said that there had been no bargaining with Dartiguenave and that he did not think that the latter knew that the United States wished him to be elected.[68] This statement is not necessarily inconsistent with the fact that Dartiguenave had earlier assured the Americans of his willingness to cooperate. At any rate there seems no reason to suppose that Dartiguenave was not the free choice of a majority of the congressmen, and it is clear that approximately a third of the congressmen felt free to vote for other candidates.

The Treaty of 1915

On the day of the election the State Department instructed the Chargé d'Affaires to present to the President-elect a draft treaty providing for American control of Haiti's finances, for the creation of a constabulary under American officers, and for the appointment of American engineers to have charge of "the sanitation and public improvement" of the republic. One article read: "The United States shall have authority to prevent any and all interference with the attainment of any of the objects comprehended in this convention as well as the right to intervene for the preservation of Haitian inde-

[68] *Hearings*, p. 316.

pendence and the maintenance of a government adequate for the protection of life, property, and individual liberty." Another obligated Haiti not to transfer any territory to any foreign power except the United States.

The draft treaty went somewhat farther than the proposals that had been urged on Haiti in July 1914 and was designed to establish virtually the same sort of control that the American government had been seeking to impose on the Jiménez administration at Santo Domingo. As Lansing took pains to point out to the Haitian government, there was no demand for the cession of the Mole St. Nicholas. This represented a change in American policy. Two years earlier, when Assistant Secretary Osborne had visited Haiti, both Bryan and Wilson had wished to acquire the Mole.[69] But in October 1914 the General Board of the Navy had expressed the opinion that the United States had no need for a naval station there. It reiterated this opinion in August 1915 when Lansing again consulted it.[70]

In submitting the draft to the President-elect, the Chargé was to say that the State Department believed that the Haitian congress, "as a guaranty of the sincerity and interest of Haitians in the orderly and peaceful development of their country," would be "pleased to pass forthwith a resolution authorizing the President-elect to conclude, without modification, the treaty submitted. . . ." After such action, the treaty could be signed and the Haitian government simultaneously recognized. Lansing and his colleagues, after their recent experiences with the Dominican government, evidently did not intend to permit the Haitians to question the program which was to be imposed on them for their own good. The new Haitian government, however, insisted on discussing the terms of the treaty, and Dartiguenave and his Cabinet threatened to resign if the United States refused to consider modifications. When the State Department told them that the United States, in that event, would either establish a military government pending the holding of elections or permit the control of the administration to pass to some other faction, the Haitians said that they could accept the treaty if a few "details" were changed. Having thus maneuvred the Americans into a negotia-

[69] Bryan to Wilson, June 20, 1913, and Wilson to Bryan June 23. Bryan-Wilson Correspondence, Vol. i, pp. 58, 61.
[70] Lansing to Wilson, August 7, 1916, 838.00/1275D.

tion, they came forward with proposals that omitted or radically altered every provision of the original draft.

Fortunately, Chargé d'Affaires Davis' firmness and tact prevented a break that might have led to the establishment of an American military government. Davis persuaded the State Department to give up its demand for a previous resolution by the congress, and after Dartiguenave removed two of the most intransigeant members of his Cabinet, a treaty containing virtually everything that the United States asked, but with minor changes to make it more palatable to the Haitians, was signed on September 16, 1915. The article that would specifically have authorized American intervention was changed to read:

> Article XIV. The high contracting parties shall have authority to take such steps as may be necessary to insure the complete attainment of any of the objects contemplated in this treaty; and, should the necessity occur, the United States will lend an efficient aid for the preservation of Haitian independence and the maintenance of a government adequate for the protection of life, property and individual liberty.

The treaty was to be in force for a period of ten years, but might be extended for a further ten years if either party felt that its purposes had not been fully accomplished. The Dartiguenave government was formally recognized when the treaty was signed.

A large segment of Haitian public opinion seems to have accepted the treaty with less hostility than one might have expected. Many of the *élite* were inclined to feel that American intervention was a lesser evil than the continuance of anarchy. Time after time during the past two years Port au Prince had been overrun by half-savage, undisciplined *caco* troops, and in the short intervals between revolutions the harsh rule of military dictators and the frequent political executions made life anything but pleasant. With one of their own class as president, and with the promise of American help in maintaining peace, the mulatto aristocracy would no longer live under a reign of terror. There were many, too, who welcomed the promise of American help in developing the country economically. For a time, especially before the American officers' wives began to arrive, personal relations between Haitians and Americans were friendly, with little evidence of the race consciousness that later manifested itself.

There were many Haitians, however, who opposed the occupation from the beginning. On September 3, anti-American propaganda and growing agitation against the proposed treaty led Caperton to proclaim martial law in Port au Prince and its immediate vicinity. Dartiguenave had secretly requested this action, but he instructed his Minister in Washington to protest and also to complain about the Admiral's seizure of the customhouses at all of the more important Haitian ports. Lansing refused to discuss either matter in Washington.[71]

Much of the interior was still controlled by armed bands of *cacos,* who prevented the country people from bringing food into the seaport towns which Caperton had occupied. The situation around Cape Haitian was especially bad. Caperton thought that he might have to move against some of the groups that had refused to turn in their arms, but Secretary of the Navy Daniels promptly ordered him not to take any offensive action against Haitians without further instructions unless it were absolutely necessary to prevent loss of life or property. Nevertheless, armed clashes occurred when marine patrols attempting to open communications with the interior were attacked near Gonaives on September 22 and near Cape Haitian on September 25. During October and November there was a considerable amount of fighting with *cacos* in northern Haiti, who were thought to be receiving arms from Desiderio Arias, the Minister of War at Santo Domingo. Reports of heavy casualties among the Haitians caused such concern in Washington that in November the Navy Department ordered Caperton to suspend offensive operations. The Admiral thought that patrolling must be continued for the protection of peaceable inhabitants, but he suspended other operations. Most of the *caco* bands had by this time been dispersed, and some of the more important opposition political leaders had agreed to cooperate in disarming them.[72] In February 1916 Caperton was able to report that brigandage had stopped and that the Haitian rural

---

[71] Caperton reported confidentially that Dartiguenave had requested the declaration of martial law, 838.00/1287.

[72] Col. Waller to the Cruiser Squadron Commander, Oct. 16, 1915, Navy Caribbean Area File.

guards and the newly formed constabulary were performing all police and patrol duty.[73]

These Haitian forces were led by American officers and were under the Admiral's command. There was no relaxation of American military control. All of the customs revenues were deposited in the National Bank to the order of the Admiral, who decided how much should be spent and for what purpose. With the rather reluctant approval of the Departments at Washington, the Admiral even ordered the National Bank not to recognize court orders obtained by speculators who had discounted the salaries of government employees. Disbursements for public works and for local government in each district were made by the local American detachment commanders. The Dartiguenave administration had for its own use only a small weekly allowance which Caperton gave it for salaries and expenses. After January 1916 even this money was not turned over to the government itself, for payments were made directly by American officers to individuals. The State Department had apparently decided to let this state of affairs continue until the treaty signed in September should have been ratified.[74]

By a large majority the Haitian Chamber of Deputies approved the treaty early in October, with an "interpretative commentary" which was not regarded as an amendment. In the Senate there was more opposition. Davis attributed this to "the desire of certain members with presidential aspirations to see present government fall" and to the "influence of certain foreigners." He was probably referring to the Germans, for the German Minister at Port au Prince had protested formally in September that Caperton's seizure of the customhouses injured German interests in Haiti. The State Department's urgent representations seemed to have little effect on the Senate, but on November 10 Caperton was instructed to tell the Haitian Cabinet, for the Senators' benefit, that the United States would retain control if the treaty were not ratified and that "those offering opposition can only expect such treatment as their conduct merits." The Admiral was also to refer to rumors of bribery and to say that those giving or accepting bribes would be vigorously prosecuted. Against a background of martial law, these threats were im-

[73] Caperton to the Navy Department, Feb. 6, 1916, 838.00/1379.
[74] See Leland Harrison's memorandum of Oct. 18, 1915, attached to 711.38/116.

pressive, and the Senate approved the treaty immediately by a substantial majority.

Since ratification at Washington would have to await the next session of the United States Senate, the two governments agreed to put the treaty in effect provisionally by a *modus vivendi* which was signed on November 29. The plan was to designate officers from Caperton's staff to serve temporarily in the new positions created by the treaty, but after this idea had been approved by all concerned it was realized that it could not be put into effect without violating the laws of the United States. The Admiral did designate officers to perform "duties somewhat similar to those provided in the treaty" [75] and went ahead especially with the organization of the new constabulary. This arrangement was not wholly satisfactory to the Haitian government, which had hoped that the signature of the *modus vivendi* would mean the end of military rule.

The United States Senate approved the treaty by a unanimous vote on February 28, 1916, and ratifications were exchanged on May 3. On June 12 an act of Congress which authorized naval and marine officers to accept paid employment under the Haitian government made it possible to appoint such officers to the new treaty services. The salaries of the principal treaty officials were fixed by an agreement signed on June 27.

The officials who were to serve under the treaty were apparently selected with some care. Addison T. Ruan, the financial adviser, was an experienced official in the Bureau of Insular Affairs in the War Department who had worked for years with the State Department in connection with financial matters in other Caribbean countries. His appointment was at first held up by President Wilson because he spoke little French, but Lansing and General McIntyre insisted that it would be difficult to find an equally qualified man who had the language.[76] Political considerations obviously entered into the choice of A. J. Maumus, who was nominated as General Receiver of Customs, but he was apparently competent and spoke French perfectly. The Deputy General Receiver, W. S. Matthews, Jr., had six years' experience in a customs office in Mississippi. All

[75] *Hearings*, p. 403.
[76] Lansing to Wilson, July 6, 1916, enclosing copy of General McIntyre's letter of July 5, 838.51/532.

of the other Americans in the customs service were apparently selected by Maumus from a list given him by Senator Broussard of Louisiana, but only a few of them turned out badly.[77] Lt. Edgar Garfield Oberlin, who was to be in charge of public works and sanitation, was a civil engineer in the navy who had been in Haiti for some time. He too spoke French.

Settlement with the Bank and Railroad

The State Department had proposed that the commission that came to Washington to negotiate agreements about the salaries of the treaty officials should attempt to settle the outstanding disputes between the Haitian government and the National Bank and National Railroad. An arrangement with the bank was especially urgent because it would be difficult to administer the finances in an orderly way or to proceed with the hoped-for foreign loan until more normal relations had been restored. An agreement between the commission and the bank's representatives was signed on July 10, 1916. The government was to go ahead with the currency reform, about which there had been so many disputes in the past. The bank retained its privilege of note-issue, and was to resume the treasury service except with respect to the customs receipts, which were to be deposited in the bank but dealt with in accord with the treaty with the United States. The bank was to receive a commission of 1 percent on moneys received and ½ percent on moneys paid out. Several minor controversial points were disposed of, but the repayment of the government's indebtedness to the bank was left for future settlement. The bank gave up its preferential rights in connection with foreign loans, insofar as new loans might be floated in the United States, and it agreed to lend the government $500,000 pending the flotation of a loan.

A settlement with the railroad proved more difficult. Caperton had urged that construction on the line, which the company had stopped in September, 1913, be resumed to relieve unemployment, and the French Embassy at Washington, in May 1916, asked that payments on the company's bonds be made. These had been in default since August 1914 because the Haitian government had failed

[77] See 838.51/593, 600, 696, 703.

to honor its guarantee of interest. The Haitian commissioners, however, did nothing, and only with difficulty did the State Department persuade the Haitian government to instruct its Minister at Washington to negotiate with the company. Each party had well-founded grievances against the other, and there were bitter exchanges of charges and countercharges. The State Department's anxiety for a settlement increased when representatives of the French bondholders threatened to institute foreclosure proceedings. Finally, in February 1917, a partial settlement was reached. The company agreed to meet one of the government's contentions by building the remainder of its line between St. Marc and Cape Haitian over a shorter route, and the government agreed to abandon the foreclosure proceedings that had been instituted in 1914. Other questions at issue, including the company's claim for exemption from customs and tonnage duties, were to be settled by the Financial Adviser. The State Department undertook to discuss with the Haitian government the two matters that were of most interest to the French bondholders: the extension of the Haitian government's guarantee to $44,600 of bonds issued in 1914 and the payment at the earliest practicable date of the arrears of interest on the company's bonds in general. The government at first claimed that the company had forfeited its right to the guarantee by suspending service, but in December 1917 it gave in on both points.

In supporting its nationals' claims on the bank and the railroad the French government showed no disposition to obstruct what the United States was doing in Haiti. In October 1915, it had asked the American government for assurances that French interests in the country would be safeguarded, and Lansing had promised that the existing contracts of the National Bank would be respected; that French citizens would receive treatment equal to that accorded to Americans; that an effort would be made to settle all pending foreign claims; and that the use of the French language and the existing ecclesiastical organization would be respected. With respect to the last point, it will be remembered that the Church in Haiti was staffed entirely by French priests. These promises were embodied in an exchange of notes entered into in July and August 1916, after the Haitian-American treaty had gone into effect.

The Treaty Services

With the appointment of the officials provided for under the treaty of 1915, the regime under which Haiti was to be governed during the next fifteen years began to take shape. Five "treaty services" were set up: the Customs Receivership, the Office of the Financial Adviser, the Constabulary, the Public Works Service, and the Public Health Service. These were attached to the appropriate Haitian ministries and, except in the case of the customs service, were theoretically to work under instructions from the Haitian government. Their principal officers were appointed by the President of Haiti upon nomination by the President of the United States.

In providing for control of Haiti's finances, the State Department had obviously been influenced by its experience in Santo Domingo. The General Receiver was to collect all customs duties and apply them to the expenses of his office, to the service of the public debt, to the expenses of the new constabulary, and to other expenses of the Haitian government, in that order. The Financial Adviser, in the words of the treaty "shall be an officer attached to the Ministry of Finance, to give effect to whose proposals and labors the Minister will lend efficient aid. The Financial Adviser shall devise an adequate system of public accounting, aid in increasing the revenues and adjusting them to the expenses, inquire into the validity of the debts of the Republic, enlighten both Governments with reference to all eventual debts, recommend improved methods of collecting and applying the revenues, and make such other recommendations to the Minister of Finance as may be deemed necessary for the welfare and prosperity of Haiti." On paper, he had less independent authority than the General Receiver, but in practice he exercised far more power.

The constabulary, or *gendarmerie,* was to be organized and officered by Americans, who were to be replaced by Haitians as the latter were found qualified. Its officers were to be clothed by the Haitian government with all necessary authority, and it was to have control of arms and military supplies throughout the country. Under the supplementary agreement signed in 1916 it was to be the sole military and police force of the republic.

The other two treaty services were established under Article XIII of the treaty which provided: "The Republic of Haiti, being desirous to further the development of its natural resources, agrees to undertake and execute such measures as in the opinion of the high contracting parties may be necessary for the sanitation and public improvement of the republic, under the supervision and direction of an engineer or engineers, to be appointed by the President of Haiti upon nomination by the President of the United States, and authorized for that purpose by the Government of Haiti."

First Years of the Treaty Regime

The Haitians had hoped that the establishment of the treaty services would bring a relaxation of military control and the inauguration of the program of economic development which the United States had promised them. Unfortunately, neither of these expectations was fulfilled. In September 1916, the State Department asked the navy to continue military control and martial law for the time being, until the *gendarmerie* had proved its efficiency and loyalty and until the other treaty services had been effectively organized. Economic development was delayed because no money was available and because the public works and public health services were slow in starting work. It was not until June 1919, that the engineer-in-chief was able to take over road and bridge building from the *gendarmerie,* which started these activities on a small scale soon after its organization.

Failure to coordinate the activities of the American officials made the treaty regime less effective than it should have been. After Admiral Caperton was transferred to another post in July 1916, no one person was responsible for American policy in Haiti. At Washington, authority was divided between the State and the Navy Departments. In Haiti, the Minister supposedly outranked the other American officials, but Bailly-Blanchard was ineffective, and the State Department could not persuade him even to keep it informed about what was going on.[78] The marine Brigade Commander was the dominant figure in the American group, especially as the *gendarmerie* remained under his direct command. He often acted as the

---

[78] Instructions to Legation, Port au Prince, Jan. 30 and June 11, 1917, 838.00/1436a, 1436a suppl.

spokesman for the American government, but he had no authority to direct the work of the other treaty officials, particularly in the case of the Financial Adviser and the General Receiver, who were civilians. Admiral Knapp, who became Commander of the Cruiser Squadron in November 1916, had some authority over the *gendarmerie* and the naval officers who headed the public works and sanitary services, but he was also Military Governor of Santo Domingo and was rarely present in Haiti. He issued orders urging the treaty services to cooperate with one another and with the American Legation,[79] but the various treaty services still acted as independent organizations and were handicapped in their dealings with the Haitian government by a lack of any definite policy-guidance from their American superiors. Sometimes there was friction between them and the head of one service urged policies on the Haitian government that embarrassed other American officials.

Especially disappointing was the failure to obtain the hoped-for foreign loan. The roads and port improvements and irrigation works that the country needed would require a substantial amount of new capital. A refunding operation was also a prerequisite for any orderly management of the government's finances, because the Financial Adviser could hardly continue indefinitely to disregard the complicated system of "affectations" by which each item of revenue was pledged for the benefit of specific creditors, or to leave unpaid the rather large amount of debts that the government owed both to natives and to foreigners. One of the obligations that was most pressing, because it caused embarrassment both to Haiti and to the United States, was the service on the external bonds held in France, which were in complete default.

The failure to pay interest on the foreign debt was the more embarrassing because it could be made to appear that the default was a direct consequence of the intervention. It was true that the Haitian government had failed to honor its guarantee on the National Railroad bonds in 1914 and had made no payments on account of sinking fund since 1905 in the case of the 1875 loan and since 1914 on the other French loans, but interest on the government bonds had been paid up to the time when Caperton took over the customhouses. Caperton had remitted some money for debt service to Paris at

[79] *Foreign Relations, 1917*, p. 810.

the request of the State Department, but the amount was not sufficient for the payment of a coupon and the money apparently remained on deposit.[80] It was clear that the curtailment of Haitian
coffee exports to France because of the war would make the resumption of full service difficult, unless a refunding loan were arranged.

Ruan began to work on a refunding plan soon after he went to
Haiti, and in the latter part of 1916 he suggested to the State Department the flotation of a loan for $30,000,000. President Wilson
was skeptical about the feasibility of the proposal, partly because
he thought that his administration did not have "access to banking
assistance that some previous administrations have had," but he
suggested that the matter be discussed with bankers and with the
French government, and also with the Chairman of the Foreign
Relations Committee of the Senate, because the flotation of so large
a loan would require the extension of American control for a longer
period than the ten years provided by the treaty.[81]

Ruan and the State Department consequently went forward with
their plans. The French government indicated that it would be willing to buy the Haitian bonds held in France and turn them in in
return for cash from a new loan. The State Department, probably
after discussing the question with interested bankers, thought that
new bonds could be sold in the United States, if the treaty of 1915
could be extended, in accord with one of its provisions, for an additional ten years. Bailly-Blanchard was consequently instructed
to support Ruan in urging the Haitian government to request such
an extension. The Haitian government was reluctant to do so, but
it gave in after Ruan indicated that he would have to curtail its
expenditures unless some plan were adopted for covering the current deficits.[82] A protocol fixing the life of the treaty at twenty years
was signed on March 28, 1917.

Ruan at once came to the United States to consult further with
the French financial commissioner and with bankers. Though the
United States' entry into the war and the flotation of the First

[80] Lansing to Secretary of Navy, Nov. 18, 1915, 838.51/436c; Caperton to Secretary
of Navy, Nov. 20, 838.51/435; Lansing to Legation, Port au Prince, Nov. 23, 838.51/
437a.
[81] Lansing to Wilson, Dec. 2, 1916, and Wilson to Lansing Dec. 3, 838.51/578½.
[82] Polk to Bailly-Blanchard, Feb. 24, 1917, 838.51/590; Bailly-Blanchard to Lansing,
March 3, 1917, and Lansing to Bailly-Blanchard, March 22, 838.51/596.

Liberty Loan made it difficult to go forward with a loan to Haiti, the National City and some other large New York banks seemed willing to lend Haiti $15,000,000 if the French government would accept additional bonds in return for those of the old loans, but would agree to hold the new bonds off the market for a period of years. The negotiations with this group went on for some time, but the Treasury Department's reluctance to see so much money leave the United States and Ruan's inability to agree with the French on the price for the old bonds prevented their successful conclusion.

The Constitution of 1918

Both governments felt that the operation of the treaty would require changes in the Haitian constitution. The United States was especially interested in the abrogation of a provision that forbade foreigners to own land, because this prohibition would be a serious obstacle to the development of the country's agriculture by outside capital. Dartiguenave, who was being criticized for cooperating as much as he did with the United States, probably hoped to free himself from the menace of a potentially hostile congress. He dissolved the Senate on April 5, 1916, and announced that the Chamber of Deputies would be convoked to act as a constituent assembly, to pass on amendments which his newly appointed Council of State would propose. It soon appeared, however, that many of the deputies had turned against the President and against the occupation. When Dartiguenave convoked the Chamber to consider a new constitution only a handful of members attended. The Haitian government consequently decided to await the election of a new congress in January 1917.

On January 6, 1917, Admiral Knapp was authorized, at his discretion, to tell the government of Haiti that it had been the policy of the United States to "support Dartiguenave so long as he conducted his administration in accordance with correct principles and the agreements entered into between Haiti and the United States." No attempt to overthrow the President would be countenanced, and any legislative attempt to annul decrees that he had issued would be regarded as the "beginning of activities of a revolutionary and disorderly political character." If the government should be defeated in the elections, however, it would be "highly desirable" that a new Cabinet in harmony with the dominant party be appointed. It is significant that the American Legation was informed of this statement but told to take no action without further instructions. The military was evidently to be left in control of Haitian affairs.

In the congressional election, the government's opponents apparently won a majority, though Dartiguenave professed to be satisfied with the result.[83] When the National Assembly met in April, its presiding officer, Stenio Vincent, made a speech expressing friendly sentiments toward the United States [84] but any hope that the body would cooperate with the occupation soon disappeared. It was impossible to obtain from it a declaration of war against Germany, which the Americans desired, and it was soon clear that there would be trouble about the new constitution.

Dartiguenave had ready a draft constitution which had been drawn up by his Council of State and modified in some respects to meet the views of the State Department at Washington, but in June an assembly committee reported a quite different draft, retaining the prohibition against foreign land-ownership and adding a clause that would have enabled the Congress to force changes in the President's Cabinet. The assembly seemed determined to adopt it, despite representations made by Bailly-Blanchard under instructions from the State Department, and Dartiguenave seemed unwilling to take any definite stand because public opinion was overwhelmingly on the side of the assembly.

Bailly-Blanchard reported on June 18 that the American officials had decided to dissolve the assembly if this action was necessary to prevent the approval of an unsatisfactory constitution. They would do this by presidential decree, if possible; otherwise by direct action. One reason for this decision was a report that the assembly was about to impeach Dartiguenave. The State Department cabled the Minister to take no action pending the receipt of further instructions, but before the cable was received the assembly had been dissolved. Dartiguenave, angered by the congressmen's personal attacks on him, issued the necessary decree, after attempting to

---

[83] Navy Department's letter of May 14, 1917, 838.00/1453.
[84] *Ibid.*

persuade the commander of the *gendarmerie* to act without authorization,[85] and the latter was ordered by the marine Brigade Commander to communicate the decree to the assembly. Lansing wrote the President on June 23 that the Haitian government was wholly responsible for the dissolution, and he attributed much of the blame for what had happened to German efforts to obtain a provision restricting land ownership to foreigners who had been in Haiti at least five years. He thought that Dartiguenave should now be left to work out the problem for himself.[86]

Both governments now thought that the best solution would be to present the constitution to the Haitian people in a plebiscite. In October, the State Department sent the Legation a new draft it had compiled from "various projects submitted to the Department by the Government of Haiti and the Legation in Port au Prince." Assistant Secretary of the Navy Franklin D. Roosevelt was perhaps referring to this draft when he claimed the authorship of the Haitian constitution in a public speech some time later. The State Department said that it was willing to consider modifications to meet the views of the Haitian government, so long as the principal provisions remained intact, and it instructed Bailly-Blanchard to discuss the matter in a "liberal spirit." The draft was submitted to the Haitian government on February 2, 1918, after the State Department had accepted several further changes urged by the Americans at Port au Prince. Dartiguenave obtained other modifications in negotiations that followed, and after Bailly-Blanchard had pointed out that "it is their constitution" the State Department agreed to the final version, though it could not give "entire approval from a legal point of view."

The constitution was submitted to a plebiscite on June 18. The *gendarmerie* was ordered to try to convince the voters of its desirability and to give receptions and barbecues, paid for from *gendarmerie* funds, to make it more popular. Any opposition that tended to incite distrust in the minds of the people was to be treated as a disturbance of the peace and those responsible were to be arrested. The *gendarmerie* officers, however, were enjoined to act with discretion and to assure a free and proper vote. The constitution was

[85] See General Butler's account in *Hearings,* pp. 536ff.
[86] 838.00/1675a.

approved by 98,225 to 768. Colonel John Russell, the brigade commander, reported candidly that there had been little enthusiasm for adoption but asserted that neither the occupation nor the *gendarmerie* had influenced the outcome. The total vote cast, he pointed out, was very small, though it was the largest in Haiti's history. Few of the intelligent class had gone to the polls and many of those who did go had no idea of the purpose of the election. One man thought that he was helping to elect a pope. All of the government employees, however, had voted at least once, and many peasants had voted for approval because they wanted peace. Those who opposed abstained from voting.[87]

The constitution was a reasonably liberal one, with ample safeguards for civil rights and provisions about the executive and legislative powers similar to those in many other American constitutions. It had "transitory" provisions, however, which would enable the President of Haiti to rule virtually as a dictator for an indefinite period. The first congressional election was to take place in January "of an even-numbered year," and the President was to decide which year it would be. In the meantime a Council of State, appointed by him and holding office at his pleasure, would exercise the legislative power. This unusual arrangement remained in effect until 1930.

Other provisions, incorporated at the instance of the United States, made treaties superior to any law enacted by Congress and ratified and validated all acts of the United States government during its military occupation. The *gendarmerie* was specifically recognized and made the only armed force of the republic. Foreigners living in Haiti and foreign companies engaged in agricultural, commercial, industrial, or educational enterprises were given the right to own land, but this right was to cease five years after the foreigner left the country or the company ceased its activities.[88]

The Caco Revolt

At the time of the constitutional plebiscite, practically all armed opposition to the American occupation seemed to have been sup-

[87] Secretary of Navy to Secretary of State, July 1, 1918, enclosing Col. Russell's report of June 17, 838.011/64.

[88] Most of the correspondence about the adoption of the Haitian constitution of 1918 is in file 838.011 or in the Navy Caribbean Area file.

pressed and the country was enjoying a peace that it had rarely known since colonial times. The new constabulary, though still not fully trained, had taken over the task of maintaining order and was apparently performing it well. The masses of the country people seemed pleased with the new state of affairs. Only a few months later, however, the situation had radically changed, and much of the interior was being laid waste in military operations that probably caused more loss of life than had occurred in a typical revolution before 1915.

The change in the attitude of the peasants, which made the revolt possible, seems to have been caused principally by the constabulary's enforcement of the *corvée* law, which required each inhabitant to contribute to the upkeep of roads either by paying a tax or by working a few days in each year. When the constabulary was first formed, its officers had realized that the building of roads was a military as well as an economic necessity. Since no funds were available for construction, they had revived the almost forgotten *corvée*, with the Haitian government's approval. At first the peasants seemed glad to cooperate, in return for the food and entertainment which the constabulary provided, and by the end of 1917 an automobile was able for the first time in Haiti's history to make the trip from Port au Prince to Cape Haitian. It was not long, unfortunately, before resentment developed. Many peasants were compelled to give more service than the law required or to work at places far from their homes. Often they were the victims of extortion or mistreatment at the hands of Haitian *gendarmes* or local officials who selected the recruits for the *corvée*. The American *gendarmerie* officials were frequently arbitrary or tactless. A realization of the growing hostility led the chief of the *gendarmerie* to order the abolition of the *corvée* on October 1, 1918, but through disobedience or misunderstanding it continued to be enforced in the district of Hinche for some months thereafter. It was in this district that the *caco* revolt began.

The principal leader was Charlemagne Peralte, who had escaped from custody in September 1918, while serving a term for banditry. Peralte was thought to have about 20,000 followers, but only about 5,000 of them, divided into many small, poorly armed bands, were actually in the field at any one time.[89] By the end of 1918 these bands were operating throughout the hilly, relatively sparsely settled regions in eastern and northeastern Haiti, occasionally attacking towns and frequently looting or destroying small villages. The insurgents received help from dissatisfied politicians in Port au Prince, and probably from some of the Germans who had financed *caco* activities in the past, and it was soon evident that the constabulary would not be able to suppress the movement without help. The American marines consequently went into action in March 1919. Port au Prince itself was attacked twice, in October 1919 and in January 1920, but on each occasion the insurgents were driven off with heavy losses.

There was more than a year of fighting before the uprising ended. Peralte was killed in October 1919, when Captain Hanneken, an American in the *gendarmerie,* entered his camp in disguise with a handful of followers; but Peralte's lieutenant, Benoît Batraville, took over the leadership. He too was killed in May 1920, and soon afterward most of the rebel bands took advantage of the amnesty offered them and surrendered. It was estimated that some fifteen hundred Haitians had been killed during the suppression of the uprising.

Most of the fighting, on the part of the marines and the *gendarmerie,* was done by small patrols led in many cases by non-commissioned officers or privates in the marine corps. Because of the expansion of the marine corps during the European war, and because many of the better elements in the corps were in Europe, some of these men in Haiti were inadequately trained and ill prepared for the difficult task of carrying on such operations in a hostile country, where they had little supervision or support by their superiors. Most of the marines, and most of the constabulary, conducted themselves in a creditable way, but there were enough reports of cruelty to shock public opinion in the United States and to strengthen the hands of the anti-imperialist groups that were by this time beginning a campaign against the continuance of the occupation. There were undoubtedly a few cases where prisoners were shot without trial. Two subsequent investigations, however, one by a naval court of

[89] James H. McCrocklin, *Garde d'Haiti* (Annapolis, 1956), p. 104. This book gives one of the best accounts of the insurrection.

373

inquiry and the other by a committee of the United States Senate, indicated that most of the atrocity charges could not be substantiated.

The Protocol of 1919 and the Currency Reform

At the end of 1918 the economic situation was hardly more satisfactory than the political situation. The hoped-for foreign loan had still not materialized. When the Haitian government finally declared war on Germany after the adoption of the constitution of 1918, the State Department suggested that the United States government might provide funds under the War Loan Act, but the Treasury replied that this was impossible.[90] Without such help, it was difficult to deal with several financial problems that urgently required solution. The State Department wished to put an end to the default on the foreign debt, which the French government pressed on its attention from time to time, and the failure to adjust the internal debt caused hardship to many persons in Haiti. Little could be done for the improvement of economic conditions until funds were available for public works. Even the currency reform, which should have been carried out with the proceeds of the 1910 loan, was held up because the National Bank had lent to the government or otherwise invested $600,000 of the $1,500,000 set aside for the reform and claimed that it could do nothing until its accounts with the government were settled.[91]

The adjustment of the bank's accounts was delayed by a controversy with the Financial Adviser, who insisted that the bank give up a substantial part of its claim for interest on previous advances to the government. The bank demanded 6 percent interest on the $1,800,000 which the government owed it, but Ruan pointed out that the bank was holding $2,300,000 of the government's money, including the funds for the currency reform, on which it paid no interest. He also insisted on an audit of the bank's accounts. Both the American and the French stockholders rejected his demands, and the bank refused to issue new notes until the matter was settled. This caused a serious situation in Haiti, because the delapidated

[90] Crosby to Lansing Oct. 12, 1917, 838.51/654.
[91] Ruan's memorandum of May 29, 1918, 838.51/876.

paper currency was completely inadequate for the country's needs when business began to revive early in 1918.

After some months during which neither the Financial Adviser nor the bank seemed disposed to make concessions, the French government, in November 1918, made representations to the State Department on behalf of the bank and complained again about the failure to resume service on the foreign debt. The Department told the Legation at Port au Prince that something must be done about both matters. Ruan then agreed to a compromise with the bank which satisfied its local representatives and its American stockholders, but the issue of the much-needed new currency was delayed for some time by the failure of the French stockholders to give their approval. The Legation also reported that $952,000 was being set aside in the budget for debt service, but Ruan insisted that no payments should be made until the validity of the various claims against the government should be determined. Full service on the debts secured by specific "affectations" of the revenues would have required approximately 75 percent of the government's entire income.[92]

Ruan's insistence that the French bondholders accept something less than the principal of their bonds in any refunding operation still made it difficult to proceed with plans for a loan. The prospect for an agreement improved when he was sent to Panama as fiscal agent in January 1919, and John A. McIlhenny was appointed to succeed him. Mr. McIlhenny was a prominent citizen of Louisiana, who had recently been chairman of the Civil Service Commission in Washington but had little experience to fit him for his new position. Before the new Financial Adviser went to Haiti, plans for the refunding of the republic's debts and a definitive plan for the currency reform were drawn up at conferences in the State Department with representatives of the French and American stockholders in the National Bank.

One obstacle to the flotation of a new loan was the fact that the treaty, even as extended, would expire in 1936. It would be impossible to sell bonds repayable after that date unless the purchasers could be given some assurance that American control of the reve-

[92] *Foreign Relations, 1919*, Vol. II, p. 341.

nues would continue. To provide this assurance, the conferees hit on the idea of a protocol which would purport to give effect to the treaty's provisions requiring the refunding of Haiti's debts and in doing so would provide for American collection of the pledged revenues during the life of the bonds. The draft agreement prepared for submission to the Haitian government established a commission which was to pass on all claims against Haiti except the external bonds, the debt to the National Bank, and a part of the debt due the P.C.S. Railway. To make possible the payment of the commission's awards and of the debts exempted from its jurisdiction, a $40,000,000, 30 year-bond issue was to be authorized, secured by the internal revenues and the customs duties, both of which would continue to be collected, after the expiration of the treaty, by officers appointed by the President of Haiti on nomination by the President of the United States. The protocol contemplated the exchange of the new bonds for the outstanding French loans, on terms to be agreed upon.

The plan for the monetary reform followed closely a draft which Ruan had prepared in March 1918. It had been accepted then by the Haitian government and the local representatives of the National Bank, but the quarrel over the debt due the bank had prevented its execution. The bank was to exchange its own notes for the outstanding paper money, charging the value of the retired bills against the portion of the 1910 loan that had been held for this purpose. In effect, this meant that the bank would pocket $1,735,000 of the government's money, assuming in return the obligation to redeem its notes at any time at the rate of five gourdes to the dollar and to maintain a reserve against its notes. This would give the bank a considerable profit, but Ruan pointed out that the new agreement merely recognized rights that the bank already had under its 1910 concession and at the same time provided many safeguards which the concession did not contemplate. Where the concession required that the bank's notes be secured by a cash reserve of 33⅓ percent, the new plan called for an additional 66⅔ percent in commercial paper. It also required the bank to pay a tax of 1 percent on its circulation in excess of 10,000,000 gourdes and to share with the government the profits from any notes that were not presented for redemption.

The Haitian government accepted the plan for the currency reform in April 1919, and within a short time the republic had a satisfactory and stable monetary system. The protocol was also agreed upon, with minor changes and with comparatively little difficulty, and was signed on October 3. It was not possible, however, to accomplish either of the principal purposes of the agreement—the establishment of a claims commission or the flotation of a foreign loan—during the seventeen months that remained of the Wilson administration.[93]

Deteriorating Relations with the Haitian Government

One reason for the failure to make progress was the increasing unfriendliness between President Dartiguenave and the American officials at Port au Prince. There can be little doubt that Dartiguenave had been sincere in his preelection statements that he wished to cooperate with the United States and that he hoped that American help would assure peace and economic progress in Haiti.[94] He had expressed the same ideas from time to time during the first years of his term, and in general showed a willingness to accept American advice. After 1918, however, his relations with the American officials became less cordial. With some reason, he complained of Haiti's failure to obtain all of the advantages promised under the treaty, and he was increasingly resentful as he realized the full extent of the authority which the American officials expected to exercise under the treaty's provisions.

The treaty services had taken over most of the government's more important functions and were spending by far the greater part of the government's income. Theoretically they worked under the President's direction, but in practice Dartiguenave found that he was expected to follow their advice in matters of policy and to refrain from interference in their daily work. He was compelled after some argument to accept the American demand for complete control of the Haitian as well as the American personnel in the services. He had relatively few government appointments at his own dis-

[93] For the texts of the protocol and the plan of monetary reform, see *Foreign Relations, 1919*, Vol. II, pp. 347, 362.

[94] For Dartiguenave's attitude, as described by his private secretary, see B. Danache, *Le President Dartiguenave et les Americains* (Port au Prince, 1950).

posal, and very little freedom in the use of government funds—a situation that was particularly galling in a country where the group in power had always used the treasury for their own benefit.

The American officials could have accomplished little if they had not had complete control over their subordinates and if they had not been able to resist the unreasonable and often improper demands of the local politicians. But they were not always tactful, and they were too often unable to conceal their belief that any opposition to their proposals was inspired by corrupt motives. Most of them were competent and deeply interested in their work, but they were handicapped by lack of funds and by their own government's failure to coordinate and guide their activities. The State Department endeavored to promote a better working arrangement in 1918, when it authorized the Legation to act as the intermediary between the United States and all the treaty officials and when it instructed Bailly-Blanchard to meet at least once a week with the heads of the treaty services and the Brigade Commander,[95] but this effort at coordination produced no notable results.

The chief source of friction was the Financial Adviser's insistence on complete control of the government's expenditures, even in connection with activities that were not covered by the treaty. After the occupation, Caperton had collected most of the government's revenue and had doled out the proceeds as he saw fit. When Ruan arrived, the Haitian government agreed that all payments from customs revenues or from loans and all contracts for supplies and services must have his approval, though it continued for the time being to use the relatively insignificant internal revenues as it saw fit. Ruan prepared the budget and allocated the funds between the treaty services and the other governmental departments. During his first two years in Haiti, he had relatively little trouble with the government because he was able to work harmoniously with M. Heraux, the Minister of Finance, who was kept in office partly by the State Department's insistence that Dartiguenave retain him.[96]

In June 1918, when Dartiguenave appointed a new Cabinet with Louis Borno as Minister of Finance, the government at once as-

---

[95] Lansing to Bailly-Blanchard, July 3, 1918, *Foreign Relations, 1918*, p. 305–6.
[96] Bailly-Blanchard to Lansing, March 31, 1917, and Lansing to Bailly-Blanchard, April 2, 838.002/58.

sumed a more aggressive and independent attitude toward the American officials. In November the Council of State refused to accept the budget which Ruan had prepared and challenged the Financial Adviser's right to control its expenditures. To avoid a situation where the treaty services would be without funds, the American officials decided to invoke the authority of martial law, and Colonel John H. Russell, the brigade commander, ordered the National Bank to make no payments except by his order.[97] A few days later, when the Council of State was still defiant and the American officials thought that Borno was inspiring unfriendly articles in the newspapers, Russell and Bailly-Blanchard called on Dartiguenave and demanded the Minister's removal. The appointment of a new Minister of Finance made an agreement possible. The chief point at issue was settled by an exchange of notes providing that no payments for the account of the Haitian government should be made without the "visa" of the Financial Adviser, an arrangement that gave the latter practically complete control of the government's finances.

Dartiguenave now made a determined effort to change the American policy by direct appeals to the higher authorities of the American government. Lengthy formal complaints by the Legation at Washington went without reply for several months and then brought forth only an unsympathetic rebuttal. He had little more success in January 1919 in presenting his case to Wilson and Lansing at the Paris peace conference, where Haiti was represented because of its declaration of war after the adoption of the Constitution of 1918. At that time Dartiguenave instructed his Minister in France to talk with the President and the Secretary of State and to ask especially for the abolition of martial law and the recognition of the Haitian government's right to appoint and discharge employees in the customhouses. The Minister was to suggest that the United States might prefer not to have Haiti complain to the full peace conference about the injustice of the United States "just at the moment when . . . President Wilson is giving the assurance that one of the principal reasons for his personal presence at the table of the Conference is to bring about the triumph of the principle of respect for the rights of the small nations by the strong." The Minister saw Lansing, who was evidently impressed by the thought that the

[97] Bailly-Blanchard to Lansing, Nov. 15, 1918, 838.51/741.

United States would be subject to criticism if it continued the military occupation and who suggested to the State Department at Washington that the marine brigade might be transformed into a legation guard when the peace treaty was signed. Both the Acting Secretary of State and the American officials in Haiti, however, pointed out that such a change would be inadvisable at a time when the marines were being called on to support the *gendarmerie* in suppressing the *caco* revolt.

There were no further serious conflicts for nearly two years. The *caco* uprising doubtless made Dartiguenave realize his dependence on American support. A dispute about the budget in 1919 was settled by agreement, and another of Dartiguenave's ministers had to be removed at the demand of the American officials, but there was relatively little difficulty in obtaining the Haitian government's approval of the protocol of 1919 and the plan for currency reform. By the summer of 1920, however, a strongly organized opposition to the occupation was developing among the Haitian *élite* and the movement was being encouraged by anti-imperialist activities in the United States, where Wilson's Haitian policy was being criticized by the Republicans during the presidential campaign. This situation, and perhaps a desire to strengthen his political position as the end of his term approached, encouraged Dartiguenave to make another attempt to assert a measure of independence.

The immediate occasion was a dispute over the terms of a new charter for the National Bank. The National City Bank of New York, which had bought the shares held by the other American stockholders in 1916, had arranged in 1919 to buy the bank itself from the French corporation that owned it. The State Department, for obvious reasons welcomed the elimination of the French interests. The terms of a new charter which Haiti would give to the American-controlled bank were worked out at conferences in the State Department late in 1919 and early in 1920 and were agreed to by Haitian representatives who participated in the conferences. The State Department insisted on a number of provisions that made the new concession less profitable to the bank than its existing charter.

After the conferences, the National City Bank and the Financial Adviser apparently agreed on an additional article which would require the Haitian government, after consultation between the National Bank and the Financial Adviser, to restrict the importation of foreign currency into Haiti.[98] This would perpetuate, in a different form, a provision of the currency reform agreement, which had restricted trade in other currencies during the period when the government's paper money was being retired. The bank thought that the importation of dollars might lessen the value of its right to issue banknotes, and McIlhenny feared that the circulation of dollars might tend to increase wages and thus make the country less attractive to foreign capital.[99]

The provision was opposed by the American Foreign Banking Corporation [100] and by the Royal Bank of Canada, both of which were doing business in Haiti, and also by the Haitian government, which at the same time refused to put into operation the similar provision in the currency reform agreement. McIlhenny insisted that the government follow his advice on both matters, and, when Dartiguenave persisted in his negative attitude, the Financial Adviser told the government that he was suspending the study of the budget until other affairs of great national importance should be settled to his satisfaction. The Haitian Chargé d'Affaires protested in Washington but got no satisfaction.

In provoking a showdown, the Financial Adviser sought also to settle another and basically more important question that had been the subject of controversy. In 1918, after the adoption of the new constitution, the two governments had agreed that projects of law bearing on any of the objects of the treaty of 1915 would be communicated to the American Legation and, if necessary, discussed between the two governments before enactment.[101] The United States insisted that this included all legislative proposals, and in 1919, when several laws were enacted without previous consultation, the American Minister instructed the treaty officials to disregard them. Dartiguenave then agreed to a procedure that should have assured the submission of all laws to the American Legation

---

[98] The record does not show clearly the history of the additional amendment. See *Foreign Relations, 1920,* Vol. II, p. 817n.

[99] Mr. McIlhenny frequently expressed this idea in conversation with me.

[100] For the American Foreign Banking Corporation's protest, see 838.516/146. McIlhenny was evidently mistaken when he wrote Dr. Rowe (*Foreign Relations, 1920,* Vol. II, p. 767) that this company had no objection to the provision.

[101] *Foreign Relations, 1919,* Vol. II, pp. 304–305.

before enactment by the Council of State, but he soon proceeded to disregard this procedure in at least nine or ten cases. The Americans disapproved especially of a law regulating the right of foreigners to own real estate and insisted that it be replaced by a draft that they had prepared.

Bailly-Blanchard, as was too often the case, had not informed the State Department fully about the events that had led up to the crisis, and the State Department perhaps thought that it was settling the matter when it consented late in July to the National City Bank's taking over the bank in Haiti under its existing concession, with the understanding that the desired changes in the charter would be made when the Haitian government gave its consent to the establishment of a new company. The Department's decision was motivated, partly, by the fact that the National City Bank's option on the French-owned shares was expiring and that the Royal Bank of Canada seemed disposed to buy the shares if the deal with the National City Bank fell through.[102] The American Minister, the Brigade Commander, and the Financial Adviser all protested that the State Department's action had weakened their position in dealing with the Haitian government, but they were told that the Department could not withdraw its consent and Bailly-Blanchard was reprimanded for not keeping the Department better informed.[103]

The American officials in Haiti continued to insist that the laws they urged must be enacted and the objectionable ones repealed; and, when the Council of State adjourned without action on August 4, the Financial Adviser obtained instructions from Bailly-Blanchard to suspend the payment of the salaries of its members and also the salaries of the President and the Cabinet. The State Department was surprised and angered. It rebuked the Minister for acting without instructions, but it was not prepared to destroy the Legation's influence by repudiating its action. It attempted to work out a face-saving compromise, by which the payment of salaries would be resumed if the Haitian government gave assurances of a more cooperative attitude, but with no success, apparently because there

[102] See Welles' memorandum of July 17, 1920.

[103] Bailly-Blanchard to Colby, July 16, 1920, and Colby to Bailly-Blanchard July 24, 838.516/138; McIlhenny to Colby, July 28, and Colby to McIlhenny Aug. 5, 838.516/140.

was little willingness to compromise on either side at Port au Prince. The Haitian government, meanwhile, was sending to Washington long and detailed accounts of the difficulties that it had had with the Financial Adviser. It assured the State Department of its desire to cooperate with the United States, but defended its action in enacting the laws to which the Financial Adviser had objected.

The State Department's disapproval of McIlhenny's arbitrary suspension of the salaries of the President and his advisers did not mean that it was prepared to permit the Haitian government to block measures necessary for the achievement of the purposes of the 1915 treaty. It was not prepared to support McIlhenny in his somewhat questionable position with regard to the prohibition of foreign currency imports, but it considered it essential to retain control over Haitian legislation and it wished to proceed with plans for the proposed loan, which were being held up by the conflict between the Haitian government and the Financial Adviser. At the end of August, it was considering the idea of invoking the authority of martial law to put into effect its whole program. It was reluctant, however, to resort to this sort of intervention, especially as it feared that such action might cause Dartiguenave and his Cabinet to resign.[104] As a step toward a solution, it asked Rear Admiral Harry S. Knapp, the former Military Governor of Santo Domingo, to visit Haiti as military representative of the United States early in September, with instructions to tell the Haitians that the American demands for the repeal of several laws and the enactment of others must be accepted at once.

Knapp promptly obtained Dartiguenave's promise to comply with the wishes of the United States and had McIlhenny pay the suspended salaries for July and August. When the President was inexplicably slow in carrying out his promise, the American officials again proposed to withhold salaries but were peremptorily told not to do so. The State Department had by this time decided that there was no justification under the treaty of 1915 for the Financial Adviser's action. The latter had attempted to justify the suspension by arguing that he was merely interpreting strictly Article v of the treaty, which required the General Receiver to set aside funds for debt service and the constabulary before paying the balance to the

[104] Colby to Bailly-Blanchard, Aug. 26, 1920, 838.51/948.

Haitian government. But it was clear that this did not justify the non-payment of a few selected salaries, especially when the government's revenues had reached a point where there were funds for all of the purposes specified in Article v.

The Haitian government finally complied with American demands about the disputed legislation, but when Admiral Knapp returned to Washington he gave a disturbing picture of the situation at Port au Prince. He thought that Dartiguenave's attitude toward the United States had become distinctly less friendly and that the growing hostility of the other politicians to the President made the political situation increasingly bad. He was disturbed by the "license" of the press, which the American government had been unwilling to permit the occupation to control. There was much hostility to McIlhenny, and there was little interest in the proposed loan because the politicians realized that it would afford little opportunity for graft. The discussion of Haiti in the United States presidential campaign had weakened the American position, and concessions made by the State Department were regarded as indications of weakness.[105]

During the remaining months of the Wilson administration, there was little change in the unsatisfactory situation which Knapp described. Agitation against the occupation continued both in Haiti and in the United States, and the hope that a new administration at Washington would reverse its predecessor's policies made the position of the American officials more difficult. The Haitian government's attitude, as well as the financial situation abroad, prevented any substantial progress toward the flotation of the foreign loan, upon which the success of their program largely depended. The government also withheld its approval of the new charter for the bank, so that the National City Bank was compelled for some years to operate the bank under the old concession with several French directors. The one constructive step during the last year of the administration was the resumption of full service on the outstanding French bonds, which was made possible by an increase in the government's revenues.

In the first five years, the occupation and the treaty services had thus accomplished less than the two governments had hoped to

[105] Admiral Knapp to the Secretary of State, Jan. 15, 1921, 838.00/1742.

achieve when the treaty was signed. The new regime, however, had at least eliminated the worst of the conditions that had led to the American intervention. Though the *gendarmerie,* as the new constabulary was at first called, was unable even with the support of the marines to prevent the *caco* revolt in 1918, it soon developed into an efficient police force. Revolutions and political executions became things of the past, and the country people were freed from the oppression and extortion from which they had suffered even in times of peace. The officers in charge in the smaller towns, most of them non-commissioned officers in the marine corps, acted as advisers to the local communal governments and were able to bring about a marked improvement in their administration. The prisons were cleaned up and many prisoners were taught useful trades. There were also schools for the enlisted men at each *gendarmerie* post. The *gendarmerie,* using the *corvée,* had built a number of roads, including especially the very important one between Port au Prince and Cape Haitian. Living conditions in several of the towns had been improved by sanitation and street improvements. The European war, however, by cutting the government's income and by preventing the flotation of the loan, had made it impossible to begin any large program of public works.

The war, and unsatisfactory conditions in Haiti, had also discouraged the investment of any great amount of foreign capital. Two American groups had endeavored to start large agricultural enterprises, but both had failed. One of these was said to have lost nearly $1,000,000 in an unsuccessful attempt to grow cotton.[106] The other was a group in Chicago and Indianapolis which took over the properties of the Central Railroad of Haiti in 1917 and built a large sugar mill, investing, they said, over $7,500,000.[107] The Haitian American Corporation, which they set up, was soon in difficulties of several kinds. It could not obtain enough sugar to operate the mill efficiently and it had disputes with the Financial Adviser over the concessions and claims of the P.C.S. Railway and the wharf and the electric light companies. The State Department, which suspected that the former German owners still had a concealed interest in the enterprise, refused its support. Late in 1919 the company was able to

[106] Testimony of Roger L. Farnham, *Hearings,* p. 111.
[107] See the company's printed memorandum of July 22, 1920, 838.153C73/20.

convince the War Trade Board that it had freed itself from any German influence, and some of its subsidiaries' claims were paid, but it nevertheless went into bankruptcy in 1921. It was subsequently reorganized and became one of the principal North American enterprises in Haiti.

The American officials felt that two important omissions from the treaty had prevented its complete success. One was the lack of a provision for an improvement in the administration of justice. The Haitian courts had always been notoriously venal and incredibly irresponsible in their treatment of foreigners, and there had been little change for the better when Dartiguenave reorganized them under the constitution of 1918. It was difficult for the *gendarmerie* to enforce the laws if the courts refused to convict criminals. The situation was unfortunate because it frequently made the American officials feel that they must prevent the execution of decisions of the Haitian courts and led the occupation to use its own military courts in cases where American officials felt that action was necessary. The Haitian government repeatedly complained about the alleged cruel and arbitrary conduct of the provost courts.

In general, the provost courts seem to have been used sparingly and without gross abuses. There was far less interference with freedom of speech and freedom of the press than under the Dominican military government. Much was made however of one case in 1918 where a newspaper was closed for three months and its owner, Henri Chauvet, was fined $300 for publishing a report of Ruan's impending departure and saying that his recall confirmed President Wilson's "sentiment of Right and Justice." The State Department told the Haitian government that it considered this a "proper punishment of the offense," [108] but soon afterward the restrictions on the press were modified and violent and sometimes scurrilous attacks caused the American officials much annoyance.

The other omission from the treaty was with respect to education. The children of the *élite* were educated in schools maintained by foreign religious orders, but the public school system had been shockingly neglected. If Haiti were ever to have a stable democratic government, something must be done about the universal illiteracy of the people. The State Department proposed in 1920 that a mixed

[108] *Foreign Relations, 1919,* Vol. II, p. 337.

commission with a technical adviser be appointed to recommend a program for the establishment of a better educational system, but the Haitian government replied that the United States had no responsibility for education under the treaty except to see that funds were available. It considered the Financial Adviser's failure to provide funds the chief obstacle to progress.[109]

Far-reaching changes in the American treaty organization were made under the Harding administration, and for several years after 1922, when Louis Borno succeeded Dartiguenave and General Russell became American High Commissioner, there was effective and constructive cooperation between the two governments. The occupation consequently continued in Haiti long after the withdrawal of the military government from Santo Domingo. Many Haitians, however, opposed Borno's policy, and a violent resurgence of discontent in 1929 caused President Hoover to inaugurate a plan for an orderly withdrawal, which was completely carried out during the next five years.

[109] *Foreign Relations, 1921*, Vol. ii, pp. 188, 197.

Wilsonian Dollar Diplomacy in Nicaragua

✒ One of the most urgent problems that confronted the new officers in the State Department in 1913 was the situation in Nicaragua. The expectation of a change of policy at Washington and the Nicaraguan government's political and financial weakness had encouraged both the *zelayistas* and the *chamorristas* to think about a new revolution. There was a report from San Salvador that President Araujo was planning to foment uprisings both in Nicaragua and in Honduras in the hope of uniting the three countries under his own leadership for an attack on Estrada Cabrera in Guatemala.[1] When President Wilson issued his statement of March 11, 1913, declaring that the United States would exert its influence to support constitutional government in Latin America, he evidently had Central America in mind, for he explained to his Cabinet that "the agitators in certain countries wanted revolutions and were inclined to try it on with the new Administration." He added that he would not permit revolutions if he could prevent them.[2]

The President's declaration had a good effect in Nicaragua, especially with the *chamorristas,* who voted to give up the arms they were hiding and to reaffirm their support of Díaz.[3] The continued presence of the Legation guard was a further indication that the United States would uphold the constituted government. There could be little hope for any great improvement in the Nicaraguan situation, however, until the government's financial plight could be alleviated. The salaries of many employees were still in arrears, and many other creditors, including native and foreign holders of awards by the claims commission, were clamoring for payment. Even the new currency system threatened to break down if additional money were not found for the reserve fund. The hope that all of these problems would be settled by a large loan under the 1911 treaty had

[1] Heimke to Bryan, March 17, 1913, 813.00/821.
[2] D. F. Houston, *Eight Years in Wilson's Cabinet* (Garden City, 1926), Vol. I, pp. 43–44.
[3] Weitzel to Bryan, April 4, 1913, 817.00/2251.

practically vanished. The government would have been virtually penniless if the bankers had not agreed in March to release temporarily the portion of the customs receipts that would otherwise have been applied to reduce their loans.

The Bryan-Chamorro Treaty

Secretary Bryan apparently paid little attention to Nicaragua's problems during his first two months in the State Department. When Díaz sent his Minister of Finance to seek help from the United States, the Minister was unable to get a real hearing from the Secretary until he employed Charles A. Douglas as counsel. Douglas, who enjoyed Bryan's confidence, was able to impress on the Secretary the seriousness of the situation, and he took an active part in the negotiations that followed.

A Latin American Division memorandum of May 22, 1913, gave the Secretary a brief history of the Nicaraguan problem and pointed out that ". . . if the loan convention [of 1911] cannot be ratified, or if the Department of State will not promise a certain measure of protection and support to the American bankers, it seems probable that their arrangement with Nicaragua will come to an end on the first of July. Much of the good that has already been accomplished will be lost and Nicaragua will probably look to Europe for a new loan." The writer emphasized the importance of the claims commission and the desirability of obtaining funds to pay its awards, especially in the case of European creditors. He suggested that the ratification of the pending canal option treaty might meet some of Nicaragua's needs, if the Secretary was unwilling to continue to work with the bankers.

"What Nicaragua needs and wants" the memorandum concluded "is peace. It seems doubtful whether she can secure it without some sort of support and co-operation on the part of the United States. She can certainly not secure it unless she can obtain the funds necessary to pay the awards of the Claims Commission, to refund all of her old foreign and internal debts, to pay the salaries of Government employees which are now in arrears, and to undertake much needed work in developing the resources of the country.

"Perhaps the most marked instance of the so-called dollar diplomacy of the past administration was to secure these results to Nicaragua by means of the loan convention. The time has now arrived for the present administration to define its attitude towards that loan convention and towards the Nicaraguan questions in general." [4]

Bryan laid the matter before the President on May 24. He apparently accepted without question the idea that the United States must continue to support Díaz and should help him solve his financial problems. Neither the Latin American Division's memorandum nor the Secretary's letter to the President mentioned that Díaz' was a minority government which was being kept in power by American marines. The new administration apparently accepted its predecessor's view that the liberals, by their support of Zelaya and their conduct in 1912, had shown themselves unfit to rule. For the moment, in fact, Bryan did not even suggest that the New York bankers' operations in Nicaragua should be terminated. He recommended that an effort be made to obtain ratification of the Chamorro-Weitzel treaty, which had been signed in the last days of the Taft administration, because he was "inclined to think that the purchase of the canal option might give sufficient encouragement to the bankers to loan without the conditions which were, at their request, put into the other treaty. . . ." He realized that the "other treaty," the Knox-Castrillo convention, could not be ratified and that even the canal option treaty would meet with strong opposition.[5]

The President approved the proposed course of action, and on June 16 Bryan sent to the White House a new version of the canal option treaty, drafted by Douglas. The most important change was the addition of the provision proposed by Díaz in December 1911 giving the United States a right to intervene to maintain a stable government in Nicaragua. One of the Nicaraguan representatives stated later that Senator Bacon, the Chairman of the Committee on Foreign Relations, had suggested this addition.[6] The draft also provided that the money paid for the canal option be used partly for the immediate needs of the government and partly for paying the awards of the claims commission.[7] Bryan wrote the President that he himself would have preferred that the money be used for

---

[4] *Foreign Relations, 1913,* pp. 1040–1042.

[5] R. S. Baker, *Woodrow Wilson, Life and Letters,* Vol. IV, p. 436.

[6] Pedro J. Cuadra Chamorro, *Motivos Sobre El Tratado Chamorro-Bryan* (Managua, 1950), p. 10.

[7] Douglas to Bryan, June 9, 1913, 817.812/38.

public works and education, as the Chamorro-Weitzel treaty had stipulated, but that he was more interested in obtaining the canal option and the naval bases than in the way the money was spent.[8] Bryan seemed to emphasize the importance of the treaty from the standpoint of national defense, whereas his predecessors had apparently thought of it chiefly as an expedient for giving financial help to Nicaragua.

Wilson approved the new draft, and Senator Bacon, who had severely criticized the Taft administration's policy in Nicaragua, told Bryan that he thought that the Senate would approve the treaty and the "Platt Amendment" provision.[9] When the draft was made public on July 20, the *Nation* reported that Mr. Borah seemed to be the only prominent Senator who opposed it.[10] The *Literary Digest* of August 2 thought that most of the press approved. On August 7, however, the *Nation* said that opinion in the Senate and in the country at large was unfavorable. Both periodicals mentioned the opposition that had manifested itself in other Central American countries.

When Bryan conferred with the Senate Foreign Relations Committee, he found that there was little hope for prompt ratification because the senators were "against any extension of our authority over these countries." [11] They were apparently not impressed by Bryan's assurance that the treaty did not contemplate United States control—that the President wanted Nicaragua to choose her own officials, and that the only influence which the United States would exert would be in assuring free elections.[12] The Committee on Foreign Relations not only rejected the idea of a "Platt Amendment" but refused even to consider the canal option treaty in its original form.[13]

When it became evident that the treaty could not be ratified in time to relieve Nicaragua's pressing need for money, Bryan turned to another idea, which seemed more extraordinary to his contem-

[8] Bryan to Wilson, June 16, 1913, 817.812/30a.
[9] Bryan to Wilson, June 16, 1913, 817.812/30a.
[10] *The Nation,* June 24, 1913.
[11] Bryan to Wilson, July 31, 1913, quoted by Baker, *Woodrow Wilson,* Vol. iv, p. 437.
[12] Undated memorandum for the Senate Foreign Relations Committee, 817.812/22.
[13] Adler, "Bryan and Wilsonian Caribbean Penetration," *Hispanic American Historical Review,* Vol. xx (May 1940), p. 208. See also Holt, *Treaties Defeated by the Senate,* pp. 240–243.

poraries than it would today. On July 17, when he was seeking a solution for the problems arising from Ecuador's default on her foreign debt, Bryan suggested to Wilson that the United States should lend its credit to Latin American countries, by issuing its own bonds and relending the proceeds at 4½ percent. The difference between 4½ percent and the interest which the United States paid would be used to retire the debt. This arrangement would save the Latin Americans from what seemed to Bryan the extortionate demands of private bankers and would provide funds for internal development. Also it "would give our country such an increased influence . . . that we could prevent revolutions, promote education, and advance stable and just government." He now proposed to apply this idea in Nicaragua.[14] The President, however, thought that the idea "would strike the whole country . . . as a novel and radical proposal."[15]

The 1913 Loan Negotiations

The only alternative was to permit Nicaragua to obtain a loan from private sources. Brown Brothers and Seligman, who had agreed in June to continue until October 15 the arrangement for the release of the customs revenues, were willing to help, but Bryan was reluctant to deal with them because he thought that they had exacted onerous terms for their earlier loans. He was given a somewhat distorted picture of these transactions by the Nicaraguan Minister of Finance, who told him that the expense of collecting the customs was "enormous," that the currency reform had brought on "a commercial crisis . . . such as the history of our country has never seen," and that the reconstruction of the Pacific Railroad had intensified the crisis because it retired from circulation the money used in the work.[16]

Bryan wrote Wilson that Nicaragua, which owed the bankers about $711,000, had given them not only the customs and the returns from the railroad and other properties but an option on 51 percent of the railroad's stock, at a figure that would give them a profit of

[14] Bryan to Wilson, Aug. 16, 1913, Wilson Papers, Library of Congress.

[15] Wilson to Bryan, March 20, 1914, Bryan-Wilson Correspondence, Vol. I, p. 434. See also Baker, *Woodrow Wilson*, Vol. IV, pp. 433ff., and Adler, "Bryan and Wilsonian Caribbean Penetration," pp. 208–209.

[16] Cuadra to Bryan, Aug. 30, 1913, *Foreign Relations, 1913*, p. 1047.

about $1,500,000. The bankers were willing to increase their loan to a total of $2,000,000, at 6 percent, but were asking an option on the whole railroad line. "I mention this," the Secretary wrote, "to illustrate what I said in a letter the other day about our being in the position of a good Samaritan and helping those who have fallen among thieves." [17]

Bryan was consequently disposed to look sympathetically upon a proposal from Samuel Jarvis, the banker whose operations in the Dominican Republic were mentioned in earlier chapters. It was apparently the Latin American Division in the State Department that put Jarvis in touch with the Nicaraguans. He could not make a large loan himself, but he proposed to buy a controlling interest in the National Bank of Nicaragua and to serve as "Finance Commissioner" of the republic in return for a commission of 1 percent of any loans that he might negotiate, plus an unspecified amount of compensation for other services. He assured the Nicaraguans that he could raise $2,000,000–$3,500,000 and perhaps more, and that he could himself put up $1,000,000, which would make it possible to pay all debts to the New York bankers before floating the new loan. He apparently expected to float the new loan in England.[18]

On August 18 Bryan wrote the President that Jarvis had worked out a tentative contract with the Nicaraguan representatives, who preferred his terms—6 percent interest and 1 percent commission—to the New York bankers' proposal. The Secretary intended to make further inquiries about Jarvis but thought that Jarvis seemed more interested in the welfare of Nicaragua than anyone he had yet met.[19] Two weeks later Bryan sent the President a letter from the Nicaraguan representatives outlining the proposed arrangement. This had apparently been drafted by Bryan himself, for the Secretary assured Wilson that he had put in everything he could think of to protect the Nicaraguans, even including some provisions that the Nicaraguans had not wanted. Jarvis, he wrote, had not seen the documents in their final form.[20]

In the meantime Brown Brothers and Seligman had made their

[17] Bryan to Wilson, Aug. 13, 1913, cited above.
[18] Long's memorandum to Bryan, Aug. 30, 1913, 817.51/556½.
[19] 817.51/1780b.
[20] Bryan to Wilson, Sept. 3, 1913, 817.51/565. The letter from the Nicaraguan representatives is printed in *Foreign Relations, 1913*, p. 1050.

own proposal, which Bryan had described to the President in his letter of August 13. The New York bankers evidently wished to maintain their relationship with Nicaragua if the State Department's policy made it possible for them to do so. Besides the $700,000 that Nicaragua owed the two firms, Brown Brothers had an investment of more than $400,000 in the Emery claim, which was not likely to be paid until Nicaragua's finances were in better shape. The bankers' option on 51 percent of the stock of the Pacific Railroad might eventually be valuable, for the line was already beginning to show a profit under their management. Undoubtedly, too, they had a less selfish interest in the success of the whole program of financial rehabilitation, and especially in the currency reform—an interest which they had demonstrated by advancing an additional $100,000 for the reserve fund in June. They had responsibility for the customs collectorship, which would have to continue under their arrangement with the British bondholders even if the treasury notes were paid. They had been unwilling to make further commitments until they saw what the policy of the new administration would be, but when it became clear that Díaz would continue to have the American government's support they were prepared to make a new loan.

Bryan, with Wilson's approval, wrote the bankers that he did not like the "concealed profit" involved in the railroad option which they demanded, and he asked them to make a proposal without the option.[21] The bankers indignantly repudiated the idea that there was any concealment but, as an alternative, offered to buy the railroad stock already under option for $1,000,000 and to advance an additional $1,000,000, from which the $711,000 already owed them would be deducted. They still insisted on a preferential right to buy the remaining 49 percent of the railroad stock at the price offered by any other prospective purchaser. It will be remembered that they felt that they should have been given an option on this stock under the 1912 contract. They also stipulated that at least $500,000 of the new money should be used to increase the capital of the National Bank and to strengthen the currency reserve.[22]

[21] Bryan to the bankers, Aug. 27, 1913, 817.51/560. For Wilson's approval see his letter to Bryan of Aug. 25, 1913, 817.51/781.
[22] Foreign Relations, 1913, p. 1052.

Bryan was probably surprised to learn that President Díaz wanted to accept the bankers' proposal. Díaz evidently had little confidence in Jarvis' efforts. He needed money, and he was not so unfriendly to the bankers as one might have supposed from reading the complaints laid before the State Department by the Minister of Finance. When the State Department questioned the fairness of the price offered for the railroad stock, Díaz agreed that the stock might be worth more but insisted that he wished to sell it.[23] Bryan asked him to wait ten days to give Jarvis a chance to arrange a loan in London, but the Nicaraguan President replied that the situation was "horrible," and the $200,000, which was all that Jarvis could offer immediately, would not help.[24] Jarvis himself cabled the State Department from London that he could not negotiate effectively because the Nicaraguan government had not given him adequate authority.[25]

The Nicaraguan representatives consequently negotiated a new contract with Brown Brothers and Seligman. Despite Bryan's objections, the bankers insisted on an option on the remaining 49 percent of the railroad stock. The Nicaraguan government, on the other hand, turned down Bryan's request that $400,000 of the proceeds of the loan be set aside to pay the awards of the claims commission. The contracting parties did agree to Bryan's proposal that the Secretary of State appoint a man who would serve on the boards of directors of the railroad and the National Bank and act as "examiner" for both companies. The loan contracts, at the Secretary's request, were submitted to him before signature, and he formally approved them, with the reservation that he felt that the bankers had imposed unreasonably severe terms.[26]

The contracts were signed on October 8, 1913. The bankers bought 51 percent of the stock of the Pacific Railroad for $1,000,000 and obtained a preferential right to buy the other 49 percent at the price offered by any other prospective purchaser. On their own account, they provided $153,000 to increase the capital of the National Bank, thus becoming owners of 51 percent of the stock of that institution.

[23] *Ibid.*, p. 1053.

[24] Copies of cables exchanged between Díaz and the Nicaraguan Minister, 817.51/-583.

[25] Jarvis to Long, Sept. 22, 1913, 817.51/564.

[26] For the negotiations, see *Foreign Relations, 1913*, pp. 1054ff. Copies of the contracts are in Arana, *op. cit.*, Vol. I, pp. 314ff.

Each company was to have nine directors, of whom six would be appointed by the bankers, two by the Minister of Finance of Nicaragua, and one by the Secretary of State of the United States. The bankers agreed to lend the railroad $500,000 for extensions and improvements and to arrange that all of the company's net earnings up to October 1 be paid to the government as a dividend. They also bought new one-year treasury bills to a face amount of $1,060,000 for $1,000,000, an arrangement that made the interest rate a fraction more than 6 percent, but with no commission. The treasury bills were secured by liens on the customs and on the stock which the government continued to own in the railroad and the National Bank. From the funds which it received, the government paid its existing debts to the bankers and the National Bank and added $350,000 to the currency reserve fund.

The terms which the bankers exacted were probably less unreasonable than Bryan thought. Six-percent interest, without commission, was not excessive for a loan to a virtually bankrupt government whose recent history made it anything but an attractive risk, and the bankers' demand for security could be defended. The customs revenues, despite the American collectorship, were hardly adequate because experience had shown that the bankers could not reimburse themselves out of the collections without crippling the Nicaraguan government. It is more difficult to say whether the price paid for the railroad stock was a fair one. The hundred-mile single track line, with its run-down equipment, was gradually being converted into a more valuable property under the bankers' management, and in 1913–1914 it made a net profit of $244,706, or about 12 percent on the capital.[27] Seven years later the bankers sold the stock back to the government for $1,750,000. Its value was probably substantially greater in 1920 than in 1913, because Nicaragua's economic condition had improved notably in the meantime and because a part of the railroad's earnings had been invested in improvements.

The October 1913 contracts committed the new regime in the State Department to the same policy of dollar diplomacy for which its predecessor had been criticized. The failure to adopt a new policy cannot be attributed to the influence of personnel held over from the previous administration, because nearly all of the officials who

[27] Munro, *The Five Republics of Central America* (New York, 1918), p. 261.

dealt with Latin American affairs, from the Chief of the Latin American Division up, were newcomers. The State Department's records, in fact, indicate that Bryan himself made the important decisions about Nicaraguan matters, after consulting the President, and handled the negotiations, sometimes without informing his subordinates about them.[28] He approved the 1913 contracts because he saw no other way to obtain the financial help which Nicaragua needed. In agreeing to appoint a director and examiner for the National Bank and the railroad, he accepted a responsibility which his predecessors would probably have sought to avoid, for Knox, as we have seen, had maintained the position that the bankers' loans to Nicaragua were private business transactions.

Central American Opposition to the Canal Treaty

Unfortunately the 1913 contracts promised only a temporary and inadequate relief. Much of the proceeds went to refund earlier advances and very little was available for the government's expenses or for the payment of the claims commission's awards. Some more permanent arrangement was needed. The only solution in sight was the proposed canal option treaty. This, however, was still opposed in the Senate, and the opposition increased as it became evident that the proposed agreement had aroused much resentment in Central America.

Central American resentment of the United States' policy in Nicaragua had increased when Bryan's proposal to incorporate a "Platt Amendment" provision in the proposed treaty became known. In the summer of 1913 the State Department was forced to take note of hostile demonstrations in Costa Rica and El Salvador.[29] Soon afterward, the government of El Salvador invited Guatemala, Honduras, and Costa Rica to a conference to discuss the policy of the United States—a step that brought forth a sharp protest from Bryan and met with a negative reception from the other Central American states.[30]

While all of the neighboring countries objected to the proposed

[28] This is mentioned in a Latin American Division memorandum of Aug. 8, 1916, 817.51/264. Several important papers dealt with by Bryan show no indication of having been seen by the Latin American Division.

[29] *Foreign Relations, 1913*, p. 1024.

[30] *Ibid.*, pp. 1025–1027.

protectorate over Nicaragua, some of them also objected to the treaty for other reasons. Costa Rica, which owned much of the south bank of the San Juan River, had formally protested against the Chamorro-Weitzel Treaty in April 1913 on the ground that an arbitral award made by President Cleveland in 1888 had stipulated that Nicaragua should make no grants for canal purposes without consulting her. El Salvador objected to the proposed naval base in the Gulf of Fonseca, asserting that the waters of the gulf belonged jointly to Nicaragua, Honduras, and herself. El Salvador's protest, in October 1913, set forth this claim and also asserted that the existence of the base would endanger the neighboring countries in the event of war. Even the government of Colombia came forward with a claim that the Corn Islands belonged to it and not to Nicaragua.[31]

President Wilson was somewhat doubtful about going ahead with the treaty in the face of this Central American opposition,[32] but Bryan insisted that Nicaragua should have the assistance which the treaty would provide. He pointed out to the President that "Nicaragua has gone farther than any other Central American state in asking us to take part in her affairs, and by so doing has not only cut herself off from European aid but has aroused antagonism among her neighbors."[33]

The State Department refused to admit that the Central American protests had any validity. In his reply to El Salvador, on February 18, 1914, Bryan argued that neither Nicaragua nor Honduras considered that the waters of the Gulf of Fonseca were the undivided property of the three states bordering on it, and that El Salvador had recognized their division in a treaty signed in 1884 but never ratified. He assured El Salvador that one of the purposes of the treaty would be to safeguard the sovereignty of the Central American states, and offered to consider similar treaties with El Salvador and Honduras. Costa Rica's protest was not formally answered until August 1, 1914, when the United States took the position that the sale of a mere option to build a canal could not affect Costa Rica's

---

[31] For Costa Rica's protest, see *Foreign Relations, 1913*, p. 1022; for El Salvador's, *ibid.*, p. 1027. Colombia protested to the Nicaraguan government, *ibid.*, pp. 1031–1034.

[32] Wilson to J. B. Moore, Nov. 21, 1913, and Wilson to Bryan, Jan. 20, 1914, both in Wilson Papers, Library of Congress.

[33] Bryan to Wilson, Feb. 11, 1914, 817.51/630A.

rights, and that it was not certain that the canal would not be entirely within Nicaragua's territory. Furthermore, Bryan wrote, Costa Rica in the protocol of 1900 had accepted the principle that the two governments would negotiate separately with the United States on the canal question. Neither El Salvador nor Costa Rica was satisfied, and both reiterated their protests.[34]

In the meantime, Bryan was still trying to persuade the Senate Foreign Relations Committee of the need for a Nicaraguan treaty that would include provisions similar to the Platt Amendment. He had little success, even though President Díaz cabled President Wilson that: "The effect of the Platt Amendment on Cuba has been so satisfactory that, since your government is considering a canal convention with Nicaragua, I respectfully request that said convention be made to embody the substance of the Platt Amendment, so that my countrymen may see Nicaragua's credit improved, her natural resources developed, and peace assured throughout the land. I believe that revolutions will cease if your Government can see its way clear to grant the addition of the Amendment as requested." [35]

By this time both governments seemed to feel that the chief purpose of the proposed treaty was to provide much needed funds for the Díaz administration. In February the Nicaraguan Minister urged that the treaty would be the best solution for his country's "terrible economic situation," which was complicated by European diplomatic pressure for the payment of claims.[36] There seemed to be no other solution, because the bankers were unwilling to make a new loan, though Bryan at least twice asked them to do so.[37] When they learned that Díaz faced bankruptcy because he had been using his own money to meet government expenses, they agreed to protect some drafts that he had drawn on New York; [38] and they reluctantly authorized the National Bank to lend the government a total of $205,000 between March and June, 1914. They pointed out to the

[34] For the replies to El Salvador and Costa Rica, see *Foreign Relations, 1914*, pp. 954 and 964. The Protocol of 1900 with Costa Rica is discussed in Chapter II above.

[35] Díaz to Wilson, Feb. 4, 1914. *Foreign Relations, 1914*, p. 953.

[36] *Ibid.*

[37] Bryan to the bankers, Jan. 13, 1914, *ibid.*, p. 944, and March 7, 1914, 817.51/-639.

[38] Bryan to the bankers, March 7, 1914, and the bankers' reply of March 10, 817.51/638, 639.

State Department that these advances only made the ultimate situation worse by imposing new charges on the customs receipts.[39]

When the State Department asked the American Minister to give it a full description of Nicaragua's financial situation, in order to consider how a complete financial reorganization of the country could be effected in connection with the canal treaty, the Minister replied that "the chaotic mismanagement of the government's accounts and the deplorable and almost incomprehensible state of its finances" made it difficult to get reliable figures.[40] It became increasingly clear, however, that help was needed. The salaries of public employees were months in arrears, and the government's inability to pay its debts to local merchants contributed to a business depression that affected the customs revenues.

In the hope of making the treaty more acceptable to the Senate, Bryan finally decided to give up the "Platt Amendment" provision. On August 5, 1914, he and Emiliano Chamorro, the Nicaraguan Minister at Washington, signed a treaty that closely resembled the earlier Chamorro-Weitzel Treaty, with essentially the same provisions about the canal option, the naval base in the Gulf of Fonseca, and the Corn Islands. The new agreement was only slightly less objectionable to Costa Rica and El Salvador than the draft that had been under discussion during the past year. It met with a less hostile reception in the United States Senate, but there was enough opposition to delay approval for more than eighteen months.

While the treaty was pending, Bryan endeavored to placate Costa Rica and El Salvador. Both governments seemed willing to discuss arrangements based on monetary compensation, but public opinion in both countries had been stirred up to a point where an agreement with the United States would have been politically dangerous. The Costa Ricans resented the American government's failure to consult them before concluding the agreement with Nicaragua, and they were insulted when Bryan offered to make a similar treaty with them because they thought that he was suggesting one with a

[39] The bankers to the Secretary of State, March 2, 1914, 817.51/636. The texts of the contracts with the National Bank, dated March 16, June 12, and June 30, 1914, are in Arana, *op. cit.* Vol. I.

[40] Bryan to Jefferson, Jan. 17, 1914, *Foreign Relations, 1914*, p. 945. Jefferson to Bryan, Feb. 8, 1914, 817.51/635. A part of Jefferson's reply, altering "mismanagement" to "management" is printed in *Foreign Relations, 1914*, p. 945–946.

"Platt Amendment" provision. After this misunderstanding was cleared up, the Costa Rican government still sought some assurance that the option granted by Nicaragua would not mean that no canal would ever be built.[41] The President of El Salvador suggested that opposition in his country might be overcome if the United States would help to put the country "on a gold basis" and would arrange for the establishment of an American bank "with large capital." He also proposed that an American school, open to students from all of Central America, might be set up at the proposed naval station.[42]

Shortly before Bryan left the State Department in July 1915, he instructed Boaz Long, the American Minister in El Salvador, to visit the other Central American states to discuss their attitude toward the treaty. In December Secretary Lansing sent the President a rather elaborate plan that Long had worked out. In addition to buying a canal option from Costa Rica and naval base rights from El Salvador, the United States would establish a school for Central American youths and would endeavor to interest American bankers in providing funds for the development of El Salvador and Honduras. Honduras had not joined in the protest against the treaty, because the government did not consider that the Gulf of Fonseca belonged jointly to the states that bordered on it,[43] but her territory would be affected, and Long proposed that the United States should build a new port for her on the gulf, in order to destroy the monopoly of the German firms that controlled trade through Amapala.[44] The President seems to have taken no action on Long's plan. When the Senate finally approved the Bryan-Chamorro Treaty on February 18, 1916, after Wilson had exercised a considerable amount of pressure on some of the Democratic senators,[45] the best opportunity for a negotiated settlement had passed.

The Senate added a clause similar to one that had been incorporated at Díaz' suggestion in the unratified 1913 agreement pro-

[41] *Foreign Relations, 1915*, pp. 1104–1112.

[42] Long to Bryan, March 26, 1915, *ibid.*, p. 1115.

[43] Honduras, in December 1916, formally objected to El Salvador's contention that the Gulf was undivided property, *Foreign Relations, 1916*, p. 890.

[44] Lansing to Wilson, Dec. 11, 1915, 817.812/174. For the draft treaty with El Salvador see 817.812/176.

[45] Holt, *Treaties Defeated by the Senate*, p. 243.

viding that the money paid to Nicaragua was "to be applied by Nicaragua upon its indebtedness or other public purposes for the advancement of the welfare of Nicaragua in a manner to be determined by the two High Contracting Parties, all such disbursements to be made by orders drawn by the Minister of Finance of the Republic of Nicaragua and approved by the Secretary of State of the United States or by such person as he may designate." This and another minor change were promptly accepted by Nicaragua, and ratifications were exchanged on June 24.

The Senate in consenting to ratification had stipulated that nothing in the treaty was "intended to affect any existing right of Costa Rica, El Salvador, or Honduras," but its action angered the Central American governments because they had been under the impression that ratification was being delayed as a courtesy to them.[46] Senator Stone had suggested in December that a further delay might be advisable, but Lansing preferred to go ahead because the President had not decided whether to undertake negotiations on the basis of Long's plan.[47] When the treaty was favorably reported by the Committee on Foreign Relations, Costa Rica and El Salvador promptly presented new protests, which were rather curtly rejected by the State Department.[48]

On March 24, 1916, Costa Rica asked the Central American Court of Justice to declare the Bryan-Chamorro Treaty null and void because it violated the Cleveland award and her boundary treaty with Nicaragua. Lansing immediately informed all of the American representatives in Central America for their "discreet use" that the United States felt that the Court had no right to "attempt jurisdiction of any matter of diplomatic relation" between it and a Central American country, and added that the "attempt by Costa Rica to interfere with freedom of action of Nicaragua in this matter cannot but be viewed by the United States as an unjustifiable effort to prevent Nicaragua from fulfilling her contractual obligations." [49] Despite the American government's attitude, El Salvador also appealed to the Court in August 1916, alleging that a naval base close to one of

[46] Long mentioned this impression to Bryan in a memorandum of June 5, 1915, 817.812/172.
[47] Latin American Division memorandum of Dec. 16, 1915, 817.812/175.
[48] *Foreign Relations, 1916*, pp. 811ff.
[49] *Ibid.*, p. 831–832.

her most important ports would imperil her autonomy and that the treaty violated her proprietary rights in the Gulf of Fonseca. Nicaragua denied that the Court had jurisdiction and refused to be a party to either suit.

The Court handed down its decision in Costa Rica's case on September 30, 1916, and in El Salvador's on March 9, 1917. It declined to declare the Bryan-Chamorro Treaty null and void, but it held that Nicaragua had violated the rights of the other two countries. Immediately after the announcement of the second decision, the Nicaraguan government denounced the treaty under which the Court had been established, and the tribunal soon afterward went out of existence.[50]

It was unfortunate that the United States should have been put in a position where it could be held responsible for the Court's destruction. It is true that the Court had not lived up to the expectations of its founders. The hope that it would be an impartial tribunal, acting independently of the governments that set it up, was hardly realistic in countries where the local courts were expected to take orders from the president in any matter involving politics. In the first case that came before it, in fact, when Nicaragua and Honduras complained that Guatemala and El Salvador were fomenting a revolution in Honduras, four of the judges clearly voted as their governments wished them to.[51] In 1911 the Court's prestige was further impaired when the conservative government was permitted to replace the Nicaraguan judge in outright violation of the 1907 treaty. In general, the Court's record of accomplishment was not impressive. It had helped to prevent a Central American war in 1908, but its efforts for peace in Nicaragua in 1910 and again in 1912 had produced no result. In the few cases brought before it by private citizens between 1908 and 1916 it had refused, perhaps properly, to assume jurisdiction.[52] Nevertheless, its dissolution weak-

---

[50] Translations of Costa Rica's complaint to the Court and of the Court's decision in the case of Costa Rica were published by the Costa Rican Legation in Washington in 1916. For the text of El Salvador's complaint, see *Foreign Relations, 1916*, pp. 853ff., and for the decision in the case of El Salvador, *Foreign Relations, 1917*, pp. 1101ff. Nicaragua's position with respect to the decision was stated in a circular note of Nov. 24, 1917, *ibid.*, p. 1104.

[51] See Chapter IV, *supra*.

[52] For a brief history of the Central American Court, see Munro, *The Five Republics of Central America*, p. 221–225.

ened the whole structure set up by the Central Americans with Secretary Root's help at the Washington Conference of 1907; and in the eyes of most Central Americans and of many people elsewhere the United States was to blame.

Wilson and Lansing probably insisted on the prompt ratification of the canal option treaty because it seemed the only way to save Nicaragua from financial collapse and political chaos. It seems doubtful that either of them thought that the canal option and the proposed naval bases were very important from the standpoint of the national security of the United States. Bryan, as we have seen, was interested in this aspect of the treaty, but a memorandum written in June 1914 suggests that Lansing, while he was still counselor of the State Department, was at least doubtful about it. When Wilson read this memorandum, he admitted that the United States was perhaps giving more than it was receiving but wrote that he thought that the treaty was on the whole wise and necessary.[53] In November 1915, in reply to an inquiry, Lansing was told that the General Board of the Navy thought that a coaling station in the Gulf of Fonseca would be useful, but the tone of the recommendation did not suggest any great feeling of urgency. The General Board did, however, think that it would be undesirable to have any foreign base in the gulf, and it is probable that a desire to forestall any European effort to get a foothold in Central America influenced Lansing's attitude.[54] There had been vague stories about British and Japanese interest in a Nicaraguan canal, and in May 1914 the German Chargé d'Affaires at Managua told Díaz that the price offered by the United States for the canal option was very small, and suggested negotiation with other governments.[55]

The State Department seems to have been convinced that the complaints of Costa Rica and El Salvador had no real merit, and that the action of the Central American Court was improper. It doubted the sincerity of the protesting governments. Long, who was probably the best informed of the Department's representatives, thought that their real purpose was to weaken the Nicaraguan gov-

[53] Bryan to Wilson, June 12, and Wilson to Bryan, June 13, 1914, 817.812/168.

[54] Secretary of State to Secretary of Navy, Nov. 16, 1915, 817.812/141a. Secretary of Navy to Secretary of State, Nov. 18, 1914, 817.812/142.

[55] Telegram from Legation, Managua, May 27, 1914, 817.812/74. President Díaz confirmed the story in conversation with me several years later.

ernment's position and foment anti-American feeling.[56] It could hardly be denied, however, that both Costa Rica and El Salvador had reason to feel that the treaty affected their interests and it seems regrettable that there was not a more effective effort to meet their objections.

Ironically, the treaty gave little immediate financial relief to the Díaz government because a dispute over the application of the $3,000,000 held up the disbursement of the money. The government's situation had grown even worse after the war in Europe closed the principal markets for Nicaragua's products. In December 1914 the bankers were compelled to consent to a small new issue of paper money, with a temporary abandonment of the gold exchange standard. The *córdoba* was brought back to par in 1915,[57] but the government would have had virtually no money if the bankers and the British bondholders had not agreed to a series of temporary suspensions of payments to them from the customs. Díaz promised to make up the back payments on the treasury bills and the British bonds as soon as he received the treaty money, and he obtained credit from the National Bank and from the government's purchasing agent in New York by similar promises.

While the treaty was under consideration in the Senate, however, the State Department had begun to realize that $3,000,000 would meet only a part of Nicaragua's most pressing obligations. The British government had repeatedly warned the United States that it would object to any distribution of the treaty fund that did not provide for approximately $100,000 of British claims that had been recognized by Nicaragua in 1912, and Lansing had promised that these claims would receive consideration.[58] Similar promises had apparently been made informally to other European governments. All holders of awards of the claims commission, which totaled $1,840,000, would have good cause to complain if they were not paid. Furthermore, many other North American creditors of the

---

[56] Long to Lansing, March 26, 1916, 817.812/178. A portion of this message is printed in *Foreign Relations, 1916,* without indication that anything is omitted.

[57] Munro, *The Five Republics of Central America,* pp. 247–249.

[58] The British Ambassador to the Secretary of State, Oct. 28, 1915, *Foreign Relations, 1915,* p. 1118; April 12 and May 21, 1916, *Foreign Relations, 1916,* pp. 833 and 836. The Secretary of State to the British Ambassador, May 5, 1916, *ibid.,* p. 836.

Nicaraguan government had served notice on the State Department that they expected to share in the treaty fund and had enlisted the support of members of Congress. When the Department realized that the agreements under which Nicaragua had been permitted to use the customs receipts would mean that a few claimants would receive nearly $2,400,000 of the $3,000,000, it refused to recognize them. It maintained this position even after the bankers produced a letter from Bryan, dated October 13, 1914, explicitly approving their arrangement with Nicaragua.[59]

The Nicaraguan government wished to honor its contracts. It probably realized that the United States Congress had not yet appropriated the money due under the treaty and that its situation would be desperate if it could not use the customs receipts after July 1, 1916, when its agreement with the bankers would expire. The need for continuing help from the bankers became greater when the British bondholders refused to consent to a further suspension of payments to them. This compelled the Collector General to withhold a portion of the customs receipts after July 1, but the government was able to make new agreements with the bankers on July 31 and October 26, in both of which it promised not to consent to any application of the treaty funds which conflicted with its obligations to them. These called forth severe rebukes from the State Department,[60] and the Department refused to approve any payments from the treaty fund after the money was finally appropriated. Relations between the Department and the bankers were increasingly strained. The deadlock continued during the remainder of Díaz' term, so that his administration received nothing from the treaty fund.

The Nicaraguan Election of 1916

Several months before the ratification of the Bryan-Chamorro Treaty, the State Department had begun to consider what its policy should be when the time came to elect Díaz' successor. It was generally recognized that Díaz had been able to stay in office only because the continued presence of the legation guard meant that

---

[59] The letter, which had apparently not been in the State Department's files, is printed in Foreign Relations, 1916, p. 905.

[60] Ibid., pp. 908, 912.

the United States would not permit another revolution, and it was clear that Díaz' group would remain in power by controlling the election if the United States took no action. This would be unsatisfactory for several reasons. Discontent in Nicaragua had manifested itself only in minor disturbances, most of them provoked by dissident conservatives or by foreign adventurers, but the political situation was clearly unstable and continuing rivalry between Díaz' friends and the *chamorristas* made the conservatives' hold on the government precarious. There had been many reports of inefficiency and graft in the Díaz regime. More especially, the State Department was sensitive to charges that it was supporting a minority government by force, and it would be further criticized if the same group continued in power by stealing the election. It was difficult to deny the liberals a fair chance to participate in the election, even though their hostility to the United States and their association with the Zelaya regime made many of the Department's officials unwilling to see them regain control.

Rather surprisingly, Lansing himself received Julián Irías, who had been Zelaya's right-hand man, when Irías came to Washington in July 1915 to ask whether the United States would object to his being a candidate for the presidency. The Secretary did not reply immediately,[61] but during the next few months other officials carried on conversations with J. Reuben Clark, the former solicitor of the State Department, who was employed as the liberals' counsel. Through Clark, Irías asked that the United States supervise the election, and he promised to cooperate in the American government's policy if he became president. He would accept a canal option treaty, with Platt Amendment provisions, and would agree to the appointment of an American financial adviser and the establishment of a rural guard under American instructors. He also undertook to consult the United States before granting concessions to foreigners. Even the terms of the proposed treaties were discussed.[62] These would have set up in Nicaragua a regime somewhat similar to that which the United States was then imposing on Haiti and that which it was trying to impose on the Dominican Republic.

[61] For a memorandum of the conversation, see 817.00/2534.
[62] J. R. Clark to Lansing, June 10, 1916, 817.00/2545. See also a memorandum by Leland Harrison of the Latin American Division, dated Sept. 5, 1915, 817.00/2536.

The State Department made no promises but telegraphed Minister Jefferson on October 29, 1915, that it wanted to discuss the Nicaraguan situation with him in Washington, mentioning the criticism of its Nicaraguan policy and saying that it wanted to withdraw the marines and have a free election. It suggested that it might consider the organization of a constabulary under American officers to replace the marines, if Díaz asked it to, and inquired in rather vague language whether Díaz would request American supervision of the election. The Department thought that it would be inadvisable to support Díaz as a candidate, but it asked whether another candidate might be able to unite the conservative party and mentioned Emiliano Chamorro in this connection.[63]

There is no record of decisions made during Jefferson's ensuing visit to Washington. It is clear that the State Department continued to feel that there ought to be a free election in Nicaragua, but at the same time wished that a conservative victory could be assured. In January 1916 the Latin American Division seemed to be reaching the conclusion that Chamorro would be the candidate most likely to assure a conservative victory. General Chamorro was clearly the party's most popular leader. He had sacrificed his presidential aspirations in 1912 for the sake of harmony and had probably had an understanding with Díaz at that time that he would be the official candidate in 1916.[64] Since 1913, he had been Minister at Washington and had made an excellent impression in the State Department. Secretary Lansing himself told Chamorro on January 15, 1916, that the United States would view his candidacy with great pleasure, at the same time pointing out to him that an arrangement for American supervision of the election seemed the only honorable course for both governments.[65]

When the Chargé d'Affaires at Managua approached Díaz on the question of supervising the election, the President flatly rejected the proposal. He said frankly that free elections would be inadvisable. As the Chargé put it, "he regards opponents of his admin-

[63] Telegram to Managua, Oct. 29, 1915, 817.00/2422a.
[64] The State Department's pamphlet, *The United States and Nicaragua* (Washington, 1932), p. 32, states that there was such an understanding, but I have found nothing about it in the file.
[65] Latin American Division memorandum of Jan. 14, 1916, with endorsement showing the Secretary's action, 817.00/2439.

istration in majority and undesirable characters might be chosen by ignorant voters." [66] Díaz' subordinates, in fact, were preventing both liberals and *chamorristas* from registering as voters, and the President was actively supporting the presidential candidacy of his associate Pedro Rafael Cuadra.[67] Díaz became more cooperative, however, after Jefferson's return to Managua. He extended the period for registration and lifted the "state of siege" that had discouraged political meetings; and a few days later he promised to have a fair election and to permit American marines to act as observers at each polling place, unless Irías or another extreme *zelayista* should be a candidate.[68] The State Department was gratified and agreed with the Minister that no further action should be taken until after the Nicaraguan congress had ratified the Bryan-Chamorro Treaty.[69]

The American government had not yet defined its attitude toward the liberal party. Perhaps because of a change in personnel, the Latin American Division seems to have lost any interest that it may once have had in the assurances obtained through Clark from Irías.[70] It evidently felt that it would be unfortunate if the liberals returned to power. On March 29, Lansing sent the President a long memorandum by J. Butler Wright, the Acting Chief of the Division, which went into the history of Nicaragua in some detail and expressed the opinion that Irías should not be permitted to become president, despite his promises, because he was a *zelayista* and at heart an enemy of the United States. Contrary to the opinion of most observers, Wright thought that the two political parties in Nicaragua were about equal numerically, but he said that the conservatives included the pro-American and more respectable classes in the community while the liberals had the support of the ignorant masses. He saw four possible courses of action: (1) to remove the marines, which was clearly undesirable, (2) to supervise the election, which was impracticable because of Díaz' refusal to consent, (3) to main-

---

[66] Wicker to Lansing, Feb. 10, 1916, 817.51/767.

[67] Wicker to Lansing, Feb. 17, 1916, 817.00/2434.

[68] Jefferson to Lansing, March 10 and March 13, 1916, 817.00/2437, 2438.

[69] Lansing to Jefferson, March 15, 1916, 817.00/2438.

[70] Boaz Long, though still Minister to El Salvador, was directing Latin American affairs in the State Department until late in 1915, when J. Butler Wright became Acting Chief of the Latin American Division. ·

tain order while the Díaz administration ran the election, a course that would leave the country with a weak, unpopular government, or (4) to support the candidacy of Chamorro. This last was the course which Wright, and apparently Lansing, advocated.[71] The President replied that he had only vague recollections about our Nicaraguan relations, based on "desultory conversations" with Mr. Bryan, and that he wanted to talk with Lansing about them.[72] The State Department's files do not indicate what instructions, if any, he gave in subsequent conversations.

The State Department, however, followed essentially the course Wright recommended. In April, Wright told Clark, for Irías' benefit, that the United States would not supervise the election, but that Díaz had promised to assure fair play and to permit observation by the American marines. He told Clark of Díaz' statement that his promises would not be valid if Irías were a candidate, but apparently did not say that the United States would object to Irías.[73] In May, when Chamorro returned to Nicaragua to carry on his campaign, he was carried to Corinto on an American warship, a courtesy which meant a great deal in a situation where all of the politicians were anxiously awaiting some indication of the United States government's intentions. Jefferson was told to urge the conservatives to unite on one candidate,[74] and he hardly needed to be told who the candidate should be.

Díaz and his friends were nevertheless hard to convince, because the more moderate groups in the conservative party feared that Chamorro would institute an illiberal and militaristic regime that might lead to civil war. They had been unable to muster much support for Pedro Rafael Cuadra, but in June, after the other faction had formally nominated Chamorro, they held a convention which proclaimed the candidacy of Carlos Cuadra Pasos. Jefferson's efforts on behalf of Chamorro were hampered by the State Department's reluctance to take a definite stand with Díaz' representative in Washington,[75] for the Department, while willing to advise the con-

[71] Lansing to Wilson, March 29, 1916, 817.00/2440a. Wright's memorandum was dated Feb. 28 and is filed under 817.00/2435½.
[72] Wilson to Lansing, April 2, 1916, 817.00/2444½.
[73] Latin American Division memorandum of April 22, 1916, 817.00/2543.
[74] Lansing to Jefferson, May 5, 1916, 817.00/2444a.
[75] Jefferson to Lansing, July 18, 1916, 817.00/2453.

servatives for their own good, did not want to seem to impose a candidate on them. For some months the outcome was in doubt. Chamorro complained to the State Department that the government was arresting and intimidating his supporters and that Jefferson was giving him no help,[76] while Díaz protested still more vigorously about the Minister's partiality to Chamorro.[77]

The division in the conservative party seemed likely to help Irías, whose followers were carrying on an active campaign with less interference from the government than an opposition party would normally expect in Central America. Jefferson, however, had suggested to the State Department in April that the Legation let it be known that the United States would not recognize any candidate who would "resort to the old and bad order of things," even if he were elected. The State Department replied several weeks later that "any repetition of Zelaya regime cannot expect approbation of this Government," though otherwise the United States was neutral between the two parties.[78] Jefferson apparently took this as authorization to say to the liberals that no candidate who had been associated with the Zelaya regime would be recognized if elected.[79] The liberals suffered another blow when Irías landed at Corinto on August 5 but was not allowed to remain on shore. The treatment that he received was hardly compatible with electoral freedom, but the State Department took no position either for or against his entering Nicaragua when Clark asked that it use its influence to have him admitted.[80]

On August 10 Jefferson reported that Díaz had agreed to let Lansing choose the conservative candidate.[81] A few days later, however, Díaz indicated through his Chargé d'Affaires at Washington that Chamorro would not be acceptable. When Lansing saw the Chargé and told him that Chamorro would be a proper person to unite the conservative party, adding a warning that the United

[76] Charles A. Douglas to Polk, June 13, 1916, enclosing a copy of a cable from Chamorro, 817.00/2456.

[77] Lansing to Jefferson, July 28, 1916, 817.00/2458a.

[78] Jefferson to Lansing, April 27, 1916, and Lansing to Jefferson, June 16, 1916, 817.00/2445.

[79] When I was in Nicaragua in July 1916 it was a matter of common knowledge that Jefferson had made this statement to the liberal leaders.

[80] Latin American Division memorandum, Aug. 1, 1916, 817.00/2460.

[81] Jefferson to Lansing, Aug. 10, 1916, 817.00/2465.

States might consider withdrawing the legation guard, Díaz replied that he could not support Chamorro. He said that he knew that the guard might be withdrawn, but that his government could maintain itself.[82]

Jefferson was promptly instructed to say that the Secretary of State was "loath to believe" that Díaz would not honor his offer to let the Secretary choose the conservative candidate and to say further that the United States expected the Nicaraguan government to fulfill its promise of a free election and to maintain order. It would be contrary to the "spirit of this Government's attitude toward Nicaragua" to recognize the next president if the election were not absolutely free. The United States would also be unwilling to countenance any regime that would not bring about economic reforms. Díaz was warned that any disorder would lead to grave consequences.[83] Jefferson was authorized on September 7 to make public the last part of this message and to intimate that the United States would not pay the canal treaty money to an unrecognized government.[84]

In the meantime Jefferson was talking with some of the liberals, and thought that they might ask him to designate a candidate for their party. He planned, if they did, to nominate José María Moncada, who had been one of the leaders of the Bluefields revolution of 1909–1910; but he found that Moncada had little support in the party because he was too "pro-American." [85] Irías continued to be the official liberal candidate.

The reason for Díaz' defiant attitude soon became apparent. When Irías returned to Nicaragua on September 5, obviously with the government's consent, it was evident that the President and the liberals had reached some understanding. Lansing told the Nicaraguan Chargé that he was "greatly disquieted." [86] Jefferson seemed to have lost control of the situation. He regained control, however, when Admiral Caperton arrived at Corinto with two additional American warships. On September 16 the Admiral was able to re-

[82] Díaz' telegram of Aug. 17 to Nicaraguan Chargé d'Affaires, 817.00/2474.
[83] Lansing to Jefferson, Aug. 25, 1916, 817.00/2475a.
[84] Lansing to Jefferson, Sept. 7, 1916, 817.00/2481.
[85] Jefferson to Lansing, Aug. 24, Sept. 7, and Sept. 21, 1916. 817.00/2472, 2483, 2493.
[86] Memorandum of conversation, Sept. 11, 1916, 817.00/2496.

port that "the political leaders are again giving the usual weight to the Minister's words and are less inclined to fractiousness"; [87] and on September 21 Jefferson telegraphed that Díaz said that the conservative party had united behind Chamorro.[88]

The Minister told Irías, in Caperton's presence, that any liberal candidate would have to respect all existing arrangements and would have to furnish satisfactory proof that he had not taken an active, objectionable part in Zelaya's administration or in any revolutionary movement since 1910.[89] Irías promptly withdrew from the contest and advised his followers to abstain from registering or voting. When the elections were held a few days later Chamorro received practically all of the votes cast. Jefferson reported that everything had gone off quietly except for a few street fights in which four or five persons were killed.[90]

The Financial Plan of 1917

The deadlock over the disposition of the treaty fund continued until the last few days of Díaz' term in office. The State Department, in its resentment at Brown Brothers and Seligman, even tried secretly, and unsuccessfully, to interest other bankers in taking over their interests in Nicaragua.[91] It was determined not to let the greater part of the treaty money go to the bankers and the British bondholders, even though it could hardly compel the Nicaraguan government to disregard its contracts with them. Lansing and his advisers, however, evidently realized the weakness of their position, and President Wilson, when Lansing consulted him, felt that the administration could not simply "brush aside" the assurances that Bryan had given the bankers in 1914.[92] A compromise was finally worked out through the good offices of the "Permanent Nicaraguan Group," one of the national committees established by the Pan American Financial Conference that had recently met in Washington.

At a meeting with the bankers on December 18, 1916, the State

[87] "Review of Conditions," Sept. 16, 1916, 817.00/2510.
[88] 817.00/2493.
[89] Ibid.
[90] Jefferson to Lansing, Oct. 2 and Oct. 3, 1916, 817.00/2499, 2502.
[91] Latin American Division memorandum of Nov. 22, 1916, 817.51/879.
[92] Wilson to Lansing, Dec. 8, 1916, 817.51/883.

Department recognized the validity of the Nicaraguan government's promises to them and to the British bondholders, and the bankers indicated that they would be willing to postpone a part of the payment due them if a general refunding of Nicaragua's debts could be effected. It was agreed that a new joint commission should adjudicate and scale down all claims against Nicaragua, including even the unpaid awards of the earlier mixed claims commission, many of which were thought to have passed into the hands of speculators. The new commission's awards would be paid partly in cash and partly with an issue of bonds secured by a second lien on the customs. A continuance of the financial mismanagement that had made the situation what it was would be prevented by the installation of an American financial adviser. In reporting the result of the conference to Minister Jefferson, Lansing urged that the new President should announce the program in his inaugural address and said that the appointment of a financial adviser was "very imperative." He considered Colonel Ham, the collector of customs, the best man for the position.[93]

Chamorro did not commit himself to the plan, but he did not immediately reject it. Taking office with no money in the treasury and an accumulation of pressing debts that included $500,000 in back salaries, he was not in a strong bargaining position. He objected to a reopening of the awards of the old claims commission, but when the State Department said that it had in mind only the reconsideration of awards that had passed into the hands of speculators he had the congress pass an act creating the new commission, with one Nicaraguan and two North American members. He also seemed to accept in principle the proposal for a financial adviser but said that he would await a favorable opportunity to present the matter to the congress.[94] The State Department consequently let him have $250,000 from the treaty fund early in February.

Soon afterward, however, it became clear that Chamorro did not intend to accept the financial control which the State Department and the bankers sought to impose. He encouraged violent newspaper

[93] Lansing to Jefferson, Dec. 22, 1916. Part of this telegram, omitting reference to the financial adviser, was published in *Foreign Relations, 1916*, p. 916. See also the Latin American Division memorandum of Dec. 18, 817.51/880.

[94] The Nicaraguan Chargé d'Affaires to the Secretary of State, Jan. 31, 1917, 817.51/886.

attacks on the bankers and their agents in Nicaragua,[95] and he repeatedly refused to go forward with the appointment of a financial adviser. The State Department found itself dealing with a self-confident, stubborn leader who was less amenable to pressure than Díaz because he felt more secure in his political and military position.

After long and painful negotiations, during which Chamorro at one time threatened to seize the customhouses,[96] the two governments and the bankers agreed on a compromise. A series of contracts signed on October 20 put into effect the Financial Plan of 1917.[97] The Nicaraguan government agreed to limit its budget to $95,000 per month, but additional expenditures up to $26,666.66 per month could be made with the approval of a high commission, composed of the Minister of Finance, a resident American commissioner, and an umpire named by the Secretary of State of the United States. Of the receipts above these amounts, referred to as the "surplus revenues," half would be used to reduce the debt to the bankers and the British bondholders and the remainder for public works. The High Commission would be fiscal agent for a new issue of "guaranteed customs bonds," the proceeds of which would be used to pay a portion of the awards of the new claims commission. The Nicaraguan government agreed that the Collector General should continue to collect the customs so long as any of the British bonds or the bankers' treasury bills should be outstanding, and that he should also take over the collection of the republic's internal revenues if their product under Nicaraguan administration should fall below a certain point. In view of these arrangements, the bankers agreed to extend the maturity of half of their outstanding treasury bills, and the British bondholders agreed to a partial suspension of service during the next three years.

It thus became possible for the United States to disburse the treaty fund. The British bondholders received $799,720.23 to cover their arrears of interest, and the New York bankers $767,696.80 for half of the principal of the treasury bills plus interest and expenses;

[95] The bankers to the Secretary of State, Feb. 8 and March 14, 1917, 817.51/896, 907.

[96] Jefferson to Lansing, June 18, 1917, 817.51/969.

[97] For the text see 817.51/1017, 1018, or Arana, *op. cit.* Vol. II, pp. 20–64.

$111,404.83 went to repay the government's debt to the National Bank of Nicaragua. In addition, the holders of the Emery claim received four-fifths of their principal, or $485,000. Neither the Nicaraguan government nor the State Department wished to make this payment out of the treaty fund, but Brown Brothers and Company were able to exact preferential treatment because their claim, as an arbitral award, was technically a debt of Nicaragua to the United States, and federal law forbade payment from the treasury to persons owing money to the United States without first deducting the indebtedness.[98] The Nicaraguan government received a total of $500,000 for its own use in paying back salaries, and the balance of $336,178.14 was held by the Collector General of Customs to be applied to the payment of claims.[99]

The Financial Plan of 1920

Nicaragua's financial situation, which had caused the State Department so much concern since 1910, improved rapidly after 1917. The Financial Plan forced the government to live within its budget. A. F. Lindberg, the resident American commissioner, who had formerly been in the Nicaraguan customs service, was able and tactful, and his control over a part of the government's expenditures enabled him to discourage bad practices and to bring about some administrative reforms. The surplus revenues rapidly paid off the treasury bills and the back interest on the British bonds. The political situation was also better. The liberals were still unhappy, but Chamorro's firm hand and the continued presence of the legation guard discouraged any attempt at revolt. The country was comparatively prosperous during the last years of the world war.

By 1919 it was clear that the government would soon have a considerable surplus of unobligated funds. Chamorro decided to use some of this to build the long desired railroad to the Atlantic Coast and sent his Minister of Finance and Colonel Ham, the Collector General of Customs, to discuss his plan with the New York bankers. The State Department expressed a very lively interest, both in the building of the proposed railroad and in the refunding

[98] Foreign Relations, 1917, pp. 1134, 1135.
[99] Ibid., pp. 1149, 1150.

of the existing foreign debt, which was part of the plan,[100] but the bankers were less enthusiastic. The condition of the bond market would make a large refunding loan difficult, and the proposed new railroad might impair the value of their stock in the Pacific line.

The bankers nevertheless agreed to help Nicaragua work out a new financial plan under which the Atlantic railroad might eventually be financed. They insisted, however, that the government first take off their hands the railroad stock which they had bought in 1913. The State Department criticized their original proposals as one-sided and onerous to Nicaragua and obtained some changes,[101] but it took a far less active part in the negotiations than it had in some of the earlier transactions.

The result of the negotiations was the Financial Plan of 1920, which was approved by the Nicaraguan congress in December. Under this, the customs service and the High Commission continued as before, but the government's monthly allowance was increased to $105,000, plus $26,666.66 controlled by the High Commission. The republic repurchased the bankers' stock in the Pacific Railroad, paying $300,000 in cash and giving treasury bills bearing 9-percent interest for the remainder of the purchase price of $1,750,000. This represented a substantial profit over the $1,000,000 that they had paid for the stock, but the bankers claimed that the road had become a much more valuable property under their management. Unfortunately, the most important feature of the plan, a new loan for railroad construction, was never carried out because the situation in the bond market made it impossible for the bankers to take the bonds on any terms that Nicaragua considered reasonable.[102] The Financial Plan of 1920 nevertheless remained in effect for several years.

The Presidential Election of 1920

Two years before the end of his term it was evident that General Chamorro was planning his own reelection. The State Department

---

[100] Latin American Division memorandum of Oct. 18, 1919, 817.51/1182.

[101] Trade Adviser's Office memorandum of Feb. 21, 1920, 817.51/1249; Mallet-Prevost to Rowe, March 3, 1920, 817.51/1250.

[102] For the Financial Plan of 1920 see Arana, *op. cit.*, Vol. ii, pp. 123–229.

pointed out twice during 1919 that the Nicaraguan constitution provided that "no citizen who holds the office of President, either as the duly elected incumbent or accidentally, shall be eligible to the office of President or Vice President for the next term." Stabler told the Nicaraguan Minister that the United States was "strongly convinced that the constitution of Nicaragua must be complied with, and that if after a study of the constitution, the Government of the United States was convinced that it was against the constitution for General Chamorro to come up for re-election, this Government would be guided accordingly in its views." On February 12, 1920, after Chamorro had publicly suggested the possibility that he might be a candidate, the State Department took a more definite stand and sent word to Chamorro that it was convinced that the constitutional provisions "absolutely forbid his candidacy" and that "any deviation from this strictly constitutional course would create a most unfortunate impression in the United States." [103]

Whoever the conservative candidate might be, he would almost certainly be elected if the Nicaraguan government controlled the voting and the continuing presence of the legation guard discouraged armed resistance by the liberals. A new group of officers in the Latin American Division of the State Department felt that the United States should not help what was apparently a minority party to stay in power through another election like that of 1916. They proposed that the United States insist on some form of supervision, but Assistant Secretary Adee, who was still a power in the Department despite the obvious effects of increasing age, vetoed the idea as an improper intervention in Nicaragua's internal affairs. The illness of President Wilson and changes in the highest positions in the State Department made it difficult to obtain any adequate consideration of the question of policy involved.[104]

The State Department nevertheless made an effort to see that the election was better than the preceding one had been. General Enoch Crowder, who had recently drafted a new electoral code for Cuba, was asked to examine the Nicaraguan electoral law, and he

---

[103] Except where otherwise noted, the correspondence about the 1920 election is in *Foreign Relations, 1920*, Vol. III, pp. 292ff.

[104] There seems to be no record of this incident in the State Department's files. This account is based on my own recollection of what happened.

reported that it was completely inadequate. Jefferson was consequently instructed on May 29, 1920, to propose to Chamorro that he invite Crowder to come to Nicaragua to study the Nicaraguan law and suggest amendments which would "give assurance to all parties that their voting strength will be actually registered in the elections, thus contributing to the development of democratic institutions in Nicaragua." Chamorro declined to consider the idea, but Jefferson still hoped to be able to obtain some reforms and thought that there would be trouble if the election was not satisfactory. He consequently obtained the State Department's permission to issue a statement on July 1 expressing the American government's interest in a free election and emphasizing that it had no preference as to possible candidates.

The State Department was the more concerned about the situation in Nicaragua because the political situation throughout Central America seemed to be deteriorating. After the American intervention in Nicaragua in 1912, and partly as a result of that intervention, the isthmus had had some years of relative peace. More recently, however, the Tinoco affair in Costa Rica, where a government which the United States openly opposed was able to stay in power for more than two years, and a successful revolution in 1919 in Honduras had seemed to encourage the dissatisfied elements in several Central American countries to test the determination of the United States to support constituted governments. The new regime in Honduras was unfriendly both with the Nicaraguan government and with the government of El Salvador, and several border incidents had suggested that each government was encouraging revolutionary activities against the others. On July 12, 1920, the State Department thought it necessary to warn all three to behave and to say that it would not look with favor on any government "not brought into power by constitutional methods or retained in power by extra-constitutional methods." [105]

The prospect of trouble from an unfair election had increased after Chamorro brought about the nomination of his relative Diego Manuel Chamorro as the conservative candidate early in May. Other leaders in his own party were angered, and the liberals were less than ever disposed to acquiesce in the imposition of a new president

[105] 817.00/2668a.

whom they considered ultra-clerical and reactionary. Realizing that the situation was becoming more threatening, the State Department on July 13 tentatively suggested to Jefferson that a coalition candidate might be chosen, saying that this would avoid many of the dangers in the existing situation. Some observers had urged this solution of the Nicaraguan problem in 1916 when both the Díaz government and the liberals might have accepted it, but there was little chance of its acceptance by a vigorously partisan president like General Chamorro. Jefferson replied that there had been some suggestion of such a compromise but that nothing had come of it.[106] Meanwhile, in the first days of August, the liberals and some of the anti-Chamorro conservatives nominated a wealthy coffee planter named José Esteban González for the presidency.

The State Department still felt that it must make an effort to assure a fair election. It disapproved of Jefferson's idea of secretly sending small parties of marines in civilian dress to observe the electoral procedure,[107] but on August 9 Sumner Welles, chief of the Latin American Division, pointed out that an illegal election might cause a revolution that would force the United States to intervene in Nicaragua, and he urged that Major Jesse I. Miller be sent to Managua as Military Attaché with instructions to attempt to procure fair play.[108] Miller, who had served under General Crowder in the Provost Marshal General's Office, started for Nicaragua a few days later with instructions that authorized him to travel through the country and if necessary to call on General Chamorro, with the American Minister, to make representations about any abuses that he observed. He was told that it appeared that the opposition candidate might have a large majority and that the government might resort to fraud and intimidation, which could cause a revolution. The American government would need to know the facts.[109]

The first test of the electoral machinery came with the registration of voters, which took place just before Miller arrived. There were disturbances at several places, including Managua, and press reports indicated that intimidation and violence prevented thou-

[106] Merle-Smith to Jefferson, July 13, 1920, 817.00/2649; Jefferson to Colby, Sept. 9, 1920, 817.00/2704.
[107] Colby to Jefferson, Aug. 19, 1920, 817.00/2673.
[108] Welles to the Undersecretary, Aug. 9, 1920, 817.00/2675.
[109] For Miller's instructions, see 817.00/2728a.

sands of citizens from registering. Several persons were killed, and twenty-four liberals, among them four prominent leaders, were imprisoned. Jefferson was told to make it clear that the United States government vigorously disapproved and to say that the United States expected that "the Government of Nicaragua will take steps immediately to dispel the impression created by the arrest of these political leaders and will take no further action which will cause this Government to feel that the people of Nicaragua will not be able to vote freely, without constraint or hindrance of any kind, in the coming elections." Jefferson was first to say this to Chamorro, but he was to publish the statement if its communication to the President did not produce the desired result.[110]

When Miller arrived, he made a careful study of the registration books. He concluded that the lists were "enormously padded," presumably for the benefit of the conservatives, and that a great number of adherents of the opposition "coalition party" were not inscribed. Since there was no time for remedial action by the congress, he suggested that the State Department authorize him to urge Chamorro to decree that any citizen could be permitted to vote if his name appeared in any registration catalogue since that of 1906, which had been made up while the liberals were in power. He proposed too that the electoral boards should be appointed, with representatives from both parties, instead of being chosen in a popular election in which the government party would obtain all the seats. He thought that each person who cast a ballot should be marked with indelible ink, to prevent conservatives from voting more than once.

The State Department did not approve Miller's proposal to use the old electoral registers, and it thought that the proposal to mark the voters would "involve a degree of personal indignity." It did agree with his proposal about the electoral boards, but Chamorro asserted that a change in the electoral law by presidential decree would be unconstitutional. When the members of the electoral boards were chosen on September 20, the coalitionists voted in only a few places, so that the overwhelming majority of the boards were controlled by the government party.

Shortly before the election, however, Chamorro announced that

[110] *Foreign Relations, 1920*, Vol. III, pp. 296–298.

the coalition party would be permitted to have an inspector at each polling place with the same rights and immunities as a member of the electoral board and that every citizen would be allowed to cast a ballot whether registered or not, but with the proviso that the votes of those whose names did not appear in the official catalogues would not be counted. Miller considered this arrangement "fairly satisfactory" because it would expedite the voting and would show the actual voting strength of each party as well as the number of each party that was registered. The State Department would then be able to decide whether it wished to take any further action before the final canvas of the vote by the congress in December.

The coalitionists' decision not to take part in the elections for members of the electoral boards aroused fears that they might also abstain in the general election. Jefferson sought to reassure them by issuing a statement on September 18 reiterating the United States' interest in a fair election and its impartiality as between candidates. Chamorro's concessions probably also encouraged them to remain in the race. Neither party seemed much interested when the Guatemalan and Cuban Ministers, acting probably on their own initiative, offered their good offices to settle the electoral problem by dividing all positions equally between the two parties and drawing lots for the presidency. The government party was inclined to resent the suggestion, and the liberals told Jefferson that "if they wanted intervention they would request it of the United States."

The elections were held on October 3 and 4. There was no serious disorder, but the coalitionists complained that many of their adherents were not permitted to vote. Preliminary reports from all departments except the east coast gave the conservatives 69,900 votes and the coalition 40,800, but the numbers were reduced to 59,000 and 28,000 after the elimination of ballots of voters not on the registration lists. Dr. J. A. Urtecho, an independent conservative candidate who had been expected to cut into Chamorro's support, received only about 1,500 votes. Miller cabled the Department that each party was accusing the other of fraud but that the country was quiet because neither thought that the election was decided until the State Department had passed on it.[111]

[111] Miller's telegram of Oct. 8, 1920, 817.00/2722.

Miller's final report made it clear that there had been much fraud and much improper use of the government's power. Citizens had been disfranchized by arrest for minor offenses or intimidated by threats of induction into the army. The soldiers and police had prevented many from voting when they came to the polls. The ballots of 50 percent of the coalitionists who did vote were rejected on the ground that the voters were not registered. The election clearly did not meet the State Department's "requirements." Miller thought nevertheless that the absence of violence made it a "unique achievement in Nicaraguan self-government." [112]

Miller did not think that the abuses that had occurred would warrant the American government's taking the position that González had really won the election. His study of the relative strength of the two parties led him to believe that the liberals did not have the overwhelming popular support which they had always claimed and with which most foreign observers and even many conservatives had credited them.[113] He thought that a fair election would have been close. He reported, however, that the coalitionists were angry and were refraining from violence only because they hoped for relief from the American government. He thought that they would revolt after the inauguration of the new president on January 1, and that the United States would be confronted by a choice between giving its support to a minority government or permitting a civil war.

There was little that the State Department could do about the situation. The abuses in the election could not be corrected, because the Nicaraguan electoral law provided no machinery for their correction. Welles thought that to insist on the holding of a new election would be "an interference in the internal affairs of Nicaragua which the relations between the two governments would not justify," and that any such action would "prove most harmful to our relations with Latin America generally." [114] The United States might perhaps have withdrawn the legation guard and left the liberals free to start a revolution, but this would have been a sad end to ten

[112] For Miller's report, see 817.00/2760.
[113] *Foreign Relations, 1920,* Vol. III, p. 302.
[114] Welles to the Acting Secretary, Dec. 28, 1920, 817.00/2771.

years of effort to promote stable government and economic progress in Nicaragua. The only practical course seemed to be to recognize Diego Manuel Chamorro as president-elect.

Before indicating that it would do so, however, the State Department endeavored to make sure that it would not again be confronted with a similar situation. Miller reported that no fair election would have been possible under the vague and unworkable provisions of the existing law. Jefferson was consequently instructed on December 1 to make clear the American government's dissatisfaction with the conduct of the election and to insist that President Emiliano Chamorro appoint an expert to draft a new law which the Nicaraguan congress would approve before the end of its current session. Chamorro agreed to do so, after being assured that the American government did not intend that the law should apply retroactively to the 1920 election. At the same time the State Department suggested that the incoming President might avert revolutionary disturbances by including some of the coalition leaders in his Cabinet, but this idea seems to have been received with little enthusiasm by either party.

President Wilson does not seem to have been consulted about the decision to recognize Diego Manuel Chamorro as president.[115] Jefferson was simply instructed to attend the inauguration on January 1, without any public announcement of the American government's position. The liberals made no serious effort to revolt. The new government was less effective and less secure in its position than had been the previous administration, but the presence of the American legation guard continued to be regarded as an indication that the United States would not tolerate any serious disorder.

There was some delay in naming the electoral expert. Both the State Department and the Nicaraguan government had thought that General Crowder would undertake the work, but at the end of December the General was ordered to Cuba as President Wilson's special representative in that country. It was not until after the

---

[115] After Chamorro's inauguration, Acting Secretary of State Davis wrote Tumulty that a refusal to recognize Chamorro, merely on the ground of fraud in the election, would be an "unwarranted interference" in Nicaragua's internal affairs. Davis to Tumulty, Jan. 21, 1921, 817.00/2755.

change in administration at Washington that Dr. Harold W. Dodds was selected to draft a new electoral law for Nicaragua.

The State Department hoped that the election of 1924 would install a government satisfactory to a majority of the Nicaraguan people, and in 1923 it announced that it would withdraw the legation guard when the new government took office. The marines left Nicaragua in 1925, but the disastrous civil war that ensued led to a second American intervention which would not be terminated until 1932.

◄ 10 ►

Non-Recognition of Revolutionary Governments

The Case of Costa Rica

🖋 Non-recognition, or the threat of non-recognition, was one of the chief means by which the United States attempted to discourage revolutionary changes of government in the Caribbean after 1909. Before that time, the traditional policy had been to recognize a new government as soon as the new authorities seemed to have established an effective and generally accepted control and to be able and willing to discharge their international obligations. The Taft administration departed from this policy to bring about the overthrow of the Madriz regime in Nicaragua, and it twice delayed recognition of governments in Haiti until its obtained assurances about the treatment of American interests. President Wilson, in dealing with Huerta in Mexico, introduced a new concept in American policy when he made recognition a matter of principle. Under his administration, and under those of his immediate successors, recognition of a new regime, especially in the Caribbean, came to signify that the regime had the moral support of the United States, and non-recognition or the threat of non-recognition was repeatedly used to discourage revolution and to compel political leaders to respect constitutional procedures. The recognition policy became one of the important instruments through which the United States influenced the course of internal politics.

In Central America, after the events of 1909–1910, it was generally believed that a regime that failed to obtain American recognition had little chance for survival. Political leaders were consequently reluctant to align themselves with an unrecognized government, and native and foreign business interests were unwilling to advance credit to it because its acts could more easily be repudiated by its successors than in the case of a government that was recognized. The attitude of the United States was the more important because European and other Central American governments usually followed its example, either as a matter of policy or under pressure from Washington.

THE TINOCO COUP D'ÉTAT

No question of recognition arose in Central America during the first years of the Wilson administration, because there were no successful revolutions. After the intervention in Nicaragua in 1912, few political leaders were disposed to challenge the American government's announced determination to maintain peace in the isthmus, and when disorder threatened, the timely appearance of an American warship was usually enough to discourage a revolt. The first serious disturbance of the constitutional order came, curiously enough, in Costa Rica, which had not had a revolution for nearly half a century, and which seemed to be the one Central American state that had achieved a truly republican government.

In the Costa Rican presidential election of 1914, none of the three candidates received a majority of the vote, and the final decision was thrown into the congress. The constitution required that the choice be made between the two candidates who had received the highest popular vote, but instead of following the constitutional procedure some of the party leaders made a deal by which Alfredo González Flores, who had not been on the ballot at all, was installed in the presidency as First *Designado*. González, inexperienced politically and with little personal following, soon found himself in a difficult position. Many questioned the legality of his election, and the dislocation of trade during the first months of the European war confronted him with serious financial problems. When he attempted to solve these by proposing a property tax and a progressive income tax, the number of his enemies greatly increased.

There was consequently very little opposition when Federico Tinoco, the Minister of War, suddenly seized control of the government on January 27, 1917. González and ten or fifteen other frightened officials took refuge in the American Legation, crowding the small building to a point where the Minister had to move his office to the pantry. The *coup* was an unmitigated act of treachery, for the President had complete confidence in Tinoco's loyalty up to the very minute of his betrayal, but the new government seemed to meet with rather general popular acceptance.

The revolt took the State Department by surprise. The American Minister, Edward J. Hale, was a 77-year-old political appointee, who had reported practically nothing about political conditions in Costa Rica during the past two years. He had apparently ignored warnings of the impending revolt, which had been expected by many well-informed people,[1] and he gave the State Department little information about it after it occurred. When questioned about his violation of the standing instructions about political asylum, he explained that it was "the government" that had sought refuge.[2] On January 29 he expressed the opinion that an administration satisfactory to all parties could be established and asked that no warships be sent. Reports that ships were coming had caused much excitement, and in the belief that American lives might be endangered Hale issued a statement on his own authority saying that there would be no intervention. The Minister clearly had little understanding of the Wilson administration's attitude toward Central American revolutions, for on February 5 he sent two cables urging recognition of the provisional government.[3]

At Washington there was no disposition to countenance so flagrant a violation of the standards of conduct that the American government had been endeavoring to impose in Central America. In a memorandum for the President, Stabler pointed out that González had been friendly to some of the Germans in Costa Rica, but recommended against any support of Tinoco. He feared that what had happened would have a bad effect in other countries, and expressed a suspicion that the United Fruit Company had encouraged the *coup d'état*. Wilson accepted the State Department's recommendation that he refuse to recognize Tinoco and that the United Fruit Company be warned not to interfere in Costa Rican affairs. Under his instructions, the language of the statement which Stabler proposed to issue was made more emphatic.[4]

The statement, which was sent to all of the American Legations in Central America on February 9, declared that illegal acts like Tinoco's revolt "tend to disturb the peace of Central America and

[1] Johnson to Lansing, May 2, 1917, 818.00/147.
[2] *Foreign Relations, 1917*, p. 305. Except where otherwise indicated, the correspondence referred to in this section is found in *Foreign Relations, 1917*, 301ff; *1918*, 229ff.; and *1919*, Vol. i, pp. 803ff.
[3] 818.00/172, 173.
[4] Lansing to Wilson, Feb. 7, 1917, 818.00/105½; Wilson to Lansing, Feb. 7, 818.00/106½.

to disrupt the unity of the American continent." The United States would not give recognition or support to any government that might be established in Costa Rica unless it was clearly shown that it was elected by legal and constitutional means. Hale was told to hand the statement personally to Tinoco and to say that no government set up by him would be recognized. When the usurper asked whether this would be true even if he were elected president by a free vote, Wilson authorized Lansing to reply that it would.

Another public statement, on February 22, was evidently issued in compliance with the President's instruction that a warning be given to the United Fruit Company. It read: "In order that citizens of the United States may have definite information as to the position of this government in regard to any financial aid which they may give to, or any business transactions which they may have with those persons who overthrew the Constitutional Government of Costa Rica by an act of armed rebellion, the Government of the United States desires to advise them that it will not consider any claims which may in the future arise from such dealings, worthy of its diplomatic support."

The suspicion that the Fruit Company was partly responsible for Tinoco's revolt was based on circumstantial evidence. The company had frequently been accused of interfering in internal politics in the Central American states, and it had naturally been opposed to González' tax program. Minor C. Keith, who was vice president of the company, had large interests of his own in Costa Rica and was known to have close personal relations with the Tinoco family. Against this background, an incident that occurred at the time of the revolt convinced the State Department and the President of the company's guilt. Hale's first report of the *coup* was delayed for two days because the company's San José office refused to transmit it over its own lines when the Minister found that he could not use the ordinary telegraph service, and in the meantime the company was sending the State Department copies of cables that Keith had received from Tinoco and was urging that there was no cause for intervention. The President later wrote that he was "painfully impressed" by the fact that the State Department had received the first news of the revolt from a representative of the Fruit Company and that this was coupled with an urgent request to recognize

Tinoco.[5] The company explained that a subordinate official had refused to send Hale's message because the action would have violated specific orders of the government and would have endangered the company's concession, and it pointed out that it had furnished a special train to carry the Legation's courier to Port Limon.[6]

Subsequent investigations failed to reveal any definite evidence that either the company or Keith personally had any part in instigating the revolt, but President Wilson remained convinced that the Fruit Company was back of the Tinoco regime. It is in fact clear that Minor Keith did help Tinoco while he was head of the government, with advice and money, and that he obtained valuable concessions in return. Both the State Department and the President, at different times, asked the Department of Justice to consider prosecuting Keith, but no action seems to have been taken, probably because it was difficult to find legal grounds for prosecution.[7]

Neither Wilson nor the State Department seem to have realized that there was another American company that could reasonably be suspected of an interest in Tinoco's revolt. González later claimed that one of the reasons for his fall was his opposition to an oil concession which an American group wished to obtain. The State Department had known of the competition for oil rights in Costa Rica, but it apparently did not realize that this competition might have a connection with González' overthrow.

The possibility that there might be oil in Costa Rica had aroused the interest of several promoters. In 1913 the Pearson interests of London, who controlled much of the oil production in Mexico, attempted to get a concession in Costa Rica. When their proposals were rejected by the congress, they attempted to buy some oil rights held by a local Costa Rican group but were outbid by a Dr. Greulich of New York. In 1915 Dr. Greulich sought to strengthen his position

[5] Letter to Senator Joseph E. Ransdell, March 5, 1918, Wilson Papers, Library of Congress.

[6] Penfield to Lansing, May 15, 1917, 818.00/149.

[7] See Wilson's letters to the State Department, March 8, March 25, April 5, and April 10, 1918 (818.00/1015, 1017, 1018), and J. F. Dulles' personal letter to Charles Warren, Aug. 24, 1917, 818.00/234a. There are two memoranda in which the solicitor of the State Department discussed the matter: March 13, 1918 (818.00/-1010) and April 16, 1918 (818.00/1011).

by negotiating a concession for exclusive rights to explore for oil in three Costa Rican provinces.

The State Department, when it learned of the Pearson project, sent Minister Hale a copy of Wilson's Mobile speech, which had been directed largely against the operations of the Pearson group in Mexico, and told him that the question of oil concessions in Costa Rica was of "unusual interest because of its relation to naval bases and the proximity of Costa Rica to the Panama Canal." [8] When Hale suggested that he be authorized to support Greulich's concession, however, the Department was definitely unenthusiastic. Frank Polk, the counselor, pointed out that President Wilson had denounced monopolistic concessions of this sort.[9] There were doubts about Greulich's American citizenship and his connections, and there was some unfriendly feeling toward Lincoln Valentine, who was one of Greulich's associates. Valentine, as one official put it, had caused the State Department "considerable inconvenience" by his claims in Honduras and his alleged support of revolutionary activities there; also he had recently severely criticized the American government's Nicaraguan policy in an article in the *Century* magazine.[10] Furthermore, A. B. Butler of Washington, D.C., represented by Minor Keith's brother-in-law, Robert Crespi, informed the State Department that he also was interested in Costa Rican oil and protested against the monopolistic nature of the Greulich concession.[11] The Department consequently requested further information from Hale and declined to help Greulich's representatives when they asked it to urge that a special session of the Costa Rican congress be called to approve the concession.[12]

Butler and Crespi, as it later appeared, were working for Pearson, and their efforts to defeat the Greulich concession were ably seconded by the British Minister in Costa Rica, who seems to have persuaded President González to withdraw his support of the project.[13] At any rate the President publicly opposed the concession, which he himself had signed, and the government also interfered

[8] Moore to Hale, Dec. 2, 1913, *Foreign Relations, 1919*, Vol. i, p. 866.
[9] Long's memorandum of Dec. 16, 1915, 818.6363/8.
[10] Wright's memorandum of Dec. 2, 1915, 818.6363/9.
[11] Wright to Adee, Dec. 6, 1915, *ibid.*
[12] Wright's memorandum of Dec. 29, 1915, 818.6363/12.
[13] Hale to Lansing, Jan. 7, 1916, *Foreign Relations, 1919*, Vol. i, p. 868.

with Greulich's enjoyment of the oil rights which he already held. The State Department declined to interfere because there was no evidence that Greulich had been denied justice in the courts.[14]

The State Department suspected that Greulich was working for German interests. Its further investigation showed that he had an unsavory record, and in March 1916 Lansing instructed Hale to refrain from facilitating his project in any way. The Secretary pointed out that the State Department usually supported American interests only when they encountered difficulties, and referred to the "unusually comprehensive nature" of the concession. In the same instruction he discussed Butler's and Crespi's interest in Costa Rican oil. He evidently had learned something by this time of Butler's English connections, but he told Hale that "while the exclusive participation of British interests in Costa Rican development would be viewed with apprehension by the Department, there appears no reason to believe that Mr. Butler contemplates such participation, or that British interests will be predominant in such contracts as he may submit or retain." [15]

The Costa Rican congress approved Greulich's concession in November 1916, but González returned it with his veto. The congress then ordered its publication, on the ground that the veto message had not been countersigned by one of the Cabinet. Though the legality of the concession was thus doubtful, a company organized by the Sinclair Oil interests in New York bought it from Valentine and his associates in December 1916, and after the revolution Tinoco recognized the concession as valid. Hale gave the State Department little information about these proceedings, but in November 1918 González published in the New York *Herald* several letters said to have been written by Valentine which indicated that bribery had been used to obtain favorable action by the congress and that the Tinoco family were financially interested in the concession.[16]

Lansing and Wilson were convinced that they had been right in refusing to recognize Tinoco when González came to Washington in February 1917 and gave them his version of the background

[14] Solicitor's memorandum of June 21, 1916, 818.6363/21.

[15] Instruction of March 25, 1916, 818.6363/14. A portion of this instruction was printed in *Foreign Relations, 1919*, Vol. I, p. 869.

[16] Much of the correspondence about the oil concessions was printed in *Foreign Relations* for 1919.

of the revolt. The ex-President made it clear that he did not ask that the United States intervene by force. He thought that non-recognition and the bad economic situation that would inevitably result would bring about the usurper's fall within two or three months and that it would then be possible to agree on a compromise government acceptable to all parties. Lansing assured him that the policy of the United States would not be changed.

In Costa Rica, however, the new regime seemed to be accepted by a majority of the people. The seven living ex-Presidents, who traditionally were called on for advice in times of national crisis, agreed to participate in drafting a new constitution; and when Hale, under Lansing's instructions, undertook to explain the American government's position to them most of the group joined in a statement that they supported "the present order of affairs which is upheld by the will of the people. . . ." There was no opposition when Tinoco was elected president on April 1, though the cynical way in which the voting was conducted aroused some hostile comment.

Minister Hale left San José in April, leaving Stewart Johnson, an intelligent but inexperienced junior secretary, in charge of the Legation. In May Lansing's nephew, John Foster Dulles, who was traveling ostensibly on private legal business but in reality on a mission to Panama for the State Department, visited Costa Rica and brought back a more complete report on conditions there than the State Department had yet had. Tinoco, he said, was in undisputed control of the country. Though he was increasingly unpopular, it was not likely that the "slow pressure" of non-recognition would force him out for some months. Meanwhile, non-recognition would bring on an economic collapse and perhaps serious disorder, with little hope for the establishment of a better government. Tinoco was friendly to the Allies, and had offered the United States the use of Costa Rican ports and waters for military purposes immediately after the American declaration of war on Germany. Any government that replaced him would probably be pro-German. Dulles thought that Tinoco should be recognized, if he would agree to the election of a constituent assembly or to the institution of a senate or an advisory council that would give respectability to his government.[17]

[17] Dulles to Lansing, May 1, 1917, 818.00/142.

Lansing was convinced that Tinoco's willingness to help the Allies and the pro-German attitude of his opponents made recognition advisable. There were in fact well-founded reports that the Germans were financing a projected revolutionary movement by the ex-President's friends. The British and French governments and the American military men in the Canal Zone thought that recognition would be useful from a military point of view. Wilson, however, would not be moved by an "argument of present expediency." "I am clear," he wrote, "that we can in no circumstances extend recognition to his government or to any other in Latin America that may have a similar beginning and origin." Lansing must tell the Costa Ricans that they had to set up a real constitutional government, and must tell the revolutionists that the United States would oppose any government that they might establish.[18]

In view of the President's attitude, Johnson was told that Tinoco would not be recognized and was asked to recommend a course of action that might lead to the prompt and peaceful selection of a new president. In reply the Chargé suggested that the United States give González moral and financial support for a counterrevolution. He thought that many people would join the ex-President if he made a "manly effort" and landed with a few men at a Costa Rican port. Johnson pointed out that the government was becoming more unpopular because of its corrupt and oppressive conduct. On the other hand, rather inconsistently perhaps, he expressed the opinion that the opposition could accomplish little so long as the government had money to pay the police and the greatly expanded army.[19]

Johnson's proposal was, of course, inconsistent with President Wilson's policy, which excluded any approval of an attempt to oust Tinoco by force. Stabler in fact told González' representative on June 12 that the United States would openly and effectively oppose a revolution in the interest of any individual.[20] Meanwhile, on June 9, Lansing instructed Johnson to reiterate to Tinoco the President's determination not to recognize him and to urge that he withdraw so that a new government could be set up in an orderly manner.

[18] Lansing to Wilson, May 23, 1917, 818.00/200. Wilson to Lansing, May 28, filed with 818.00/196.
[19] Telegram to Johnson, May 29, 1917, 818.00/162a; Johnson's reply, June 2, 818.00/164.
[20] Stabler's memorandum of June 12, 1917, 818.00/184.

Tinoco courteously refused to give up the presidency and soon afterward formally withdrew his request for American recognition, saying that a survey of the situation had shown that Costa Rica could get along without economic help from the United States.[21]

The use of non-recognition as a means of discouraging violent changes of government always entailed the risk that the United States would find itself in an embarrassing situation if an unrecognized government proved able to maintain itself in power. Non-recognition encouraged the opposition and forced the unrecognized administration to resort to oppressive methods to maintain its authority, but the United States' opposition to revolutions made it more difficult for the opposition to resort to the one method of effecting a change which was likely to be effective. Meanwhile internal dissension and uncertainty about the future were apt to bring on economic difficulties that caused hardship to the people as well as to the government, and which created pressures from American business interests for a change in policy. This was the situation that developed in Costa Rica, and there was the additional fact, as Lansing pointed out, that the policy of non-recognition ran "directly contrary to our interests in prosecuting the war." [22] Tinoco was eager to cooperate with the Allies, while many of the opposition leaders were known to be pro-German.

By the end of 1917, both the economic and the political situations in Costa Rica were rapidly deteriorating. Tinoco's reckless financial policies and his evident determination to establish the sort of military dictatorship which the Costa Ricans had believed no longer possible in their country, had dismayed many of the leaders who were at first inclined to support him. The general public had acquiesced, though without any great enthusiasm, in his election as constitutional president in April, but he had little popular support a few months later. The Costa Ricans, however, were a peaceful people with a strong tradition against revolution, and it seemed unlikely that any movement within the country could defeat the government's well-armed military forces.

The State Department tried in various ways to make the dictator's position more difficult. In September 1917, it warned the other Cen-

[21] R. Fernández Guardia to Lansing, June 28, 1917, 818.00/175.
[22] Lansing Papers, Vol. ii, p. 521.

tral American governments that it would not regard their recognition of Tinoco as evidence of a friendly feeling to the United States. All except Nicaragua, however, did recognize him, and there was some evidence that Estrada Cabrera was giving him active support. American bankers were discouraged from lending money to the Costa Rican government, but an effort to embarrass Tinoco by urging the local representative of the foreign bondholders to insist on a more rigorous observance of the 1910 loan contracts was unsuccessful.[23]

Attempts to organize a revolution, on the other hand, met with no encouragement from the United States. In August 1917, John Foster Dulles proposed that González and his friends be permitted to load a vessel with arms and go to Costa Rica, pointing out that the United States still recognized González as President;[24] but this was not approved. In December, Alfredo Volio appeared in Panama with several armed companions and told the American Minister that he planned to invade Costa Rica from Nicaragua and hoped to have support from the Nicaraguan government. Volio admitted that he expected the Germans in Costa Rica to help him, but he promised a pro-American, pro-Ally administration. Johnson urged that the Panamanian authorities be "influenced" to permit him to proceed;[25] but Lansing instructed Minister Price to inform Volio that "the Government of the United States will not countenance armed activities such as he contemplates, inasmuch as this Government feels that only by moral force can a constitutional and duly legalized government be set up in Costa Rica." He asked that the government of Panama and the authorities in the Canal Zone take steps to prevent any armed expedition against Costa Rica.[26] The Secretary must have been surprised when the President himself tentatively suggested that the United States might support Volio. Wilson had evidently forgotten the policy which he had so explicitly laid down, but he hastily withdrew his suggestion when Lansing told him what the State Department had done.[27]

[23] 818.00/105, 143.
[24] Memorandum to Lansing, Aug. 27, 1917, 818.00/315.
[25] Telegram of Dec. 14, 1917, 818.00/270.
[26] Lansing to Price, Dec. 29, 1917, *Foreign Relations, 1917*, p. 349.
[27] Wilson to Lansing, Dec. 29, 1917, 818.00/287½; Lansing to Wilson, Dec. 31, 818.00/280; Wilson to Lansing, Jan. 1, 1918, 818.00/28½.

Lansing's action frustrated Volio's plans, and a small uprising in Costa Rica in February 1918 was easily suppressed. The alleged murder of the leader and some other participants in the revolt horrified Costa Rican public opinion and made Tinoco's situation more critical. Nevertheless another uprising in April also failed, partly because the Panamanian government again refused to permit revolutionists to pass through its territory.

Despite Tinoco's defiant attitude, it was as clear to him as it was to his opponents that his regime could never attain any real stability until he was recognized by the United States. In April 1918, Johnson reported that the American authorities' action in restraining Volio at Panama had revived the usurper's hope for recognition. He suggested that a categorical statement reiterating the American government's position might lead Tinoco to resign, and Lansing cabled the text of a statement for the Chargé to make. When Johnson talked with Tinoco and his brother, who was a powerful figure in the administration, he found both men thoroughly discouraged and scared, and he attempted to force their withdrawal by threatening to make the statement public if they remained in office. This effort failed when it was learned that the statement had already been published elsewhere, and during the next few weeks the Tinocos apparently regained some of their confidence. In May they forced through congress a declaration of war on Germany, but this made no change in the attitude of the United States.

When Volio was released from detention in Panama, he went to Nicaragua, where he had reason to hope that he would get help from Emiliano Chamorro. Tinoco had angered the Nicaraguan President by giving Julián Irías and other Nicaraguan liberals positions in his administration, and since the first months of 1918 it had been assumed that any revolt in Costa Rica would have the Nicaraguan government's support. In May of that year, when Chamorro told Minister Jefferson of the increasing tension between the two countries and asked the American government's advice, the State Department urged him to exercise "all possible patience and forbearance." In October, the Minister at Tegucigalpa reported that Chamorro was urging that Nicaragua and Honduras jointly support a revolution against Tinoco. Lansing told both governments that the United States ". . . cannot approve of any armed activities such as would appear to be contemplated inasmuch as it considers that a constitutional and duly legalized government can only be set up in Costa Rica by such moral forces as can be exerted by the people of that country." The plan for joint intervention was dropped, but Chamorro continued to harbor and probably continued to help the Costa Rican refugees who were making plans for an invasion from Nicaragua.

While these events were occurring, the Pearson oil interests were again endeavoring to obtain a foothold in Costa Rica. In June 1918, Tinoco granted John M. Amory and Son of New York a concession for exploration in the provinces not covered by the Sinclair contract. The company purported to be American, but Valentine showed Johnson a purloined letter which indicated that it was backed by British capital. When Johnson reported this, the State Department told him that it considered it "most important that only approved American interests should possess oil concessions in the neighborhood of Panama Canal," and that he should use his best efforts to block the concession,[28] but in the meantime Tinoco obtained congress' approval of the Amory concession. Johnson thought that he could have prevented final action if he had received the instruction earlier.

Tinoco had rushed the matter through because he knew of the letter that Valentine had. He was indignant with Valentine, and Johnson thought that he might move to cancel the Sinclair concession. When the Chargé asked for instructions, the State Department told him that it regarded "the concession held by the Sinclair Oil interests as held by Americans in good repute." Sinclair's office in New York was even permitted to send Valentine a cable through the Legation, because, as Stabler wrote, "it looks as if . . . the one way to retain American control of the oil is through Sinclair." [29] Tinoco started to prosecute Valentine for violating the Costa Rican mails, and was apparently supported in this action by most of the American colony in San José, but Valentine left Costa Rica while the case was pending.

Wilson's policy toward Tinoco aroused much controversy in the United States. Agents of both Costa Rican factions not only bom-

[28] For this correspondence, see *Foreign Relations, 1919*, Vol. I, pp. 872–875.
[29] Penciled note attached to Department's telegram of July 20, 1918, 818.6363 Am 6/9.

barded the State Department with letters and memoranda but attempted to influence public opinion by sensational revelations in the press. At Washington, after the first few months, there was little sympathy for either group. Wilson wrote Lansing in April 1918 that González' representative must not be allowed to draw the United States into any of the "miserable intrigue down there." The President reiterated that his own course toward Tinoco was unchangeably fixed and that the intrigues of Tinoco's predecessor were "none of our business." [30] At the same time he again urged action against Minor Keith and his associates for "shamelessly playing against their own government" and told Lansing that "we cannot go too far in bagging such disloyal men." [31] To William J. Bryan, who had secretly been employed to plead Tinoco's case, the President wrote:

"I feel obliged to retain immovably my position that I will not and cannot recognize a government which originated in individual unconstitutional action. This is a test case, and I am sure that my yielding in it would break down the whole morale of our relations, particularly with Central America.

"Behind it all . . . there are contending business interests in the United States which we ought to be very careful to disappoint in what is nothing less than an attempt on their part to use the Government of Costa Rica for their own benefit." [32]

Several of the American businessmen in Costa Rica continued to urge the recognition of Tinoco as the only practical course of action, and they were able to obtain some support in the United States Congress. From time to time various Republican senators introduced resolutions calling for an investigation or questioning the propriety of the President's policy. Senator George H. Moses of New Hampshire was especially active on Tinoco's behalf, and his efforts undoubtedly did much to encourage Tinoco to attempt to remain in power, though conditions in Costa Rica were going from bad to worse.

The State Department maintained informal contact with Tinoco through Johnson until November 1918, when it closed the Legation because a demonstration of friendship to the United States

[30] Wilson to Lansing, April 3, 1918, 818.00/398½.
[31] Wilson to Lansing, May 20, 1918, 818.00/493.
[32] Wilson to Bryan, July 13, 1918, Wilson Papers, Library of Congress.

after the Armistice was brutally broken up by the police. After Johnson's withdrawal, the American representative at San José was Consul Benjamin Chase, an erratic and impetuous officer who sent alarming and often exaggerated reports about Tinoco's conduct and his alleged threats against the consulate and against American citizens in general. His animosity to Tinoco, which seems to have been fully reciprocated, made hopeless any attempt to carry on further negotiations with the *de facto* government.

The State Department still refused to countenance the activities of the revolutionists who were operating from Nicaragua. In April 1919, when Tinoco's agent complained that Chamorro was helping the exiles there, the Department expressed a hope that the Nicaraguan President would be "governed in his actions by the principles of international comity." A few days later it warned Jefferson that it did not wish to be placed in a position where it could be criticized for a failure to urge the maintenance of a strict neutrality. These representations were not particularly forceful, and their tone suggests that some of the State Department's officials hoped in their hearts that actions of which they could not officially approve might put an end to an increasingly intolerable situation; but, on May 12, Acting Secretary of State Frank Polk directed Jefferson "to urge upon President Chamorro in the strongest manner possible, that he take all means in his power to prevent the departure from Nicaragua of armed expeditions into Costa Rica." Polk pointed out that an outbreak of warfare in Central America would be especially regrettable at a time when a conference was about to convene in Paris to establish a permanent peace. Chamorro emphatically denied that he was giving the revolutionists any assistance. He nevertheless permitted them to recross the frontier and prepare for a new invasion when they were defeated by Tinoco's army on Costa Rican soil a few days later.[33]

At San José opposition to Tinoco continued to increase, and the government resorted to more and more oppressive policies to prevent an outbreak. Chase cabled on May 12, 1919, that threats were being made against Americans and asked that warships be sent to both coasts of Costa Rica "and if possible soldiers for San José." The State Department replied that there were ships at Bluefields

[33] For these events, see *Foreign Relations, 1919*, Vol. i.

and Amapala, but that it did not wish to send them to Costa Rican waters because this might be misunderstood in Costa Rica. In a personal cable to Chase, Polk explained that the presence of warships would be construed as an effort to undermine the influence of Tinoco and said that sending marines to San José was out of the question unless some actual danger threatened the consul or the American colony. The State Department obviously did not take Chase's reports very seriously, but it warned Tinoco's agents in Washington that nothing must happen to the consul or to other American citizens.[34] The explosion of a bomb in front of the American Legation on May 19 suggested that there was some basis for Chase's fears.

On June 12 Chase reported that the police had broken up a demonstration in front of the consulate and had fired into the building when some of the crowd took refuge there. The next day he cabled: "Have called gunboat Castine, everybody in danger. Marines needed here at once. City in turmoil. Revolution growing." Polk replied that the State Department could not send ships or marines in the absence of specific acts against Americans. The *Castine* went to Port Limón, in response to Chase's call, but the Captain refrained from landing marines when he learned that the situation was not so bad as Chase had pictured it. Meanwhile the State Department had ordered Consul E. M. Lawton to San José to "assist" Chase, and after Lawton's arrival on June 21 it was better informed about the situation.

Though Tinoco's forces inflicted several defeats on the revolutionists on the Nicaraguan frontier, and he still seemed to be in complete control at San José, it was becoming increasingly evident that his government could not last. The Chilean Ambassador at Washington told the State Department on June 25 that Tinoco would withdraw if Chase were put in jail and the *Castine* were withdrawn from Port Limón, and if the United States would recognize Mariano Quirós as provisional president. Henry Fletcher, who was handling many important Latin American questions in the State Department, thought that the United States might make a counterproposal by which Chase would be brought to the United States on a gun boat and the new provisional president would agree to hold immediate

[34] Polk's memorandum of May 28, 1919, 818.00/674.

441

elections under the constitution that had been in force before Tinoco's *coup*. Polk cabled this suggestion to Paris for Wilson's consideration but apparently received no reply.[35] In July an effort by El Salvador to persuade the other Central American countries to intervene diplomatically to preserve peace in Costa Rica came to nothing, although the United States expressed its mild approval of the project.

The realization that the other Central American States were now against him, combined with the increasingly bad situation in Costa Rica and the constant threat from the Nicaraguan frontier, seem to have convinced Tinoco that his position was untenable. On August 1, 1919, he asked the congress' permission to leave the country because of illness, saying nothing about a resignation. Some days later his brother Joaquín resigned as *Designado*, and Juan B. Quirós was elected in his place. Almost immediately afterward, Joaquín Tinoco was murdered on the street in San José. This terrified his brother, who precipitately turned over the presidency to Quirós and fled from Costa Rica on August 12. There was no serious disorder.

THE RESTORATION OF CONSTITUTIONAL GOVERNMENT

Quirós expected to remain in office until 1923, when Tinoco's term would have expired, and when the congress accepted Tinoco's resignation on August 20 it stipulated that he should do so. The State Department, however, considered the new regime merely "a creature of Tinoco." Chase was instructed to tell Quirós of the attitude that the United States had assumed in February 1917, and to say that "any person elected to the position of president of Costa Rica in free, open elections held under the constitution of Costa Rica, violated by Federico Tinoco, would appear to [have] good claim to recognition." Quirós, who said that he had not known of the 1917 declaration, promised to consult with an assembly of leading citizens about holding elections as soon as the country was tranquil, but this did not meet the State Department's views. It seemed probable, too, that it would not satisfy the revolutionists in Nicaragua, for Alfredo González wrote the Secretary of State on August 13 that their leaders had instructed him to demand that the govern-

[35] Fletcher's memorandum of June 25, 1919, 818.00/715.

ment be turned over to Francisco Aguilar Barquero, whom he regarded as his constitutional successor.

González, when his presidential term expired on May 1, 1918, had issued a proclamation in New York extending his term until a new government should be installed. He stipulated, however, that Aguilar Barquero, who had been Third *Designado,* should act in his place after the constitutional order was reestablished, in order to arrange for the lawful election of another president. Though this procedure was of doubtful legality, there were precedents for it in the history of other Latin American countries. The State Department, which had continued to recognize González' appointees in the Washington Legation as the official representatives of Costa Rica, could feel that Aguilar Barquero came closer to representing the constitutional order than either Quirós or Julio Acosta, the revolutionary leader, who cabled from a village on the Nicaraguan border to ask recognition.

Chase was consequently instructed on August 30 to make public the decision of the United States not to recognize Quirós and to say that "the governmental power should be deposited in the hands of Francisco Barquero," who should hold presidential elections at the earliest possible date. "Were this done," Lansing wrote, "it would appear that the necessary legal formalities had been complied with to constitute a legitimate government worthy of recognition by the Government of the United States." Quirós, after consulting many prominent citizens, decided to withdraw, and he issued an executive decree turning the government over to Aguilar Barquero. Julio Acosta telegraphed his adherence to the new regime. Through the good offices of the State Department and President Chamorro, the revolutionists were persuaded to return to Costa Rica unarmed and were given an enthusiastic welcome.

The new government naturally hoped for prompt acceptance by the United States, and in November the State Department recommended that the President accord recognition. Wilson had approved Lansing's action in insisting on Quirós' withdrawal,[36] but in September he had fallen ill and it was almost impossible to consult him

[36] See Lansing's notation on his letter to the President of Aug. 27, 1919, filed with 818.00/903a.

about matters of policy. He apparently did not grasp the fact that the situation in Costa Rica had changed, and no one who understood the situation had access to his bedside. He refused to approve Lansing's recommendation, and another approach, through Tumulty on November 26, brought no result. The State Department was consequently compelled to tell Chase on November 29 that recognition would be delayed pending the President's convalescence.[37] On two other occasions in the months that followed the State Department urged recognition, but the President, who was quoted as saying that he would never recognize the government of Costa Rica, refused to act.[38]

Julio Acosta was elected president of Costa Rica by a great majority on December 3, 1919. With his inauguration on May 8, 1920, the constitutional order seemed to have been fully reinstated, and the failure to accord recognition was increasingly embarrassing to both governments. In June 1920, Wilson was apparently more ready to consider the matter, and Norman Davis, who had just become Undersecretary of State, sent him several letters and memoranda answering questions that he evidently raised. The United Fruit Company, Davis said, had not been "instrumental" in the election of Acosta, who was not "favored" by the moneyed classes but was favored by the common people. Acosta was not believed to be anti-American. Davis consequently diffidently recommended recognition, and Secretary Colby repeated the recommendation on July 31 when he learned that the British government was about to resume normal relations with Costa Rica.[39]

Many Costa Ricans had resented the American refusal to recognize Tinoco as an unjustified interference in the country's internal affairs. This feeling, which had probably died down as Tinoco's conduct became more intolerable, was revived when the United States required them to accept a new regime of very doubtful legality. The peremptory manner in which the demand was presented was particularly offensive, and it was exceedingly unfortunate, after

[37] 818.00/940a.
[38] Lansing to Wilson, Dec. 13, 1919, 81800/955a; Polk to Wilson, March 6, 1920, 818.00/963a. The statement about what the President is reported to have said is based on my own recollection of conversations in the State Department.
[39] Davis to Wilson, June 25, July 9, and July 13, 1920. 818.00/986, 1035a. Colby to Wilson, July 31, 1920, 818.00/1004a.

what had happened, that recognition of the new government should have been so long delayed.

THE PETROLEUM CONCESSIONS

President Wilson's unwillingness to accord recognition to Acosta was especially distressing to the State Department because Costa Rica was taking on a minor role in the competition for oil rights that troubled British-American relations in the years just after the World War. Both Sinclair and the British Controlled Oil Fields, which had the Amory grant, had done at least some preliminary work under their concessions, but it was clear that both companies would face attack after the fall of Tinoco. González' friends, who were now in power, claimed that the ex-President's opposition to the Sinclair concession had been one cause of his overthrow, and they opposed the British concession because it had been granted by Tinoco.

The State Department, which had sought to prevent the approval of the Amory concession, would have been glad to see it annulled, but the Solicitor warned his colleagues that it would not be proper for the United States to make any effort to persuade the Costa Rican government to annul it.[40] It was still held nominally by an American company, though there was more than a suspicion of British ownership. Consul Chase was rebuked when he told the Costa Ricans that the United States would be pleased if all contracts or concessions granted by Tinoco to American citizens were canceled.[41] In July 1920, however, when Congressman George S. Graham asked that the American government oppose a measure passed by the Costa Rican congress annulling the Amory concession and other acts of the Tinoco government, the State Department declined to act and asked for proof that the concession was owned and controlled by American citizens.[42]

While the annulment law was pending in the congress, the British government protested, and for the first time officially revealed the British interest in the Amory concession. When this occurred, Chase

[40] Solicitor's Office memoranda of Oct. 3 and Nov. 11, 1919, 818.6363 Am 6/35, 37.
[41] Instruction to Chase, March 1, 1920, 818.00/1959.
[42] Graham to Colby, July 2, 1920, Davis to Graham, July 6, and Colby to Graham July 20, 818.6363 Am 6/41.

was warned to exercise extreme discretion in discussing the concession and to make no further suggestions about it for the present.[43] When the congress passed the law, which not only affected the Amory concession but invalidated some $200,000 worth of irregularly issued paper money that the Royal Bank of Canada had accepted from Tinoco in payment for drafts on New York just before the dictator's flight, the British government again protested and persuaded Acosta not to sign it. The law was nevertheless passed over the President's veto on August 10.

The British Minister, who came to Costa Rica on a warship in December 1920, defended both the Amory concession and the Royal Bank's claim with more vehemence than tact. Acosta was especially alarmed by the threat of a commercial boycott, which would have cut off the principal market for Costa Rica's coffee. He consequently agreed to a settlement by arbitration, in February 1921, but the congress refused to approve his action.

The State Department rather cautiously encouraged Costa Rica's resistance. It pointed out to the Costa Rican Minister at Washington that the Amory concession was clouded by bad faith because the nationality of the interests concerned had been misrepresented. The Chargé d'Affaires at San José was told to maintain the discreet attitude that had been enjoined on Chase, but he was permitted to say that the Amory concern was controlled by British interests and to mention the stand that the American government had taken with regard to business transactions with Tinoco. He was told confidentially that the State Department hoped that the concession would not be confirmed.[44] The controversy was still going on when the new administration took office at Washington, but it was settled in January 1922 by an agreement for arbitration. The arbitrator, Chief Justice Taft, decided against the British both in the case of the Amory concession and in the case of the Royal Bank.[45]

While the American government was expressing its guarded approval of Costa Rica's annulment of the British oil concession, it was at the same time opposing similar action against the Sinclair

[43] Telegram to Chase, July 21, 1920, 818.6363 Am 6/42.
[44] Colby to Thurston, Feb. 28, 1921, 818.6363 Am 6/62.
[45] For the decision, see *American Journal of International Law*, Vol. xviii (1924), p. 147.

concession. It will be remembered that the Sinclair contract had been signed by President González, but then vetoed by him, and that González had claimed that its promoters had encouraged the Tinoco *coup d'état* in order to obtain governmental recognition of its validity. In view of this history, and in view of President Wilson's warnings against business dealings with Tinoco, it seems somewhat strange that the State Department should have supported the concession. The control of foreign oil deposits, however, was considered an extremely important objective of policy in the years just after the first world war.

The validity of the Sinclair concession was attacked in the Costa Rican congress immediately after the installation of the constitutional government. The State Department, contrary to its usual practice in such cases, took the initiative in asking the Sinclair Company whether it wished diplomatic support,[46] and, receiving an affirmative reply, it asked Chase to make a full report. It told the consul that the company was a "responsible concern of standing," which had invested large sums under the concession, and that any action looking to cancelation would be "a source of concern and a subject of inquiry." Since there were no diplomatic relations between the two governments, Chase could not make formal representations, but he seems to have persuaded the Costa Rican government that immediate action against the company would be unwise.

The Solicitor of the State Department expressed the opinion that the concession was valid because González' veto had not been in proper form,[47] and President Acosta seems to have reached the same conclusion after consulting seven prominent lawyers in San José. Acosta consequently took no action when the congress asked him in June 1920 and again in August to seek to have the Costa Rican courts annul the concession. In August, however, the situation was complicated by the intervention of the United Fruit Company, which was working with the Standard Oil Company of California and which claimed that it owned the subsoil rights in its extensive landholdings in some of the areas covered by the Sinclair grant. The Fruit Company appealed to the State Department for protection. While the legal situation was not clear, the State Department

---

[46] Colby to Sinclair Oil and Refining Company, June 2, 1920, 818.6363/30.
[47] Memorandum of June 22, 1920, 818.6363/45.

could not ignore a claim based on a principle which was so importantly involved in its current disputes with Mexico, and it was compelled to instruct Chase to ask the Costa Rican government's opinion about the matter. The government dismissed the Fruit Company's contention by asserting that subsoil rights had always belonged to the state.

Acosta had been unwilling to proceed against the Sinclair Company while his government was still seeking recognition from the United States, but in October he felt free to act. As a first step, his government demanded a full report about the company's operations, implying that the transfer of control to Sinclair had been unauthorized and suggesting that the company had not complied with the concession in other respects. A few days later the Costa Rican Attorney General initiated an investigation of González' charge that Valentine had originally obtained the concession by bribery. The Chargé d'Affaires, John F. Martin, thought that these proceedings had been inspired by the United Fruit Company and the Standard Oil Company of California, which were still pressing for the recognition of subsoil rights, and it was difficult for the State Department to take a stand, where rival American interests were involved. In December, each group was presenting arguments and memoranda seeking to support its contentions, and Martin was informed that the Department was awaiting still further memoranda before attempting to reach a conclusion. The matter was still pending in March 1921. As time went on, however, and it began to appear that there was no oil of commercial value in Costa Rica, the whole question of oil rights there became of less interest to the foreign companies and to their governments.[48]

Revolutionary Activity in Honduras

President Wilson's strong statements about the Tinoco regime in Costa Rica seemed to commit the United States to a policy of refusing recognition to any government set up by force in Central America. The President probably did not intend to apply the policy to countries farther from the United States, or at least did not intend to apply it rigorously, for in 1919 he recognized President Leguía,

[48] The more important correspondence about the oil concessions in 1920 and 1921 is printed in *Foreign Relations* for those years.

who had seized power by a *coup d'état* in Peru when his partisans feared that the incumbent administration would not permit him to take office after winning the election. Even in Central America, it would be difficult to maintain a ban on forceful changes of government, for in most of the states of the isthmus free elections were unknown and revolt was often the only way to oust an unacceptable regime. Except in Costa Rica North American influence prevented serious disorders in Central America between 1912 and 1919, but in 1919 and 1920 successful revolutions in Honduras and Guatemala showed that the non-recognition policy could not always be applied.

Francisco Bertrand, who succeeded to the presidency in Honduras when Bonilla died in March 1913, was not a strong ruler, but his tolerant treatment of opponents and the moral support of the United States enabled him to give the country several years of relative peace. Subversive movements were discouraged because American warships regularly appeared on the coast at the first report of impending revolt. The neighboring countries, which had been chiefly responsible for the instability of the Honduran government in the past, were deterred from interfering by the United States' insistence on their observance of the provisions of the 1907 treaties. The overthrow of Zelaya and the intervention in Nicaragua in 1912 seemed to have convinced most of the Central American leaders that warnings from Washington must be taken seriously.

There was a threat of revolt when Bertrand decided to be a candidate to succeed himself in 1915. General Máximo Rosales, who had expected to be the official candidate, resigned from the Cabinet, and in July 1915 it was reported that he and other opposition leaders were preparing to invade Honduras from Guatemala. It was said that Estrada Cabrera, who had helped Bonilla in the revolution of 1910, was less satisfied with Bertrand, especially after Bertrand, early in 1915, removed several local officials who had been friendly to and presumably in the pay of the Guatemalan dictator. Among these was the American soldier of fortune Lee Christmas, who had controlled an important part of the north coast as *comandante* at Puerto Cortés.

There were reports too that Rosales was receiving help from the United Fruit Company or some of its subsidiaries. Though Minor Keith's loan project had failed in 1913, the American Consul at

Puerto Cortés reported that the Fruit Company was apparently still trying to get control of the National Railroad and was withholding banana shipments on the line so as to make the government more ready to part with it.[49] In August 1915 the Honduran Legation at Washington produced evidence that seemed to indicate that Rosales, who was then in New Orleans, was receiving help from Estrada Cabrera, the Fruit Company, Zemurray, and also from Valentine.[50]

The State Department, which had already told Estrada Cabrera that it would view with "grave concern" any effort to disturb peace in Honduras, made new representations to Guatemala and took the matter up with the Department of Justice. The persons who were accused of conniving with Rosales at New Orleans were kept under surveillance. At the same time, warships were sent to Honduras with orders to prevent revolutionary landings or shipments of arms. As often happened, Estrada Cabrera was able to persuade an incompetent American Minister that he was innocent of any wrongdoing. At the same time he evidently heeded the American warning, for there was no invasion of Honduras and Bertrand was peacefully reelected. When Rosales visited Washington just afterward, Long told him that the United States would look with disfavor on any revolution, but sidestepped his effort to find out whether the United States would actually intervene if one occurred.[51]

Rosales told Long that the American fruit companies were his friends because they had been badly treated by Bertrand. How far any of them was actually involved in the movement, it is impossible to say. Apparently there was less basis for the charge that Valentine was involved. At any rate Valentine was able to convince an official of the State Department a few months later that he wanted only peace in Honduras and was supporting the Bertrand government.[52]

During the next four years, although there were periodic reports that Rosales was about to invade Honduras with a revolutionary army, the chief threat to the country's peace came from a revival

[49] Consul Myers to the Secretary of State, Oct. 31, 1913, 815.00/1528.
[50] 815.00/1604, 1607.
[51] Long's memorandum of Nov. 3, 1915, 815.00/1637.
[52] J. B. Wright's memorandum of May 1, 1916, 815.00/1671.

of long-standing boundary controversies with two of its stronger neighbors. The dispute with Guatemala involved a strip of potential banana lands on both banks of the lower Motagua River, which had been almost uninhabited jungle until the Cuyamel Fruit Company started to build a railroad into it from the Honduran side early in 1917. Estrada Cabrera sent troops to stop the construction, and Honduras appealed to the United States. After both parties accepted American mediation, a conference met in Washington in 1918, but no settlement was reached and the dispute continued to cause trouble from time to time until it was settled with the aid of the United States in 1930. The other dispute, with Nicaragua, led to several minor but dangerous border incidents in 1918. The United States offered its mediation and prevented a serious conflict from developing, but no agreement could be reached about a boundary line.

Honduras' relations with her third neighbor, El Salvador, were more friendly, and there was a revival of the project to unite the two countries. President Meléndez of El Salvador took the matter up very secretly with the State Department in July 1918, and three months later the government of Honduras, which was perhaps less enthusiastic, also approached the United States. The two governments proposed to give the United States limited rights in the Gulf of Fonseca in return for its support. This would have settled, so far as they were concerned, the controversy over the Bryan-Chamorro Treaty, and the Navy Department was inclined to welcome the proposal.[53] Some of the officials in the State Department also seemed sympathetic to the plan at first, but the final decision was to give it no encouragement. There was some reason to think that the plan had originated with the Mexican government, and Lansing suspected that German influence might also be at work. Furthermore, the State Department feared that the union might lead to war with other Central American states, as attempts at union had in the past, and that the proposal might affect the Department's efforts to settle the Honduras-Guatemala boundary.[54] The project, which probably would have had little chance for success in any event, was soon dropped.

[53] Daniels to Lansing, Nov. 15, 1918, 813.00/918.
[54] Polk to Jones, Nov. 13, 1918, 813.00/911.

What happened at the end of Bertrand's second term showed how difficult it would be to prevent revolutions in countries where free elections were not held. Bertrand might have been able to pass on the government to a successor of his own choosing if he had selected and consistently supported a candidate who had some political strength; but after he had come out for and then abandoned one candidate, and his next choice had died, he threw his support to his own brother-in-law, Nazario Soriano. Soriano was opposed by other leaders who had been prominent in Bertrand's administration, including General Rafael López Gutiérrez, the former governor of Tegucigalpa, and Alberto Membreño, who had been the official candidate earlier in the campaign. In February 1919 the American Legation reported that the government was adopting high-handed measures to assure Soriano's success.[55]

The State Department told the American Minister to intimate orally to Bertrand that the United States expected a free election, but for some months it took no further action. While it suspected that El Salvador and Mexico were back of Soriano's candidacy, it could not be sure about the accuracy of the information that it was receiving from the Legation, especially after it learned that the elderly Minister, T. Sambola Jones, had recently married the 17-year old daughter of one of the opposition leaders. In July, however, Jones reported that the situation was "extremely grave"; that Bertrand had assumed a dictatorship, and that political opponents were being arrested and beaten. At the same time, the government placed troops around the American Legation, where the Minister had given asylum to a number of political refugees. The State Department instructed the Minister to reiterate orally the American government's interest in a free election and to say that its friendship for the people of Honduras and its desire for peace throughout the Western Hemisphere "necessitate its very close scrutiny of the present conditions and require that its future attitude toward those in control of the political destinies of that country be guided by their actions." Bertrand, who evidently felt that Jones was working with his enemies, refused to consider this communication unless it was put in writing.

Meanwhile, General López Gutiérrez had started a revolution.

[55] Except as otherwise indicated, this account of the 1919 revolution is based on documents printed in *Foreign Relations* for that year, and on personal recollection.

On July 25, Lansing laid the whole situation before President Wilson, recommending that the United States invite Bertrand and López Gutiérrez to meet on an American warship in an effort to reach an agreement through the good offices of the United States.[56] The President does not seem to have approved this idea, for the State Department took no action during the four weeks that followed. The civil war continued in Honduras.

On August 29, Lansing consulted the President again. He said that the revolution was apparently going to succeed, and that if it did the United States would confront the same sort of problem that it had recently confronted in Costa Rica, with an added danger in this case of complications arising from Bertrand's secret agreements with Mexico and El Salvador. He thought that the revolution would stop if the United States used its influence for a free election. The President approved this suggestion,[57] and on September 5 Acting Secretary Phillips instructed Jones to tell Bertrand in writing that there must be an immediate agreement in Honduras to end the war and to guarantee free elections. Bertrand was invited to ask the United States to use its good offices to this end, as it had in the 1911 revolution. He was warned that if he did not do so the United States would "be obliged to consider actively assisting in the reestablishment of order and in the overseeing of the coming presidential elections."

Bertrand immediately resigned and left Honduras, turning the presidential authority over to his Cabinet. This unexpected development created a new problem. If López Gutiérrez simply assumed control, as he seemed likely to do, the United States would be confronted with a revolutionary regime. The State Department acted promptly to avoid this by urging that Francisco Bográn, the second *Designado*, be recognized as provisional president. The suggestion was logical because Membreño, the vice president, was an active candidate, and the first *Designado* was Soriano, who had left the country with Bertrand. The Council of Ministers accepted it, though apparently not without a considerable amount of argument, and Bográn was invited to come to Tegucigalpa to take office.

Before Bográn could reach Tegucigalpa, however, López Gutiér-

[56] 815.00/1924a.
[57] Lansing to Wilson, Aug. 29, 1919, 815.00/2033a; Wilson to Lansing, Sept. 1, 1919, 815.00/2090.

rez had taken possession of the capital and had made it clear that, while he accepted Bográn as provisional president, he intended to be the *de facto* ruler. He permitted Bográn to name three members of the new Cabinet but named the other three himself. The Provisional President thus had little authority after he was inaugurated on October 5. Though he was not friendly to López Gutiérrez, and told Jones that the latter's accession to the presidency would be a disaster,[58] he was in no position to interfere with the victorious revolutionists' preparations to control the approaching election.

In urging that Bográn be asked to take over the government, the State Department had also proposed that all of the presidential candidates be invited to a conference to discuss measures to assure that the election would be free. The Council of Ministers agreed to this, but López Gutiérrez, though he promised a free election, told Jones that Membreño, who was now the only other important candidate, would not be permitted to run. The State Department told Jones to say that it hoped that López Gutiérrez would cooperate in inviting Membreño to attend a conference at which plans for guaranteeing a free election could be made, but the Minister apparently failed to press the matter.

The American government was thus confronted by a situation where the leader of a victorious revolution was about to take over the presidency after what could only be a pretense of a free election. To permit this seemed inconsistent with the policy that Wilson had enunciated in dealing with Costa Rica, but there was no way short of armed intervention to prevent it. The prospect was the more unattractive because López Gutiérrez was thought to be unfriendly to the United States; Jones had reported that the Germans in Honduras were celebrating his victory because they counted on him to reverse the war measures that had recently been taken against them.[59] Nevertheless, the State Department was evidently not disposed to become involved in another situation of non-recognition. The moral issue was not entirely clear, because Bertrand's conduct had given some justification for the revolution and because the forthcoming election would presumably be no different from any other in Honduras' history. From a practical standpoint, it would probably be

[58] Jones to Lansing, Oct. 7, 1919, 815.00/2072.
[59] Jones to Lansing, Sept. 20, 1919, 815.00/2026.

to the best interests of Honduras and of the United States to let matters take their course.

The officials at Washington who handled the problem would not perhaps have admitted that this was their attitude. They continued to impress on all concerned the fact that the election must be free. On September 25, the State Department expressed the hope that López Gutiérrez would do nothing to make it difficult for the United States to recognize him, as it would be inclined to do if he were chosen in a free and constitutional election open to all candidates. The State Department went on to say that, if López Gutiérrez respected the constitution, the United States would use its good offices to check any revolutionary activity.[60] Soon afterward Consul Lawton was moved from San José to take charge of the American Legation at Tegucigalpa so that all parties might feel that the conduct of the Legation during the election was absolutely impartial.[61] Lawton was instructed to use all of his influence to ensure a free election, and he worked with Bográn in the latter's apparently honest effort to assure fair play. Bográn admitted, however, that he could not control the pro-López officials in many parts of the country, and Membreño and his followers stayed in the race only because Lawton urged them to do so.

The election was held late in October 1919 without causing any serious disturbances. López Gutiérrez obtained 76,000 votes and Membreño 18,000. For a time it seemed possible that there might be trouble before the President-elect took office. When Membreño returned to Honduras on October 30, there was some question whether he should not assume the provisional presidency as Bertrand's constitutional successor. The American government, however, urged Bográn to remain in office until the end of the presidential term, and on December 11, Lawton was authorized to announce that the United States regarded López Gutiérrez "as entitled to assume the executive power" at the beginning of the next presidential term. In January the Honduran government asked the United States to take action to dissuade the Nicaraguan government from helping a revolt which Membreño's followers were organizing. Lansing sent appropriate instructions to Managua, where Chamorro denied that

[60] Phillips to Jones, Sept. 25, 1919, 815.00/2051a.
[61] Lansing to Lawton, Oct. 13, 1919, 815.00/2083a.

he was assisting the rebels in any way. The revolution made no progress, and on February 2, 1920, when President López Gutiérrez was inaugurated, Lawton reported that "general conditions" were good and that Nicaragua and El Salvador were apparently cooperating with Honduras in preventing attacks across the borders.

In the interim, the State Department had revived the idea of helping Honduras to achieve more political stability through financial reforms—a matter in which it had shown little interest during the war years. In December 1919, Lansing instructed Lawton to endeavor to have Bográn ask the American government to nominate an expert to report on the "financial system with a view to eventually placing Honduran finances on a satisfactory basis." Bográn consulted López Gutiérrez, who approved the idea, and in July 1920 Dr. Arthur N. Young, one of the ablest of the State Department's economists, went to Tegucigalpa as Financial Adviser under a six months' contract. His position was quite different from that of the financial officials who had earlier been imposed on the governments of Nicaragua, the Dominican Republic, and Haiti, because the State Department did not insist that he be given any specific authority and he was in fact an adviser and not a controller.

For a time the Honduran government seemed willing to accept much of the sound and constructive advice that Young gave it. After the first six months, he was asked to stay on, but before the end of the Wilson administration it was already clear that the Honduran congress' opposition to López Gutiérrez, and the opposition to reform by persons who profited from the status quo, would defeat much of his program. One of Young's chief objectives was a great reduction in the size of the army, which was consuming a disproportionate part of the government's income, and the creation of an effective police force to replace it, a change that was especially appropriate in Honduras because of the country's neutral position under the 1907 treaties. He apparently obtained López Gutiérrez' approval of this idea, but the expert who was selected in Washington to train the new police turned out to be an unfortunate choice. Efforts to reduce the army were frustrated by the increasing international tensions in Central America and by the influence of the President's nephew, who was Minister of War, and little had been accomplished when Young left Tegucigalpa in August 1921.

The Fall of Estrada Cabrera

The overthrow of Estrada Cabrera had greater repercussions in Central American politics than the revolutions in Costa Rica and Honduras. For more than twenty years, the crafty and unprincipled Guatemalan dictator had been interfering openly or secretly in the affairs of the other countries of the isthmus, usually with the sole purpose of making his own position more secure at home. In Guatemala his rule had been a disaster. The Indians had been forced more and more into practical slavery and the upper class had been demoralized and humiliated by police surveillance and terrorism. No opposition or criticism was permitted, and it was dangerous for a Guatemalan even to mention the President's name in a private conversation. One of the worst features of the regime was the depreciation of the currency, which had depressed standards of living and had forced all government officials to resort to corruption if they were to survive.

Estrada Cabrera had gone to great lengths to create a favorable image abroad, through paid propaganda and the support of foreigners and natives who benefited from his system. He had posed especially as a friend of the United States. He had taken in some American diplomats and some members of the United States Congress, but most of the officials who dealt with Latin American affairs were aware that his regime was a particularly detestable despotism. They also knew of his frequent underhand violations of the 1907 treaties and other actions that showed little desire to be helpful to American policy. After 1917, there was much reason to suppose that he had encouraged and aided Tinoco in Costa Rica. In such a situation, it would be difficult not to feel some sympathy for any movement that sought to overthrow the dictatorship, however strongly the State Department disapproved of revolutions in general.

Early in 1919 when Estrada Cabrera's poor health and reports of increasing discontent in Guatemala made it seem that a change of government might be imminent, the State Department asked the American Legation for a considered report on the situation that might develop if the President should die. The tenor of the instruction suggests that its author was hoping for the accession of a new ruler who would be able to maintain order and would be friendly

457

to the United States, and it is interesting to note that he asked especially for a report on Jorge Ubico, who was one of Estrada Cabrera's lieutenants, and who would become dictator of Guatemala many years later. There was apparently little thought that a new government could be established through democratic processes. Walter Thurston, an able career officer who was Chargé d'Affaires, replied that the President was less likely to die in office than to be ousted by revolution because he seemed to be losing his grip on the government and a movement against him was already under way.[62]

The opposition movement, which was at first a very small conspiracy, took shape rather slowly. The first public manifestation of discontent occurred in May 1919, when Bishop Piñol y Batres preached a number of sermons deploring conditions in Guatemala and by implication criticizing the dictatorship. He attracted large and enthusiastic audiences, but the excitement he aroused seemed to die down when the government put him in jail. It was clear that the people were still abjectly afraid of Estrada Cabrera. Thurston reported that he had carefully avoided any expression of opinion that might encourage the Bishop's supporters to resist the government, but he requested and obtained the State Department's permission to say to the President that the United States would deprecate "harsh, repressive and undemocratic measures" that might restrict freedom of speech.[63] Influenced perhaps by this statement, the President did not take the brutal measures with which he had usually suppressed any suggestion of discontent. The Bishop was released in August and three weeks later was permitted to leave the country.

While these events were occurring, the State Department was initiating a project to improve conditions in Guatemala by bringing about a much needed reform of the currency. As a first step it offered in April 1919 to suggest an expert who would draw up a plan for reform and promised to use its good offices with American bankers to get the necessary loan. Estrada Cabrera accepted the idea, and Professor E. W. Kemmerer of Princeton submitted a comprehensive

[62] Phillips to Thurston, Feb. 14, 1919, 814.00/295a; Thurston's reply, April 7, 1919, 814.00/300.

[63] Most of the important correspondence about the Guatemalan revolution is printed in *Foreign Relations, 1919*, Vol. II, pp. 263ff., and *Foreign Relations, 1920*, pp. 718ff.

report on Guatemalan monetary problems in September. The State Department was prepared to go farther with its project and to endeavor to enlist the interest of American bankers, but Estrada Cabrera showed no great desire to push the matter and the deteriorating political situation soon made further consideration of a loan impossible.

Estrada Cabrera was equally uncooperative in his attitude toward the liquidation of enemy property in Guatemala. The American government was trying to persuade both Guatemala and Honduras to take over and sell to new owners several of the enterprises formerly held by Germans, and two or three groups of Americans were interested in buying the Guatemala Electric Company, which Estrada Cabrera had seized. The State Department wished to see it sold to the highest bidder, but Estrada Cabrera did not do business that way. In May 1919, without awaiting other offers, he leased it to the American and Foreign Power Company for an annual rental of $40,000. Thurston commented that it was the general opinion among well-informed foreigners that the President would "only comply with any suggestion or request emanating from Washington when he can find no [convenient] way of disregarding it." In the months that followed, the State Department continued to urge that all of the former enemy properties be sold under conditions that would give all interested parties an opportunity to bid, but little was actually sold. The American and Foreign Power Company, however, bought most of the stock in the electric company from Estrada Cabrera just before he was driven from office.

The little group of courageous people who had secretly been organizing an opposition party were greatly encouraged when they learned that the New York *Herald,* on August 18, 1919, had published an article asserting that the United States government had told Estrada Cabrera that it would oppose his reelection at the end of his term in 1923. This complete fabrication was apparently the work of W. H. Field, who had been one of the most active propagandists for González Flores of Costa Rica. It aroused indignation among some United States senators who were friendly to Estrada Cabrera, but the State Department assured them that it had no basis in fact.[64] In Guatemala, where people learned of it in spite of

[64] Breckinridge Long to Senator Thos. J. Walsh, undated, 814.00/323a.

the censorship, the opposition leaders were so emboldened that they proposed to Thurston that they would participate actively in the approaching election of members of congress if the United States would assure them of protection. The Chargé naturally could give them no assurances, but the erroneous belief that the United States had turned against the President seems to have been an important factor in the rapid growth of the opposition movement.

Up to this time the movement had drawn most of its members from the upper class and especially from among the more devout Catholics, but in October 1919 it made contact with a number of labor groups who greatly increased its strength. On January 1, 1920, the new party announced its existence, not ostensibly as an opposition party but as a movement for the reestablishment of the Central American union. The pamphlets which it distributed caused a sensation in a community where no discussion of any political subject had been permitted for many years.

Estrada Cabrera again failed to react with his usual ferocity. His police seized the unionists' printing press and arrested several of their leaders, but he did not interfere when the party held a large meeting on January 25. A few days later, however, Benton McMillin, the new American Minister, cabled that the President was thought to be planning to provoke disturbances that would provide an excuse to terrorize the city and kill the unionist leaders. Lansing at once instructed the Minister to warn Estrada Cabrera against any summary executions and to insist that anyone accused of conspiracy be given a fair, public trial. This was hardly the sort of protection for which the unionists had hoped, but the message very possibly increased the President's suspicion that the State Department was in sympathy with his opponents and consequently made him more cautious. On the same day, however, Lansing assured the Guatemalan Minister in Washington that there was no truth in reports that the United States was in sympathy with the unionist movement.[65]

McMillin, when he discovered that the unionists were attempting to create the impression that the United States was friendly to them, "immediately took the necessary measures to counteract this." The State Department evidently did not wish him to go too far in this

[65] Lansing to McMillin, Feb. 6, 1920, 813.00/956a.

direction, and on February 14 it told him to avoid any action that might be construed as support for either side.[66] McMillin seemed chiefly concerned at the prospect of an uprising that would endanger American lives and property, and on February 21 he asked for authority to try to bring about a peaceful agreement between the unionists and the government. He was told that the State Department wished "to hold itself completely aloof from any action that might be construed as indicating that this Government was taking any position in what is for the present a purely domestic matter." [67]

If the State Department really intended to remain aloof, it did not succeed in doing so. By this time the unionists had grown so bold and had gained so much popular following that a bloody conflict seemed inevitable if Estrada Cabrera did not yield to their demands for greater political freedom. Unless the American government was to abandon its support of democratic principles, it could not acquiesce in the violent suppression of a movement that had been careful to avoid any breach of the peace. On the other hand, it did not wish to countenance the forceful overthrow even of a despotism like Estrada Cabrera's. Both of these considerations were evident in a telegram that it sent to the Legation on March 9. It listed 23 unionists who were reported to be in prison and instructed McMillin to point out to Estrada Cabrera the "unfortunate impression which would be created throughout the American continent by any action designed to suppress normal political activities in any American republic"; and at the same time it told the Minister to "mention incidentally" to the unionist leaders the unfavorable impression that would be caused in the United States by any attempt on their part to overthrow the government by violence.

The Guatemalan congress met on February 28 in an atmosphere of great tension. On March 4 it adopted a resolution approving the idea of a Central American union. On March 11 when a great parade of men, women, and children marched to congress' meeting place to present a message of congratulations, Estrada Cabrera's secret police provoked disorders in which at least two persons were killed.

---

[66] McMillin's telegram of Feb. 10, 1920, and Polk's reply of Feb. 14, 1920, 814.00/-346.

[67] McMillin's telegram of Feb. 21, 1920, 814.00/349. The reply is printed in *Foreign Relations, 1920*, Vol. II, p. 722.

Only the interposition of some of the foreign diplomats prevented a much greater slaughter. After this affair the unionist leaders told McMillin that they were planning a much larger demonstration at which the President's resignation would be demanded. The Minister told them that the admission that their program was "revolutionary" would prevent him from having any further "political communication" with them, but a few days later he was engaged in two separate and to some extent conflicting efforts to mediate between them and the President.

Immediately after the affair of March 11 both the unionists and the President asked the diplomatic corps to act as mediators in an effort to prevent further bloodshed. The corps agreed to do so unofficially, and McMillin was designated to represent it. The unionists presented a list of demands, most of which Estrada Cabrera accepted, but the unionists' unwillingness to trust the President, and the fact that many of them were now determined that he must go, made it seem improbable that any agreement could be effected. On March 16, while these negotiations were still going on, Estrada Cabrera told McMillin that he would place himself in the hands of the United States government and abide by any decision that it might make. Without having given the State Department any specific information about the points that had been under discussion in the other mediation, the Minister transmitted this proposal to Washington.

The State Department, before it received the Minister's cable, had already prepared a message telling McMillin to say very confidentially to Estrada Cabrera that the United States felt that "the success of his administration" was "in danger of being marred unless—1st, President Estrada Cabrera recognizes all rights guaranteed by the Constitution; 2nd, that no attempt be made to repress the normal political activities of the people; 3rd, that no further arrests be made for political reasons; 4th, that in no circumstances and under no conditions should prisoners be subjected to torture or even flogging; 5th, that the policy pursued by President Estrada during the recent demonstration which resulted in disturbances and loss of life had aroused grave concern in this country." This somewhat ungrammatical message went forward, and on the next day, in a more direct response to Estrada Cabrera's plea for help, Acting Secretary

Polk cabled McMillin that "The two objects which the Department desires to obtain are prevention of a revolution and the faithful meeting of the just demands of the Unionists on the part of Estrada Cabrera." The State Department suggested that the President issue a proclamation granting what he and the Minister considered the just demands of the unionists. This should include the first four points of the Department's cable of the preceding day, and a promise that all purely political prisoners would be immediately released. If the President complied with this suggestion, McMillin would issue a statement expressing the United States government's approval of the President's action and stating that this action left no excuse for a revolution in Guatemala. At the same time McMillin would tell the unionists that the United States would not countenance any revolt.

Characteristically, Estrada Cabrera proposed changes in the text of the proposed proclamation and raised other difficulties which delayed its appearance until April 5. McMillin then published his statement and warned the unionists that the United States would not countenance a revolt. By this time, the situation had reached a point where it seemed unlikely that the American government's action would have a great effect. Estrada Cabrera had concluded a direct agreement with the unionists, covering far more ground than the State Department's plan, on March 27, but neither party seemed to regard it as a final settlement of the conflict. The government continued to make political arrests, in violation of its promises, and the unionists were more than ever convinced that the President must go. McMillin himself thought that peace could only be preserved if Estrada Cabrera resigned, but the State Department refused to entertain the idea of suggesting a resignation. By this time the increasing size and enthusiasm of the unionist demonstrations, which were conducted with marvelous discipline, showed that the people of Guatemala City were determined that the President must go.

The State Department still hoped that the constitutional order could be preserved, and on April 8 Colby instructed McMillin to observe carefully to see who was responsible for any revolutionary activities that might occur.[68] This message, which suggests a failure

[68] 814.00/379.

to realize just what was happening in Guatemala, can only be interpreted as an indication that the American government planned to try to prevent anyone who resorted to force from holding office in a new government. It did not wish to be confronted with a situation where it would have to seem to approve a revolution.

The revolution nevertheless occurred. On April 8 the congress, every one of whose members had been personally selected by Estrada Cabrera, yielded to popular pressure and declared the President insane. It elected Carlos Herrera, a wealthy and generally respected civilian, as president. Estrada Cabrera still had the support of part of the army, which held several strong points around the capital, and for some days there was danger of a disastrous struggle in and around the city. McMillin, without authorization from Washington, sent for marines from the American warships on both coasts. The diplomatic corps endeavored to bring about an agreement between the President and the unionists and succeeded in arranging a truce which was only partly effective.

McMillin apparently took no very active part in his colleagues' efforts. On April 11 the State Department authorized him to offer his good offices to the contending parties and to propose a conference on an American warship or at the Legation, but this message was delayed in transmission and was not received until April 14, a few hours before the negotiations already in progress ended with an agreement for Estrada Cabrera's surrender. The unionists guaranteed the ex-President's life and the diplomatic corps accompanied him from his residence to a place of detention, where he was heavily guarded for his own protection.

The State Department urged the unionists to avoid harsh treatment of the defeated party. It thought that Estrada Cabrera should be permitted to leave Guatemala and offered to provide an escort to take him to the coast, but the new government was unwilling to release him before he had disgorged the great amount of wealth that he was supposed to have accumulated. He was, however, treated surprisingly well, when one considers the cruel treatment that many Guatemalans had suffered at his hands, and he was eventually released and lived quietly in Guatemala City until his death in 1924.

It could hardly be said that the new government had been established by orderly constitutional procedures as understood in the

United States, but it would have been somewhat ridiculous to express disapproval of a change that was accepted with enthusiasm in Guatemala and with general satisfaction elsewhere. The new government, after all, could claim that it had been established in accord with the constitution of Guatemala, for the congress, realizing that its original action in electing Herrera president was questionable, reversed itself a few days later and named him first *Designado*, so that he succeeded to the presidency when Estrada Cabrera resigned. Herrera further strengthened his moral position when he called for new presidential elections to take place at the end of August. The United States did not act precipitately in recognizing him, but on June 21 McMillin was told that the President had decided to deal with the new government as Estrada Cabrera's constitutional successor.

Efforts to Unite Central America, 1920–1921

During the last months of the Wilson administration it was evident that the relatively peaceful conditions that had prevailed in Central America since the American intervention in Nicaragua might not continue. The governmental overturns in Honduras and Guatemala showed that revolutions could still be successful despite the American government's condemnation of the use of force, and there was evidence of an increasing tendency for the Central American governments to interfere in one another's affairs. In many parts of the isthmus there was a growing resentment of North American influence and a growing feeling of hostility to the United States. The fact that the United States had been represented in several of the Central American countries since 1913 by incompetent ministers had not helped American prestige.

One important element in the policy of the United States had been its insistence on a strict observance of the provisions of the 1907 treaties, which neutralized Honduras and forbade the Central American governments to aid revolutionary movements against neighboring states. These treaties lost much of their usefulness after the disappearance of the Central American Court cast doubt on the continued validity of the whole system of which the Court had been a central feature. Between April and June 1920, new disturbances along the Honduran-Nicaraguan frontier and serious friction between Honduras and El Salvador created a situation reminiscent of the conditions existing before 1907. The State Department frequently warned the governments to behave themselves, and on July 12 it formally called the attention of all three governments to their obligation to refrain from any assistance to revolutionary movements against neighboring states. At the same time the American representatives were told to "intimate discreetly and informally" that the United States would not "look with favor on any government in Central America which is not brought into power by constitutional methods or retained in power by extra Constitutional methods." Evidently the State Department did not wish the Central Americans to think that recent developments signified any change in its policy.[69]

A new element came into the Central American picture with the victory of the unionists in Guatemala. While the party's chief purpose had been to oust Estrada Cabrera, many of its leaders were sincere in their advocacy of a Central American federation. The party's propaganda had met with much response elsewhere in the isthmus and especially in El Salvador and Honduras, where unionist sentiment was always strong. In June 1920 the government of El Salvador suggested a Central American conference to establish closer relations, and in July the Guatemalan Foreign Minister told McMillin that Costa Rica, Honduras, and El Salvador were in favor of a federation and that the two latter countries were willing to make Herrera its first president.[70] Meetings of the Central American liberal parties in September and of representatives of the Central American municipalities in November gave added impetus to the movement.[71]

When the Guatemalan congress voted in favor of a union on March 4, 1920, before Estrada Cabrera fell, its President had asked for an expression of the United States government's views. A few days later the Minister of Foreign Affairs of Honduras made a similar inquiry. Secretary Colby replied in both cases that the United States thought that a union would be desirable if it were based on the wishes of the peoples of Central America and if the plan responded

[69] *Foreign Relations, 1920*, Vol. II, p. 867.
[70] McMillin to Colby, July 17, 1920, 813.00/967.
[71] Goold to Colby, Nov. 3, 1920, 814.00/512.

to the freely expressed will of the nations concerned.[72] In August 1920, however, when there was a suggestion that the proposed Central American conference might meet in Washington, the Under-secretary of State told the Chief of the Latin American Division that it was not deemed advisable to encourage any federation.[73] In November, shortly before the meeting of the conference which El Salvador had proposed, Colby responded to another inquiry from the Guatemalan government in much the same language he had used in April, but intimated that the meeting might well consider constructive measures for other forms of closer cooperation if a union were not effected.[74]

The State Department presumably knew that all previous attempts at Central American union had ended in bloodshed, and it may have suspected that the movement was inspired by political groups that wished to diminish the influence of the United States in Central America. It could foresee that the special relationship between the United States and Nicaragua would come in for criticism when the Central American conference met. John Martin, the American Chargé d'Affaires in Costa Rica, proposed that the United States forestall any unpleasant discussion by announcing that it would withdraw the legation guard from Managua if an effective union were formed, but this suggestion was not well received. The State Department replied that the political situation was too precarious and furthermore that its information forced it to assume that a federation was impossible at that time.[75]

When representatives of all of the Central American states met at San José, Costa Rica, early in December 1920 to draw up a Pact of Union, Nicaragua precipitated a controversy by demanding that the treaty specifically recognize the validity of the Bryan-Chamorro Treaty. The other states were apparently willing to accept a provision recognizing the validity of all treaties in force, pending their revision, and this provision would apparently have met with no objection from the United States.[76] But Nicaragua nevertheless with-

[72] Telegram to Tegucigalpa, March 13, 1920, 813.00/958; to Guatemala, April 8, 813.00/957.
[73] Davis to Welles, Aug. 23, 1920, 813.00/994.
[74] Colby to Goold, Nov. 18, 1920, 813.00/1010.
[75] Martin to Colby, Nov. 23, 1920, and Colby's reply of Nov. 27. 813.00/1024.
[76] See note attached to 813.00/1050.

drew her delegates. The other four states signed a treaty on January 19, 1921. Subsequently Costa Rica, which had traditionally held aloof from efforts to reestablish a Central American union, failed to ratify the agreement, but Guatemala, Honduras, and El Salvador went ahead with the project.

The Wilson administration went out of office before there was an opportunity to determine the policy of the United States toward the venture. The three northern states set up a provisional federal council at Tegucigalpa in June 1921 and convened a constituent assembly in the same city a month later, but the new government had not really assumed any authority when a revolution in Guatemala put an end to the effort in December.

◄ 11 ►

Relations with Cuba, 1909–1921

◪ In dealing with Cuba, after the reestablishment of the Cuban government in 1909, the chief objective of American policy was to prevent the rise of conditions that would again confront the United States with the distasteful and politically unpopular task of intervention. There was no other country in the Caribbean where the maintenance of a stable and effective government was of so much interest to the United States. Aside from the island's unique strategic situation and the special responsibility that the American government had assumed under the Platt Amendment, Cuba was by far the most important of the Caribbean states from the standpoint of foreign trade and investment. Disorder there could imperil great numbers of resident Americans and great amounts of American property, and still greater amounts of other foreign capital. In the effort to avert disorder, both the Taft and the Wilson administrations frequently thought it necessary to advise or admonish the Cuban government about matters of internal policy.

Conditions that developed in Cuba after 1909 afforded some justification for the American government's solicitude. In the first years of independence, the tradition of corruption inherited from the Spanish regime had to some extent been kept in the background by Estrada Palma's honesty and frugality. Under José Miguel Gómez, who became president when the provisional government was withdrawn in 1909, there was graft and political favoritism in all branches of the administration. Gómez himself is said to have amassed a fortune of several million dollars, and his associates shared in the profits from granting concessions and other favors to business concerns.[1] A general prosperity increased the opportunities for such transactions and also increased the government's revenues, so that it was possible to create great numbers of new government jobs. Many of these were *botellas,* or positions in which the occupant rendered no services.

Politics, in fact, seemed to become little more than a competition

[1] Chapman, *History of the Cuban Republic,* pp. 286–287.

for the opportunity to live and grow rich at the expense of the community. The Cuban political parties were remarkably frank in their emphasis on jobs rather than issues as the purpose of their existence, and the fact that so many politicians had jobs or other lucrative opportunities made for more discontent among those who were not favored. This dissatisfaction, in a country where there was no confidence in the electoral process, could only find expression in attempts at revolt. The realization that the uprising which forced American intervention in 1906 had ultimately brought into power the party that started it also encouraged subversive activities, and some influential groups who were not primarily interested in Cuban politics were suspected of hoping for a revolution because they thought that it might bring on another and this time a more lasting intervention.

The American government clearly had no desire to assume permanent control of Cuba. In May 1910, when the new American Minister, John B. Jackson, requested a statement of policy, Knox replied that the United States would be unwilling to intervene again unless it became absolutely necessary, after an existing government had shown an incapacity to maintain order.[2] A month later, the State Department thought it necessary to take cognizance of "vague rumors regarding possible contemplated political disturbances, with the suggestion that such disturbances might not be viewed with disfavor by this Government" and to instruct the American Minister to make it clear that the United States would support the constituted authorities.[3] Nevertheless, with the accumulation of evidence about the Gómez government's conduct, some of the officials in the State Department began to feel that intervention was inevitable unless matters improved and that the best way to avoid intervention was to check tendencies that were dangerous to Cuba's financial and political stability.

The Cuban Ports Company Affair

The first important application of what Huntington Wilson called the "Preventive Policy"[4] was in the case of the Cuban Ports Com-

[2] Knox to Jackson, May 11, 1910, 837.00/380.
[3] Knox to Jackson, June 21, 1910, *Foreign Relations, 1910*, p. 416.
[4] This phrase was used on several occasions. See, for example, Huntington Wilson's suggestion that the President use it in making an oral statement to the Cuban Minister in 1912, 837.00/777a.

pany. A bill authorizing the improvement of Habana and several other ports was introduced in the Cuban congress in January 1911. The improvement was needed, and the work was to be done by a large American engineering firm domiciled in Habana; but it was to be paid for by increasing the port dues to one dollar per ton on general merchandise, with a 20 percent reduction in the case of imports from the United States. The money collected would be turned over to the company for a period of thirty years. Since the work would cost $10,000,000–$12,000,000, and the port dues could be expected to produce $50,000,000–$60,000,000 during the life of the concession,[5] and since the project would be financed by issuing bonds abroad, the Cuban politicians who held the stock in the company could expect to make a large profit with little or no investment of their own money.

When the American Consul General pointed out the doubtful aspects of the pending bill, Wilson instructed the Legation to inquire about the project. He asked that the State Department have an opportunity to see the bill before it was enacted,[6] but the measure was rushed through both houses of congress and signed by Gómez with a haste that forestalled any effort to interfere. In response to protests from many sources, however, Gómez insisted that the amount of the port dues be reduced to 88 cents per ton.

When the text of the concession reached the State Department, the Solicitor, J. Reuben Clark, urged a protest, on the ground that the measure was "improvident." He wrote that all recent visitors to Cuba thought that the United States could not long "escape another intervention" there, and he thought that the United States would not want to find Cuba's finances tied up by improvident contracts when it intervened. Wilson instructed the Legation to say discreetly that the contract seemed improvident and to bring the matter earnestly to the attention of the Cuban government, suggesting that some other arrangement be made for dredging the ports.[7] When Jackson replied that it would not be "discreet" to make these representations, because the company was already at work, the State Department, though it disagreed, told him to take no action for the time being.[8]

[5] These estimates are based on several papers in the file.
[6] Wilson to Jackson, Feb. 16, 1911, 837.156/9.
[7] Clark to Doyle, March 17, 1911, 837.156/29; Wilson to Jackson, March 25, 1911, 837.156/31A.
[8] Jackson to Knox, March 27, 1911, 837.156/32.

Wilson warned the Minister, however, that "the Government of the United States feels it its duty, when occasion may demand, to caution the Government of Cuba against enacting improvident legislation or granting burdensome concessions which may adversely affect the future." [9]

Jackson was obviously reluctant to interfere in the Ports Company case. He insisted that the project, in his opinion, would be beneficial to Cuba, and he doubted the propriety of interfering in a purely internal matter. Before he received Wilson's reply to his refusal to act, he asked the State Department for guidance as to his responsibility in connection with Cuban legislation in general. Many people, he wrote, thought that he should be a "moral adviser." At the moment there seemed to be almost a concerted effort to realize on all possible government assets and to compromise all sources of revenue in order to protect the concessionaires if the country should suddenly cease to be independent. Improvident and ill-advised legislation was frequently adopted, but it was difficult and risky for the Legation to attempt to give advice without more expert assistance than it had.[10]

Knox's reply was an important statement of policy: ". . . because of its special treaty relations with Cuba, and its interest in the welfare of the Cuban Republic, the Department considers that besides the direct protection of American interests you are to endeavor, by friendly representations and advice, to deter the Cuban Government from enacting legislation which appears to you of an undesirable or improvident character, even though it seem improvident or ill-advised purely from the Cuban standpoint, especially if it is likely in any degree to jeopardize the future welfare or revenue of Cuba." [11]

In the Ports Company case, the State Department evidently felt that it confronted a *fait accompli* and could do nothing further for the moment. Before long, however, it had an opportunity to take action that forced the company to consider its views. The company was financing its work by selling $6,000,000 of its bonds in England and another $1,000,000 in Cuba, and on May 12 an English banker wrote to the Secretary of State to ask whether the American govern-

[9] Wilson tc Jackson, April 20, 1911, 837.156/34.
[10] Jackson to Knox, confidential, April 22, 1911, 837.00/473.
[11] Knox to Jackson, May 6, 1911, 837.00/473.

ment would raise any objection to the issue under the Platt Amendment: Wilson replied that the Ports Company contract was so manifestly improvident and one-sided as to raise grave doubts about its ultimate validity and legality.[12] In the face of such a statement, further sales of bonds would obviously be difficult.

Meanwhile, when it learned that a bill authorizing certain changes in the concession was before the Cuban congress, the State Department had expressed its views about the concession to the Cuban Minister at Washington. The project, Knox wrote, affected the government's ordinary revenues, which were already scarely adequate, and reflected "a highly imprudent and dangerous fiscal policy which threatens to brings Cuba to a condition of national bankruptcy and consequent inability to maintain a government adequate efficiently to serve the nation's needs." The interests of Cuba demanded changes in the contract.[13]

The principal Americans connected with the Ports Company were Captain Tillinghast L'Hommedieu Huston, formerly of the United States Army and more recently one of the most successful foreign businessmen in Habana, and Norman Davis of the Trust Company of Cuba. Both were to become prominent later in the United States, Huston in baseball circles as part owner of the New York Yankees and Davis as Undersecretary of State. Both asserted that they had been told by Jackson, when they first undertook the project, that the United States would not object to it, and they said that they had agreed to changes which Jackson had suggested in the original contract.[14] They must have known of the State Department's disapproval, but they went ahead with their plans until the letter to Kleinwort threatened to place them in an impossible position. Then they expressed a willingness to discuss changes in the contract to meet the American government's views. At about the same time Minister Jackson was replaced by Arthur M. Beaupré, who had been Minister to Colombia at the time of the Panama affair.

The discussions with the Ports Company dragged on for more

[12] Kleinwort Sons and Co. to the Department of State, May 12, 1911, 837.156/47. Part of Wilson's reply of June 12, which was addressed to Goldman Sachs and Co. of New York, is missing from the file, but a copy was sent to the Legation at Habana on July 27, 837.156/66.

[13] Knox to Cuban Minister, June 23, 1911, 837.156/56.

[14] See their printed pamphlet of July 25, 1911, filed under 837.156/69.

than a year. The State Department objected to the contract principally because it felt that the Cuban government should not give up a substantial part of its ordinary revenues for a period of thirty years and because it thought that the amount of money which the company would collect would be far greater than the cost of the work. The company apparently agreed with the Department on a number of changes, and in June 1912, in an instruction that was submitted to President Taft for approval, Knox instructed Beaupré to urge the Cuban government to accept these and also to amend the contract so that the government would have a right to terminate the concession with compensation to the owners. Knox said that this would make the contract conform to Article II of the Platt Amendment.[15]

The company seemed willing to accept in principle a provision permitting cancelation, but it suggested terms that would be highly advantageous to the holders of its stocks and bonds, and the American Chargé d'Affaires thought that the government was so "closely identified" with the company that no real improvement in the contract was likely.[16] Finally, at Knox's insistence, the company agreed to an arrangement by which the United States government would appoint three appraisers to fix the amount of compensation if the concession were canceled and would have the right to approve or disapprove their decision.[17] This ended the matter for the time being.

The Veterans' Movement

The Ports Company concession, as Jackson indicated, was but one of many acts of the Gómez regime that showed a reckless disregard for the interests of the Cuban taxpayer. In the summer of 1911, after Jackson's withdrawal, the State Department asked Chargé d'Affaires Hugh Gibson to gather data that would show how far the Cuban government had gone in the direction of national insolvency.[18] Gibson's reply showed a disturbing state of affairs. The government's estimated expenses had increased by 50 percent since the last budget under the provisional government, and a great num-

[15] Knox to Beaupré, June 5, 1912, 837.156/105A; Knox to the Ports Co., June 11, 1912, 837.156/105B. Article II of the Platt Amendment provided that the Cuban government should not contract any debt which could not be served from the ordinary revenues of the island.

[16] Gibson to Knox, Oct. 4, 1912, 837.156/110.

[17] Knox to Beaupré, Feb. 18, 1913, 837.156/133.

[18] Wilson to Gibson, Aug. 30, 1911, 837.51/142.

ber of new jobs had been created. The tax burden was heavy, but only a small sum was available for public works. The report nevertheless contained little that would seem to justify any extraordinary action by the American government, and no action was taken.[19]

A few months later, however, the political situation in Cuba again brought the preventive policy into play. By this time the political leaders were maneuvering for advantage in the presidential elections that were to take place in 1912. Many leaders in both parties opposed Gómez' apparent desire for reelection, and a wish to discredit the President seems to have been one of the motives for the noisy agitation begun by the association of veterans of the war for independence in November 1911.

The veterans' principal demand was for the removal of all officeholders who had sided with Spain during the war. Gómez at first refused to comply, but then agreed that the congress should suspend the civil service laws to permit the discharge of the persons to whom the veterans objected. The veterans still questioned his good faith, and in January 1912 the President provoked a new crisis by ordering army and rural guard officers not to participate in politics or to attend veterans' meetings. Both the American Minister and the Consul General reported that there was danger of serious disorders. When Beaupré urged that the American government issue a solemn warning to all concerned, Knox authorized him to make public a note to the Cuban government saying that:

"The situation in Cuba as now reported causes grave concern to the Government of the United States.

"That the laws intended to safeguard free republican government shall be enforced and not defied is obviously essential to the maintenance of the law, order and stability indispensable to the status of the Republic of Cuba, in the continued well-being of which the United States has always evinced and can not escape a vital interest.

"The President of the United States therefore looks to the President and Government of Cuba to prevent a threatened situation which would compel the Government of the United States, much against its desires, to consider what measures it must take in pursuance of the obligation of its relations to Cuba."[20]

Beaupré reported that the statement was well received by the

[19] Gibson to Knox, Sept. 22, 1911, 837.51/146.
[20] Foreign Relations, 1912, pp. 240–241.

local press and public opinion, though some groups were misrepresenting its intent in the hope of causing further trouble. The situation quieted, and at a meeting on January 20 the veterans agreed to cease their agitation, with the understanding that the government would continue to eliminate officeholders who had been actively pro-Spanish during the war for independence. Gómez' execution of the agreement gave the State Department some concern, because he seemingly took advantage of the opportunity to replace a large number of civil service appointees with veterans who would be useful to him politically; and the State Department at the end of February authorized the Legation to remonstrate at his delay in reinstating the suspended civil service law.[21]

Beaupré thought that the American interposition had been the more effective because there had been no show of force. There was an implied rebuke to the United States in one clause of the agreement between Gómez and the veterans, providing that its text be published to show that there would be "no justification for any intervention in our internal affairs by the United States, to whose honor and loyalty as well as its own patriotism the Cuban people trusts its peaceful development." But there was little evidence of resentment on the part of the Cuban government during the first months of 1912. The Cuban Secretary of State, in welcoming Knox to Habana during the Secretary's tour of the Caribbean, spoke in friendly terms of the "policy of prevention"; "there being nothing reprehensible," he went on, "in your exercise of an office operated for our own preservation and profit. . . ."[22] A few weeks later, Gómez himself declared that the ceremonies attending the removal of the wreck of the *Maine* "demonstrated to the entire world the close ties of affection which bind us to the American people."[23]

During this period, the negotiations for the enlargement of the Guantánamo naval station, which had begun many months earlier, seem to have been carried on in a friendly atmosphere. In return for the lands it needed, the United States offered to relinquish the right to establish another base at Bahía Honda. The negotiations

[21] The more important part of the correspondence about the veterans' movement is in *Foreign Relations, 1912*, pp. 236–242. For the remainder, see 837.00/502ff.

[22] *Foreign Relations, 1912*, p. 301.

[23] Message to the Cuban Congress, April 2, 1912, *Foreign Relations, 1912*, pp. 308–309.

made slow progress, partly because of confusion and indecision at Washington, but an agreement was finally signed on December 27, 1912.[24]

The Negro Revolt

Later in 1912, unfortunately, the preventive policy caused more bad feeling. The veterans' agitation had barely subsided when the State Department was forced to consider what it could do about a much graver threat to the stability of the Cuban government.

During the second American intervention, Evaristo Estenoz had organized an "Independent Party of Color," which demanded that Negroes be given a larger number of government positions in recognition of the prominent role they had played in the war for independence and in the revolution of 1906. Only a part of the Negro voters joined the party, but its formation disturbed the liberals, who counted on the colored people for much of their support. Gómez imprisoned Estenoz and several of his followers in 1910 when their agitation became troublesome but soon released them. Although a law proposed by another Negro leader in May 1910 outlawed parties based on race or color, Estenoz continued his agitation. For a time Gómez seems to have tolerated if not encouraged it, possibly because he hoped that a threat of civil war would make easier his own reelection.[25]

Early in 1912, the veterans' success in forcing concessions from the government apparently encouraged Estenoz to make more insistent demands, and rumors of an impending revolt began to circulate. Some of the Negro leaders appealed to President Taft in March, through the Minister at Habana, to stop the outrages that the Cuban government was alleged to be inflicting on them, invoking "the protection of your Government under article three of the Platt Amendment." On May 20 armed bands started a revolt in several parts of the island. The government soon suppressed most of them, but guerrilla operations continued in the sparsely settled mountainous Oriente province.

Many of the foreigners in Cuba were greatly alarmed. There were

[24] The text is in *Foreign Relations, 1912*, p. 295. For the negotiations, see file 811.34537.

[25] Chapman, *History of the Cuban Republic*, pp. 309–310.

widely believed rumors that the revolt was being fomented and
financed by persons who wished to provoke American intervention
and that systematic destruction of foreign property, to compel intervention, might be expected. The former Consul General Frank Steinhart was one of the persons suspected.[26] Beaupré reported on May
23, apparently with little or no foundation in fact, that destruction
of property was the Negroes' "first object." He said that Gómez
hoped to crush the movement within ten days, but he feared that
the government would not be able to guarantee "absolute protection" to all foreign properties in the meantime.

The State Department immediately announced to the press that
it was sending warships and marines to Guantánamo for the protection of Americans, and on May 25 it informed the Cuban government that war vessels were being sent to Habana and Nipe Bay
and that a large naval force would be assembled at some nearby
American port. The note added that forces would be landed if the
Cuban government failed to protect American lives and property,
but it emphasized that "this is not intervention." Four companies
of marines were landed at Guantánamo some days later, and on
June 9, when attacks by white mobs on Negroes created a tense
situation at Habana, additional warships were sent to that city.

The Cuban government regarded this show of force with mixed
emotions. In conversations with the American Minister, Gómez and
his advisers expressed gratification at the landing of the marines
and said that the Cuban troops that were relieved from the duty
of protecting American property would be available for operations
against the rebels. For the record, however, they registered formal
protests. In response to the American government's communication
of May 25, Gómez cabled Taft that the United States' action "alarms
and injures the feelings of a people jealous of their independence,
above all when such measures were not even decided upon by previous agreement between both Governments, which places the Government of Cuba in a humiliating inferiority through a neglect of
its national rights, causing it discredit within and without the country." He insisted that the Cuban government was doing everything
that could be expected of it in its efforts to suppress the revolt.

Another communication from the State Department on June 5,

[26] Beaupré to Knox, May 22, 1912, 837.00/595.

reporting the landing of the marines and warning the Cubans that a "continued failure . . . adequately to protect life and property will inevitably compel this Government to intervene in Cuba under and in response to its treaty rights and obligations," called forth a long and eloquent remonstrance. Politely, but with evident emotion, the Minister for Foreign Affairs maintained that "the intervention which has been initiated and which is being prepared is in no sense justified." He asserted that the marines had been landed before any American property had been destroyed or any American lives endangered and that the Cuban government had "performed wonders" in restricting the revolt to one small section of the country within two weeks after its outbreak. The pressure for protection of foreign interests had seriously impeded military operations, "while the natives, without legations to which to appeal, were left completely unprotected." The government's problem, he said, was the more difficult because the rebels hoped that burning foreign property would force intervention and that the United States, as in 1906, would then "enter into arrangements with them after first turning out the Government that opposed them." Before preparing to intervene, the United States might well give the Cuban government a reasonable amount of time to deal with the situation—"the time that the American Government itself would need were it in our place."

From the beginning of the revolt, Beaupré's reports gave an alarming picture of the situation and expressed a lack of confidence in the Cuban government's ability to deal with it. He gave little credence to the information that he received from official sources. It was probably his unfriendly attitude, as well as a suspicion of the State Department's intentions, that led Gómez to send Orestes Ferrara as his personal representative to Washington early in June. Ferrara's representations may have helped to convince the State Department that its public criticism of the Cuban government and its threats of intervention were making the suppression of the revolt more rather than less difficult. At any rate, in a statement published on June 14 under instructions from Washington, Beaupré declared that "the United States is not contemplating intervention in Cuba, but hopes and believes the Cuban Government will, by prompt and active measures, be able to suppress the insurrection."

Subsequent events seemed to indicate that the Cuban government's estimate of the situation had been more accurate than Beaupré's. Few if any Americans or other foreigners were actually injured during the revolt, and little foreign property was destroyed. Though the Negroes had about 4,000 men under arms, the government defeated them, and after the death of Estenoz on June 27 the movement collapsed. By the end of June, most of the American warships were withdrawn.[27]

The Zapata Swamp Concession

Knox's policy in the veterans affair and the Negro revolt was quite different from his predecessors'. Root, in 1901, had assured the Cubans that the Platt Amendment would not be used as an excuse for "intermeddling" in their affairs, and Roosevelt had refused to intervene under the amendment in 1906 until the Cubans themselves forced him to act. The events of 1906, however, seemed to demonstrate the advisability of acting to correct a bad situation before actual intervention should become necessary. There was a real danger that the Cuban government's opponents might provoke disorder in the hope of achieving what the liberals had achieved in 1906. The State Department's threats probably helped to avert trouble in the veterans affair, but they were less helpful in the Negro revolt, and in both cases they aroused suspicion and hostility in Cuba. The Cubans' apprehension that the American government was interpreting the Platt Amendment in a way that endangered their independence was increased by the free discussion of a possible third intervention in the American press and in Congress during both episodes, even though this discussion revealed little enthusiasm for intervention. This apprehension was intensified by the State Department's ill-judged interference in the Zapata Swamp affair.

In July 1912, Beaupré reported that the Cuban government was about to grant a concession for the reclamation of the Zapata Swamp, a marshy area covering approximately 1,000 square miles on the south coast of the island. He understood that the project would give away "incalculable millions" in timber and charcoal wood, and he considered it a "gigantic and barefaced steal" in which the President

[27] For the correspondence about the Negro revolt, see *Foreign Relations, 1912*, pp. 242–268.

and his friends undoubtedly had an interest.[28] There had been a "strong outburst of public opinion against the concession." The Minister urged that he be authorized to protest to President Gómez. He was told to say that the concession seemed "so clearly ill-advised a project, so improvident and reckless a waste of revenue and natural resources" that the American government was compelled to express "emphatic disapproval." [29]

When Beaupré conveyed this message in a curt personal note to Gómez, the President made an angry reply. He denied the accuracy of the Minister's information and asserted, in rather provocative language, that the Platt Amendment did not justify "systematic intervention" by the United States in Cuba's internal affairs.[30] Gómez was obviously referring not only to the Minister's recent note but to the position taken by the United States during the Negro revolt and in connection with the Ports Company. The State Department evidently felt that this raised an issue which it could not ignore and cabled Beaupré to tell Gómez that it was "making full reservation in the premises" pending "the announcement of its determination and purpose" in connection with the position that he had taken.[31]

On July 26, Knox discussed the Cuban problem at a Cabinet meeting and obtained approval for a draft note that would have asserted forcefully the right of the United States to give advice and the duty of Cuba to follow it. The draft described in some detail the improvident and improper actions of the Gómez administration and pointed out that the United States was seeking by its advice to avoid the necessity for intervention. Knox proposed to assert the right of the United States to take measures, "peaceful or otherwise," to correct bad conditions if the Cuban government did not follow its advice and to warn the Cubans that the American government reserved the right to cancel improper concessions if it should have to intervene.[32]

The note was not sent, possibly because despatches from Beaupré,

[28] Beaupré to Knox, July 5, 1912. 837.6112. Part of this dispatch is printed in *Foreign Relations, 1912,* p. 309.

[29] *Foreign Relations, 1912,* p. 311.

[30] *Ibid.,* p. 312.

[31] *Ibid.,* p. 313.

[32] The draft note is filed with 837.6112.

making new suggestions, were received on July 29. The Minister reported that the Cuban government was planning to seek a loan of $11,000,000 for public works, and he urged the United States to assume more control over Cuba's financial affairs. The first essential, he thought, was to supervise all public contracts, concessions, and other legislation. If the United States announced that it proposed to exercise "broad supervisory powers" and that its advice must be accepted, the Cubans would acquiesce, after an outburst of indignation. The Minister urged prompt action to save as much as possible from the "rapidly disintegrating financial and legislative wreck." [33]

The State Department was evidently not prepared to go so far as Beaupré suggested, but on August 15 Knox instructed the Minister to deliver a modified version of the note drafted three weeks before. "This Government believes" he wrote, "that the Cuban Government is pursuing a fiscal policy which will ultimately lead to a situation requiring intervention, and therefore, inasmuch as from the standpoint of both Governments intervention is not desired, it must be evident to the Cuban Government that the United States is not only justified but is acting in accordance with its rights and obligations in warning the Cuban Government against the course it is pursuing." The Secretary discussed the United States' right of intervention under the Platt Amendment, and continued "it is evident that in case intervention becomes necessary, questions will arise as to the legality of any concessions or fiscal measures which by their own consequences or in connection with general conditions in Cuba have made intervention necessary. The legality of such acts cannot be permitted to go unchallenged, and the United States will be at liberty in the event of intervention to take such steps as may be appropriate and necessary to undo and redress any wrongs which the Cuban people may have suffered at the hands of the Cuban Government."

Gómez, in his reply, made clear his disagreement with the State Department's views about the right of intervention but indicated that he would not continue the discussion. Meanwhile, on August 14, he had sent word to Washington that he would not approve the Zapata Swamp concession.

With the passage of time, it became apparent that Beaupré's criti-

[33] Beaupré to Knox, July 23, 1912, 837.51/167, 168.

cism of the concession had been based on misinformation. An American who was interested in the project told the Legation that the sole purpose was to reclaim land for agricultural use and that there was no valuable timber in the swamp. He offered, too, to accept changes in the concession which would define the boundaries of the grant and protect the rights of private owners. When Consul General Rodgers visited the swamp at the State Department's request, he reported that there was little or no valuable timber there and that the reclamation project would be a useful one.[34] The American government consequently withdraw its objections, and Gómez reinstated the concession with the amendments.

The Last Months of the Gómez Administration

The Ports Company and the Zapata Swamp affairs were but two of several cases where the American government attempted to curb Gómez' reckless economic policies. In June 1912, for example, Knox authorized Beaupré discreetly to oppose the grant of a monopoly for the importation of crude petroleum and petroleum products, which the Minister had described as particularly "iniquitous" and "injurious." [35] Frequently the persons interested in such projects were American citizens, and the projects were opposed by other American citizens whose interests would suffer.

The growing resentment of North American interference was reflected in the hostile attitude of some of the newspapers toward the American representatives at Habana. An unpleasant incident occurred in August 1912 when a reporter on one of the papers brutally assaulted Hugh Gibson, who was at the time Chargé d'Affaires. The State Department brusquely told the Cuban Minister at Washington that the assailant must be punished, and when the Cuban government failed to make a prompt formal apology Huntington Wilson told the Minister that "this Government is shocked at the seeming acquiescence of the Government of Cuba in the attacks upon the Legation, to be inferred by its silence thus far. . . ." President Gómez sent an appropriate telegram to President Taft on September 1, four days after the incident occurred, and a few

[34] His report, dated Nov. 20, 1912, is filed under 837.6112/14. There is a brief summary in Foreign Relations, 1912, p. 321.
[35] Beaupré to Knox, June 28, 1912, 637.003/187.

days later the Cuban Secretary of State prevailed on most of the Habana newspapers to desist from their campaign of abuse. Gibson's assailant was sentenced to two years and six months' imprisonment.

When it became known soon afterward that Gibson was being transferred to Brussels, some of the Habana newspapers suggested that the transfer was an indication of the State Department's dissatisfaction with his conduct. Huntington Wilson promptly wrote to Taft to urge that the transfer be canceled. The Legation at Habana, he said, had for the first time "forced itself into that strong position of authority and influence which our Legation in Cuba for so many years has lacked." [36] On October 13, the State Department announced that Gibson would remain at Habana because of his special familiarity with American interests in Cuba.

A portion of the Habana press continued to publish attacks on the American government and its representatives in Cuba, and on February 5, 1913, the newspaper *Cuba* started a series of scurrilous articles charging Beaupré and Gibson with gross corruption. Knox immediately instructed Beaupré to demand the prompt and "adequate" prosecution of those responsible. The Cuban government expressed regret and promised to act, but alleged that it was hampered in doing so because the nominal editor of the paper was a congressman who enjoyed immunity under the constitution. It asked the congress to consent to a prosecution, but Beaupré was doubtful about the outcome because the congress already had before it 35 or more requests to permit prosecutions of congressmen for crimes committed in Habana province alone. The Minister urged that a vigorous insistence on the punishment of the guilty parties would "render an important and much needed service to individuals and business interests in Cuba which have, by the ridiculous scope accorded to Congressional immunity, been subjected to every form of extortion, blackmail, and libel." [37] Knox and Huntington Wilson left the State Department while the matter was pending, and their successors seemed less inclined to make an issue of it; but before Beaupré left Habana in June the new administration in Cuba persuaded the offending newspaper to publish a retraction of its charges.

[36] H. Wilson to Taft, Oct. 4, 1912, Taft Papers, Library of Congress.
[37] Beaupré to Bryan, March 18, 1913, *Foreign Relations, 1913*, p. 411.

The Cuban Election of 1912

With relations between the two governments in so unsatisfactory a state, it was fortunate that the Cuban presidential elections, which were held in November 1912, went off without causing further complications. The outcome was a victory for the conservatives, who won because dissensions among the liberals deprived their candidate of the usual measure of official assistance. Gómez, who apparently hoped until late in the campaign to find some excuse for running for reelection himself, pretended to support the liberal nominee, Alfredo Zayas, but he did so with an obvious lack of enthusiasm. Governor Asbert, the powerful liberal boss in Habana province, and General Monteagudo, the commander in chief of the armed forces, both supported Mario García Menocal, who was again the conservative candidate. Both sides resorted to the intimidation and fraud that always marked Cuban elections, but there was no great amount of disorder. The State Department apparently did not involve itself in the contest in any way, though it asked the War and Navy Departments just before the voting to be ready for any necessary action if serious disorders should occur.[38]

The Amnesty Bill, 1912–1913

In December 1912, the Cuban House of Representatives passed an amnesty bill, ostensibly for the benefit of persons implicated in the Negro revolt but also covering many minor offenses and all crimes committed by public officials or employees before August 12, 1912. Amnesties for common crimes as well as for political offenses had frequently been granted in Cuba both under Estrada Palma and under Gómez, and they usually had strong political support because many of the persons in prison were there for crimes connected in one way or another with political activity. A particularly sweeping jail-delivery had been sponsored by Gómez at the beginning of his administration in 1909. The American government apparently did not object to the earlier amnesty laws but by the end of 1912 its "preventive policy" had developed to a point where it felt that it had to interfere if any legislation that it considered harmful was proposed.

[38] Secretary of State to Secretary of War and Secretary of Navy, Oct. 30, 1912, 837.00/942 a and b.

When the New York Life Insurance Company brought the matter to the State Department's attention in a letter which complained that the proposed law would put an end to the company's attempt to prosecute some persons who had been involved in a particularly brazen insurance fraud in 1909, the Department cabled the American Legation that it was "obviously undesirable to have any such legislation." [39] Some days later, Wilson instructed Beaupré to point out, orally, that an amnesty that included other than political offenders "would create an unfortunate impression that common crimes were allowed to go unpunished in Cuba, and that thus crime was not dealt with in the manner found necessary in all countries to the adequate protection of life, property, and individual liberty." [40] Gómez appeared to agree and promised that he would have the bill changed to apply only to political offenses, but Beaupré learned that the bill was still under consideration and was being amended so as to make it more rather than less objectionable.

On March 4, the day when the new administration took office in Washington, Beaupré telegraphed that the bill had passed congress. Secretary Bryan told him to express the hope that Gómez would see that the measure was limited to political offenses, but on March 6 Gómez told the Minister that he would sign the bill as it stood. When Beaupré reported that it would affect various American interests, including a contractor who was suing an official for embezzling funds,[41] he was instructed to say that the bill seemed "to be not only an injustice to the American citizens affected but also to effect such a withdrawal of due protection of property and individual liberty of Cuba as to excite this Government's concern" and to refer pointedly to the rights and obligations of the United States under the Platt Amendment. When Bryan was informed that Gómez had nevertheless signed the bill, he expressed regret and serious concern, and reserved the right to hold the Cuban government responsible for any injury to American citizens.

Gómez, like many other political leaders in the Caribbean, had evidently hoped that there would be a change in policy at Washington under the new administration. When he found that there had

[39] Dec. 23, 1912, 337.115 N 48/14.
[40] Wilson to Beaupré, Jan. 6, 1913, *Foreign Relations, 1913*, p. 355.
[41] Beaupré to Bryan, March 6, 1913, 837.13/7.

apparently been no change, he returned the amnesty bill to the congress and recommended that it be restricted to political offenses. The House of Representatives complied with his recommendation, but added clauses including crimes "committed in connection with or in consequence of political or electoral struggles." During the debate there was much evidence of resentment at the interference of the United States, and the Speaker and other members introduced resolutions calling for an investigation. When Beaupré reported this, Bryan showed his cable to the President, and on March 18 the State Department instructed the Minister not to press further objections to the amnesty bill. As it turned out, the Cuban congress took no final action on the bill at that session.[42]

Menocal's First Term

With the inauguration of Menocal in May 1913, there was a marked change in the tone of Cuban-American relations. The new President was a Cornell graduate who had become wealthy through his connection with American sugar interests. He was considered personally honest and unusually able, and Beaupré, in his despatches to the State Department, had predicted that he would be a better president than Gómez. It seemed unlikely that he would give the United States any reason to maintain the suspicious and critical attitude toward the Cuban government that had made friendly relations difficult during the preceding administration. He was working, too, with a new American Minister. William E. Gonzales, who succeeded Beaupré, was a newspaper editor from Columbia, South Carolina, who had had no previous diplomatic experience. He was himself of Cuban descent, though he spoke little Spanish. He was less aggressive than Beaupré, and less inclined to take a vigorous stand in controversial matters.

One of the first problems that arose after the change in administrations was a financial one. Work under the old McGivney and Rokeby contract for paving streets and laying sewers in Habana had finally got under way during Magoon's administration and had continued under Gómez, using funds from a $16,500,000 loan which had been authorized by Magoon and obtained by Gómez in 1909.

[42] The principal correspondence about the amnesty bill is in *Foreign Relations, 1913*, pp. 354ff.

In the latter part of 1912 the funds were running out. The State Department had repeatedly urged the completion of the work, but its dislike of Gómez' financial policies made it hesitate to approve the President's proposal for a large new loan to carry on and extend the operation. In January 1912, however, J. P. Morgan and Company were permitted to make a short term advance of $1,500,000, with the understanding that it would be refunded when the Cuban Congress approved a larger loan.

The United States agreed to a further advance of $1,000,000 by Morgan in July 1913, and on July 21 the Cuban Minister formally asked that the United States give its consent to a long-term loan of $15,000,000. The State Department asked for the full information about Cuba's financial situation which would be needed to decide whether the loan could be approved under the Platt Amendment. While the matter was under consideration, Speyer and Company, which had floated the 1909 loan, complained that the contracts with Morgan violated preferential rights granted under the 1909 contract with respect to any Cuban loans floated before 1919. When the complaint was rejected by Menocal, who asserted that Gómez had had no legal authority to accept the preferential clause, Bryan refused to support Speyer, telling Menocal through Gonzales that such clauses should not be inserted in loan contracts.

On September 5, after receiving the information that it had requested, the State Department gave its consent for the $15,000,000 loan. There was opposition to the project in the Cuban congress, and Menocal was compelled to reduce the amount to $10,000,000 in order to obtain its approval. The bonds, with a 5-percent coupon, were sold to J. P. Morgan and Company at 94 after Speyer had refused to submit a bid. It is interesting to note that the State Department apparently approved the transaction without the careful examination of the contract upon which Knox had insisted in the case of loans to other Caribbean countries.[43]

A new dispute, involving the Cuban Ports Company, caused somewhat more trouble. Menocal canceled the company's concession soon after he took office, and when the government began to collect the port dues the company was unable to maintain the service of the bonds which it had sold in England. Both the company and the

[43] The correspondence about this loan is in file 837.51.

bondholders appealed to the Cuban courts. The State Department urged a compromise settlement, and Menocal professed a willingness to accept one, but could not obtain approval in the congress for the plan that he suggested. After the courts decided against the company, the State Department pressed more vigorously for a settlement, because it wished to head off a diplomatic controversy between Cuba and Great Britain, but for some time it could obtain no satisfaction. Finally, in July 1917, Menocal pushed through the congress a plan by which the Cuban government exchanged its own 5-percent bonds at par for those of the company, and allowed the company's stockholders to retain its assets, which included a large amount of valuable real estate.[44]

The Election of 1916

The first crisis that confronted the Wilson administration in Cuba arose when Menocal brought about his own reelection in 1916. By the end of his first term, the President's position was weaker than it had been in 1912, partly beecause he had lost the support of the Habana liberals led by Governor Asbert. Asbert and a congressman had murdered the chief of police of Habana in 1913, and the Governor's followers had been angered and surprised when Menocal did nothing to prevent his conviction and imprisonment. The President's opponents obtained a majority in Congress in 1914, and in 1916 they patched up their factional quarrels and nominated Alfredo Zayas for the presidency. Many conservatives also opposed Menocal, but he was able to obtain the conservative nomination by a rather questionable manipulation of the party convention.

The State Department apparently did not anticipate any serious trouble. Lansing expressed his own views about the election in a letter he wrote to Wilson's private secretary in May 1916, when a Habana newspaper asked the President for a statement to be published in a special number on Cuba's independence day. Menocal, he said, did not seem to have the political support needed to assure his reelection, but he was well-disposed to the United States and would probably be able to accomplish much that would be useful if he had a second term. The opposition were of a "different calibre," and some of them were already making revolutionary threats. Lansing advised

[44] *Foreign Relations, 1917*, pp. 431–456.

the President to send a letter urging the Cubans to uphold the constitutional authority and to maintain order.[45]

Gonzales informed the State Department three months later that "the prospect for peaceful elections and of abidance by the result has never been brighter on the eve of any presidential election since the first one in 1902." He was sure that there would be no uprising like that of 1906.[46] There was, however, at least the usual amount of violence during the campaign. Both parties were responsible, and conservative writers pointed to the fact that 42 of their partisans were killed, and only 7 liberals, as evidence of the government's impartiality.[47] There was also much fraud on election day, November 1, for it was evident that the number of votes cast was greater than any possible number of bona fide voters. Here, too, both sides seem to have been to blame.

It seemed certain at first that Zayas had been elected, but within a day or two the government began to intercept the returns sent from the local electoral boards to the central board at Habana and to withhold them from publication. The liberals were alarmed and excited, and the American Chargé d'Affaires reported on November 7 that there would be trouble if Menocal went through with his apparent plan to steal the election. He suggested that the United States interfere, and if necessary offer its good offices for an amicable settlement,[48] but Lansing did not consider the time "opportune" for such action. Gonzales, who was in Washington, doubted that there would be a serious revolt and questioned the advisability of undertaking to insure honest elections and investigate frauds in Cuba. He pointed out that American intervention at the inception of a revolution would encourage an uprising by the losing side in every election, and he thought that the Cuban government should have an opportunity to show that it could put down disorders by itself.[49] The Minister's recommendations suggested that he was not particularly concerned about the working of democracy in Cuba, but there was much logic in what he said.

For a time it seemed probable that the Cubans would settle the

[45] Lansing to Tumulty, May 4, 1916, 837.00/1784.
[46] Gonzales to Lansing, Aug. 3, 1916, 837.00/1028.
[47] Chapman, *History of the Cuban Republic*, p. 352.
[48] Scholle to Lansing, Nov. 7, 1916, 837.00/1039.
[49] Gonzales' memorandum of Nov. 9, 1916, 837.00/1044.

matter in an orderly way. The Central Electoral Board upheld many of the liberals' protests, and the Cuban Supreme Court, on January 12, 1917, sustained the board's action. As the result of these decisions, each side was given the electoral vote of two provinces, and new elections were ordered in a few districts in each of the other two: in Santa Clara on February 14 and in Oriente some days later.

A victory in either province would give the liberals a majority of the electoral vote. In Oriente, the conservatives had a small majority in the first election, but in Santa Clara they could win only if the new election in six precincts, containing about 2,400 registered voters, gave them enough votes to overcome a liberal majority of 1,164 in the rest of the province. Since the voters in the six precincts had been rather equally divided between the parties in the past, it seemed impossible for the conservatives to win unless they resorted to grossly unfair tactics. After what the government had already done, however, the liberals were sure that it would resort to unfair tactics.

When Gonzales returned to Cuba he apparently changed his ideas about the seriousness of the situation. The liberals were charging that Menocal was sending troops into the districts where the new elections were to be held and generally endeavoring to intimidate the voters. Gonzales reported on January 22 that the President seemed ready to do anything necessary to win the election, and that his conduct might well bring on a revolution worse that than of 1906. Even if it did not, the Minister thought that Menocal's success by such methods would be "an enduring calamity to Cuba." [50]

The State Department authorized Gonzales to say informally that the American government was interested in an orderly settlement and would regret any action that might lead to disturbances; and on February 10 Lansing issued a long statement, to be published in Cuba, expressing the interest of the United States in the way in which the Santa Clara elections would be carried out. He appealed to Cuban patriotism to effect a peaceful solution and said that the American government was "anxious that all the parties should know that their course is being followed by the United States with the closest observance and in the confident expectation that the means

[50] *Foreign Relations, 1917*, p. 350. Most of the important correspondence about the 1917 revolution will be found in this volume.

provided for by the Cuban constitution and the laws enacted for this very purpose will bring as a logical result a satisfactory and peaceable settlement of the present difficulties." At the same time, Gonzales was instructed to tell Menocal personally that the United States was confident that the President would use every means to prevent any disturbance and that it was "observing with the closest scrutiny every act of each of the parties which might indicate intimidating action by armed forces or illegal pressure exerted by the military or the police at the time of elections." As first drafted this message contained a threat that recognition might be withheld if the American government's views were not heeded, but this was crossed out before the telegram was signed.[51]

The American government's action came too late, for the liberals had started a revolution on February 11. Ex-President Gómez, who assumed the leadership, expected to have the support of the Cuban army, which had been created during his administration. He did win over a large part of the troops in the eastern part of the island, but those at Habana and in the western part of the island generally remained loyal to the government. Menocal's energy and military ability made the situation quite different from that which had confronted Estrada Palma in 1906.

On February 13 Lansing instructed Gonzales to issue another statement expressing the seriousness with which the United States viewed the resort to violence and emphasizing the American government's policy of withholding recognition from governments coming into power through revolution. On the same day he told Gonzales to urge that the elections in Santa Clara be postponed until peace was restored, but Menocal insisted that only the Central Electoral Board could order a postponement and that the board had refused to do so. The Santa Clara elections were held on February 14, as planned, and gave the conservative candidates 2,427 votes and the liberals 33.[52] The new elections in Oriente had to be postponed because the insurgents had occupied Santiago.

At the outbreak of the war, the United States demonstrated its support of Menocal by selling him 10,000 rifles and 2,000,000 cartridges, and on February 18, after consulting the President, Lansing instructed Gonzales to make a public statement saying:

[51] See the original of the telegram, 837.00/1059.
[52] Riera, *Cuba Política, 1899–1955* (Habana, 1955), p. 223.

1. The Government of the United States supports and sustains the Constitutional Government of the Republic of Cuba.

2. The armed revolt against the Constitutional Government of Cuba is considered by the Government of the United States as a lawless and unconstitutional act and will not be countenanced.

3. The leaders of the revolt will be held responsible for injury to foreign nationals and for destruction of foreign property.

4. The Government of the United States will give careful consideration to its future attitude towards those persons connected with and concerned in the present disturbance of peace in the Republic of Cuba.

When they learned of the American government's attitude, many liberals decided not to join the revolution, and those already under arms were discouraged. Gonzales reported on February 25 that the expected general uprising had failed to materialize and that the great bulk of the army had remained loyal. In the little fighting that had occurred, the government had suffered no reverses. Nevertheless, he said, transportation in Camaguey and Oriente provinces was paralyzed, and the rebels held Santiago. American lives and property were still in danger. Though Gonzales thought personally that Gómez was "as likely to fly from the country as resort to destruction" if he were defeated, most people in Cuba thought that the rebels would resort to a systematic destruction of sugar mills and cane in order to force the United States to intervene. If they did, only very prompt action by the American government could prevent "huge material losses."

Though its statement of February 18 seemed to indicate that Menocal would have its unqualified support, the American government could not but feel that a compromise settlement would be preferable to a continuation of the war. The danger to Americans and other foreigners would increase rather than decrease if the rebel armies were defeated and broken up into irresponsible bands of guerrillas. The State Department was already receiving many pleas for protection and was evidently not satisfied with Menocal's response to its insistent demands that he provide more adequate protection. Furthermore, the American government did not intend simply to help Menocal to stay in office as the result of a crooked election. It had little sympathy for the rebels, but it was aware that the great majority of the liberals, including Zayas himself, were not taking part in the revolt.

President Wilson suggested the possibility of mediation when he replied on February 23 to a telegram from the Chamber of Commerce of Santiago begging him to use his good offices to restore peace. The United States, Wilson said, could have no communication with the leaders of the rebellion while they continued to fight. It would "exert every means in its power as the friend of the Cuban Republic" to bring about the settlement of disputes through constitutional methods, but could take no further steps until the rebels laid down their arms. On March 1 Lansing asked Gonzales to give Menocal a copy of this message. He instructed the Minister to congratulate the President on the "crushing" of the rebellion and to offer the good offices of the United States for a settlement that would prevent further loss of life and property.

To make these good offices effective, Lansing urged Menocal to issue a proclamation promising that there would be a general amnesty and that new elections would be held in Santa Clara and Oriente as soon as order was restored. Gonzales was told that the matter was "of great urgency," and that he should press for immediate compliance with Lansing's suggestion, pointing out that the destruction of property that had already occurred and that was bound to result from the continuation of guerrilla warfare after the dispersal of the larger insurgent bands would probably force the United States "to take such action as might destroy the moral effect of the Constitutional Government's successes."

Menocal flatly rejected this proposal. "This is not a revolution of the people," he wrote, "but is almost wholly a military sedition of officers who have been disloyal to the Government. . . ." To negotiate about an "indiscriminate pardon" would disastrously affect the morale of the loyal troops. Furthermore, the suggestions about the holding of elections were "inconsistent with the facts." The elections in Santa Clara had already taken place, and the elections in Oriente would be held as soon as the government regained control of Santiago. Gonzales also opposed any compromise with the rebels, and it seems unlikely that he urged the proposal on Menocal with any vigor. He asserted that he had received no complaints about the elections in Santa Clara and that if there were complaints they should be considered by the Supreme Court. In view of his attitude and Menocal's, the State Department rather reluctantly dropped its plan, though it urged Menocal at least to proceed with the elections in Oriente province after peace was restored.

On March 10 Lansing made another proposal. Gonzales had reported that Menocal, in discussing the earlier offer of mediation, had said that he would be willing to have General Crowder investigate and pass on the whole electoral question. The President had probably not meant this statement to be taken seriously, but Lansing now told Gonzales to say that the President and the Secretary of State had suggested that peace might be sooner restored if General Crowder and "other representative Americans" were invited to investigate and adjust "the election question." Menocal rejected this proposal also because he thought that the liberals would regard its adoption as a moral victory for them.[53]

The American government's congratulations on the crushing of the rebellion had been somewhat premature, for the fighting continued in Camaguey and Oriente provinces. The end was brought nearer when José Miguel Gómez and his staff were captured on March 7, but other leaders remained in the field. The situation was particularly bad in Oriente, where many of the largest American sugar properties were situated, and the danger to these was increased by the rebels' growing resentment at the policy of the United States.

This resentment increased after the American naval commanders permitted Menocal's forces to occupy Santiago in March. The rebels had occupied that city at the beginning of the revolution and had attempted to close the harbor by sinking two merchant ships in its narrow mouth. An American naval officer prevented this action, which would have kept the nearby sugar mills from obtaining coal and other necessary supplies; and American forces were landed at Santiago and Guantánamo and a few other ports to maintain order. Their commanders insisted that there be no fighting in Santiago[54] and that the rebels withdraw their forces from the city, but they did not interfere with its administration by the revolutionary civil authorities. Both the naval commanders and the American Consul seem to have sympathized rather openly with the liberals in

[53] Gonzales to Lansing, March 12, 1917, 837.00/1208.
[54] Navy Dept. to State Dept., March 17, 1917, 837.00/1478.

their desire for American intervention to settle the electoral questions, and their attitude distressed Gonzales, who thought that any compromise with rebels in arms would set a vicious precedent.[55] On March 16, however, the naval commanders permitted Menocal's forces to reoccupy Santiago. Their action seems to have been proper, but the revolutionary leaders and many of their followers felt that they had been betrayed.[56]

The State Department and the Legation at Habana had maintained their refusal to approve any concessions to rebels under arms even though their policy made the situation of Americans in Cuba more precarious, but they could not be indifferent to the danger that confronted Americans and their property. From the beginning of the revolt, the State Department had been beset by urgent demands for protection, and it had pressed Menocal more and more vigorously to take effective action to prevent injury to foreigners and their property. On March 13, Gonzales had been instructed to ask Menocal whether he realized how much American and other foreign property was being destroyed and whether he could furnish adequate protection, and to say that "the action of this government is contingent upon his reply to these questions." As the situation grew worse, the State Department considered the possibility of armed intervention to restore order, but was restrained by the fear that the landing of troops would be the signal for still more destruction of American property.

Gonzales and Menocal continued to be troubled by the actions of some of the American naval commanders, who still seemed inclined to listen to the rebels' pleas for intervention or mediation by the United States. On March 23, the Minister reported that persistent rumors of American intervention were again circulating in Habana and suggested that another "unequivocal declaration" of the State Department's policy might result in the immediate collapse of the revolution. Lansing authorized him to publish a statement that the United States was supporting the constitutional government and would have no communication with the rebels until they laid down their arms. This may have further discouraged the liberal leaders, who could by this time have had little hope of vic-

---

[55] This attitude is evident in several of Gonzales' dispatches.
[56] Chapman, *History of the Cuban Republic*, pp. 377–379.

tory. At any rate, many of the revolutionary bands surrendered during the next four weeks, and on April 21 the government's forces won a decisive victory in Camaguey province. A number of guerrilla bands continued to terrorize the countryside in Oriente, but the revolution was no longer a formidable political movement.

Although some of the revolutionary leaders were condemned to death, Menocal did not permit any of them to be executed. After the restoration of peace, however, many former rebels are said to have been murdered by personal or political enemies with the apparent connivance of public officials.[57] At Washington, there was much interest in what might happen to Gómez. Several members of Congress asked Wilson or Lansing to intercede on his behalf, and in October 1917 Lansing cabled privately to the Cuban Foreign Minister to suggest that his trial be postponed until the end of the World War in the interest of Cuban unity. The Minister replied that the trial could not take place for several months at the earliest, and that in the meantime Gómez was being allowed to live in his own house, though still under arrest.[58] Gómez and the other participants in the revolution were freed under a general amnesty enacted in March 1918.

The postponed partial elections were held in Oriente on April 9, but both parties seem to have regarded them as a mere matter of form. Gonzales did not even report how they came out. When the Cuban congress met on May 7, enough liberal members attended to make a quorum, and Menocal was duly declared elected for a second term. Gonzales reported that there were no speeches "or semblance of bad feeling." Many of the liberal politicians evidently thought it better to dissociate themselves as far as possible from the rebellion. Zayas himself had withdrawn from the movement when it became clear that it was not likely to succeed and had been living in Habana.

The American government could hardly feel that its policy with respect to the election and the revolution had been a complete success. It had shown the liberals that they could not provoke intervention by revolting and destroying property, and that political

[57] Consul General Morgan to Herbert Hoover, Aug. 27, 1917, 817.61351/32.

[58] Tumulty to Lansing, Oct 3, 1917, and Lansing to Gonzales Oct. 4, 837.00/1422. Gonzales to Lansing, personal, Oct. 12, 837.00/1438.

disputes in Cuba must be settled by legal means and not by force; but the result had been to keep Menocal in office after an election won by questionable methods. The liberals were of course at fault in resorting to rebellion when legal means of asserting their rights were still open to them. The partial elections that would have determined the outcome had not been held, and any complaints about the way in which they were held could have been taken to the electoral boards and the Supreme Court, which had already demonstrated their impartiality. On the other hand, the Cuban government's attitude and conduct gave the liberals some reason to suppose that it would be futile to pursue their legal remedies. The American government had recognized this in its proposals for mediation, and several of the more prominent American businessmen in Cuba had urged that the best way to restore peace would be to insist on a fair settlement of the electoral question.[59] A fair settlement, however, could only have been attained if the matter had been pushed much more vigorously from Washington and if the State Department's proposals had been supported by vigorous and competent diplomacy in Habana. They clearly did not get effective support from Gonzales, who was convinced that any concession to the insurgents would be a mistake.

Cuba and the First World War

Before the end of the "Revolution of February" both the United States and Cuba declared war on Germany, and the depredations of the guerrilla bands that continued to operate after the principal revolutionary leaders surrendered took on the aspect of efforts to help the common enemy. The State Department emphasized this in a statement that was published on May 15, expressing gratification at Cuba's declaration of war and urging the rebels to lay aside internal political quarrels "in the face of the grave international danger." It said that the United States and the Allied Powers must "depend to a large extent upon the sugar production of Cuba" and warned those still under arms that disturbances that interfered with

[59] See, for example, Stabler's memorandum of March 12, 1917, about his talk with Rionda, 837.00/1246; J. G. White's letter of March 12 to Henry Morgenthau, 837.00/1231; and Steinhart's opinion as reported by J. F. Dulles in the latter's memorandum of Feb. 27, 1917, 837.00/1222.

production must be considered as hostile acts. It might be necessary for the United States to regard those who did not immediately return to their allegiance as enemies and to deal with them accordingly.

Though Menocal and Gonzales insisted that the situation was rapidly clearing up, reports from some of the American consuls and naval officers showed that there was still much disorder in the eastern part of the island. Consul General Henry N. Morgan, who was sent to Cuba in May as a representative of the National Council of Defense, reported that the lack of protection was discouraging the planters from clearing areas where cane had been burned, and that the coming year's sugar crop would be greatly reduced. He urged that more marines be sent to Cuba to restore confidence.[60] Menocal insisted that this was unnecessary, but early in July, after consulting President Wilson,[61] Lansing instructed Gonzales to take the matter up again. The Minister was to explain that the sugar situation was very serious and that the United States wished to send troops to Cuba as a war measure, and with Menocal's full understanding. Lansing pointed out, however, that the United States had a right under treaty arrangements to send troops to Guantánamo at any time and that he was not establishing a precedent by asking Menocal's permission. Menocal at once gave his consent and offered to provide areas for training camps in places outside of Guantánamo if the United States wished to train its forces in a warm climate. The 2,000–3,000 marines who came to Cuba, some of whom remained in Oriente and Camaguey provinces throughout the remainder of the Wilson administration, were consequently there ostensibly for training, at the invitation of the Cuban government. Their presence did much to stabilize the situation. Despite the widespread efforts of German agents to cause the burning of cane in the fields, the prospect for the 1917–1918 crop rapidly improved.

Sugar beet production had been greatly reduced in Europe, and other supplies, including the North American beet and cane crops, fell far short of meeting the needs of the United States and its allies. There was in fact reason to fear that the supply would be inadequate even with good crops in Cuba. The Allied Powers consequently set

[60] Telegram of May 30, 1917, 837.61351/12.
[61] Lansing to Wilson, July 5, 1917, 837.00/1394.

up an International Sugar Commission, to control the distribution of sugar among them. To protect the American consumer, the United States Food Administration made an agreement with American refiners to limit the margin between the cost of raw and the selling price of refined sugar. It also proposed to fix the price of Cuban raw sugar, which determined the price of all sugar in the American market, by agreement with the Cuban government and the planters.

The Cubans were willing to cooperate, but there was naturally disagreement as to what would be a fair price. The cost of production varied greatly from mill to mill. Consul General Morgan, who was the Food Administrator's representative in Cuba, thought that the average was not less than 4¾ cents per pound and that any price under 5½ cents might discourage future production.[62] This estimate was evidently high, because the planters asked 5 cents and the Cuban government was willing to accept any price between 4¾ and 5.[63] British representatives on the International Sugar Commission, however, insisted that 4½ cents would be adequate, because they had been buying South American and other West Indian sugar at this price or less.[64] They finally agreed reluctantly that the Cuban planters be offered 4.60.

Herbert Hoover, the Food Administrator, did not wish to set a precedent of governmental price-fixing for imports, and he took the position that the price of sugar should be determined between the buyers and sellers, the buyers being a committee of American refiners working with the International Sugar Commission. The Cuban Minister, however, pointed out that his government and the planters were in fact dealing with the allied governments, and he continued to ask the State Department's assistance in obtaining a price of 4¾ cents. President Wilson supported Hoover in his position that the matter should not be dealt with through diplomatic channels,[65] and soon afterward the Cubans accepted the price of 4.60 for the 1917–1918 crop. The following year the entire 1918–1919 crop was purchased by the United States Sugar Equalization Board at a price of 5½ cents.

[62] Morgan to Lansing, Sept. 4, 1917, 837.61351/35.
[63] H. de Mesa to the Federal Food Commission, Oct. 22, 1917, 837.61351/50; De Céspedes to Lansing, Oct. 26, 1917, *Foreign Relations, 1918*, p. 345.
[64] See Stabler's memorandum of Nov. 19, 1917, 837.61351/58.
[65] Wilson to Lansing, Nov. 24, 1917, 837.61351/60.

Some Cubans complained that the control of the market by the United States deprived them of the very great profits which they might have made if they had been left free to sell sugar for what it would bring, but it is hard to see that they were unfairly treated. The United States was compelled to control other foods and to control shipping during the war, and the Cubans would have been in desperate straits if the American government had not allocated to them the supplies they needed and the ships to carry them. The American government also helped them to deal with serious difficulties that arose in connection with the storage of sugar awaiting export and the financing of the harvest. The prices paid for sugar were high enough to give the industry a substantial profit and to encourage a very large increase in production.

While the purchase of the 1917–1918 crop was being negotiated, Menocal sent a commission to Washington to ask a $15,000,000 war loan from the United States Treasury. The Treasury Department was sympathetic to the proposal, but Lansing pointed out that the requirements of the Platt Amendment must be satisfied, and he thought too that two pending controversial matters ought to be settled before the loan was granted. One of these was the Ports Company matter, which was then still pending, and the other the claims of the American-owned Cuba Railroad Company for damages suffered during the revolution. The State Department considered it urgent that a part of this company's claim be paid so that it could rehabilitate its line in time to haul the approaching sugar crop. The Treasury Department agreed to delay action on the loan until the State Department should be satisfied on these points.[66]

When John Foster Dulles discussed the matter with the Cuban representatives on August 29, he mentioned only the need for more adequate information about Cuba's financial situation and the American government's interest in the rehabilitation of the Cuba railroad. He said that the United States would probably wish to supervise the expenditure of funds by the railroad to make sure that they were used for the benefit of the entire island and not solely to benefit the railroad itself or certain favored companies. Menocal was annoyed and hurt when he learned of the State Department's conditions. He had already loaned the railroad company $1,000,000, but he was

[66] Lansing to McAdoo, Aug. 13, 1917, *Foreign Relations, 1918*, p. 298.

unwilling to acknowledge claims for damages without further investigation, and he resented the suggestion that the American government should supervise the work of rehabilitation. Nevertheless he agreed some days later to an arrangement that Gonzales and the president of the railroad company considered satisfactory.

Consequently, after the Bureau of Insular Affairs had examined the data submitted by the Cuban government and reported that a loan could be approved under the Platt Amendment, provided that the current expenditures of the Cuban government were not increased, the State Department formally gave its consent to the loan. It was evidently satisfied by this time that the Ports Company matter would be settled, as it was in fact settled early in October. Soon, however, a new difficulty arose. The act of Congress under which the United States made war loans required that the interest rate must be increased if the United States should ever have to pay a higher rate on its own obligations, whereas the Cuban law authorizing a bond issue stipulated a 6-percent rate. The Treasury Department suggested that the Cuban law be amended, but on October 29 the Cuban Minister told the State Department that this was impossible.

Since the Cuban government had already promised the railroad company about $3,000,000 and had arranged to buy a considerable amount of material from the United States Navy for coast defenses, both the Treasury and the State Department thought that there was a moral obligation to provide funds for these commitments. McAdoo consequently now proposed to arrange a loan on a different basis and to give the Cuban government a lesser amount, perhaps $5,000,-000 against demand notes which would be secured by bonds. Gonzales was instructed to discuss this idea with Menocal and to find out how much Cuba needed. For some months, however, the Cuban government seemed to show little interest in the matter, and in January the president of the Cuba railroad reported that he had to suspend work on the line for lack of funds.[67] Gonzales finally reported on February 18, 1918, that Menocal again requested a loan of $15,-000,000.

The Treasury Department set up a credit for $15,000,000 and, after some delay caused by legal technicalities, advanced $5,000,000

[67] Whigham to Stabler, Jan. 9, 1918, 837.51/286.

to the Cuban government on March 17. It made another advance on November 4, 1918, but only after the State Department had demanded much additional information from Habana and had made it clear that it was watching the Cuban government's financial operations with increasing concern. General McIntyre of the Bureau of Insular Affairs had called attention to what he thought were excessive expenditures for the army and navy, and on August 29 Lansing approved a memorandum by the Solicitor of the State Department urging that such expenditures should not be encouraged and that the Cuban government should be made to feel that it could not get money from the United States without searching inquiry.[68] No further advances were made.

The State Department's attitude revealed its growing dissatisfaction with Menocal's conduct of the Cuban government. Although the President perhaps did not take graft himself, he was surrounded by associates and relatives whose morals seemed little better than those of their liberal predecessors. Gonzales had reported as early as November 1915 that the government was making no effort to keep expenses within its income and that there was much corruption and favoritism. He thought that the United States might sooner or later have to exert an influence to discourage excessive expenditures.[69] After 1917 prosperity caused by good sugar prices had increased the government's income and had encouraged greater waste and extravagance. The national lottery, where a few thousand favored persons could buy tickets from the government and sell them at a profit, because the public was willing to pay more than the legal price, was being used to buy political support in both parties. The State Department's relations with Menocal were still far more friendly than its relations with Gómez had been, but there was a growing realization in Washington that the situation in Cuba was far from satisfactory.

The Cuban Election of 1920

The darkest cloud on the Cuban horizon at the end of the European war was the probability that there would be trouble if the liberals were again deprived of the presidency by a crooked election

[68] 837.51/318.
[69] Gonzales to Lansing, Nov. 26, 1915, 837.51/242.

in 1920. The American government could not afford to permit a repetition of the events of 1916–1917. However much it disliked the principal liberal leaders, whom it had denounced for their rebellion and who were considered hostile to the United States, it felt that it had an obligation to see that they had fair play. The State Department had begun to work on the problem nearly two years before the election. When Gonzales was in Washington late in 1918, Polk and Stabler discussed it with him and instructed him to tell Menocal that the United States felt that the electoral laws must be amended and that there should be a new census which would make it possible to correct the registers of voters. The Minister was to endeavor to persuade Menocal to invite the United States to send a commission to Cuba to supervise the elections and to persuade him to issue a public statement promising a free and fair vote. Gonzales was to have made these representations on his return to his post, but the receipt of a telegram from the Naval attaché at Habana, saying that serious trouble could be expected within the next few days, led the State Department to instruct the Chargé d'Affaires on January 15, 1919, to present the matter at once. He did so in a formal note to the Minister of Foreign Affairs, and after Gonzales returned the Legation received a formal reply, saying that Menocal had already endeavored to have the electoral law amended and to have a new census but had been blocked by his opponents in congress. The President was confident, however, that he could obtain the desired reforms at the forthcoming session of congress, and he declined the offer of an American commission to supervise the elections.[70]

The State Department refused to drop the matter. It said that it regarded the "situation throughout Cuba as extremely serious and dangerous to best interests of United States and Allies" and told Gonzales to intimate that the United States could not support governments that denied free elections. The Minister persuaded Menocal to reverse his position, and on February 13 the Legation transmitted an invitation to General E. H. Crowder to come to Cuba to assist in formulating amendments to the electoral law.

[70] Except where otherwise indicated documents referred to in this section are printed in *Foreign Relations, 1919*, Vol. II, pp. 1–84, and in *Foreign Relations, 1920*, Vol. II, pp. 1–43.

General Crowder was already known and respected in Cuba because of his work as chairman of the Advisory Commission during the American occupation of 1906–1909. He had been largely responsible for the existing Cuban electoral law and had directed its application in the election of 1908. He now went to Habana with added prestige from his service as Provost Marshal General of the United States during the World War. After his arrival on March 18, he made a careful study of the electoral evils that had developed since 1909 and then drew up a series of reform measures, working in consultation with a bi-partisan group representing both houses of the Cuban congress. All of these were enacted into law before his departure on August 8.

The most conspicuous feature of the customary electoral procedure was the outrageous padding of the registers of voters. In each recent election, the number of votes cast had exceeded, and often greatly exceeded, the number of adult male citizens. The local boards had failed to remove from the registers the names of deceased or absent persons, and had permitted the addition of many fraudulent names. This often resulted from collusion between representatives of the political parties, who were interested in maintaining the apparent following of their own factions at the expense of rival groups in the same party. Local conservative and liberal bosses were often the more willing to work together because the system of proportional representation, under which congressmen and some other officials were elected at large in the province or municipality rather than by districts, had encouraged the fraudulent trading and counting of votes. A new census taken with the help of American experts made possible the revision of the electoral registers and the new code made provision for checking the registers in any case where the number of names seemed to exceed the probable number of qualified voters.

The new electoral law contained several other provisions designed to make the electoral machinery more impartial and efficient and to prevent abuses in canvassing the vote. One of the most important regulated the organization and required the periodic reorganization of the political parties. Crowder found that there had been little change since 1908 in the membership of the groups that had been making nominations for national, provincial, and municipal offices—a situation that deprived the rank and file of any control over party affairs and encouraged corrupt deals between the bosses.

The provisions of the electoral law were reinforced by other laws which Crowder helped to draft. One of these sought to assure the tenure and the independence of the municipal judges, who were to be the presidents of the municipal electoral boards, and another provided that pardons should be granted only after careful investigation and with adequate publicity. Criminals were often released before elections, either to obtain the votes of their friends or because the violence that characterized local political contests made their talents useful; and the members of the winning party, at least, could commit criminal offenses with impunity during the election because they could expect to be pardoned if convicted.

No one could suppose that the new laws, by themselves, would assure a free vote, but Crowder thought that they would achieve their purpose if they were honestly applied. He hoped that the Cuban courts could deal with any violations that occurred. To prevent a recurrence of the abuses that had marked recent elections, he suggested in his report to the Secretary of State that the American Legation closely supervise the procedure under the new code. The State Department, after considering his report, felt that something more would be needed. On October 23, 1919, it instructed Gonzales to present to Menocal "in a forceful manner" a suggestion that he ask Crowder to supervise the approaching presidential election, working through the Cuban agencies provided for in the law. The Department pointed out that the liberals were apparently going to demand some sort of outside supervision, and that apparently there was "no way to escape some such supervision, without the alternative of facing serious political disturbances or a condition equally serious, as a result of failure to supervise."

Gonzales, who was about to leave Cuba for his new post as Ambassador to Peru, obviously did not press the State Department's suggestion with any enthusiasm. He was sure before he presented it that Menocal would turn it down. Gonzales himself had always opposed any idea of electoral supervision. "My view," he wrote, "is positive that if Cuba cannot hold fairly honest elections under the new electoral laws, it would be much preferable frankly to take over the government for a long period and institute the many reforms possible under such conditions, than to undertake the doubtful, endless and thankless task of guaranteeing honest elections. That form of invasion of sovereignty promises little for the future of this country." The Minister felt that the liberals were entitled to no sympathy after their own fraudulent conduct in the 1916 elections and their subsequent resort to revolution, and he pointed out that no one could speak for the various factions into which the party was divided.

Under these circumstances it is not surprising that Menocal refused to accept the suggestion. He also turned down Gonzales' suggestion that he invite Crowder simply to observe how the electoral law was carried out. He would have been willing to do so, he said, but for the fact that Fernando Ortiz, a liberal with whom some officials of the State Department had been talking, had publicly announced that Crowder was coming to supervise the election. After this, the General's arrival in any capacity could only strengthen the position of the Gómez wing of the liberal party, which Ortiz represented.

The State Department did not press its suggestion. On December 1, it told Gonzales to inform Menocal that it had received with pleasure his assurance that the electoral law "would be carried out not only to the letter but in the spirit in which it was drafted" and his assurance that he was "fully cognizant of the responsibility which he assumes." General Crowder, it added, was pleased that it would be unnecessary for him to go to Cuba in connection with the elections. When the liberals continued to assert that the United States would supervise the elections, Gonzales suggested that a statement of the Department's attitude "might be beneficial." Lansing asked him to outline a statement "which, in view of Department's present attitude, would not be construed as injuring any political party," but on December 8, probably before he received this cable, the Minister issued a statement of his own saying that reports about American supervision were entirely without foundation. The State Department rebuked him [71] but the statement could not be recalled.

Up to the end of 1919 neither party had united behind a candidate. Both had planned to hold their nominating conventions in May of that year, but Crowder, with vigorous support from the

[71] Adee to Gonzales, Dec. 29, 1919, 837.00/1600.

State Department, had insisted that the electoral law require the nominations to be made after January 1, 1920, and by party conventions reorganized in accord with the law. The conservatives postponed their meeting in deference to Crowder's views, but the liberals met on May 10 as planned. Most of Zayas' followers, however, refused to attend when it became evident that the Gómez faction would be in control.

The enactment of the electoral law with the provision that Crowder advocated invalidated Gómez' nomination, but he still seemed to have the support of a majority in the party. Many liberals were disgusted with Zayas' equivocal position during the 1917 revolution and were unwilling to support him even though they feared that the United States might oppose Gómez' candidacy. Crowder, before he went to Cuba, had urged that the United States take a definite position on this question and had suggested that it should express disapproval of Gómez, both because of his corrupt conduct while president and because of his leadership in the revolution.[72] But the State Department apparently decided to make no statement. By the fall of 1919 the liberals could see that the American government was not going to veto the ex-President's candidacy.

The conservatives seemed to have no very strong candidate. Menocal at first supported General Rafael Montalvo, but it was clear that Montalvo did not have a great deal of following. In January 1920, the American Chargé d'Affaires, after Gonzales' departure, reported that Menocal would welcome a confidential hint from the United States before deciding definitely on a candidate, but Lansing replied that the United States' attitude toward the election made it inadvisable to express any opinion. He added that the State Department expected Menocal to carry out the electoral law in letter and spirit.[73] Soon afterward the conservatives decided that the only way to defeat Gómez, whom they hated, was to form a coalition with the Zayas liberals. This required a change in the electoral law which had sought to prevent one of the commoner forms of corrupt political deals by forbidding a candidate to appear on the ticket of more than one party.

[72] See H. Johnson's memorandum to Polk, June 12, 1919, 837.51/339.
[73] Williamson to Lansing, Jan. 1, and Lansing to Williamson, Jan. 12, 1920, 837.00/1612.

Boaz Long, who succeeded Gonzales as American Minister, informed the State Department on February 13 of reports that such an amendment was under consideration and suggested that the Department urge that Crowder be invited to come to Habana to discuss it, saying that Crowder might then remain until after the election. Long thought that this would "be satisfying" to the liberals, who were threatening not to take part in the elections unless they were supervised. Polk replied that the State Department had concluded that it would be highly undesirable to amend the electoral law unless such action seemed indispensable for a fair and free election. If any amendment were necessary, the Department and General Crowder should have an opportunity to consider it carefully before it was presented to the Cuban congress. At the same time he emphasized that the Department "does not feel that any expression as to the advisability of the nomination of certain individuals for the Presidency of Cuba comes within its province" and asked the Minister to prevent any misunderstanding of the Department's attitude.

The conservatives said nothing further about amendments until March 10, when they suddenly announced that the law would be changed to permit a conservative-*zayista* coalition. The State Department again instructed Long to oppose a change and reiterated these instructions after it had studied the proposed amendments, which would have made several other undesirable changes in Crowder's law. The congress nevertheless passed them, and Menocal signed them, alleging to Long that he had been unable to resist pressure from the members of congress. The State Department could only express its surprise and disapproval and urge Long to prevent "any further tinkering" with the electoral law.

Gómez' followers were more convinced than ever that the conservatives planned to win by force or fraud. They proposed to send representatives to Washington to discuss the situation, but the State Department discouraged them, saying that "any attempt to transfer the forum of political activity from the Island of Cuba to Washington is harmful to the best interests of Cuba and is fruitful of endless misunderstandings." On March 31, Colby authorized Long to tell the liberal leaders, if necessary, that their withdrawal from the election would be regarded "not only as undemocratic, but as tending to undermine the foundations of popular government." They were to be warned that a withdrawal would be regarded as evidence of their incapacity to participate in Cuba's political life and would in no way influence "the policy of the United States to regard the result of a fair election as expressive of the national will." The State Department reiterated this position in April when Long reported that the president of the liberal party threatened that it would remain away from the polls if there was no supervision. The American government, Adee wrote, was still relying on Menocal's assurance that the election would be fair.

The liberals refused to believe that the United States would not ultimately agree to supervision, and they threatened to revolt if it did not.[74] The State Department was still determined that the Cubans must run their own election, but it was disturbed by Long's reports of liberal complaints about the conduct of the registration of voters.[75] On June 4 it instructed the Minister to present a note which Menocal was asked to make public, urging that all complaints about electoral procedure be carefully investigated and promptly dealt with and rather pointedly suggesting that the United States might ultimately have to decide whether the election had been fair. The message was intended as a warning to the liberals that they could not expect supervision and must avail themselves of the remedies provided by the electoral law, and as a warning to Menocal that the United States would hold him to his assurances of fair play.

Menocal was unwilling to publish the note because he alleged that it would hurt his prestige. He agreed to give out his own statement to the same effect, but for some weeks he found pretexts for failing to do so. Meanwhile there were increasing reports of violence in the electoral campaign. When Gómez complained in July that a liberal judge had been murdered by a congressman and that the matter was treated as an ordinary crime, with no investigation by the electoral board, Long was instructed to make vigorous representations, recalling Menocal's promises and saying that the affair had caused an "unfortunate impression" at Washington, which only the most diligent activity could remove.[76]

[74] Long to Colby, May 11, 1920, 837.00/1667.
[75] Long sent several reports on this matter, filed in 837.00.
[76] Colby to White, July 30, 1920, 837.00/1710.

By this time, the State Department realized that it must do more than it had been doing if a repetition of the events of 1916 were to be avoided. In the latter part of July it decided to send agents to each province in Cuba to observe the way in which the electoral procedure was carried out. This fell far short of the supervision for which the liberals had been asking, but it met Long's repeated complaints that he had no adequate staff to investigate reports of abuses. The Secretary of War refused to detail army officers for this task,[77] but civilian observers were sent to cover four provinces, and members of the staff of the Legation's military attaché covered the other two.

Norman Davis, who had succeeded Polk as Undersecretary of State in June 1920, was particularly interested in Cuba, where he had been a successful banker, and was perhaps responsible for the decision to provide Long with additional help. Davis, in fact, proposed that Crowder be sent back to Cuba immediately to attempt to check the abuses that were going on during the electoral campaign.[78] Colby apparently did not agree. On July 28 he proposed to the President that the United States announce that it would "observe" but not supervise the election. At the same time, he recommended that a special representative of the President of the United States be sent after the election to confer with the President-elect of Cuba about the general corruption, the neglect of sanitation, and the abuses in the national lottery, which were flagrant during Menocal's administration. Wilson approved both suggestions.[79]

The announcement of the American government's intention to "observe" the elections was withheld for a time to give Menocal a chance to publish the statement which the State Department had been urging him to make. On August 29, Menocal finally issued a proclamation containing the essential points of the Department's instruction of June 4; he promised a free election and urged that electoral complaints be dealt with through the machinery provided by law. The next day, Francis White, the American Chargé d'Affaires, gave out a statement which set forth the policy of the United States:

[77] See L. S. Rowe's memorandum of July 23, 1920, 837.00/1770.
[78] See his memorandum of August 31, 1920, 837.00/1860b.
[79] Colby to Wilson, July 28, 1920, 837.00/1860a.

"During the past few months" he said, "there have appeared in the Cuban newspapers various statements to the effect that the Government of the United States favored certain designated persons for the presidency of Cuba. My Government has authorized me to state that the sole interest of the Government of the United States in the approaching presidential elections in Cuba is that these elections shall be conducted in such a way as to secure the freest and fairest expression of the popular will of the Cuban people, and that the candidate thus securing the highest popular vote shall be declared President-elect of Cuba.

"When the United States Government was requested to pass judgment on the 1916 elections, it found a woeful lack of properly taken evidence to serve as the basis for reaching a decision. The new electoral law supplies the machinery for collecting evidence of irregularities, and it is hoped that the Cuban people will make use of the agencies thus placed at their disposal.

"When the United States Government was requested by one of the political parties in Cuba (October 1919) to supervise the 1920 presidential elections, the American Legation consulted with President Menocal and accepted his assurance that he would answer for the strict fulfillment of the new electoral law in the 1920 elections, in so far as such fulfillment depends upon the Government.

"The responsibility of a free and fair election thus rests with the Government and people of Cuba. The United States Government hopes and believes that there will result from this new procedure that clear definition of each and every electoral situation which will eliminate all controversies as to the actual facts and facilitate a conclusion upon the issues raised by those facts.

"Notwithstanding the expectation of this Government that the new procedure will be followed by the Government of Cuba, still the exceptionally close relations existing between Cuba and the United States; the fact that the new electoral law is for the first time being put to the test; and the further fact that the United States may again be called upon by the Cuban people for a decision regarding the fairness of the election, makes it incumbent upon the Government of the United States to use all available means to observe the conduct of the electoral procedure in Cuba, as well as the spirit in which the electoral law is being enforced.

"The Government of the United States does not propose actually to supervise the elections. However, *it is by treaty pledged* to 'the maintenance of a government in Cuba adequate for the protection of life, property and individual liberty.' It is, therefore, unalterably opposed to any attempt to substitute violence and revolution for the processes of government. I am desired to emphasize the fact, however, that it is no less opposed to intimidation and fraud in the conduct of elections as such procedure might be effective in depriving the people of Cuba of their right to choose their own government.

"The Government of the United States hopes and expects that the Government and people of Cuba will profit by the new electoral machinery and by the lessons of the past to hold elections which may be recognized as just and fair, and which may inspire confidence for the future."

Gómez was formally nominated for the presidency by his supporters in the liberal party on July 12, and on August 27 Zayas, who was already the candidate of his own *partido popular cubano*, was also named as the conservative candidate. The announcement of the coalition caused new talk of abstention among the liberals. White was consequently authorized to show some of the leaders, in confidence, the statement which the Legation was about to publish and also to call their attention to the State Department's telegram of March 31, condemning the idea of abstaining. On August 30 he was able to report that the liberal assembly had decided to go to the polls.

Up to the end of August there had been no lack of the murderous violence that normally characterized Cuban electoral campaigns, but there was apparently little evidence that the conservatives were more at fault than the liberals.[80] It was clear, however, that the electoral machinery was not working well, and the State Department felt that Menocal was not living up to his agreements. All available information suggested that Gómez would have a majority in a free vote.[81] If he lost, there was grave danger that his followers, despite their experience in 1917, would revolt in an effort to compel the United States to intervene.

General Crowder discussed the situation with Sumner Welles,

---

[80] See Spinden's report, transmitted by White, Aug. 13, 1920, 837.00/1740.

[81] The Cuban Subsecretary of State told Francis White confidentially in August that a majority of the voters favored Gómez, 837.00/1741.

the chief of the Latin American Division, at the end of August, saying that he was convinced that Zayas could not legally be elected and that he thought that the American government's statements had done little good. He believed that "radical measures on our part are now all that can save the situation." Welles, in reporting the General's views to the Undersecretary, recommended that Crowder be sent to Cuba immediately as Special Representative of the President of the United States to see that the electoral law was complied with. If this caused Menocal to resign, the Vice President might prove more amenable. Welles realized that Menocal's resignation would cause an unfortunate impression in other Latin American countries, but ultimate intervention would be worse.[82]

At Welles' suggestion, Long was ordered to cut short his leave and return to Cuba at once. When he broached to Menocal the idea of inviting Crowder to come to Habana, the President vigorously objected. The General's arrival, he said, would be interpreted as a victory for the liberals and a reflection on himself; he would not be able to remain in office if the General came. The State Department evidently did not wish to force the issue. When Welles made his proposal, he had perhaps not realized that Emilio Nuñez, the Vice President, had broken with Menocal and was supporting Gómez, so that the President's resignation would have had more sensational consequences than the State Department was probably willing to face.

The increasing possibility of disorder during or after the election caused Long to recommend that 350 more marines be sent to Camaguey, where the American force which had been there since 1917 had now been reduced to 150 men. He pointed out that there were important American properties in the four eastern provinces of Cuba and that everyone predicted that these would be the first to be destroyed if disturbances occurred. He also wanted to use a number of marines to aid him in obtaining information about the elections. The State Department vetoed this latter suggestion and was extremely reluctant to send more marines to protect American property unless Menocal requested them; and when Menocal insisted that Cuban forces could provide all needed protection the matter was dropped. Three weeks before the election, the State

[82] Welles to Davis, Aug. 27, 1920, 837.00/1764.

Department was ready to reconsider if Long still thought that the Marines were needed. It also was disposed to approve Long's proposal that warships be sent to three of the principal Cuban ports to discourage revolutionary outbreaks, but President Wilson refused to approve either action.

In October it became increasingly clear that the conservative administration did not intend to have an honest election. On October 5, after the arbitrary and illegal removal of the liberal Mayor of Habana, the State Department told the Cuban Minister at Washington that it was being forced regretfully to the conclusion that Menocal was unable or unwilling to fulfill his assurances of fair play. Though Long thought that the government was complying at least with the letter of the electoral law, and that the liberals, by their threats of rebellion and destruction of property, were "exercising the strongest kind of moral intimidation," [83] his reports showed that the conservatives were systematically taking over the control of the police in districts where the liberals controlled the municipal governments. This was accomplished through "military supervisors," officers detached from the Army to serve under the Secretary of the Interior in places where the President considered it advisable to interfere in a municipality's affairs. In some cases, Long thought, these appointments were justifiable, in view of the prevailing unrest, but the fact that they were usually made in liberal strongholds gave the opposition cause for complaint. By election day 73 out of 112 municipalities were under military control.[84] Menocal rather plausibly defended the appointment of so large a number by pointing out that the liberals were persistently threatening that they might revolt and that he did not wish to be caught unprepared as he had been in 1917.

The liberals' mistrust of the supervisors was the more understandable because they were under the direction of Colonel Charles Hernández, who had helped to steal the 1916 election while in charge of posts and telegraphs, and who now headed both the Interior Department and the War Department. Long reported on October 8 that the government was using the army and the rural

[83] *Foreign Relations, 1920*, Vol. ii, p. 26.

[84] H. J. Spinden, "Shall the United States Intervene in Cuba?" *Worlds Work*, Vol. xli (March 1921), p. 473.

guards and the local police to intimidate the voters and that it was also availing itself of the services of great numbers of recently released criminals.[85] Menocal granted 335 pardons between March 1 and October 6, 1920; 44 of them to murderers.[86]

The State Department apparently still hoped that the safeguards provided in Crowder's electoral law, combined with diplomatic pressure on Menocal, might bring about a passable election. There was some justification for this hope in the fact that both parties were still actively campaigning and that nothing had occurred to convince the liberals that they could not win. During the fortnight before election day, the Department's anxiety about the situation was evident in several messages which Long was instructed to deliver to Menocal. On October 20 it warned the President to make sure that election returns were promptly made public, so as to avoid any trickery like that which had occurred in 1916. Two days later it advised him to stop the practice of buying or forcefully taking identity cards from voters and urged him to publish a circular instruction to the military supervisors enjoining an attitude of strict impartiality. On October 27 it remonstrated vigorously because the conservative who had illegally been made Mayor of Habana was kept in office in defiance of decisions of the Central Electoral Board and the Supreme Court.[87]

A long telegraphic instruction sent to the Legation on October 25 seemed to indicate that the officials at Washington were still optimistic. Acting Secretary Davis said that the statements issued by Menocal and by the American Legation at the end of August had "effectively relieved the tension in the United States as well as in Cuba which had existed from fear that the Government would resort to unfair methods in the election," and he cited the fact that each party expected to win as an evidence of confidence. The pre-election period had been marked by disorders and crimes, but these were not sufficiently numerous or significant to "indicate as great a proportion of unfairness in electoral methods as had existed hitherto at election periods." The State Department trusted that the President had already issued a proclamation which would offset

[85] Long to Secretary of State, Oct. 8, 1920, 837.00/1818.
[86] Spinden, "Shall the U.S. Intervene in Cuba?" p. 476.
[87] Colby to Long, Oct. 27, 1920, 837.00/1826.

the bad situation caused by the appointment of so many military supervisors. It thought now that he should issue a further proclamation explaining in detail how the electoral machinery ought to operate and what remedies were available to persons who had complaints. The President was asked to "make it clear beyond any question that the provisions of the Electoral Code, in everything relating to the military and police forces, have been faithfully observed and will be maintained with the same fidelity."

Menocal had not in fact issued the desired instructions to the military supervisors, though he had agreed with Long that some such action would be helpful. On October 28, however, he issued a statement to the Cuban people, covering in rather general terms some of the points which the State Department had urged him to stress.

The election was held on November 1, 1920. The voters of both parties turned out in great numbers. Except in Pinar del Rio, where its man was driven out by a military supervisor, the Legation had observers in each province. Long thought that their influence had been salutary,[88] but their reports indicated that there had been many cases where liberals had been prevented from voting by intimidation or trickery.[89] On the face of the returns, Gómez won in Habana and Zayas had rather small majorities in each of the other five provinces. Some weeks elapsed before the final count of the vote was available, because the local electoral boards were unable to complete the canvass within the periods prescribed by the law.

The liberal leaders, who were certain that they would have won in a free vote, proposed to send a commission to Washington to demand that the elections be annulled. The State Department, however, instructed Long to tell them that it could not consider their complaints until they had availed themselves of the recourses provided by the electoral law. To hear their case before the Cuban courts had acted would be "an uncalled for and unwarranted intervention in the internal affairs of Cuba and could not but be regarded as a hurtful precedent which would tend to render more difficult in the future the determination by the Cuban people themselves of the problems which confront them in the development of a demo-

[88] Long to Colby, Nov. 5, 1920, 837.00/1870.
[89] Long to Colby, Nov. 5, 1920, 837.00/1873.

cratic and independent government." The Minister was to endeavor to discourage the departure for Washington of any liberal commission "or any other attempts which may be made to transfer the center of Cuban political activity from Cuba to Washington."

Gómez and his advisers consequently decided to pursue their legal remedies, explaining to their followers that the United States would not countenance even the most justifiable rebellion. A great number of complaints about the conduct of the voting in specific districts was submitted to the provincial electoral boards and then, on appeal, to the Central Electoral Board and to the courts. This procedure inevitably took time, and in many cases decisions seemed to be unnecessarily delayed by excessive red tape and procrastination. It began to look as though there might be no final solution before the dates when the new officials should take office. The situation seemed potentially as dangerous as that of 1917.

The "Dance of the Millions" and The Financial Crisis

The political problem, dangerous though it was, was overshadowed by the financial crisis that suddenly arose in the last weeks of the electoral campaign. The removal of wartime controls on sugar, in 1919, had been followed by a rapid rise in sugar prices in the first months of 1920, until sugar sold in New York in May at more than 20 cents per pound. This meant unheard-of wealth for Cuba and encouraged a period of wild speculation, both in sugar and in other forms of property. The Cuban government, with phenomenally large revenues at its disposal, became even more extravagant and corrupt than it had been during the World War. The State Department had watched the situation with growing concern. As early as January 1919, it asked Gonzales for a report on the government's finances, pointing out that there would be serious trouble when the price of sugar fell, as it must when beet production was resumed in Europe. The Minister was told that the American government would have to consider suggesting some form of financial supervision and invoking its treaty rights if reforms were not effected. Gonzales replied, however, that there was "nothing immediately alarming in situation." [90]

[90] Telegram to Habana, Jan. 16, 1919, and Gonzales' reply of Feb. 2, 837.51/329a, 332.

The speculation had been financed by the already none-too-sound local banks, and when the price of sugar fell as sharply as it had risen, reaching 7 cents early in October, the banks were in serious trouble. The crisis materialized suddenly when one of the largest of the local institutions suspended payments on October 9, and runs started on two of the others.

To save the banks, Menocal decreed a fifty-day moratorium on all debts. This immediately threatened to paralyze the country's commerce, for Long estimated that 80 percent of the Cuban merchants and industrialists were dependent on the three local banks that were in difficulties. If employers were unable to withdraw money to pay wages, thousands of people would soon be out of work, and it would be impossible to harvest the approaching sugar crop if no credit were available.

In the emergency, Menocal asked the American government's advice. He wished that the American banks which had branches in Cuba might provide funds to help the local banks, and he asked about the possibility of having a branch of the United States Federal Reserve System in Cuba. He thought that a fixed price for sugar—he suggested 10 cents—would also be helpful.[91]

Davis replied that it would be difficult if not impossible for the United States government to do anything to help, but he convened a large meeting of sugar producers, sugar brokers, bankers, and government officials to discuss the matter. The consensus was that the chief cause of the crisis was the large amount of loans carried on sugar which could not now be sold, and that the first step would be to provide a market for this sugar, to an amount estimated at 300,000 tons. Those present thought that it would be possible for the Cuban government to borrow $50,000,000 in the United States with which it could purchase the unsold sugar at a stabilized price; 7 cents was suggested. If such an arrangement were made, the conferees thought that the orderly financing of the approaching crop would be possible.[92]

Menocal apparently wanted to accept this recommendation, but he said that it would be impossible to obtain approval from the congress until the political passions aroused by the electoral campaign had quieted. He proposed to make the loan under his war powers,

[91] Long to Colby, Oct. 8, 1920, 837.156/25.
[92] Davis to Long, Oct. 14, 1920, 837.516/25; and Oct. 18, 837.516/30.

but the bankers were reluctant to proceed on this basis.[93] Despite the increasing distress in Cuba, no definite remedial action was taken, and the moratorium was extended when the original fifty days expired. In the meantime, various schemes, some of them obviously unsound, were urged on Menocal by groups in Cuba. The State Department objected especially to a plan to issue a sort of emergency currency and insisted that the only solution was a loan to buy the surplus sugar and to make advances to help the banks which were basically solvent.[94]

In the first days of the crisis, Long with Menocal's approval had suggested that the American government send a financial expert or experts to help devise remedial measures. Davis at the time thought this unnecessary and inadvisable,[95] but subsequently the American government suggested that Menocal employ Albert Rathbone, recently Assistant Secretary of the Treasury, to advise him in connection with the loan negotiations. In December, when the arrangement of a loan had proved more difficult than had been expected, Rathbone went to Cuba to look into the situation and to propose a solution.

Just before Rathbone's arrival at Habana, Long reported that a bill had been submitted to the Cuban congress authorizing the President to expropriate the surplus sugar, paying for it in certificates which would be legal tender, and to control the sale of the next crop. A loan of $100,000,000 would be authorized. Menocal apparently supported the measure, and it seemed likely to be adopted despite Long's and Rathbone's opposition, but it was dropped when the State Department objected vigorously to some of its provisions and told Long to say that its adoption would make impossible the flotation of a loan in the United States.[96]

Rathbone stayed only a few days in Cuba and apparently did not accomplish very much. Long thought that it was unfortunate that his coming had been delayed so long and that his visit was so short.

[93] Long to Davis, Oct. 28, and Davis to Long Oct. 29, 1920, 837.516/45.

[94] Davis to Long, Nov. 22, 1920, 837.51/366a. Part of this telegram is printed in *Foreign Relations, 1920*, Vol. II, p. 47.

[95] Long to Davis, Oct. 15, 1920, and Davis to Long Oct. 18, 837.516/32.

[96] Long to Davis, Dec. 10, 1920, and Davis to Long Dec. 14, 837.51/378; Davis to Long Dec. 17, 837.51/393. A part of this correspondence appears in *Foreign Relations, 1920*, Vol. II, pp. 49ff.

Menocal apparently made no effort to persuade him to stay longer.[97] Rathbone's report to Menocal, submitted on December 17, recommended that the Cuban government borrow $50,000,000 to be used for advances to solvent banks, in order to make possible the lifting of the moratorium. The money would be administered by a commission which would also take over and liquidate those banks which it found to be insolvent. The surplus sugar should be sold, preferably in one block, and no effort should be made to control the coming crop. These recommendations were doubtless sound, but they were not carried out.

General Crowder's Mission

The Cuban government seemed unable to find a way out of a situation that threatened to become utterly disastrous unless the approaching sugar crop could be financed and sold. The political situation continued to be tense, and the settlement of the electoral question was being delayed by the slow procedures of the boards that were passing on disputes. There was danger of a collapse that might raise the question of intervention under the Platt Amendment —a question that the administration did not care to face after the attacks on its Caribbean policy during the recent presidential campaign in the United States. The American government had not been able to give very much help, and the Cubans, if left to themselves, seemed likely to adopt remedial measures which the State Department would consider unsound and objectionable.

In these circumstances, the State Department revived, in somewhat different form, the proposal, which President Wilson had approved in July, to send a special representative of the President to Cuba to urge reforms. On December 31 the press reported that General Crowder would probably return to Cuba,[98] and a cable sent on the same day told Long that the General was being sent to Cuba on special mission as the personal representative of the President of the United States to inform Menocal of the grave anxiety with which the American government regarded the political and financial situation in Cuba, and to discuss remedial measures. The Minister

[97] See Long's dispatch of Dec. 21, 1920, 837.51/399.
[98] New York *Times*, Dec. 31, 1920.

was instructed to say to Menocal, without comment, that Crowder was coming by special order of the President.[99]

Unfortunately, this message was not delivered until January 4, after the Cubans and Long had learned from other sources that the General was about to arrive on the *U.S.S. Minnesota*. The liberals were jubilant, because they thought that the mission was a blow to Menocal's prestige,[100] and Menocal was so resentful that he at first threatened to refuse to receive Crowder. The State Department, however, insisted that the special relations between Cuba and the United States made it unnecessary for the President of the United States to obtain the consent of the President of Cuba before sending a representative to consult with him, and it intimated that the United States might have to resort to some sort of intervention if Menocal refused to cooperate. A press statement from the White House, explaining that the General was being sent to confer with Menocal about the best means of dealing with Cuba's political situation and the economic crisis, and assurances to the Cuban Minister at Washington that the purpose was not to investigate Menocal's acts, helped to mollify the President, and Crowder was received in a friendly way when he called at the Palace on January 6.

Crowder's original instructions emphasized particularly the need to settle the electoral problem, but in a cable sent on January 7 he was told to endeavor also to bring about the earliest possible suspension of the moratorium.[101] He went to work immediately on both problems, and within a few days of his arrival amendments to the electoral law and economic measures that he had drafted or approved were on their way through the Cuban congress.

The amendments to the electoral law were designed to expedite the procedure of the electoral boards and the courts in dealing with complaints. It was becoming evident that there would have to be new elections in enough districts to make the final outcome doubtful, but, until the complaints were acted on, it would be impossible to decide when these elections could be held. Crowder pointed out to the Cubans, very explicitly, that a failure to settle the matter in

[99] Davis to Long, Dec. 31, 1920, *Foreign Relations, 1920*, Vol. II, p. 43.

[100] Except as otherwise indicated, this account of General Crowder's mission is based on correspondence published in *Foreign Relations, 1921*, Vol. I, pp. 670ff.

[101] Colby to Crowder, Jan. 7, 1921, 837.00/1952. The original instructions are printed in *Foreign Relations, 1920*, Vol. II, p. 41.

time for the new authorities to take office in accord with the constitution would create a situation where it would be "very difficult if not impossible to avoid actual intervention." [102] In response to his prodding, the electoral boards and the courts speeded up their work and it was soon possible to set March 12 as the date for new elections in all of the disputed provinces except Oriente.

The new elections would of course mean little unless they could be held under satisfactory conditions. Crowder pointed out to Menocal that most of the verified complaints against the November elections had to do with violence rather than fraud, and he insisted on amendments to the electoral law and to the regulations of the Central Electoral Board designed to check many of the most notorious abuses. He also successfully pressed Menocal to remove most of the military supervisors and some of the other army officers who had been responsible for intimidating the voters.

The liberals hoped that the new elections would reverse the conservative majorities in at least two provinces, which would give Gómez enough electoral votes to win, and they were disappointed when the Supreme Court in February ordered new elections in only fourteen districts in Camaguey, which was one of the provinces on which they had counted. In their discouragement, some of them began to look for another solution, and on February 16 Crowder was told that the liberals had suggested that both Gómez and Zayas withdraw and that the electoral colleges should vote for a compromise candidate to be designated by Menocal. Crowder was doubtful about the propriety of the plan, but when he asked for instructions Colby told him that the matter was one for the Cubans to decide. "The people of Cuba" Colby said, "should not be permitted to feel that we claim any voice in their selection of a president or other public official, or that this government expects them in any way to be influenced by any preferences on our part as to candidates. We shall endeavor not even to feel a preference and scrupulously to refrain from expressing one." [103] At Colby's suggestion, Crowder published this statement in Cuba on March 3.[104]

Nothing came of the suggestion for a compromise candidate, but

---

[102] *Foreign Relations, 1921*, Vol. I, p. 675.
[103] *Foreign Relations, 1921*, Vol. I, p. 677.
[104] Crowder to Colby, March 3, 1921, 837.00/2020.

a few days later the liberals proposed the appointment of "conciliation committees" to discuss measures that would assure order and fair play in the new elections. Menocal agreed, but the first meeting of the two committees broke up because the conservatives demanded that the liberals renounce "all direct or indirect, public or private, effort near the American Government with regard to the electoral problem of Cuba." This demand was dropped when Crowder protested to Menocal, and the two committees met again on February 26. The result was an apparently satisfactory agreement on the way in which the elections would be conducted.

By this time the new elections had been postponed until March 15, except in Santiago where they were to be held on March 26. Crowder was well satisfied with what had been accomplished. He thought that the decisions of the Cuban courts had been in the main correct and that the President and the Central Electoral Board had provided all proper safeguards for the elections and had met nearly all of the liberals' demands for safeguards.[105] Early in March he visited what he considered the "pivotal provinces," Matanzas, Santa Clara, and Camaguey, and found conditions generally satisfactory. He had arranged to have a large number of competent inspectors in the districts where elections would take place, and he was confident that there would be no organized intimidation or violence.

The liberals, however, were disappointed at the outcome of their suits in the courts and were still resentful because the United States had not taken over the conduct of the new elections. By this time, furthermore, it seemed unlikely that these elections would change the conservative majority in enough provinces to affect the result, even if they were fairly conducted. At the last minute, consequently, Gómez and his followers seized on minor disturbances, which they apparently organized themselves, as an excuse to withdraw from the contest. The new elections thus merely confirmed Zayas' victory.

There was a new administration at Washington after March 4, but President Harding asked Crowder to stay in Cuba as his personal representative and there was no immediate change in the policy of the United States. On April 16 the American Minister at Habana was authorized to issue a statement saying that the liberals

[105] Crowder to Hughes, March 7, 1921, 837.00/2017.

had had every opportunity to avail themselves of the provisions of the Cuban electoral law and that the American government saw no reason why they should not have relied on the courts to deal with any abuses that might have been committed in the new elections, just as they had relied on the courts to deal with their earlier complaints. The United States considered that Zayas had been elected president and that the Cuban people should accept this decision as final. When Gómez visited Washington, Secretary Hughes received him courteously but said that the United States would view with regret and apprehension any attempt by the liberal party to prevent the proclamation of Zayas as president. Gómez accepted this decision, saying that his party was forced to submit to any decision that the American government might reach.

The liberals had again put themselves in the wrong by withdrawing from the electoral process before they exhausted the remedies that the electoral law gave them. They had less excuse in 1921 than in 1917, because Crowder's efforts had assured them a fair hearing in the courts and had made it more probable that the new elections would be properly conducted. They were perhaps right in asserting that the government's actions during the November election had placed them at a disadvantage which could not be overcome simply by holding new elections in districts where gross improprieties could be proved. Intimidation and coercion had probably deprived them of many votes in other districts where it was difficult to assemble convincing evidence or to persuade witnesses to testify, for the ignorant country people were easily influenced by fear or threats, and the voting was often conducted in a way that nullified the legal provisions for secrecy. Fair play, however, could really have been assured only by an outside supervision that would have involved control of the police and army as well as the electoral machinery. There were good reasons for the United States government to refuse to undertake any such supervision, among them the fact that the psychological effect of imposing supervision would almost certainly cause the defeat of the government party.

Efforts to Settle the Financial Crisis

While he was dealing with the electoral matter, Crowder was also endeavoring to help the Cuban government to emerge from the financial crisis. When he reached Habana, Menocal and his advisers were apparently less interested than they had been in the plan for a loan and were working instead on a plan devised by Senator Cosme de la Torriente for the gradual lifting of the moratorium and the liquidation of banks that proved to be insolvent. Crowder found that public opinion in Cuba was "clamorous and undivided" in its demand that the moratorium should not continue after January 31, when its most recent extension would expire; [106] and he thought that the Torriente plan would be acceptable with certain modifications. He had doubts about the proposed loan because he thought that the current crop and the sugar held over from the last crop ought to be sold promptly and he feared that the loan would encourage those who had sugar to hold it off the market in the hope of obtaining a higher price.[107] The State Department, which regretted that the Cuban government had not followed Rathbone's advice, was more skeptical, but it reluctantly acceded to Crowder's views, with the proviso that a commission be set up to liquidate any banks that proved insolvent.[108]

Crowder consequently drafted several amendments to the measure known as Torriente Law No. 1, and he almost completely rewrote Torriente Law No. 2. Both were passed by the Cuban congress and signed by Menocal before the end of January. The first provided for the gradual lifting of the moratorium. Debtors were to be permitted to meet their obligations gradually over a period of 105 days, and banks were given 135 days to pay their deposits, but only on condition that they met stated portions of their obligations within definite periods. If a bank wished to take advantage of the delay, however, it would at once be placed under government supervision and control. Torriente Law No. 2, as redrafted by Crowder, provided that banks which could not meet their obligations should be liquidated by a commission composed of the Cuban Secretary of the Treasury and two members named by the President. The State Department had stipulated, and Menocal had agreed, that one of these should be nominated by all of the banks in Cuba and the other by the United

---

[106] See his report of March 12, 1921, in *Foreign Relations, 1921*, Vol. I, pp. 775ff.
[107] *Ibid.*, pp. 777–778.
[108] Davis to Crowder, Jan. 20, Crowder to the Secretary of State, Jan. 21, Davis to Crowder, Jan. 22, 1921, 837.51/420,422.

States Federal Reserve Board.[109] Another measure, known as Torriente Law No. 3, created a commission to frame a new banking law. The bad practices that had made the financial crisis so serious could hardly have existed if Cuba had had any adequate banking legislation.

With the moratorium taken care of, Crowder turned his attention to the situation in the sugar industry. In December the price of sugar had dropped below 4 cents, which was less than the cost of production, and it seemed unlikely that the producers could get money to grind the 1920–1921 crop even if the banks resumed operations. Menocal proposed to set up a Sugar Finance Commission which would take over the sale and shipment of the entire crop, and Crowder supported the plan. The General thought that the bankers would furnish credit if there was assurance of a fair price for sugar and that it was imperatively necessary that the current crop be harvested. The State Department disliked the plan because it feared that it would result in high prices to the American consumer, but it consented to it provisionally, reserving the right to oppose it at a later date if prices rose unduly. It stipulated, however, that the makeup of the proposed commission be changed so that it would not be completely controlled by representatives of the sugar industry. Menocal accepted this change and promised that he would abolish the commission whenever the price of sugar rose to between 5½ and 6 cents. Menocal issued a decree establishing the commission on February 11.[110]

The price of sugar immediately rose from less than 4 to more than 5 cents. This greatly improved the situation in Cuba but led to criticism in the United States. The United States Senate passed a resolution asking about a reported plan to "pool" Cuban sugar; and Arbuckle Brothers, the refiners, who had protested to Colby on February 11 against the establishment of the commission, apparently tried to bypass it when it got into operation.[111]

[109] Davis to Crowder, Jan. 21, 1921, 837.51/422. Crowder to the Secretary of State, Jan. 24, 1921, 837.51/428. For translations of the Torriente Laws, see Crowder's reports of Jan. 30 and Feb. 1, 1921, 837.51/436, 451.

[110] *Foreign Relations, 1921*, Vol. I, pp. 793–799. For a translation of the presidential decree establishing the commission, see Crowder's dispatch of Feb. 11, 1921, 837.61351/214.

[111] *Foreign Relations, 1921*, Vol. I, p. 799.

Since only a few months remained of Menocal's term, Crowder apparently did not attempt to take up with him in any general way the Cuban government's own financial situation, which was to give much trouble later on. He did, however, urge that the State Department prevent the enactment of the budget which Menocal had submitted to the congress in November, which would have authorized expenditures of more than $136,000,000; and Long was instructed to express the American government's grave anxiety. Menocal assured Long that there would be no effort to pass the proposed budget, and that the government would continue to operate under the 1918–1919 budget, which had authorized expenditures of less than $65,000,000.[112]

By March 12 Crowder was able to make a final report, and a rather optimistic one, on the financial aspects of his mission. The moratorium was gradually being ended and the soundness of the general business situation was shown by the fact that very few merchants had availed themselves of the provisions of Torriente Law No. 1. Eight banks had taken advantage of the provisions authorizing delayed payments of deposits, but most of them, including the three largest Cuban institutions, had thus far avoided being placed under the supervision of the liquidation commission. The operations of the Sugar Finance Commission had had a good effect.[113]

Apparently all of this, as well as the settlement of the electoral question, had been accomplished through a fairly harmonious cooperation between Crowder and President Menocal. The circumstances under which Crowder's mission began were unfortunate, but the high respect in which the General was held in Cuba and his obvious single-minded concern for Cuban interests helped to dispel the government's resentment. He frankly pointed out the danger of American intervention if the electoral problems were not settled, but the Cubans knew that he was sincerely trying to prevent the need for intervention from arising. The economic measures that he sponsored were in the main measures devised and supported by

[112] Crowder to the Secretary of State, Feb. 6, 1921, 837.51/447. Colby's instruction of Feb. 11 to Long and Long's dispatch of Feb. 18 are printed in *Foreign Relations, 1921*, Vol. I, p. 697.

[113] Crowder to the Secretary of State, March 12, 1921, *Foreign Relations, 1921*, Vol. I, p. 775.

Cubans rather than solutions proposed from outside. It was not until after the change in administrations at Washington and at Habana that his mission took on a somewhat different aspect.

There was of course unfriendly comment in Cuba from the time of Crowder's arrival, even though the always present anti-American sentiment was less apt to find expression when both parties were hoping for help from the United States. The fact that Crowder traveled and made his headquarters on an American battleship inspired unpleasant allusions to military pressure, and Menocal felt it necessary to issue a proclamation on February 1 saying that the Cuban congress had acted freely in considering the Torriente laws and paying tribute to Crowder's assistance and the respect that he had shown for Cuba's sovereignty.[114] Some of the sniping at Crowder, like the frequent, concerted newspaper attacks on the foreign banks in Habana, was probably inspired by the large Cuban banks which were opposed to the Torriente laws because they would find it difficult to avoid liquidation under them.

General Crowder remained at Habana for several years, as Personal Representative of the President of the United States and after 1923 as American Ambassador. Shortly after the events that have just been described, the financial situation in Cuba took a turn for the worse. All of the banks in the island, except the branches of three foreign institutions, collapsed in the spring of 1921, and the Cuban government's finances were disastrously affected by the loss of the large deposits that it had had in the Banco Nacional. Crowder found himself endeavoring to help the new administration to deal with a situation that was hardly less serious than that which had existed late in 1920, but we cannot here go into the long story of his relations with the Zayas regime.

[114] Long to the Secretary of State, Feb. 5, 1921, 837.51/452.

◄ 12 ►

Intervention and Dollar Diplomacy in Retrospect

To many observers the policy which culminated in the military occupation of Haiti and the Dominican Republic and interference to a lesser degree in the internal affairs of other nearby countries seemed little different from the imperialism of European powers in Africa and the Far East. The American intervention in the Caribbean aroused a hostility throughout Latin America that still affects our relations with the other countries of the hemisphere. What happened might have been forgotten after the repudiation of the intervention policy by Presidents Hoover and Franklin Roosevelt, had it not been for the belief that the policy was inspired by sinister and sordid motives, which might well reassert themselves at some future time. This belief has contributed materially to the myth of North American imperialism, political and economic, which is assiduously kept alive today by hostile propaganda.

The persistence of this belief in Latin America is not surprising, because the same ideas about the motives behind the intervention policy have often found expression in the United States. Many liberal North Americans were shocked when they realized that American marines were killing Haitians and Dominicans who resisted the occupation of their countries by foreign forces, and thought that the policy which led to such a situation must be wrong. Writing at a time when historians were prone to assume that all governments were unprincipled and that governmental actions must be explained by economic considerations, "anti-imperialist" authors assumed that the United States could only have been acting for the benefit of American financial interests, and they found enough in the story of dollar diplomacy to convince them that their assumption was correct. One still hears it said that the marines were sent to the Caribbean "to collect debts," an idea that seems somewhat incongruous when one reflects that it was Woodrow Wilson who ordered the more important interventions. For several years after 1920 most of the books written about Caribbean affairs, some of them the work of honest and competent historians, reflected this point of view.

It would be impossible to deny that many of the American government's actions were ill-judged and unfortunate in their results. As we look back on the story, however, it seems clear that the motives that inspired its policy were basically political rather than economic. What the United States was trying to do, throughout the period with which this study has dealt, was to put an end to conditions that threatened the independence of some of the Caribbean states and were consequently a potential danger to the security of the United States. Revolutions must be discouraged; the bad financial practices that weakened the governments and involved them in trouble with foreigners must be reformed; and general economic and social conditions, which were a basic cause of instability, must be improved. The Platt Amendment was an effort to achieve these purposes in Cuba, and the Roosevelt Corollary to the Monroe Doctrine meant that the United States would seek to achieve them in other Caribbean states.

The same purposes inspired the policy of successive administrations from Theodore Roosevelt to Woodrow Wilson. The methods used in attempting to achieve them varied from one administration to another, but more because of accumulating experience and increasing involvement than because.of any difference in the ultimate goals. Each successive Secretary of State took up Caribbean problems where his predecessor had left them, in most cases making no abrupt change in the way in which they were being handled.

As time went on, there was more and more active interference in the internal affairs of some of the states that seemed most in need of help. When Roosevelt first took office, he certainly did not contemplate any extensive effort by the United States to better political and economic conditions in the Caribbean. The Cubans had already been compelled to accept the Platt Amendment, but this, as its sponsors conceived it, was essentially a negative measure, designed to give the United States a legal basis for any action that might some day prove necessary. It seems clear that neither Roosevelt nor Root, who had been chiefly responsible for the amendment, thought that it should serve as an excuse for any avoidable interference in the island's internal affairs. There were, moreover, special reasons why the United States felt responsible for the welfare of Cuba. It was not until after the Anglo-German attack on Venezuela that Roosevelt came to feel that European intervention in any Caribbean state must be prevented. With the formulation of his Corollary to the Monroe Doctrine, he committed the United States to a policy of helping its neighbors to correct conditions that exposed them to possible aggression.

Roosevelt offered such help only where it was urgently needed and usually avoided any appearance of coercion. By the time when he became president, he seems to have given up the somewhat imperialist ideas that he had expressed as a younger man. The Panama affair showed that he was capable of aggressive and arbitrary action in what he considered a good cause, but he thought that public opinion would not support him in any general policy of intervention in the Caribbean. He clearly seems to have been less willing than were his successors to assume responsibilities in connection with the internal affairs of Caribbean states. He apparently looked on the establishment of the customs collectorship in Santo Domingo as an unfortunate necessity, and he endeavored to avoid intervention in Cuba in 1906.

Root, who directed Latin American policy in Roosevelt's second administration, had helped to formulate the President's Corollary to the Monroe Doctrine and believed in its validity, but he realized that injudicious efforts to bring about more orderly conditions and better government in the Caribbean states would arouse opposition and resentment. In dealing with threats of war in Central America, he enlisted the cooperation of Mexico to avoid the suspicion that would have been aroused by unilateral North American intervention, and he encouraged the Central Americans to devise their own program for maintaining peace, instead of putting forward his ideas. In the Dominican Republic the permanent establishment of the customs collectorship and the adjustment of the foreign debt were carried out in friendly cooperation with the local government. Unfortunately, subsequent developments both in Central America and in Santo Domingo undid much of what he seemed to have accomplished, and the problems that confronted his successors were the more troublesome because of the new commitments which the United States had assumed under his leadership.

In Cuba, Central America, and Santo Domingo, Roosevelt and Root did not act until they were faced with emergencies where action seemed necessary to prevent further bloodshed or to ward off

European intervention. Their successors began to urge fiscal and political reforms which would prevent such emergencies from arising. In the somewhat naïve belief that the chief goal of revolutions was the customs receipts, they hoped that the establishment of customs collectorships would give the Central American states the same stability and economic progress that the Dominican Republic enjoyed between 1907 and 1911. Their efforts to substitute North American for European financial influence were intended to do away with a potential source of conflict with European states. In Cuba, the purpose of the Taft administration's preventive policy was to correct conditions that threatened to bring on another intervention. Knox and Huntington Wilson were not very successful in what they attempted to do, partly because they did not have Root's sympathetic understanding of the people with whom they were dealing. Their dollar diplomacy miscarried when the United States Senate rejected the loan treaties. The Dominican Republic, where the customs receivership seemed to have had such good results, sank into anarchy, and the government with which they were working in Nicaragua was kept in office only by American armed intervention.

The problems that confronted the Taft administration, however, were to a considerable extent the logical consequence of what Roosevelt and Root had done. In Central America, after the United States' sponsorship of the 1907 treaties and its vigorous diplomatic efforts to persuade the Central American governments to respect them, it would have been difficult to tolerate Zelaya's blatant repudiation of his treaty obligations, even if he had not made himself still more offensive by murdering Cannon and Groce. In Santo Domingo the existence of the receivership made it impossible to remain indifferent when civil war occurred; and in Cuba there was real reason for concern about the possibility of a third intervention because the previous one had been profitable to the party whose revolt had forced the United States to act.

The Wilson administration also had to take up Caribbean problems where its predecessor left them. There was little immediate change in policy, but there was a still greater disposition to insist on peace and internal reform in the more disorderly states and to use force if necessary to compel the acceptance of measures that the United States thought beneficial. By 1913 it had become evident that some of the Caribbean governments could not maintain order by their own efforts and that even the establishment of customs collectorships did little to assure financial solvency if the local officials were free to spend the revenues as they sought fit. The new administration consequently began to urge more thoroughgoing reforms, to be carried out under the actual control of North Americans designated by the United States, and it resorted to the military occupation of Haiti and the Dominican Republic when the governments of those countries refused to accept such control.

Despite Wilson's emphasis on the duty of the United States to promote constitutional government in the Caribbean, the Roosevelt Corollary to the Monroe Doctrine, though rarely mentioned, was still the basis of American policy. President Wilson expressed his full agreement when Secretary Lansing wrote in November 1915: [1]

"The possession of the Panama Canal and its defense have in a measure given to the territories in and about the Caribbean Sea a new importance from the standpoint of our national safety. It is vital to the interests of this country that European political domination should in no way be extended over these regions. As it happens within this area lie the small republics of America which have been and to an extent still are the prey of revolutionists, of corrupt governments and of predatory foreigners.

"Because of this state of affairs, our national safety, in my opinion, requires that the United States should intervene and aid in the establishment and maintenance of a stable and honest government, if no other way seems possible to attain that end."

Throughout the period between 1901 and 1921, the first objective of American policy in the Caribbean was to discourage revolutions. Revolutions, and the interstate wars that often rose out of them, were the chief cause of controversies with European powers because they endangered foreign lives and property and disrupted the government's finances so that it could not meet foreign claims. Frequent civil wars were also an obstacle to any sort of material or social progress. A government that had to devote all of its resources simply to maintaining itself in power could do little road building and little for public education, and an atmosphere of insecurity discouraged private enterprise in agriculture or industry.

[1] *Lansing Papers*, Vol. II, pp. 467, 470.

The improvement of economic conditions was a second objective. There could be little basic improvement in the political situation while the masses of the people were poverty stricken and illiterate. A part of the Dominican bond issue of 1908 was used for public works, though little was accomplished, and the proposed loan for Nicaragua was to have provided funds to build a railroad. In Haiti and the Dominican Republic the occupation authorities had ambitious programs of roadbuilding, port improvement, and sanitation. All economic development, however, had to be carried on with the limited funds available from the countries' own revenues or from loans, because it would hardly have been possible before 1921 to ask the United States Congress to make grants of aid to another country.

In discussing their policy, officials in the State Department sometimes held out the hope of increased trade and new fields for American investment as a third objective. It is doubtful, however, whether these considerations really had any great influence in the formulation of policy. There is little evidence that the American government made any important effort to promote trade, and with the exception of Cuba the countries which the United States tried particularly to help were too small and too poor in natural resources to offer attractive opportunities for foreign enterprises.

These objectives, whatever we may think of the way in which the American government tried to attain them, were neither sinister nor sordid. Many critics of the United States' policy, however, maintained that there was a fourth purpose: to forward the selfish interests of American businessmen and bankers. To what extent this charge is justified is one of the questions that must be considered in any study of dollar diplomacy and intervention.

Certainly many American citizens who lived in Caribbean countries did benefit from the establishment of more orderly conditions and from the increased influence and prestige of the United States, which made their lives and property more secure. The American government, like other governments, thought that it had a duty to intercede for its nationals when they were the victims of violence or injustice in a foreign country, and it showed somewhat more interest in protecting them after 1900 than it had in the past. Warships were sent to Caribbean ports not only to influence the local political situation but to prevent injury to Americans and other foreigners. The State Department also tried to bring about the settlement of American claims, and in Nicaragua, Haiti, and Santo Domingo it urged the establishment of mixed commissions for this purpose. The benefits derived from these, however, were dubious, for all claims, and especially those of Americans and other foreigners, were usually arbitrarily scaled down and many claimants were compelled to accept awards which they considered unfair. A study of the work of the claims commissions hardly supports the idea that the purpose of the Caribbean interventions was to collect debts.

It is also true that controversies between certain American companies and the local governments played an important part in the chain of events that led up to each intervention. The arbitral award in favor of the San Domingo Improvement Company helped to bring on the crisis that led to the establishment of the Dominican customs receivership, and the dispute over the Emery claim aggravated the already bad relations between the United States and Nicaragua. In Haiti the disputes between the government and the National Bank and the National Railroad made the situation more exasperating and helped to convince Wilson and Bryan that the United States should intervene. In each case, however, other considerations had far more weight in determining policy: the danger of European intervention, in Santo Domingo; the determination to make the 1907 treaties effective, in Central America; and the feeling that the United States must do something about the political chaos, in Haiti. It should be noted that the companies involved profited little from the interventions. The San Domingo Improvement Company was treated less kindly than many of the Dominican government's other creditors, and the Emery claim was paid only after a delay of several years and then because a legal technicality forced the State Department to agree to its payment. In Haiti the railroad never prospered, and the occupation compelled the National Bank to give up some of the privileges that it enjoyed under its concession.

Except in Cuba, little new American capital went into the countries where the United States intervened. The occupation in Santo Domingo and the treaty officials in Haiti tried to encourage investment in new agricultural or industrial enterprises, in Santo Domingo by setting up the land courts, which improved the chaotic state of land titles, and in Haiti by abrogating the constitutional provision against foreign land ownership. The results were not particularly impressive, though the sugar companies in Santo Domingo, some of which were American, found it easier to obtain new acreage and considerably increased their production. A few new foreign agricultural enterprises were started in Haiti, most of them after 1921, but only one or two of them were ever profitable. Little foreign capital went into Nicaragua.

Dollar diplomacy might have brought profits to American bankers if it had been more successful, but its purpose, under Taft as well as under Wilson, was purely political. Both administrations were interested in loans as a means of stabilizing Caribbean governments and bringing about the establishment of American customs collectorships, and as a way to provide funds for economic development. They also wished to eliminate European financial influence in the area. Disputes over unpaid debts were always likely to provide an excuse for European intervention, and it was thought that the exploitation of the Caribbean countries by European interests was one cause of their backwardness.

In most cases, it was the State Department that took the initiative in bringing forward projects for loans. The bankers, however, were usually glad to participate in them and sometimes competed for the privilege, because they assumed that they would be sound business ventures. At times, a desire to cooperate with the State Department and the fascination exerted by projects for the development of strange and distant countries led the bankers into ventures which at least cost them far more in time and trouble than the profits could justify, but they would have been subject to merited criticism if they had gone into transactions where there was not a prospect of a reasonable profit.

The State Department, as we have seen, endeavored to make sure that the profit was reasonable and not excessive. Knox, who realized that anything that savored of exploitation would invite criticism, insisted on a careful scrutiny of the proposed Honduras and Nicaragua loan contracts by a disinterested law firm to make sure that the interests of the borrowing government were properly safeguarded. Under the proposed contracts, the Morgan firm and its associates would have bought $7,500,000 5-percent bonds from Honduras at 88, and Brown Brothers and Seligman would have taken

$12,000,000 5-percent Nicaraguan bonds at 90½. The bankers' profits would of course have depended on the spread between these prices and the figure at which they could have sold them to the public. Brazilian 5-percent bonds were selling around par on the stock exchange in the first months of 1911, and Cuban 5's between 102½ and 103½. If the bankers had been able to sell the Honduran and Nicaraguan bonds at these prices, they would have had a substantial profit, but perhaps not an unreasonable one in view of the smallness of the issues and the great amount of work involved in setting them up. It is impossible to say whether Central American bonds, even when secured by customs receiverships, would have been equally attractive to investors. It is at least clear that the two governments were obtaining better terms than they could have without the help of the United States, for the 6-percent bonds of the Ethelburga loan, contracted by Zelaya in 1909, were taken by the bankers at 75 and were offered to the public at 92 in London and 93½ in Paris.

In Honduras, the time and effort expended by the bankers in working out the contract were wasted. In Nicaragua, Brown Brothers and Seligman agreed to finance the very urgent currency reform without waiting for the loan treaty to be ratified, and their purchase of $1,500,000 in treasury bills was the first of a series of transactions that continued for many years. None of these, during the Taft administration at least, were unconscionably profitable. On the treasury bills and on the small loans made in 1912 Nicaragua paid 6 percent interest, with an additional commission of 1 percent on the two smaller loans. These terms were certainly not onerous in view of political and economic conditions in Nicaragua. Some of the bankers' transactions in Nicaragua after 1913 were probably somewhat more profitable, but hardly profitable enough to make the bankers feel that the Nicaraguan venture had been worthwhile from a purely financial standpoint.

If we dismiss as unfounded the charge that the purpose of dollar diplomacy was to enrich a few North American businessmen, we must still inquire whether the broader Caribbean policy of which it was a part was wise and profitable. The policy did eliminate, for the time being, the danger of European intervention. Perhaps neither Germany nor any other power seriously entertained the idea of territorial expansion in the Caribbean, but there is little doubt that European interference would have taken forms unacceptable to the United States and possibly dangerous to the independence of the countries involved if the American government had not acted as it did in Santo Domingo in 1905 and in Haiti after 1910. Before 1914 the vital importance of defending the approaches to the Panama Canal made any unfriendly activity in the Caribbean a much more serious matter than it seemed to be after the First World War, when the naval power of the United States was so much greater.

It is more difficult to assess the benefits and disadvantages to the Caribbean countries themselves. The policy of the United States certainly reduced, though it did not end, the bloodshed and turmoil that had kept the Caribbean states so backward before 1900. It stopped international wars between the five Central American states and made internal revolutions less frequent and destructive. Except for the *caco* uprising in Haiti, that country and the Dominican Republic had a long period of peace. Unless one has seen something of the terror and the misery caused by a civil war in a small Caribbean country, it is difficult to appreciate what peace meant to all classes of the people. It was certainly the first requisite for any sort of economic progress.

We have seen that the amount of economic progress actually achieved down to 1921 in the countries where the United States intervened was not very great. There were, nevertheless, some material benefits. The customs receiverships, which continued in Nicaragua, Haiti, and Santo Domingo for several years after 1921, helped commerce by eliminating favoritism and corruption in the customhouses and strengthened the financial position of the governments. These three countries were among the very few in Latin America that continued to pay interest on their foreign bonds during the depression.[2] Some other administrative reforms introduced by American officials and advisers were of lasting value. Much-needed roads were built in Haiti and the Dominican Republic, and there was a notable improvement in sanitary conditions in the larger cities of both countries. More might have been achieved if the public works programs had not had to be financed entirely from the scanty re-

[2] In Nicaragua, however, interest on the Ethelburga bonds was reduced from 5 to 4% in 1937 by agreement with the British bondholders.

sources of the local governments. For various reasons, the substantial foreign loans which the customs receiverships were to have made possible did not materialize, and the United States government could give little help.

The replacement of the old inefficient and corrupt armies by better-trained police forces, in Haiti and the Dominican Republic, helped to maintain peace but had unfortunate consequences after the American occupations ended. The efficiency and discipline of these organizations gave their officers a potential political power which only the ablest of the old style *caudillos* had had. In Santo Domingo, General Trujillo, the chief of the new force, took control of the government in 1930 and ruled the country despotically until 1961. In Haiti, too, the *Garde* has at times been the master of the government rather than its servant. It is perhaps less unpleasant to live under the tyranny of a comparatively efficient military force than under the equally tyrannical but irresponsible and inefficient rule of the old type of local *comandantes,* but the evolution of the constabularies was a disappointment to those who hoped that they would help to promote republican government.

It can hardly be said, in fact, that the American government's policy did very much to promote republican government in other ways, except insofar as the maintenance of peace and some economic progress created an atmosphere more conducive to the gradual development of democratic institutions. The support of constituted governments and the discouragement of revolutions meant in practice that one party might stay in power indefinitely. A government that felt secure in its position was less likely to mistreat its opponents or to curtail civil rights, and it could devote more energy and resources to constructive work; but it would be no more inclined to permit its opponents to win elections.

Roosevelt and Taft dealt with the governments in power without questioning how they had attained power and seemed to deprecate revolutions not so much on moral grounds as because of their harmful effects. They endeavored to find ways of making revolutions less frequent, and at times, as in Honduras and Santo Domingo, the Taft administration interposed to end a civil war by compromise. Wilson was much more emphatic in his denunciation of all revolutionary action on moral grounds. He effectively discouraged political uprisings in Central America and attempted to prevent them in Santo Domingo. His policy of refusing to recognize any government that came into office by force was difficult to enforce, but it greatly strengthened the position of governments that were already in power.

If Wilson did not always seem to inquire very closely into the character of the regimes that he was supporting against revolution, he did on several occasions attempt to see that changes of government took place in a democratic way. In 1914 he insisted on a free election in Santo Domingo, so that there would be a government there which the United States could consistently maintain in office by force if it needed such help. In 1916 and again in 1920 he tried, without great success, to see that fair elections were held in Cuba. On the other hand, governments that were obviously opposed by a majority of the people were kept in power in Nicaragua, where the American government decided who should be the president in 1916 and made only a feeble attempt to bring about a fair election in 1920. In Haiti, where real elections were obviously impossible, there was no pretense of consulting the voters after the plebiscite on the constitution of 1918.

The failure to insist on fair elections in Cuba and in Nicaragua unquestionably gave the opposition parties reason to feel that they were unfairly treated. The opposition parties in several other Caribbean states could likewise complain that the discouragement of revolutions and the policy of refusing recognition to governments coming into office by force was unreasonable when they had no other means of changing an unsatisfactory regime. Officials at Washington, however, might well have hesitated before committing themselves to any general policy of compelling the holding of fair elections. No supervision could be effective without assuming control of or supplanting the military forces and the civil authorities and the courts in all functions connected with the electoral process. The governments in power would have had to be coerced into accepting this sort of intervention, and this would be unfair because it would hurt the prestige and probably cause the defeat of the government party, even in cases where it might otherwise have majority support. It would be difficult to find qualified people to conduct the supervision, and there was a practical problem: the State Department had very little money which it could use for such purposes. It is not surprising that there was not a more strenuous effort to change the way in which the Caribbean governments had always conducted their elections, even though there was an inconsistency in preventing revolutions against governments that perpetuated their control in obviously undemocratic ways. It could be argued that the maintenance of peace was the first requisite for the sort of progress that would ultimately make real elections possible, and that it would be futile to try to force democratic practices on people who were not ready for them.

One unfortunate consequence of the American government's efforts to improve political conditions in the Caribbean was that the local leaders got into the habit of looking to Washington for the settlement of political problems. A belief that the faction favored by the United States would usually come out on top, and even that an established government which the United States disliked might not be able to stay in office, gave an excessive importance to every indication or fancied indication of the attitude of American officials. Rumors about American policy were fabricated and circulated for political effect, and even ordinary courtesies extended by the State Department or the American legations were given an exaggerated significance. Under such conditions, many of the local leaders tended to feel less responsibility for the settlement of their own problems.

The willingness of many political leaders to accept American help made it more difficult for the State Department and its representatives to appreciate the resentment their actions were causing. If the American government's policy after 1909, as we look back on it, seems increasingly callous in its disregard of local sentiment, we must remember that those who directed it thought that they had the support of important groups in the countries with which they were dealing. In the State Department's correspondence, one frequently encounters the idea that the truly patriotic leaders, and most of the solid and intelligent people, wanted peace and reform, and that the opposition came from "corrupt politicians" and "professional revolutionists." Had it not been for the belief that the United States must help the decent element against evil men who wished for their own selfish reasons to perpetuate anarchy and misgovernment, it would have been more difficult for Taft to send the Marines into Nicaragua in 1912 and for Wilson to order the military occupation of Haiti and Santo Domingo.

Important groups in the community often did welcome American interposition. In countries where there had been long periods of disorder, property owners and businessmen were glad to have peace restored, and many humbler citizens were glad to be free from the oppression and hardship that always accompanied civil strife. When the United States prevented a revolution, only those who had hoped to get possession of the government were really distressed. There were many patriotic people who approved of the reforms which the State Department urged and who wished for American help in road-building and education and economic development. The spirit of economic nationalism, which had already made its appearance in Mexico after 1910, was much less evident in the smaller Caribbean republics, where many people hoped that the development of their natural resources by foreign capital would help them to emerge from the backward conditions that made their lives unattractive.

As the American policy developed, however, it met with increasing opposition. There had always been much distrust and traditional dislike of the United States and some suspicion of American motives. This suspicion grew stronger as the American government intervened more and more in purely internal affairs and began to seek actual control of important governmental functions. The use of force or the threat of force to settle political problems or to compel reforms was offensive to people who were jealous of their independence. The occupation of the country by American military forces, in Haiti and the Dominican Republic, was of course still more offensive.

The hostility and distrust that it aroused, not only in the Caribbean but throughout Latin America, was the worst result of the intervention policy. The full extent of this feeling was not apparent until after the First World War, when Haitian and Dominican opponents of the American occupations began to carry on a propaganda campaign in South America and in the United States. A realization of the reaction in Latin America and of the unpopularity of intervention at home led to a gradual change of policy at Washington after 1921, but suspicion of North American "imperialism" continued to be a major obstacle to inter-American cooperation throughout the 1920's. Even today the recollection of what happened in the first decades of the century provides useful material for anti-American propaganda.

The American government was necessarily interested in what happened in the Caribbean, especially after the decision to build the Panama Canal, and it had sound reasons for wishing to do away with the internal disorder and financial mismanagement that endangered the independence of some of the Central American and West Indian republics and the security of the United States. In trying to correct these conditions the statesmen who directed the policy of the United States in the Roosevelt, Taft, and Wilson administrations were dealing with exasperatingly difficult situations, where their best efforts were often defeated by the unpredictable and irresponsible conduct of local *caudillos* and their followers. We may well hesitate to criticize them too severely, but since it is clear that their policies had bad results, and since we are still faced with similar problems, it would be regrettable if we did not learn something from the story.

One fact that stands out is the inadvisability of sending incompetent diplomatic representatives to countries where the United States had great interests and heavy responsibilities. No policy could succeed when its implementation was in the hands of ministers who were too ignorant or too senile to command respect. The State Department repeatedly had to make decisions on the basis of information and recommendations received from persons who knew little about what was really happening, and it had to entrust these same persons with the conduct of its negotiations. Several of its representatives were, of course, not so incompetent, but few of them, especially after 1913, were fitted for their positions by training or experience. Many mistakes and unfortunate incidents could have been avoided if there had been able ministers at each post.

The bad results of the American government's policy, however, cannot be attributed wholly to diplomatic ineptitude. What made the policy offensive, in the Caribbean and in South America, was the use of coercion to compel the acceptance of American control in internal affairs and to obtain reforms that the United States considered desirable. Imposition of this sort would have been intolerable, however efficiently and tactfully it was carried out. Knox, Bryan, and Lansing might have achieved more, with less bad feeling, if they had attempted, as Root did, to help the people of the Caribbean states to solve their problems in their own way, instead of insisting that they place their financial administration and their military forces under the direction of foreign officials. With a policy of persuasion and cooperation the moral influence of the United States might have accomplished more than attempted compulsion did.

Had it not been for the effort to impose controls unacceptable to any people who prized their independence, there would have been less resentment of the vast influence which the United States necessarily exercised, and less resentment even when the American government used force to back up its efforts to end armed strife and to protect foreigners. Natives, as well as foreigners, were usually glad to see a warship appear at a port where fighting was imminent, and a show of force to stop a war caused little lasting bad feeling if it led to a fair settlement with no continuing offensive American interference in the government's affairs.

With tactful persuasion, much could have been done to promote better administration and economic progress. Caribbean governments often voluntarily accepted the help and advice of foreign experts, though they naturally resisted efforts to give experts authority over their own officials. Aid in roadbuilding and education and sanitation would have been welcome if it was not accompanied by efforts to impose foreign control. In Haiti and Santo Domingo there would probably have been less progress in these fields than there was under the military occupations, but the gains that were made might have been more lasting. If the American government could have provided funds for economic development, as it does today, a great deal could have been accomplished.

A policy that relied on cooperation rather than compulsion would have required patience and self-restraint. Its success would have depended on the quality of the American diplomatic representation in the Caribbean, but the diplomats would not have had to be supermen. A minister or even a young chargé d'affaires could exercise a great influence in a Caribbean country simply because he was the representative of the United States, and this influence was still greater if he was liked and respected. It was dangerous to have an incompetent man in such a position, but a moderately able man could accomplish a great deal, both for his own government and for the people of the country where he was serving.

Such a policy would also have required a willingness to accept and to live with situations in some Caribbean countries that were far from satisfactory from the American point of view. American influence could not bring about free and fair elections in countries where the people had not learned to demand them and to run them; and so long as elections were not satisfactory governments would inevitably be ousted by force or threats of force from time to time. Other evils, like corruption and oppression of political opponents, would have continued to exist. The United States could have exercised a very great influence for better and more democratic government and for the peaceful settlement of political conflicts, but in countries which were and must remain independent political progress had to be made primarily through the efforts of the people themselves. Stable democratic government cannot be imposed by exhortation or outside pressure.

Index

Abbott, John T., 96
Acosta, Julio, 443, 444ff.
Adee, Alvey A., 21, 151–52, 175, 186, 199
Advisory Law Commission (Cuba), 136, 139
"Affectations" (Haiti), 366
Aguilar Barquero, Francisco, 443
Amador Guerrero, Manuel, 51ff.
Amapala, 401
American and Foreign Power Co., 459
Amory concession, 438, 445ff.
anti-imperialist activity, 372, 380, 530, 543–44
Arbuckle Brothers, 527
Arias, Desiderio, 95, 97, 102, 260, 265, 276–77, 285, 294, 297ff., 305ff., 311, 316, 341, 352, 359
Asbert, 128, 485, 489
Auguste, Tancrède, 259, 329

Bacon, Robert, mission to Cuba, 130ff.
Báez, Ramón, 293–95
Bahia Honda, 476
Bailly-Blanchard, Arthur, 337ff.
Banco Nacional (Santo Domingo), see Jarvis, Samuel
bankers in Nicaragua, 194, 195–97, 392ff., 405ff., 413ff., 420, 537–38
Batraville, Benoît, 373
Baxter, Clarence H., 299
Beaupré, Arthur M., 47, 473ff.
Bertrand, Francisco, 449ff.
Bluefields, events of 1910, 183–84
Bluefields Fruit and Steamship Co., 18, 172–73
Bobo, Ronsalvo, 351, 354, 355
Bográn, Francisco, 453ff.
Bonilla, Manuel, 143, 148, 225ff.
Bordas Valdés, José, 274ff.
Borno, Louis, 344, 378–79, 387
botellas, 469
Bowen, Herbert W., 70, 72
Bradford, Admiral, 106, 110
British Controlled Oil Fields Ltd., 445

Brown Brothers, see bankers in Nicaragua
Brown, Philip Marshall, 149, 170, 219ff.
Bryan, William J., appointed Secretary of State, 269; employed as attorney for Tinoco, 439
Bryan-Chamorro Treaty, 400ff., 467–68
Buchanan, William J., 152, 155, 157
Bunau-Varilla, Philippe, 42, 51ff., 60
Bureau of Insular Affairs, 122, 502
Butler, A. B., 431
Butler, Smedley, 206, 370

Cabrera, Manuel Estrada, see Estrada Cabrera, Manuel
Cáceres, Ramón, 95, 117, 124, 144, 260
cacos, 330, 359, 371ff.
Cannon, Lee Roy, 175, 214–15
Caperton, Admiral, 306ff., 352ff., 365, 366, 412
Carden, Lionel, 30, 240, 244
Cárdenas, Adán, 179
Carnegie, Andrew, 154
Castrillo, Salvador, 187
Castro, Cipriano, 66ff.
Castro, Jacinto de, 321
censorship of press, under Dominican Military Government, 314–15, 321, 323; in Haiti, 386
Central America, conditions in 1900, 141ff.; unionist sentiment, 142; interstate wars, 1906–7, 144ff.; Washington Conference and treaties of 1907, 151ff.; war of 1908, 155ff.; Knox plan for new treaties, 164ff.; effort for union 1920–1, 460ff., 465
Central American Court of Justice, 152–53, 154, 157, 183, 185, 207, 402–03
Central Railroad of Haiti, 331, 385
Céspedes, governor of Puerto Plata, 277–79
Chamorro, Diego Manuel, 419ff.
Chamorro, Emiliano, 188, 190, 199, 205, 211, 408ff., 417ff., 437, 440, 443
Chamorro-Weitzel Treaty, 213–14, 390
Chase, Benjamin, 440ff.

Chauvet, Henri, 386
Christmas, Lee, 156, 225ff., 449
Clark, J. Reuben, 252, 407, 410, 471
Clayton-Bulwer Treaty, 4, 37
Cleveland, Grover, award in Costa Rica-Nicaragua boundary arbitration, 398
Clyde Line, 17, 85, 109
Colombia, canal negotiations, 43ff.; claim to Corn Islands, 398
Colton, George R., 106, 110, 123
Coombs, Leslie, 143
commissaries (Panama), 63ff.
Conant, Charles A., 223, 225
Concha, Vicente José, 44
Coolidge, John Gardner, 168
Corn Islands, 213, 398
corvée, 372
Costa Rica: canal protocol, 38–39; 1910 loan negotiations, 235ff.; opposition to Nicaragua canal treaty, 397ff.; election of 1914, 427; Tinoco's revolt, 427; relation of oil companies to revolt, 430ff.; efforts to force Tinoco's withdrawal, 433ff.; declaration of war on Germany, 437; opposition to U.S. policy, 438ff.; revolutionary movements against Tinoco, 440ff.; fall of Tinoco, 442; U.S. insistence on Aguilar Barquero as president, 443; delay in recognition, 443–45; efforts to cancel oil concessions, 445ff.; Royal Bank of Canada claim, 446
Council of Foreign Bondholders (London), 202, 217, 237
Creel, Enrique, 150, 152, 155, 179
Crespi, Robert, 431
Cromwell, William Nelson, 39, 42ff., 103
Crowder, Enoch H., 139, 418–19, 424, 495, 504ff., 513, 521ff.
Cuadra, Pedro Rafael, 409, 410
Cuadra Pasos, Carlos, 410
Cuba: in 19th century, 3–4; independence, 24; Platt Amendment, 25–26; election of 1901, 27; U.S. withdrawal, 28; reciprocity treaty, 29ff.; effects of reciprocity, 31–33; naval bases and the Isle of Pines, 34–36; Platt Amendment treaty, 36; sanitation, 36–37; revolution of 1906, 127ff.; Taft-Bacon mission, 129ff.; provisional government, 133ff.; election of 1908, 139–40; corruption after 1909, 469–70; Cuban Ports Company affair, 470ff.; Veterans' move-

ment, 474ff.; Negro revolt, 477ff.; Zapata Swamp concession, 480ff.; hostility to U.S., 483–84; election of 1912, 485; amnesty bill, 485–87; loan questions, 487ff.; election of 1916, 489ff.; revolution of 1917, 492ff.; in the first world war, 498ff.; war loans, 501–03; Crowder electoral law, 504; proposals for electoral supervision, 506ff.; election of 1920, 517ff.; "dance of the millions," 518; moratorium, 519; Crowder mission, 521ff.; effort to settle financial crisis, 525ff.; Torriente laws, 526–27; effort to stabilize sugar prices, 527
Cuban Ports Company, 470ff., 488–89, 501–02
Cuba Railroad Company, 501–02
currency reform, in Haiti, 374, 376; in Nicaragua, 196–97, 202
customs receiverships: in Dominican Republic, 102, 299–300; in Nicaragua, 180, 199; proposed in Honduras, 180
Cuyamel Fruit Co., 451. See also Zemurray, Samuel

Danish West Indies, 6
Dartiguenave, Sudre, 354ff., 368, 377
Dávila, Miguel, 149, 150, 151, 156
Davis, Norman, 473, 511
Dawson, Thomas C., 94ff., 161, 182, 187–89, 221, 230ff.
Dawson agreements, 188–89
De Lesseps, Ferdinand, 39
Dexter, Osborn, and Fleming, 223
Díaz, Adolfo, 173, 174, 188, 190, 388ff.
Díaz, Porfirio, see Mexico
Dillingham, Commander, 94–95, 100, 102
Diskonto Gesellschaft (Berlin), 67
Dollar Diplomacy, origin of expression, 162–63; discussion of, 530ff.
Dominican Republic: in 19th century, 4, 78–79; controversy with San Domingo Improvement Co., 82ff.; establishment of customs receivership, 87ff.; debts in 1905, 118; treaty and loan of 1907, 116ff.; appointment of customs personnel, 123–24; disorder 1911–13, 259ff.; loan of 1913, 266ff.; renewed disorder, 274ff.; appointment of controller, 289–90; "Wilson Plan," 291ff.; election of 1915, 294; Jiménez administration, 295ff.; U.S. demand for reforms, 302ff.; American intervention, 307ff.; military

government, 316ff.; effort to withdraw, 322ff.

Dodds, Harold W., 425

Douglas, Charles A., 389ff.

Doyle, William Tecumseh Sherman, 180, 263-65

Dulles, John Foster, 433, 436, 501

Edwards, J. H., 308

El Salvador: war with Guatemala, 1906, 144–46; with Nicaragua, 1907, 147; Nicaraguan interference, 155; protest against U.S. intervention in Nicaragua, 206; offer of financial aid to Honduras, 234; oppositon to Nicaragua canal treaty, 397ff.; proposed union with Honduras, 451

Emery claim, 168, 169, 194, 394

Estenoz, Evaristo, 477, 480

Estrada, Juan J., 173ff., 187

Estrada Cabrera, Manuel, 144, 174, 436, 457ff.

Estrada Palma, Tomás, 27ff., 126, 132

Ethelburga loan, Nicaragua, 169, 538, 539n.

Ethelburga Syndicate in Haiti, 256, 331

Farnham, Roger L., 255, 258, 332, 334, 337–38, 348

Federal Republic of Central America, 141

Ferrara, Orestes, 479

Fiallo, Fabio, 322

Field, W. H., 459

Figueroa, Fernando, 155

Financial Adviser, Haiti, powers of, 364; control of expenditures, 378

Fletcher, Henry, 441

Foreign Service of the U.S., 20ff.

Fort mission to Dominican Republic, 292–93; to Haiti, 346–48

France, influence in Haiti, 246, 326, 333, 335, 339, 348–49, 363, 375

Fruit Despatch Company, 19

Fuller, Paul, 349–51

Furniss, Henry Watson, 247ff.

Gendarmerie d' Haiti, 364, 385

Germany: U.S. apprehension of, 6–7; Venezuela blockade, 66ff.; claims in Dominican Republic, 98; influence in Haiti, 246–47, 257, 326–27, 333, 335, 339, 348–49, 360, 373; intrigues in

Mexico, 270; pro-German elements in Dominican Republic, 313; opposition to Nicaragua canal treaty, 404; influence in Costa Rica, 428, 433, 434, 436; suspected interference in Central America, 1918, 451, 454; sabotage in Cuba, 1917–18, 499

Gibson, Hugh, 281, 474, 483, 484

Gómez, José Miguel, 126, 128, 139–40, 469ff., 492, 495, 497, 508, 513

Gómez, Máximo, 27

Gonzales, William E., 487ff.

González, José Esteban, 420

González Flores, Alfredo, 427ff., 432–33, 442

Gorgas, William C., 62

Grace, W. R. and Co., 256, 331

Greater Republic of Central America, 142

Greulich concession, Costa Rica, 430ff.

Greytown, 4

Groce, Leonard, 175, 214–15

Guantánamo, 34, 476–77

Guatemala: debt defaults, 143; Estrada Cabrera's dictatorship, 144; war with El Salvador, 1906, 144–46; loan negotiations, 1909–13, 238ff.; opposition to Estrada Cabrera, 457ff.; Kemmerer mission, 458–59; sale of enemy property, 459; growth of unionist movement, 459ff.; overthrow of Estrada Cabrera, 464

Guatemala Electric Co., 459

Guatemala-Honduras boundary dispute, 451

Guillaume Sam, Vilbrun, 346ff.

Gulf of Fonseca, 404. See also Chamorro-Weitzel Treaty and Bryan-Chamorro Treaty

Gunther, Franklin Mott, 192, 198

Habana, sanitation of, 36–37, 487

Hague Court, opinion in Venezuela case, 74–76

Haiti: early history, 245–46; loan of 1910, 245ff.; National Railroad, 255ff.; bank and railroad problems, 1911–13, 257ff.; politics before 1915, 327ff.; American financial interests, 331ff.; increasing disorder and efforts to establish financial control, 333ff.; Fort-Smith Commission, 346ff.; Fuller mission, 349ff.; prison massacre, 352; American intervention, 352ff.; treaty of 1915, 356ff.;

Haiti (*continued*)
selection of treaty officials, 361–62; settlement with bank and railroad, 362; functions of treaty services, 364–65; deficiencies in treaty regime, 365ff.; efforts to obtain loan, 366–67; constitution of 1918, 368ff.; *caco* revolt, 371ff.; declaration of war on Germany, 374; protocol of 1919, 374ff.; currency reform, 376; deteriorating relations, 1918–19, 377; dispute over bank charter, 380; control of legislation by American legation, 381ff.; suspension of salaries, 382; accomplishments of treaty services, 384ff.; investment of American capital, 385–86; justice and education, 386–87
Haitian-American Corporation, 385–86
Hale, Edward J., 427–28
Hallgarten and Co., 247ff.
Ham, Clifford D., 199, 414
Hannekin, Captain, 373
Hartmont Loan, 80
Hay, John, attitude toward Germany, 6
Hay-Herrán Treaty, 45ff.
Hay-Pauncefote treaties, 37ff.
Henríquez y Carbajal, Federico, 307–08
Henríquez y Carbajal, Francisco, 309ff., 320, 321, 322
Hepburn Bill, 41
Hernández, Charles, 515
Herrán, Thomás, 45
Herrera, Carlos, 464–65, 466
Heureaux, Ulises, 79ff.
Hollander, Jacob H., 105, 118, 119, 123
Honduras: war with Nicaragua, 1907, 147ff.; neutralization under 1907 treaty, 153; revolution of 1908, 155ff.; Knox's plan for financial reform, 164ff.; loan treaty with U.S., 193–94, 203, 217ff., 223ff.; revolution of 1911, 225ff.; failure of Dollar Diplomacy, 231ff.; attitude toward Nicaragua canal treaty, 401; political conditions after 1913, 448ff.; boundary disputes, 451; proposed union with El Salvador, 451; revolution of 1919, 452ff.; appointment of financial adviser, 456
Hoover, Herbert, 500
Hornet, 226–28
Hubbard-Zemurray Steamship Co., 18–19
Huston, T. L., 473

International Railways of Central America, 18
International Sugar Commission, 500
Investments in Caribbean, 16ff., 536–37
Irías, Julián, 407, 410ff., 437
Isle of Pines, 34–36
Italy, intervention in Venezuela, 70; threat of intervention in Dominican Republic, 93, 98, 104

Jackson, John B., 470ff.
Jarvis, Samuel, 267, 275, 283, 295, 301, 393ff.
Jefferson, Benjamin, 408ff.
Jiménez, Juan Isidro, 82, 274, 293ff.
Jiménez, Ricardo, 236
Johnson, Stewart, 433
Johnston, Charles M., 290, 296ff., 305, 308
Jones, T. Sambola, 452

Keilhauer, René, 231
Keith, Minor C., 17, 142, 146, 235, 236ff., 239ff., 429ff., 439
Kemmerer, E. W., 458–59
Kleinwort and Co., 472–73
Knapp, H. S., 314ff., 366, 368, 383–84
Knox, Philander C., attitude toward Latin Americans, 160–63
Kuhn Loeb and Co., 120, 121, 122

Ladenburg Thalmann and Co., 247ff.
land title reform, in Dominican Republic, 318
landownership in Haiti, 368, 371, 382
Lane, Rufus H., 317
Lansing, Robert, views on Roosevelt Corollary, 434
Lawton, E. M., 441, 455
Leconte, Cincinnatus, 257–59, 329
legations established in each Central American state, 156
Legation guard, Nicaragua, 388, 424, 425
Long, Boaz, 273, 401, 509
Loomis, Francis B., 90, 91
López Gutiérrez, Rafael, 452ff.
lottery in Cuba, 503, 511

MacDonald, J. P., 255, 256
Machias incident, 344–45
Madriz, José, 179ff.
Magoon, Charles E., 136–40

Mahan, Alfred, 5
Marblehead Treaty, 1906, 145
Margarita Island, 6
Maritime Canal Co. of Nicaragua, 38
Marroquín, José Manuel, 45ff.
Martin, John F., 448, 467
Masó, Bartolomé, 27
Maumus, A. J., 361
Máximo Jeréz, see Venus
McCreery, Fenton, 222
McGiveney and Rokeby contract, 36–37, 487
McIlhenny, John A., 375ff.
McIntyre, Frank, 263–65, 503
McMillin, Benton, 460ff.
Membreño, Alfredo, 452, 453, 455
Memphis, U.S.S., 310
Mena, Luis, 188, 190ff.
Menocal, Mario García, 127, 140, 485, 487ff.
Merry, W. L., 40–41, 143, 168, 178
Mexico: policy in Central America, 1906–7, 145, 147, 151, 157; breakdown of cooperation with U.S., 164–66, 171; policy in Nicaragua, 1909–10, 177–78, 181, 185; influence on President Wilson's policy, 269ff.; suspected interference in Central America, 1918, 451, 452–53
Michelena, Santiago, 101, 104, 283, 295
military supervisors, Cuba, 515
Miller, Jesse I., 420ff.
Mixed Claims Commission, Nicaragua, 188, 189, 197–98, 199
modus vivendi, Dominican Republic, 104, 106, 110
Moffat, 174, 190
Mole St. Nicholas, 327, 335, 337, 354, 357
Moncada, José María, 412
Monroe Doctrine 3, 5
Montalvo, Rafael, 508
Moore, John Bassett, 12, 50
Morales, Carlos, 88ff., 117, 260
Morgan, Edwin V., 129
Morgan, Henry M., 499, 500
Morgan, J. P. and Co., 163, 220ff., 488, 537
Moses, George H., 439
Mosquito Indians, 172

Namasigue, battle of, 147
National Bank of Haiti, 246, 250, 257ff., 331, 336, 344ff., 350, 362, 374ff., 380, 382, 384
National Bank of Nicaragua, 195, 196, 199, 211, 395, 399
National City Bank of New York, 224, 248ff., 255, 256, 267, 331, 380, 382, 384
National Railroad of Haiti, 255–56, 257ff., 334, 340, 362ff.
New York Life Insurance Co., 486
Nicaragua: canal negotiations with U.S., 37ff., 40–41, 46; Zelaya's dictatorship, 146; his attack on Honduras, 147; strained relations with U.S., 167ff.; Emery claim, 168–69; Ethelburga loan, 169; political conditions in 1909, 171–72; revolution of 1909–10, 173ff.; political affairs, 1910–12, 186ff.; loan treaty with U.S., 193; 1911 loan contracts, 195–96; 1912 loan, 201–02; currency reform, 202; defeat of loan treaty, 203; revolution of 1912, 204ff.; establishment of legation guard, 210, 216; canal option treaty, 213–14; situation in 1913, 388; Bryan-Chamorro Treaty, 389ff.; 1913 loan, 392ff.; Central American opposition to canal treaties, 397ff.; decision of Central American Court, 402–03; dispute over application of treaty fund, 405ff.; election of 1916, 406ff.; 1917 financial plan, 413ff.; 1920 financial plan, 416–17; election of 1920, 417ff.
Nicaragua-Honduras boundary dispute, 451
Nord Alexis, 329
Northcott, Elliott, 189ff.
Nouel, Adolfo, 264ff., 274, 306, 308, 321
Nuñez, Emilio, 514

Oberlin, Edgar G., 362
Oil concessions, in Costa Rica, 430ff.
Oregon, U.S.S., 37
Oreste, Michel, 329
Ortiz, Fernando, 507
Ostend Manifesto, 3

Panama: work of French Canal Company, 39; comparison of Panama and Nicaragua Canal routes, 39–40; independence, 49ff.; Canal Treaty, 55ff., 60ff.; tri-partite treaties of 1909, 158–59

Panama Railroad, 40, 51, 53, 60
Paredes, Juan, 223, 224
P.C.S. Railroad (Haiti), 246, 248, 331, 385
Pearson oil interests, 430, 438
Peralte, Charlemagne, 372ff.
Peynado, Francisco, 321
Phelan, James D., 301
Piñol y Batres, Bishop, 458
Platt Amendment, 25ff., 36
"Platt Amendment" proposed for Nicaragua, 390ff., 398, 399, 407
Pond, Admiral, 310ff.
Powell, Wm. F., 84ff.
"preventive policy," 470
provost courts in Dominican Republic, 321, 322, 323; in Haiti, 386
Pulliam, William E., 123, 275

Quirós, Juan B., 442, 443
Quirós, Mariano, 441

Rathbone, Albert, 520
Reader, Mrs. Ella Rawls, 103, 106
Reciprocity Treaty (Cuba), 29ff.
Regalado, Tomás, 143, 145
Regie, 81, 82
Reyes, Rafael, 54, 60
Roosevelt, Franklin D., 370
Roosevelt Corollary, 7, 65ff.
Root, Elihu, policy, 113–16; South American trip, 112, 115–16; summary of accomplishments, 158–59
Rosales, Máximo, 449ff.
Royal Bank of Canada, claim against Costa Rica, 446
Ruan, Addison T., 361, 367ff., 375, 378
Russell, John H., 379, 387
Russell, W. W., 261, 302

Salvador, see El Salvador
Samaná Bay, 79, 84, 86, 88
Sánchez, Juan F., 90ff.
San Domingo Improvement Co., 79ff., 95, 104–05, 106, 118, 119
sanitation, in Cuba, 36–37, 511; in Haiti, 364
Santo Domingo, see Dominican Republic
Seligman, J. and W. and Co., 238ff. See also bankers in Nicaragua
Simon, Antoine, 247ff., 256, 329
Sinclair oil concession, Costa Rica, 432, 438, 445ff.

Smith, Charles Cogswell, 292–93, 346–48
Smith, Madison, 329
Snowden, Thomas, 320ff.
Solórzano, Fernando, 189, 199
Soriano, Nazario, 452
Southerland, Admiral, 208–09
Speyer, James, 120, 194, 195, 220, 236, 237, 239ff., 248ff., 256, 331, 488
Spooner Act, 42
Squiers, Herbert G., 29ff., 35, 128
Stabler, J. Herbert, 281, 312
Stahl, Adolfo, 239
Steinhart, Frank, 129–30, 478
sugar producers, in Dominican Republic, 109, 537
Sugar Finance Commission, 527, 528
Sullivan, James M., 275ff.; removal, 301

Taft, William H., mission to Cuba, 130ff.; policy in Central America, 160–63
Taft Agreement (Panama), 63–64
Theodore, Davilmar, 333, 341, 343ff.
Thurston, Walter, 458ff.
Tinoco, Federico, 427ff.
Tinoco, Joaquín, 442
Torriente laws (Cuba), 526–27, 529
Trujillo, Rafael Leonidas, 325

Ubico, Jorge, 458
United Fruit Co. 17, 18–19, 142, 156, 172, 226–27, 235, 422, 428ff., 444, 447–48, 449–50
Urtecho, J. Andrés, 422

Vaccaro Brothers, 18–19
Valentine, Lincoln, 431, 432, 438
Valentine, Washington, 20, 150, 218ff., 225, 233, 450
Vásquez, Horacio, 84, 124, 265, 274, 277, 293–95, 325
Velásquez, Federico, 119, 124, 260, 274, 276, 293–94, 308, 321
Venezuela blockade 66ff.
Venus, 183–84
Vick, Walter C., 275, 299
Victoria, Alfredo, 260ff.
Victoria, Eladio, 260ff.
Vincent, Stenio, 369
Volio, Alfredo, 436ff.
voudou, 328

Wands, Ernest H., 192, 194, 195
Weil claim, 167–68

Welles, Sumner, 420, 513
Westendorp Co., 80
White, Francis, 511ff.
Wilson, F. M. Huntington, background and views on policy, 161–63
Wilson, Woodrow, general Latin American policy, 269ff.; Mobile speech, 271–72
"Wilson Plan" in Dominican Republic, 292–93; in Haiti, 341, 342
Wood, Leonard, 25ff.
Wright, J. Butler, 409

yellow fever, 26
Young, Arthur, N., 456

Zamor, Charles, 337, 338, 341
Zamor, Oreste, 333ff.
Zapata Swamp, 480ff.
Zayas, Alfredo, 130, 132, 140, 485, 489–90, 494, 497, 508, 513
Zelaya, José Santos, 40–41, 146ff., 171–72, 176–78
Zeledón, 209
Zemurray, Samuel, 18–19, 227, 231ff., 450